Major Figures		Events and Publications	
Seneca	c. 4 B.C.–65 A.D.		
Epictetus	c. 50–130		
Ptolemy	c. 90–168	Domitian banishes philosophers from Rome	c. 89
Marcus Aurelius	121–180		
Sextus Empiricus	c. 200		
Diogenes Läertius	c. 200		
Augustine of Hippo	354–430	Fall of the Roman Empire	c. 476
Boethius	c. 480–524	*Consolation of Philosophy* (Boethius)	523
Anselm	1033–1109	Ontological argument appears in the *Proslogion* (Anselm)	1088
Abu Hamid al-Ghazali	1058–1111		
Albertus Magnus	c. 1200–1280	Formal charter of the University of Paris	1215
Thomas Aquinas	1225–1274		
		Renaissance begins in Italy	c. 1300
Nicolaus Copernicus	1473–1543		
Martin Luther	1483–1546	Protestant Reformation begins	1517
		Copernican Revolution begins	1543
Francis Bacon	1561–1626		
Galileo Galilei	1564–1642		
Thomas Hobbes	1588–1679		
René Descartes	1596–1650		
Baruch Spinoza	1632–1677	Galileo tried by the Inquisition	1632
John Locke	1632–1704	*Discourse on Method* (Descartes)	1637
Isaac Newton	1642–1727	The Enlightenment begins with the publication of Descartes' *Meditations on First Philosophy*	1641
George Berkeley	1685–1753	*An Essay Concerning Human Understanding* (Locke)	1690
		A Treatise Concerning the Principles of Human Knowledge (Berkeley)	1710
David Hume	1711–1776	*Three Dialogues between Hylas and Philonous* (Berkeley)	1713
Adam Smith	1723–1790		
Immanuel Kant	1724–1804	*Treatise of Human Nature* (Hume)	1737
Jeremy Bentham	1748–1832	*An Enquiry Concerning Human Understanding* (Hume)	1748
Comte de Saint-Simon	1760–1825		
Thomas Malthus	1766–1834		
G. W. F. Hegel	1770–1831	American Revolution	1775–1783
		Dialogues Concerning Natural Religion (Hume)	1779
		Industrial Revolution begins in England	c. 1780

www.wadsworth.com

wadsworth.com is the World Wide Web site for Wadsworth Publishing Company and is your direct source to dozens of online resources.

At *wadsworth.com* you can find out about supplements, demonstration software, and student resources. You can also send e-mail to many of our authors and preview new publications and exciting new technologies.

wadsworth.com
Changing the way the world learns®

Douglas J. Soccio

SHASTA COLLEGE

Archetypes
of Wisdom

An Introduction to Philosophy

THIRD EDITION

I T P® Wadsworth Publishing Company

An International Thomson Publishing Company

Belmont, CA • Albany, NY • Bonn • Boston • Cincinnati • Detroit •
Johannesburg • London • Madrid • Melbourne • Mexico City •
New York • Paris • Singapore • Tokyo • Toronto • Washington

Philosophy Editor: Peter Adams
Assistant Editor: Kerri Abdinoor
Editorial Assistants: Kelly Bush and Greg Brueck
Production Editor: Hal Lockwood
Designer: Andrew Ogus, Book Design
Marketing Manager: Dave Garrison
Print Buyer: Barbara Britton
Copy Editor: Adrienne Armstrong
Cover Design: Andrew H. Ogus, Book Design
Photo Research: Stephen Forsling
Permissions Editor: Robert Kauser
Compositor: Thompson Type
Printer: Courier Companies
Cover: Detail of "The Dispute Over the Trinity" by Raphael/Scala/Art Resource, New York

Printed in the United States of America
3 4 5 6 7 8 9 10

For more information, contact Wadsworth Publishing Company, 10 Davis Drive, Belmont, CA 94002, or electronically at
http://www.wadsworth.com/wadsworth.html

International Thomson Publishing Europe
Berkshire House 168-173
High Holborn
London, WC1V7AA, England

International Thomson Editores
Campos Eliseos 385, Piso 7
Col. Polanco
11560 México D.F. México

Thomas Nelson Australia
102 Dodds Street
South Melbourne 3205
Victoria, Australia

International Thomson Publishing Asia
221 Henderson Road
#05-10 Henderson Building
Singapore 0315

Nelson Canada
1120 Birchmount Road
Scarborough, Ontario
Canada M1K 5G4

International Thomson Publishing Japan
Hirakawacho Kyowa Building, 3F
2-2-1 Hirakawacho
Chiyoda-ku, Tokyo 102, Japan

International Thomson Publishing GmbH
Königswinterer Strasse 418
53227 Bonn, Germany

International Thomson Publishing Southern Africa
Building 18, Constantia Park
240 Old Pretoria Road
Halfway House, 1685 South Africa

Library of Congress Cataloging-in-Publication Data
Soccio, Douglas J.
     Archetypes of wisdom : an introduction to philosophy / Douglas J.
Soccio. — 3rd ed.
        p.   cm.
     Includes bibliographical references and indexes.
     ISBN 0-534-52443-5
     1. Philosophy—Introductions.   I. Title.
BD21.S616   1997
100—dc21   97-19987

Edward M. Soccio
(1919–1996)

For my fatherless father, Edward M. Soccio, a modest man who, without fully realizing it, gave his family, his friends, and his community the father he never had

Contents

Preface

Archetypes of Wisdom evolved out of my identification of a serious gap in the current, crowded introduction to philosophy textbook market: The need for a text that combines a clear, integrated sense of historical continuity with individually modest, but cumulatively substantial, passages from primary sources and secondary commentary—written with attention to style as well as content.

No longer can philosophy instructors assume that most of our students share a common fund of knowledge or even a relatively similar range of language skills. Most introductory students are, understandably, unfamiliar with critical analysis and argument. Consequently, even the most readable primary sources can seem forbidding to them.

Students from divergent backgrounds like *Archetypes of Wisdom* because it shows respect for them by presenting difficult material in a manageable form. It talks to and with them, not over their heads or down to them in a trendy, pandering way. They can and will read it. Philosophical material varies in degree of difficulty, and sophisticated philosophical arguments are presented as part of a cultural context. Philosophical passages are explained in a manner that unobtrusively teaches students how to read critically and carefully by asking them pointed questions and connecting philosophical issues to students' current interests in a natural, unforced, and nontrivializing way.

Archetypes of Wisdom is a unique blend of philosophy, history, social science, and anecdote. The generous and positive response to the first two editions puts me at a loss for words (a rare condition, indeed) and nourishes my hope that *Archetypes of Wisdom* stands on its own as a "good read."

I am pleased when reviewers indicate that the form and content are seamlessly integrated, but I am profoundly affected by the many students who have written to tell me that they are going to keep *Archetypes of Wisdom* in their personal libraries. Their comments are generous and kind, and their enthusiasm for philosophy is a bracing confirmation of my faith that exposure to first-rate philosophy is a natural antidote for apathy and cultural barbarism.

About the Third Edition

This third edition of *Archetypes of Wisdom* is a substantial revision that combines the strengths of the first two editions with improvements suggested by professors and students based on three principles: (1) The best teaching begins where students are, not where they "should" be. (2) If a book is worth writing, make it a book worth keeping. (3) Philosophy matters to more than philosophers.

In light of this third principle, *Archetypes of Wisdom* remains unique among introductory philosophy textbooks in the respect it pays to the common conception of "the search for wisdom." This revision enhances that motif and its treatment of the more technical philosophical issues:

- *The entire text is more polished.*
- *Philosophical themes and issues are linked structurally via three new Overviews and textually via more cross-references.*
- *Substantial, new material from Susan Bordo's critique of modern philosophy is part of a more integrated treatment of women philosophers.*
- *New, balanced discussions of modernity, postmodernism, and philosophical advocacy add contemporary perspective.*
- *New 15-chapter configuration* more closely conforms to the length of the typical semester and improves reader accessibility.
- *Three new Overviews* identify key concepts and themes associated with the philosophical issues to be covered in subsequent chapters and interludes, and provide needed context for today's students; Overviews also enhance the storytelling qualities of *Archetypes of Wisdom*.
- *Four Interludes* are back at the well-reasoned request of reviewers and adopters. First edition users are already familiar with these less formal treatments of selected philosophical archetypes. Because they're structurally less formal, many instructors assign them as independent work or use them as sources of paper topics, reports, and presentations.

Third Edition Improvements and Additions

- *Chapter 1: Philosophy and the Search for Wisdom* Tighter, cleaner, and more inviting opening gets off to a fast, affirmative start; new section Why Study Philosophy?; clearer acknowledgment of the selective nature of *Archetypes of Wisdom* and the historical limits and biases of Western philosophy.
- *Overview of Classical Themes* New section sets the stage for the emergence of philosophy from mythology, development of rational discourse, and search for explanations.
- *First Interlude: The Presocratic Sophos* Streamlined treatment of the Presocratics; retains significant philosophical material for those instructors who discuss the Presocratics as antecedents to the develop-

ment of Sophistry, Plato's theory of forms, and Aristotle's treatment of form, matter, and causality.

- *Chapter 2: The Sophist: Protagoras* Streamlined.

- *Chapter 3: The Wise Man: Socrates* Reorganized with more philosophical content; Socrates' encounter with Thrasymachus has been expanded and moved to this chapter.

- *Chapter 4: The Philosopher-King: Plato* Significantly improved treatment of the theory of forms.

- *Chapter 5: The Naturalist: Aristotle* New sections on form, matter, and cause anticipate Aquinas's Five Ways.

- *Second Interlude: The Hedonist* Edited treatment of hedonism with a shorter look at Aristippus; fuller treatment of Epicurus is retained.

- *Chapter 6: The Stoic: Epictetus and Marcus Aurelius* Minor modifications.

- *Chapter 7: The Scholar: Thomas Aquinas* Minor modifications in light of new Aristotle material; new section: Why Do People Argue About Spiritual Matters?

- *Overview of Modern Themes* New section introduces students to modern philosophers' emphases on epistemology, method, science, rationalism, empiricism, objectivity, and universality.

- *Chapter 8: The Rationalist: René Descartes* Minor modifications.

- *Third Interlude: The Buddha* Significantly edited treatment of the Asian sage, concentrating on Buddha; some interesting Taoist material retained in boxes; placed as intriguing contrast to Western rationalism and the Humean bundle theory of the self.

- *Chapter 9: The Skeptic: David Hume* Minor modifications.

- *Chapter 10: The Universalist: Immanuel Kant* Modifications include the reintroduction of regulative ideas from the first edition, and a new section on The Objectivity of Experience; the title change anticipates contemporary challenges to "universal truths."

- *Chapter 11: The Materialist: Karl Marx* Minor modifications.

- *Fourth Interlude: The Utilitarians* Significantly edited treatment of Bentham and Mill; anticipates Chapter 15 discussion of philosophers as advocates and prophets (philosophical reformers).

- *Chapter 12: The Existentialist: Søren Kierkegaard and Jean-Paul Sartre* Improved recombination of second edition material in response to reviewers' thoughtful suggestions; this restructuring is related to the new treatment of Nietzsche.

- *Chapter 13: The Pragmatist: William James* Minor modifications; a new section, Truth Is Always Personal.

- *Overview of Postmodern Themes* New material prepares students for Nietzsche's influential critique of modernity and feminist challenges to certain aspects of modern philosophy; shows philosophical underpinnings of "postmodern" ideas held by many students; encourages respectful discussion of controversial ideas.

- *Chapter 14: The Anti-Philosopher: Friedrich Nietzsche* Major additions; expanded chapter-length treatment of Nietzsche serves as a bridge to Chapter 15 discussion of Susan Bordo's assessment of feminist critiques of modern philosophy.

- *Chapter 15: Emerging Archetypes* This new, improved treatment of feminism and prophetic philosophy avoids any suggestion that *Archetypes of Wisdom* has identified new archetypes; contains additional, substantial philosophical material from Susan Bordo's critique of Cartesian masculinization of thought, and new sections on the public-private issue and philosophical advocacy.

- *Continuative* New, brief, informal note of encouragement; a warm and welcoming invitation to join the search for wisdom; picks up Chapter 1 question Why Study Philosophy? in light of all we have learned.

About Pedagogy

- *Chapter Commentaries* Chapters conclude with clearly identified brief commentaries that include general evaluations or personal reflections concerning the philosophical ideas covered in the chapter; they often connect chapter ideas to contemporary issues.

- *Summary of Main Points* Highlights of key ideas can be used as a handy preview, review, and discussion aid for each chapter.

- *Study Questions* Each chapter contains questions keyed to the text. Questions range from specific to general, and can function as review questions, can be used as test or essay questions, or may be modified for use as paper topics.

- *Two Glossaries* In addition to the handy margin glossary, which defines key terms in the margins, highlighting their importance and facilitating text reviews, the alphabetical glossary makes it easy to find key terms and chapter and page references.

- *Bibliography of Interesting Sources* This collection of texts contains some real gems, as well as the more usual philosophy texts. A Notes section documents the major philosophical sources.

- *Index to Margin Quotes* This helps students locate authors of interesting margin quotes featured throughout the text.

Ancillary materials available to accompany this text include:

- *Unique Instructor's Manual* In addition to the usual sections containing Test Questions and Essay Questions, this manual includes a section on the Philosophy of Testing (how to prepare tests), Lecture and Discussion Tips for all chapters, Tips for New Philosophy Teachers (which are useful for all teachers), and a discussion of the Special Pedagogical Features of *Archetypes of Wisdom*. Few, if any, other manuals are as practical or complete; this is not a cursory job, but a true *instructor's* manual of useful tips and timesaving test questions and lecture guides.

- *New Interactive CD-ROM Study Guide* This optional supplement consists of an overview of key concepts, sample test questions, flash cards, a pronunciation guide, and mini-lectures for each chapter and interlude, presented in an engaging interactive format that encourages active studying. Available for both Macintosh and Windows.

- *How to Get the Most Out of Philosophy, 3E* This unique handbook for philosophy students proved to be the success surprise of the first edition. Many instructors, counselors, and students now use *How to Get the Most Out of Philosophy* as a general "student success" manual. The third edition includes new material on electronic citations and sources, and advice for using the Internet. *How to Get the Most Out of Philosophy, 3E* is available as an optional supplement at a significantly reduced cost for adopters of *Archetypes of Wisdom*, or as an independent text.

What Has Been Retained from the Second Edition?

- *Inviting, visually appealing format* A large format allows for illustrations, margin quotes, a margin glossary, and boxed quotes. Responses from readers indicate that many students enjoy browsing through the text and reading margin and boxed material for pleasure.

- *Integrated margin quotes and boxed passages* Most margin quotes are from the central figures in the chapters. Margin quotes are chosen to add spice and information to the body of the text. Browsing through them is a painless introduction to a philosopher's ideas. Margin quotes and boxed passages make excellent discussion material.

- *The call of stories* Even the most uninterested and resistant students respond to personal anecdotes about philosophers. Each chapter contains a brief but engaging philosophical biography of one or two main figures. These biographies provide cultural and historical context for the philosophical ideas covered in the chapter, showing students how philosophers respond to important concerns of their times. A story-telling approach avoids depersonalization and the distancing effect of texts that treat issues and arguments as somehow independent of time, place, and person.

- *Accessible depth* *Archetypes of Wisdom* solves the problem of choosing between accessibility and depth by covering fewer philosophers and philosophical ideas on a more fundamental level. Primary sources are integrated with secondary explanations in passages of varying length. Secondary commentary teaches students how to read philosophical literature.

- *Cultural breadth* *Archetypes of Wisdom* blends traditional Western philosophy, non-Western and nontraditional philosophy, and contemporary issues. The figure of the *sophos* (sage) links traditional philosophical concerns with "everyday meaning needs." Nontraditional, non-Western selections include: Buddhism, existential iconoclasm (Søren Kierkegaard and Friedrich Nietzsche), prophetic philosophy (Martin Luther King, Jr., and Malcolm X, Cornell West, Henry David Thoreau, Mahatma Gandhi), and philosophical feminism (Susan Bordo, Carol Gilligan, Susan Moller Okin, Alison Jaggar, Betty Friedan, Simone de Beauvoir).

- *Ongoing student involvement* The Philosophical Query is a unique feature of *Archetypes of Wisdom*. Philosophical Queries are topical questions that directly address the reader, prompting her or him to react critically to specific passages of text. They range from the personal to the controversial and can be readily modified for use as essay questions or to focus class discussion.

- *A wide range of contemporary sources* *Archetypes of Wisdom* contains a variety of contemporary sources that address philosophical issues from beyond academic philosophy. These show—rather than merely tell—students that philosophy occurs outside of philosophy class and under other guises.

- *Flexible structure* Each chapter and interlude is a self-contained unit. It is not necessary to cover sections in chronological order or to cover every chapter or interlude in order to have an effective class. Material not covered by the instructor can be used for independent writing assignments, group presentations, and the like.

Acknowledgments

I thank the many reviewers who have worked on each edition of this text for their thoughtful, timely, and helpful advice, which often went well beyond the call of duty. I hope this revision lives up to their high standards. I am grateful to third edition reviewers Ronald R. Cox, San Antonio College, and Arnold A. McMahon, Saddleback College. I offer extra special thanks to Philip Jung, Grand Rapids Community College, and Scott A. Olsen, Central Florida Community College, for the considerable thought and effort they put into their fair but firm reviews. Lastly, I pay special tribute to the superb professional advice and personal support provided by my friend and colleague Joe Mellon.

Among the people who worked on earlier editions, I remain grateful to Ken King for his enthusiasm for my original proposal and his willingness to produce a complicated, unique text, and to Mary Arbogast, whose insight, intelligence, and sensitivity improved the initial text beyond measure.

Among the folks at Wadsworth Publishing Company whom I especially wish to thank, I begin with Peter Adams (aka Petaradamus the Seer) for his support, encouragement, gracious good humor, solid advice, hard work, and care packages. Peter's enthusiasm has been a joy and blessing. Adrienne Armstrong, my "which hunter" and copyeditor, has cleaned up unwieldy passages and saved me from much embarrassment. The care put into the proofreading by Martha Ghent provided my wife, Margaret, and me with much-needed peace of mind. Once again, permissions editor Bob Kauser deserves extra-special recognition and appreciation for helping me work my way through the maze of permission conditions. My sincerest thanks also to Hal Humphrey, who coordinated the entire Wadsworth end of the production. Dick Cole's great line drawings add distinction and verve; they are an integral part of the text.

Hal Lockwood of Penmarin Books deserves some sort of medal for juggling so many tasks so well—with patience, foresight, and energy, and for the judicious use of that awful threat: "Or we'll have to leave you out of the loop." Hal coordinated a very complex project with aplomb. I also thank Stephen Forsling for the care he put into finding photos and illustrations for abstract ideas, never an easy task.

Lastly, I cannot begin to express my gratitude at my good fortune for having Andrew Ogus design yet another edition of *Archetypes of Wisdom*. I think of Andrew as an essential part of this book. With each edition, we come a bit closer to expressing the vision I had more than fifteen years ago for "an elegant, integrated, and affective as well as effective philosophy book." Andrew's aesthetic sensitivities and talent help make *Archetypes of Wisdom* the kind of book students want to keep.

Among my many kind and supportive friends, the following continue to provide special support and encouragement: At Shasta College, Ross Fetters and Joe Vargas keep me from despair as the technocrats and bottom-liners persist in their efforts to turn education into a commodity and students into customers. My friend George Linville, the "Nietzsche of Shasta County," continues to remind me that at least one *sophos* is still among us—although dangerously close to running amok. I remain grateful for the "long-distance friendship" with Admiral Jim Stockdale that has resulted from the publication of the first edition of this book.

I have reached that stage of life where I mark each revision by changes in my family. Since the publication of the second edition, both my father, Ed Soccio, and my stepson, Raymond T. Borst, died. Each of these men taught me the same thing, but each in his unique way: Profound love can transform the meanest of circumstances into fields of grandeur. Ed and Ray tried so hard to stay among those they loved, and when that was no longer possible, they left with sadness, but without bitterness. In their gratitude for the smallest of favors—a cool touch, a bit of broth, a silent companion—they reinforced the teachings of the sages, and convinced me more than ever that wisdom does matter, that it is real, and that ordinary individuals express it all the time. During this revision, I have also been reminded of the sweetness of life by the welcome arrival of my newest niece, Abby Hickerson, and my newest nephew, Michael Pesavento, who give me joy and hope just by being here.

I continue to watch in wonder as my brother and sisters, Mike, Gina, and Lucianna, grow in love, courage, and wisdom, and with pride as my stepdaughter Patricia C. Borst embarks on her new teaching career. I also want to thank Elizabeth Borst for taking the time to catch mistakes in the text and study guide.

Supporting my father as he left this world, and welcoming her grandchildren as they entered it, my mother, Helon Musick Soccio, showed me (once again) that generosity can thrive in the face of adversity, willingness in the midst of change, faith in the mere possibility of faith, and, most of all, that once rooted, unconditional love is invincible.

Lastly, I owe my wife, Margaret L. Malone, more than I can ever repay for loving and supporting me through yet another complicated, exhausting, and exhilarating revision of this book, of which she remains so much a part. *Archetypes of Wisdom* would be much less without her. And so would my life.

Philosophy and the Search for Wisdom

I do not know how to teach philosophy without becoming a disturber of the peace.
Baruch Spinoza

Y ou are about to embark on the study of a subject that is unlike any other. Historically, most academic subjects began as
some aspect of philosophy and branched off as knowledge became specialized. Philosophy resembles history and social science when it studies the development of ideas in terms of the social climate
from which they emerged. It resembles art criticism when it analyzes the
meaning and function of poetry, painting, or music, the nature of beauty,
or the moral qualities of art. It resembles physics and chemistry in its efforts to describe ultimate reality. It resembles linguistics and semantics in
its analyses of language, communication, and meaning. It resembles geometry and algebra in the theorems and proofs of symbolic logic. Informal
logic may remind you of English or communications classes in its identification of fallacies and of persuasive maneuvers.

The word **philosophy** comes from Greek roots meaning "the love of wisdom." The earliest philosophers were considered wise men and women, or
sages, because they devoted themselves to asking "big questions": What is
the meaning of life? Where did everything come from? What is the nature of
reality? For a long time, most philosophers were wisdom-seeking amateurs.
Philosophy was a way of living for them, not a way of making a living.

We often use the term *philosophy* in just that sense, when we think of a
person's basic philosophy as the code of values and beliefs by which he or she
lives. Sometimes we talk about Abby's philosophy of cooking or Mikey's philosophy of betting on the horses. In such instances, we are thinking of philosophy as involving general principles or guidelines. Technically, that's known
as *having a philosophy*; it is not the same thing as *being a philosopher*. Philosophy is all around us, even if we don't recognize it or agree on what it is.

Why Study Philosophy?

Why study philosophy? Because you can't avoid philosophizing if you're
the least bit conscious or reflective. That is, thoughtful people do not live
without wondering about THE BIG QUESTIONS: Does God exist? Does

life in general have a purpose? Does *my* life have a purpose? Why do innocent people suffer? Is everything a matter of opinion? How can we know? Can we know that we know that we know? Are all people really "equal"? In what sense? What is the best form of government? Is it better to try to make the majority happy at the expense of the few, or the few at the expense of the many? How are minds connected to bodies? Is there one standard of right and wrong for everyone, or are all judgments relative? Is beauty in the eye of the beholder? Does might make right? Is everyone biased, acting from self-interest and ulterior motives? Can stuff make people happy? Is it better to try to have as much pleasure as possible or is it smarter to try to avoid pain and hardship?

The preceding are samples of philosophical questions that have been tackled by philosophers we'll encounter in our studies together. I'll bet you've pondered many of them. I can promise that if you study carefully, and as much as possible without prejudgment, you will be hooked by the vitality, power, and intrinsic interest of many, if not all, of the philosophical issues and arguments presented in the representative sampling of philosophical archetypes included in this text.

Although the idea of studying selected highlights of nearly three thousand years of (mostly) Western philosophizing may seem *exhausting*, this is not meant to be an *exhaustive* history of philosophy or survey of philosophical topics. That is, *Archetypes of Wisdom* was never meant to be "complete," covering every significant philosopher or every significant contribution of the philosophers it does include. Rather, it's meant to be *a philosophy textbook with a heart*, a text that respects both the fundamental and original human need "to make sense of our lives as a whole" and a more rigorous, specialized, "professional" level of "doing philosophy."

Whether or not you become a professional (or "real") philosopher, you will benefit from studying philosophy: You'll learn about the intellectual roots of Western civilization. You'll learn about a subject that's much discussed but infrequently studied in an organized, methodical way. You'll encounter fascinating individuals and intriguing ideas. You'll find yourself having intellectual discussions, and perhaps even arguments, with important philosophers. You'll find yourself engaged or involved in a subject that is inherently "relevant" to thoughtful living. You may even discover a deeper understanding of yourself and your goals.

> Beggars get handouts before philosophers because people have some idea of what it's like to be blind and lame.
>
> *Diogenes*

> Specialization is the price we pay for the advancement of knowledge. A price, because the path of specialization leads away from the ordinary and concrete acts of understanding in terms of which man actually lives his day-to-day life.
>
> *William Barrett*

Philosophy in a Technological Age

I recommend treating your philosophy class as an intellectual retreat from the mundane goal of getting good grades in order to get a degree in order to get a "good job" as soon as possible. Take this opportunity to reflect more deeply and broadly than most other classes permit. For many students, philosophy class is an unfortunately too-rare encouragement to

Surely, Life Is Not Merely a Job

Why do we go through the struggle to be educated? Is it merely in order to pass some examinations and get a job? Or is it the function of education to prepare us while we are young to understand the whole process of life? Having a job and earning one's livelihood is necessary—but is that all? Are we being educated only for that? Surely, life is not merely a job, an occupation; life is wide and profound, it is a great mystery, a vast realm in which we function as human beings. If we merely prepare ourselves to earn a livelihood, we shall miss the whole point of life; and to understand life is much more important than merely to prepare for examinations and become very proficient in mathematics, physics, or what you will.

Jiddu Krishnamurti
"The Function of Education," in Daniel Kolak and Raymond Martin, *The Experience of Philosophy* (Belmont, Calif.: Wadsworth, 1990), pp. 20–21.

I see many people die because they judge that life is not worth living. I see others paradoxically getting killed for the ideas and illusions that give them a reason for living (what is called a reason for living is also an excellent reason for dying). I therefore conclude that the meaning of life is the most urgent of questions.

Albert Camus

think about your life as a whole; it can even be a counterweight to the formidable forces arrayed on the more technical, specialized, so-called practical side of life, forces that say: "Get a major. Don't delay. Be practical. Think ahead to the job market. Find your niche. Focus, focus, focus. And don't delay; the competition's not waiting for you."

In Chapter 5 we'll take a closer look at identifying our "true selves"—our life's proper goal—but this might be the place to paraphrase an intriguing line from the late mythologist Joseph Campbell: "There may be no greater tragedy in life than to reach the top of the wall only to discover you're on the wrong wall." The sort of tragedy Campbell had in mind results from overemphasis on means and techniques for accomplishing our goals while trivializing or ignoring the need to know ourselves before we set off to climb walls selected by other people, mass media, and conventions and customs we take for granted.

You have no doubt recognized the increasingly specialized nature of your courses as you progress through the educational maze. A *technique* is nothing more than a way of doing something. There is a technique for solving a certain kind of math problem; there is one technique for writing English 1A papers and another for writing Psychology 1A papers. There are techniques for getting dates or painting cars or casting statues. Many Americans express contradictory fears concerning technology: that we are falling behind other countries technologically and that we are being destroyed by an overreliance on technology.

One of the things philosophers do is point out such contradictions. Then we analyze them to see if they are resolvable. Technical specialists, by contrast, understandably concentrate on a clearly defined area of study and can usually identify inconsistencies and contradictions within that area. But specializing makes it hard to see more general contradictions and implications among the values and needs of different specialties. All

Is it possible to justify the study of philosophy considering the urgent needs of such overwhelming contemporary problems as world hunger? "Philosophy bakes no bread," and people need bread to live.

sorts of common human complications make it difficult for us to see inconsistencies and contradictions in our own lives. Enter the philosopher.

Of course, there's a difference between sitting around saying philosophical-sounding things and actually philosophizing. One vital difference involves the degree of rigor and discipline applied to our reflections. A simple way to make the point is by an analogy with swimming: Compare someone who swims a few laps in the backyard pool fairly regularly to an Olympic swimmer. They are both swimmers, but there's being a swimmer and being a *swimmer*.

We are probably all philosophers once in a while, and some of us are even *philosophers*. When we face a difficult change, we reflect on life, death, loss, and growth. But when things are going well, we tend to just enjoy. Perhaps we articulately express our beliefs about affirmative action, human nature, justice, or medically assisted suicide. But do we study and restudy these issues, consulting a wide array of opinions and doing our best to suspend final judgment until we are clear about all key terms and facts? Do we always remain willing to modify our strongest beliefs should new evidence warrant that? *Philosophers* do.

Without philosophy we would be little above the animals.

Voltaire

Timely Questions

Technical thinking is concerned chiefly with the means to achieve particular ends: curing AIDS, stopping automobile exhaust pollution, teaching people to read. These are different from what philosophers sometimes call **ultimate ends**.

ULTIMATE ENDS

Goals that are valued for their own sake, not as means to something else.

The Prejudices of Practical Men

If we are not to fail in our endeavour to determine the value of philosophy, we must first free our minds from the prejudices of what are wrongly called "practical" men. The "practical" man, as this word is often used, is one who recognizes only material needs, who realizes that men must have food for the body, but is oblivious of the necessity of providing food for the mind. If all men were well off, if poverty and disease had been reduced to their lowest possible point, there would still remain much to be done to produce a valuable society; and even in the existing world the goods of the mind are at least as important as the goods of the body. It is exclusively among the goods of the mind that the value of philosophy is to be found; and only those who are not indifferent to these goods can be persuaded that the study of philosophy is not a waste of time.

. . . Philosophy is to be studied, not for the sake of any definite answers to its questions, since no definite answers can, as a rule, be known to be true, but rather for the sake of the questions themselves; because these questions enlarge our conception of what is possible, enrich our intellectual imagination and diminish the dogmatic assurance which closes the mind against speculation; but above all because, through the greatness of the universe which philosophy contemplates, the mind also is rendered great, and becomes capable of that union with the universe which constitutes its highest good.

Bertrand Russell
The Problems of Philosophy (Oxford: Oxford University Press, 1912), selections from Chapters 1, 14, and 15.

Having a job at a fast-food restaurant, for example, is probably not your idea of an ultimate end. You have the job to make money. But money is probably not your ultimate goal either. You want it to pay for clothes, food, or a car. These in turn are supposed to make you happy. Happiness is an example of an ultimate end. It makes sense to ask, "Why do you want that money?" because for most people money is important only as a means to other things. But we do not ask, "Why do you want to be happy?" because we see happiness as an ultimate end, an end in itself, and not merely a means to something else.

Technology is chiefly concerned with means to specific ends, not with ultimate ends. As important as this kind of knowledge is, it cannot make us happy. For instance, many people see the global problems of oil spills, destruction of the atmosphere and the rain forests, terrorism, the breakdown of family values, high crime rates, drug abuse, and so on as evidence of a world crisis. A growing number of social commentators attribute this crisis in part to the fact that we concentrate too much on technical solutions, too much on factual information and statistics, and too little on basic thinking skills, moral reasoning, and sensitivity to ultimate ends.

It may be that we expend too much of our energy and intelligence addressing **timely questions**. Timely questions involve current issues, issues

TIMELY QUESTIONS

Questions involving issues that are important to a particular time or place.

Reprinted by permission of NEA, Inc.

that are important to a particular time or place. They focus on strategies for solving technical or specific problems: Can we find a substitute for fossil fuel? How can we improve the quality of education? Where's the best place to invest my lottery winnings? Timely questions can be very important, but they address only part of the human condition. How and in what order we answer today's timely questions should depend on our ultimate goals and most basic values. We can discover what they are only by asking another kind of question.

First learn, then form opinions.

The Talmud

Timeless Questions

A **timeless question** is one that has been asked in virtually every culture for which we have historical records. Timeless questions concern ultimate values, general principles, and the very nature of reality, knowledge, justice, happiness, truth, God, beauty, and morality. Philosophy addresses the timeless questions that other kinds of thinking cannot.

Timeless philosophical questions include some of the "big questions" referred to above: Does life have any purpose? Does my life have a purpose? Is there a God? If so, how should I live? If not, how should I live? Is it possible to escape suffering? Why not commit suicide? Is it really better to be good than evil? Are people basically good or bad? Does might make right? Is pleasure the same thing as good? Is the happiness of the greatest number always to be pursued? Are we free or the products of fate? Is it possible to turn the other cheek? Is it desirable? Are we part of nature or overlords of it? Is truth relative?

Such questions cannot be answered in the sense that a mathematical or factual question can be answered with "4" or "A.D. 1066." Timeless questions must be asked and answered anew by each culture and by any person who awakens to what Plato and Aristotle called the philosophical

TIMELESS QUESTIONS

Questions concerning ultimate values, general principles, and the very nature of reality, knowledge, justice, happiness, truth, God, beauty, and morality; asked in virtually every culture.

sense of wonder. Indeed, individuals must wrestle with these most basic questions throughout their lives.

In my own case, many of the answers to timeless questions I found as a freshman have long since ceased to satisfy me. In fact, today I have more questions and fewer answers than I did thirty-plus years ago when I was bitten by a philosophical gadfly named Socrates (Chapter 3). And yet my questions of today are more satisfying than my answers of yesterday. If this pattern keeps up, I'll have fewer and fewer answers but more and better questions for the rest of my life. Of course, this pattern unsettles lots of folks. There's an enormous industry based on providing them with "the answer." It has a religion branch, a psychology branch, a biology department. And let's not forget the astrologers and psychics or all those friends and acquaintances who know exactly how things are—and answer us before we even realize we have any questions.

Philosophical Query

Do you agree that timeless questions are important in a practical way? That is, do you think that a person needs to address timeless issues in order to be happy? Is being happy the same thing as living a good life? Is it the same as living a full life? If you had the choice of being happy and unaware or aware but not always happy, which would you choose? Discuss and explain your answers to these questions. Are any of them timeless questions? Why or why not?

Areas of Philosophy

In general, philosophy consists of the systematic, comprehensive study of certain questions. For the most part, philosophical questions involve meaning, interpretation, evaluation, and logical or rational consistency. The primary areas of philosophy are delineated below.

Metaphysics addresses the problem of what is real. Metaphysical questions concern whether or not we have free will; how the mind and body are related to each other; whether there can be a supernatural, immaterial level of existence; whether personal immortality is possible; and what the nature of reality is.

Epistemology, the study of knowledge, poses questions about the relationship of faith to reason; the difference between knowing that we know and believing that we know; whether all knowledge comes from the senses; the roles of reason and experience in determining the truth; the characteristics of artificial intelligence; and the nature of truth.

Axiology, the study of values, questions whether or not value judgments are more than matters of opinion, the relation between facts and values, and to what extent, if any, values can be objective.

METAPHYSICS

Branch of philosophy that addresses the problem of what is real.

EPISTEMOLOGY

Branch of philosophy that studies the nature and possibility of knowledge.

AXIOLOGY

Branch of philosophy that studies values in general.

Ethics includes the careful analysis of moral problems such as capital punishment, suicide, lying, sexual conduct, and unfair discrimination; the possibility of a universal moral code; and the characteristics of the good life.

Aesthetics is the study of art and raises questions about the nature of beauty, the proper uses of art, and whether or not the artist's opinion of her artwork is always correct.

Political philosophy includes the study of the state and the nature of sovereignty. It addresses the right to exercise power and the limits of the state or government.

Social philosophy is concerned with the effects of social institutions on individuals, race and gender relations, and comparisons of various types of societies.

Logic, the study of the rules of correct reasoning, includes the analysis of different kinds of evidence; the study of analogies and comparisons; precise standards of proof; the relationship between what we say and what we mean; the adequacy of feelings of certainty; and the identification of misleading arguments and reasoning errors.

Philosophers sometimes concentrate on one primary area or another. Today some philosophers go so far as to reject whole areas of philosophy as unfit for study. For example, a logician might view metaphysics as overly abstract and confused; a moral philosopher might see the study of symbolic logic as belonging to mathematics, not philosophy. Whenever philosophers concern themselves with the meaning of life or the general search for wisdom, however, all of these primary areas are involved, even if some are not dealt with explicitly.

Contemporary academic philosophers tend to specialize within these primary areas, concentrating on historical periods, certain philosophers, the philosophy of music, religion, or law, for example, or on particular philosophical issues. More than two hundred areas of specialization are currently listed by the Philosophical Documentation Center.

ETHICS

Branch of philosophy concerned with the good life and with moral value and moral reasoning.

AESTHETICS

Branch of philosophy that studies all forms of art.

POLITICAL PHILOSOPHY

Branch of philosophy concerned with the state and issues of sovereignty.

SOCIAL PHILOSOPHY

Branch of philosophy concerned with social institutions and relations.

LOGIC

Branch of philosophy that studies the rules of correct reasoning.

Philosophical Archetypes

In cartoons a sage or guru is often depicted wearing a robe of some sort, maybe carrying a staff, and sporting a long white beard. Why do you suppose that is? One possibility is that cartoonists have tapped into a basic image shared by many cultures.

In China and Japan, the sage is a "wise guide"; in some other parts of Asia, a yogi or guru; in parts of Africa, a witch doctor; among Native Americans and the nomadic tribes of Asia, a shaman. In the Bible, the prophets were people of wisdom. In many cultures, the "grandmother"

No Age Is Forbidden Us

The only people who are really at leisure are those who take time for philosophy. They alone really live. It is not their lifetime alone of which they are careful stewards: they annex every age to their own and exploit all the years that have gone before. Unless we prove ingrate, it was for us that the illustrious founders of divine schools of thought came into being, for they prepared a way of life. . . . No age is forbidden us, we have admittance to all, and if we choose to transcend the narrow bounds of human frailty by loftiness of mind, there is a vast stretch of time for us to roam. We may dispute with Socrates, doubt with Carneades, repose with Epicurus, transcend human nature with the Stoics, defy it with the Cynics. Since nature allows us to participate in any age, why should we not betake ourselves in mind from this petty and ephemeral span to the boundless and timeless region we can share with our betters? . . . The philosopher's life is therefore spacious; he is not hemmed in and constricted like others. . . . all ages are at his service.

Seneca
The Stoic Philosophy of Seneca,
trans. Moses Hadas (New York:
W. W. Norton, 1958), pp. 65–67.

ARCHETYPE

Basic image that represents our conception of the essence of a certain type of person; according to psychologist C. G. Jung, some of the images have been shared by the whole human race from the earliest times.

PHILOSOPHICAL ARCHETYPE

A philosopher who represents an original or influential point of view in a way that significantly affects philosophers and nonphilosophers: cynic, saint, pessimist, optimist, atheist, rationalist, idealist, and such.

or "grandfather" or some other elder also represents this basic image. In the West, the wise person is often depicted as a male, but not always.

What I have referred to as a basic image is also known as an **archetype**. According to psychologist C. G. Jung, an archetype is an image that has been shared by the whole human race from the earliest times. In its more traditional sense, an archetype represents our conception of the essence of a certain kind of person. An archetype is a fundamental, original model of some type: cynic, saint, pessimist, optimist, atheist, rationalist, idealist, and so on. A **philosophical archetype** is a philosopher who expresses an original or influential point of view in a way that significantly affects subsequent philosophers and nonphilosophers.

The difference between an archetype and an *ideal* is that the archetype need not be good or perfect. The difference between an archetype and a *stereotype* is one of depth. A stereotype is a simplistic distortion of a type of person. An archetype, by contrast, is a powerful representation of a fundamental response to universal experiences. Archetypes exemplify essential ways of coping with the universal aspects of life (suffering, death, loss, society, wealth, knowledge, love, purpose) in uncommonly pure ways. There are archetypes of evil as well as good and of foolish as well as wise responses to life.

This book is an introduction to philosophy in its original, *archetypal* sense—the search for wisdom—organized around philosophical archetypes. Philosophy in this sense is philosophy that confronts life by offering consolation or criticism, ways to succeed in the world, or ways to withdraw from it. Even those people who have not studied philosophy recognize the basic qualities of many philosophical archetypes. Most likely

Archetypes of wisdom appear in many forms, from the rational Greek sophos *(above) to the whirling Sufi dervish (right).*

you have already encountered individuals who resemble some of them. Two brief examples will show you what I mean.

One philosophical archetype is the skeptic (Chapter 9). Skeptics believe that any claim to knowledge must be personally verified by their own sense experience. They want to see, touch, taste, or measure everything. The New Testament contains an excellent example of this archetype in the person of Doubting Thomas, the disciple who would not believe that Jesus had risen from the grave until he carefully examined Jesus' wounds for himself. Another philosophical archetype is the unreflective hedonist (Second Interlude). Unreflective hedonists live only for intense, immediate pleasure. They seek instant gratification and don't worry about the long-range consequences of what they do. They are pretty easy to identify.

The philosophers we will meet include archetypes of these and other significant philosophical schools and orientations. These archetypes are often the founders of the schools they represent; if not, they are important exponents of them. In addition to their significance in the history of philosophy, the archetypes confront timeless questions in ways that remain uniquely interesting and engaging in light of today's timely concerns.

A special virtue of archetypes is their intensity and purity in relation to their philosophies. They are strict advocates of a philosophical worldview or philosophical method. The intensity with which they hold to their views, combined with philosophical depth and rigor, almost always challenges our own, often unclarified beliefs—whether we want it to or not. Never fear. You alone always remain responsible for what you choose,

To be a philosopher is not merely to have subtle thoughts, nor even to found a school, but to so love wisdom as to live, according to its dictates, a life of simplicity, independence, magnanimity, and trust.

Henry David Thoreau

There is a principle which is a bar against all information, which is proof against all arguments and which cannot fail to keep a man in everlasting ignorance—that principle is contempt prior to investigation.

Herbert Spencer

Since ignorance is no guarantee of security, and in fact only makes our insecurity still worse, it is probably better despite our fear to know where the danger lies. To ask the right question is already half the solution of a problem. . . . Discerning persons have realized for some time that external . . . conditions, of whatever kind, are only . . . jumping-off grounds, for the real dangers that threaten our lives.

C. G. Jung

reject, or modify. If you give them a chance, the archetypes can give you a clear picture of both a philosophy and the kind of philosopher who tries to live it. They may also give you a better sense of your own present philosophy of life, or at least some aspects of it.

The heart of philosophy in this archetypal sense always includes the search for wisdom. That's the common theme in this book. Philosophers may do battle over what is and is not wisdom, but all philosophers remain lovers: lovers of truth, lovers of clarity, lovers of wisdom and the pursuit of it.

Are Philosophers Always Men?

The history of Western philosophy contains mostly male representatives, most of them of European ancestry. This has led to the sarcastic but important charge that Western philosophy is nothing but the study of "dead white males." Even though there are increasing numbers of women and other non-European minorities entering the ranks of professional philosophy today, men still outnumber women among professional philosophers.

Although throughout history individual women were recognized for their insight and brilliance, most of them remained—or were kept—outside of the formal history of philosophy. In our own time things are a little better. Although Susanne Langer, L. Susan Stebbing, Simone de Beauvoir, Simone Weil, Ayn Rand, Christina Hoff Sommers, Alison Jaggar, and Susan Moller Okin, among many others, have achieved renown as philosophers, philosophy has lagged behind the social sciences in providing opportunities for women. Ruth Benedict, Margaret Mead, Marie Louise von Franz, Karen Horney, and Carol Gilligan are well-known examples of more widely influential women in such fields as anthropology and psychology. (In Chapter 15, we'll take a look at the work of some contemporary women philosophers.) We can expect to see more and more women philosophers, until at last philosophy becomes a truly *human* pursuit of wisdom.

Because the history of Western philosophy has been increasingly dominated by an emphasis on logical reasoning and written argument, other expressions of wisdom have been given less attention. Also, until the eighteenth century, most Western philosophers represented a small class of highly educated men, able to support themselves independently or associated with the church or some other source of income. Only with the increasing influence of great public universities were higher education and philosophy open to people from ever-widening backgrounds. And even then, philosophers tended to remain members of an educated male elite.

Consequently, wisdom found among other cultures or expressed in other ways has been overlooked by many philosophers. Only relatively recently have professional philosophers begun to recognize other rich expressions of philosophical ideas: the shamanic traditions of Native American, South American, African, and Asian cultures; the oral traditions of Eastern European Hasidic Judaism, Sufism; and so forth. There has also always been a powerful tradition of applied philosophy, which challenges the status quo and confronts social institutions. In recent times it has found especially effective and powerful expression among philosophers concerned with the environment, animal rights, family structure, racism, and sexism.

But there is no escaping the fact that the history of Western philosophy is predominantly male-influenced, shaped by a strong preference for rational and objective evidence as opposed to more holistic and intuitive approaches to problems. The pervasiveness of this orientation makes it imperative that we at least acknowledge this problem.

Mary Ellen Waithe of the University of Minnesota is the head of a team of scholars that has compiled a valuable four-volume series called *A History of Women Philosophers*. In the following passage she notes firsthand the difficulty of filling in gaps in the history of philosophy:

> On a sweltering October afternoon in 1980 . . . I sought comfort in the basement library of City University of New York's Graduate Center. I came upon a reference to a work by Aegidius Menagius [on the history of women philosophers] published in 1690 and 1692. I had never heard of any women philosophers prior to the 20th century with the exceptions of Queen Christina of Sweden, known as Descartes' student, and Hildegard von Bingen, who lived in the 12th century. . . .
>
> It took sixteen months to obtain a copy of Menagius' book. . . . As it turns out, many of the women he listed as philosophers were astronomers, astrologers, gynecologists, or simply relatives of male philosophers. Nevertheless, the list of women alleged to have been philosophers was impressive.
>
> . . . By the end of 1981 I had concluded that the accomplishments of some one hundred or more women philosophers had been omitted from the standard philosophic reference works and histories of philosophy. Just check sources such as *The Encyclopedia of Philosophy*, Copleston, Zeller, Bury, Grote and others. If the women are mentioned at all, it is in passing, in a footnote.[1]

Most of our sources will reflect the historical limits of Western philosophy, but that will not prevent us from looking at such interesting and important non-Western philosophers as Buddha, Chuang-tzu, and Lao-tzu in the Third Interlude. In Chapter 15, we'll look at intriguing "postmodern" challenges to traditional ways of philosophizing as we consider the matter of emerging archetypes. We'll discuss questions being raised about whether or not it's possible to be objective, and if it is possible,

Let no one be slow to seek wisdom when he is young, nor weary in the search thereof when he is grown old. For no age is too early or too late for the health of the soul. And to say that the season for studying philosophy has not yet come, or that it is past and gone, is like saying that the season for happiness is not yet or that it is now no more.

Epicurus

One may view the history of philosophy as a history of heresy.

Walter Kaufmann

There is no such crime as a
crime of thought; there are
only crimes of action.

Clarence Darrow

whether it is desirable. We'll ask if philosophers can justify standing back
and commenting on life, or are obligated to become activists and reformers. We'll look at Martin Luther King, Jr., Malcolm X, and Cornell West
as possible exemplars of the contemporary prophet archetype and see if,
perhaps, the feminist is emerging as an archetype.

The history of philosophy is a living thing. It is still being written. Perhaps you will contribute to it. Eventually all facets of wisdom may be
equally welcome—and future textbooks will not have sections like this
one. And as you will quickly see, the ultimate issue is not who said something or who said it first, but whether it is true and worthwhile. Wisdom,
it seems, knows no color or gender.

The Pursuit of Wisdom

Where can we go to study wisdom? We don't find "Wise People" listed in
the Yellow Pages. We don't even find "Philosophers" listed, though things
may be changing—at least in Amsterdam, where "practicing philosophers" charge more than fifty dollars an hour. One of them is Ad Hoogen-
dijk, who says, "There's a new generation of philosophers who want to
take part in society, not just work in ivory towers . . . [who help people]
answer very basic questions like: 'Who are you, and what do you want
out of life?'" [2]

But even if we did find "practicing philosophers," we would still face
the problem of deciding whether to consult them. What criteria could we
use? After all, if I am not yet wise, how can I recognize a genuine wise
person?

Sometimes people cannot recognize wisdom, and then they get taken
in by a cult leader or other guru type claiming to show them "the" way to
happiness. And let's not forget that many of those who get taken are
highly educated, successful people. Clearly, then, there is a difference between knowledge and wisdom, just as there is between success and happiness. An underlying theme of this book involves distinguishing between
knowledge and wisdom.

Let's begin by seeing how knowledge differs from belief.

It is said that when Empedocles told Xenophanes that
it was impossible to find a
wise man, Xenophanes
replied: "Naturally, for it
takes a wise man to recognize a wise man."

philophaster: a pretender
or dabbler in philosophy.

Knowledge, Belief, and Ignorance

Trusting X to be true and knowing for ourselves that X is true are two
very different things. Intellectual honesty demands that I distinguish between what I know and what I think I know. Sadly, some people do not

Philosophy Is an Axe

There is a frozen sea within us. Philosophy is an axe.

Everything you believe is questionable. How deeply have you questioned it? The uncritical acceptance of beliefs handed down by parents, teachers, politicians, and religious leaders is dangerous. Many of these beliefs are simply false. Some of them are lies designed to control you.

Even when what has been handed down is true, it is not your truth. To merely accept anything without questioning it is to be somebody else's puppet, a second-hand person.

Beliefs can be handed down. Knowledge can perhaps be handed down. Wisdom can never be handed down. The goal of philosophy is wisdom. Trying to hand down philosophy is unphilosophical. Wisdom requires questioning what is questionable. Since everything is questionable, wisdom requires questioning everything. That is what philosophy is: the art of questioning everything.

Daniel Kolak and Raymond Martin
The Experience of Philosophy (Belmont, Calif.: Wadsworth, 1990), p. 2.

make this distinction. They confuse the quality of their beliefs with the intensity of their beliefs. In other words, they equate knowledge with belief.

Philosophers generally define **knowledge** as justified true belief. Thus, to know X means, first, that X actually is true; second, that I believe X to be true; and third, that I can justify my belief in X by providing "adequate evidence." Of course, these requirements raise some interesting questions. Is a strong personal feeling adequate evidence? How much proof is enough? According to whose criteria? The philosopher demands that we be able to articulate reasons to justify claims to knowledge.

Belief refers to the subjective mental acceptance that a claim is true. Beliefs—as distinct from knowledge—need not be true or adequately justified. Since beliefs are subjective mental states, it is possible to be firmly convinced that a belief is correct when it is not. Sometimes we are correct in our beliefs but cannot offer adequate evidence for them. We can have true and false beliefs, but technically speaking we cannot have false knowledge. Rather, what we thought we knew turns out to be mistaken. **Mere belief** is a conviction that something is true for which the only evidence is the sincere conviction of the believer.

If any position is sound and worth holding, there will be ample reasons for believing it. Questioning our beliefs is frightening only if we don't think they will survive serious study. If a position cannot survive reasonable questioning and cannot hold up against counterevidence, then the rational thing to do is to reject it. Yet it is quite common to encounter a wall of resistance to the spirit of wonder and inquiry: "I don't care what anybody says, nobody can convince me of X." "No, I haven't read the book. I know it's obscene without having to read it." "Nothing you can say will make me change my mind." "Once a Z always a Z, as far as I'm concerned."

KNOWLEDGE

Justified true belief.

BELIEF

Conviction or trust that a claim is true; an individual's subjective mental state; distinct from knowledge.

MERE BELIEF

A conviction that something is true for which the only evidence is the sincerity of the believer.

Even more subtly, we can shut off challenging questions by prejudging them, by being inattentive and bored when they come up, or by mocking other points of view without investigating them. When we do this, we hold on to a position regardless of the facts; we are indifferent to the possibility of error or enlightenment. Such an attitude is called **willed ignorance**, and it is as opposite from the love of wisdom as any attitude I can think of.

Philosophical Query

Have you ever been guilty of willed ignorance? If so, why do you think you were? Are you still? Why? What do you suppose the relationships between willed ignorance and arrogance and between willed ignorance and bored disinterest might be? What's the difference between willed ignorance and simply having made up your mind about something?

WILLED IGNORANCE

An attitude of indifference to the possibility of error or enlightenment that holds on to beliefs regardless of the facts.

"Isn't It All Really Just a Matter of Opinion?"

Does it ever occur to you that there's no way to ever settle certain kinds of disagreements because they're only about beliefs and opinions? Perhaps you don't have a problem with willed ignorance because, as you see it, "What's right for you may not be right for me. You believe whatever you want, and I'll believe whatever I want." This "mellow" relativism is almost the opposite of rigidly dogmatic willed ignorance. **Relativism** is the name for the belief that knowledge is determined by specific qualities of the observer. In other words, absolute (universal) knowledge of *the* truth is impossible—one opinion is as good as another.

Consider what many people think of as *the* "philosophical" question: What is the meaning of life? After all, there seem to be nearly as many answers as there are lifestyles. For some people, the meaning of life is fun, for others it's devotion to God, or learning as much as possible, or having a family, or being loved, or getting rich. Others insist that the very question is meaningless and a waste of time!

And what about the seemingly endless differences of opinion surrounding abortion, the right to die, capital punishment, the existence and nature of God, affirmative action, immigration policies, President Bill Clinton's moral character and whether or not Hillary Rodham Clinton is acting properly, and who's the greatest rock and roll singer in history. We haven't even gotten to evolution, alien autopsies, whether men are from Mars and women are from Venus, whether one race or gender is "superior" to another, or whether homosexuals are fit to raise children.

Amateur relativists can be heard saying things like: "Well, there's no way to decide if this particular affirmative action policy is better than that one. African Americans, women, and members of other protected classes favor it because they'll get first crack at all the good jobs, government grants, and scholarships. Middle-aged white males don't like it because

RELATIVISM

Belief that knowledge is determined by specific qualities of the observer, including age, race, gender, cultural conditioning.

now it's their turn to ride in the back of the social bus. It's always a matter of perspective." And "Professor, I think my essay grade is unfair. It's only your opinion. I mean this is not like science or math. Here in philosophy class, there's no real way to determine which opinion about Plato's theory of justice is true. Just because you've got a Ph.D. doesn't mean you're right. You're still just giving your opinion."

Somewhat more sophisticated versions of this line of reasoning are made by some social scientists along the lines that there is no way for one culture to judge another. In America, for instance, most of us think it's wrong to treat women as second-class citizens who should defer to their fathers, brothers, and husbands. But in some Middle Eastern countries, the notion that women should have social equality is viewed as absolutely wrong. Who are we, the relativist asks, to judge a completely different way of life?

> A closed mind is a dying mind.
>
> *Edna Ferber*

Various forms of relativism seem to be especially popular today. Sometimes relativism is advocated as a form of tolerance, a way of "honoring diversity." Thus, it is considered "elitist" or "racist" to insist that specific cultural, sexual, or religious values are the only correct ones or that some views are "better than" or "superior to" others and are thereby "entitled" to "impose" their standards on others. ("Who are you to correct my grammar?")

This is not the place to "settle" these perennial issues, but you'd do well at this stage to suspend any relativistic tendencies to resist thinking deeply and respectfully about the many philosophical positions we're going to examine. I suspect that sometimes relativism is the result of intellectual laziness: It's easier to accept all opinions than it is to sort through them thoughtfully. Further, by refusing to assert and defend a firm, thoughtful point of view we can avoid unpleasant or threatening disagreements. By refusing to take sides, we may hope to evade giving offense to or being excluded by those who disagree with us.

> Wisdom outweighs any wealth.
>
> *Sophocles*

It will be much more difficult to interest yourself in philosophy if you begin with an indifferent relativistic attitude. Philosophical relativism is much more interesting and challenging than simple, unreflective relativism, and we'll visit the issue throughout this text, beginning in Chapter 2 with the Sophists and continuing into discussions in Chapters 3 and 4 concerning Socrates' and Plato's efforts to refute sophistry right up to our look at contemporary or "postmodern" philosophies in Chapter 15.

And just in case you do think that right and wrong are entirely relative, let me just mention, without further comment, the Holocaust of World War II, child abuse, and my observation that every relativist I have so far met argues for his relativism or at least tries to give reasons why my nonrelativism is "inferior," "misguided," or "mistaken"—and usually gets angry when logical inconsistencies or contradictions in his position are identified.

So let's do our best to be tolerant in the sense of being willing to give philosophers a chance to make their case before we accept or reject it, but let's also resist any temptation toward cool indifference because everything's only an opinion anyway. If we give in this soon to either willed ignorance or relativism, we will fail to engage in philosophical speculation and will, at most, skim the surface of deep and invigorating waters.

I take the search for wisdom seriously, and I invite you to join me. It's time to take a closer look at wisdom.

Wisdom and Knowledge

WISDOM

General knowledge of what does and does not produce human happiness, including the difference between right and wrong combined with the desire and ability to act in basic accord with that knowledge.

THEORETICAL KNOWLEDGE

The accurate compilation and assessment of factual and systematic relationships.

PRACTICAL KNOWLEDGE

Consists of skills needed to do things like play the piano, use a band saw, remove a tumor, or bake a cake.

Wisdom is general knowledge of what does and does not produce human happiness. Wisdom requires knowing the difference between right and wrong combined with the desire and ability to act in basic accord with that knowledge. Unlike forms of knowledge based primarily on education and intelligence, wisdom involves an accumulation of experiences beyond the intellectual or theoretical variety. **Theoretical knowledge**, by contrast, is the accurate compilation and assessment of factual and systematic information and relationships. **Practical knowledge** consists of skills needed to do things, such as play the piano, use a band saw, remove a tumor, or bake a cake. All knowledge involves identification and justification in the form of logical arguments, scientific predictions, or the demonstration of skillful performance, depending on the kind of knowledge.

Philosophers generally separate knowledge from personality traits and moral character. This seems correct, for it is possible to be knowledgeable in one or many areas and foolish in others. It is also possible to be wise without being knowledgeable in many areas. A person may be wise without knowing the periodic table of elements or how to spell, balance a checkbook, remove a tumor, or bake a cake.

Traditionally, wisdom has been associated with maturity and experience in a way that knowledge has not. That is probably why wisdom is so often associated with the elders of a tribe or clan. Yet, clearly, age alone does not guarantee wisdom. Wisdom is also a function of personal, moral, intellectual, and spiritual growth. It is associated with personal virtue in a way that knowledge is not.

Philosophical Query

What is the relationship of increased awareness to wisdom? Is wisdom merely a matter of being more aware? What are some of the factors that may encourage or inhibit the development of wisdom? Some young people seem to be "wise beyond their years." What do you think might account for wisdom at an early age? On the other side of life, some older people seem exceptionally foolish for their age. What factors might account for this?

The Skills We Need Most

I cannot accept the idea that our proper schooling lies in the urbane skills of making conversation and making a living, each in its preferred style and time. Rather, the skills we need most are the skills of mortality—the soul and the spittle to accept and to share, decently, even nobly, even more graciously, a common human calling and a common human fate. The proper aim of education is then, above all else, not competence but wisdom, which has always been seen to be at one with holiness. It is fitting that education should undertake the discipline demanded for the full and decent living of one's life and dying of one's death. This wisdom and holiness and their attending discipline are not the preserve or the preoccupation of a single generation or time of life or period of history. They are the concern of the young when one is young and the concern of the old when one is old.

Robert E. Meagher
Cave Notes: First Reflections on Sense and Spirit (Philadelphia: Fortress Press, 1975), p. 3.

Learning Wisdom

Wisdom is not neat and orderly; it addresses the whole range of life, slopping over the boundaries of academic specialties. Further complicating the academic study of wisdom is the fact that wisdom is always concerned with the practical conduct of life; everything else is viewed in terms of its helpfulness to this purpose, including collecting facts and creating theories to explain them. Wisdom is not scientific or technical knowledge, though it may borrow from them. It involves insight and the capacity to learn from experience, but wisdom is not the same thing as educated intelligence. Albert Hakim puts it this way:

> Wisdom stands for more than the kind of knowledge a pilot has who knows how to set a compass for direction or the sociologist who knows the right sampling device for making a survey. We do not call the pilot or the sociologist "wise" because each knows how to use the compass or the sampling device. Wisdom looks for more; it touches a level where separate things can be seen in unity, or disparate things in interrelatedness.[3]

The sense of unity and interrelatedness that Hakim attributes to wisdom must be acquired through living as well as through thinking. Wisdom looks past accidental differences to the essences of things. Thus the pain of discrimination felt by a woman of color can give her a feeling of relatedness with the man who wasn't hired because he is too fat or the teenagers who are always unwelcome at the corner store, in a way that merely intellectual knowledge cannot provide. Passing on knowledge is the primary aim of education. When we go beyond education, beyond

The only important problem of philosophy, the only problem which concerns us and our fellow men, is the problem of the wisdom of living. Wisdom is not wisdom unless it knows its own subject and scope.

Lin Yutang

There is only one wisdom: to recognize the intelligence who steers all things through all things.

Heraclitus

learning what others have known, and try to apply their insights to life, we enter the realm of wisdom. The popular historian of ideas, Will Durant, knew this:

> Our culture is superficial today, and our knowledge dangerous, because we are rich in mechanisms and poor in purposes. The balance of mind which once came of a warm religious faith is gone; science has taken from us the supernatural bases of our morality, and all the world seems consumed in a disorderly individualism that reflects the chaotic fragmentation of our character. . . . We move about the earth with unprecedented speed, but we do not know, and have not thought, where we are going, or whether we shall find any happiness there for our harassed souls. We are being destroyed by our knowledge, which has made us drunk with our power. And we shall not be saved without wisdom.[4]

The Pursuit of Wisdom Can Be Dangerous

Serious thinking will inevitably challenge some of our present beliefs. The serious pursuit of wisdom demands that we question and perhaps reject some of the values we currently hold dear. This often makes other people uncomfortable, for it can reveal the weaknesses of their own ideas or their own complacency.

Over the years, students have told me about friends, advisers, or family members who warned them not to take philosophy classes, for reasons as old as the history of philosophy: "Philosophy will destroy your faith." "All philosophers do is criticize and tear down." "Philosophers are elitist; they make fun of democracy and America." "You'll only get stirred up. Philosophy questions everything, and then leaves you without any answers."

Such criticisms, though overly general and vague, are based on a sense of another, more personal kind of danger that is also part of thinking deeply. It is the danger of tearing down inadequate ideas and then finding nothing to replace them. This is a form of fear of the unknown. I know that sounds like a cliché, but fear of the unknown is a real, severely limiting fear. The pursuit of wisdom makes a direct assault on the unknown. No area is off-limits, no important question unasked.

Philosophical Query

Have you encountered any criticism of the dangers of philosophy? Was it informed or uninformed criticism? How did/would you respond to it?

Suppose that after taking a philosophy class, you lose your religious faith or change your attitude toward America or democracy. Would that mean philosophy had destroyed your beliefs? Is there another way to interpret what happened?

Can we not understand that all the outward tinkerings and improvements do not touch man's inner nature, and that everything ultimately depends upon whether the man who wields the science and the techniques is capable of responsibility or not?

C. G. Jung

Of what use is a philosopher who doesn't hurt anybody's feelings?

Diogenes

It Is a Shameful Question

The busy reader will ask, is all this philosophy useful? It is a shameful question: we do not ask it of poetry, which is also an imaginative construction of a world incompletely known. If poetry reveals to us the beauty our untaught eyes have missed, and philosophy gives us the wisdom to understand and forgive, it is enough, and more than the world's wealth. Philosophy will not fatten our purses, nor lift us to dizzy dignities in a democratic state; it may even make us a little careless of these things. For what if we should fatten our purses, or rise to high office, and yet all the while remain ignorantly naive, coarsely unfurnished in the mind, brutal in behavior, unstable in character, chaotic in desire, and blindly miserable?

. . . Perhaps philosophy will give us, if we are faithful to it, a healing unity of soul. We are so slovenly and self-contradictory in our thinking; it may be that we shall clarify ourselves, and pull ourselves together into consistency, and be ashamed to harbor contradictory desires or beliefs. And through unity of mind may come that unity of purpose and character which makes a personality, and lends some order and dignity to our existence.

Will Durant
The Mansions of Philosophy (New York: Simon & Schuster, 1929), p. x.

We ultimately suffer when we fail to address the fundamental issues of our lives: purpose, unity, and value. In a world of limited choices, given a life span of uncertain and finite scope, one of the most tragic wastes of a life is to settle for simply passing time from one event to another: drifting into a college major or a job or a marriage—in other words, living without a coherent vision. Without philosophizing at least a little bit, we do not live our lives—circumstances live us.

Once wisdom becomes our goal, we are dangerous to a social order that encourages conformity; to an educational system that exists primarily to train specialists; to a church that regards certain questions as blasphemous and heretical; to a society that pays an actor millions of dollars to appear in a film or an athlete millions of dollars to throw a ball a few months a year, yet pays its grade school teachers a comparably negligible amount; to a society that esteems as its highest bastions of learning universities whose most important professors sometimes resent having to do undergraduate teaching, and whose faculties cannot even agree on what the educated person must know.

Philosophy is dangerous whenever it is taken seriously. But so is life. *Safety is not an option.* Our choices, then, are not between risk and security, but between a life lived consciously, fully, humanly in the most complete sense and a life that just happens. In the end, as the poet says, the grave claims each of us. The issue, then, is how to live. No longer just what *can* I do, but what *should* I do? No longer just what is *true*, but what is *valuable* and *worthwhile*? Because of its fragility and finiteness, life is too important not to wonder about.

The effect of life in society is to complicate our existence, making us forget who we really are by causing us to become obsessed with what we are not.

Chuang-tzu

The recipe for perpetual ignorance is: be satisfied with your opinions and content with your knowledge.

Elbert Hubbard

© 1994 The Washington Post Writers Group. Reprinted with permission.

When you no longer just look but also notice, when you are no longer content to settle for never-questioned beliefs, when you are at last troubled by the inconsistencies among your own beliefs and actions, when the wind of wonder raises the hair on the back of your neck, then the spirit of the ancient wise ones catches fire one more time.

Summary of Main Points

1. The word *philosophy* comes from Greek roots meaning "the love of wisdom." The difference between expressing philosophical opinions and actually philosophizing involves the degree of rigor and discipline applied to our reflections. Philosophy in the original sense always includes the search for wisdom.

2. Ultimate ends are valued for their own sake, not as means to something else. Happiness is an example of an ultimate end.

3. Timely questions are concerned with means to specific ends and involve current issues that are important to a particular time or place.

4. Timeless questions have been asked in virtually every culture and concern ultimate values, general principles, and the very nature of reality, knowledge, justice, happiness, truth, God, beauty, and morality. Philosophy addresses timeless questions.

5. Philosophy in the original, archetypal sense is an activity as well as a fixed body of knowledge. A philosopher is a lover of wisdom, someone who has a compelling need to pursue wisdom.

6. Bertrand Russell said that philosophy is valuable because its emphasis on questions reveals unsuspected possibilities and because the greatness of the objects it contemplates frees us from narrow, personally limited perspectives.

7. The primary areas of philosophy are metaphysics (which addresses the problem of what is real), epistemology (the study of knowledge), axiology (the study of values in gen-

eral), ethics (which is concerned with the good life and moral reasoning), aesthetics (the study of art in all its forms), political philosophy (the study of the state), social philosophy (the study of social institutions and relations), and logic (the study of the rules of correct reasoning).

8. Philosophical archetypes are philosophers who express an original or influential point of view in a way that significantly affects subsequent philosophers and nonphilosophers. They are powerful representations of fundamental responses to universal experiences of suffering, death, loss, society, wealth, knowledge, love, and purpose.

9. The history of Western philosophy has been dominated by males of European ancestry, but increasing interest in women and non-European philosophers is expanding the scope and nature of philosophy.

10. Philosophers distinguish between knowledge (justified true belief), belief (an individual's subjective mental state), and mere belief (a conviction that something is true for which the only evidence is the sincerity of the believer).

11. Willed ignorance is an attitude of indifference to the possibility of error or enlightenment that holds onto beliefs regardless of the facts.

12. In contrast to willed ignorance, relativism is the name for the belief that knowledge is determined by specific qualities of the observer. In other words, absolute (universal) knowledge of the truth is impossible; "one opinion is as good as another."

13. Wisdom is general knowledge of what does and does not produce human happiness, including the difference between right and wrong, combined with the desire and ability to act in basic accord with that knowledge. Traditionally, wisdom has been associated with maturity (experience) and moral character.

14. Theoretical knowledge is the accurate compilation and assessment of factual and systematic relationships. Practical knowledge consists of skills needed to do things. Knowledge requires demonstration in the form of arguments, predictions, or performance, depending on the kind of knowledge.

15. Because wisdom involves insight and the capacity to learn from experience, it differs from educated intelligence. Wisdom is associated with a sense of unity that comes from living. Formal education is chiefly concerned with the transmission of knowledge and social skills. Wisdom goes beyond learning what others have known and applies their insights to life.

16. The pursuit of wisdom always changes us because serious thinking will inevitably challenge some of our present beliefs. No questions are off-limits to philosophy in the original sense, and this makes philosophical inquiry threatening to those whose allegiance is to their current beliefs. Philosophy is dangerous because it threatens to change our lives.

Study Questions

1. Distinguish between timely and timeless questions. Define each, and give examples.

2. How would you explain what philosophy is to someone who did not know?

3. Identify the primary areas of philosophy and give an example of the kinds of questions covered in each.

4. What does Bertrand Russell mean by "practical men"?

5. What is the value of philosophy, according to Russell?

6. What is an archetype? How does it differ from a stereotype? Give examples of each.

7. What are the advantages of studying philosophical archetypes?

8. Make the case that our culture is suffering from a kind of philosophical illiteracy. Don't be overly general. Cite examples and identify patterns. Why study philosophy?

9. Do you think that there should be "practicing philosophers"? Would they be more like priests or psychologists? Explain. Would you ever consult one? Why or why not?

10. What is wisdom? Explain how it is related to knowledge.

11. What do people mean when they say that philosophy is dangerous? Are they correct? Explain.

12. Do you think a universal hunger for meaning really exists? How good are we at satisfying it? Support your position.

13. Analyze your own education up to this point. In what ways has it hindered and in what ways has it supported your love of wisdom?

14. If you could make only one improvement in the American educational system, what would it be and why?

15. To what extent do you think gender and ethnic background should be considered in evaluating an individual's beliefs? Do gender, ethnic background, and other factors (age, income, and so on) control what we think?

Overview of
Classical Themes

Empty is the philosopher's argument by which no human suffering is therapeutically treated. For just as there is no use in a medical art that does not cast out the sicknesses of the bodies, so too there is no use in philosophy, unless it casts out the suffering of the soul.

Epicurus

There is, I assure you, a medical art for the soul. It is philosophy, whose aid need not be sought, as in bodily diseases, from outside ourselves. We must endeavor with all our strength to become capable of doctoring ourselves.

Cicero

We must not make a pretense of doing philosophy, but really do it; for what we need is not the semblance of health but real health.

Epicurus

The true lover of knowledge naturally strives for truth, and is not content with common opinion, but soars with undimmed and unwearied passion till he grasps the essential nature of things.

Plato

The unexamined life is not worth living.

Socrates

Western philosophy began in ancient Greece about eight hundred years before the time of Christ. At that time, the chief component of Greek culture was a powerful religious mythology. These early myths offered primitive explanations of natural phenomena, human history, and the gods. They provided standards of conduct, morality, social obligations, education, art, religious practices, and so on. The most important mythical view of life was expressed in the *Iliad* and the *Odyssey*, two epic poems attributed to the ancient Greek poet **Homer (c. eighth century B.C.)**.

For the Greeks of Homer's era, everything happened through some kind of divine agency. They believed, for example, that the sun was carried around the heavens by Apollo's golden chariot, that thunder and lightning were hurled down from the top of Mount Olympus by Zeus, and that the motion of Poseidon's trident created waves. Other natural phenomena were thought to have similar divine origins. The nature of the community, victory or defeat in war, the course of love, and other human affairs were also directly tied to the gods.

The ancient Greek gods were exaggerated human beings: bigger, stronger, faster, and so forth. Like human beings, they were also jealous, sneaky, biased, lazy, promiscuous, and violent. They were not, however, morally or spiritually superior to humans. In fact, the gods were often indifferent to human affairs, including human suffering, because they were involved in complicated soap operas of their own. Occasionally the gods took an interest in an individual human being or involved themselves in wars or politics, often treating people as pieces in an elaborate chesslike game.

Although the ancient Greeks' mythological accounting of events ultimately failed, it established two crucial principles:

1. There is a difference between the way things *appear* and the way *they really are*.
2. There are unseen causes of events; things happen as they do for some reason.

These insights marked a major advance beyond earlier, less critical characterizations of nature and society.

Greek mythology was not sheer fantasy; it was the product of a desire to find explanations. Science grew out of this search for explanations, and philosophy grew out of attempts to provide rational justification for these early prescientific explanations.

As ancient Greece developed, its social structure became less restrictive (though by no means democratic in the modern sense). Colonization of outlying cities and communities contributed to the rise of philosophy, as increased social and political freedom combined with an established culture to permit increasingly free inquiry and exchange of ideas.

Explaining events with "the gods willed it" may have been good enough when people had very little understanding of and control over their environment, but as Greek civilization grew, and as colonization led to increas-

Homer's Iliad *had a major impact on ancient Greek culture. This powerful tale of the Trojan war intertwined the lives of humans with the whims of Olympian gods and provided a mythical ideal of the hero.*

ing interaction with sophisticated nearby Eastern cultures, the mythological worldview became less effective.

The Presocratic philosophers challenged the mythological worldview by asking for rational explanations of questions that mythology could not adequately answer: "Why doesn't the earth fall out of the sky like an apple from a tree?" "What holds it up? And what holds that up?" "Why don't the stars fall out of the sky?" Or, more subtly yet, "How come if I eat fish and grain, I don't look like a fish or stalk of wheat? How does 'fish stuff' become fingernail 'stuff'? Where does the stone go that is worn away by the waterfall? I cannot see it being chipped away. What is this invisible 'stuff' that 'goes away'?" And, again: "Where did 'stuff' come from? Where does it go?" (See First Interlude for a fuller account of this stage of philosophical development.)

Nature and Convention

In their efforts to provide *unified* rational explanations, these early philosophers first concentrated on the "world order," *kosmos* in Greek, and "nature," *phusis* or *physis* in Greek. You may recognize the roots of the English words *cosmos* and *physics* in these ancient Greek terms.

Around the fifth century, an element of specialization emerged. Actually, the word "division" is probably more accurate than "specialization," since philosophers began to distinguish between **nature** (*physis*) and **convention** (*nomos*), rather than to specialize along narrower lines. The terms "norm," "normative," and "normal" derive from the Greek root *nomos*. Humanistic philosophers known as *Sophists* (Chapter 2) turned away from the study of nature and toward the study of "man."

Contemporary Lessons from the Past

You're right to wonder about the use of the word "man" here: The ancient Greek world was socially hierarchical and chauvinistic. It was hierarchical in its divisions of people into social classes of varying status, influence, and power according to nationality, bloodlines (a crude form of "racial" thinking), gender, language and dialect, talent, and beauty.

For many—but not all—classical philosophers, women were, by nature, not capable of philosophical reasoning and living. Of course, in this, the philosophers were not alone; they reflected the norms of their times, as did many women. Plato, arguably the single most influential Western philosopher, thought of women as "lesser men," although he also allows women in the ranks of the philosopher-kings who occupy the highest strata in his ideal state (Chapter 4). Aristotle (Chapter 5), one of the most significant thinkers in the history of Western philosophy, thought of women as "mistakes" of nature—"incomplete" or "misbegotten" men. Epicurus, the hedonist, on the other hand, made no philosophical distinctions between men and women (Second Interlude).

One of the most important and complex questions philosophers ask today concerns proper attitudes toward thinkers from the past. The Overview of Postmodern Themes addresses this issue directly, and reference to it recurs throughout our philosophical journey together. But at the beginning of this inquiry, let me encourage you to seek *empathetic understanding before passing judgment*.

FALLACY OF
ANACHRONISM

Error in reasoning that results from uncritically and rigidly applying contemporary values to past practices and ideas.

Practicing this principle helps avoid committing the **fallacy of anachronism**. We commit the fallacy of anachronism when we uncritically and rigidly apply our contemporary values to past practices and ideas by ignoring the historical, technological, cultural, and scientific context of those practices and ideas.

Even though we can never be sure that our current understanding of the past is "accurate," we can make good-faith efforts to understand the conditions that affected people's thinking and acting. This does not commit us to some form of *relativism* that prevents evaluating and ranking points of view and philosophical values. Rather, understanding the historical context that gives rise to philosophical expression can prevent us from overlooking the richness and complexity of the human condition. Further, we do not need to reject an entire philosophical enterprise just because we

Persons and Arguments

If we reject a philosopher's arguments because we object to that philosopher's personal habits or beliefs, we are guilty of the **ad hominem fallacy.** *We commit the ad hominem fallacy whenever we confuse an attack on the charac-* *ter of the arguer with a criticism of the argument. Ad hominem is* Latin for "at the man." In this context it means "against the arguer, against the person making the argument." Ironically and neatly, however, the term *ad* *hominem* presents us with one more case of the pervasiveness and ambiguity of terms based on the root "man": "mankind," "human," "chairman," "humanistic," even "woman."

find some aspect of it unacceptable—unless what's unacceptable is the heart of the enterprise or entailed by essential components of it.

The Search for Excellence

"Excellent" is a trendy term today. It pops up in a species slang ("Most excellent hat, dude!") and even gave rise to two movies celebrating *Bill and Ted's Excellent Adventures.* "Hey, they do pal around with Socrates, a most excellent philosopher!" (Chapter 3) At my college, as at many other schools, stodgy old departments and divisions have been transformed into *Centers of Excellence.*

One of the major themes in classical Greek philosophy is the search for virtue, *aretē* in Greek. *Aretē* also means "excellence" and is associated with potency, ability—functionality, in short. Thus, something lacking in "virtue" can be said to fail to function well or at all. In other words, without virtue, things are "dysfunctional."

The philosophical search for human excellence links the Sophists (Chapter 2) to Socrates (Chapter 3), Plato (Chapter 4), Aristotle (Chapter 5), the Stoics (Chapter 6), and the Hedonist (Second Interlude).

The Search for Happiness

Classical philosophers did not distinguish between "being good" and "being happy" the way many of us do today. Rather, they thought of "living the good life" as "living well," in the sense of thriving, of being healthy. *Eudaimonia* is the Greek word that most translators translate as "happy."

Today, most of us seem to equate "being happy" with some form of "personal satisfaction." Thus, if I *feel* happy I *am* happy. Let's think of that view as the contemporary view of happiness—happiness as a purely subjective experience. The classical notion of happiness is more complicated because it includes rational and objective components. According to this view, the individual is not the determiner of what is true, logical, or real. He or she only recognizes, deduces, infers, or experiences truth and reality.

A helpful analogy here is between *being healthy* and *feeling healthy* and *being happy* and *feeling happy*. It's easy to understand that Margaret may not be well just because Margaret feels well. In other words, Margaret can be unhealthy and feel fine. Conversely, Joe can be convinced that he is dying from cancer even though he is cancer-free. Further, unhealthy individuals can—because they are unhealthy—get used to being sick. Thus, the smoker "feels good" when she poisons herself with a puff on a cigar, but "feels bad" when she acts wisely and refrains from smoking.

Personally, I find the classical discussions of virtue, excellence, well-being, "living the good life"—living the best life possible for a human being—rich, illuminating, inspiring, and consoling. The addition of an objective component to the notion of happiness forces me, at least temporarily, to look beyond my feelings and ask myself if what I am satisfied with is worthy, is good enough, is "excellent."

Philosophy as a Way of Life

In the Continuative we'll look at the possibility of "philosophy as a way of life" today. For now, as you enter the world of classical philosophy, note the seriousness, the sacredness, with which many of these early philosophers viewed the personal, *engaged*, and *committed* pursuit of wisdom. Perhaps they had the "advantage" of living in "simpler times," ignorant of DNA, psychobiology, cultural diversity, and so forth; free of the complicated social, political, and economic factors that toss us about; free of the "cynical" effects of the widespread dissemination of contemporary knowledge and information via the Internet and mass media. Perhaps their optimistic love of wisdom and faith in the possibility of human excellence rested on ignorance and bias.

Perhaps so. But then again, perhaps there is some basic, fundamental human condition, some set of life circumstances and problems that underlie cultural and technological changes. And if so, perhaps the ancient "physicians of the soul" are worth a visit.

First Interlude
The Presocratic Sophos

Heraclitus

All things which have life, both the greater and the less, are ruled by mind.

Anaxagoras

The shaman and prophet are the two direct ancestors of the sage, the oldest philosophical archetype. The **sage** is an archetypal figure who combines religious inspiration with a love of wisdom. The word *sage* is derived from the Latin *sapiens*, meaning "wise." Today, the term *sage* is often used to refer to masters associated with religious traditions or to the wise elders of a group or tribe. Sages understand and teach the requirements of the good life, when the good life is understood to include peace of mind, compassion, social harmony, and respect for nature.

The sage has no exact equivalent in our society today. Sages perform a complex function: part therapist, part prophet, part philosopher, part friend. They appeal to our hearts and minds in their efforts to dissolve fragmentation and to heal alienation from our true selves, from each other, and from nature.

According to anthropologist Mircea Eliade, the **shaman** specializes in techniques for making contact with the sacred forces that govern the world by going "outside of" him- or herself.[1] In most tribal cultures, the shaman receives wisdom through a public initiation ceremony that involves ritualized suffering and ecstatic trance. Depending on the culture, a shaman may fly to heaven, walk on a rainbow, climb a sacred pole symbolizing the *axis mundi* that connects the earth to heaven, soar as a bird, become a fish, and so forth. In Asian cultures especially, the gods come to

SAGE

Derived from the Latin *sapiens*, meaning "wise"; in Asian traditions, an archetypal figure who combines religious inspiration with a love of wisdom; gurus, *yogis*, and Zen *roshis* are examples of sages; in Western traditions, the *sophos* and Hasidic *rebbe* fulfill the role of sage.

SHAMAN

A specialist in techniques for making contact with the sacred forces that govern the world by going "outside of" him- or herself; in tribal cultures the shaman usually receives wisdom through a public initiation ceremony that involves "ritualized suffering" and ecstatic trance, though in some cultures the gods come to the shaman.

31

Woman as Sophos

Aesara of Lucania (c. third century B.C.–first century A.D.) was a Pythagorean philosopher who has only recently attracted any attention. In the single existing fragment of her book, *On Human Nature*, she says that through the introspection and contemplation of our own souls we can discover the "natural" foundation of all law and the structure of morality. In the following passage, Aesara wisely acknowledges the importance of reason as a guide, without overlooking the importance of emotions. Reading it, we cannot help but wonder what philosophy may have lost by overlooking the contributions of women philosophers for so long.

By following the tracks within himself whoever seeks will make a discovery: Law is in him and justice, which is the orderly arrangement of the soul. Being threefold, it is organized in accordance with triple functions: That which effects judgment and thoughtfulness is [the mind] . . . that which effects strength and ability is [high spirit] . . . and that which effects love and kindness is desire. These are all so disposed relatively to one another that the best part is in command, the most inferior part is governed, and the one in between holds a middle place; it both governs and is governed.

. . . And indeed, a certain unanimity and agreement in sentiment accompanies such an arrangement. This sort would justly be called good

---

I have heard many men talk, but none who realized that understanding is distinct from other knowledge.

Heraclitus

PROPHET

From the Greek roots *pro* (before) and *phanai* (to speak), originally a prophet was a person who spoke with divine guidance and who was said to be able to predict the course of events; prophets functioned as religious leaders and teachers, as advisers to rulers, and cried out for justice and mercy in the face of tyranny.

the shaman. Among Native Americans, the "vision quest" is a regular part of moving from adolescence to adulthood.[2]

Though primarily a healer and a link between the living and dead for his or her tribe, the shaman's reports of visionary experiences reaffirm, clarify, and shape the tribe's fundamental beliefs about the nature of the universe and the people's relationship to it. The shaman expresses the sacred wisdom of nonliterate cultures.

The term **prophet** comes from the Greek roots *pro* (before) and *phanai* (to speak). Originally, a prophet was a person who spoke with divine guidance and who was said to be able to predict the course of events. Prophets functioned as religious leaders, teachers, or advisers to rulers, and often cried out for justice and mercy in the face of tyranny.

Shamans and prophets appear in both Western and Eastern cultures. In ancient Egypt, the priest filled the role of shaman-prophet, and in Persia (now Iran), Zoroastrian prophets known as *magi* were highly respected for their wisdom. Prophets such as Elijah, Jeremiah, and Hosea were the conduits of God's will (wisdom) in Old Testament Judaism. Muhammad was known as the *rasul* of early Islam, the prophet of God, the messenger commanded to recite Allah's sacred *Qur'an*. In early Christianity, Jesus fulfilled the role of a prophet—communicating the divine will to nonliterate people. In prephilosophical ancient Greece, priests and oracles performed the shamanistic-prophetic role when the Olympian religion dominated Greek culture.[3] The prephilosophical shaman-prophet developed order, whichever, due to the better part's ruling and the inferior part's being ruled, should add the strength of virtue to itself. Friendship and love and kindliness, cognate and kindred, will sprout from these parts. For closely-inspecting mind persuades, desire loves, and high spirit is filled with strength; once seething with hatred, it becomes friendly to desire.

Mind having fitted the pleasant together with the painful, mingling also the tense and robust with the slight and relaxed portion of the soul, each part is distributed in accordance with its kindred and suitable concern for each thing: mind closely inspecting and tracking out things, high spirit adding impetuosity and strength to what is closely inspected, and desire, being kin to affection, adapts to the mind, preserving the pleasant as its own and giving up [reasoning] to the thoughtful part of the soul. By virtue of these things the best life for man seems to me to be whenever the pleasant should be mixed with the earnest, and pleasure with virtue. Mind is able to fit these things to itself, becoming lovely through systematic education and virtue.

Holger Thesleff, "Pythagorean Texts of the Hellenistic Period," in Mary Ellen Waithe, ed., *Introduction to the Series, A History of Women Philosophers*, vol. 1, 600 B.C.–A.D. 500, trans. Vicki Lynn Harper (Dordrecht: Martinus Nijhoff Publishers, 1987), pp. 20–21.

into the wise person known as the **sophos,** or sage, from the Greek word for "wise." What we know of them is fragmentary and intriguing.

Philo-Sophia: Strangeness and Wonder

In his book *Philosophy as a Way of Life*, French philosopher Pierre Hadot says that in the ancient world, to be a philosopher implied "a rupture with . . . *bios,* that is daily life." Signs of this rupture included ignoring or challenging convention by refusing to do such expected and "normal" things as practicing a trade (having a regular job) or pursuing wealth and fame. In other words, one common image of the original philosopher is the stereotype of the shabby, unkempt, "absent-minded," starry-eyed dreamer and asker of silly questions. Whether such a figure is viewed as "eccentric" and "amusing," or "subversive" and "dangerous," he (very rarely she) lived and spoke in ways that were interpreted as showing disregard for conventional values, and that set him or her apart from "regular folks" living "normal" lives.[4]

This "strangeness" would have been seen as even more disturbing, more abnormal, even "perverse," in the cases of ancient women philosophers. Sometimes, for both females and males, even a slight resemblance to being "a philosopher" provokes uneasy, mixed reactions: "Yep, my son's really bright. I just can't figure out why he wants to major in *philosophy*! When

SOPHOS

Sage or wise man; term applied to the first philosophers; from the Greek word for "wise."

The decrees of the people are in large measure repealed by the sages.

Seneca

I was in college, the philosophy majors were really weird. Kind of scruffy. Snooty. Probably couldn't cut it in the real world. You know, couldn't get dates. Couldn't make the team. Kind of lazy—didn't care if they could get a job or not. Weird!"

Unfortunately, it seems as if a similar attitude reflecting suspicion of philosophers is still with us, at least in some quarters. During their 1996 presidential election campaigns, for example, both Bill Clinton and Bob Dole criticized "cynicism," one of the sophos-based philosophies we will examine in Chapter 6. The common notion of "cynics" seems to be of unwholesomely negative and distrustful individuals who stand outside of the American mainstream, who may even be "anti-American" for refusing to "join the team." ("If you're not an active part of the solution, if you're only sitting on the sidelines criticizing, then you're part of the problem.") And, of course, understandable economic pressures to get the kind of education that will make graduates "marketable in the twenty-first century" reinforces the idea that any college student preferring a philosophical education to a "practical" one is "unrealistic" and "self-indulgent"—strange. "There's something 'not quite right' about people who aren't particularly interested in the pursuit of success, popularity, and wealth."

As the platitude reminds us, however, "The more things change, they more they stay the same." Consider this intriguing passage from Hadot referring to a legal decree from third-century Rome:

> Jurists too considered philosophers a race apart. According to [the third-century jurist] Ulpian, in the litigation between professors and their debtors the authorities did not need to concern themselves with philosophers, for these people professed to despise money. A regulation made by the emperor Antoninus Pious on salaries and compensations notes that if a philosopher haggles over his possessions, he shows he is no philosopher. Thus philosophers are strange, a race apart. Strange indeed those Epicureans [Second Interlude], who lead a frugal life, practicing total equality between the men and women inside their philosophical circle—and even between married women and courtesans; strange, too, those Roman Stoics [Chapter 6] who disinterestedly administer the provinces of the empire entrusted to them and are the only ones to take seriously the laws promulgated against excess. . . . Strange indeed all those philosophers whose behavior, without being inspired by religion, nonetheless completely breaks with the customs and habits of most mortals.[5]

Socrates (Chapter 3), perhaps the most-recognized example of the ancient Western *sophos*, was called *atopos* ("unclassifiable") because he was a "philo-sopher" in the archetypal sense: a person in love with wisdom. In Plato's *Symposium*, Diotima, an ancient woman philosopher whom Socrates refers to as one of his teachers, says that wisdom is not a human state; it is a level of perfection and knowledge that can only be "divine." In

Men have talked about the world without paying attention to the world or to their own minds, as if they were asleep or absent-minded.

Heraclitus

In Greece wise men speak and fools decide.

Anacharsis

Reason is immortal, all else is mortal.

Pythagoras

other words, falling in love with wisdom is foreign to the ways of the world, and the *sophos* will always be a "stranger to the world."[6]

First Philosophers

The very first Western thinkers identified as philosophers were initially concerned with questions about the nature of nature (*physis*) and the "world order" (*kosmos*). Today, we would classify many of their concerns as scientific. Thus, we notice an ambiguity in the early use of the word "philosopher" that carries over into the present day. On the one hand, the *sophos*, who is wise, is seen as a kind of prophet-priest-therapist, whereas the *philosopher*, who is in love with wisdom but not necessarily wise, is seen as an unusual sort of thinker or truth-seeker. As you read the various fragments from the Presocratic philosophers, note how frequently they refer to the natural ordering of the cosmos in mytho-ethical terms that retain the poetic resonance of the *sophos*. Although it is common to refer to the Presocratics as philosophers, we must not overlook their dual natures during this period when the division between the philosopher and the sage first appears.

The earliest philosophers are referred to as the *Presocratics* because they appeared prior to Socrates, the first major figure in the Western philosophical tradition. The Presocratics are also known as *proto-scientists* because they took steps to transform mythology into rational inquiry about nature and the cosmos. Originally, the difference between a *sophos* who became a *philosopher* and one who became a *proto-scientist* was one of subject matter; later it became one of method. In Chapter 2, we will see how this difference in focus resulted in the emergence of philosophers chiefly interested in human behavior and customs.

A general understanding of the development of Presocratic philosophy is helpful for placing subsequent philosophical issues and disagreements in context. And a sense of context is needed if we are to apply our principle of "understanding before evaluating" to the philosophies we will meet later.

As significant and interesting as the Presocratics are, they lived and thought in a radically different world from ours. Consequently, what is obvious to us may have been unthinkable in their world, and what was obvious to them may be obscure or unfathomable to us.[7]

> The sage probes, not the fact of survival, but the reasons.
>
> *Guan Yin*

> Nature loves to hide.
>
> *Heraclitus*

> There are in fact two things, science and opinion: the former begets knowledge, the latter ignorance.
>
> *Hippocrates*

The Search for a Common Principle

Traditionally, the first Western philosopher is said to have been **Thales (c. 624–545 B.C.).** Thales lived in the city of Miletus, part of a Greek colony on the Asian coast in an area known as Ionia. His parents are thought to have been Phoenician.

The Olympian god Atlas was said to support the world on his shoulders. Growing dissatisfied with such mythological accounts of natural phenomena, Presocratic philosophers sought rational explanations.

Thales so surpassed those who preceded him that everyone has forgotten them.

Simplicius

MONISM

General name for the belief that everything consists of only one, ultimate, unique substance such as matter or spirit.

RATIONAL DISCOURSE

The interplay of carefully argued ideas; the use of reason to order, clarify, and identify reality and truth according to agreed-upon standards of verification.

For the most part, it seems that Thales was absorbed in his speculative studies, devoting only the minimum effort necessary to his financial affairs. In one of the earliest "absent-minded professor" stories, Plato records that Thales fell into a well "when he was looking up to study the stars . . . being so eager to know what was happening in the sky that he could not see what lay at his feet."[8]

Philosophically, Thales is significant for his attempt to find a common source, a single substance underlying all things. For him, this basic "stuff" was water. Aristotle says that Thales "observed" that "the nutriment of everything is moist, and that . . . the seeds of everything have a moist nature; . . . and that from which everything is generated is always its first principle."[9]

The great power of Thales' insight was not his specific conclusion that all things are water, but his reduction of all things to one substance. The name for such single-substance philosophies is **monism**, the belief that reality is essentially one—either one reality, one process, one substance, one structure, or one "ground."

Thales' belief that everything is composed of water was a major move beyond mythological accounts of nature because it rested on systematic, rational evidence and careful observation, rather than mythical stories and poetic images. Thales tried to "figure out" or reason his way to a theoretical explanation of the changes he saw throughout nature. His ideas inspired others to refine or reject them—based on carefully *reasoned* arguments. The resulting interplay of carefully argued ideas became known as **rational discourse**: the use of reason to order, clarify, and identify reality and truth according to agreed-upon standards of verification. In his last years, Thales was accorded the title *sophos* by common opinion.

But what "holds up" the water that Thales claimed the earth floats on? Thales' pupil **Anaximander (611–546 B.C.)**, who was also from Miletus, made a major step forward in philosophical reasoning when he offered a purely rational explanation for what holds the earth in place, an explanation that does not rest on experience. According to Anaximander, the earth stays where it is because where it is is at the precise center of the cosmos, "not supported by anything but resting where it is because of its equal distance from everything."[10]

According to Aristotle, Anaximander's reasoning rested on what is now known as the **Principle of Sufficient Reason** (nothing happens without a reason) and went like this: "There is no reason why what is situated in the middle and is similarly related to the edges should move upwards rather than downwards or sideways. But it cannot move in opposite directions at the same time. So it necessarily rests where it is."[11]

Anaximander developed Thales' recognition of the need for a unifying principle to explain natural occurrences by providing *a systematic explanation* of the origin of life. He thought that in the beginning the earth was fluid, and that an external source of heat dried some of it. The dried sections became land. Variations in temperature caused winds, and living organisms arose at varying stages of this drying-out process.[12]

The Problem of Change

Anaximander thought that particular "stuffs" emerged in pairs of opposites (hot-cold, dry-wet, hard-soft, and so on) from a vast "Indefinite-Infinite" called the **apeiron**. He believed that a continuous exchange of opposites can be seen throughout nature, as cold winter becomes warm spring, which becomes hot summer, which becomes cool fall, which becomes cold winter, and on and on. When, for example, hot comes into existence, cold returns to the apeiron, and vice versa. The single surviving fragment of Anaximander's actual words refers to this continuous, mutual destruction of opposites: "They give justice and reparation to one another for their injustice in accordance with the arrangement of time."[13]

Thales' direct legacy culminated in Anaximander's pupil, **Anaximenes (died c. 500 B.C.)**, the third of the Presocratic Milesian philosophers. Anaximenes' notion that the first, universal, underlying element is *air*, or *pneuma*, was yet a further refinement of philosophical reasoning. **Pneuma** is the ultimate, pervasive spirit that holds the world together.

Just as Anaximander identified problems in Thales' thinking, Anaximenes recognized an important question raised by Anaximander's doctrine: On one hand, Anaximander characterized the apeiron as indefinite or "boundless"; on the other hand, he insisted that the apeiron is one thing.

PRINCIPLE OF SUFFICIENT REASON

The principle that nothing happens without a reason; consequently, no adequate theory or explanation can contain any brute, crude, unexplained facts. First specifically encountered in the work of the medieval philosopher Peter Abelard (1079–1142), it is usually associated with the rationalist philosopher Gottfried Wilhelm Leibniz (1646–1716), who used it in his famous "best of all possible worlds" argument.

APEIRON

According to Anaximander, the first principle from which all existing things develop, a vast "Indefinite–Infinite"; the apeiron is an infinite mass of forces with no specific qualities.

PNEUMA

According to Anaximenes, the ultimate, pervasive spirit that holds the world together; all things are produced by either "rarefaction" of the *pneuma*, which creates fire, or condensation of the *pneuma*, which creates (in order of density) wind, cloud, water, earth, and stone.

How can *one thing* contain *many particular things* and still be only one thing? In what sense is it "one thing" then? If it is indefinite, limitless, how can it be a "single thing"?

Anaximenes advanced the search for a common principle with the introduction of the argument that *qualitative* differences can result from *quantitative* changes. Rather than pairs of opposite stuffs, Anaximenes proposed two opposing *processes of exchange: condensation and rarefaction*. In Anaximenes' cosmology, in its pure, original state, air (*pneuma*) is invisible. Pure air becomes progressively denser through the process of condensation, in the following stages: air → fire → wind → cloud → water → earth → stone. Matter becomes progressively lighter during the process of rarefaction: stone → earth → water → cloud → wind → fire → air. Thus, the ongoing cosmic and natural cycle of generation and destruction provides a single underlying world order that itself stays the same throughout all change: air ↔ fire ↔ wind ↔ cloud ↔ water ↔ earth ↔ stone.

If correct, Anaximenes' argument could account for the *process* of change, but it is not clear that it can account for the problem of "the one and the many," the problem of explaining how completely different kinds of things ("stuffs") can "come from" a single primal "stuff." What sort of primal "stuff" could account for the generation of secondary "stuffs"? Let's see how the most important of the Presocratic philosophers addressed the problem of "the one and the many."

> You cannot conceive the many without the one.
>
> *Plato*

> Things perish into those from which they have been born.
>
> *Anaximander*

Parmenides

> [The path] that it is not . . . is bound not to be: this I tell you is a path that cannot be explored; for you could neither recognize that which is not, nor express it.
>
> *Parmenides*

Parmenides of Elea (fl. fifth century B.C.) radically transformed the early philosophers' interest in cosmology, the study of the universe as a rationally ordered system (cosmos), into ontology, the study of "being." Parmenides was probably born around 515 B.C. in Elea, a Greek colony in southern Italy. His work was a major influence on Plato, who suggests that Parmenides and his pupil Zeno (see box, pages 40–41) came to Athens, where they met young Socrates.[14]

According to Parmenides, none of his predecessors adequately accounted for the process by which the one basic stuff of the cosmos changes into the many individual things we experience everyday. In his search for a solution to the problem of "the one and the many," Parmenides turned to an analysis of the process of change itself.

What Is Not, Is Not, and What Is, Is

Parmenides presented his philosophy in the form of a poem called *On Nature*, which recounts how a goddess revealed "the whole truth" to Parmenides. In this poem, the goddess identifies three possible "paths" of study and understanding and indicates that only one is true.

Parmenides' reasoning is based on two key premises: "What is, is" and "What is not, is not." "What is not" equals "not being"—nothing, or not anything at all. In other words, the term *nothing* does not name anything. It is impossible to even imagine nothing. According to Parmenides, strictly speaking, "nothing" can never refer to any thing or object. Thus, strictly speaking, the sentence "Nothing exists" is self-contradictory. The Parmenidean nothing paralyzes reason: Lacking any content whatsoever, it cannot be comprehended at all. Since it cannot be comprehended, it cannot be described—there is nothing to refer to.

Parmenides was a monist who characterized the one real thing as *being*. "What is" equals being. According to Parmenides, being is purely positive, simple, and unconditioned. That is, being is one, eternal, and indivisible; it is the "unchanging one." *Not-being*, in contrast, is negative, complex, and impure. Being ("what is") can be conceived of and expressed. Not-being ("what is not"), as we have seen, is unintelligible; it "paralyzes" thought and is inexpressible.

> It is both necessary to say and think that *being* is; for to be is possible, and nothingness is not possible.
>
> *Parmenides*

> How could being perish? How could it come into being? If it came into being, it is not; and so too if it is about to be at some future time.
>
> *Parmenides*

Being and Change

According to Parmenides, change and variety (the many) are only *appearances*; they are not *real*. Parmenides placed all sensations in the realm of appearance. In other words, *reality* cannot be apprehended by the senses. If this is true, then our most commonly held opinions are "mere opinions," and most of us are unaware of reality, which is one being.

Parmenides associated being with correct thinking and not-being with illusion. Correct thinking is always about being, according to Parmenides, because we can only think about subjects that exist, that *are*: "In fact it is the same thing to think and to be."[15]

Being must be eternal because to come from something other than being would be to come from not-being—which would be to come from nothing, and nothing can come from nothing. Being cannot change into something else because to do so would require being to be not-being—a clear impossibility.

Being is not a "principle" or fundamental "stuff" like the basic principles of the earlier Presocratic philosophers. Parmenides thought that being is perfect and complete, or "whole." Thus, it cannot move or change. Philosophical historian Giovanni Reale characterizes Parmenidean being as "the being of the visible cosmos, immobilized, and to a great extent purified, but still clearly recognizable."[16]

Being is recognized by *reason* as a perfect whole, as One. Yet our senses only experience *becoming*: living and dying, moving, changing. The *senses cannot recognize being*, much less can they discover that being is One. In other words, you cannot see, touch, taste, hear, or smell being. In

> The unnameable is the eternally real.
>
> *Lao-tzu*

> [T]here are many signposts . . . that being has no coming-into-being and no destruction, for it is whole of limb, without motion, and without end. And it never was, nor will be, because it is now, a whole all together, one, continuous; for what creation of it will you look for? How, whence sprung? Nor shall I allow you to speak or think of it as springing from not being; for it is neither expressible nor thinkable that what is not is.
>
> *Parmenides*

Zeno's Paradoxes

Zeno of Elea (c. 490–430 B.C.) forcefully defended the idea that change in the form of motion is impossible. These intriguing paradoxes present one of the earliest examples of a particular method of proof known as a **reductio ad absurdum** (reduce to absurdity). In a *reductio*, an opponent's position is refuted by showing that accepting it leads to absurd, unacceptable, or contradictory conclusions. Zeno is credited with perfecting a way of revealing an idea's absurdity by: (1) showing that accepting it leads to a logical contradiction, or (2) showing that it leads to a logical conclusion that is somehow obviously ridiculous because it offends either our reason or common sense.

Using a form of the *reductio*, Zeno tried to show that the Her-aclitean claim that everything is always changing is absurd because the very idea of change or motion is absurd. The paradoxes also reveal the ultimate inadequacy of the Presocratic notion of the continuum.

Zeno's paradoxes were admired by ancient philosophers and continue to generate lively discussions among contemporary philosophers. See what you make of the three most famous.

The Dichotomy

The first argument is this: if movement exists, it is necessary that the mobile [moving thing] traverse an infinite number of points in a finite time; but this is impossible, hence movement does not exist. Zeno demonstrated his position affirming that whatever is moved must traverse a certain distance: but any distance is divisible to infinity, what is moved must first traverse half of the distance and then the whole of it. But first he must traverse the entire half of the distance, and the half of that and the new half of the previous half. But if the halves are infinite in number, since for every whole taken it is possible to take half, then it is impossible to traverse in a finite time an infinite number of points. . . . Then, given that every magnitude admits of infinite divisions, it is impossible to traverse any magnitude in a finite time.

Simplicius
In Aristotle's Physics, 1013.4ff.; quoted in Giovanni Reale, *A History of Ancient Philosophy vol. 1, From the Origins to Socrates*, trans. John

REDUCTIO AD ABSURDUM

From the Latin for "reduce to absurdity"; form of argument that refutes an opponent's position by showing that accepting it leads to absurd, unacceptable, or contradictory conclusions because: (1) accepting it leads to a logical contradiction, or (2) it leads to a logical conclusion that is somehow obviously ridiculous because it offends either our reason or common sense.

his poem, the goddess advises Parmenides to follow reason rather than the senses because only by reasoning can being be recognized as One. The senses can only perceive things as discrete, as many. Parmenides' poem views the world of the senses as corrupted by appearances and by "mere belief" in the reality of not-being.

Most startling of all, Parmenides "solved" the problem of the *appearance of change* by concluding that the very concept of change is self-contradictory. What we think of as change is really an illusion. The reasoning runs as follows: "Change" equals transformation into something else. When a thing becomes "something else," it becomes what it is not. But since it is impossible for "nothing" (what is not) to exist, there is no "nothing" into which the old thing can disappear. (There is no "no place" for the thing to go into.) Therefore, change cannot occur.[17]

Whatever the power of Parmenides' vision of being as One, change and motion remain basic facts of experience for most of us. The unpopu-

R. Catan (Albany: State University of New York Press, 1987), p. 91.

Achilles and the Tortoise

The second [paradox] is the so-called "Achilles," and it amounts to this, that in a race the quickest runner can never overtake the slowest, since the pursuer must first reach the point whence the pursued started, so that the slower must always hold a lead. This argument is the same in principle as that which depends on bisection [cutting the distance in half], though it differs from it in that the spaces with which we successively have to deal are not divided into halves. The result of the argument is that the slower is not overtaken: but it proceeds along the same lines as the dichotomy argument (for in both,

a division of the space in a certain way leads to the result that the goal is not reached, though the Achilles goes further in that it affirms that even the quickest runner in legendary tradition must fail in his pursuit of the slowest). . . .

Aristotle, *Physics*, Hardie and Gaye translation, 239B.14ff.

The Flying Arrow

The argument of Zeno, beginning from the premise that everything which occupies a space equal to itself either is in motion or is at rest, that nothing is moved in an instant, and that the mobile always occupies in each instant a space equal to itself, seems to adjust itself in this way: the flying arrow in every instant occupies a place equal to itself, and thus,

for the whole time of its motion. But what occupies in an instant a place equal to itself does not move because nothing is moved in an instant. Hence the flying arrow, as long as it is in motion, does not move for the whole time of its flight.

Simplicius, *In Aristotle's Physics*, 1015.19ff.; in Reale, *A History of Ancient Philosophy vol. 1, From the Origins to Socrates*, trans. John R. Catan (Albany: State University of New York Press, 1987), p. 93.

larity of an opinion is not a measure of its merit, however. And Parmenides' position was the product of careful reasoning in a way that "common sense" rarely is. Further, Parmenides' contemporaries took his arguments seriously, and Parmenides' notion of being played an important part in the development of Plato's theory of forms (Chapter 4).

The Pluralists

The next major shift in Presocratic philosophy was the emergence of **pluralism**, the belief that there exist many realities or substances. Building on Parmenides' belief that motion is impossible because there is no empty space (no "what is not"), **Empedocles (c. fifth century B.C.)** concluded that reality must be "completely full." According to Empedocles, reality is a *plenum* without any gaps.

PLURALISM

The belief that there exist many realities or substances.

Because he agreed with Parmenides that nothing comes into existence or goes out of existence, Empedocles decided that all motion and change take place *within* existing reality. Things do not move into empty space but exchange places with each other.

According to Empedocles, rather than an unmoving One (*being*), reality consists of six basic components: four basic "roots" and two basic "motions." The roots are: earth, air, fire, and water. Each root is eternal—uncreated, indestructible, and unchanging. The two basic motions are *Love*, which unites different things, and *Strife*, which breaks things up into their basic elements. Wisdom falls under the domain of Love, being of "like by like," and ignorance falls under the domain of Strife, being of "unlike by unlike."[18]

According to Empedocles, at the beginning of the "world cycle," the four roots were all mixed together, under the motion of Love. Eventually, Strife took over and the four roots separated into their own individual domains. Once Strife dominates and the four elements are completely separate, Love reemerges and the process repeats itself.[19]

In the beginning of the separation process, according to Empedocles, certain "mixtures" of elements could not survive. But in the course of the great random "mixing together" of different combinations, survivable combinations would eventually result. It is chance, in the form of "random combinations," then, that accounts for human beings and all other things that are part of this particular world cycle.

Empedocles was not consistent in his attitude toward the evolutionary cycle he describes. Although he sometimes talks about "accidental" combinations, his whole tone shifts when he talks about the world cycle or process itself. He uses the term *god* for the process—which he worships. The god of Empedocles lacks a body and is "only a sacred and unutterable mind flashing through the whole world with rapid thoughts."[20]

Mind

Anaxagoras (c. 500–428 B.C.) realized that Empedocles' four basic roots were no more helpful in explaining change and transformation than water, apeiron, or pneuma were. "How," he wondered, "could hair come from what is not hair or flesh from what is not flesh?"[21]

Anaxagoras rejected Empedocles' two fundamental motions, Love and Strife. In their place he posited **Nous** (Greek for "mind"). Nous is the "all-pervading Mind which imposes (brings about) an intelligible pattern in an otherwise unintelligible universe." Nous affects all things without being in them, but it is not a process or force in the contemporary scientific sense. The fragments of Anaxagoras reveal difficulty in clearly articulating the nature of Nous. Some passages stress that Nous "sets all things in order," but others treat it as purely mechanical.[22]

Many a head came to birth without a neck.

Empedocles

For already have I once been a boy and a girl, a bush and a bird and a dumb sea fish.

Empedocles

NOUS

From the Greek for "mind"; according to Anaxagoras, "the all-pervading Mind which imposes (brings about) an intelligible pattern in an otherwise unintelligible universe"; a material being that affects all things without being in them.

According to Anaxagoras, in the beginning everything was so evenly distributed that it would have been impossible to recognize things as we now know them. Then Nous produced a kind of "shuffling" in which individual things were separated out, much like separating out the suits of a deck of cards that have been randomly put together.

Anaxagoras's concept of Nous provided "one of the most powerful intuitions . . . in the whole course of Presocratic philosophy . . . that the [basic] principle is an infinite reality, separate from everything else."[23] The beautiful and haunting Fragment 12 is worth reading carefully:

> All things which have life, both the greater and the less, are ruled by mind. Mind took command of the universal revolution, so as to make (things) revolve at the outset. At first things began to revolve from some small point, but now the revolution extends over a greater area, and will spread even further. And the things which were mixed together, and separated off, and divided, were all understood by mind. And whatever they were going to be, and whatever things were then in existence that are not now, and all things that now exist and whatever shall exist—all were arranged by mind, as also the revolution now followed by the stars, the sun and moon, and the air and aither [ether] which were separated off. It was this revolution which caused the separation off. And dense separates from rare, and hot from cold, and bright from dark, and dry from wet. There are many portions of many things. And nothing is absolutely separated off or divided the one from the other except mind. Mind is all alike, both the greater and the less. But nothing else is like anything else. . . .[24]

If "nothing is absolutely separated off or divided the one from the other except mind," then change is not the transformation of one kind of stuff into another kind, but the combining or mixing of "ultimate stuffs" according to the operations of Mind (Nous).

Anaxagoras believed that "in everything there is a portion of everything."[25] A fingernail, for example, contains bits of whale and plum. Any given sensible stuff contains bits of an infinite variety of ultimate stuffs or "seeds." What we see when we look at a fingernail "or at anything" is the dominant stuff in the mixture. Our eyes and other senses are too gross (unrefined) to see everything: "From the weakness of our sense we are not able to judge the truth. What appears is a vision of the unseen."[26]

If there are seeds of every kind of stuff in every sensible thing, clearly they must be very, very small. Indeed, in order for a very small thing like a speck of dust or diamond chip to contain seeds of *every* other kind of thing, these seeds must be infinitely small. If this is so, then things as we perceive them must be composed of tiny "bits" or seeds that we cannot see individually. We can see things only when seeds are combined in sufficient quantity. The wedge between appearance and reality has been driven in another notch.

Mind began to revolve first from a small beginning; but the revolution now extends over a larger space, and will extend over a larger still. . . . And this revolution caused the separating off, and the rare is separated off from the dense, the warm from the cold, the light from the dark, and the dry from the moist.

Anaxagoras

How can you hide from what never goes away?

Heraclitus

Our knowledge of matter at this level is no longer derived from direct sensory experience, and therefore ordinary language is no longer adequate to describe the observed phenomena.

Fritjof Capra

The Atomists

Although Anaxagoras and Empedocles did not solve the problem of "the one and the many," they helped further clarify it by drawing more refined attention to the key questions that any adequate explanation must answer: How does the world of things as we ordinarily perceive them "emerge from" some kind of basic stuff that is quite different in its characteristics from the things of our experience? How can the variety of colors, textures, odors, densities, and so on that we see all around us "come from" a single, completely different something else?

The Parmenidean assault on the senses was not adequately "resolved" until the middle of the fifth century B.C., when **Leucippus of Miletus (c. fifth century** B.C.**)** and **Democritus of Abdera (c. 460–370** B.C.**)** argued that there are many "ones." Leucippus is credited with being the originator of atomism, and Democritus further developed his ideas. **Atomism** is the materialistic view that the universe consists entirely of empty space and ultimately simple entities that combine to form objects. The most thorough expression of early atomism occurs in the Roman poet **Lucretius's (c. 98–55** B.C.**)** great poem, *De Rerum Natura*. Lucretius's poem helped popularize the ideas of both Democritus and Epicurus (Second Interlude).

Atoms and the Void

Rather than reject Parmenidean being by denying the obvious—the existence of motion, variety, and change—Leucippus argued that there are many "ones," or beings. According to Leucippus, being is infinite. Democritus termed these "ones" atoms.

The word *atom* comes from the Greek *atomos*, meaning "indivisible," "having no parts," or "uncuttable." **Atoms** are minute material particles, the ultimate material constituents of all things. According to Democritus, atoms have properties such as size, shape, position, arrangement (combination), and motion, but they do not possess sensible qualities like color, taste, temperature, or smell. However, combinations (compounds and composites) of atoms can grow large enough for us to perceive.

Democritus argued that atoms must be so small that they are invisible to the naked eye. Being so small, they are "uncuttable"—thus they cannot be destroyed. In other words, atoms are eternal. Because motion is an inherent property of atoms, they are constantly moving, bumping into each other and bouncing away or quivering in one spot.

Accepting Parmenides' fundamental division between being and not-being, Democritus reasoned that not-being cannot exist since it "is not." Further, Democritus argued, the absence of not-being is not the same thing as the absence of empty space. Space is empty, Democritus stated, when it

---

ATOMISM

Early Greek philosophy developed by Leucippus and Democritus and later refined by Epicurus and Lucretius; materialistic view that the universe consists entirely of empty space and ultimately simple entities that combine to form objects.

ATOMS

From the Greek *atomos*, meaning "indivisible," "having no parts," or "uncuttable"; minute material particles; the ultimate material constituents of all things. Atoms have such properties as size, shape, position, arrangement (combination), and motion, but lack qualities like color, taste, temperature, or smell.

PARMENIDES

Being   Not-Being
(What Is)   (What Is Not)

DEMOCRITUS

Being   Not-Being
(What Is)   (What Is Not)

Atoms   Void
(Things)   (No-Things)

Figure I1.1 *Comparison of two conceptions of reality.*

does not contain "things" or "bodies." Space can be empty of bodies without being empty of being.

Democritus further reasoned that it is possible to separate "ones" from each other by empty space devoid of any bodies. The **void** is Democritus's term for no-thing (no-bodies), or empty space. *No-thing* is not the same as *nothing*. Parmenides failed to make this important distinction, according to Democritus. Perhaps the profound significance of Democritus's argument can be better grasped if we compare a Parmenidean picture of reality with a Democritean picture, shown in Figure I1.1.

Reason and Necessity

According to Democritus, things come into existence when atoms combine in certain ways, and they go out of existence when their parts or atoms separate. Stable substances and things are composed of highly compatible atoms, and less stable ones are composed of less compatible atoms. Marble, for instance, contains more stable atoms than nitroglycerin.

If we ask why certain things exist, Democritus's answer is that given the eternal swirling of atoms, some collisions are bound to stick due to the nature of the atoms involved. There is no divine order, no Nous or intelligence guiding or combining these atoms. All that exists in this view are atoms and the void—nothing else. There is no intentional order or *purpose* to the universe, though there is *predictability*. That is, "nothing occurs at random." Mechanical laws of motion explain everything; there is no deeper or higher explanation. What appears to be chance is simply a lack of information and knowledge. If we could observe a long sequence of atomistic behavior the way we might observe a game of billiards, we could—in theory—predict the future positions and combinations of various atoms.

Nature and Convention

We never experience atoms directly, according to Democritus. Shape, taste, and other sensible properties are the result of "effluences" and "images"

VOID

Democritus's term for no-thing (no-bodies); empty space in Atomist theory.

Not even the gods fight against necessity.

Diogenes Laertius

Knowledge is not intelligence.

Heraclitus

One ought not to talk or act as if he were asleep.

Heraclitus

Not I but the world says it: All is one.

Heraclitus

Through the Logos all things are understood yet men do not understand as you shall see when you put acts and words to the test I am going to propose: One must talk about everything according to its nature, how it comes to be and how it grows.

Heraclitus

as we sense atoms striking the eye, ear, skin, tongue, and so on. Thus, we are "cut off from the real" because our sensations are products of our own particular condition: our sensory acuity, whether we are sick, and so forth.

Not only do we never experience atoms directly, even perceptual qualities—like sweet and sour, hot and cold, smooth and rough, hard and soft—are matters of convention, not nature: "Sweet exists by convention, bitter by convention, color by convention; but in reality atoms and the void alone exist," according to Democritus.

Although Democritus rejected the skeptical implications of this insight, subsequent philosophers have elaborated on them with stunning effect. In subsequent chapters we shall look at some of the far-reaching consequences engendered by the issue of what is true by nature and what is true by convention. (See especially Chapters 2–4, which cover some of the most exciting aspects of this struggle, and Chapters 8–10, which concern the modern search for an answer to skepticism.)

Heraclitus of Ephesus

A native of Ephesus, a city on the Ionian coast north of Miletus, **Heraclitus (fl. 500 B.C., d. 510–480 B.C.)** is one of the most important and enigmatic of the Presocratics. Although virtually nothing is known of his life, the extant written fragments of Heraclitus reveal a powerful intellect, a profound artist, and a withering social critic.[27] Greatly admired by the Cynics and Stoics (Chapter 6), Heraclitus was claimed by Nietzsche (Chapter 14) as a philosophical ancestor. The Sophists, Plato, and Aristotle (Chapters 2, 4, and 5) were also influenced by Heraclitus's ideas. Because the available fragments of Heraclitus's work are pronouncements rather than arguments, philosophers profoundly disagree over their meaning. The summary that follows concentrates on the Heraclitean emphasis on the power of discourse, the underlying "tension" or struggle between opposites that sustains all existing things, and the compelling and disturbing use of "war" as a dominant philosophical motif.

The *Logos*

According to Heraclitus, ignorance occurs when people do not comprehend the basic structure of the human *psyche* (soul) and its relationship to the universal principle through which all things come to exist. Heraclitus called this universal principle *logos*.

The Greek word *logos* is rich and complex, meaning all of the following: "intelligence," "speech," "discourse," "thought," "reason," "word," "meaning," "study of," "the record of," "the science of," "the fundamental principles of," "the basic principles and procedures of a particular discipline," "those features of a thing that make it intelligible to us," and "the rationale for a thing."

Although *logos* retains these associated meanings for Heraclitus, in its most important sense the **Logos** was *the rule according to which all things are accomplished and the law which is found in all things.*[28] Heraclitus says that there is one *Logos* to which everyone ought to listen, although he thinks that most people are unable to comprehend it. Some recent commentators suggest that the Heraclitean *Logos* is both *an account of reality* and *that which is revealed by* the account. The *Logos* is the fundamental reason for things being as they are; it is the fundamental principle of the world.[29]

The Heraclitean capital-L *Logos* is like God, only without the anthropomorphizing (humanizing) of the earlier philosophers and poets who attributed human qualities to the gods. According to Heraclitus's impersonal view of God, the *Logos* is a process, not an entity. As such, the *Logos* is unconcerned with individuals and human affairs, in much the same way that gravity affects us but is unconcerned with us.

Heraclitus's rich use of language reflects his attempts to express the "universal law" of the *Logos*. His use of the imagery of fire, thunderbolt (lightning), war, perpetual change, and so forth add a mystical quality to fragments about the *Logos*, which may account for some of Heraclitus's persistent appeal. Another possible source of this persistent appeal may be rooted in a widespread, transcultural affinity with Heraclitus's conviction that the world order must be intelligent, that a nonintelligent world order is impossible.

Heraclitus distinguished "comprehension" and "understanding" from "knowledge," and being "asleep" or "dreaming" (ignorance and foolishness) from being "awake" (seeing through ignorance to the wisdom that comes only from recognizing the *Logos*).

Heraclitus thought that the *Logos* is very close to us. For Heraclitus, the love and pursuit of wisdom is the love and pursuit of the *Logos*. He rejected all other conceptions of wisdom because they were not based on comprehension of the *Logos* as it operates in all things: "There is only one wisdom: to recognize the intelligence who steers all things through all things."[30]

Appearance and Reality

According to Heraclitus, even though many things appear to remain the same, "Change alone is unchanging."[31] Traditionally it has been held that Heraclitus went so far as to claim that *everything is always changing all the time.* But whether he really meant that everything is always changing, or that individual things are held together by energy (change), remains unclear.

LOGOS

One of the richest and most complex terms in ancient philosophy; associated meanings include: "intelligence," "speech," "discourse," "thought," "reason," "word," "meaning"; the root of "log" (record), "logo," "logic," and the "ology" suffix found in terms like sociology and physiology; according to Heraclitus, the rule according to which all things are accomplished and the law which is found in all things; according to the Stoics, World Reason, also referred to as Cosmic Mind, God, Zeus, Nature, Fate: the force that governs the world.

Man, who is an organic continuation of the *Logos*, thinks he can sever that continuity and exist apart from it.

Heraclitus

One cannot step twice into the same river, for the water into which you first step has flowed on.

Heraclitus

The Cosmic Music of the Spheres

About 530 B.C., **Pythagoras of Samos** (sixth century B.C.) left the Greek mainland for the Greek colony of Crotona in southern Italy, where he established a religious community that existed in one form or another for hundreds of years. The Pythagorean community eventually developed important mathematical and philosophical ideas that grew out of efforts to purify the psyche.

Although we know that Pythagoras was a historical figure, it is difficult to determine exactly what Pythagoras himself taught. He wrote nothing, and the ideas of other members of the community were attributed to him as a sign of respect and as a way of lending weight to the ideas. Plato and Aristotle rarely assign ideas to Pythagoras himself, although Pythagorean ideas seem to have influenced Plato's philosophy.

Pythagoreans asserted that number is the first principle of all things. They were the first systematic developers of mathematics in the West, and discovered that natural events could be described in mathematical terms, especially as ratios.

To the Pythagoreans, the "principle of number" accounted for everything. Number was a real thing. Somehow, numbers existed in space, and not just as mental constructs. *One*, for instance, was a point, *two* a line, *three* a surface, *four* a solid, and so forth. The earth, being a solid, was associated with the cube; fire was associated with the pyramid, air the octahedron, and water the icosahedron. From this perspective, all things "follow rules," and are "ordered."

According to Pythagorean doctrine, the entire universe is an ordered whole consisting of harmonies of contrasting elements. The Greek for "ordered whole" is **cosmos**. The Pythagoreans were the first philosophers to use the term *cosmos* to refer to the universe in this way. In contrast to the nearly mystical quality of the Heraclitean Logos, the Pythagorean cosmos is acces-

---

COSMOS

Greek term for "ordered whole"; first used by the Pythagoreans to characterize the universe as an ordered whole consisting of harmonies of contrasting elements.

Heraclitus's concept of change is not what you and I usually mean by change. Remember, he implied that *everything is always changing*. Our common experience suggests that, on the contrary, many things "stay the same" for very long periods of time; most things do not change all the time. In order to reconcile the common perception of permanence with his belief that everything is always changing, Heraclitus distinguished between *appearance* and *reality* in a way that contrasted *apparent permanence* with the *hidden reality* of continuous change.[32] According to Heraclitus, the harmonious quality of the "hidden reality" cannot be grasped by the senses, but only by "seeing" or "hearing" the *Logos*: "The unseen design of things is more harmonious than the seen."[33] The harmony that Heraclitus refers to is not, as you might expect, a pleasant and gentle mixing or commingling of complementary forces. Rather, it is harmony created by tension.

War and Strife

Heraclitus claimed that the world exists in a constant struggle between opposing forces. He compared stability (permanence) to the kind of tension a bent bow or stringed musical instrument is under: "We do not nosible to arithmetic, geometry, and rationality on a far greater scale. Rationality and truth are both functions of number.

The "celestial music of the spheres" is the hauntingly beautiful phrase the Pythagoreans coined to describe the sound of the heavens as they rotate according to cosmic number and harmony. One point of view held that because we have been exposed to the music of the spheres from birth we do not hear it. Other Pythagoreans thought that the music of the spheres was beyond the range of human hearing. Aristotle says:

> Some thinkers [Pythagoreans] suppose that the motion of bodies of that size must produce a noise, since on our earth the motion of bodies far inferior in size and speed of movement has that effect. Also, when the sun and moon, they say, and all the stars, so great in number and in size, are moving with so rapid a motion, how should they not produce a sound immensely great? Starting from this argument and from the observation that their speeds, as measured by their distances, are in the same ratios as musical concordances, they assert that the sound given forth by the circular movement of the stars is a harmony. Since, however, it appears unaccountable that we should not hear this music, they explain this by saying that the sound is in our ears from the very moment of birth and is thus indistinguishable from its contrary silence, since sound and silence are discriminated by mutual contrast. What happens . . . then, is just what happens to coppersmiths, who are so accustomed to the noise of the smithy that it makes no difference to them.

Aristotle, *De Caelo*, trans. J. L. Stocks, 290B12; in G. S. Kirk and J. E. Raven, *The Presocratic Philosophers* (Cambridge: Cambridge University Press, 1957), pp. 258–9.

tice how opposing forces agree. Look at the bow and lyre."[34] A bow appears to be "at rest" only because the bowstring and bow pull "equally" against each other. According to Heraclitus, throughout nature and society (convention), stability (permanence) is actually a state of tension between equal and opposite forces.

For example, peace and stability exist only when equal opposing forces or pressures hold each other in check. Social struggle is the maneuvering of various "forces" for domination. Social stability is thus analogous to two equally powerful wrestlers pushing in opposite directions. So long as their strength, angle of attack, and so forth are identical, they will appear to be immobile—even though they are locked in a mighty struggle—a war.

Some of Heraclitus's most famous fragments deal with strife and contention. His powerful language and use of the rhetoric of war and opposition make him controversial and difficult to interpret, but nonetheless intriguing and compelling. Consider the following:

> War is father of us all and our king. War discloses who is godlike and who but a man, who is a slave and who is freeman.

> It must be seen clearly that war is the natural state of man. Justice is contention. Through contention all things come to be.

> God is day night winter summer war peace enough too little, but disguised in each and known in each by a separate flavor.
>
> *Heraclitus*

> This world, which is always the same for all men, neither god nor man made; it has always been, it is, and always shall be: an everlasting fire rhythmically dying and flaring up again.
>
> *Heraclitus*

The "celestial music of the spheres" is the hauntingly beautiful phrase the Pythagoreans coined to describe the sound of heavenly bodies as they rotate according to cosmic number and harmony. One point of view held that, because we have been exposed to the music of the spheres from birth, we do not hear it.

When Homer said that he wished war might disappear from the lives of gods and men, he forgot that without opposition all things would cease to exist.

Opposites cooperate. The beautifullest harmonies come from opposition. All things repel each other.

We know health by illness, good by evil, satisfaction by hunger, leisure by failure.[35]

From Sophos to Sophist

To God all is beautiful, good, and as it should be. Man must see things as either good or bad.

Heraclitus

When the *sophos* first emerged from the mists of prehistory, knowledge and wisdom were not neatly divided. As early Greek civilization became more refined and sophisticated, mythology and religion developed into philosophy and philosophers began to concentrate on the study of nature and the cosmos or the study of human behavior and values. Social historian Amaury de Riencourt describes the early history of philosophy as a series of increasingly abstract steps, until a "fanatical concern" with logical consistency and rules of thinking led to theories that, though logically consistent, did not match observed facts.[36] The result, de Riencourt says, was "The absolute predominance of the dissociating, analytical . . . principle in Greek thought . . . its strength and its weakness."[37]

Philosophical speculation became increasingly alienated from common experience, and unemotional, implacable reason threatened to dominate other sources of wisdom. Seemingly bizarre theories and countertheories struggled for dominance as the first principle of existence. Challenging one another's explanations of the world order and reality, the *Presocratics* variously claimed that everything was composed of or could be explained by such disparate forces and principles as water, "the indefinite-infinite," air, earth, fire, love, strife, being, mind, or atoms.

Distinguishing between appearance and reality, these first philosophers rejected common opinion and the evidence of the senses as products of ignorance and illusion. Reason was exalted as being the only reliable way to understand the "real" world.

As the ideas of these philosophers became widely known, at least in second- and third-hand variations, more and more people decided that the philosophers were the ones utterly out of touch with reality. Philosophical speculation was sometimes viewed as an indulgence suitable only for those not fit for "real life"—individuals supported by other people, or else absorbed in pointless "intellectual squabbles." Philosophy—as popularly understood—became a subject of both confusion and ridicule and awe and respect.

"What," people asked, "is philosophy good for, if philosophers can hold contradictory and absurd ideas that bear no resemblance to common sense? How can we take seriously charges that we can never experience reality, that our most cherished and widely held beliefs are merely illusions?" If careful thinkers end up in such tangles, maybe it's better to think less and live more.

This suspicious attitude toward philosophy contributed to a kind of philosophical revolution that occurred when the first "professional" thinkers, known as *Sophists*, turned from the study of the cosmos to the study of human beings. The Sophists' demands for practical philosophy blew through the early history of philosophy like a bracing wind. They are the subject of Chapter 2.

You would not by your going discover the limits of soul though you traveled over every path, so deep has it a *Logos*.

Heraclitus

The intellect can understand any part of a thing as a part, but not as a whole.

R. H. Blyth

The struggle against desire is difficult, because it must be purchased at the soul's expense.

Heraclitus

Everything flows; nothing remains.

Heraclitus

2

The Sophist

Protagoras

Man is the measure of all things, of the things that are, [how] they are, and the things that are not, [how] they are not.

Protagoras of Abdera

T he scene: A society showing signs of tension and strain, yet still exciting and important. The privileges of the establishment are being challenged by more liberal democratic groups. Wealthy parents pay outrageous tuitions to have their children taught by prestigious educators, only to have these very same children then reject their parents' ideals and beliefs. People complain that atheistic, relativistic trends are permeating the schools and that basic values are breaking down. Traditional religions and beliefs are challenged by intellectuals, by occult practices, and by competing Eastern religions. Scientific, mathematical, and intellectual advances compete for social control and influence with conservative, fundamentalist religious and moral tenets. Political corruption is pervasive and public. People take one another to court for a variety of real and inflated slights and transgressions. Success, prestige, and power become the overriding goals of many. Consider one commentator's description:

> It seems as if the dominant drive of more and more citizens is the objective of getting as rich as possible. . . . Meanwhile the money-makers, bent on their business, . . . continue to inject their poisoned loans wherever they can, and to demand high rates of interest, with the result that drones and beggars multiply. . . . Yet even when the evil becomes flagrant [the rulers] will do nothing to quench it. . . . This being so, won't everyone arrange his life as pleases him best? It's a wonderfully pleasant way of carrying on in the short-run, isn't it? It's an agreeable, anarchic form of society, with plenty of variety, which treats all men as equal, whether they are or not.
>
> It is a picture easy to recognize.[1]

America today? No. You have just read Plato's characterization of the "democratic" state. Because of their sophisticated, successful civilization, the Athenian people had long viewed themselves as unique, special, superior to all others. But the Athens of around 500–400 B.C. attracted aspiring entrepreneurs from all over Greece and parts of Asia. Those who considered themselves to be "original, true Athenians" grew uncomfortable

Ancients of our culture sought clarity: Plato portrays Socrates tirelessly splitting hairs to extract essential truth from the ambiguities of language and thought. Two thousand years later we are reversing that, for now we pay intellectual talent a high price to amplify ambiguities, distort thought, and bury reality. . . . One of the discoveries of the twentieth century is the enormous variety of ways of compelling language to lie.

Jules Henry

53

But if cattle and horses or lions had hands, or were able to draw with their hands and do the works that men can do, horses would draw the forms of the gods like horses, and cattle like cattle, and they would make their [the gods'] bodies such as they each had themselves.

Xenophanes

Drawing by S. Harris; © 1992 *The New Yorker Magazine*, Inc.

ETHNOCENTRISM

From Greek roots meaning "the race is the center"; belief that the customs and beliefs of one's own culture are inherently superior to all others.

and defensive. Social scientists call this attitude **ethnocentrism** (from Greek roots meaning "the race or group is the center"). Ethnocentric individuals see their ways as inherently superior to all others: Their religion is the one true religion. Their science, music, tastes in all areas of life are unsurpassed. The ethnocentric person thinks: "The gods speak *our* language, look like *us*, are *our* color. *Our* family practices are *natural*, others are *deviant*."

For instance, in some Hindu cultures, eating the flesh of a cow is forbidden. In other cultures, it is not. Some people get sick at the mere idea of eating a dog or monkey; to others, such culinary practices are normal. Ethnocentrism is what makes us laugh at the way other people dress or talk. We can even do this to other citizens of our own country. Some Southerners make fun of people with a "New York accent," and New Yorkers in their turn may mock those with "Southern accents." The ethnocentric person thinks that he or she doesn't even have an accent!

The Greeks of this time were so ethnocentric they invented the term **barbarian** to mock people who spoke in other languages. They mimicked the way foreigners talked by making a sound something like "bar, bar, bar." Today we would probably say, "blah, blah, blah." So the outsiders were bar-bar-ians (or blah-blah-ians), people whose language sounded like noise or nonsense to the Greeks. To these Greeks, other cultures were simply "uncivilized," "less human." But what happens when a closed-off culture begins to interact with other highly civilized cultures on a regular basis?

Philosophical Query

Can you think of any ways you are ethnocentric? What are some close parallels between Athens of the fifth century B.C. and America today? Discuss.

> **BARBARIAN**
>
> From a rude "bar-bar" noise used to mock dialects considered crude by the ancient Athenians; originally referred to other cultures considered "less than human" or uncivilized.

The Advent of Professional Educators

Ancient Athens was chauvinistic in many respects. For example, full citizenship was originally confined to males from certain aristocratic families. The ambitious, talented young immigrants from throughout the Mediterranean area who were attracted by Athens's vitality as a trading center had fewer rights and opportunities than Athenian citizens. Regardless of their ability, it was difficult, if not impossible, for them to achieve the same levels of success as those lucky enough to have been born into the right families.

As the number of capable immigrants settling in and around Athens grew, tension and conflict became inevitable. The Athenians' snobbery was challenged. Some Persians and Spartans and Milesians were smarter, quicker, stronger, more attractive; some of their goods were of higher quality; their traders sometimes outfoxed Athenians. Thus the Athenians' image of themselves as unique and superior people became increasingly difficult to maintain as interaction with people from other cultures increased (as is always ultimately the case). Indeed, great deliberate effort was required to maintain a view of unquestioned superiority.

As the lively trade center flourished, the privileges of birth were challenged by the emergence of a wealthy new business class. Good business sense, personal charm and persuasiveness, willingness to work hard, and individual ability began to compete with merely having been born in the right place to the right kind of family.[2]

In this changing climate, more and more individuals were allowed both to speak before the Athenian Assembly and to sue one another over business and personal matters. The ability to think clearly and speak persuasively

> If a man were really able to instruct mankind, to receive money for giving instruction would, in my opinion, be an honour to him.
>
> *Socrates*

> The art of the Sophist is the semblance of wisdom without the reality, and the Sophist is one who makes money from an apparent but unreal wisdom.
>
> *Aristotle*

Reality has nothing to do with reputation, reputation has nothing to do with reality. Reputation is nothing but pretence.

Lie Zi

was a means for members of the new middle class to enter political life and to improve their social status. These conditions combined to create a demand for something unknown in the Mediterranean world before this time: formal, specialized higher education in such subjects as letters, rhetoric (persuasive speaking), science, statesmanship, and philosophy.[3]

While these social changes were taking place, philosophy was also affected by growth. Presocratic philosophers had asserted that everything was fundamentally composed of water, or air, or earth, or fire, or flux, or number, or one, or many, or some combination of these. Thales, for example, said, "the [basic] principle is water." Anaximander disagreed, claiming, "It is neither water nor any other of those things that are called elements." Anaximenes thought it was air: "The other things are then derived from air." Heraclitus said, "Lightning is lord over all." And Pythagoras saw ultimate reality as being mathematical in nature: "All things which can be known have a number; without this nothing could possibly be thought or known." And that's only a partial list. (See the First Interlude to learn more about the Presocratics.)

Each theory was flawed. Each philosopher's position was criticized logically by a newer point of view, which was in turn criticized. Even good logic and sound reasoning seemed ultimately unhelpful in sorting things out. One problem was with the characteristics of arguments themselves. All arguments consist of two aspects, their logical structure and the truth or falsity of their content. Sound arguments consist of good reasoning based on true premises. If one or more premises of an argument are false, the conclusion will be unreliable. Thus, *if its starting point is flawed, even the most tightly reasoned argument or theory will be flawed.*

Overwhelmed by so many conflicting theories, the "new *sophos*" of the fifth century B.C., now called a **Sophist**, concluded that it was impossible to discover "The Truth." If good reasoning could lead to inconsistent results, then the difference between a "good" argument and a "bad" argument was just a matter of the starting point. And the only difference between one starting point and another, according to the Sophists, was custom and individual preference.

SOPHISTS

Fifth-century B.C. paid teachers of rhetoric; relativists who taught that might makes right, truth is a matter of appearance and convention, and power is the ultimate value.

The Sophists

The Sophists were a group of wandering teachers who gravitated toward Athens during this fertile period. They were the first professional teachers, charging a fee to teach any who wished to study with them. They made Athenian education democratic at least in the sense that all who could pay were equal. It was no longer necessary to belong to a certain family— as long as you had enough money to pay high tuitions. The *sophos*, in contrast, had followers and disciples, not paying students.

The Sophists also differed from the *sophos* in that the Sophists turned increasingly from the study of nature to the formal study of human life and conduct. Many of them had traveled rather widely and thus were "*sophist*-icated," or worldly-wise. We get that word from them. The Sophists knew firsthand about various cultures; they had witnessed a variety of religious practices, and had experienced a variety of tastes in clothing, food, family patterns, legal values, and morals. They might be thought of as the first social scientists, combining, as it were, anthropology, psychology, and sociology to produce a particular view of social life and human nature. Their sophistication was a direct threat to the chauvinistic elite that ruled Athens. The idea that anyone with the fee could be educated was offensive to those who saw themselves as inherently superior.

> The Sophists speak in order to deceive, and they write for their own gain, and in no way to be of use to anyone.
>
> *Xenophon*

Power and Education

The Sophists looked closely at what worked in various cultures and concluded that virtually nothing was good or bad by nature, but that good and bad were matters of custom and preference. Further, they noticed that although different individuals desire different things, everyone seeks some form of power. Indeed, every living thing seeks to be happy and to survive as long as possible, and so the only "natural" good is power, because power increases control over the conditions of happiness and survival. For instance, getting a new car won't make you happy if you cannot keep it. Being right about something at work won't help if you lack the ability (power) to get your boss to recognize it. Based on such observations, the Sophists concluded: So-called truth is subservient to power.[4]

> There is no definite right or wrong human principle. To be able to adapt to the changing times is true wisdom.
>
> *Lie Zi*

The Sophists remained professionals, in the sense of always demanding payment, eventually becoming infamous for their insistence on being well paid. It was widely believed that the worst of them would teach anything they could get someone to pay for. The Sophists' reputation also suffered because of their emphasis on winning debates in and out of court. Since they believed that power was the ultimate value, the key issue became not right or wrong, but getting your own way. The Sophists became expert debaters and advertisers; they learned to use emotional appeals, physical appearance, and clever language to "sell" their particular point of view. These characteristics have led to the modern meaning of **sophistry** as subtle, plausible, but fallacious reasoning. Plato characterizes the Sophist this way:

> First, I believe he was found to be a paid hunter after the young and wealthy . . . secondly a kind of merchant in articles of knowledge for the soul . . . third did he not turn up as a retailer of these same articles of knowledge? . . . and in the fourth place we found he was a seller of his own products of knowledge . . . and in the fifth he was an athlete in contests of words, who had taken for his own the art of

SOPHISTRY

The teachings and practices of the original Sophists; modern usage refers to subtle, plausible, but fallacious reasoning used to persuade rather than discover truth.

disputation . . . the sixth case was doubtful, but nevertheless we agreed to consider him a purger of souls, who removes opinions that obstruct learning.[5]

Socrates, the first great Western philosopher, lived at the same time as the Sophists and was also a famous educator. He often had what he claimed were discussions with Sophists; the Sophists, however, thought they were contests. Many Athenians weren't sure whether or not Socrates was a Sophist or a *sophos*. Socrates himself, though, was clear on one thing: It is wrong to charge money for teaching philosophy. He said:

> [I believe] that it is possible to dispose of beauty or of wisdom alike honorably or dishonorably; for if a person sells his beauty for money to anyone who wishes to purchase it, men call him a male prostitute; but if anyone makes a friend of a person whom he knows to be an honorable and worthy admirer, we regard him as prudent. In like manner those who sell their wisdom for money to any that will buy, men call sophists, or, as it were, prostitutes of wisdom; but whoever makes a friend of a person whom he knows to be deserving, and teaches him all the good that he knows, we consider him to act the part which becomes a good and honorable citizen.[6]

Philosophical Query

Discuss some of the pros and cons of personal education versus professional education. Try to consider a variety of factors: efficiency; effects of money on pupils, teachers, and institutions; mediocrity; conformity. Do you agree that it is wrong to "sell wisdom"? Is it realistic to expect teachers (or philosophers) to teach for free, for love only? Can't any source of financial support lead to bias? Must it?

Relativism

The Sophists were among the first systematic thinkers to conclude that the truth is relative. **Relativism** is the belief that knowledge is determined by specific qualities of the observer. The Sophists, for example, claimed that place of birth, family habits, personal abilities and preferences, religious training, age, and so forth control an individual's beliefs, values, and even perceptions. (Don't confuse relativism with subjectivism. See page 197 for a discussion of subjectivism—the belief that we can only know our own sensations.)

Based on this tenet, they argued that we need only accept what *seems* true at the moment, according to our culture. The most extreme Sophists claimed that even within the same culture, individuals have their own

For all their shameless accusations, my accusers have not been able in all their impudence to bring forward a single witness to say I have ever received a fee or asked for one. I, on the other hand, have a convincing witness that I speak the truth, my poverty.

Socrates

RELATIVISM

Belief that knowledge is determined by specific qualities of the observer, including age, race, gender, cultural conditioning.

Comparing the lifestyles and beliefs of these contemporary Islamic women to those of contemporary American women shows how difficult it is to dispute the Sophists' claim that all values are culturally determined.

truths. The consequences of this position can be unsettling, to say the least. If no ultimate truth exists, no moral code is universally correct or absolutely superior to any other. The Sophists taught that each culture (or individual!) only *believes* that its ways are best, but the person who has studied many cultures knows better: One is as good as another if you believe in it.

There are two basic variants of what is known as *moral relativism*: cultural and individual. Cultural relativism is the belief that all values are culturally determined. Values do not reflect a divine order or a natural pattern, but merely the customs and preferences that develop in a given culture. Thus what is right in 1990s America is not necessarily right in South Africa or Brazil. Your grandmother's sexual morality was right for a particular person at a particular time and place, but not for all people all the time and in every place. What is right for a twenty-year-old African-American woman will be different from what is right for a ninety-year-old Chinese-American man, and so on. Consequently, what's right for you may very well be different from what's right for people of different ages and backgrounds.

The narrower, more radical view of moral relativism, called individual relativism, simply carries the logic of cultural relativism to a more refined conclusion. It goes like this: Even in the same place and time, right and wrong are relative to the unique experiences and preferences of the individual. There is no unbiased way to say that one standard is better than another, for the standard used to make *that* claim is itself the reflection of

Traditions and customs are set by people. Therefore what people regard as "truth" tends to be a subjective matter.

Lie Zi

The Ring of Gyges

The technical name for the view that all morality reduces to self-interest is *egoism*. It is usually associated with moral skepticism, since it is the only source of values left for the moral skeptic. One of the earliest and most interesting presentations of the egoist's position occurs in Plato's *Republic*:

> Even those who practise justice do so against their will because they lack the power to do wrong. This we would realize if we clearly imagined ourselves granting to both the just and the unjust the freedom to do whatever they liked. We could then follow both of them and observe where their desires led them, and we would catch the just man redhanded travelling the same road as the unjust. The reason is the desire for undue gain which every organism by nature pursues as good, but the law forcibly sidetracks him to honour equality. The freedom I just mentioned would most easily occur if these men had the power which they say the ancestor of the Lydian Gyges possessed. The story is that he was a shepherd in the service of the ruler of Lydia. There was a violent rainstorm and an earthquake which broke open the ground and created a chasm at the place where he was tending sheep. Seeing this and marvelling, he went down into it. He saw, besides many other wonders of which we are told, a hollow bronze horse. There were window-like openings in it; he climbed through one of them and caught sight of a corpse which seemed of more than human stature, wearing nothing but a ring of gold on its finger. This ring the shepherd put on

a preference, ad infinitum. No matter how far back we push "ultimate" reasons, they always reduce to someone's preference. Hence, moral values are matters of individual taste and opinion.

Philosophical Query

Some English teachers hesitate to impose standards of English grammar. They see all grammar as "preferences." Do you agree? Ask your English teacher about this.

Protagoras

Protagoras the Pragmatist

Perhaps the greatest of the Sophists was **Protagoras of Abdera (481–411 B.C.).** Attracted to Athens around the middle of the fifth century, he became a famous teacher there. He was befriended by wealthy and powerful Athenians, and as a consequence became rich and powerful himself. Plato even named a dialogue after him.

Protagoras was an archetypal Sophist: an active traveler and first-rate observer of other cultures who noted that although there are a variety of and came out. He arrived at the usual monthly meeting which reported to the king on the state of the flocks, wearing the ring. As he was sitting among the others he happened to twist the hoop of the ring towards himself, to the inside of his hand, and as he did this he became invisible to those sitting near him and they went off talking as if he had gone. He marvelled at this and, fingering the ring, turned the hoop outward again and became visible. Perceiving this he tested whether the ring had this power and so it happened: if he turned the hoop inwards he became invisible, but he was visible when he turned it outwards. When he realized this, he at once arranged to become one of the messengers of the king. He went, committed adultery with the king's wife, attacked the king with her help, killed him, and took over the kingdom.

Now if there were two such rings, one worn by the just man, the other by the unjust, no one, as these people think, would be so incorruptible that he would stay on the path of justice or bring himself to keep away from other people's property and not touch it, when he could with impunity take whatever he wanted from the market, go into houses and have sexual relations with anyone he wanted, kill anyone, free all those he wished from prison, and do other things which would make him like a god among men.

Plato
The Republic, trans. G. M. A. Grube (Indianapolis: Hackett, 1974), p. 32ff.

customs and beliefs, each culture believes unquestioningly that its own ways are right—and roundly condemns (or at least criticizes) views that differ from its own. So he asked himself: What really makes something right or wrong? Is anything *really* right or wrong? What is truth? Can we know it? Can we *know that we know it*, or are we limited to mere beliefs? His answers may strike you as surprisingly contemporary. And they are—as the term *Sophist* suggests—quite sophisticated.

Based on his observations and travels, Protagoras concluded that morals were nothing more than the social traditions, or mores, of a society or group. What makes the Athenian way right for someone living in Athens is the fact that following the mores of one's place is the best way to live successfully and well—in that place. The task of the truly wise observer is to record accurately and describe without bias what works and what does not work. Hence the famous remark quoted at the beginning of this chapter: *Man is the measure of all things.* Here is how Plato reported Socrates' characterization of what Protagoras meant:

> Well, is not this what [Protagoras] means, that individual things are for me such as they appear to me, and for you in turn such as they appear to you—you and I being "man"? . . . Is it not true that sometimes, when the same wind blows, one of us feels cold and the other

We recognize that morality differs in every society, and is a convenient term for socially approved habits. Mankind has always preferred to say, "It is morally good," rather than "It is habitual," and the fact of this preference is matter enough for a critical science of ethics. But historically the two phrases are synonymous.

Ruth Benedict

does not? or one feels slightly and the other exceedingly cold? . . . Then in that case, shall we say that the wind is in itself cold or not cold; or shall we accept Protagoras' saying that it is cold for him who feels cold, not for him who does not?[7]

Since we do not have complete texts of Protagoras's actual essays available, we must rely on fragments and commentaries. One of the clearest presentations of Protagoras's relativism is a partial reconstruction of his philosophy by Gregory Vlastos, a contemporary scholar who specializes in ancient philosophy. Using the form of a dialogue between himself and Protagoras, Vlastos begins with a reference to the famous opening sentence of Protagoras's essay "Truth." In Vlastos's translation the opening sentence reads: "Of all things man is the measure: both of things that are (man is the measure) that they are, and of things that are not (man is the measure) that they are not."

Protagoras: Appearance *is* reality. Even what you philosophers call "reality" is just what appears true to them.

Vlastos: But appearances are not consistent. The same wind often feels warm to me, cold to you.

Protagoras: Then it *is* warm for you, cold for me.

Vlastos: But what is it in itself?

Protagoras: "Wind-in-itself"? I know of no such thing. Do you? The only wind you can know is the one you can feel: this is the wind for you, and you are its measure.

Vlastos: If that is the way you reason, you might as well hold that all beliefs are true.

Protagoras: I do. All beliefs *are* true for those who believe them.

Vlastos: I suppose you have no scruples about applying your appearance-is-reality doctrine to morals.

Protagoras: Are you insinuating there is something unscrupulous about that? . . . anything held right and just in a given state is right and just for it.

Vlastos: But there is often disagreement *within* a state. Is the minority view wrong when it conflicts with the official doctrine?

Protagoras: Not wrong for the minority.

Vlastos: So you would require the minority to act in ways that seem unjust to them, and are unjust for them?

Protagoras: I see no logical inconsistency in that, but if you mean that it would be very awkward, I quite agree. When people differ in their moral judgments, it is very hard for them to avoid acting out their disagreements, and then the very purpose for which morality

---

"Pick the right time and flourish, miss the right time and perish." Nowhere is there a principle which is right in all circumstances, or an action that is wrong in all circumstances. The method we used yesterday we may discard today and use again in the future. There is no fixed right and wrong to decide whether we use it or not.

Lie Zi

The Ethiopians say that their gods are snub-nosed and black, the Thracians that theirs have light blue eyes and red hair.

Xenophanes

was invented—to facilitate friendly and harmonious social relations—would be defeated. This is a practical problem, and it calls for a practical answer. On my view, moral disagreement is like a disease. You don't argue about it. You cure it.

Vlastos: How do you propose to do that?

Protagoras: The way it is done in every civilized community. Just think how many of the things you do are concerned with the *prevention* of disagreement in the first place, and then if this fails, with its *cure.* You start with the child telling him, "This is just, that is unjust . . . ; do this, don't do that," and if he goes along with you the problem has been forestalled. If not, then, "like a bent and warped wood," you "straighten it out by blows."

Vlastos: By "straightening" it out, you mean you bring it into line with the mores of its elders?

Protagoras: What else? Or are you hankering after straight-in-itself?

Vlastos: But isn't what the little rebel thinks straight, straight for him?

Protagoras: Certainly. But you are missing the point. The point is not, who is right—the child or his parents? There is no sense to that question: there never is, in any case of moral disagreement. The only question that makes sense is how to get rid of the disagreement. And the answer to this is obvious. The parents can straighten the child according to their views, while the child is in no position to impose his on them.[8]

Protagoras predicted a crucial tenet of modern social science: Our values are determined by our culture, our conditioning, our experience, and our particular biopsychology. It is, according to Protagoras, utterly impossible to form a culture-free or context-free belief. For instance, philosophy students born, raised, and educated in Moscow, Russia, cannot help but "see" a different world than those born, raised, and educated in Moscow, Idaho.

Thus the real issue is not what is true, since true always means "true for the believer," and if Student A believes something, that alone makes it true from her perspective. The worthwhile issue is what works for Student A, not what is universally true or what works for Student B. The point of view that beliefs are to be interpreted in terms of "whether they work" (their usefulness) is called **pragmatism**, from the Greek *pragma*, "deed." Ideas have meaning or truth value to the extent that they produce practical results and are effective in furthering our aims.

Plato criticized Protagoras for—in Plato's view—reducing the concept of what is "useful" to whatever people think is useful. Of course Protagoras could respond to Plato this way: "What is useful if not useful to some particular individual, at some particular place and time? What sense is

---

The religion of one seems madness unto another.

Sir Thomas Browne

When Aesop's lion was shown a painting in which a man was depicted killing a lion, he commented contemptuously, "The artist was obviously a man."

B. F. Skinner

PRAGMATISM

From the Greek for "deed"; ideas have meaning or truth value to the extent that they produce practical results and effectively further our aims; empirically based philosophy that defines knowledge and truth in terms of practical consequences.

But if a man arises endowed with a nature sufficiently strong he will, I believe, shake off these controls, burst his fetters, and break loose. And trampling upon our scraps of paper, our spells and incantations, and all our unnatural conventions, he rises up and reveals himself our master who was once our slave, and there shines forth nature's true justice.

Callicles

there in talking about 'useful in general'? Useful always means useful for the specific purposes and desires of an individual. And even for individuals, what is useful changes."

In a speech Plato attributes to Protagoras, the Sophist makes the case that *wisdom is what works*:

For I maintain that the truth is as I have written; each one of us is the measure of the things that are and those that are not; but each person differs immeasurably from every other in just this, that to one person some things appear and are, and to another person other things . . . do not lay too much stress upon the words of my argument, but get a clearer understanding of my meaning from what I am going to say. Recall to your mind what was said before, that his food appears and is bitter to the sick man, but appears and is the opposite of bitter to the man in health. Now neither of these two is to be made wiser than he is—that is not possible—nor should the claim be made that the sick man is ignorant because his opinions are ignorant, or the healthy man wise because his opinions are different; but a change must be made from the one condition to the other, for the other is better. So, too, in education a change has to be made from a worse condition to

Protagoras maintained that "each one of us is the measure." Is your reaction to the sumo wrestlers more negative than to Dennis Rodman? If so, why is one extreme more desirable than the other? If you do not care for either extreme, is your preference more "reasonable," "healthier," or just your preference?

a better condition; but the physician causes the change by means of drugs, and the teacher of wisdom by means of words. . . . And on the same principle the teacher who is able to train his pupils in this manner is not only wise but is also entitled to receive high pay from them when their education is finished. And in this sense it is true that some men are wiser than others, and that no one thinks falsely, and that you, whether you will or no, must . . . be a measure. Upon these positions my doctrine stands firm.[9]

> We are what we think, having become what we thought.
>
> *The Dhammapada*

Philosophical Query

Analyze Protagoras's speech. Has he convinced you? Explain. See if you can explain the trick used by both Protagoras and his pupil in the *Wager* (see page 66).

Protagoras was a rather tame Sophist. He reasoned that the most intelligent thing to do is to accept the customs and beliefs of your own

Protagoras's Wager

Among the consequences of the Sophists' emphasis on power, winning, and relativism are the aggressive competitiveness and boldness that flourish in such a climate. Because the Sophists chose to be public figures, seeking fame and influence, they were always eager to show off their abilities. They used their speaking skills to attack one another and attract students. Whenever possible, they spoke to large audiences, whether in the Assembly or in the public square. The average Athenian found these sparring matches entertaining at first. But as you will learn, the audience soon regarded the Sophists as disturbing and dangerous. A famous example of sophistic sparring is the story known as *Protagoras's Wager*.

Protagoras had a pupil named Eulathus, who arranged to take Protagoras's course in rhetoric and sophistry, a kind of law school, for partial tuition. So sure was Protagoras of his abilities as a teacher that he told Eulathus he did not have to pay the balance until Eulathus won his first court case. In fact, Pro-

tagoras guaranteed that Eulathus would win his first case.

Time dragged on and Eulathus neither paid up nor argued any cases in court. Not only was Protagoras out the money, he looked bad to his students and to other Sophists. After all, if winning is what counts, and if appearance is reality, and if the pupil can outmaneuver the old master, why should anyone continue to pay his high fees? Protagoras was compelled to take action.

Confronting Eulathus (probably in a public place where he could use his crowd-pleasing skills), Protagoras demanded payment in the form of this dilemma: "Eulathus, you might as well pay me, since I am going to sue you for the rest of the tuition. If I win in court, the court will rule that you owe me the money; if I lose in court, you will have won your first case, and you will owe me the money. Either I win in court or I lose, so either you owe me the money or you owe me the money."

Protagoras, alas, was a good teacher, and Eulathus was ready for him. He shot back with a

counterdilemma: "No, sir, you have it backwards. If you defeat me in court, then I have lost my first case and so do not owe the money; if I defeat you, the court will rule that I do not owe you the money. Either I defeat you or you defeat me. In either case, I do not owe you the money."

Who won? The story does not say. And besides, Sophists being what they were, neither Eulathus nor Protagoras would have wanted to lose big in a highly publicized trial. *Protagoras's Wager* gives us an instructive glimpse of sophistry in action. Such encounters were common, as Sophists vied for students and reputation. To the general citizenry, they were sometimes amusing entertainment. Men like Protagoras lived rather mild lives considering what they taught and the reactions their excitable pupils had to their ideas. But when the same kinds of tricks were used for high stakes, say to convict innocent citizens, to control democracy, to wrest property away from people, no one laughed. Sophistry's reputation grew darker.

community. By understanding that the mores of the community are not universal absolutes, you will develop a relaxed, effective attitude about them. This in turn will allow you to use them rather than being controlled by them. Openly flouting convention is most likely to be counterproductive. With the rare exceptions of talented and charismatic individuals, *behaving in a generally conventional way affords us the most social power*.

Dress the way that will get you promoted at work, or get you a date at the club. Write the kind of essay your teacher wants and you'll get a good grade; write your own creative masterpiece and you may not. Drive with the flow of traffic—neither too fast nor too slow—and you'll lower your insurance rates. If you want to get elected, go to church and keep your hair neat and conservative.

Tradition has it that Protagoras did not always follow his own advice. The story goes that at the home of a friend, Protagoras gave a reading of one of his own treatises called *On the Gods*. This particular work applied the principle of relativism to religious belief, apparently holding religion to the pragmatic standard. There was no separation of church and state in Athens at this time. Failure to believe in and respect "the gods of the state" was considered to be a form of treason known as impiety. One of the other guests, a conservative army officer, was so offended by Protagoras's ideas that he consequently had Protagoras indicted for impiety. Protagoras was found guilty. All copies of *On the Gods* were confiscated and burned, and the authorities set out to confiscate Protagoras, too. Facing death or exile, he attempted to escape on a ship headed for Sicily. The ship was wrecked and Protagoras drowned.

Moral Realism: Might Makes Right

In contrast to Protagoras, the next generation of Sophists carried moral relativism to a more radical level, proposing a pragmatic social philosophy unfettered by any moral considerations.

The laws of every society, says the moral realist, turn out to reflect the interests of those in power. The U.S. Constitution, for example, places great emphasis on property rights and protections because most of its chief architects were landed gentry: persons with property. Hence their view of the "ideal" state reflected and furthered their material interests. Each new Supreme Court reflects the values of the majority of its members, now liberal, now conservative. The "right" view is the view held by those currently in power. The rest of us, says the moral realist, ultimately obey because we have to; we have no other choice: Regardless of whether we believe that what is legal is also right, the average person obeys anyway because he or she lacks sufficient power (and courage) not to obey.

From a certain perspective, history seems to support the view that might and power determine right. But what about counterexamples like the civil rights movement of the 1960s? Here "right" finally prevailed, even against centuries of custom and habit supporting racist practices. This example seems to show that moral progress is possible and that not everyone acts from limited self-interest.

A contemporary Sophist could point out, however, that civil rights changes occurred in this country only after members of the powerful white middle class began to support the position of the racial minorities. The view of the most powerful faction of the time won: Civil might made civil

The majority of just acts according to the law are prescribed contrary to nature. For there is legislation about the eyes, what they must see and what not; and about the ears, what they must hear and what not; and about the tongue, what it must speak and what not; and about the hands, what they must do and what not; and about the feet, where they must go and where not. And about the soul, what it must desire and what not.

Antiphon

And how many legions does the Pope have?

Joseph Stalin, at Yalta

Calvin and Hobbes. Copyright © 1991 Universal Press Syndicate. Reprinted with permission.

rights. The same is true of women's rights. Women's rights have increased in proportion to women's power. African Americans, Hispanic Americans, Asian Americans, and other groups have rights in direct proportion to their might. The elderly will have more rights in the future because by the year 2000 they will outnumber members of other age groups. And so it goes. Your philosophy instructor has more power over your philosophy course than you do. Thus—ultimately—her interpretation of your test is more "right" than yours. Her answers are more "useful" than yours. Parents are "right" about many things simply because they have more power than children. Whoever has power gets to be right.

Philosophical Query

Is "might makes right" the only explanation for social changes like the civil rights movement? Could other factors besides self-interest account for a shift in basic social values? What factors? Is anything lost by accepting a might-makes-right interpretation? Is anything gained?

Convention is the ruler
of all.

    Pindar

The Doctrine of the Superior Individual

Not everybody willingly submits to those in power or depends on a group for clout. Those who do not are well represented by a Sophist named **Callicles (c. 435 B.C.).** His point of view goes by different names: the doctrine of the superior individual, the true man, the natural man, the superman. You may recognize foreshadowings of Nazism and racism in it. It is always elitist, but it is not always a racial doctrine. Indeed, in its most compelling form it is highly individualistic. A person is superior not because of racial or cultural background but only because of individual virtues and traits. (We will study one of the most notorious expressions of this view in Chapter 14.)

The moral realist distinguished what is right by nature from what is right by convention. In the following selection from Plato's *Gorgias*, Callicles asserts that by nature the strong dominate the weak, whereas conventional morality tries to restrain the superior, the strong, the truly powerful individual. In nature, the survival of the fittest is the rule. This, said such Sophists, shows that power is the ultimate value, and that *the superior and powerful individual has a natural right to dominate others. All people are no more created equal than all animals are.*

For to suffer wrong is not the part of a man at all, but that of a slave for whom it is better to be dead than alive, as it is for anyone who is unable to come either to his own assistance when he is wronged or mistreated or to that of anyone he cares about. I can quite imagine that the manufacturers of laws and conventions are the weak, the majority, in fact. It is for themselves and their own advantage that they make their laws and distribute their praises and their censures. It is to frighten men who are stronger than they and able to enforce superiority that they keep declaring, to prevent aggrandizement, that this is ugly and unjust, that injustice consists in seeking to get the better of one's neighbor. They are quite content, I suppose, to be on equal terms with others since they are themselves inferior.

This, then, is the reason why convention declares that it is unjust and ugly to seek to get the better of the majority. But my opinion is that nature herself reveals it to be only just and proper that the better man should lord it over his inferior: it will be the stronger over the weaker. Nature, further, makes it quite clear in a great many instances that this is the true state of affairs, not only in the other animals, but also in whole states and communities. This is, in fact, how justice is determined: the stronger shall rule and have the advantage over his inferior. . . .

. . . Now, my dear friend, take my advice: stop your [philosophy], take up the Fine Art of Business, and cultivate something that will give you a reputation for good sense. Leave all these oversubtleties to someone else. Should one call them frivolities or just plain nonsense? They'll only land you in a house where you'll be the only visitor! You must emulate, not those whose very refutations are paltry, but men of substance and high repute and everything else that is good.[10]

Where there is no vision, the people perish; where there is no framework of moral reasoning, the people close ranks in a war of all against all.

Cornel West

"What is right in one group is wrong in another," he says. But what exactly is a group? and which group is one to select? Every person is a member of many different groups—his nation, his state, his city, his club, his school, church, fraternity, or athletic association. Suppose that most of the people in his club think that a certain kind of act is wrong and that most of the people in his nation think it is right; what then?

John Hospers

There are two sides to every question.

Protagoras

Darrow's Cigar

An apocryphal story about the legendary lawyer Clarence Darrow circulates among law students: Darrow had to defend an especially unsavory client. This was a hard case to make. As the prosecutor ranted and raved to the jury about the heinous nature of the crime and the plight of the suffering victims, Darrow paid him close and courteous attention, puffing distractedly on a large cigar. The ash grew, an eighth of an inch, a quarter, a half, an inch or more—yet did not fall. Darrow didn't seem to notice. He just politely concentrated on the prosecutor's words. But the jury noticed. Instead of paying full attention to the prosecutor, they were drawn again and again to Darrow's cigar—into which he had secretly inserted a thin piece of wire.

One sophistry used by contemporary Darrows is having their clients dress "persuasively." Erik and Lyle Menendez often wore "college boy" crewneck sweaters at their trials for killing their parents. O. J. Simpson testified that he could not pay the 30 million dollar civil judgment against him while uncharacteristically wearing inexpensive shoes—and slacks with a hole in the backside.

Philosophical Query

Is some part of you stirred by all this talk of power and superiority? The Sophists would say that if you can be honest, you'll answer in the affirmative. What might prevent you (in the Sophists' view) from admitting that you agree with them? Are they correct? Even if you personally reject Callicles' position, how common do you think it is? What's your evidence?

If ethical relativism is correct, it is clearly impossible for the moral beliefs of a society to be mistaken because the certainty of the majority that its beliefs were right would prove that those beliefs were right for that society at that time. The minority view would therefore be mistaken, no matter what it was. Needless to say, most people who state that "in morals everything is relative" and who proceed to call themselves ethical relativists are unaware of these implications of their theory.

John Hospers

Commentary

The questions raised by the Sophists are important, not just in the dusty archives of scholarly concerns but also for the continuing influence sophistic ideas exert on our lives and beliefs. Sophists helped free the Greeks to think on new, less restricted levels. From this beginning emerged a nonreligious (amoral) scientific method as well as a philosophic method of questioning, both of which are free to pursue knowledge for its own sake and wherever it leads. In other words, the Sophists helped break the shackles of dogma and superstition. For that we remain in their debt. They laid the cornerstone for the scientific study of human behavior— what would become the social, psychological, political, and anthropological sciences.

The Sophists' emphasis on the individual as determiner of value and the challenges they posed to the possibility of a moral absolute were contributing factors to increasing democracy in Athens. Thus, the Sophists were perceived as a direct threat by the "establishment" of privileged aristocrats.

The youth of Athens responded with gusto to these ideas as a call to unrestrained self-assertion and personal freedom. It was stimulating to challenge the stuffy, square, straight, uptight values of the establishment. The glorification of the "superior individual" or "natural man" has always appealed to adolescent cravings for power, fame, freedom, and identity. Logic and the rhetorical devices refined by the Sophists were liberally applied to legal maneuvering, politics, techniques of manipulation, and control of the marketplace. By the third generation, Sophists no longer claimed to be *sophistai*, teachers of wisdom, but advertised shortcuts to guaranteed social, political, financial, and personal success. These were the forerunners of today's how-to-succeed, you-can-have-it-all books, courses, and techniques. Freed of any moral anchor, the Sophists were often deadly and effective. They took no responsibility for the ways people might use their ideas, as the great Sophist Gorgias reminds us:

> And if a man learns rhetoric, and then does injustice through the power of his art, we shall not be right, in my opinion, in detesting and banishing his teacher. For while the teacher imparted instruction to be used rightly, the pupil made a contrary use of it. Therefore, it is only right to detest the misuser and banish and kill him, not his teacher.[11]

Although they were attacked by Plato and others on moral grounds, most Sophists were actually amoral (nonmoral) rather than immoral. Like the caricature of a mob attorney who uses all her persuasive skills to vigorously and lucratively defend known drug dealers and Mafia bosses, the Sophists made no moral judgments. They were concerned only with "what worked." They saw the world as hard and brutal, a jungle. Because the restraints and inhibitions of morality weaken us, they refused to acknowledge them. In contemporary terms they were masters of "effective" thinking, communicating, and acting.

Many sophistic techniques, like Darrow's cigar (see box), are genuinely clever and clearly effective. The Sophists of ancient Athens inspired mixed feelings of awe and admiration, anger and disgust. They raised vital, ongoing questions: When the stakes are high, is playing fair the smart thing to do? Just how important is winning? And how should we be judged? On the conventional morals most of us profess? Or on the values we actually practice and (secretly?) admire: strength, power, daring, attractiveness, social contacts, success? Can we ever have objective knowledge or escape the limits of culture? In the absence of certainty, might it be better to allow more individual choice rather than less?

As you reflect on the archetype of the Sophist, think about its place in today's world. As you are probably realizing, the similarities between the cultural climate of ancient Athens and that of America in the 1990s are widespread and deeply rooted. The Sophists represent one side of the

Go about with your middle finger up and people will say you're daft; go about with your little finger out, and they will cultivate your company.

Diogenes

Probably most people who call themselves ethical relativists are not so at all, for they believe in one moral standard which applies in different ways to different societies because of the various conditions in which they live. One might as well talk about gravitational relativism because a stone falls and a balloon rises; yet both events are equally instances of one law of universal gravitation.

John Hospers

Of what value is smartness of speech? Opposing a man with the mouth excites anger.

Confucius

timeless struggle between "the world" and wisdom. We all face this struggle. So we're not just learning about the past, about dead ideas. We are learning about living issues.

As the original Sophists grew in numbers and boldness, they attracted more and more enemies. Unable to distinguish sophistic philosophies from other forms, the citizens of Athens began to agree with each other that philosophy itself was unacceptably subversive. Philosophy's reputation for being somehow unpatriotic and dangerous was established. Into this breach stepped perhaps the single most influential and arresting philosopher of all, the first major philosopher of the West: Socrates.

Summary of Main Points

1. As Athens grew in influence it attracted more and more people from other city-states and countries. Those who considered themselves to be "original, true Athenians" grew uncomfortable and defensive. They became increasingly ethnocentric. Ethnocentrism includes the often unconscious tendency to consider one's own customs, foods, and social patterns as superior to all others. This leads the ethnocentric person to condemn other customs as "unnatural."

2. The emergence of a new middle class combined with opportunities for a growing number of Athenians to speak before the Assembly created a demand for formal, specialized higher education in subjects such as letters, rhetoric, science, statesmanship, and philosophy.

3. Social and cultural changes also affect philosophy. Competing points of view criticized one another, yet failed to withstand criticism. Overwhelmed by so many conflicting theories and cultural viewpoints, a new kind of *sophos* emerged known as a *Sophist*.

4. Sophists concluded that if good reasoning could lead to inconsistent results, then the difference between a "good" argument and a "bad" argument was just a matter of the starting point. And the only difference between one starting point and another, according to the Sophists, was custom and individual preference.

5. The Sophists were a group of wandering teachers who were the first professional teachers, charging a fee to teach any who wished to study with them. They made Athenian education democratic at least in the sense that all who could pay were equal.

6. The Sophists believed that virtually nothing is good or bad by nature, but that good and bad are matters of custom and preference. They claimed that although different individuals desire different things, everyone seeks some form of power. The Sophists taught that so-called truth is subservient to power.

7. The early Sophists argued that the truth is relative. They were relativists who believed that knowledge is determined by specific qualities of the observer—for example, place of birth, family habits, personal abilities and preferences, religious training, age, and so forth control an individual's beliefs, values, and even perceptions.

8. There are two basic variants of what is known as *moral relativism*: cultural and individual. Cultural relativism is the belief that all values are culturally determined. Individual rela-

tivism carries the logic of cultural relativism to a more refined conclusion: Even in the same place and time, right and wrong are relative to the unique experiences and preferences of the individual.

9. Protagoras of Abdera was one of the most influential of the Sophists. Protagoras said that morals are nothing more than the social traditions, or mores, of a society or group. Therefore, following the mores of one's place is the best way to live successfully and well—in that place. According to Protagoras, the task of the truly wise observer is to record accurately and describe without bias what works and what does not work. Hence his famous remark: *Man is the measure of all things.*

10. The next generation of Sophists carried moral relativism to a more radical level, proposing a social philosophy unfettered by any moral considerations. According to the moral realist, the values that prevail in all areas of life—economic, political, racial, educational—reflect the interests of the strong. Certain values dominate not because they are in some absolute sense "right," but because they are the views preferred by the most powerful individual or group. Moral realism distinguishes what is right by "nature" from what is right by "convention."

11. Callicles was a Sophist associated with an aspect of moral realism known as the doctrine of the superior individual. He asserted that by nature the strong dominate the weak, whereas conventional morality tries to restrain the superior, truly powerful individual. In nature, the "survival of the fittest" is the rule. This, Callicles claimed, shows that the superior and powerful individual has a natural right to dominate others.

Study Questions

1. What is ethnocentrism? Give a few current examples from your own experience.

2. Describe the circumstances that led to the change from *sophos* to *Sophist*.

3. What is a Sophist?

4. Identify and explain three or four specific sophistic ideas.

5. Make a convincing case that advertisers are Sophists. Are they? What would nonsophistic advertising be like?

6. Is there any merit to the claim that modern colleges and universities are sophistic in their attempts to compete for students? What other trends in contemporary education might be viewed as sophistic? Analyze.

7. Briefly distinguish different kinds of relativism.

8. Is there something logically peculiar about the claim that *all* values are relative? Analyze carefully.

9. If all opinions are true, as Protagoras claimed, why discuss them? What grounds does a relativist have for being angry when others dispute her beliefs? Does she need any grounds? If not, what follows?

10. Discuss Protagoras's notion that disagreements can be "cured."

11. What's wrong with believing whatever makes you happy? Are there any truly harmful consequences to believing in astrology or crystal power? How can we question the beliefs of others just because we haven't had similar experiences?

12. On the one hand, it seems as if we should not base a moral position on how people actually behave. If we did, we'd have to condone lying regularly, cheating now and then, and so forth. On the other hand, it seems foolish, and perhaps cold and arrogant, to ignore our basic conduct and weaknesses. What do you think? Explain. (Note: This is an important ethical issue that we will see again.)

13. Do you think that society stifles the "superior individual"?

14. Is there a contradiction involved in the way the Sophists present their doctrine that "justice is in the interest of the stronger"? Can you present a better version of it?

15. Is there any way to refute the idea that might makes right? Explain why or why not.

16. Are lawyers Sophists? Do the ends justify the means? Discuss.

17. Try to find a few current examples of sophistry. What do you think of them and why?

18. Today, the term *sophist* is often used as a criticism. Have the Sophists been given a bad rap? Why or why not?

The Wise Man

Socrates

Socrates: Tell me, Euthydemus, have you ever gone to Delphi?

Euthydemus: Yes, twice.

Socrates: And did you observe what is written on the temple wall—"Know thyself"?

Euthydemus: I did.

Socrates: And did you take no thought of that inscription, or did you attend to it, and try to examine yourself, and ascertain what sort of character you are?

Xenophon

Socrates

Never mind the manner, which may or may not be good, but think only of the truth of my words, and give heed to that: let the speaker speak truly and the judge decide justly.

Socrates

Y ou are about to meet one of the most powerful, intriguing, annoying, inspiring, widely known, and yet misunderstood figures in the history of philosophy: **Socrates** (c. 470–399 B.C.). He has been called the greatest of philosophers and also the cleverest of Sophists. Stoics, Hedonists, and Cynics (each of whom we shall study in other chapters) have all claimed him as their chief inspiration and model. He was a pagan who is seen by many Jews and Christians as a man of God. His Holiness Tenzin Gyatso, the fourteenth Dalai Lama of Tibetan Buddhism, has expressed respect for him as an enlightened individual. Socrates claimed to have devoted his life to serving his country but was executed as a traitor. He attracted faithful and adoring admirers and was idolized by many young followers, yet the second charge at his trial was "corrupting the youth of Athens." Although he wrote no philosophy himself, he taught and inspired one of the two most influential philosophers in Western history, who in turn taught the other: Plato and Aristotle.

In his impressive book *Socrates*, the renowned classical scholar W. K. C. Guthrie says, "Any account must begin with the admission that there is, and always will be, a 'Socratic problem.'"[1] In the first place, Socrates wrote nothing. (Or at least nothing philosophical. In *Phaedo*, Plato asserted that Socrates wrote a hymn to Apollo and versified some of Aesop's fables while in prison.[2]) Our two main sources of information about Socrates are the dialogues of his most brilliant and famous pupil, Plato, and the anecdotes and memoirs of the less philosophical soldier, Xenophon. Additionally, briefer references to Socrates appear in Aristotle, Aristophanes, and elsewhere. The "Socratic problem" is compounded because Socrates' philosophy was nearly inseparable from the way his whole personality was reflected in his spoken teachings and the conduct of his life. Guthrie says, "In spite of the most scientific methods, in the end we must all have to some extent our own Socrates, who will not be precisely like anyone else's."[3]

What will *your* Socrates be like? Perhaps you too will be "stung" by the man who referred to himself as a gadfly (horsefly) sent by "the god" to keep his drowsy fellows alert. Perhaps you too will give birth to a brain-child with the aid of this ancient *sophos* who claimed to "teach nothing" but merely to act as a "kind of midwife," helping others draw out the wisdom hidden within them. Or perhaps you too will be annoyed—even angered—at the sophistic arrogance and logical tricks of a dangerous enemy of conventional morality, democracy, and religion. These are just some of the documented reactions to Socrates.

"The fact is," Guthrie says, "that no one was left indifferent by this altogether unusual character: everyone who has written about him was also reacting to him in one way or another."[4] It is still possible to get a basic picture of Socrates, however. For example, even though Plato and Xenophon present almost completely different views of him, we can treat their accounts as honest reflections of Socrates filtered through the minds and experiences of two completely different admirers. Neither account is "inaccurate" so much as incomplete and perhaps exaggerated. By comparing and evaluating various accounts of Socrates, we can get some idea of the man as well as the philosophy. So let me introduce you to my Socrates.

> It is not the knowledge of the wise we acknowledge to be special but the value they place and invite us to place on it. In some sense, the recognition of wisdom is the recognition of that which we, the unwise, not only have known but should have known all along.
>
> *Stanley Godlovitch*

The General Character of Socrates

As noted above, it is almost impossible to separate what Socrates taught from his whole personality. This accounts for much of his influence and charisma. Not only were his teachings challenging and powerful, he actually seemed to live up to them. Put in today's terms, he seems to have practiced what he preached.

The psychological term for this is *integration*. The opposite of an *alienated* or *fragmented* person, an integrated person has a clear sense of identity. She knows what she values and why, and is therefore strong. When we don't know who we really are or what is most important to us, we keep changing our minds. We get something we wanted very badly and then decide we don't like it. We have trouble making decisions because we are afraid of losing out on something better later. Living in a society that gives us many choices makes it especially difficult to find a clear identity. But it has never been easy. That is why Socrates' guiding motive of "Know thyself" has been so challenging to people all over the world and in all historical periods. Socrates struggled with one of the great problems of our time: Who am I? How can I discover my true identity? How shall *I* live?

Plato presents Socrates as an integrated, essentially unambivalent individual who stood clearly for some values and clearly against others. Then, as now, such personal clarity, such strong sense of direction and purpose, were attractive to young (or any) people confused as to who they are or

> In spite of being in sympathy with the sages, I am well aware of not having been one of them. As a person I was too self-indulgent and not heroic enough: as a writer I was too miscellaneous: as a thinker I was born at the wrong time and bred in the wrong way.
>
> *George Santayana*

This nineteenth-century sculpture of Socrates teaching in the agora shows the contrast between Socrates' inner beauty and outer ugliness.

want to be. Then, as now, Socrates' consistent respect for justice, integrity, courage, temperance, decency, beauty, and balance was especially appealing in a cultural climate of dizzy excesses, crass materialism, and cut-throat competition for money, power, and prestige. In a complex, sophisticated society in which old values were under siege, the simplicity and clarity of an individual with Socrates' obvious abilities were intriguing, even when they were upsetting.

The Ugliest Man in Athens

Against the popular notion of his time (and ours), Socrates taught that beauty and goodness should be determined by usefulness and fitness of function, rather than by mere appearance or personal feelings of delight. An interesting illustration of this can be found in his own appearance. He was universally acknowledged to be "extraordinarily ugly"—so ugly, in fact, that he fascinated people.

His most notable physical features were a broad, flat, turned-up nose, protruding, staring eyes, thick, fleshy lips, and a belly that he himself characterized in Xenophon's *Symposium* as "a stomach rather too large for convenience,"[5] and that he elsewhere announced plans to "dance off." His friends compared him to a satyr or an electric eel, whose penetrating questions stunned his listeners, "shocked" them into higher awareness.

He made his appearance serve him well. His humorous references to it reflect his good nature and modesty, as well as his hierarchy of values. After all, if, as he taught, the true self is not the body but the soul (psyche), and if all *virtue* implies *excellence of function*, then the appearance of the body is less important than how well it functions. True beauty is inner beauty, beauty of spirit and character. Socrates' friends certainly came to see the "true Socrates," and so, for them, the beauty of who he was transcended and transformed the ugliness of his body.

Beauty in things exists in the mind which contemplates them.

David Hume

In Plato's *Gorgias*, Socrates says that we cannot know whether a person is happy just because his external condition is attractive to us. He insists that happiness, like goodness, is a matter of inner qualities:

> Then doubtless you will say, Socrates, that you do not know that even the Great King is happy.
>
> Yes, and I shall be speaking the truth; for I do not know how he stands *in point of interior formation* and justice.
>
> Why, does happiness entirely consist of that?
>
> Yes, by my account, Polus; for a good and honorable man or woman, I say, is happy, and an unjust and wicked one is wretched.[6]

Philosophical Query

Everyone I like and love seems quite "attractive" to me. Yet one of my friends resembled Socrates. Before I ever met him I had noticed him in the college cafeteria. I thought he was one of the most unfortunate-looking persons I had ever seen. He was friends with some acquaintances of mine, and so I eventually met him. I initially felt uncomfortable even being around him because of his looks, I'm sorry to say. But slowly I discovered an intelligent, funny, kind, strong, and courageous man. Over the years of our friendship, I actually lost the capacity to *see* him as ugly. Sadly, the converse has been true in my experience as well. A beautiful or handsome countenance that belongs to a slothful or self-centered or shallow or cruel person over time becomes less handsome or beautiful to me. Have you noticed this pattern? Analyze it, if you have.

Don't think Socrates was a prude. He was not. He was tempted by physical attractiveness, but he governed his life according to "true beauty and goodness," preferring a good and beautiful soul to a pleasing body that housed a lesser self.

An informative and humorous passage from Chapter 5 of Xenophon's *Symposium* illustrates how Socrates could incorporate philosophy into anything, even joking around with friends. Socrates is engaged in a good-natured "beauty contest" with a handsome young man named Critobulus. Critobulus has challenged Socrates to use his famous question-and-answer method (we'll look at this shortly) to prove that Socrates is "more beautiful" than Critobulus.

Critobulus: All right, but which of our noses is the more beautiful?

Socrates: Mine, I should say, if the gods give us noses to smell with, for your nostrils point to earth, but mine are spread out widely to receive odours from every quarter.

Critobulus: But how can a snub nose be more beautiful than a straight one?

Socrates: Because it does not get in the way but allows the eyes to see what they will, whereas a high bridge walls them off, as if to spite them.

I'm tired of all this nonsense about beauty being only skin deep. What do you want—an adorable pancreas?

Jean Kerr

Many are ruined by admirers whose heads are turned by the sight of a pretty face; many are led by their strength to attempt tasks too heavy for them, and meet serious evils; many by their wealth are corrupted, and fall victims to conspiracies; many through glory and political power have suffered great evils.

Socrates

Critobulus: As for the mouth, I give in, for if mouths are made for biting you could take a much larger bite than I.

Socrates: And with my thick lips don't you think I could give a softer kiss?

Critobulus: By your account I seem to have a mouth uglier than an ass's. . . . I give up. Let's put it to the vote, so that I may know as quickly as possible the forfeit I have to pay.[7]

When the votes were counted, Socrates lost unanimously, prompting him to accuse Critobulus of bribing the judges.

Barefoot in Athens

Socrates was also well known for his indifference to fashion and ordinary comforts. He was usually barefoot and apparently had only one tattered coat, about which his friends joked. His enemies accused him of being "unwashed," and even his friends admitted that it was a surprise to see Socrates freshly bathed.

One of his most noted characteristics was hardiness, reflected in remarkable self-control, or *temperance*. Temperance in this sense means indifference to both the presence and absence of material pleasures; it does not mean total abstinence from pleasure or extreme asceticism. In Xenophon's *Memorabilia*, Socrates put it like this:

> You seem, Antiphon, to imagine that happiness consists in luxury and extravagance. But my belief is that *to have no wants is divine*; *to have as few as possible comes next to the divine*; and as that which is divine is supreme, so that which approaches nearest to its nature is nearest to supreme [emphasis added].[8]

Socrates' self-control included indifference to fear. During a battle at Delium he is said to have been the last Athenian soldier to give way before the advancing Spartans. In the Potidaean military campaign, Socrates is reported to have walked about barefoot on the icy winter ground of Thrace, dressed as he customarily was back home. In Plato's *Symposium*, Alcibiades claims that this irritated the other soldiers, who, bundled and muffled against the fierce winter with their feet wrapped in felt and sheepskin, thought Socrates was trying to humiliate them.

In Xenophon's *Memorabilia*, Socrates talks about self-control and self-discipline with his friend Euthydemus. He uses the term *incontinence* in its original sense to mean lack of self-control, especially concerning appetites and passions. Socrates argues that self-control—not self-indulgence and weakness of will—leads to pleasure. Lack of self-control, he asserts, prevents us from the finest expressions of pleasure in eating, drinking, resting, and making love. If we gratify every urge as soon as it arises, we must often settle for fast food, cheap drink, sleeping all day, or crude sexual en-

The Sophos at Large

When Socrates prayed, he asked only for "good gifts, for the gods know best what things are good."

According to Diogenes Läertius, Socrates' style of arguing was sometimes so intense that his opponents frequently attacked him with their fists or tore his hair out, "yet he bore all this ill-usage patiently."

When Alcibiades offered Socrates a large site on which to build a house, he replied, "Suppose, then, I wanted shoes and you offered me a whole hide to make a pair, would it not be ridiculous of me to take it?"

Socrates used to say that he most enjoyed the food that was least in need of seasoning, and the drink that made him feel the least desire for another drink, adding that he was as the gods because he had few wants.

When someone asked Socrates whether he should marry or not, the *sophos* replied, "Whichever you do you will repent it."

When Socrates invited some rich men to dinner, his wife Xanthippe said she was embarrassed by the meal she had prepared. "Never mind," he said. "If they are reasonable they will put up with it, if they are good for nothing, we shall not trouble ourselves about them."

When someone said, "Socrates, you are condemned by Athens to die," he responded, "So are you, by nature."

---

counters. We will be little more than animals. Without self-control we have no hope of learning how to moderate ourselves and our lives:

> "The delights of learning something good and excellent, and of studying some of the means whereby a man knows how to regulate his body well and manage his household successfully, to be useful to his friends and city and to defeat his enemies—knowledge that yields not only very great benefits but very great pleasures—these are the delights of the self-controlled; but the incontinent have no part in them. For who should we say has less concern with these than he who has no power of cultivating them because all his serious purposes are centered in the pleasures that lie nearest?"
>
> "Socrates," said Euthydemus, "I think you mean that he who is at the mercy of the bodily pleasures has no concern whatever with virtue in any form?"
>
> "Yes, Euthydemus," said Socrates.[9]

Part of Socrates' appeal comes from the fact that he had the same desires as the rest of us. They may even have been more intense. So we respond to the effort he must have exerted to keep all his appetites and passions under strict control. His philosophical searching was, consequently, based on a full involvement with life. It was not the product of a withered, passionless mentality. Nor was it based on a naive goody-goody view of the human condition. He knew and loved life at its fullest, wrestling with it and challenging others to join his "enduring quest."

There is no doubt that in one form or another, Socrates and Buddha, Jesus and St. Paul, Plotinus and Spinoza, taught that . . . without renunciation of many of the ordinary appetites, no man can really live well.

Walter Lippmann

Philosophical **Query**

What do you think of Socrates' views on self-control? Does the current concern with healthy diets, exercise, and so on seem to be in line with what Socrates thought? Discuss.

A Most Unusual Father and Husband

Socrates was married to Xanthippe and had three sons. He was seventy years old at the time of his execution; his oldest son was not yet twenty, and the youngest was said to be a small child.[10] We know relatively little of Socrates' home life, but Xanthippe probably had aristocratic connections.

Although he was probably apprenticed as a stonecutter or sculptor by his father, Socrates worked only now and then. He lived off a modest inheritance from his father, consisting of a house and some money, which his best friend Crito invested for him.[11] And while he never took money for teaching (as the Sophists did), he occasionally accepted gifts from his wealthy friends and admirers.

His well-known contempt for indiscriminate social approval made it a simple matter for him to live comfortably without shoes and with an old coat. But what effect would Socrates' uncommon values have had on his wife and sons? Here was an obviously brilliant, physically powerful man who spent his time wandering about the marketplace asking philosophical questions all day. He seems to have had ample opportunity to eat and drink and mingle with the movers and shakers of Athens, yet he refused to seek political, social, or financial influence. Even (especially?) today it is easier to preach nonmaterialistic spiritual and philosophical values than to actually live as if the soul is more important than the body.

Imagine a philosophy professor today being indifferent to prestige, salary, and possessions. Also consider the effect this might have on her unphilosophical husband. Imagine the effect on her children: "Mommy cannot afford to buy you new shoes. She's busy searching for the meaning of life." Although a bit oversimplified, the point is important. An encounter with Socrates, likened to an "electric shock," is centered at just such tension: His life and teachings are at once inspiring and frustrating to us, as they were to his contemporaries.

Philosophical **Query**

How might we explain the fact that many churches and schools are luxurious? Don't both educators and preachers (not to mention gurus and therapists) *say* that material success does not guarantee happiness? Don't many of them *say* that the life of the mind or soul is most important? Why, then, do they *look* as if they don't believe it? There are plenty of famous examples of this inconsistency. Discuss one or two of them. If the Socratic view is wrong, why do so many people give it lip service?

In the world, one cannot have it both ways. If he wants to maintain his good reputation, he must not think of pursuing status and wealth. But if he wants status and riches, he must bear in mind that it will be at the expense of his integrity.

Lie Zi

Asked what was very difficult, Thales replied: "To know thyself."
Asked what was very easy, he answered: "To give advice."

The Archetypal Individual

The combined portraits of Plato and Xenophon reveal Socrates as a master teacher, a man of awesome intellectual force, possessing an integrated self, whose charisma and personal power sprang from more than either mere intellect or personality. In other words, Socrates is a genuine **archetypal individual,** or, in a term coined by philosopher and psychologist Karl Jaspers, a **paradigmatic individual.** Jaspers applied the term to a special class of teachers, philosophers, and religious figures whose nature becomes a standard by which a culture judges the "ideal" human being.

An archetypal or paradigmatic individual is a rare human being whose very nature represents something elemental about the human condition. "The historical reality of [the paradigmatic individual]," says Jaspers, "can be discerned only in [his] extraordinary impact on those who knew [him] and in [his] later echoes."[12] In any encounter with an archetypal individual, the power or force of the whole person is galvanic. This power does not come from a rational argument. It is an experience that almost goes beyond words and cannot be ignored. It triggers not just personal but deep philosophical and spiritual responses in others.

These human paradigms possess a timeless quality, according to Jaspers. They serve as *archetypal images* for their cultures, and usually speak to other cultures as well. Although different cultures and eras produce different archetypes (Jaspers used as his examples Socrates, Confucius, Buddha, and Jesus), *the archetypal individual's very nature demands a response*: What is it to be a human being? What is most important? What is good? How should *I* live?

Jaspers says:

> A radical change is experienced and demanded [by paradigmatic individuals]. They are stirred to their depths, by what we do not know. They express what there is no appropriate way of saying. They speak in parables, dialectical contradictions, conversational replies. . . .
>
> Socrates seeks himself and his relation to other men. By his extreme questioning he arouses a real, living certainty that is *not mere knowledge* of something. He transcends the world without negating it. He forges total knowledge, total judgments, contenting himself with a nonknowledge in which truth and reality are actualized [emphasis added].[13]

That is, Socrates continued to develop and grow as a person because of his philosophical search. He did not "fragment" himself into two parts, the thinker and the real person. He did not force himself to stick to a rigid theory. He responded anew to each experience. When Jaspers refers to "a nonknowledge" he means that Socrates always insisted that his "wisdom" lay in knowing what he did not know. (We'll look into this important concept shortly.)

ARCHETYPAL INDIVIDUAL OR PARADIGMATIC INDIVIDUAL

A special class of teachers, philosophers, and religious figures whose nature becomes a standard by which a culture judges the "ideal" human being; a rare human being whose very nature represents something elemental about the human condition.

The Old Boy and the World

The people of the world are
    merry-making,
As if partaking of the sacrificial
    feasts,
As if mounting the terrace in
    spring;
I alone am mild, like one
    unemployed,
Like a new-born babe that
    cannot yet smile,
Unattached, like one without a
    home.

The people of the world have
    enough and to spare,
But I am like one left out,
My heart must be that of a fool,
Being muddled and nebulous!
The vulgar are knowing,
    luminous;
I alone am dull, confused.
The vulgar are clever, self-
    assured;
I alone, depressed.
Patient as the sea,
Adrift, seemingly aimless.

The people of the world all have
    a purpose;
I alone appear stubborn and
    uncouth.
I alone differ from other people,
And value drawing sustenance
    from the Mother.

Lao-tzu
The Wisdom of Laotse, trans. and
ed. Lin Yutang (New York: Modern
Library, 1976), pp. 128–29.

Every man is enlightened,
but wishes he wasn't.

    R. H. Blyth

Because their very natures "demand response," community reactions to paradigmatic individuals can be extreme: love and embrace them or reject and exclude them. The paradigmatic individual is more challenging and intense than the mere sage. We saw in the First Interlude that the sage was considered "strange" and "alien," *atopos* in Greek. But this kind of strangeness can be trivialized or dismissed as merely "odd" or "eccentric." The paradigmatic individual may be just as "strange" as the sage, but in a manner that is more personally disturbing, more deeply unsettling to our everyday habits and values.

Something about a paradigmatic teacher "shocks" us into a state of uncomfortable, reflective alertness. By actually "living up to" principles that we, too, profess to see as worthy—and by living up to them with remarkable consistency and courage—the mere existence of a "human paradigm" provokes us into wondering how well our own lives reflect our beliefs. In other words, the *life* and *teachings* of the paradigmatic individual form a whole, a harmony that precludes the "safe distance" that exists between the lives of more ordinary teachers and their teachings. The paradigmatic figure invites us to close the gap by calling on us to live courageously and honestly according to articulated principles—without excusing ourselves.

For the most part, paradigmatic teachers stand in opposition to moral compromises to our integrity—however that is understood. But living without significant compromise is dangerous. In the first place, there is the risk that what appears to be integrity is, in fact, dogmatic rigidity, self-satisfied and self-righteous fanaticism. Then, too, by holding him- or herself to the highest standards, paradigmatic teachers step outside the "norm," become estranged from the more modest or common standards and goals of the community. This "outsider" position is, itself, seen as a threat to conformity and group identity. This threat is amplified whenever a sage or prophet refuses to stop with mere questioning, and throws down the gauntlet of living with fearless integrity.

One contemporary educational philosophy advises teachers not to pretend to be "perfect"; to admit their failings and "share" their weaknesses with their students to make it easier for the students to "relate" to the teachers. And from a certain perspective, it does seem "safer" (easier) to admire the *lessons* of teachers who are "just like us." The weaknesses of teachers who are "just like us" protect us from feeling deeply challenged: We are not confronted by the power of the kind of teacher whose teaching is completely reflected in his or her *being*. By actually "living up to" their teachings, integrated teachers deny us the safety of believing that the standard is set too high to reach, the notion that *no one really lives like that.*

And so, on one level, we actually prefer the pastor who humbly admits to—and indulges in—a love of fine automobiles or sailboarding, willingly paid for out of the collection plate; the ethics professor who copies colleagues' new software and uses the school's equipment to play on the Internet; the psychology instructor who lectures while intoxicated and dates students (only "mature" students, of course); the activist professor whose passionate indictments of elitism or racism or sexism are simply virulent forms of the very same "isms," only in reverse; and so on.

So ingrained is contemporary suspicion of the possibility of healthy expressions of "paradigmatic integrity," that I am uncomfortable writing this passage and listing these commonplace examples of apparent gaps between teachers and what they teach. So let's be honest: The historical Socrates was probably not such a fine fellow, anyway. Plato probably just invented him to get back at the Sophists (Chapter 2). Once we grow up, we see through these romanticized, Sunday-school type lessons. This sophisticated, "honest" attitude toward "perfectionism" provides us with a safety zone between the ideal and the realistic. Nobody could really live like Socrates today. But what if . . .

> But I shall be asked, Why do people delight in continually conversing with you? I have told you already, Athenians, the whole truth about this matter: they like to hear the cross-examination of the pretenders to wisdom; there is amusement in it.
>
> *Socrates*

Philosophical Query

Can you think of other paradigmatic individuals? Remember, a paradigmatic individual is more than a merely influential teacher, adviser, social reformer, or significant religious figure. Do you think that contemporary America, with its present sense of diversity, can produce archetypal philosophers? Or must each community, ethnic group, or race have its own human paradigms? What qualities do you think a contemporary "American *sophos*" must possess?

The Teacher and His Teachings

As presented by Plato, the harmony between Socrates' life and teachings transformed him from a truth-seeker into a sage, from a sage into a paradigm of the teacher-as-more-than-sage. Pierre Hadot says:

> There were several reasons for the fact that my research on the sage as a model gradually became fixed upon Socrates. In the first place, I found in him a figure who exercised a widespread influence of the greatest importance on the entire Western tradition. Secondly, and most importantly, the figure of Socrates—as sketched by Plato, at any rate—had it seemed to me one unique advantage. It is the portrait of a mediator between the transcendent ideal of wisdom and concrete human reality. It is a paradox of highly Socratic irony that Socrates was not a sage, but a "philo-sopher": that is, a lover of wisdom.[14]

For reasons that remain controversial to this day, Socrates' "electric shock" effect on Athens resulted in his indictment, conviction, and execution as a traitorous blasphemer. Speaking for the last time as a public figure, on trial for his life, the seventy-year-old philosopher repeated what he had *always* insisted, "I neither know nor think that I know."

As we learn more about Socrates' teachings and teaching method, let's see if we can gain some understanding of how it came to pass that a philosopher who insisted, under threat of death, that his wisdom consisted of knowing what he did not know still stands as *the* archetypal *wise man* in Western philosophy.

The Dialectic

Socrates argued that one of the chief reasons many people cannot think clearly is that they do not even know what they are talking about. Consequently, the first order of business is to define our terms. The early dialogues of Plato reveal a Socrates constantly pushing and searching for clearer and more precise definitions of key terms. Time after time he lures a confused individual from one muddled definition to another. Then, using skillful (some would even say loaded or leading) questions, he attempts to guide his "opponent" closer to the truth by allowing the opponent to experience the logical inconsistencies in his own stated positions. Socrates was so effective with this method of philosophical teaching and inquiry that it came to be known as the **Socratic dialectic**, also known as the **Socratic method**.

The Socratic method begins with the assumption that the function of education is to draw the truth out of the pupil rather than "fill an empty vessel." In practice, it is a series of guided questions known as the dialectical method of inquiry. Claims are continually refined, definitions required for all key terms, logical inconsistencies brought to light and resolved. A

SOCRATIC METHOD OR SOCRATIC DIALECTIC

Question-and-answer technique perfected by Socrates to draw truth out of his pupils, often by means of achieving a clearer, more precise definition of a key term or concept.

vital aspect of Socratic teaching is the active involvement of the audience (pupils, listeners), hence the use of questions rather than straight lectures.

The dialectical process as Socrates practiced it was dynamic and hopeful. At worst, the participants learned that although they may not have found *the* answer, or *the* meaning of justice, *the* good life, or courage, they were each at least a bit clearer than before. At any rate, this was Socrates' experience—others were often angered and frustrated, if not humiliated, as their confusion and ignorance were exposed.

Socrates believed that the truth was somehow in each of us. The teacher's role, then, isn't to put knowledge into an empty mind, but to draw wisdom and clarity out of a disordered and confused soul. Just as a midwife does not herself give birth, but aids the mother, Socrates claimed to aid others in giving birth to their own insights by *drawing out what was already there*. And just as a midwife is of no help until the mother has conceived a child, Socrates was of no help until the other person had conceived at least a sketchy idea.

For Socrates, the most important order of business was to *engage* the other person. The Socratic method in full form is more than just questions and answers. It is a highly personal activity, guided by one who knows both the general direction of the inquiry (but not "the answers") as well as the nature and needs of the individual student. It works only if the other "participant" actively listens and responds.

Socratic Irony

A key element in keeping his pupils engaged, and calling attention to meaning, was Socrates' use of **irony**, a way of communicating on more than one level. An ironic utterance has at least two levels of meaning, *the literal level*, also known as the obvious level, and *the hidden level*, also known as the real level. As a rule, the two meanings are near opposites, as in the case of the sarcastic professor who writes on a woefully inadequate term paper: "Beautiful job! You've never done better!"

By using words in unexpected ways, by meaning more than one obvious, surface-level thing, Socrates hoped to keep his listeners alert. Further, the use of irony underscored his belief that things are not always as they first appear, that there is a deeper reality than may be apparent. Socrates used irony to keep his listeners on their toes and to avoid putting answers in their mouths. For instance, he begins his *Apology* (his defense at his trial) by referring to the "persuasive" abilities of his immediate accusers, who are Sophists. Of course, his remark is actually an ironic way of showing that these Sophists have not persuaded him of anything. His use of irony in his opening remarks gets the audience's immediate attention:

> How you, O Athenians, have been affected by my accusers, I cannot tell; but I know that they almost made me forget who I was—so

> Wise men profit more from fools than fools from wise men; for the wise men shun the mistakes of fools, but fools do not imitate the successes of wise men.
>
> *Cato the Elder*

IRONY

Communication on at least two levels, a literal or obvious level and a hidden or real level; favored by Socrates as a technique for keeping his listeners alert and involved.

What an Extraordinary Effect His Words Have Had on Me . . .

In Plato's *Symposium*, Alcibiades notes the staggering power of Socrates:

. . . when we listen to you, or to someone else repeating what you've said, even if he puts it ever so badly, and never mind whether the person who's listening is man, woman, or child, we're absolutely staggered and bewitched. And speaking for myself, gentlemen, if I wasn't afraid you'd tell me that I was completely bottled, I'd swear on oath what an extraordinary effect his words have had on me—and still do if it comes to that. For the moment I hear him speak I am smitten with a kind of sacred rage . . . oh, and not only me, but lots of other men.

. . . He makes me admit that while I'm spending time on politics I am neglecting all the things crying for attention in myself. So I just refuse to listen to him—as if he were one of those Sirens, you know—and get out of earshot as quick as I can, for fear he will keep me sitting listening till I'm positively senile.

And there's one thing I've never felt with anybody else—not the kind of thing you'd expect to find in me, either—and that is a sense of shame. Socrates is the only man in the world that can make me feel ashamed. Because there's no getting away from it, I know I ought to do the things he tells me to, and yet the moment I'm out of his sight I

don't care what I do to keep in with the mob. So I dash off like a runaway slave, and keep out of his way as long as I can, and the next time I meet him I remember all that I had to admit the time before, and naturally I feel ashamed. There are times when I'd honestly be glad to hear that he's dead, and yet I know that if he did die I'd be more upset than ever—so I ask you, what is a man to do?

Plato, *Symposium*, 215D–16C, in Edith Hamilton and Huntington Cairns, eds., *Plato: The Collected Dialogues*, trans. Michael Joyce (New York: Pantheon Books, Bollingen Series 71, 1966), p. 567.

I do not suppose that I know.

Socrates

persuasively did they speak; and yet they have hardly uttered a word of truth. But of the many falsehoods told by them, there was one which quite amazed me;—I mean when they said that you should be upon your guard and not allow yourselves to be deceived by the force of my eloquence. To say this, when they were certain to be detected as soon as I opened my lips and proved myself to be anything but a great speaker, did indeed appear to me most shameless—unless by the force of eloquence they mean the force of truth; for if such is their meaning, I admit that I am eloquent. But in how different a way from theirs! Well, as I was saying, they have scarcely spoken the truth at all; but from me you shall hear the whole truth: not, however, delivered after their manner in a set oration duly ornamented with words and phrases . . . at my time of life I ought not be appearing before you, O men of Athens, in the character of a juvenile orator—let no one expect it of me.[15]

Ironic communication confuses those who are inattentive or not "in on" the key to the hidden meaning. For instance, most members of Socrates' jury would have been familiar with his wranglings with Sophists and with sophistic emphasis on the arts of persuasion. A smaller group would have also responded to the irony of Socrates, whose life was devoted to following the command "Know thyself," forgetting who he was. Irony was both a crucial component of Socrates' method and a contributing factor to his ultimate trouble, since to many observers, Socrates' use of irony was just another sophistic trick.

Philosophical Query

See how many ironic references to Sophists you can find in the preceding passage from Plato's *Apology*.

Dialectic in Action: Socrates versus Thrasymachus

To some critics, Socrates' entire "philosophical career" was what vaudeville performers used to call a "shtick," a gimmick that gives a performer a recognizable identity to hide behind and a repertoire of set (predictable) routines. In Socrates' case, Sophists and other critics saw him as merely pretending to be a simple fellow, poor and modest, on a sincere quest for wisdom. According to this view, Socrates was simply a clever—and often cleverer—Sophist; his "Aw, shucks," seemingly meek mask was thought to be a ruse designed to set opponents up for the fall. That is, by lulling people into a false sense of security and trust, Socrates was able to catch them off guard and "shock" them with sneaky word tricks and leading questions. Whether there is merit to such a picture of Socrates is something you must wrestle with for yourself.

> The doer of injustice is unhappier than the sufferer.
>
> *Democritus*

Before we look further into some specific Socratic doctrines, let's enrich our sense of the dialectic as a potentially interpersonal philosophical method. We can do that by taking an extended look at the kind of dialectical exchange with a Sophist that Socrates became famous for: precisely the sort of explosive encounter that fueled his ambiguous reputation and contributed to the animosity between Socrates and certain sophists.

Plato provides one of the most intriguing examples of the Socratic dialectic in action early in his masterpiece, *The Republic* (Chapter 4). The passage that follows concerns an encounter between Socrates and the Sophist Thrasymachus. **Thrasymachus (c. 450 B.C.)** is an archetype of the kind of Sophist who is less interested in theories and philosophy than in political and social action. In Book I, section 3, of *The Republic*, Plato paints a vivid portrait of the volatile, aggressive style Thrasymachus used in confronting his opponents.

The Republic consists of a series of dialogues between Socrates and various individuals, chiefly about the nature of justice. By skillful

Sometimes it seems as if might does indeed make right—at least that's what some observers of the 1992 Los Angeles riots claimed. They argued that the riots brought attention, financial aid, business loans, and so forth to the riot-torn communities. Do you agree with this assessment?

questioning, Socrates "reveals" that conventional notions of morality are confused and "muddleheaded." After Socrates has rejected a number of attempts to define justice, Thrasymachus literally bursts onto the scene. With energy and sarcasm, he categorically denies that any one moral standard can be equally applicable to rich and poor, strong and weak, "superior" and "inferior."

Thrasymachus's Moral Realism

Thrasymachus goes well beyond Socrates' rejection of common conceptions of justice as repaying debts or giving persons their "due." Thrasymachus substitutes unabashed self-interest for any other view of justice. He thereby transforms *moral relativism* into a hard-edged *moral realism*, contending that an unsentimental view of life shows quite clearly that *might makes right*. Whether we like it or not, according to Thrasymachus, the values that prevail in all areas of life—economic, political, racial, educational—reflect the *interests of the strong*. Certain values dominate not because they are in some absolute sense "right," but because they are the views preferred by the most powerful individual or group. And since nature rewards power, the powerful individual is always the superior type, the "true individual," gloriously free in his or her indifference to the puny concerns of conventional morality.

Reflecting Socrates' harsh opinion of moral realism, Plato portrays Thrasymachus as loud, offensive, and often on the verge of resorting to force. From the very start, we know we are in for an interesting experience as Thrasymachus disrupts the courteous, "philosophical" tone of the discussion.

Encounter with a Sophos

As you read the following passage from *The Republic*, look for examples of irony (and sarcasm). Reflect on Thrasymachus's accusations against Socrates and his method. Study Socrates' responses. Note, too, how Socrates manages to draw Thrasymachus into his preferred question-and-answer process—in spite of Thrasymachus's apparent awareness of the dialectic's effects and his own strong assertions that he will not participate. Be alert for the possible interpersonal consequences that might result from a "losing" encounter with Socrates. (And add some zest to your reading by mentally picturing the two protagonists: the volatile, younger, stronger, hotheaded Thrasymachus and the confident old master of the cross-examination.)

As our drama opens, Socrates is describing Thrasymachus's impatient interruption of a discussion he was having with Polemarchus:

> While we had been talking Thrasymachus had often tried to interrupt, but had been prevented by those sitting near him, who wanted to hear the argument concluded; but when we paused . . . he was no longer able to contain himself and gathered himself together and sprang on us like a wild beast, as if he wanted to tear us in pieces. Polemarchus and I were scared stiff, as Thrasymachus burst out and said, "What is all this nonsense, Socrates? Why do you go on in this childish way being so polite about each other's opinions? If you really want to know what justice is, stop asking questions and then playing to the gallery by refuting anyone who answers you. You know perfectly well that it is easier to ask questions than to answer them. Give us an answer yourself, and tell us what you think justice is. And don't tell me that it's duty, or expediency, or advantage, or profit, or interest. I won't put up with nonsense of that sort; give me a clear and precise definition."
>
> I was staggered by his attack and looked at him in dismay. If I had not seen him first I believe I should have been struck dumb; but I had noticed him when our argument first began to annoy him, and so managed to answer him, saying diffidently: "Don't be hard on us, Thrasymachus. If we have made any mistake in the course of our

But if a man arises endowed with a nature sufficiently strong he will, I believe, shake off these controls, burst his fetters, and break loose. And trampling upon our scraps of paper, our spells and incantations, and all our unnatural conventions, he rises up and reveals himself our master who was once our slave, and there shines forth nature's true justice.

Callicles

The majority of just acts according to the law are prescribed contrary to nature. For there is legislation about the eyes, what they must see and what not; and about the ears, what they must hear and what not; and about the tongue, what it must speak and what not; and about the hands, what they must do and what not; and about the feet, where they must go and where not. And about the soul, what it must desire and what not.

Antiphon

And how many legions does the Pope have?

Stalin, at Yalta

argument, I assure you we have not done so on purpose. For if we were looking for gold, you can't suppose that we would willingly let mutual politeness hinder our search and prevent our finding it. Justice is much more valuable than gold, and we aren't likely to cramp our efforts to find it by any idiotic deference to each other. I assure you we are doing our best. It's the ability that we lack, and clever chaps like you ought to be sorry for us and not get annoyed with us."

Thrasymachus laughed sarcastically, and replied, "There you go with your old affectation, Socrates. I knew it, and I told the others that you would never let yourself be questioned, but go on shamming ignorance and do anything rather than give a straight answer."

"That's because you're so clever, Thrasymachus," I replied, "and you know it. You ask someone for a definition of twelve and add, 'I don't want to be told that it's twice six, or three times four, or six times two, or four times three; that sort of nonsense won't do.' You know perfectly well that no one would answer you on those terms. He would reply, 'What do you mean, Thrasymachus; am I to give none of the answers you mention? If one of them happens to be true, do you want me to give a false one?' And how would you answer him?"

"That's not a fair parallel," he replied.

"I don't see why not," I said: "but even if it is not, we shan't stop anyone else answering like that if he thinks it fair, whether we like it or not."

"So I suppose that is what you are going to do," he said; "you're going to give one of the answers I barred."

"I would not be surprised," said I, "if it seemed to me on reflection to be the right one."

"What if I give you a quite different and far better definition of justice? What plea will you enter then?"

"The plea of ignorance: for those who don't know must learn from those who do."

"You must have your joke," said he, "but you must pay your costs as well." [The Sophists always charged for their instruction; and Thrasymachus is having his own joke by demanding a fee for "instructing" Socrates.]

"I will when I have any cash."

"The money's all right," said Glaucon; "we'll pay up for Socrates. So let us have your definition, Thrasymachus."

"I know," he replied, "so that Socrates can play his usual tricks, never giving us his own views but always asking others to explain theirs and refuting them."

"But what am I to do?" I asked. "I neither know nor profess to know anything about the subject, and even if I did I've been forbidden to say what I think by no mean [insignificant] antagonist. It's much more reasonable for you to say something, because you say you know, and really have something to say. Do please do me a favour and give me an answer, and don't grudge your instruction to Glaucon and the others here."

Glaucon and the others backed up what I had said, and it was obvious that Thrasymachus was anxious to get the credit for the striking answer he thought he could give: but he went on pretending he wanted to win his point and make me reply. In the end, however, he gave in, remarking, "So this is the wisdom of Socrates: he won't teach anyone anything, but goes round learning from others and is not even grateful."

To which I replied, "It's quite true, Thrasymachus, to say I learn from others, but it's not true to say I'm not grateful. I am generous with my praise—the only return I can give, as I have no money. You'll see in a moment how ready I am to praise any view I think well founded, for I'm sure the answer you're going to give will be that."

"Listen then," [Thrasymachus] replied. "I define justice or right as what is in the interest of the stronger party. Now where is your praise? I can see you're going to refuse it."

"You shall have it when I [Socrates] understand what you mean, which at present I don't. You say that what is in the interest of the stronger party is right; but what do you mean by interest? For instance, Polydamas the athlete is stronger than us, and it's in his interest to eat beef to keep it; we are weaker than he, but you can't mean that the same diet is in our interest and so right for us."

"You're being tiresome, Socrates," he returned, "and taking my definition in the sense most likely to damage it."

"I assure you I'm not," [Socrates] said; "you must explain your meaning more clearly."

"Well then, you know that some states are tyrannies, some democracies, some aristocracies? And that in each city power is in the hands of the ruling class?"

"Yes."

"Each ruling class makes laws that are in its own interest, a democracy democratic laws, a tyranny tyrannical ones and so on; and in making these laws they define as 'right' for their subjects what is in the interest of themselves, the rulers, and if anyone breaks their laws he is punished as a 'wrongdoer.' That is what I mean when I say that 'right' is the same thing in all states, namely the interest of the established ruling class; and this ruling class is the 'strongest' element in each state, and so if we argue correctly we see that 'right' is always the same, the interest of the stronger party.

". . . Consider how the just man always comes off worse than the unjust. For instance, in any business relations between them, you won't find the just man better off at the end of the deal than the

Speak softly but carry a big stick.

Theodore Roosevelt

The gods help them that help themselves.

Aesop

Convention is the ruler of all.

Pindar

unjust. Again, in their relations with the state, when there are taxes
to be paid the unjust man will pay less on the same income, and when
there's anything to be got he'll get it all. Thus if it's a question of office, if the just man loses nothing else he will suffer from neglecting
his private affairs; his honesty will prevent him appropriating public
funds, and his relations and friends will detest him because his principles will not allow him to push their interests. But quite the reverse is
true of the unjust man . . . the man . . . who can make profits in a big
way: he's the man to study if you want to find how much more private profit there is in wrong than in right. . . . *So we see that injustice,
given scope, has greater strength and freedom and power than justice;
which proves what I started by saying, that justice is the interest of
the stronger party, injustice the interest and profit of oneself*" [empha-
sis added].

"Now," I said, "I understand your meaning, and we must try to
find out whether you are right or not. Your answer defines 'right' and
'interest' . . . but adds the qualification "of the stronger party.""

"An insignificant qualification, I suppose you will say."

"Its significance is not yet clear; what is clear is that we must consider whether your definition is true. For I quite agree that what is
right is an 'interest'; but you add that it is the interest 'of the stronger
party,' and that's what I don't know about and want you to consider."

"Let us hear you."

"You shall," said I. "You say that obedience to the ruling power is
right and just?"

"I do."

"And are those in power in the various states infallible or not?"

"They are, of course, liable to make mistakes," he replied.

"When they proceed to make laws, then, they may do the job well
or badly."

"I suppose so."

"And if they do it well the laws will be in their interest, and if they
do it badly they won't, I take it."

"I agree."

"But their subjects must obey the laws they make, for to do so is
right."

"Of course."

"Then according to your argument it is *right* not only to do what is
in the interest of the stronger party but also the opposite."

"What do you mean?" he asked.

"My meaning is the same as yours, I think. Let us look at it more
closely. Did we not agree that when the ruling powers order their
subjects to do something they are sometimes mistaken about their
own best interest, and yet that it is *right* for the subject to do what
his ruler enjoins?"

"I suppose we did."

"Then you must admit that it is *right* to do things that are *not* in the interest of the rulers, who are the *stronger* party; that is, when the rulers mistakenly give orders that will harm them and yet (so you say) it is right for their subjects to obey those orders. For surely, my dear Thrasymachus, in those circumstances it follows that it is 'right' to do the opposite of what you say is right, in that the weaker are *ordered* to do what is against the interest of the stronger."[16]

Philosophical Query

Statistically, poorer, less educated people make up a disproportionate segment of our prison population. Just how relevant to Thrasymachus's position is it that white-collar and celebrity criminals are often punished less severely than poor or obscure defendants? Other studies suggest that physically attractive job candidates are most likely to be hired. Have you ever noticed how some students seem to get by mostly on cleverness and charm? Should we draw conclusions about the nature of justice from these cases or just chalk them up to the way things sometimes go? Try to separate our lip-service moral values from those we practice. Try to separate a storybook conception of life from a realistic one. Are moral realists onto something or not? Explain.

The Unexamined Life

Among Socratic teachings, the most persistent command was "Know thyself." The significance to Socrates of this command is underscored by the fact that he stressed its importance to his life and mission during his *Apology*. Facing the end of a long life, Socrates uttered one of the most famous statements in the history of ideas: "The unexamined life is not worth living." By this he meant, among other things, that a life devoid of philosophical speculation is hardly a *human life*. That is, it is incomplete; it is not fully functioning and so lacks virtue or excellence.

Socrates believed that the human psyche is the essence of humanness. The **psyche** was a combination of what we think of as the mind and soul: consciousness, the capacity to reason, and the ability to reflect, known as *reflective thinking*. An "unexamined" life is, in a sense, an unconscious life. It is lived on the minimal level: Thinking never rises above practical concerns; desires are rarely pondered; custom, habit, and unquestioned beliefs substitute for reflection and assessment. Consequently, it is possible for a very intelligent, materially successful individual to live an unexamined life.

Giovanni Reale says, "As has recently come to light, no one prior to Socrates had understood by *soul* what Socrates understood by it, and after

PSYCHE

Greek for "soul"; in today's terms, combination of mind and soul, including capacity for reflective thinking.

Calvin and Hobbes. Copyright 1993 Watterson. Reprinted with permission. All rights reserved. Dist. by Universal Press Syndicate.

Socrates the whole of the West . . . the soul for Socrates was identified *with our consciousness when it thinks and acts with our reason and with the source of our thinking activity and our ethical activity.* In short, for Socrates the soul *is the conscious self, it is intellectual and moral personhood.*"[17]

An unexamined life is a life that takes the psyche for granted. It ignores the "true self." Interestingly, using Socrates' case as an example, we discover that the examined life does not produce "all the answers." Instead, it results in a life devoted to knowing more; a life in which progress means shedding false beliefs; a life in which pretense is continually reduced. The examined life is lived in conscious awareness of the human condition; it is not merely spent in an uncritical attempt to satisfy various needs and desires.

Philosophical Query

The relationship of reason to faith is a troublesome question for many. Do some informal research among your friends to get a sense of some contemporary conceptions of the soul. Compare and contrast what you discover with Socrates' conception of the psyche. How might a person's conception of the soul influence his or her response to the issue of the unexamined life?

Socratic Ignorance

I am not wise.

Socrates

When Socrates was probably in his thirties, his friend Chaerephon went to the Oracle at Delphi with a question: Is anyone wiser than Socrates? The Oracle was believed to have the gift of prophecy. Either through divine guidance or cleverness, it gave this famous, ambiguous reply: *No man is wiser than Socrates.* This can be taken to mean either (a) Socrates is the wisest man in Athens, or (b) even though Socrates is not very wise, he is as wise as anybody gets. The first interpretation makes Socrates unique. The second makes him an archetype of the human condition.

Socrates took the Oracle's reply quite seriously, claiming that it was the turning point in his life. His first reaction to hearing the god Apollo's reply was confusion:

> I said to myself, What can the god mean? and what is the interpretation of his riddle? for I know that I have no wisdom, small or great. What then can he mean when he says that I am the wisest of men? And yet he is a god, and cannot lie; that would be against his nature. After long consideration, I thought of a method of trying the question. I reflected that if I could only find a man wiser than myself, then I might go to the god with a refutation in my hand. I should say to him, "Here is a man wiser than I am; but you said I was the wisest." Accordingly I went to one who had a reputation of wisdom, and observed him—his name I need not mention; he was a politician whom I selected for examination—and the result was as follows: When I began to talk with him, I could not help thinking that he was not really wise, although he was thought wise by many, and still wiser by himself; and thereupon I tried to explain to him that he thought himself wise, but was not really wise; and the consequence was that he hated me, and his enmity was shared by several who were present and heard me. So I left him, saying to myself, as I went away: Well, although I do not suppose that either of us knows anything really beautiful and good, I am better off than he is—for he knows nothing, and thinks that he knows; I neither know nor think that I know. In this . . . , then, I seem to have slightly the advantage of him. Then I went to another who had still higher pretensions to wisdom, and my conclusion was exactly the same. Whereupon I made another enemy of him, and of many others besides him.[18]

One of the most intriguing aspects of Socrates' teachings is his profession of ignorance. (This is what Jaspers meant by "nonknowledge.") Plato's portrait of him suggests that Socrates continually reached "negative" conclusions of the form "This idea is faulty," or "That definition is inadequate." As we have seen, Socrates used the dialectical method to draw wisdom out of the minds of his listeners.

What point could Plato have been making? Clearly—it seems—Socrates possessed some kind of wisdom. Just as clearly—it seems—he was a basically good and honest man. He must have believed in his own ignorance, since he alluded to it on many occasions. If we allow for an element of irony in this, it then becomes clear that Socrates was challenging our notions of wisdom and knowledge. To certain sorts of people, Socrates' statements will remain clouded, perhaps beyond comprehension. Among them are young people whose "minds have not conceived at all," or older ones whose thoughts are already so firmly set that they can see only a phony technique used to avoid answering questions. Such people cannot conceive of their own ignorance. They are firmly convinced that

> I found that the men in most repute were all but the most foolish; and that others less esteemed were really wiser and better.
>
> *Socrates*

> Socrates is guilty of rejecting the gods acknowledged by the state and of bringing in strange deities; he is also guilty of corrupting the youth.
>
> *Indictment brought against Socrates*

they know everything important. To the Sophists, Socrates' use of "fake ignorance" was merely a clever psychological ploy to keep them off balance and on the spot. It's the sort of thing that made Thrasymachus so angry.

Since the Socratic method employs guided questions, we can conclude that Socrates *does* have some ideas about the general direction the search for answers will take and the adequacy of certain lines of analysis. But he refuses to reveal these in dogmatic form. Socrates' "ignorance" was part of his whole mission, which he saw as bringing home to others *their own* intellectual needs. Once that was accomplished, they were invited to join the search for truth using the dialectical method of question-and-answer. The essence of the Socratic method is to convince the learner that, although he thought he knew something, in fact he may not.

Socrates was also sharing his own honest doubt. Even if he knew more than he let on, he was much more aware of the uncertain nature and limits of knowledge (his own included) than most of us probably are. In this, he was wiser than the average person in two ways. First, many of us tend to think that we know much more than we do. Second, all human knowledge is tentative and limited: we are not gods, though we sometimes act as if we were.

> Shall I tell you what knowledge is? It is to know both what one knows and what one does not know.
>
> *Confucius*

The Power of Human Wisdom

Perhaps the best way to glimpse the power of Socratic ignorance is to look once more to the *Apology*, this time where Socrates makes tantalizing statements regarding his "wisdom."

> I dare say, Athenians, that some of you will reply, "Yes, Socrates, but what is the origin of these accusations which are brought against you; there must have been something strange which you have been doing? All these rumours and this talk about you would never have arisen if you had been like other men: tell us, then, what is the cause of them, for we should be sorry to judge hastily of you." Now I regard this as a fair challenge, and I will endeavour to explain to you the reason why I am called wise and have such evil fame. Please to attend then. And although some of you may think that I am joking, I declare that I will tell you the entire truth. Men of Athens, this reputation of mine has come of a certain sort of wisdom which I possess. If you ask me what kind of wisdom, I reply, wisdom such as may perhaps be attained by man, for to that extent I am inclined to believe that I am wise; whereas the persons to whom I was speaking have a superhuman wisdom, which I may fail to describe, because I have it not myself; and he who says I have, speaks falsely, and is taking away my character.[19]

The Socratic distinction between "human wisdom" and "more-than-human wisdom" is a powerful one. Similar distinctions are made in Asian philosophies (see the Third Interlude).

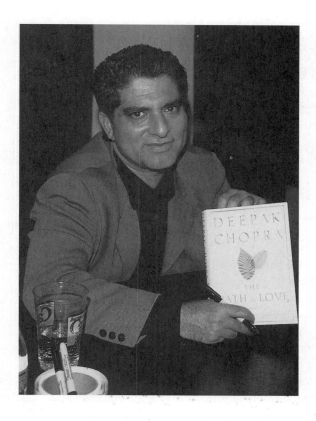

It is fascinating to imagine encounters between Socrates and such contemporary "sages" and professional advice-givers as "New Age guru" Deepak Chopra. How do you think Chopra (and other celebrity gurus) would fare with Socrates as a guest?

In his effort to understand why the god said no one was wiser than he, Socrates discovered how easy it is to become deluded by our own special skills. The modern tendency to compartmentalize rather than integrate our lives, combined with the respect we have for specialized skills and knowledge, may make us especially susceptible to self-delusion. Television talk shows are a parade of individuals expressing their "insights" and "discoveries" in all areas of life. Psychologists discuss morals, entertainers lecture on food additives, preachers propose legislation, all sorts of people write books generalizing from their own experience to the human condition. They—and we—seem to assume that if you have a degree, sell lots of books, get rich, have a television or radio show, or become famous, then you *must know what you're talking about no matter what you're talking about*. Things haven't changed:

> At last I went to the artisans, for I was conscious that I knew nothing at all, as I may say, and I was sure that they knew many fine things; and here I was not mistaken, for they did know many things of which I was ignorant, and in this they certainly were wiser than I was. But I observed that even the good artisans fell into the same error as the poets—because they were good workmen they thought that they also knew all sorts of high matters, and this defect in them overshadowed their wisdom; and therefore I asked myself whether I would like to be

The oldest sage would admit at the close of a life of study his wisdom was as a raindrop to the sea. Nor is this idea new. . . . anthropologists have traced its presence in the legends and indigenous ideas of nearly every country in the world.

Christmas Humphreys

Reprinted with permission of King Features Syndicate, Inc.

as I was, neither having their knowledge nor their ignorance, or like them in both; and I made answer to myself and to the oracle that I was better off as I was.

This inquisition has led to my having many enemies of the worst and most dangerous kind, and has given occasion to many calumnies. And I am called wise, for my hearers always imagine that I possess the wisdom which I find wanting in others; but the truth is, O men of Athens, that God only is wise; and by his answer he intends to show that the wisdom of men is worth little or nothing; he is not speaking of Socrates, he is only using my name by way of illustration, as if he said, He, O men, is wisest, who, like Socrates, knows that his wisdom is in truth worth nothing. And so I go about the world, obedient to the god, and search and make enquiry into the wisdom of anyone, whether citizen or stranger, who appears to be wise; and if he is not wise, then in vindication of the oracle I show him that he is not wise; and my occupation quite absorbs me, and I have no time to give either to any public matter or interest or to any concern of my own, but I am in utter poverty by reason of my devotion to the god.[20]

Philosophical Query

Have you ever met a highly educated specialist (physician, biochemist, psychologist, philosophy teacher, preacher) who thinks nothing of pontificating on the economy, sex education, and how you should raise your child? Discuss in light of Socratic statements concerning human wisdom.

The Physician of the Soul

Socrates' entire teaching mission centered on his conviction that *we are our souls*. That is, the "real person" is not the body, but the *psyche*. Perhaps the most important passage in the *Apology* concerns Socrates' sense

To know what you do not know is best. To pretend to know what you do not know is a disease.

Lao-tzu

of himself as a kind of "physician of the soul." In Socrates' sense, "seeking my own welfare" means "seeking the welfare of my soul." Note how in the following passage Socrates implies that he does indeed know something (that the most important thing is care of the soul) and that he views his whole public career as a teacher in light of his expanded notion of the self as the soul:

> Men of Athens, I honour and love you; but I shall obey God rather than you, and while I have strength I shall never cease from the practice and teaching of philosophy, exhorting any one whom I meet and saying to him after my manner: You, my friend,—a citizen of the great and mighty and wise city of Athens,—are you not ashamed of heaping the greatest amount of money and honour and reputation, and caring so little about wisdom and truth and the greatest improvement of the soul, which you never regard or heed at all? And if the person with whom I am arguing, says: Yes, but I do care; then I do not leave him or let him go at once; but I proceed to interrogate and examine and cross-examine him, and if I think that he has no virtue in him, but only says that he has, I reproach him with undervaluing the greater, and overvaluing the less. And I shall repeat the same words to everyone I meet, young and old, citizen and alien, but especially to the citizens. . . . For know that this is the command of the god; and I believe no greater good has happened to this state than my service to the god. For I do nothing but go about persuading you all, old and young alike, not to take thought for your persons or your properties, but first and chiefly to care about the greatest improvement of your soul. I tell you that virtue is not given by money, but that from virtue comes money and every other good of man, public as well as private. This is my teaching.[21]

He who enjoins a knowledge of oneself bids us become acquainted with the soul.

Plato

Philosophical Query

Compare Socrates' attitude toward the soul with your own. With your church's, if you go to church. What do you see as the main differences? What are some advantages and disadvantages of Socrates' view?

No One Knowingly Does Evil

The fundamental Socratic imperative "Know thyself" takes on special significance in light of Socrates' view that human beings always seek what they believe to be their own welfare and cannot deliberately do otherwise. In the *Gorgias*, Socrates points out that when people do what appear to be bad or distasteful things, it is always with some ultimate good in mind:

> So it is for the sake of the good that people do all these [distasteful] actions?
>
>   Yes, it is.

> And we have admitted that when we act for any purpose, we do not desire the action itself but the object of the action?
>
> Yes.
>
> Then we do not desire . . . these [distasteful] actions themselves; but if they are advantageous, we desire to do them; and if they are harmful, we do not. For we desire what is good . . . but things that are neither bad nor good we do not desire, nor things that are bad either.[22]

For Socrates, the good or harm in question is always determined by what benefits or harms the soul. In order to seek my soul's welfare I have to "know myself." And in order to "know myself," I have to know what kind of thing I am. Without this knowledge, I cannot know what is really good for me.

In the *Protagoras*, Socrates reinforces his conviction that no one knowingly does evil:

> For no wise man, I believe, will allow that any human being errs voluntarily, or voluntarily does evil or base actions; but they are very well aware that all who do evil and base things do them against their will.[23]

Philosophical Query

Do you agree that no one knowingly does evil? Explain. You might want to read the box about the Ring of Gyges in Chapter 2 and the discussion of egoism in the Fourth Interlude before you answer.

Virtue Is Wisdom

The Sophists claimed to be "teachers of human excellence," with excellence meaning "excellence of function" or **virtue** (*arete* in Greek). Too often, however, the result, as we saw in Chapter 2, was might-makes-right moral relativism and a radical this-worldly egoism—in contrast to Socratic egoism, which centers on the soul as the real self. The Sophists looked outward for markers of well-being and success, whereas Socrates looked inward at character.

Socrates believed that human excellence (virtue for short) is a special kind of knowledge that combines technical understanding with the skill and character to apply that knowledge. One of the words Socrates used for this kind of knowledge was **techne**, the Greek term for practical knowledge of how to do things. At various times, *techne* meant art, skill, craft, technique, trade, system, or method of doing something. It is the root of English words such as technique, technical, and technology. Techne is knowledge of what to do and how to do it. Thus, it is knowledge of both means and ultimate ends. Plato accused the Sophists of developing per-

---

VIRTUE

From the Greek *arete*, meaning "that at which something excels," or "excellence of function."

TECHNE

From the Greek for "art," "skill," "craft," "technique," "trade," "system," or "method of doing something"; root of English words such as "technique," "technical," and "technology"; term Socrates used when he asserted that virtue (*arete*) is knowledge or wisdom (*techne*).

suasive skills (rhetoric) without acquiring a corresponding knowledge of what ought to be done or avoided—that is without knowledge of ultimate ends.

According to Socrates, a knowledgeable physician, for example, has both theoretical understanding and practical skill. Her *techne* is manifest by the fact that she makes her patients well. If she made them worse, we would conclude that she was not really a physician, that she lacked medical knowledge. Techne is not like mere knowledge of a cake recipe; it also requires certain skill (character) to bake a good cake.

According to Socrates, the Sophists' lack of techne was evident because their teachings made people worse. Their own pupils attacked them and tried to cheat them out of their fees or engaged in corrupt business practices and destructive political schemes. Thus, the Sophists lacked knowledge of human excellence, or virtue.

In other words, for Socrates, knowledge of virtue is wisdom; it goes beyond theoretical understanding of justice or right and wrong, and includes *living* justly, living honorably and well in the highest sense. In the following passage from the *Meno*, Socrates argues that virtue is wisdom and that all things "hang upon" wisdom:

> *Socrates*: The next question is, whether virtue is knowledge or of another species?
>
> *Meno*: Certainly.
>
> *Socrates*: Do we not say that virtue is good? . . .
>
> *Meno*: Certainly. . . .
>
> *Socrates*: Then virtue is profitable?
>
> *Meno*: That is the only inference. . . .
>
> *Socrates*: And what is the guiding principle which makes [things] profitable or the reverse? Are they not profitable when they are rightly used, and hurtful when they are not rightfully used?
>
> *Meno*: Certainly.
>
> *Socrates*: Next, let us consider the goods of the soul: they are temperance, justice, courage, quickness of apprehension, memory, magnanimity, and the like?
>
> *Meno*: Surely.
>
> *Socrates*: And such of these as are not knowledge, but of another sort, are sometimes profitable and sometimes hurtful; as, for example, courage wanting prudence, which is only a sort of confidence? When a man has no sense he is harmed by courage, but when he has sense he is profited?
>
> *Meno*: True.
>
> *Socrates*: And . . . whatever things are learned or done with sense are profitable, but when done without sense they are hurtful?

I think that all men have a choice between various courses, and choose and follow the one which they think conduces most to their advantage.

Socrates

To live is not itself an evil, as has been claimed, but to lead a worthless life is.

Diogenes

Yes, Socrates, I stand in amazement when I reflect on the questions that men ask. By the Gods, I do! I want to know more and more about such questions, and there are times when I become almost dizzy just thinking about them.

Plato

Meno: Very true.

Socrates: And in general, all that the soul attempts or endures, when under the guidance of wisdom, ends in happiness; but when she is under the guidance of folly, the opposite?

Meno: That appears to be true.

Socrates: If then virtue is a quality of the soul, and is admitted to be profitable, it must be wisdom or prudence, since none of the things of the soul are either profitable or hurtful in themselves, but they are all made profitable or hurtful by the addition of wisdom or folly; and therefore if virtue is profitable, virtue must be a sort of wisdom or prudence?

Meno: I quite agree. . . .

Socrates: And is this not universally true of human nature? All other things hang upon the soul, and the things of the soul herself hang upon wisdom, if they are to be good; and so wisdom is inferred to be that which profits—and virtue, as we say, is profitable?

Meno: Certainly.

Socrates: And thus we arrive at the conclusion that virtue is either wholly or partly wisdom?

Meno: I think that what you are saying, Socrates, is very true.[24]

All Evil Is Ignorance

Socrates believed that knowledge (wisdom) always produces behavioral results, because behavior is always guided by beliefs. For instance, if I believe that the glass of water in front of me is poisoned, I will not drink it—unless I also believe that dying will be better for me than living, given my present circumstances, say terminal cancer of a painful sort. This rationalistic view that behavior is always controlled by beliefs about what is good and the means to that good is sometimes called **intellectualism**. Intellectualism differs from egoism in its emphasis on cognitive states (beliefs) whereas egoism is usually expressed in terms of desires.

Socrates' intellectualism was part of his unusual claim that no one knowingly does wrong. According to Socrates, when we "admit" (state) that our choices are wrong, we are playing word games. To take an extreme example, a satanist who glories in "choosing" *evil* really believes in the superiority of what he is calling evil. Perhaps according to Jews or Christians what he is choosing is wrong, but to the satanist, it is *really good*. If he honestly believed (knew) that X was wrong (fatal to his soul), our hypothetical satanist could not choose X, according to Socrates.

INTELLECTUALISM

Term used to refer to the claim that behavior is always controlled by beliefs about what is good and the means to that good.

In other words, there is no such thing as true *weakness of will*. We are, implies Socrates, psychologically incapable of knowing what is good and not doing it. Conversely, we are psychologically incapable of doing what we really know (and believe wholeheartedly) will harm us. Socrates' simple psychology and intellectualism led him to the conviction that all evil is a form of ignorance, because no one knowingly wills harm to herself.

Socrates: . . . Do not all men . . . desire the good?

Meno: I think not.

Socrates: There are some who desire evil?

Meno: Yes.

Socrates: Do you mean that they think the evils which they desire, to be good; or do they know that they are evil and yet desire them?

Meno: Both, I think.

Socrates: And do you really imagine, Meno, that a man knows evils to be evils and desires them notwithstanding?

Meno: Certainly I do.

Socrates: And desire is [for] possession?

Meno: Yes, [for] possession. . . .

Socrates: Well, and do those who, as they say, desire evils, and think that evils are hurtful to the possessor of them, know that they will be hurt by them?

Meno: They must know it.

Socrates: And must they not suppose that those who are hurt are miserable in proportion to the hurt which is inflicted upon them?

Meno: How can it be otherwise?

Socrates: But are not the miserable ill-fated?

Meno: Yes, indeed.

Socrates: And does any one desire to be miserable and ill-fated?

Meno: I should say not, Socrates.

Socrates: But if there is no one who desires to be miserable, there is no one, Meno, who desires evil; for what is misery but the desire and possession of evil?

Meno: That appears to be the truth, Socrates, and I admit that nobody desires evil.[25]

Philosophical Query

What do you think of Socrates' claim that all evil is ignorance? Do you think it is possible to knowingly choose (will) evil? If all evil is ignorance, can we ever justly punish evildoers? Discuss.

> The cause of error is ignorance of the better.
>
> *Democritus*

> The striving to find meaning in one's life is the primary motivational force in man.
>
> *Viktor Frankl*

The Trial and Death of Socrates

Socrates' philosophy cannot be separated from his life. Neither can it be separated from his death. As with other great sages, much of what Socrates *said* has wide appeal. The difficulty, as many of us know, is trying to live in accordance with what we say we believe. Socrates not only lived his philosophy, he died for it. And in the act of dying, he reaffirmed it one more time.

For most of his long life Socrates was able to function as a critic at large, questioning Athenian values and occasionally annoying important and powerful people in the process. He acquired a mixed reputation, being viewed on the one hand as a harmless, irrelevant eccentric, and on the other as a dangerous social critic and "freethinker"—in short, a Sophist. Socrates' philosophic method consisted of raising question after question, calling into doubt cherished, often unchallenged, beliefs to see if they were worthy of allegiance. Many Athenians found this skeptical attitude disrespectful and threatening; they preferred unwavering loyalty to the status quo and to conventional beliefs. To these citizens, the very process of questioning fundamental values was subversive, perhaps even traitorous.

Socrates' status changed from mere annoyance to overt threat as a result of events associated with the bitter Peloponnesian Wars between Athens and Sparta. One of Socrates' students, Alcibiades, went to Sparta, where he advised the Spartans during the war. In some people's minds, as the teacher, Socrates was responsible for the student's act of betrayal.

Socrates further alienated himself from powerful Athenians when he resisted efforts to judge eight Athenian generals accused of poor military strategy as a group, rather than as individuals, as was their right under the Athenian constitution. Socrates was the *one member* of the Committee of the Senate of Five Hundred *to refuse*. The other 499 members initially agreed with Socrates' position, but backed down when aggressive prosecutors threatened to add to the indictment the names of Committee members who refused to ignore the constitution. The threat worked, the generals were found guilty, and the six who were already in custody were executed on the same day. This is another example of Socrates' willingness to put his principles above all other considerations (including, perhaps, his family's).

Sparta defeated Athens in 404 B.C., and set up a Commission of Thirty to form a new Athenian government. The Thirty turned out to be a ruthless dictatorship that executed supporters of the earlier Periclean democracy and greedily confiscated their property. The Thirty lasted about eight months before being removed from power by force. Unfortunately for Socrates, among the Thirty were his close friends Critias and Charmides. Once again, in the minds of many Athenians, Socrates was guilty of treason by association.

No other trial, except that of Jesus, has left so vivid an impression on the imagination of Western man as that of Socrates.

I. F. Stone

Finally, resentment, distrust, and hostility against Socrates grew to such proportions that he was brought to trial for "not worshiping the gods of the state" and "corrupting the young." These were potentially capital offenses, and Socrates' prosecutor, Meletus, demanded death. At the time, it was customary for individuals charged with such crimes to submit to voluntary exile. Had Socrates chosen this option, there would have been no trial. Socrates, however, remained to answer his accuser before a jury of his peers.

Athenian trials consisted of two parts. First, the jury determined whether or not the accused was guilty as charged. If guilty, the second stage of the trial determined the most appropriate punishment. Socrates' jury consisted of 501 members. There was no way such a large group could reasonably debate various penalty options, so if a defendant was convicted, the prosecutor proposed a penalty and the defendant proposed a counter-penalty. Then the jury voted once more, choosing one or the other. The hope was that both sides would be moderate in their demands.

Socrates defended himself and was judged guilty by a rather close vote. The custom of the time was for those convicted to show some contrition. The greater the prosecutor's proposed penalty, the more remorse the condemned man was expected to express. In cases where death was asked, the proposed counterpenalty was supposed to be stiff. It might include leaving Athens forever and giving up most or all of one's property as fines. Public humiliation was also part of the price of escaping death. Defendants were expected to tear at their clothes, roll on the ground, and throw dirt on themselves while crying and wailing. They would usually have their wives and children and friends cry and plead for their lives. An important function of the trial involved making peace with those one had offended.

Instead of following custom, Socrates pointed out that it would be undignified at his age to grovel for life. He refused to allow his friends and family to crawl either. To make things even worse, he reminded the jury that many of them believed he was not guilty and had been falsely convicted. Thus Socrates offered to redeem the jury! At one point, he considered that since he had given up opportunities to make money because he was trying to help others, he should perhaps be given free meals for the rest of his life. Ultimately, he made only a modest, inadequate concession to the jury by offering to let his friends pay a fine for him. His conviction did not upset him, for a divine sign had led him throughout:

O my judges—for you I may truly call judges—I should like to tell you of a wonderful circumstance. Hitherto the divine faculty of which the internal oracle is the source has constantly been in the habit of opposing me even about trifles, if I was going to make a slip or error in any matter; and now you see there has come upon me that which may be thought, and is generally believed to be, the last and worst evil. But the oracle made no sign of opposition, either when I was

If I had engaged in politics, I should have perished long ago . . . for the truth is, that no man who goes to war with you or any other multitude, honestly striving against the many lawless and unrighteous deeds which are done in a state, will save his life; he who will fight for the right, if he would live even for a brief space, must have a private station and not a public one.

Socrates

And this, O men of Athens, is the truth and the whole truth; I have concealed nothing, I have dissembled nothing. And yet, I know that my plainness of speech makes them hate me, and what is their hatred but a proof that I am speaking the truth?

Socrates

Either acquit me or not;
but whichever you do,
understand that I shall
never alter my ways, not
even if I have to die many
times.

Socrates

His martyrdom, and the
genius of Plato, made him a
secular saint, the superior
man confronting the igno-
rant mob with serenity and
humor. This was Socrates'
triumph and Plato's masterpiece. Socrates needed the
hemlock, as Jesus needed
the Crucifixion, to fulfill a
mission. The mission left a
stain forever on democracy.
That remains Athens' tragic
crime.

I. F. Stone

leaving my house in the morning, or I was on my way to the court, or
while I was speaking, at anything which I was going to say; and yet I
have often been stopped in the middle of a speech. . . . What do I take
to be the explanation of this silence? I will tell you. It is an intimation
that what has happened to me is good, and that those of us who think
that death is an evil are in error. For the customary sign would surely
have opposed me had I been going to evil and not to good.[26]

Though we cannot know the exact nature of Socrates' "divine sign,"
we know that he took it seriously. One result was that Socrates himself
had a clear sense of purpose, a vocation. His teaching was part of the
whole person; it was not a way to *make* a living, but a way *of* living.

At his trial he said, "My service to the god has brought me into great
poverty." Just as for Socrates real beauty was beauty of soul, real riches
were riches of soul. Socrates appeared poor only by conventional standards. By his own sense of things, his service to the god brought real
riches, rather than apparent ones.

Philosophical Query

Some people argue that Socrates committed suicide by provoking the
jury. By insisting that he was right and by refusing to show fear or at least
some repentance, he drove them to execute him. He knew they would get
carried away and yet he insulted them. So it is his own fault that he was
executed. What do you think? Is there a defense for Socrates' actions?
Who is responsible for the vote?

The Death of Socrates

Socrates could not be executed on the day of the trial, as was customary,
because the trial had lasted longer than usual, extending into late afternoon, the beginning of a holy period. Socrates was put in prison to await
the end of the holy period, in this case about a month. While there, he continued to pursue his philosophical questions. He was offered the opportunity to escape, the officials going so far as to make it clear they would not
stop him. He refused, until finally the holy period ended and word came
that Socrates must die before sundown.

A number of Socrates' friends visited him in prison on the last day of
his life. He discussed the nature of the soul with them and told a mythical
story about the soul's immortality. When his friend Crito asked how they
should bury him, Socrates jokingly replied, "In any way you like; but you
must get hold of *me*, and take care that I do not run away from you."
Plato described what happened next:

Then he turned to us and added with a smile:—I cannot make Crito
believe that I am the same Socrates who has been talking and con-

THE WISE MAN: SOCRATES 109

Hemlock

Conine is the toxic component of the plant commonly known as *hemlock*. Hemlock is a coarse, biennial plant that looks like a carrot or parsnip plant when young. Mature hemlock stands four to ten feet tall, has small white flowers, and has small grayish-brown fruit that contains seeds. Native to Europe and Asia, hemlock can be found in waste areas throughout the eastern United States, the Rocky Mountains, southern Canada, and the Pacific coast.

Depending on the dose, initial symptoms can be vomiting, confusion, respiratory depression, even muscle paralysis. Other possible effects include salivat-ing, thirst, double vision, loss of vision, slow heartbeat, seizures, burning sensations of mouth, throat, and abdomen, and kidney failure. Ultimately, hemlock poisoning results in paralysis of the skeletal muscles and intense, diffuse muscle pain. . . .

Source: *POISINDEX®*, Vol. 86, © 1974–1995 Micromedia Inc.

ducting the argument; he fancies that I am the other Socrates whom he will soon see, a dead body—and he asks, How shall you bury me? And though I have spoken many words in the endeavour to show that when I have drunk the poison I shall leave you and go to the joys of the blessed. . . . I shall not remain, but go away and depart; . . . I would not have [you] sorrow at my hard lot, or say at the burial, Thus we lay out Socrates, or, Thus we follow him to the grave or bury him; for false words are not only evil in themselves, but they infect the soul with evil. Be of good cheer then, . . . and say that you are burying my body only, and do with that whatever is usual, and what you think best.[27]

Socrates went to bathe, while his friends talked about what he had said. Plato reported that his friends felt as if they were losing a father and would be orphans for the rest of their lives. After Socrates' bath, his children and the women of his household were brought in. When he finally sent the women and children away, it was close to sunset—the end of the day, by which time he was officially supposed to be dead. The jailer came in while he was talking, and said that it was time. Most condemned men resisted drinking the hemlock until late into the evening, getting drunk and putting off the inevitable for as long as they could, but Socrates asked that the poison be prepared and brought to him. Socrates' jailer noted how different Socrates was and, weeping, he thanked Socrates for talking with him and treating him as a friend. Crito begged him to delay, but Socrates said that there was nothing to be gained by it. Rather, there was much to lose by degrading himself. To evade and fear death would have made a mockery out of his entire life, for Socrates had long taught that death was not an evil.

When Rabbi Bunam lay dying his wife burst into tears. He said: "What are you crying for? My whole life was only that I might learn how to die."

Martin Buber

Jacques-Louis David's 1787 painting The Death of Socrates *is perhaps the most famous artistic depiction of that significant event. Does it reflect your conception of Socrates' death?*

If you think that by killing men you can prevent someone from censuring your evil lives, you are mistaken; that is not a way of escape which is either possible or honorable; the easiest and the noblest way is not to be disabling others, but to be improving yourselves. This is the prophecy which I utter before my departure to the judges who have condemned me.

Socrates

When the jailer returned with the cup, Socrates asked what he had to do and was told to just drink it and then walk around a bit. Plato's account continues:

Then raising the cup to his lips, quite readily and cheerfully he drank off the poison. And hitherto most of us had been able to control our sorrow; but now when we saw him drinking, and saw too that he had finished the draught, we could no longer forbear, and in spite of myself my own tears were flowing fast; so that I covered my face and wept, not for him, but for the thought of my own calamity in having to part with such a friend. Nor was I the first; for Crito, when he found himself unable to restrain his tears, had got up, and I followed; and at that moment Apollodorus, who had been weeping all the time, broke out in a loud and passionate cry which made cowards of us all. Socrates alone retained his calmness: What is this strange outcry? he said. I sent away the women mainly in order that they might not misbehave in this way, for I have been told that a man should die in peace. Be quiet then and have patience. When we heard his words we were ashamed, and refrained our tears; and he walked about until, as he said, his legs began to fail, and then he lay on his back, according to the directions, and the man who gave him the poison now and then looked at his feet and legs; and after a while he pressed his foot hard, and asked him if he could feel; and he said, No; and then his leg, and so upwards and upwards, and showed us that he was cold and stiff. And he felt them himself, and said: When the poison reaches the heart, that will be the end. He was beginning to grow cold about the groin, when he uncovered his face, for he had covered himself up, and said—they were his last words—he said: Crito, I owe a cock to Asclepius [the god of healing]; you will remember to pay the debt? The debt shall be paid, said Crito; is there anything else? There was no answer to this question; but in a minute or two a movement was heard, and the attendants uncovered him; his eyes were set, and Crito closed his eyes and mouth.

Such was the end . . . of our friend; concerning whom I may truly say, that of all the men of his time whom I have known, he was the wisest and justest and best.[28]

Philosophical Query

Although complex political reasons lay behind some of the animosity that led to Socrates' execution, it is likely that bad feelings of a deeper, more primitive nature were also important factors. Whatever reasons there may have been for trying Socrates on capital charges, recall that he was seventy years old at the time of his trial. What is the significance of this fact? Why bother to try, convict, and execute a seventy-year-old man whose behavior had been remarkably consistent and publicly observed for perhaps fifty years? There was nothing "new" about Socrates. So what was it?

I will tell you something, Socrates [said Aristides, the son of Lysimachus and grandson of the great Aristides], something quite incredible but true. I have never learned a single thing from you, as you know yourself; but whenever I was with you I improved, even if I was only in the same house but not in the same room. . . .

Plato, Theages

Commentary

Although Socrates was probably correct in his belief that no normally reasonable person willingly does himself harm, he was surely wrong in his rejection of the possibility of weakness of will. His limited knowledge of the complexities of human psychology prevented him from recognizing what is a very common experience for most of us: We lack the will to do the good we know or to resist the bad that tempts us. Jesus' oft-quoted line that "the spirit is willing, but the flesh is weak" probably comes closer to our experiences than Socrates' intellectualistic optimism.

Socrates was, after all, quite an optimist. He was convinced that genuine knowledge would make us good. The social qualities of the dialectic are predicated on the belief that by working together, two or more honest, well-meaning, and reasonable people can move steadily from ignorance to virtue (goodness and happiness).

Perhaps the best way to approach the seeming paradoxes of Socrates' rejection of the weak will and insistence that virtue is knowledge lies in not imposing our contemporary sense of the soul and lack of respect for wisdom on the ancient *sophos*. The common counterexamples used to show that we often know the good but choose what we know is bad (smoking, acts of malice, dishonesty) are only counterexamples when we separate knowledge from wisdom.

Reason or a halter.

Diogenes

If, as they say, I am only an ignorant man trying to be a philosopher, then that may be what a philosopher is.

Diogenes

If by "know the good," we mean, for example, to cognitively understand that smoking leads to impaired health, then it is possible to know the good and do the bad. But if by "know the good" we mean value and love the soul, then perhaps Socrates is correct. Perhaps we choose to smoke or lie in ignorance of their effects on our souls.

We might also find Socrates' ideas difficult to accept because—like the Sophists and many Greeks of his time—we grant primacy to the external physical and social world rather than to the soul. We more easily recognize harm to our reputations and physical health than we do harm to our souls. Using the physical and deductive sciences as our paradigms of knowledge makes it difficult to recognize the possibility of wisdom.

When Socrates said that "human wisdom" is "worthless," his point was that while the benefits of technical knowledge are apparent, its limits often escape us. It might be a fine thing to discover the physical origin of the universe or develop safer automobiles, and so forth. But does that kind of knowledge help our psyches? Does it help us be better and happier people? Cures for AIDS and cancer will bring a certain peace of mind to us, because living longer seems to be a good thing. But how long? Would you like to live three hundred years, trying to plan for your retirement in another two hundred and fifty years? How will living longer make your life better if you are often bored or lonely now? Will more of the same be an improvement?

Contemporary psychologists are rediscovering both the soul and wisdom. Thomas Moore's book *Care of the Soul* was a surprise best-seller in 1993. Solomon Schimmel's *The Seven Deadly Sins*, Robert J. Sternberg's *Wisdom: Its Nature, Origins, and Development*, and T. Byram's *Wisdom in the Practice of Psychotherapy* are three of the most significant recent books by clinical and research psychologists dealing with wisdom. More recently, the contemporary rediscovery of wisdom is reflected in such works as Pierre Hadot's *Philosophy as a Way of Life*, Julia Annas's *The Morality of Happiness*, Martha E. Nussbaum's *The Therapy of Desire*, and Mary Nicholas's *The Mystery of Goodness*. Whether this new interest will result in actually taking better care of the soul remains to be seen, but at least wisdom is once again being taken seriously outside the academy.

Human wisdom rests on the courage to change what should be changed combined with the maturity and insight to accept what cannot be changed. I have no hope of doing either until I know myself. This, of course, means that I must discover the difference between what I cannot do and what I so far have only failed to do. So long as I think that I know more than I know, I will learn less than I can. The unexamined life—whatever its causes—is always a tragedy.

By professing his ignorance, Socrates has achieved a kind of immortality. He is one of the few great philosophers to whom people of many cultures, eras, abilities, and interests have looked for wisdom. The Socratic mission has not ended. Socrates' power to provoke, challenge, and awaken lives on.

For me, Socrates remains fresh. I return to him repeatedly. Slow learner that I must be, I am again and again caught up short by the force of his insight into *human* wisdom. Like Athens, I doze, forgetting to question myself. In a dreamlike condition, I imagine that I know what I do not know. I may fool myself. Perhaps I even fool others. But I cannot fool the old *sophos*. In moments of clarity, I long for human wisdom.

> One ought not to talk or act as if he were asleep.
>
> *Heraclitus*

Summary of Main Points

1. Socrates is the first major Western philosopher. He wrote no philosophy, and what we know of him comes chiefly from his pupils Plato and Xenophon.

2. Socrates challenged the Sophist doctrines of relativism, moral realism, and might makes right. He also insisted that no one who took money for teaching could teach the truth.

3. Socrates' teaching and life were so fully integrated that the power or force of his whole person galvanized others. Socrates possessed a power that went beyond rational argument. An encounter with him could trigger not just personal but deep philosophical and spiritual responses in others. Individuals of this sort are known as paradigmatic or archetypal individuals, rare human beings whose very nature represents something elemental about the human condition.

4. Socrates' dialectical encounters with powerful Sophists, his use of irony, his disdain for the trappings of material success, and his contempt for paid teachers angered and offended Sophists and those whom they taught. Encounters such as the one he had with the Sophist Thrasymachus led many Athenians to believe that Socrates was just another Sophist. In 399 B.C. he was condemned and executed.

5. Socrates perfected a style of philosophical inquiry known today as the Socratic method or Socratic dialectic. The method is based on the assumption that the function of education is to draw the truth out of the pupil rather than "fill an empty vessel." A series of guided questions continually refines the ideas under scrutiny; definitions are required for all key terms and logical inconsistencies brought to light and resolved. Because the active involvement of the audience is essential, questions are preferred to straight lectures.

6. Socrates used irony to encourage active listening by his pupils or dialectical partners. An ironic utterance is a way of communicating that has at least two levels of meaning, the literal level, also known as the obvious level, and the hidden level, also known as the real level.

7. Among Socratic teachings, the most persistent command was "Know thyself." By this he meant, among other things, that a life devoid of philosophical speculation is hardly a human life, because only philosophical reflection can help us discover what is real and important from the standpoint of the psyche, the uniquely human soul-mind. The unexamined life takes the psyche for granted.

8. Socrates insisted that his only wisdom consisted of a kind of "nonknowledge": He knew what he did not know. Acknowledgment of ignorance, Socrates taught, is a fundamental characteristic of the examined life.

9. Socrates saw himself as a kind of "physician of the soul." He believed that we are our souls, that the "real person" is not the body, but the *psyche*.

10. Socrates believed that human excellence or virtue is a special kind of knowledge (*techne*) that combines technical understanding with the skill and character to apply that knowledge. *Techne* is knowledge of what to do and how to do it.

11. Socrates believed that knowledge (wisdom) always produces behavioral results, because behavior is always guided by beliefs. This view is sometimes called intellectualism. Socrates' intellectualism committed him to the unusual claim that no one knowingly does wrong. In other words, there is no such thing as weakness of will. We are, implies Socrates, incapable of knowing what is good and not doing it.

Study Questions

1. Discuss what is meant by the "Socratic problem." Be sure to include strategies for dealing with it.

2. What do you see as the relevance of Socrates' life to his teachings? Explain.

3. Suppose it were discovered that Socrates secretly violated many of his teachings. How would this affect your attitude toward his philosophy? Which do you see as more important, the man or the ideas? Explain.

4. Explain how Socrates used his physical appearance to support his general theory of virtue.

5. Explain Socrates' views of self-control. Reconstruct his argument in your own words.

6. Use Socratic principles to defend Socrates against the charge of being a bad husband and father.

7. Explain what Jaspers meant by a paradigmatic individual. Then think about meeting one. Would it be a pleasant experience?

8. Thoroughly describe the Socratic dialectic. Then explain its significance to Socrates' claims of ignorance.

9. What is irony? Give one or two examples. Explain its function in the Socratic method.

10. Many Athenians thought that Socrates was a Sophist. Using the encounter between Socrates and Thrasymachus, identify ways in which Socrates and the Sophists were alike. Then make your case that he was or was not a Sophist. Be sure to justify your counterargument with specific examples.

11. Analyze Socrates' claim that "the unexamined life is not worth living." What did he mean? Was he correct? Why or why not?

12. Explain "human wisdom."

13. What is Socratic intellectualism? How does it relate to Socrates' rejection of weakness of will and belief that evil is ignorance?

14. Fully explain what Socrates meant when he said that virtue is knowledge. What kind of knowledge? What is virtue?

15. What is the function of ignorance in Socratic philosophy?

16. In your own words, describe Socrates' mission.

17. How are Socrates' ideas about wealth and possessions connected to other aspects of his teaching?

18. Socrates thought it very important not to teach for money. Why? What kind of teaching did he mean? Was he right? Can this principle be extended to priests, rabbis, and preachers? Explain.

19. What individual or group (if any) provides a Socratic function for our society? Explain. If none, explain that.

The Philosopher-King
Plato

Until philosophers are kings, or the kings and princes of this world have the spirit and power of philosophy . . . cities will never have rest from their evils . . . nor the human race . . . and then only will our State . . . behold the light of day.

Plato, The Republic

Democracy is the best form of government. Can there be any doubt? One of the great traditions of American history has been that "any boy can grow up to be president." And certainly our history suggests a continuous (if sometimes painfully slow) movement toward extending greater and greater choices and opportunities to all our citizens. Now it's no longer "any *boy* can grow up to be president," but "any *person*." Visible and invisible barriers of race, creed, and social class are being removed. Increasingly, the only limits on our dreams are our own. And someday even these barriers may be removed by educators, scientists, and therapists who seek special techniques and discoveries to abolish as many disadvantages of birth or background as possible.

As citizens of a democracy, we are free to seek any position we wish in society. The highest public office has only three entrance requirements: citizenship, age, and a majority of the votes. If in practice our presidents come from the wealthier, more educated classes, they still do not need to meet any stringent requirements of self-discipline, character, or wisdom. Nor do we who elect them. This is the glory of democracy.

Picture now a November morning. A line of voters waits to elect the next president of the United States. You have spent weeks studying the televised debates (you've even read the written transcripts). You've subscribed to liberal and conservative magazines and newspapers in order to get as complete a picture of the candidates' records and the issues as you can. You've read those long political editorials in the newspaper, as well as your voter's pamphlet. Because there are a number of lesser offices, bond issues, and legislative amendments on the ballot, you've brought a written list of your carefully reasoned decisions with you to the polls.

Patiently waiting your turn, you overhear a small group of people standing in line behind you. A woman announces, "I'm voting for *X*. She's a woman, and that's good enough for me." Someone else says, "My dad always voted Republican, so I'm voting Democrat!" A third person chimes in, "I'm not voting for *Y*. He's a jerk." Someone asks about "all those propositions and stuff," and the group laughs. "Who cares?" someone else snaps. "None of that stuff makes any difference." "Yeah," another responds, "there are too many to keep straight anyway. I just vote yes, no, yes, at random." Yet another says, "As a single parent, I'm only interested in Prop. M, since I need money for child care. I'll just guess at the rest."

Disturbed by this, you suddenly notice that the man in front of you is weaving. You ask if he's sick, and he laughingly answers, with the unmistakable smell of beer on his breath: "Heck, no. I'm loaded. It's the only way to vote." You vote anyway, but can't shake your anger for a long time. It doesn't seem fair that these irresponsible votes should equal your carefully researched and reasoned decisions. They might even cancel your vote out. It's worse than unfair. It's dumb. It's not *reasonable*, you think. There should be *some* requirement for voting. Not anything unfair or "discriminatory," just *reasonable*. And come to think of it, there should be some kind of test or something for politicians. They're a pretty unethical and dumb lot, too.

If you have ever had thoughts like this, your disgust and annoyance at "the way things are run around here" have probably triggered a desire for a "more ideal" society. As we all know, however, no such ideal society exists in this world, so where did you get the idea for it? It's as if you have seen beyond the way things are, seen a *higher* possibility.

Anyone who has visualized a fairer, more ideal society has already shared at least some ideas with perhaps the greatest, and certainly one of the most imposing and influential, philosophers in the Western world: Plato.

Philosophical Query

Americans have reason to be wary of requirements for voting. In the past they have been used to prevent women and people of certain ethnic groups from voting. On the other hand, a case might be made that by not having some minimal standard of preparedness and awareness, we make a mockery of "choosing." How can an ignorant voter "choose" anything? Discuss from both sides.

Plato's Life and Work

Our chief source of information regarding Plato's philosophy is Plato himself. We still have all the works attributed to him by ancient scholars. The most important of these are philosophical dialogues. We have already seen material from some of these in Chapters 2 and 3: the *Apology*, *Crito*, *Phaedo*, *Theaetetus*, *Timaeus*, *Gorgias*, *Protagoras*, *Meno*, and *The Republic*. We also have the summaries and analyses of some of Plato's doctrines left by his greatest student, Aristotle. We probably have more biographical information about Plato than of any other ancient philosopher, much of it from Diogenes Laërtius's *Life of Plato*. Last is a controversial

The truth is that the common man's love of liberty, like his love of sense, justice and truth, is almost wholly imaginary.

H. L. Mencken

Plato has exerted a greater influence over human thought than any other individual with the possible exception of Aristotle.

Raphael Demos

Perictione: Plato's Philosopher-Mother

In *On the Harmony of Women*, Perictione (c. 450–350 B.C.) calls women to philosophy in terms reminiscent of Socrates (Chapter 3), Epicurus (Second Interlude), and Epictetus (Chapter 6). Perictione is believed to have been Plato's mother, and we hear in her work echoes of Socrates' disdain for vanity, his ideal of self-control, and his affirmation of the superiority of inner or essential beauty over mere physical attractiveness. We must wonder about the influence Perictione had on her son, as well as about the influence other forgotten and overlooked women philosophers may have had on their more fa-mous peers. In the passage quoted here, Perictione argues that wisdom and self-control in an individual woman generate other virtues, which in turn lead to harmony and happiness for the entire community:

> One must deem the harmonious woman to be full of wisdom and self-control; a soul must be exceedingly conscious of goodness to be just and courageous and wise, embellished with self-sufficiency and hating empty opinion. Worthwhile things come to a woman from these—for herself, her hus-band, her children, her household, perhaps even for a city. . . .
>
> But one must also train the body to natural measures concerning nourishment and clothing, baths and anointings, the arrangement of the hair, and ornaments of gold and precious stone. Women who eat and drink every costly thing, who dress extravagantly and wear the things that women wear, are ready for the sin of every vice both with respect to the marriage bed and the rest of wrongdoing. It is necessary merely to appease hunger and

collection of thirteen letters and some dialogues whose authenticity some scholars dispute. One of these, *Letter: VII*, is of special interest because of its comments regarding the mature Plato's attitudes toward democracy in view of the way Socrates was treated by it.

Probably no single work of Western philosophy has been read by as many people as Plato's *Republic*. It is considered by most philosophers to be Plato's most impressive and important work because it presents his overall philosophy in a dramatic, organized, and brilliant form. We'll use *The Republic* as the basis for our introduction to this genuinely great archetype of the philosopher-king, but first let us start with a brief sketch of Plato's life.

Plato

The Aristocrat

Plato (c. 427–348 B.C.) is actually the nickname of Aristocles, the son of one of the oldest and most elite Athenian families. Through his mother's family he was related to a celebrated lawgiver named Solon. His father's family traced its lineage to the ancient kings of Athens and even further back to Poseidon, the god of the sea. His given name, Aristocles, meant "best, most renowned." He is said to have done well at practically every-thirst, even if this be done by frugal means; in the case of cold, even a goat-skin or rough garment would suffice. . . . So the harmonious woman will not wrap herself in gold or precious stone from India or anywhere else, nor will she braid her hair with artful skills or anoint herself with infusions of Arabian scent, nor will she paint her face, whitening or rouging it, darkening her eye-brows and lashes and treating her gray hair with dye; nor will she be forever bathing. The woman who seeks these things seeks an admirer for feminine weakness. It is the beauty that comes from wisdom, not from these, that gratifies women who are well-born. . . .

But I think a woman is harmonious in the following way: if she becomes full of wisdom and self-control. For this benefits not only her husband, but also the children, relatives, slaves; the whole house, including possessions and friends, both fellow-citizens and foreign guest friends. Artlessly, she will keep their house, speaking and hearing fair things, and obeying her husband in the unanimity of their common life, attending upon the relatives and friends whom he extolls, and thinking the same things sweet and bitter as he—lest she be out of tune in relation to the whole.

Holger Thesleff, "Pythagorean Texts of the Hellenistic Period," *Acta Academiae Aboensis, Humaniora,* trans. Vicki Lynn Harper, in *A History of Women Philosophers,* vol. 1, 600 B.C.–500 A.D., ed. Mary Ellen Waithe (Dordrecht: Martinus Nijhoff Publishers, 1987), pp. 20–21.

thing as a young man: music, logic, debate, math, poetry. He was attractive and made his mark as a wrestler. In the military he distinguished himself in three battles, and even won a prize for bravery.[1] His nickname, Platon, means "broad" or "wide"; one story is that he had wide shoulders, another that he had a wide forehead.

Plato was born two years after the death of Pericles, the great architect of Athenian democracy. Athens was fighting Sparta in the Peloponnesian Wars, which lasted more than twenty years. During all that time Athens was in a state of turmoil, not unlike America during the Vietnam War. Great energy and expense were drained off by the war itself, as well as by disagreements over whether Athens should continue to fight, and if so, how. As we learned in Chapter 3, Athens finally surrendered to Sparta in 404 B.C.

The Spartan army supported a group of nobles, known as the Thirty, who overthrew the democracy and ruled Athens for a short time. Plato's family were members of this group. This is the same Thirty Socrates resisted when ordered to condemn and execute Leon of Salamis in violation of the Athenian constitution. Looking back on this time, Plato recalled:

Of course I saw in a short time that [the Thirty] made the former government look in comparison like an age of gold. Among other

The decrees of the people are in large measure repealed by the sages.

Seneca

Do you think I would have survived all these years if I were engaged in public affairs and, acting as good man must, came to the help of justice and considered this the most important thing? Far from it . . . nor would any other man.

Socrates

things they sent an elderly man, Socrates, a friend of mine, who I should hardly be ashamed to say was the justest man of his time . . . against one of the citizens. . . . Their purpose was to connect Socrates to their government whether he wished or not. . . . When I observed all this—and some other similar matters of importance—I withdrew in disgust from the abuses of those days.[2]

The impact of these events never left Plato, who was in his early twenties at the time. The nobles who formed the Thirty had no doubt been disturbed by changes in Athenian society brought about by the long war and the loss of elitist privilege that accompanied increased democracy: the breakdown of tradition; the Sophists' use of debaters' tricks to sway the mob; the rule of passion and emotion. In a democracy, the cleverest, most persuasive, and most attractive speakers could control the state. The great privileges of being born into a special class disappeared. Moreover, the emerging business class had created a power base built on money and aggressiveness rather than tradition and social status.[3]

The Thirty, however, failed in their efforts to restore rule by an elite based on bloodlines, not character or wisdom. Their reign lasted only about eight months before democracy was restored. It was the restored democracy, however, that tried and condemned Socrates.

Plato's Disillusionment

The status of Plato as the greatest of Western philosophers lies not in the soundness of the answers he provides, but rather in his unequaled perception of what questions must be asked, in his shaping of the language to allow the asking, and in the vast range of possibilities suggested in his exploration of every problem.

Alexander Sesonske

This turmoil caused Plato to become discouraged by both the "mob" and the status "elite." The mob, represented by the jury at Socrates' trial, was irrational and dangerous; it was swayed by sophistic appeals to emotion, not by reason. Rule by the status elite, represented by the behavior of the Thirty, was cruel, self-centered, and greedy. When Plato saw that neither the aristocracy nor the common citizenry was capable of superior rule, his "disillusionment [was] fearful and wonderful to behold."[4]

Plato concluded that most people are unfit by training and ability to make the difficult and necessary decisions that would result in a just society. The "average person" lacks wisdom and self-restraint. As Plato saw things, most people make emotional responses based on personal gain and sentiment, rather than rational choices based on an objective, long-term view of what is genuinely good for the individual and society. What, he wondered, could be clearer proof of the mob's deficiencies than its utter failure to recognize the truth of Socrates' message? The trial and death of Socrates showed Plato what happens when "justice" is reduced to a majority vote.

Now as I considered these matters, as well as the sort of men who were active in politics, and the laws and the customs, the more I examined them and the more I advanced in years, the harder it appeared

Plato's Academy was created as a school for philosopher-kings.

to me to administer the government correctly. . . . The result was that I, who had at first been full of eagerness for a public career, as I gazed upon the whirlpool of public life and saw the incessant movement of shifting currents, at last felt dizzy, and . . . *finally saw clearly in regard to all states now existing that without exception their system of government is bad* [emphasis added].[5]

Socrates would be avenged—but by philosophy rather than by political action.

After the revolt of the Thirty and the execution of Socrates, Plato left Athens and wandered for nearly twelve years. He studied with Euclid (the great pioneer of geometry) and possibly with the hedonist Aristippus (Second Interlude). He seems also to have gone to Egypt. During his travels he studied mathematics and mysticism, both of which influenced his later philosophy. He studied Pythagorean philosophy and was deeply influenced by its emphasis on mathematics as the basis of all things (see box, pages 48–49).

How can any man be a democrat who is sincerely a democrat?

H. L. Mencken

The Academy

Plato was probably forty years old when he founded the Academy (around 388 B.C.). Ironically, considering the importance and influence the Academy was to exert, we have no solid evidence concerning when it was founded, how it was organized, what exactly was studied, or what educational techniques were used. Most of Plato's writing seems to have been finished before he founded the Academy, with the exception of a few works completed when he was an old man. His chief function at the Academy was probably as a teacher and administrator.[6] Here Plato lived for another forty years, lecturing "without notes," until he died.

The chief purpose of the Academy was probably to educate people who would be fit to rule the just state. Plato's ideal educational program was a progressive one in which the study of mathematics, geometry, music, and so forth introduced discipline into the student's overall character, and order into the mind. Only after the mind and soul were disciplined were a select few allowed to study ultimate philosophical principles.

Because, in Plato's view, "no present government [was] suitable for philosophy," the Academy was established as a philosophic retreat, isolated from the turmoil of Athenian politics, safe from the fate of Socrates. Let's see what philosophy Plato thought could produce the just state.

Plato's Epistemology

Socrates' death, the revolt of the Thirty, sophistic abuses, and other factors convinced Plato that a corrupt state produces corrupt citizens. He thus turned to the development of a theory of knowledge that could refute sophistic skepticism and moral relativism. Plato believed that if he could identify and articulate the difference between mere opinion and genuine knowledge, it would then be possible to identify the structure of the ideal state, a state based on knowledge and truth rather than the mere appearance of truth and personal whim.

Plato correctly understood that before he could provide satisfactory answers to ethical, social, political, and other philosophical questions, he must first tackle the problem of knowledge. We have seen how the conflicting opinions of the Presocratics first led to philosophical confusion and then to ethical and political abuses in the hands of the most extreme of the Sophists. Socrates' heroic effort to refute ignorance and relativism was most successful in its exposure of error and inconsistency. It was less successful in establishing any positive knowledge.

Thus, Plato could not avoid the challenge of sophistic skepticism or ignore philosophy's reputation for generating ludicrous doctrines that contradicted each other—and themselves. Though the Presocratics, the

He was buried in the Academy, where he spent the greatest part of his life in philosophical study. And hence the school which he founded was called the Academic school. And all the students joined in the funeral procession.

Diogenes Läertius

Plato's genius is exhibited in the fact that he succeeded in eliciting from his observations of the Athenian state reflections on society and government that are true everywhere.

Raphael Demos

Sophists, and Socrates had all made use of the distinction between appearance and reality, the exact nature of reality and clear rational criteria for distinguishing reality from appearance had eluded them.

Attempts to explain how one kind of thing changes into another generated ambiguities and seeming contradictions: How could "one thing" somehow change into something else? In what sense can my twelve-year-old dog Daiquiri be the "same" dog she was five years ago? Does this mean that Daiquiri is both the same dog she was *and* a different dog? In what sense did the "same person" change from an infant into a philosophy student?

Plato recognized the full importance of the questions raised by the Presocratics concerning coherent explanations of how things change, how reality "becomes" appearance, how appearances are related to reality, and other fundamental issues. The relation between appearance and reality, the problem of "the one and the many," and the nature of change needed to be clarified before any answer to the sophistic assault on rationality was possible.

Plato's Dualistic Solution

Plato concluded that the solution to the basic problem of knowledge lay in acknowledging that both Heraclitus and Parmenides were partially correct in their efforts to characterize reality (First Interlude). Heraclitus asserted that the "one" is some kind of orderly cycle or process of change. He said that "change alone is unchanging." Parmenides, in contrast, referred to the "one" as *being*. Parmenides argued that being is perfect and complete or "whole." It cannot move or change. Parmenidian being is material, "it is the being of the visible cosmos, immobilized, and to a great extent purified, but still clearly recognizable." (See First Interlude.)

According to Plato, Heraclitus and Parmenides probably thought they were discussing things that could be sensed or perceived as part of the physical world. (We can refer to such things as "sensibles," for short.) The Sophists' skeptical arguments were also aimed at contradictions and difficulties generated by problems of sensation and perception. (See Chapter 2.)

Suppose, Plato wondered, that reality is not a single thing (a monism) but is rather a dualism. One reality might be Heraclitean and another Parmenidian; one reality in constant change and the other eternally changeless.

Of course a supposition is not evidence. Plato needed to prove the dual nature of reality. Part of the "proof" seemed easy enough: it seems obvious that the world of "sensibles" exists. And the sensible world certainly seems to be one of change: growth cycles, soil erosion, flowing rivers, wear and tear of the implements of daily living, and so on. Further, this change is orderly: the same seasons follow the same seasons, dogs do not give birth to stones, objects fall down not up, and so forth. So, as far as the world of sensibles is concerned, Heraclitus seems to be basically correct.

For as all nature is akin, and the soul has [already] learned all things, there is no difficulty in . . . learning . . . all the rest, if a man is strenuous and does not faint; for all enquiry is but recollection.

Plato

Wise men say . . . that heaven and earth, gods and men, are held together by the principles of sharing, by friendship and order, by self-control and justice; that, my friend, is the reason they call the universe "cosmos," and not disorder or licentiousness . . . what a mighty power is exercised, both among men and gods, by geometrical equality.

Plato

But a completely Heraclitean world of observable change, for all its "obviousness," would be a world devoid of the possibility of knowledge and certainty, according to Plato. Such a world would be a world of appearances only, a realm of opinion, not knowledge. Plato called this condition the world of *becoming*.

Knowledge and Being

According to Plato, the very essence of time is change but the very essence of knowledge is unchanging. What is true is always true. Therefore, whatever is relative and always changing cannot be true. The Sophists could not discover truth because they were only concerned with the Heraclitean world of sensibles, the world of ever-changing perceptions and customs. Truth and knowledge are found in another realm of reality: the level of being that Parmenides tried to characterize.

Plato believed that this second reality, while closely related to the world of becoming, exists independently of it. This other reality has many of the qualities Parmenides ascribed to the one (being): It is not physical and it is not affected by space and time. What is eternal is *real*; what changes is only *appearance*. Thus, we can have *knowledge* of what is eternal; of appearances there can be only *opinions*. To repeat: Opinions change; knowledge is timeless. Plato insisted that whatever is permanent is superior to whatever is not. Reality is superior to appearance, and knowledge (reality) is superior to opinion (appearance), in Plato's view.

The Theory of Forms

In Plato's metaphysics, the level of being consists of timeless essences or entities called *forms*. Such a metaphysics is sometimes called transcendental because it asserts that there is a plane of existence "above and beyond" our ordinary existence. To transcend anything is to go so far beyond it as to reach a qualitatively different level.

The **Platonic forms** are independently existing, nonspatial, nontemporal "somethings" ("kinds," "types," or "sorts") that cannot be known through the senses. Known in thought, the forms are not ideas in the usual sense. Knowledge is always about forms.

It may be helpful to think about other meanings of the word *form*. By form we sometimes mean the shape or manner or style or type of something. We make forms from which to mold dishes or statues, for example. We fill in business forms. The very notion of form implies something that provides general or essential order, structure, or shape for a particular instance. Thus, the form of something is sometimes called its structure or essence, or even its "basic nature." Many of these everyday meanings in-

PLATONIC FORMS

Independently existing, nonspatial, nontemporal "somethings" ("kinds," "types," or "sorts") known only through thought and that cannot be known through the senses; independently existing objects of thought; that which makes a particular thing uniquely and essentially what it is.

volve the essence of a thing, the quality that makes it what it is. In Platonic terms, a thing's form is what it uniquely and essentially is.

However, *exactly what Plato meant* by "forms" has remained a subject of intense philosophical debate and disagreement from Plato's time to ours. For the last forty years, the theory of forms has probably been the most discussed part of Plato's philosophy among English-speaking philosophers. And, still, philosophers cannot agree on exactly what Plato meant. The complexity of the problem is further compounded by the fact that, although Plato places great importance on the forms, he does not seem to have a very well worked out theory of forms.[7]

Nevertheless, since Plato's theory of forms is central to the rest of his philosophy, and thus the basis for his theory of the ideal state, we need to take the time to develop a general sense of what Plato hoped to show by appealing to the theory of forms.

What Are Forms?

Because the Greek root for "form" (*eidos*) is sometimes translated as "idea," philosophers can slip into the error of thinking of forms as the kinds of mental entities (ideas) that only exist in our minds. Plato thinks the forms are part of reality, independent of any minds.[8] Two other terms used by translators for *eidos* are "archetype" or "essence."

According to Plato, each form actually exists—pure and unchanging—regardless of continuous shifts in human opinions and alterations in the (physical) world of sensibles. Each form is a pure, unmixed, essence that exists independently of human consciousness. It is important to be very clear about this: Although the forms actually exist, they are not physical objects.

Forms are universal types or kinds that exist outside space and time. The physical world contains particular sensible instances or examples of the various universal forms. Forms are what we today might call abstract objects, but Plato considers such abstract objects more real than mere concrete physical objects.

The sorts of things Plato refers to as forms include geometrical, mathematical, and logical relations (triangularity, equivalence, identity); virtues (goodness, wisdom, courage); and sensible properties (roundness, beauty, redness). The physical sensations we associate with such qualities as roundness and redness are not the same thing as *roundness* and *redness* in and of themselves.

Particular things will differ in terms of what Plato variously refers to as their "participation in," "sharing in," "resembling," or "reflecting" the form roundness or the form redness. There is only one essential form of *redness*, for instance, although there may be a virtually infinite number of particular things that "share" some element or degree of *redness*, that "resemble" or "reflect" the essence of pure *redness*. But *redness* (the form) is

It is hard, too, to see how a weaver or a carpenter will be benefitted in regard to his own craft by knowing this [a form], or how the man who has viewed the Idea itself will be a better doctor or general thereby. For a doctor seems not even to study health in this way, but the health of man, or perhaps rather the health of a particular man; it is individuals that he is healing.

Aristotle

If a man . . . does away with Forms of things and will not admit that every individual thing has its own determinate Form which is always one and the same, he will have nothing on which his mind can rest; and so he will utterly destroy the power of reasoning.

Plato

always the same regardless of any changes that occur in some particular object. When, for example, a red flower fades to pale pink, its participation in the form *redness* decreases. There is, however, no decrease in the form *redness*.

What might Plato have meant by saying that particular things "resemble," "share in," "participate in," or "reflect" different forms? Consider two apparently identical glass beads, each "reflecting" *roundness* and *identity*. Yet no sensible object is ever absolutely, truly, perfectly round, because sensible objects always contain "mixtures," "impurities," even "opposites." Under microscopic scrutiny, we would expect to find that the surface of the smoothest, purest glass bead ever discovered was minutely pitted or uneven—microscopically pitted or uneven—yet pitted or uneven nonetheless, hence not absolutely, truly, perfectly round; at most, it might be "as round as possible."

According to Plato, no physical object is, or ever can be, perfectly round. "Aha!" you may think, "but two glass beads can be identical—especially given today's computerized technologies and sophisticated manufacturing techniques."

Stop and think a little further, though. What would it mean for two physical objects to be genuinely, absolutely, perfectly *identical*? In the strictest sense, "Two things are identical if all the characteristics of one are also possessed by the other and vice versa."[9] Is it possible for two glass beads to be *absolutely identical*? No, because in order to be identical (not very, very similar) they would have to contain exactly the same silica molecules, atoms, quarks, neutrinos, and such—in exactly the same place at exactly the same time. Of course they cannot do so, for if that were the case, there would be only one glass bead. Two very, very similar glass beads must be in two distinct places. By being in two distinct places at precisely the same moment, they are different from one another in respect to location. Thus, they are not—strictly speaking—identical.

Lastly, consider the kinds of reasons Plato might offer to support the claim that forms exist independently of human consciousness: We have good reasons to believe that round objects existed before any perceivers (animals or people) did. Hence, roundness is not a property that depends on human minds for existence; *roundness* is more than just a human idea. *Roundness* itself—as distinct from any particular round thing—is unchanging. It cannot change from being *roundness* to, say, *nearly roundness* or *oblongness* or *rectilinearity*. Following basic laws of rationality, *roundness* is either *roundness* or it is not. And so for all forms. (For a different view of whether or not objects and properties can exist independently of perceivers, see Chapter 9.)

In general, the truths about mathematical objects exist whether we know those truths or not. Plato thinks the same is true for moral and aesthetic facts.

I had a dream, and I heard in my dream that the primeval letters or elements out of which you and I and all other things are compounded have no reason or explanation; you can only name them, but no predicate can be either affirmed or denied of them . . . if you mean to speak of this or that thing by itself alone.

Plato

Philosophical Query

Reflect on the following objection to the preceding paragraphs. See if you can respond to it on Plato's behalf: "The glass bead example is only playing with semantics. When we talk about two physical objects being 'identical,' we don't mean literally identical—we mean so similar that human beings are unable to distinguish one object from the other. Obviously we can distinguish different things from each other when they're right next to each other. But if we find no differences when we analyze them one at a time, we are justified in saying that they are identical, 'indistinguishable.' Identical means indistinguishable to human beings; that is, so closely resembling one another that we cannot tell them apart."

Why Did Plato Need the Forms?

Among other things, Plato wanted the theory of forms to provide a *rational explanation* of how knowledge is possible. The forms are the foundation of Plato's bold answer to the Sophists' skeptical assault on knowledge and to their relativistic rejection of universal (absolute) truths. Defense of absolute, unchanging truths is difficult under the best of circumstances; it is especially difficult if we wish to move beyond merely heartfelt assertions of belief in absolutes, and beyond appeals to the widespread popularity of belief in absolutes. Sincerity and popularity only tell us about believers, not about beliefs. Plato knew that unless he could offer more than *faith* in the existence of absolutes, more than authoritarian and dogmatic pronouncements, he would fail, as a philosopher, to meet the challenge of relativism.

Plato's forms provide stable objects of knowledge for the mind to latch onto in a world of change and uncertainty. In this way Plato is able to reconcile Parmenides' world of stability with Heraclitus's world of flux.

Plato's task here is of more than mere historical interest to us; it bears on some of the most basic philosophical and human questions: *Is everything a matter of opinion?* If not: 1) Is there any way to *show* that knowledge is possible? and 2) Is there any way those of us who are not wise or enlightened can identify those who are? That is, if we cannot always grasp the truth, can we at least identify those who can, and thereby benefit from their counsel? If the answer to 2 is "no," then we are at the mercy of unverifiable beliefs, rule by force, rhetoric, and seduction. If one opinion is as ultimately good as any other, then one form of government is no better than any other, and there is no point in seeking truth or wisdom. All that matters is surviving as comfortably as possible (in my opinion).

On the other hand, if knowledge is possible, and if some opinions really are better than others, how can we justify democracy, a form of government that treats all citizens as equal, and thus treats all opinions as

To what purpose is it for philosophy to decide against common sense in this or any other matter? The material world is older, and of more authority, than any principles of philosophy. It declines the tribunal of reason, and laughs at the artillery of the logician.

Thomas Reid

equal? Put more forcefully: If knowledge exists, what would justify ignoring it? Can there be any reasonable justification for ignoring the difference between knowledge and opinion?

In this context, we can see that Plato's task is of more than merely academic or historical interest. It cuts to the heart of controversial issues facing us today. In struggling to develop his theory of forms, Plato was struggling to refute—not just reject—relativism and preserve the distinction between knowledge and opinion. Plato reasoned that if he could solidly establish that knowledge is possible, and that knowledge exists, then he could also justify and preserve a worldview that admitted of real (objective) distinctions between right and wrong, true and false, better and worse.

All around us we see that the consequences of accepting or rejecting such hierarchical distinctions are enormous. They shape our attitudes and actions concerning education, morality, family life, gender issues, government, and more. In other words, metaphysical and epistemological positions underlie real-life controversies and hard choices. (At least that is one opinion.)

Philosophical Query

Is it possible to know that no one does know? Is it possible to know that no one does know that no one does know? Is it possible to know that no one can know that no one does know? Is it possible to know that no one can know that no one can know? How do you know? Or, how do you know that you don't know?

Knowledge and Opinion

For Plato, the chief distinction between knowledge and opinion is that knowledge is fixed, absolutely and eternally true (correct), whereas opinions are changeable and "unanchored." According to Plato, *scientific knowledge of particulars is impossible*. That is, fundamental knowledge of reality must always be knowledge of forms. What we often think of as knowledge of particulars—that Janet is older than Methuselah—Plato thought of as *opinion*.

Knowledge is always of forms, and is acquired by deductive reasoning and deep contemplation. Opinion, in contrast, is always about perceptions, particulars. Thus, a "science" consists of necessary and universal truths about the objects (forms) that the science studies. In all scientific subject areas, the physical objects, formal relationships, particular individuals, societies, or governments studied represent forms. The particular things themselves are never "as real" as the forms they participate in or resemble.

Remember, too, that for Plato, that which changes is less real than that which does not. That which changes is "lower" than that which does not. And since all particular things change, when Protagoras said that the individual is "the measure," he was, from Plato's view, talking about the level of *becoming*, about the lower level of perceptions of particular things, about the personal and individual rather than the public and universal.

In Plato's metaphysics, the level of change is the level of growth and decay, life and death—change and *becoming*. Only in the realm of *becoming*, can opinions change from true to false. In the *Timaeus* Plato says:

> That which is apprehended by intelligence and reason is always in the same state, but that which is conceived by opinion with the help of sensation and without reason is always in a process of becoming and perishing and never really is.[10]

Because as a particular person, living in a particular place during a specific span of time, I can have better—or worse—opinions today than I did yesterday. I change, material and social conditions change, but truth and knowledge themselves cannot and do not change.

What Happens When People Disagree About Knowledge?

Granted that people and conditions change; granted that we disagree among ourselves over what is true and what is real; what happens when we disagree about knowledge?

Suppose, for example, that Michael simply cannot "see" or "understand" that 2 × 3 does not equal 4. In other words, for Michael, 2 × 3 = 4. We can say, then, that Michael has a false belief or opinion; we can also say, however, that the product of 2 × 3 is not a matter of opinion (Michael's or anyone's), but of fixed mathematical properties and relationships. We know this because in order to understand concepts such as number, three, two, product, equivalence, and such, we have to "glimpse" their forms. This "glimpse" of recognition is what understanding the concept is.

Next, consider the case of Michael's aunt, Patricia. Asked the product of 2 × 3, Patricia proudly says, "I know the answer. It's six!" Asked how she knows, Patricia explains, "Because mother told me so. And because my mother's mother told her." Michael's friend, Abby, also confidently agrees that 2 × 3 = 6. When we ask her to explain why, Abby says, "Teacher told me so."

Abby does not *know* that 2 × 3 = 6 any more than Michael "knows" that 2 × 3 = 4 or Patricia "knows" that 2 × 3 = 6. Unlike Michael's belief, Patricia's and Abby's beliefs are true. But they are still just *beliefs* (opinions). Patricia and Abby are lucky this time—their beliefs are "unanchored," however.

Lacking knowledge, Michael, Patricia, and Abby have no way to *determine* who is right or wrong. If they vote, they may end up with the "correct answer"; but only by chance. What they cannot do is willingly

The Tao that can be told of
Is not the absolute Tao;
The Names that can be
    given
Are not the Absolute
    Names.
The Nameless is the origin
    of Heaven and Earth;
The Named is the Mother
    of All Things.

Lao-tzu

The true lover of knowledge naturally strives for truth, and is not content with common opinion, but soars with undimmed and unwearied passion till he grasps the essential nature of things.

Plato

choose the correct answer, because they lack sufficient understanding to make an informed determination: They don't *know* what it is!

Without knowledge, we are like Michael, Patricia, and Abby: We, too, are at the mercy of luck and uninformed preference. We are "unanchored," and so can only act based on habit, tradition, personal preference, and impulse.

Throughout *The Republic* Plato repeatedly distinguishes between knowledge and opinion, warning against even true opinions that lack grounding in knowledge. Here's a typical passage:

> "But I don't think it's right, Socrates . . . for you to be able to tell us other people's opinions but not your own, when you've given so much time to the subject."
>
> "Yes, but do you think it's right for a man to talk as if he knows what he does not?"
>
> "He has no right to talk as if he knew; but he should be prepared to say what his opinion is, so far as it goes."
>
> "Well," I [Socrates] said, "haven't you noticed that opinion without knowledge is blind—isn't anyone with a true but unthinking opinion like a blind man on the right road?"
>
> "Yes."[11]

According to Plato, the Sophists failed to understand this, confusing opinion with knowledge, perception with understanding, and the realm of *becoming* with the realm of *being*. Plato's task, then, is analogous to "proving" the existence of colors to persons born blind.

When an appeal to direct experience or common understanding is not possible, an indirect approach may prove effective. In this case, if we have yet to grasp the forms, perhaps we can get some indirect idea of them.

In *The Republic*, Plato uses three different comparisons to help express various aspects of the theory of forms: the Divided Line, the Simile of the Sun, and the Allegory of the Cave. We will study each of them. Each illustration clarifies different but interconnected aspects of the theory of forms. Do not worry if you need to take extra time with this material. Allow each of Plato's illustrations to help you better grasp the whole.

The Divided Line

Plato used the concept of a divided line to illustrate the relationship of knowledge to opinion, reality to appearance, metaphysics and epistemology, and the worlds of being and becoming. The Divided Line shows that both knowledge and opinion deal with forms, though in different ways.

The Divided Line consists of two basic sections, each unevenly divided into two segments. The four segments illustrate four ways of apprehend-

To understand Plato is to be educated; it is to see the nature of the world in which we live. The vitality of what he has to say is due to one factor. He took his starting point from what is and not from what man wants.

Huntington Cairns

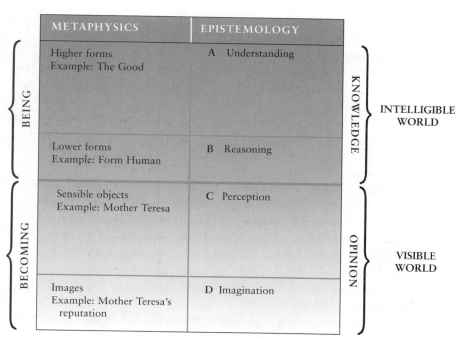

Figure 4.1   *Plato's Divided Line*

A + B = World of Forms (Being)
C + D = Physical World (Becoming)
Segments **A, B, C, D** represent decreasing degrees of truth. Each degree of truth corresponds to a different kind of thinking and different level of reality.
A: This is the level of pure intelligence or understanding. Here the soul directly apprehends truth at its highest level.
B: This is the level of reasoning; specifically, mathematical thinking and deductive reasoning.
C: This is the level of belief or common opinions about physical objects, morals, politics, practical affairs.
D: This is the level of illusion, dominated by secondhand opinions and uncritical impressions.[12]

ing four components of reality; two each of being and becoming. Here's a representation of the Divided Line to refer to as you read Plato's presentation of it. Note how the four metaphysical levels of reality correspond to four epistemological ways of apprehending the forms.

With Figure 4.1 as a guide, let's take a look at what Plato said about the Divided Line. In this passage Socrates is describing a conversation he had with Plato's older brother, Glaucon:

"Well, take a line divided into two unequal parts, corresponding to the visible and intelligible worlds, and then divide the two parts again in the same ratio, to represent degrees of clarity and obscurity. In the visible world, one section stands for images: by 'images' I mean first

Out of Plato come all things that are still written and debated among men of thought. Great havoc makes he of our originalities. We have reached the mountain from which all these drift boulders were detached.

Ralph Waldo Emerson

shadows, then reflections in water and other close grained, polished surfaces, and all that sort of thing if you understand me."

"I understand."

"Let the other section stand for the objects which are the originals of the images—animals, plants and manufactured objects of all kinds."

"Very good."

"Would you be prepared to admit that these sections differ in their degree of truth, and that the relation of image to the original is the same as that of opinion and knowledge?"

"I would."

"Then consider next how the intelligible part of the line is to be divided. In one section the mind uses the originals of the visible world in their turn as images, and has to base its inquiries on assumptions and proceed from them to its conclusions instead of going back to first principles: in the other it proceeds from assumption back to self-sufficient first principles, making no use of the images employed by the other section, but pursuing its inquiry solely by means of Forms. . . .

". . . it treats assumptions not as principles, but as assumptions in the true sense, that is, as starting points and steps in the ascent to the universal, self-sufficient first principle; when it has reached that principle it can again descend, by keeping to the consequences that follow from it, to a final conclusion. The whole procedure involves nothing in the sensible world, but deals throughout with Forms and finishes with Forms."[13]

Levels of Awareness

The lowest level of awareness, **D** on Figure 4.1, is the level of illusion. Virtually no one inhabits this level all the time, but we can occasionally slip into states of illusion. We slip into **D** on purpose and for fun when we go to magic shows or watch movies (which are really just light, shadows, and sound creating the illusion of depth and action). This is known as the "willing suspension of disbelief." But we can also slip into illusion without being aware of it when we hold opinions based solely on appearances, unanalyzed impressions, uncritically inherited beliefs, and unevaluated emotions. The image—opinion—I have of Mother Teresa is an example of Level D awareness. It is based on photographs I have seen, news clips on television, and part of a speech she gave to the United Nations, which I watched on the C-Span cable network.

C on Figure 4.1 represents the second or informed level of awareness. It involves a wider range of opinions about what most of us probably think of as reality. At this level of informed awareness, we attempt to distinguish appearance from reality, but in a kind of "everyday way." For example, I believe that my desk looks solid but it is actually made up of

Many admire, few know.

Hippocrates

countless molecules and atoms in motion. I believe that the sun looks small because of its distance from earth, but in fact, it is much larger. Strictly speaking, I do not *know* these things. I have had some science classes, looked through microscopes and telescopes, and so forth, but I do not have a scientist's sophisticated knowledge built upon rigorous deductive reasoning. At the same time, my Level C opinions are based on observations and perceptions of physical objects, not just photos or representations of them. On this informed level we realize that the way things appear may not be the way they are. Most of us spend much of our lives dealing with more or less informed opinions about most things. If I ever get to meet Mother Teresa, perhaps my Level D image of her will become a more accurate Level C informed opinion.

The next level of awareness (**B**) takes us out of the realms of becoming and opinion (**D** + **C**) and into the world of being and the first stage of knowledge acquired through deductive reasoning. As we've learned, Plato believed truth is changeless, eternal, and absolute, and that knowledge doesn't grow or decay, it just *is*. Since Mother Teresa the individual does grow and change, however, Level B knowledge must be of a form, say the Form Human. The Form Human does not change—grow or decay—according to Plato.

At the highest level of reality (**A**), the soul has no need for perception or interpretation. Plato says that it "directly apprehends" the "absolute form of the Good." At the highest level, reason does not—indeed it cannot—deduce the forms. The higher forms are directly understood, apprehended—"glimpsed"—without any mediating process or principles.

Human insight requires a turning around. . . . But when it is a question of thinking in earnest, when an . . . eternal truth . . . makes a claim on independent thinking, then there is something in man that rebels against the rigors of responsible self-clarification. He does not want to wake up but go on sleeping.

Karl Jaspers

The Simile of the Sun

Plato compared the "absolute form of the Good" to the sun: Just as the sun (light) is necessary for vision and life, so, too, the Good makes Reality, Truth, and the existence of everything else possible. The Good exists beyond becoming at the highest reaches of being. The Good cannot be observed with the five senses and can be known only by pure thought or intelligence. The Good is the source of both the value and the existence of all other forms. The Good is the Form of the Forms.

Comprehension of the Good is unlike other forms of knowing. It is holistic, not partial. The soul must deliberately work its way up from the lowest level of becoming to enlightenment. Experience of the Good so far transcends all other experiences that it cannot be clearly described, so Plato uses a comparison or simile to allude to the Good. We can represent Plato's comparison of the Good to the sun as shown in Figure 4.2.

In the following extended passage from *The Republic*, Plato (in the character of Socrates) compares the Good to the sun, and apprehension

Figure 4.2 *Figure 4.2 shows the hierarchy of being and knowledge reflected in Plato's simile of the sun.*
A = pure understanding
B = deductive thinking
C = common opinion
D = uncritical impressions

VISIBLE WORLD (C + D)	INTELLIGIBLE WORLD (A + B)
The Sun	The Good
Growth	Reality
Light	Truth
Visibility	Intelligibility

There seems to be nothing in the study of chemistry that makes you feel like a superior order of being, but you study Plato and you begin to believe you're a philosopher.

S. I. Hayakawa

of the Good to seeing. Note how strongly he expresses his ultimate regard for the Good:

"Well, [the sun] is the child of the Good. . . . The Good has begotten its own likeness, and it bears the same relation to sight and visibility in the visible world that the Good bears to intelligence in the intelligible world."

"Will you explain that a bit further?"

"You know that when we turn our eyes to objects whose colours are no longer illuminated by daylight, but only by moonlight or starlight, they see dimly and appear to be almost blind, as if they had no clear vision."

"Yes."

"But when we turn them on things on which the sun is shining, then they see clearly and their power of vision is restored."

"Certainly."

"Apply the analogy to the mind. When the mind's eye rests on objects illuminated by truth and reality, it understands and comprehends them, and functions intelligently; but when it turns to the twilight world of change and decay, it can only form opinions, its vision is confused and its beliefs shifting, and it seems to lack intelligence."

"That is true."

"Then what gives the objects of knowledge their truth and the mind the power of knowing is the Form of the Good. It is the cause of knowledge and truth, and you will be right to think of it as being itself known, and yet as being something other than, and even higher than, knowledge and truth. And just as it was right to think of light and sight as being like the sun, but wrong to think of them as being the sun itself, so here again it is right to think of knowledge and truth as being *like* the Good, but wrong to think of either of them as being the Good, which must be given still a higher place of honor."

"You are making it something remarkably exalted, if it is the source of knowledge and truth, and yet itself higher than they are. For I suppose you can't mean it to be pleasure?"

"A monstrous suggestion," I replied. "Let us pursue our analogy further. . . . The sun, I think you will agree, not only makes the things we see visible, but causes the process of generation, growth and nourishment, without itself being such a process. . . . The Good therefore may be said to be the source not only of the intelligibility of the objects of knowledge, but also of their existence and reality; yet it is not itself identical with reality, but is beyond reality, and is superior to it in dignity and power."[14]

Toward the end of the discussion of the Good, Glaucon remarks that the process of escaping from shadows to enlightenment "sounds like a long job." Plato-Socrates agrees, adding:

> And you may assume that there are, corresponding to the four sections of the line, four states of mind: to the top section [A] Intelligence, to the second [B] Reason, to the third [C] Opinion, and to the fourth [D] Illusion. And you may arrange them in a scale, and assume that they have degrees of clarity corresponding to the degree of truth and reality possessed by their subject-matter.[15]

Just as people born blind have different meanings for color words than those who have seen colors, those on one level of reality cannot recognize what is being said by those on a higher level. They have no comparable experience. Those who reach the level of comprehending the Good are forever transformed; they are en-light-ened—they are wise. And the relationship between the enlightened and the unenlightened is at the heart of Plato's whole philosophy.

> With [the Good], it is not the same as with other things we learn: it cannot be framed in words, but from protracted concentration devoted to [it] and from spending one's life with it, a light suddenly bursts forth in the soul as though kindled by a flying spark, and then it feeds on itself.
>
> *Plato*

The Allegory of the Cave

One problem common to any hierarchical enlightenment philosophy involves the gap between what the wise master knows and the pupil's initial ignorance. Different levels of experience can create communication and comprehension gaps.

We see a similar kind of difficulty in interactions between adults and young children. Most of us—at least as we mature—have no difficulty with the concept of degrees of awareness and knowledge between adults and children. We even accept the fact that there are levels of knowledge and experience dividing adults with some form of mental impairment or limit and those of average or better mental capacities.

But what about differences between average and so-called wise or enlightened people? Do such differences really exist? If they do, are they indicators of different levels of what Plato refers to as "intelligence" or "wisdom," or are they just unprovable claims made by people who think they know more than the rest of us? What reasons do we have for believing Plato's claims about levels of being and the Good? Why should we discount the views and experiences of the vast majority of people and listen to the claims of one supposedly wiser person?

> The parable [of the Cave] is unforgettable. It is a miracle of philosophical invention, providing an approach to thoughts that do not lend themselves to direct statement.
>
> *Karl Jaspers*

Plato responded to this important challenge by telling a story with a lesson, an allegory, in Book VII of *The Republic*. This allegory is offered not as a conclusive proof, but as a suggestive possibility. It is the summation of the exposition of Plato's theory of forms that includes the Divided Line and the Simile of the Sun.

The Divided Line expresses Plato's hierarchical view of reality and wisdom. The Simile of the Sun characterizes the act of apprehending highest truth in the form of the Good. In the Allegory of the Cave (Figure 4.3), Plato compares the level of becoming to living in a cave, and describes the ordeal necessary for the soul's ascent from shadowy illusion to enlightenment—from mere opinion to informed opinion to rationally based knowledge to wisdom.

The levels of awareness identified in the Allegory of the Cave correspond to the segments of the Divided Line referred to above and in Figure 4.1: those chained to the wall of shadows are imprisoned in the shadowy world of imagination and illusion (**D**); those loose within the cave occupy the "common sense" world of perception and informed opinion (**C**); those struggling through the passageway to the surface are acquiring knowledge through reason (**B**); the rich surface world of warmth and sunlight is the highest level of reality, directly grasped by pure intelligence (**A**).

The allegory illustrates the ascent of the mind from illusion to enlightenment, and alludes to the obligation of the enlightened wise person to return to the world of becoming in order to help others discern the forms.

Socrates presents the allegory as part of his continuing conversation with Glaucon:

> "I want you to go on to picture the enlightenment or ignorance of our human conditions somewhat as follows. Imagine an underground chamber, like a cave with an entrance open to the daylight and running a long way underground. In this chamber are men who have been prisoners there since they were children, their legs and necks being so fastened that they can only look straight ahead of them and cannot turn their heads. Behind them and above them a fire is burning, and between the fire and the prisoners runs a road, in front of which a curtain-wall has been built, like the screen at puppet shows between the operators and their audience, above which they show their puppets."
>
> "I see."
>
> "Imagine further that there are men carrying all sorts of gear along behind the curtain-wall, including figures of men and animals made of wood and stone and other materials, and that some of these men, as is natural, are talking and some not."
>
> "An odd picture and an odd sort of prisoner."
>
> "They are drawn from life," I replied. "For, tell me, do you think our prisoners could see anything of themselves or their fellows except the shadows thrown by the fire on the wall of the cave opposite them?"

Learning without thought brings ensnarement. Thought without learning totters.

Confucius

Every man takes the limits of his own field of vision for the limits of the world.

Arthur Schopenhauer

Figure 4.3 *The Allegory of the Cave illustrates Plato's vision of the ascent of the mind from illusion (Level D) to opinion (Level C) to reasoned knowledge (Level B) to enlightenment (Level A). These levels of awareness correspond to the segments of the Divided Line illustrated in Figure 4.1.*

"How could they see anything else if they were prevented from moving their heads all their lives?" . . .

"Then if they were able to talk to each other, would they not assume that the shadows they saw were real things?"

"Inevitably."

"And if the wall of their prison opposite them reflected sound, don't you think that they would suppose, whenever one of the passers-by on the road spoke, that the voice belonged to the shadow passing before them?"

"They would be bound to think so."

"And so they would believe that the shadows of the objects we mentioned were in all respects real."

"Yes, inevitably."

"Then think what would naturally happen to them if they were released from their bonds and cured of their delusions. Suppose one of them were let loose, and suddenly compelled to stand up and turn

Bodily exercise, when compulsory, does no harm to the body; but knowledge which is acquired under compulsion obtains no hold on the mind.

Plato

his head and look and walk towards the fire; all these actions would be painful and he would be too dazzled to see properly the objects of which he used to see the shadows. So if he was told that what he used to see was merely illusion and that he was now nearer reality and seeing more correctly, because he was turned towards objects that were more real, and if on top of that he were compelled to say what each of the passing objects was when it was pointed out to him, don't you think he would be at a loss, and think that what he used to see was more real than the objects now being pointed out to him?"

"Much more real."

. . . "And if, . . . he were forcibly dragged up the steep and rocky ascent and not let go till he had been dragged out into the sunlight, the process would be a painful one, to which he would much object, and when he emerged into the light his eyes would be so overwhelmed by the brightness of it that he wouldn't be able to see a single one of the things he was now told were real. . . . he would need to grow accustomed to the light before he could see things in the world outside the cave. . . . The thing he would be able to do last would be to look directly at the sun, and observe its nature without using reflections in water or any other medium, but just as it is."

"That must come last."

"Later on he would come to the conclusion that it is the sun that produces the changing seasons and years and controls everything in the visible world, and is in a sense responsible for everything that he and his fellow-prisoners used to see."

"That is the conclusion which he would obviously reach."[16]

Philosophical Query

The Allegory of the Cave has intrigued students of Plato since it first appeared. Do you think it accurately expresses the way we experience knowledge? For instance, in childhood, everything is black and white, but with experience, we discover rich nuances and hues, as it were.

What level are you on? Society in general? The world? Explain. Do you believe in levels of reality? In enlightenment? Why or why not?

Plato is philosophy, and philosophy Plato. . . . No wife, no children had he, and the thinkers of all civilized nations are his posterity and are tinged with his mind.

Ralph Waldo Emerson

The Rule of the Wise

Plato's fundamental vision is hierarchical and aristocratic, rather than egalitarian and democratic. His epistemology and metaphysics reflect and encourage this kind of highly discriminating orientation. Today, any non-democratic position is likely to be called "elitist." If you believe in the fundamental equality of all people, you may be suspicious of Plato's belief in the superiority of those who have supposedly escaped the Cave and seen the Good. If you are skeptical about the possibility of any human being discovering "the truth," you will probably have difficulty with the idea that only these exceptional, enlightened individuals are more fit to govern than the rest of us.

Such concerns are well-founded. We are all aware of the abuses committed by Nazis, racist supremacists, and all sorts of "true believers" who are convinced that they alone know the truth and are thus superior to the rest of us.

Plato's aristocracy of wisdom, however, is not based on gender, national origin, and the like, at least in theory. It is built on Plato's conviction that enlightenment is real and that it is more than intellectual ability isolated from moral character. With rare exceptions, Platonic enlightenment is the product of careful training, directed desire, hard work, and luck (being raised in an environment that does not prevent us from escaping the Cave).

At the end of the Allegory of the Cave, Plato echoes the teachings of another enlightenment philosophy covered in this text, Buddhism, which insists that enlightenment is always accompanied by a desire to help others escape the bonds of illusion and ignorance. Plato's philosophy, unlike Buddhism, however, stresses progression through ascending stages of rationality and posits a linear hierarchy of reality. (See Third Interlude.)

As the Allegory of the Cave draws to a close, Plato-Socrates expresses the love-based obligation of the wise person to guide and teach those less wise, helping them escape the Cave:

> "And when he [who escaped the cave] thought of his first home and what passed for wisdom there, and of his fellow-prisoners, don't you think he would congratulate himself on his good fortune and be sorry for them?"
>
> "Very much so." . . .
>
> "And if he had to discriminate between the shadows, in competition with the other prisoners, while still blinded and before his eyes got used to the darkness—a process that might take some time— wouldn't he be likely to make a fool of himself? And they would say that his visit to the upper world had ruined his sight, and that the ascent was not worth even attempting. And if anyone tried to release them and lead them up, they would kill him if they could lay hands on him."
>
> "They certainly would."
>
> "Now, my dear Glaucon," I went on, "this [allegory] must be connected, throughout, with what preceded it [the Divided Line and Simile of the Sun]. The visible realm corresponds to the prison, and the light of the fire in the prison to the power of the sun. And you won't go wrong if you connect the ascent into the upper world and the sight

Among the disciples of Socrates, Plato was the one who shone with a glory which far excelled that of the others and who not unjustly eclipsed them all.

St. Augustine

of the objects there with the upward progress of the mind into the
intelligible realm—that's my guess, which is what you are anxious to
hear. The truth of the matter is, after all, known only to God. But in
my opinion, for what it is worth, the final thing to be perceived in the
intelligible realm, and perceived only with difficulty, is the absolute
form of the Good; once seen, it is inferred to be responsible for everything right and good. . . . And anyone who is going to act rationally
either in public or private must perceive it."[17]

Although we cannot fully describe being, Plato wrote *The Republic* to show
that the levels of reality correspond to three types of people. The highest
type is the philosopher-king. This remarkable individual is fit to rule because he (or she) is not just "intelligent" in the modern sense, but wise,
too. In other words, philosopher-kings are more than clever—they are *rational* in the fullest sense: They can both *calculate means* and *wisely choose
ends*. Thus, *The Republic* is Plato's answer to who should rule, based on his
theory of reality.

The Republic

At the beginning of *The Republic*, Socrates and his friend Glaucon have
spent the day at a festival and are on their way home when another friend,
Polemarchus, stops them. The dialogue begins with good-natured banter
among friends.

> "Socrates," said Polemarchus, "I believe you are starting off on your
> way back to town."
> "You are right," I [Socrates] replied.
> "Do you see how many of us there are?" he asked.
> "I do."
> "Well, you will either have to get the better of us or stay here."
> "Oh, but there's another alternative," said I. "We might persuade
> you that you ought to let us go."
> "You can't persuade people who won't listen," he replied.[18]

You can't persuade people who won't listen. Plato is no doubt referring in part to the people who executed Socrates. But he may also be giving us a key to the rest of *The Republic*.

Socrates believed in the pursuit of wisdom through the dialectical
method of question-and-answer. This required participants willing to listen actively and to respond intelligently. But what about people who cannot or will not listen? What about people who are satisfied with life in the
Cave? What good is being reasonable in the face of ignorance? Will a mob
listen to reason?

Plato thought not. He came to believe that there were different types of human beings, with different strengths and weaknesses corresponding to each type. Not everyone is capable of participating in rational discourse. Some people lack the intellect. Some lack the will. Some may even lack both. Thus it is that a wise and wonderful individual who has escaped from the Cave, like Socrates, can be brought down by his moral and intellectual inferiors who are still in it. In Plato's view, Socrates made a mistake in going to "the people" at all. Socrates himself had even said that in matters of virtue and wisdom, the majority is usually wrong, while only a few are wise.

> Philosophy's first promise is a sense of participation, of belonging to mankind, being a member of society.
>
> *Seneca*

The Search for Justice

Plato argued that a reciprocal relationship exists between the individual and the kind of society he or she lives in. That means a certain kind of society produces a certain kind of individual, and certain kinds of individuals produce certain kinds of societies. In fact, Plato thought the relationship between the two was so close that a clear understanding of the just (ideal) society would yield a clear understanding of the just (healthy) individual. In *The Republic* he refers to society as "the individual writ large." *The Republic* is, consequently, a study of Plato's ideal society and, by extension, a study of types of individuals.

The first book of *The Republic* begins with a discussion of justice. But justice in this context doesn't mean quite what it does today. Philosophy translator H. D. P. Lee says that the Greek roots of what is usually translated as *justice* cover a cluster of meanings that no single English word does. According to Lee, *justice* in *The Republic* is a broad term covering right conduct or morality in general; the verb from the same root can mean to act "rightly" or "justly."[19] For Plato, justice involved much more than fairness under the law; it went beyond a legalistic limit. Historian of ancient Greece B. A. G. Fuller says that what Plato is interested in is nothing less than "the whole sphere of moral action, both external and internal."[20]

Various limited and specific definitions of justice are offered during the course of *The Republic*. The first one is that justice is paying our debts and telling the truth. Over the course of the dialogue a variety of modifications and alternatives are discussed and rejected.

Function and Happiness

The Republic contrasts two views of morality. One asserts that right and wrong must be determined by the consequences our acts produce, and the other holds that they can be understood only in terms of their effect on our overall functioning as human beings. The first view is sometimes called an **instrumental theory of morality**. Right and wrong are treated as

> **INSTRUMENTAL THEORY OF MORALITY**
>
> Moral position that right and wrong must be determined by the consequences of acts; right and wrong viewed as means (instruments) for getting something else.

means to, or instruments for, getting something else. Be good, get X. Be bad, get Y. Plato characterizes the instrumental view:

> For fathers tell their sons, and pastors and masters of all kinds urge their charges to be just not because they value justice for itself, but for the social prestige it brings; they want them to secure by a show of justice the power and family connexions and other things which [were] enumerated, all of which are procured by the just man of good reputation.[21]

FUNCTIONALIST
THEORY OF MORALITY

Moral position that right and wrong can be understood only in terms of their effect on anything's natural function; each kind of thing has a natural purpose (function).

Plato, by contrast, argues for a **functionalist theory of morality** in which each kind of thing (including human beings) has a "natural purpose or function." Renowned Plato scholar A. E. Taylor says that in *The Republic*, "Happiness depends on conformity to our nature [function] as active beings."[22] In other words, only virtuous people can be happy. The Greeks viewed happiness as being more than a matter of personal satisfaction. *Happiness was the result of living a fully functioning life.* It involved balance and wholeness. It required being pleased by what is good and being displeased by what is bad. For instance, under such a view, no cigarette smoker can be "happy" regardless of the pleasure derived from smoking. The reason is that no fully functioning, maximally healthy human being will enjoy polluting his or her body. (For a fuller treatment of this view of happiness, see Chapter 5.)

The rest of *The Republic* reveals Plato's view of "our nature as active beings" and what human nature needs to function properly. A good life can be lived only in a good society. No one can live the best possible life controlled and crushed by a repressive, irrational society. Conversely, no one can live a truly good life without having some social activities, obligations, and concerns. Thus a life of extreme individualism is as imbalanced as a life of individual repression. Plato's goal was to identify the kind of society that nurtures the essential nature of each individual.

The Ideal State

Plato said that society originates because no individual is self-sufficient. The most basic function of society is to provide necessities like food, shelter, and clothing. The just or ideal state meets three basic categories of needs: (1) nourishing needs (food, shelter, clothing); (2) protection needs (military, police); (3) ordering needs (leadership and government). These needs are best met by members of three corresponding classes of people: (1) workers (butcher, baker, truck driver); (2) warriors (soldiers, police officers, fire fighters); (3) guardians (philosopher-kings).

The just state functions fully. An unjust state is dysfunctional; it is not meeting some essential need. Only when all classes of people are virtuous *according to their natures* is the state whole, healthy, balanced, and just. *The good life is nothing more than each individual functioning well ac-*

Besides, this at any rate I know, that if there were to be a treatise or a lecture on the [ideal society], I could do it best.

Plato

cording to his or her own nature, in a state which is well-ordered and wisely ruled.

Injustice is a form of imbalance for Plato. It occurs whenever a state does not function properly. Some imbalance always results when one part of the state tries to fulfill the function of another part. Thus, countries in which the military governs are unjust in the Platonic sense. Justice, happiness, and the good life are interrelated *functional results* of order. Because the essence of a thing determines its proper order, function, and care, only those who have seen the forms and seen the Good can know what this essence is for the state or for individuals.

The Parts of the Soul

For Plato, **virtue** is excellence of function (which reflects form). We must identify a thing's function before we can fully evaluate it. The human soul resembles the state in that it too is divided into three parts. The healthy, good, or virtuous soul is one in which all parts function harmoniously. The three parts of the soul are *reason*, *spirit*, and *appetite*.

VIRTUE (PLATONIC)

Excellence of function.

Plato disagreed with Socrates' belief that "to know the good is to do the good." He believed in weakness of will. According to Plato, we most clearly encounter each part of our souls when we're faced with a difficult choice. Suppose you are on a date with someone who wants to go dancing and stay out late. You, on the other hand, have an important test early the next morning. Your *reason* says: "Go home, review your notes, rest. You can go dancing another time, but you cannot make up this important test." Your *appetite* says: "I'd love a pizza. I'd love to party." Your *spirit*, which is concerned with honor, says: "This is awful! I hate it! I don't know what to do. I sort of want to study—but I'd really like to go out. Oh my, oh my!"

Most of us are intimately familiar with what can be characterized as "parts" of ourselves. Plato called them parts of the soul. In the *Phaedrus* Plato compares the soul to a chariot being pulled by two horses. One horse needs no touch from the whip, responding instantly to whispers and spoken commands. The other horse is full of "insolence and pride," and "barely yields to whip and spur." The charioteer knows where he wants to go but needs the help of both horses to get there. The driver, of course, corresponds to *reason*; the horse that responds to the merest whisper corresponds to *spirit* (or will); and the bad but powerful horse represents *appetite*.

The greatest griefs are those we cause ourselves.

Sophocles

If the charioteer is unable to control both horses, he will be dragged all over the place by the stronger horse. It is the *function* and therefore the *duty* and the *right* of the charioteer to control the horses. In *The Republic*, Plato says:

> So the reason ought to rule, having the ability and foresight to act
> for the whole, and the spirit ought to obey and support it. And this

Perhaps the strongest evidence supporting Plato's belief in the three-part psyche comes in the form of everyday struggles between reason and appetite or desire—a struggle faced by many a student caught up in the throes of a strong desire to daydream.

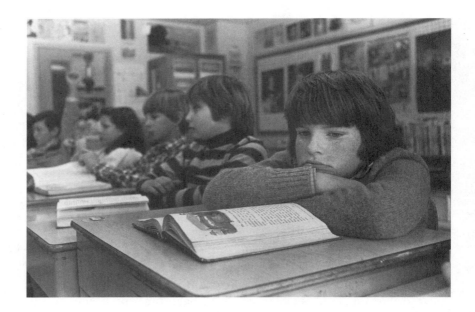

concord between them is effected, as we said, by a combination of intellectual and physical training, which tunes up the reason by intellectual training and tones down the crudeness of natural high spirits by harmony and rhythm.[23]

The Cardinal Virtues

Plato identifies four "cardinal virtues" as necessary for a good society and for a happy individual. Cardinal virtues are essential, basic virtues that provide optimal functioning for the human soul.

Temperance is another name for self-control and moderation. It is important for the worker class, but necessary for all three classes of people. The state, too, must control itself, not yielding either to the unjust demands of other states or to a lust for expansion or power. It must not give in to an excess of liberty or repression. The healthy state resembles the healthy person. Both are moderate and self-disciplined, and guided by reason. The healthy soul is not controlled by appetites.

Courage is the essential virtue of the warrior class. Courage is necessary to protect the community and to enforce the just laws of the guardians. In the individual, courage is a quality of will, an essential drive that provides a person with stamina and energy.

Wisdom is the virtue associated with the guardians who are called the philosopher-kings. In the individual, wisdom is present when the rational part of the soul is healthy and in control. Wisdom is found only in a community ruled by those fit by nature and training to guide it: the philosopher-kings who have seen the Good.

Then the master passion runs wild and takes madness into its service; any decent options or desires and any feelings of shame still left are killed or thrown out, until all discipline is swept away, and madness usurps its place.

Plato

Justice is the result of the other three cardinal virtues, in much the same way that bodily health is the result of the proper functioning of all organs and systems. **Justice** is excellence of function for the whole: Each essential element works well, and together all elements blend into a balanced system in the just state and in the just individual.

For Plato, justice extends far beyond a legal system. The just state is well, whole, vital. It nurtures each individual by providing a lifestyle appropriate to him or her.

Philosophical Query

Consider the family as a functional system: If young children are allowed to spend the money, determine bedtimes, and so on, the whole family suffers. If the parents try to live like children, the whole family suffers. If every family member is free to pick and choose what he or she feels like doing or not doing every day, there can be no family. You might try similar analyses of marriages, churches, schools, or factories. Discuss the need for hierarchy, authority, and a governing order.

> **JUSTICE (PLATONIC)**
>
> Excellence of function for the whole; in a just society each individual performs his or her natural function according to class; in a just individual, reason rules the spirit and the appetites.

Societies and Individuals

Plato's *Republic*, and a later dialogue called *Laws*, outline **utopias**, that is, perfect, ideal societies. (Although Plato originated the idea, the word *utopia* was coined by Thomas More in 1516.)

Can we create a good society that will encourage and foster inner harmony for ourselves and social harmony for the whole community? As Jesus said, "The spirit . . . is willing but the flesh is weak." Plato might add "and reason is absent." A Platonic utopia would be enormously difficult, perhaps impossible, to achieve. But a consideration of Plato's program for a utopia will prove to be worthwhile on many counts.

For Plato, the ideal form of government is the rule of philosopher-kings, not democracy. Because our current culture is democratic and individualistic in so many respects, many of us view democracy as the ideal form of government without giving any other possibilities serious consideration. For that reason alone, consideration of an elitist alternative can be illuminating. It may help us to better identify the virtues of our own society—and we may get a clearer look at its shortcomings. Let's complete this survey of Plato by looking at his vision of a better, "ideal" way of life.

> **UTOPIA**
>
> Term for a perfect or ideal society derived from Sir Thomas More's 1516 novel of the same name; the word was created from the Greek root meaning "nowhere."

The Origin of Democracy

In Book VIII of *The Republic* Plato discusses different kinds of governments and the types of souls they produce. He argues that democracy grows out of a form of government called *oligarchy*, the rule of a wealthy few.

Oligarchy: A government resting on a valuation of property, in which the rich have power and the poor man is deprived of it.

Plato

Because the chief aim of the oligarchs is to get rich, they create a constitution and form of government that encourage the acquisition of property.

But just having property isn't enough. Plato asks, "Doesn't oligarchy change into democracy because of lack of restraint in the pursuit of its objective of getting as rich as possible?"[24] The seeds of democracy, according to Plato, are the love of property and riches, and the corresponding need for a free economy. So the oligarchs must encourage trading in real estate, heavy borrowing, and lack of self-control. The "money people" need to stimulate irrational but constant consumption by everyone else. Plato declares, "It should then be clear that love of money and adequate self-discipline in its citizens are two things that can't co-exist in any society; one or the other must be neglected."[25]

Philosophical Query

Can you spot any symptoms in our society of the pattern Plato attributes to injustice in individuals and the state? Can you identify individuals or groups that "fall into sickness and dissension at the slightest provocation"? What—if anything—does justice (or a lack of justice) have to do with these reactions? Explain.

In Plato's diagnosis, as the rich get richer, the poor grow angrier until they somehow overthrow the rich, either through armed revolt or by social and legal pressure. Resentful over their status, the poor initiate a program of *equality*.

Poverty in a democracy is as much preferable to so-called prosperity in an autocracy as freedom is to slavery.

Democritus

Then democracy originates when the poor win, kill or exile their opponents, and give the rest equal rights and opportunity of office. . . . There is liberty and freedom of speech in plenty, and every individual is free to do as he likes. . . . That being so, won't everyone arrange his life as pleases him best? . . . a democracy is the most attractive of all societies. The diversity of its characters, like the different colours in a patterned dress, make it look very attractive . . . perhaps most people would, for this reason, judge it to be the best form of society . . . [if they] judge by appearances.[26]

A democratic state, Plato says, will contain every type of human temperament. But the predominant characteristic of democracy is lack of guidance and self-control, lack of wisdom, and lack of temperance. Swayed by opinion rather than grounded in knowledge, the democratic state is in a state of constant flux, always *becoming*. It is hostile to the possibility of a fixed hierarchy of being.

In a democracy . . . there's no compulsion either to exercise authority if you are capable of it, or to submit to authority if you don't want to; you needn't fight if there's a war, or you can wage a private war in peacetime if you don't like peace. . . . It's a wonderfully pleasant way of carrying on in the short run, isn't it?[27]

Not only is it pleasant, Plato points out that even those convicted of a crime in a democracy can continue "to go about among their fellows." H. D. P. Lee paraphrases Plato's description of the democratic type as "versatile but lacking principle."[28]

Most damning of all, Plato says, democracy violates the principle of functional order and rule by reason. He asserts that only very rare and exceptional individuals can grow up to be good people without good training from infancy, in a good environment. But democracy lacks the order and balance to provide this.

Plato says that at its most extreme, the disordered, democratic soul resists all limits, both internal and social:

> All pleasures are equal and should have equal rights. [Such a character] lives for the pleasure of the moment. One day it's wine, women, and song, the next bread and water; one day it's hard physical training, the next indolence and ease, and then a period of philosophic study. . . . There's no order or restraint in [this] life and [such a person] reckons [this] way of living is pleasant, free, and happy. . . . It's a life which many men and women would envy, it has so many possibilities.[29]

The Pendulum of Imbalance

Ancient philosophers were aware that one extreme often produces another, nearly opposite, extreme in a never-ending effort to achieve balance. In Plato's view, the chief objective of democracy is "excessive liberty." For Plato, the built-in excesses of democracy already contain the seeds of tyranny. **Tyranny** is a form of government in which all power rests in a single individual, the tyrant.

In one of the more interesting and perhaps prophetic passages in *The Republic*, Plato describes the effects "too much liberty" will produce. As you read what he said so long ago, take note of parallels to our own culture.

> It becomes the thing for the father and son to change places, the father standing in awe of his son, and the son neither respecting nor fearing his parents, in order to assert his independence; and there's no distinction between citizen and alien and foreigner. And there are other more trivial things. The teacher fears and panders to his pupils, who in turn despise their teachers and attendants; and the young as a whole imitate their elders, argue with them and set themselves up against them, while their elders try to avoid the reputation of being

Thus the only sort of liberty that is real under democracy is the liberty of the have-nots to destroy the liberty of the haves . . .

H. L. Mencken

TYRANNY

Form of government in which all power rests in a single individual, known as the tyrant.

Each individual is his own center, and the world centers in him.

Søren Kierkegaard

Democracy . . . is a system where anything, or almost anything, can happen. The worst, but also the best. In it one may encounter all types: the sophist and also the philosopher. That is the unique advantage of this way of life.

Andre Koyré

disagreeable or strict by aping the young and mixing with them on terms of easy good fellowship. . . .

You would never believe—unless you had seen it for yourself—how much more liberty the domestic animals have in a democracy. Love me love my dog, as the proverb has it, and the same is true of horses and donkeys as well. . . . Everything is full of this spirit of liberty. . . .

What it comes to is this, . . . that the minds of the citizens become so sensitive that the least vestige of restraint is resented as intolerable, till finally, as you know, in their determination to have no master they disregard all laws, written or unwritten.[30]

One form of shamelessness is an exaggerated sense of honor. In this condition, the individual is always "ready to take offense." Every restriction or social limit is taken personally: "The least vestige of restraint is resented as intolerable."

Plato makes the case that "from an extreme of liberty one is likely to get, in the individual and in society, a reaction to an extreme of subjection." That is, an extreme of liberty will create a corresponding demand for law and order; it will result in an extreme of control.

Certainly in the last few years we've seen some reaction against the permissiveness of the '60s and '70s, the "winner take all" excesses of the '80s, and the politically correct early '90s. As society becomes troubled by increased abuses of personal liberty in the form of high rates of venereal diseases, drug casualties, white-collar crime, and so forth, we witness demands for more restrictive sexual standards, more pressure to abstain from drugs and alcohol, more disciplined diets, more people convicted of fraud, embezzlement, and so on. As "shock jocks" push the bounds of free speech on the radio, and artists and musicians test the limits of their various media, we witness efforts to censor or ban what's on the radio, what's on television, records, and tapes, and even what's in art museums.

As we approach the twenty-first century—"the millennium"—signs of a swing toward repressive control seem to emerge: One *kindergartner* is suspended from school for patting a teacher on the bottom (sexual harassment) and another for bringing a metal nail file to school ("zero tolerance" for anything that "looks like a weapon"). A Northern California school reacts to excessive absences and poor grades by requiring students to wear uniforms—and then pressuring the staff to wear them, too—so as "not to make the students feel like they're different."

In our daily lives we see people become more undisciplined and abusive of their liberties, infringing upon one another's happiness. If we all talk in the movie theater, none of us can hear. If I insist on putting a megawatt stereo in my car and booming through your neighborhood, you will insist on laws to stop me. If bankers and real estate brokers continue to make exorbitant profits while growing numbers of families cannot buy homes, the state will be forced to exert stricter controls on everybody. If

Plato thought that excessive liberty always leads to its own destruction because demands for increasing individual freedom result in counterdemands for restrictions and control, as seen in the call for schoolchildren to wear uniforms instead of dress of their choice, which may be extreme or outlandish.

great hordes of us continue to exercise our liberty by commuting to work in our own vehicles, traffic will come to a stop and the sky will turn brown from the smog of excessive liberty.

Philosophical Query

What do you see as the good and bad points of "democratic families" in which the parents and children have essentially the same rights? What about school relationships in which teachers are "buddies" with students and the classroom is run democratically?

Are we making everything equal, including animals and the environment? Can you find support for Plato's observation about animal rights in a democracy?

Do you think absolute equality of opportunity is desirable or possible? Discuss fully.

The Tyranny of Excess

The ills of democracy were aggravated for Plato by a pattern of increasing self-indulgence, which he thought would pass from generation to generation. Sooner or later, pleasures and excesses would actually control the soul—they would tyrannize it.

> Isn't this the reason . . . why the passion of sex has for so long been called a tyrant? . . . And isn't there also a touch of the tyrant about a man who's drunk? . . . And the madman whose mind is unhinged imagines he can control gods and men and is quite ready to try. . . . Then a precise definition of a tyrannical man is one who, either by birth or habit or both, combines the characteristics of drunkenness, lust, and madness. . . . And how does he live? . . . When a master passion has absolute control of a man's mind, I suppose life is a round of holidays and dinners and parties and girl-friends and so on. . . . And there will be a formidable extra crop of desires growing all the time and needing satisfaction. . . . So whatever income he has will soon be expended, and he'll start borrowing and drawing on capital.
> . . . When these sources fail, his large brood of desires will howl aloud. . . . He *must* get something from somewhere or his life will be torment and agony.[31]

Philosophical Query

Compare Plato's description of the tyrannical soul to the life of a hard-core drug addict. The "fix" certainly *tyrannizes* the addict's soul. Identify and discuss other common examples of this tyrannical pattern.

What begins as unlimited freedom ends up as the tyranny over reason by the lower parts of the soul. The spoiled and undisciplined person grows used to playing now and paying later. When he cannot pay his own way, he turns to his parents to gratify his desires. He sees their estate as "his due," and "if they don't give in to him," Plato says, "he'll try first to get his way by fraud and deceit." But "if his old mother and father put up a resistance and show fight . . . [he will not] feel any hesitation about playing the tyrant with them."

Ultimately, enough such people (even if they are not the majority) corrupt the whole state as "they become thieves, burglars, pick-pockets . . .

No educated man stating plainly the elementary notions that every educated man holds about the matters that principally concern government, could be elected to office in a democratic state, save perhaps by a miracle. His frankness would arouse fears, and those fears would run against him; it is his business to arouse fears that will run in favour of him.

H. L. Mencken

To speak much is one thing, to speak well is another.

Sophocles

they turn informers and false witnesses and take bribes." Fed up with this turn of events, the majority demands more law and order. As more and more individuals get in one another's way, each demands protection from the others.

For Plato, the most imbalanced type of personality is the tyrant. Plato believed that happiness and goodness were inseparable, as were unhappiness and wickedness. Thus the most wicked person is the most unhappy, because he is the most imbalanced. A tyrant is always a slave to his own strong passions and desires. The tyrant who is controlled by drugs or lust is obviously a slave. But so is the politically powerful leader who is a slave to power and domination. Once again, things are not as they initially appear. What looks like power is in truth a form of enslavement. The Hitlers and Stalins and small-town bosses of the world live restricted, imbalanced lives. A "control freak" is not a happy person.

The only cure for excesses of either liberty or tyranny is justice. If the state is not just, then at least perhaps a fortunate "happy few" individuals can impose order on their own souls through the rule of reason aided by moderate appetites and a healthy spirit.

> The state, if once started well, moves with accumulating force like a wheel. For good nurture and education implant good constitutions [temperaments], and the good constitutions taking root in a good education improve more and more, and this improvement affects the breed in man as in other animals.
>
> *Plato*

Commentary

The most damning charge that can be leveled at all enlightenment philosophies is that no matter how initially intriguing or appealing they seem, they remain impractical and unrealistic in the world as most of us experience and understand it.

In Plato's case, we might ask ourselves whether we have any supportable firsthand evidence for believing in actual levels of reality. Does a story like the Allegory of the Cave really help us determine who is enlightened and who is deluded? Do the Divided Line and Simile of the Sun do anything besides reflect common psychological states?

On the other hand, who can doubt the need for order and balance in both the individual and society? Further, it would not be difficult to make Plato's case against the "excesses of democracy" using trends and events from our own time. We might even find some merit in his idea that letting each individual choose his or her occupation based solely on strength of desire and ambition leads to great overall unhappiness.

When we rank occupations by income and prestige, most of the tasks needed for a good society are less desirable than a few glamorous, less useful ones. Which, then, does more lasting harm: letting everyone who wishes scramble for the top of the heap, or carefully matching people's basic abilities and personalities with various levels of education and occupation? We might find Plato's three categories of people, guardians, warriors, and workers, too restricting, but does that rule out a more realistic division?

> Concerning the essentials I have written no book nor shall I write one.
>
> *Plato*, Letter: VII

Plato is dear to me, but
dearer still is truth.

   Aristotle

Lastly, Plato's general portrait of the soul (psyche) might be worth looking into. There is much to be said for living a well-rounded life. That includes, of course, being individually balanced. But a society that values narrow specialists and puts as much emphasis on material success as ours does makes personal growth more difficult than a society that encourages fuller personal development.

Interestingly, even though Plato's great pupil Aristotle turns away from his theory of forms, he follows the direction in which his great teacher pointed and makes perhaps the finest case for the fully functioning, whole, balanced human being. He is the subject of the next chapter.

Summary of Main Points

1. Plato was a member of the Athenian aristocracy and Socrates' most famous and important pupil. Socrates' trial and death convinced him that Athenian democracy was irrational mob rule. His experiences with the Thirty convinced him that rule by a greedy, cruel social elite was no better than mob rule.

2. Plato founded his famous Academy to educate wise rulers. His progressive educational program included mathematics, geometry, music, and philosophy.

3. In Plato's metaphysics, the highest level of reality consists of timeless "essences" or entities called ideas or forms. Such a metaphysics is sometimes called transcendental because it asserts that there is a plane of existence "above and beyond" our ordinary existence.

4. Plato divided reality into three levels. The highest level of reality is being. Being is eternal and changeless. The other two levels together make up the level of becoming, the level of change, which includes growth and decay, life and death. For Plato, knowledge is always of things in their unchanging, eternal form, of their essence. Opinion, by contrast, is like perception: limited by our individual senses, backgrounds, and cultural experiences. Disagreement is only possible on the lower level of becoming.

5. According to Plato, the very essence of knowledge is unchanging. Therefore, whatever is relative and always changing cannot be true. The Sophists could not discover truth because they were only concerned with the Heraclitean world of sensibles, the world of ever-changing perceptions and customs. Truth and knowledge are found in another realm of reality: the level of being that Parmenides tried to characterize. Plato's theory of forms was part of his refutation of sophistry.

6. Plato used the concept of the Divided Line to illustrate the relationship of knowledge to opinion, reality to appearance, and the worlds of being and becoming. The Divided Line consists of two basic sections, each unevenly divided into two segments. The four segments illustrate four states of mind or ways of apprehending four components of reality: (1) pure intelligence or understanding, (2) reasoning, (3) informed belief or ordinary opinions, and (4) illusion and imagination, dominated by secondhand opinions and uncritical impressions.

7. Plato compared the "absolute form of the Good" to the sun: Just as the sun (light) is necessary for vision and life, the Good makes the existence of everything else possible. The Good exists beyond becoming at the highest reaches of being. The Good cannot be ob-

served with the five senses and can be known only by pure thought or intelligence. The Good is the source of both the value and the existence of all other forms.

8. In the Allegory of the Cave, Plato characterizes three levels of awareness by referring to three distinct levels of reality: two levels of becoming, the literal and the informed, and one qualitatively unique and ultimate level of being—the enlightened level. The lowest level of reality is the literal level, which is inhabited by people with little or no imagination. The informed level of reality involves a wider range of basic understanding. People on this level distinguish appearance from reality. The enlightened level is the level of truth and reality. On this level the soul has no need for perception or interpretation. Plato says that it "directly apprehends" the form of the Good.

9. In *The Republic*, Plato describes the just or ideal state. Plato argued that there is a reciprocal relationship between the individual and the kind of society he or she lives in.

10. *The Republic* contrasts two views of morality. The instrumental theory of morality asserts that right and wrong must be determined by the consequences our acts produce, and the functionalist theory of morality holds that right and wrong can only be understood in terms of the way they affect our overall functioning as human beings. Plato is a functionalist, and *The Republic* is Plato's attempt to identify the kind of society that nurtures the essential nature of various types of individuals.

11. The just state functions fully. An unjust state is dysfunctional; it does not meet some essential need. Only when all classes of people are virtuous according to their natures is the state whole, healthy, balanced, and just. The good life consists of each individual functioning well according to his or her own nature, in a state that is ordered and wisely ruled.

12. The just or ideal state meets three basic categories of needs: (1) nourishing needs; (2) pro-

tection needs; (3) ordering needs. These needs are best met by members of three corresponding classes of people: (1) artisans; (2) warriors; (3) guardians or philosopher-kings.

13. The human soul resembles the state in that it too is divided into three parts: reason, spirit, and appetite. The just (healthy, good, or virtuous) soul is one in which all parts function harmoniously. The just society is one ruled by guardians in a way that each class functions at its best.

14. Plato identifies four cardinal (essential, basic) virtues necessary for a good society and for happy individuals. He defined virtue as "excellence of function." The virtue of temperance is important for the worker classes but necessary for all three classes of people and the state itself. Courage is the essential virtue of the warrior class; in the individual, courage is a quality of will, an essential drive that provides a person with stamina and energy. Wisdom is the virtue associated with the guardians and the rational part of the soul. Justice, the result of the other three cardinal virtues, is excellence of function for the whole: Each essential element works well, and together all elements blend into a balanced system in the just state and in the just individual.

15. Plato rejected democracy as unjust because rule by the majority usurps the rightful role of the guardian class. The result is an excess of liberty and rule by impulse, appetite, and emotion in which all classes suffer. Democracy violates the principle of functional order and rule by reason.

16. Plato thought that the excessive liberty found in democracies contains the seeds of an opposite impulse known as tyranny, a form of government in which all power rests in a single individual, the tyrant. Extreme liberty creates a corresponding demand for extreme control. For Plato, the most imbalanced type of personality is the tyrant.

Study Questions

1. Discuss some of the personal experiences that shaped Plato's overall idealism.

2. What is meant by Plato's "disillusionment"?

3. What was the Academy? Where did it get its name? What was its chief purpose?

4. How did Plato distinguish between knowledge and opinion?

5. What is meant by calling Plato's philosophy transcendental?

6. What are forms?

7. How do forms differ from ideas?

8. Illustrate the Divided Line and relate each segment to Plato's epistemology as it is characterized in the Allegory of the Cave.

9. How did Plato use the sun to help explain the Good?

10. Identify and explain the three basic levels of reality.

11. Distinguish the realm of being from the realm of becoming.

12. Identify and characterize the levels of reality.

13. Tell the Allegory of the Cave in your own words. Then carefully explain its purpose.

14. What is the Good?

15. What is the "key" Plato reveals at the opening of *The Republic*? What is its significance to his basic attitude toward democracy?

16. How is Plato's use of the word *justice* different from ours?

17. Explain in what sense Plato's theory of justice is "functionalist." What kind of moral theory is contrasted with functionalism?

18. How is the Greek concept of happiness different from our contemporary concept? Compare and evaluate them.

19. Describe the general structure of the ideal state as Plato presents it in *The Republic*.

20. List and discuss the cardinal virtues.

21. What is special about justice as a virtue?

22. Carefully explain the relationship of the individual to the state in *The Republic*.

23. What are the three parts of the soul and how are they related?

24. Briefly explain the origin and nature of democracy according to Plato.

25. What is the democratic soul like, according to Plato? Do you agree? Justify your answer.

26. What is the relationship between democracy and tyranny as Plato saw it? Identify some current evidence that supports his view. On balance, do you agree with him or not? Explain.

27. What does Plato see as the most unjust type of person and state? Why? Do you agree? Explain.

28. Write a general assessment of contemporary American culture from a Platonic perspective.

29. In your opinion, what is Plato's greatest philosophical weakness? Explain.

30. In your opinion, what is Plato's greatest philosophical insight? Explain.

The Naturalist

Aristotle

There is perhaps nothing worse than reaching the top of the ladder and discovering that you're on the wrong wall.

Joseph Campbell

> You need not, and in fact cannot, teach an acorn to grow into an oak tree, but when given a chance, its intrinsic potentialities will develop. Similarly, the human individual, given a chance, tends to develop his particular human potentialities. He will develop then the unique alive forces of his real self. . . . In short, he will grow . . . *toward self-realization*. And that is why I speak . . . of the *real self* as that central force, common to all human beings and yet unique in each, which is the deep source of growth.
>
> *Karen Horney*

One of the most frustrating aspects of college can be choosing a major. Sometimes students are encouraged to decide without having had much exposure to a variety of disciplines, and some of us may just not really know who we are yet. (This condition is not confined to students or persons of any particular age.) As a result, we may change our minds as sophomores or juniors or seniors, when we realize that our initial choice was wrong for the real us. Outside the campus environment, more and more people seem to be making significant career changes at mid-life or later.[1]

What prompts a forty-five-year-old person to leave a secure job, giving up seniority and retirement benefits and medical insurance, to open a cookie shop? What makes a social worker quit work and go to law school? What drives a middle-aged man or woman to leave his or her family, lose weight, buy a sports car, and become a poet? What makes a pre-med major just nine units short of graduation drop out of school and join the Peace Corps? There are many reasons; some of them may be unwise, but perhaps some of them are good reasons.

Did you ever feel that you weren't really being yourself? What does that mean? Aren't you always yourself, even if that self is confused or inconsistent or phony? Maybe that's just who you are? On the other hand, maybe the "real you" is being denied or starved. Perhaps people who walk away from their jobs or families have been false to their "true selves" for years. Does that seem possible?

Aristotle would have thought so, even though he would not have suggested that we "find ourselves" by returning to adolescence or a self-indulgent escape from responsibility. But he did believe in a natural development of the soul/self based on an inner identity or goal. He believed that the good life involves balance and fullness. And though each of us may have individually different "selves" to develop, in his view all human beings share a common nature that makes it possible to identify the general outline of the best possible life.

The good life, according to Aristotle, is broad and rich, involving full emotional, intellectual, spiritual, and physical development and health. Thus it is entirely possible to wake up one day and realize that we have grown too much in some areas and too little in others. Such a realization may explain radical changes in our lives. We may be seeking balance and completion.

But unlike many modern theorists of self-realization and balance, Aristotle did not think that each individual is free to be whoever he or she chooses to be. Instead, he advocated self-emergence according to a natural order. He attempted to base his moral and social philosophy on a practical and empirical study of human behavior. His *Nicomachean Ethics* is among the most influential books ever written on self-realization and related moral and social factors. Rather than concentrate on an "ideal world" as Plato did, Aristotle turned to a study of the natural world and our place in it.

> With regard to excellence, it is not enough to know, but we must try to have and use it.
>
> *Aristotle*

Works

Aristotle is said to have written twenty-seven dialogues on a level comparable to Plato's, and it is through these dialogues that he was best known in the ancient world.[2] Unfortunately, they were all destroyed when the barbarians sacked Rome in the year 400. What we know today as the "writings of Aristotle" are really a collection of notes. These apparently include notes Aristotle made for his lectures and possibly notes taken by students who attended his lectures. Of 360 works mentioned by Diogenes Läertius, 40 survive today.

Aristotle's works include *Organon*, a collection of six logical treatises; *Physics*; *On Generation and Corruption*; *De Anima (On the Soul)*; *On the Heavens*; *The History of Animals*; *On the Parts of Animals*; *Metaphysics*; *Politics*; *Rhetoric*; *Poetics*; and the *Nicomachean Ethics*.

What remains of Aristotle's work is complex, stiffly written, and often dry. But in spite of that, these notes reflect a genius whose range of interests, wonder, insight, and effort stands as a most remarkable testament to the human mind and spirit.

Aristotle's Life

The son of a court physician, **Aristotle (384–322 B.C.)** was born in Stagira, a Greek community in Thrace. What little we know of him comes primarily through Diogenes Läertius's compilation of the lives of ancient philosophers.

Aristotle

Aristotle probably learned basic anatomy and dissection from his father before he was sent to study at Plato's Academy in Athens at the age of eighteen. When he arrived, practically everyone noticed him, in part because he was something of a dandy. Plato is reported to have said that Aristotle paid more attention to his clothes than was proper for a philosopher. In order to be fashionable, he cultivated a deliberate lisp, the speech pattern that the Greek elite used to separate themselves from the masses. (In a similar way, some people today think of an English accent as being "higher class" than a Southern drawl or Brooklyn accent.)

Despite his affectations, Aristotle almost immediately earned a reputation as one of the Academy's finest students. Diogenes Läertius says that on one occasion when Plato read aloud a difficult treatise about the soul, Aristotle "was the only person who sat it out, while all the rest rose up and went away."[3] Aristotle remained with Plato for perhaps twenty years, and Plato is supposed to have humorously remarked that his Academy consisted of two parts: the body of his students, and the brain of Aristotle. Although Aristotle disagreed with Plato on important philosophical matters, he built an altar to Plato at his teacher's death.

Aristotle, thirty-seven years old when Plato died, expected to be the next master of the Academy. But when the trustees of the Academy picked a native Athenian instead, because they saw Aristotle as a "foreigner," he waited for the first good opportunity to leave Athens. As it turned out, a former classmate who had become a kind of philosopher-king over a rather large area in Asia Minor invited Aristotle to be his adviser.

Apparently Aristotle had little effect on his friend's rulership, but he did manage to marry the man's adopted daughter in 344 B.C. She had a large dowry, which Aristotle happily invested. Aristotle's life was disrupted the same year, however, when his political benefactor offended the king of Persia. Shortly after Aristotle and his wife fled to the island of Lesbos, Aristotle's friend was crucified by the Persian king. While on Lesbos, Aristotle studied natural history, and his wife died giving birth to their daughter. Aristotle later lived with a woman named Herpyllis. Their long, happy relationship produced Aristotle's son Nicomachus, to whom he dedicated the *Nicomachean Ethics*.

In 343 B.C. King Philip of Macedon invited Aristotle to train his thirteen-year-old son Alexander. The boy was wild and crude, but Aristotle was able to smooth his rough edges and instill in him respect for knowledge and science. As Alexander the Great, Aristotle's famous pupil ordered his soldiers to collect specimens of plant, marine, and animal life from faraway places for his old teacher.

In 340 B.C. Philip sent Aristotle back to his hometown, so that Aristotle could write a code of laws to help restore the community, which had been disrupted by a war. Aristotle did well enough that Stagira celebrated a yearly holiday in his honor. In 334 Aristotle at last returned to Athens, where he founded his own school, possibly with money from Alexander.

All men by nature desire knowledge.

Aristotle

The development of philosophic science as science, and, further, the progress from the Socratic point of view to the scientific, begins with Plato and ends with Aristotle. They of all others deserve to be called teachers of the human race.

G. W. F. Hegel

The Lyceum

Aristotle named his school after the god Apollo Lyceus. The Lyceum was built near some of the most elegant buildings in Athens, surrounded by shady groves of trees and covered walkways. Socrates used to visit the same groves, remarking on what a wonderful spot they made for reflection.

Aristotle's students were known as the *peripatetic* philosophers because he often discussed philosophy while strolling with them along tree-covered walkways called the Peripatos. In addition, Aristotle's curriculum included technical lectures for limited audiences and popular lectures of more general interest. Aristotle collected hundreds of maps, charts, and documents, forming the first important library in the West. For instance, he collected and studied 153 political constitutions.

Leadership of the Lyceum rotated among certain members of the school according to rules drawn up by Aristotle. Once a month he held a common meal and symposium at which one of the members was picked to defend a philosophical idea against criticism from everyone else. Aristotle continued to lecture and research for his entire tenure at the Lyceum.[4]

The Lyceum's students tended to be from the middle class, whereas the Academy's were more aristocratic. For a short while the two schools were bitter rivals, but as each concentrated on its own particular interests this rivalry died down. The Academy stressed mathematics and "pure" understanding, while Aristotle's students collected anthropological studies of barbarian cultures, chronologies of various wars and games, the

The actuality of thought is life.

Aristotle

When Alexander the Great met the Cynic Diogenes, he is reported to have said: "If I were not Alexander, I would be Diogenes."

organs and living habits of animals, the nature and locations of plants, and so on.[5]

Alexander the Great died in 323 B.C. Athens had smarted under a Greek unification program begun by his father Philip and continued under Alexander. With Alexander dead, Athens openly expressed its hostility and resentment toward all things Macedonian. Because of his long and favored place under the protection of both Philip and Alexander, Aristotle found himself in an uncomfortable position. He left Athens and the Lyceum the next year after being legally charged with not respecting the gods of the state—one of the same charges leveled at Socrates. Rather than stand trial like the crusty old *sophos*, Aristotle fled to the island of Euboea (his mother's birthplace), in his words, "lest Athens sin twice against philosophy."

In 322 B.C. the man who had created the first important library, tutored the greatest ruler of the ancient world, invented logic, and shaped the thinking of an entire culture died. So great was his influence on later thinkers that for hundreds of years all educated persons knew him simply as *the Philosopher*.

The Naturalist

Aristotelian philosophy is so complex in treatment and scope that no introductory survey can do justice to all of it. A good place to begin, however, is with a look at his ethics and psychology, for in addition to presenting a powerful and challenging doctrine of happiness as self-realization and personal growth, they rest on Aristotle's naturalistic metaphysics.

In Plato we saw one significant expression of the search for the good life: evaluating this life by comparing it to some ideal standard and then trying to perfect this world. In a sense, Aristotle brings to full maturity a second major expression of the search for the good life: attempting to acquire facts without bias and then using that information to make this a better world.

Although Aristotle loved and respected Plato, he saw dangers in Plato's rationalistic idealism. Partly as a reaction to Plato, and partly as a consequence of his own temperament, Aristotle is sometimes said to have brought philosophy down to earth. He combined the study of humanity and nature to a degree that was not possible again, because after Aristotle no single individual could seriously hope to contribute to so many distinct fields in a major way.

Aristotle stands alone as an archetype of the philosophical naturalist. Basically, **naturalism** is the belief that reality consists of the natural world. The naturalist's universe is ordered in that everything in it follows consis-

---

For Aristotle, the great philosopher of the classical period, reared to accept slavery and pursue self-centeredness, the Greek was human. The European barbarians were not human, because they were unskilled; nor were Asians human, because they lacked strength and character; women were not human either; women were halfway human and children were only potentially human. The human being par excellence is the free man of the *polis* of Hellas.

Enrique Dussel

NATURALISM

Belief that reality consists of the natural world; denial of the existence of a separate supernatural order of reality; belief that nature follows orderly, discoverable laws.

tent and discoverable *laws* of nature; everything can be understood in terms of those fundamental laws. Nothing exists outside of space and time. Nature always acts with a purpose, and the key to understanding anything lies in determining its essential purpose.

Philosophical naturalists deny the existence of a separate supernatural order of reality. They believe that *human beings, although special, are part of the natural order and behave according to fixed laws and principles.* Thus a clear understanding of nature is necessary to any clear conception of human behavior. Ethics and political (social) science must be based on the actual facts of life, carefully observed and collected by a scientific method—not on speculative, "otherworldly," rationalistic schemes.

Aristotle based his philosophical positions on close scrutiny of particular, actual things, not on the isolated contemplation of mathematical laws or "pure ideas." Let's see what Aristotle discovered when he turned his scientist's eye to the teeming natural world.

Natural Changes

Recall that the Presocratic philosophers struggled to explain how change is possible. In simplified form, the problem of explaining change was generated by a seemingly inescapable contradiction: In order for *X* to change into *Y*, then somehow *X* must be *both X* and *Y*. If *X is Y*, then *X* cannot be said to *become* (change into) *Y*. For example, water is not ice, yet we say that water "changes into" or "becomes" ice (and the opposite). But until the water becomes ice, it is not ice: it is water. When it is ice, it is no longer water.

"But," you may ask, "what about the in-between stages, the transitional period when some water molecules are freezing into ice molecules? There you have both ice and water!" Do we? That is, do we have some sort of "ice-water" molecule? If so, then it is not water or ice, but a third—different—thing. Further, we still need some clear explanation of *how* what once *was* water *is* now ice. (You may wish to review the problem of change in the First Interlude, as well as study the box Zeno's Paradoxes on pages 40–41.)

Aristotle is sometimes called "the father of science" because he was the first Western thinker of record to provide an adequate analysis of a *process* of change based on the claim that form is inseparable from matter, and that it is the form (essence) of nature to change in orderly and predictable ways. Later we'll see how the concept of essence, or form, led Aristotle to produce one of history's most influential theories of human excellence and well-being. Let's begin with an overview of what Aristotle meant by *form*.

> A likely impossibility is always preferable to an unconvincing possibility.
>
> *Aristotle*

> In all things of nature there is something of the marvelous.
>
> *Aristotle*

Form (Whatness)

Aristotle was troubled by Platonic dualism, the division of the universe into two worlds, or realms: the realm of becoming and the realm of being. (You may find it helpful to review the discussion of Plato's Theory of Forms in Chapter 4 at this point.)

Recall that according to Plato, only Forms (with a capital F) are truly real; objects of sense perception are mere reflections or diluted copies of Forms. Aristotle worried that dualism leads to "otherworldliness, to a chasm between the actual and the ideal . . . [which means] that discussion of what is can never amount to more than a 'likely story,' and knowledge of what *ought to be* has little or no relevance to pressing moral, political, and social problems."[6] If Aristotle's claim that there is only one world is correct, whatever "form" is can only be an aspect of this world.

Aristotle argued that form can be distinguished from content only in thought and never in fact. For instance, we can make a mental distinction between shape and color, but we never encounter shapeless colors or colorless shapes. We can mentally distinguish between mortality and living things, but we will never encounter mortality-of-and-by-itself, any more than we will encounter living things without also encountering mortality. Thus, mortality is a formal or essential aspect of living things.

Aristotle warned that we must take care not to mistake "intellectual analysis" for "ontological status." Aristotle accused Plato of doing just that by imputing actual existence to the Forms. For Aristotle, form exists *within the natural order* embedded in particular things and *cannot* exist independently.

Aristotle argued that every particular thing, considered at any given time, has two aspects. First, it shares properties with other particulars. For example, you and your philosophy professor share certain properties with each other. You also share properties with Willy the whale, with anything containing hydrogen, and so on. But there is something special, unique, or primary (basic) that you and your professor share with each other and with me. This shared quality consists of whatever answers the question "What is that?"

Aristotle characterized this basic *whatness* as the "substance" of a thing. So, "*What* are you?" You are a mammal, an animal, a vertebrate—just like your professor, Willy, and I are. But you, your professor, and I share a common *whatness* that Willy lacks: We are human beings according to Aristotle (if not to our friends!). We share qualities that Willy lacks, and Willy has qualities that we lack and that he shares with other underwater creatures. The more thorough our list of the shared, common properties that make up a thing's *whatness*, the fuller our grasp of its *whatness*.

According to Aristotle, *form* (with a lowercase f) makes a substance what it is. This kind of substance-making form is sometimes referred to as the *essence* of a thing. So we (you, your professor, and I) share a common

It is possible to fail in many ways . . . while to succeed is possible only in one way (for which reason also one is easy and the other difficult—to miss the mark easy, to hit it difficult).

Aristotle

It is absurd to suppose that purpose is not present because we do not observe the agent deliberating.

Aristotle

"form," "substance," or "essence." In each case, the answer to *what*—not who—we are is: a human being. After distinguishing among various ways that we talk about being (in reference to a thing's size, shape, and such), Aristotle says:

> Although being is used in all these ways, clearly the primary kind of being is what a thing is; for it is this alone that indicates substance. When we say what kind of thing something is, we say that it is good or bad, but not that it is three feet long or that is a man; but when we say what a thing is, we do not say that is white, hot, or three feet long, but that is a man or a god. All other things are said to be only insofar as they are quantities, qualities, affections . . . so what is primarily—not in the sense of being something, but just quite simply being—is substance.[7]

In other words, Aristotle is saying that when we characterize or define *what a thing is*, we are speaking of that thing's substance or essence. Thus, according to Aristotle, *form* is the essence of substance itself, the *whatness* that makes a substance a substance.

From the Greek word for essence (*ousia*), **Aristotelian form** is that which is *in matter* and makes a thing what it is; Aristotelian form can be abstracted from matter but cannot exist independently of matter. Although knowing what kind of thing a thing is can be useful, merely knowing a thing's form (essence) does not account for its particularness, its individuality. So, according to Aristotle, form is only one basic aspect of reality. The other is matter.

Matter (Thisness)

Navigating wisely through life requires that we recognize the common features of things, their essences, "natures," "qualities," "common characteristics," and such; it also requires dealing with specific things, with particulars. The *whatness* that you, your philosophy professor, and I share is that we are human beings; we are also, however, particular human beings. So we also need to ask about *this* specific human being (or horse, or book, or anything).

In Aristotle's view, when we ask about *this* particular thing, we are asking about the material composition of whatever constitutes that thing, the specific stuff that makes a general form (human being) into a particular instance of that form (you, your professor, me). For Aristotle, **matter**, from the Greek *hyle*, is the common material stuff found in a variety of things; matter has no distinct characteristics until some form is imparted to it or until the form inherent in a thing becomes actualized.

Thus, for Aristotle, individual things are "formed matter." His careful studies of the natural world led Aristotle to posit a *hierarchy of forms*,

FORM (ARISTOTLE)

From the Greek word for essence (*ousia*), that which is in matter and makes a thing what it is; can be abstracted from matter but cannot exist independently of matter.

MATTER (ARISTOTLE)

From the Greek *hyle*, the common material stuff found in a variety of things; it has no distinct characteristics until some form is imparted to it or until the form inherent in a thing becomes actualized.

moving from the simplest kinds of things to the most complex, based on each thing's function or purpose. At the highest levels, form is the "purpose," "goal," or "overall plan" of an object considered as a *whole*, as a *unity*.

Aristotle did *not* mean that the universe (nature) has been planned by something separate from it like God or Plato's Forms. Rather, he argued, order and purpose are inherent in nature. Nature is purposive. Matter provides "opportunity"; form provides "direction." Form does not—cannot—exist without matter; matter does not—cannot—exist without form. The Aristotelian universe is a continuum of formed matter, from the lowest, most inert things to the most complex, autonomous, and active ones. Understanding anything consists of understanding its relationships to other things on this continuum.

Change

Aristotle thought that his picture of nature as formed matter explained how it is that things can change. Let's return to the example of water changing into ice. When water changes into ice, some part of the water itself remains water, and some part of the water changes. The basic matter stays the same, but it changes form. As water becomes progressively colder, the behavior or properties of the molecules that constitute water change from liquid form to crystalline form.

The basic process of change—substitution of forms in stages—is the same from the simplest to the most complex things. As an acorn changes into an oak tree, a progressive succession of shapes occurs: acorn to sprout to sapling to tree. (And the tree stage itself consists of a series of shape changes as the trunk thickens and branches grow out and up.)

Guiding this series of changes, says Aristotle, is movement toward an inherent structure or form (oak tree). The acorn, for instance, contains a potential sprout—a form not yet "materialized." If conditions are right, the acorn's actual form is replaced by its potential form, and the *potential* sprout is *actualized*. The actualized sprout contains within itself the form of a potential sapling. Given the necessary material conditions, the sprout restructures its own matter into a sapling according to this "blueprint" (form of a sapling). The sapling, of course, contains the form of a potential tree, and so on.

So "change" is really a series of smaller changes in which matter loses and gains form. In complex organisms, change occurs as an orderly series of progressively complex forms. Such structured, systematic change, from simple to complex, accounts for the qualitative distinction between change and *development* or *growth*. Development occurs when changes follow a pattern that leads toward a "goal" or end (purpose or function).

The goal or purpose that produces growth unites or unifies the successive changes as *stages* leading to a single goal (actualization of the ulti-

> The actuality of thought is life.
>
> *Aristotle*

> Some have said that no intellectual substance can be the form of the body. . . . But this can be shown to be impossible. For the animals and men are sensible and natural things; and this would not be the case if the body and its parts did not belong to the essence of man and animal.
>
> *Thomas Aquinas*

mate form or essence). From this, Aristotle argued that in order to understand something, it is necessary to identify its function or purpose. But there is more to a thing than its function (purpose or end). The most complete analysis or understanding of anything, Aristotle believed, could only come from asking, "What accounts for the existence of this or that thing?"

We'll conclude this introductory overview of Aristotle's naturalistic metaphysics with a look at what he says about the need to link understanding to function or purpose. Then, we'll be better able to appreciate the foundations and richness of his most famous, and magnificent, account of happiness.

Aristotle's Hierarchy of Whys

You may have heard the story of the three bricklayers who are asked: "What are you doing?" The first worker says, "I am laying this brick." The second answers, "I am building an arch." The third says, "I am building a cathedral." In a sense, each worker is "correct." She has stated her view of her task, her sense of purpose or primary function. The story is often told to inspire us to set our sights on lofty goals. But it has another lesson, too. This story teaches us that the same thing can be characterized by distinctly different accounts or explanations, depending on the *purpose* of the account—and the purposes that together constitute the thing, process, or activity.

In the story of the bricklayers, each succeeding account includes the essence of the prior account. When the second bricklayer says, "I am building an arch," she implies: "I am laying this brick in order to make an arch." In other words, her goal is the arch. When the third bricklayer says, "I am building a cathedral," she implies: "I am laying this brick in order to make an arch in order to make a cathedral." Her goal is "higher" than that of the second worker, whose goal is, in turn, higher than that of the first bricklayer's more modest task.

In this simplistic example, we also see that a number of alternative explanations and accounts could have been given, depending on the focus (purposes) of the account giver. If the first bricklayer is a novice with no knowledge of arches or cathedrals, then she will be unable to grasp the ultimate purpose of her activity as part of a complex, goal-directed process. Her view is not incorrect; it is incomplete. She lacks adequate comprehension of the *end* of the construction process, which is a *means* governed by a plan.

Have you noticed, however, that even the third worker's account can be broadened. We still—naturally—want to ask, "But *why* are you building a cathedral?" Here, too, a variety of responses will be "correct": "To make money." "To honor God." "To impress my special friend."

Nature does nothing uselessly.

Aristotle

"Because I enjoy it." The first three answers don't necessarily bring a halt to the inquiry, do they? We may still need to ask: "Why do you want money? What's the money to be used for?" "Why honor God by building a cathedral?" "What's the purpose behind trying to impress your special friend?"

The fourth answer seems somehow different. What kind of answer might we expect to the question, "Why do what you enjoy?" We don't usually ask that question because pleasure (enjoyment) is capable of standing as an *end in itself*. That is, enjoyment is treated as an ultimate goal by many people, a goal that does not look forward toward a yet-higher goal.

Later in this chapter we'll see what Aristotle has to say about money and other things, including pleasure, as final goals. What's important now is the concept of hierarchical ends, a hierarchy of "whys." Aristotle's hierarchical account of causation serves as a foundation for his moral psychology, and greatly influenced subsequent thinkers.

A man is the origin of his action.

Aristotle

The Four Causes

Aristotle was the first philosopher to understand that not all "why" questions can be answered in the same way because there is more than one kind of *why*. In marked contrast to the single *why* view, Aristotle distinguished among four different kinds of *whys* that, together, constitute a complete accounting or understanding of a thing. He referred to them as *causes*. Aristotle's Greek word for cause, *aitia*, meant "the reason for something happening." According to Aristotle, complete understanding of a thing must tell us what material the thing is made of, what form the thing takes, what triggered the events that set the thing's existence into motion, and the ultimate purpose for which the thing exists.

Aristotle's "four causes" are thus offered as accounts of: (1) the material the thing is made of (*Material Cause*); (2) the form the thing takes (*Formal Cause*); (3) the "triggering" action or motion that begins the thing (*Efficient Cause*); and (4) the ultimate purpose or goal for which the thing exists (*Final Cause*). After describing the Four Causes, Aristotle says that "it is the business of the natural scientist to know about them all . . . [and to] give his answer to the question 'why?' in the manner of a natural scientist . . . [by referring] to them all—to the matter, the form, the mover, and the purpose."[8]

Let's take a closer look at each of the Four Causes.

The final cause, then, produces motion through being loved.

Aristotle

Well begun is half done.

Aristotle

Material Cause

In his *Physics*, Aristotle points out that merely identifying the material out of which, say, a bed or statue is made does not tell us how and why that bed or that statue exists:

Some people regard the nature and substance of things that exist by nature as being in each case the proximate element inherent in the thing, this being itself unshaped; thus, [according to such a view] the nature of a bed, for instance, would be wood, and that of a statue bronze. [Those who think this way offer] as evidence . . . the fact that if you were to bury a bed, and the moisture that got into it as it rotted gained enough force to throw up a shoot, it would be wood and not a bed that came into being. [According to this view, the bed's] arrangement according to the rules of an art . . . is an accidental attribute, whereas its substance is what remains permanently, and undergoes all these changes.[9]

Aristotle rejects merely identifying a thing's *matter* as a complete understanding of the "how" and "why" of that thing. After all, it is not the nature of wood to become beds or bronze to become statues. Statues and beds are made of many different things, and some bronze and wood never become statues or beds. Identifying a thing's matter is a necessary part of—but not a complete—accounting for that thing. The **Material Cause** of a thing refers to the material (substance) from which the thing comes, and in which change occurs.

Formal Cause

But what accounts for wood becoming a bed instead of, say, a table? Until wood is fashioned into some particular thing, say a bed or table, it is *potentially* but not *actually* a bed or table. Wood needs to be *formed* into beds and tables and other crafted objects "according to the rules of an art." It is not just wood (matter), then, that makes a bed or table, but the *form* the wood takes. Therefore, in addition to identifying the Material Cause of a thing, we need to know its **Formal Cause**, the shape, or form, into which "this matter" is changed.

It is easy enough to see how an artisan imposes form on matter; the bedmaker shapes wood into beds or tables. But what about "natural" things, growing things, and such? What forms natural objects? According to Aristotle, flesh and bone, for example, become flesh and bone only when their substance (matter) *forms* into "that which makes flesh, flesh" and "that which makes bone, bone." Aristotle says:

> What is potentially flesh or bone does not yet have its own nature until it acquires the form that accords with the formula, by means of which we define flesh and bone; nor can it be said at this stage to exist by nature. So in another way, nature is the shape and form of things that have a principle of movement in themselves—the form being only theoretically separable from the object in question.[10]

The basic elements that flesh or bone are made from are not—of themselves—flesh or bone. Flesh *is* (essentially and by definition) the precise

MATERIAL CAUSE

The material (substance) from which a thing comes, and in which change occurs; first of Aristotle's "four causes."

FORMAL CAUSE

The shape, or form, into which matter is changed; second of Aristotle's "four causes."

Nature, like mind, always acts for a purpose, and this purpose is its end [goal]. That it should be so is according to nature; for every part of a living body is an organ of the soul. Evidently then, all such parts are for the sake of the soul, which is their natural end.

Aristotle

"formulation" of matter-as-flesh. Bone *is* (essentially and by definition) the precise "formulation" of matter-as-bone.

Together, then, the Material and Formal Causes of a thing tell us what stuff it is composed of and how that stuff is formed. In other words, Material and Formal Causes combine to describe a particular unit of "formed matter."

Efficient Cause

But what explains *why* this bone or flesh or person or tree actually *exists*? What accounts for the potentially "formed matter" *becoming actualized*? What starts the whole process? What gets it going? What "triggers" the sequence that results in this bone or that person? Aristotle answers that a "proximate mover" "causes" a thing's "coming-to-be." Some sort of "motion" is needed to convert potentiality into actuality. Aristotle says:

> Thus the answer to the question "why?" is to be given by referring to the matter, to the essence, and to the proximate mover. In cases of coming-to-be it is mostly in this last way that people examine the causes; they ask what comes to be after what, what was the immediate thing that acted or was acted upon, and so on in order.[11]

Aristotle named a thing's "triggering" cause the **Efficient Cause**: that which initiates activity; the substance by which a change is brought about. (Although, for Aristotle, Efficient Causes, like all causes, are substances, the concept of a "triggering action" is probably closer to our contemporary notion of cause than the other "causes" Aristotle discusses.)

EFFICIENT CAUSE

The "triggering cause" that initiates activity; the substance by which a change is brought about; close to the contemporary meaning of cause; third of Aristotle's "four causes."

Final Cause

Aristotle addressed one other "why" question, a question that still confounds philosophers, scientists, and theologians, and that is the basis of certain "ultimate meaning" questions: What is the meaning of life? Does life have purpose? Why (not how) does this universe exist? Ultimate "why" questions are also asked and (usually) easily answered about crafted objects: "Why do these shoes exist? To keep our feet warm and protected." In the case of the shoes, note: The answer states the *reasons for which* the shoes were made, the *purpose, goal,* or *end* that the shoes exist to serve.

Aristotle called the *ultimate why* of a thing that thing's *telos,* or "final" goal, the purpose of its very existence. Thus, the very last answer in a series of "why" questions identifies the "final cause" needed to complete our understanding of the thing. A thing's **Final Cause** is that for which an activity or process takes place; a thing's very reason for being (*raison d'être*).

Another term for "final" cause is *end,* not in the sense of last event or action, but in the sense of *purpose* or *completed state.* In this sense, a thing is "completed" or "finished" in the way that a chair or painting or song is

FINAL CAUSE

That for which an activity or process takes place; a thing's very reason for being (*raison d'être*); fourth of Aristotle's "four causes."

finished when the artisan has accomplished his or her goal. When living things are finished in this sense, they are said to be fully realized, mature, ripe, "grown," "complete," "whole," or "perfected." Note that, from a naturalistic perspective, referring to persons as "complete," "whole," and "perfect" does *not* carry religious or moralistic connotations. Rather, the terms connote "realization," "actualization," or "reaching" our ultimate stage of development, our "end" or "purpose."

Aristotle claimed to have identified what he called an "inner urge" in each living thing to realize its end or purpose, a drive to develop, to become its unique self. Speaking this way, we can say that the acorn, for example, has an *inner urge* to become an oak tree, the baby has an *inner urge* to become a fully realized adult, and so forth. Aristotle characterized this inner urge to become what a thing is "meant to be" as "having its end within itself." The Greek word for this is **entelechy**, and it is upon the concept of entelechy that Aristotle constructs his theory of human well-being. Let's see how.

Entelechy

Aristotle thought that entelechy explained nature as a whole. Certainly the concept frames his entire practical philosophy. *Entelechy means that things do not just happen—they develop according to natural design.* That is, nature is ordered and guided "internally." Sometimes Aristotle refers to entelechy as a "creative drive." "Such principles," he says, "do not all make for the same goal, but each inner principle always makes for the same goal *of its own [kind]*, if nothing interferes" [emphasis added].[12]

We see evidence of this natural order and purpose everywhere: Cats do not give birth to puppies; cornstalks do not yield turnips. As we have already learned, life, the whole of reality, is not just *matter* and it is not just *form*. It is clearly both, and neither can be understood in isolation from the other.

The acorn will become an oak tree if nothing stops it. But the acorn lacks the power to ensure that all of its needs are met. It may fall upon rocky soil, get too much or too little water, and so forth. It might become a pretty pathetic oak tree—but it will never become any kind of cedar. Change occurs within substances. Human beings, however, are more complex than acorns. And though we must remain human beings, we may fail (for reasons to be discussed) to follow our own entelechy. We may never fulfill our ultimate purpose, to become our "true selves." We may remain incompletely "formed," in much the same way some plants "meant to blossom" never blossom. Malformed, they linger in hostile conditions, spindly, thin, unproductive. Materially, they remain petunias, azaleas, cherry trees; they grow but do not develop.

ENTELECHY

From the Greek for "having its end within itself": according to Aristotle, an inner urge that drives all things to blossom into their own unique selves; inner order or design that governs all natural processes.

I am convinced that each human being is unique and that he has a right to be his own separate self.

Aaron Ungersma

For Aristotle, life without development is all too common for human beings, too. Because we are so much more complex than acorns and azaleas, the conditions necessary for fully realized human beings are correspondingly more complex. But before we look into Aristotle's formula for thriving, we need to see how and why Aristotle applied the concept of form to the human soul.

Psyche

We must have richness of soul.

Antiphanes

We've already seen that formless existence is not possible, according to Aristotle. Things exist according to some pattern, some form. As noted earlier, the Greek term for soul is *psyche*. We get the term *psychology* from it. For Aristotle, *soul is the form of the body.* Just as we cannot even imagine a soul going to Atlanta without a body, so too, one's body is not a human being without a human soul, in Aristotle's view.

Soul is entelechy. For Aristotle, it is impossible to affect the body without affecting the soul or to affect the soul without affecting the body. There is no way to reach the soul except through the bodily organs (including the brain/mind), and there is no way for the soul to act or communicate except bodily. Recently, some scientists have lent support to the view that the mind plays a role in altering the course of various autoimmune diseases, that laughter and positive attitudes have healing power. Such ideas reflect Aristotle's insistence on the organic, holistic, inseparable union of body and the natural soul. (African, Amazonian, Native American, and other tribal cultures have long accepted this as a fact.)

Human beings are not the only *besouled* creatures (to use one translator's beautiful word), and each kind of substance requires a different kind of study.

The Hierarchy of Souls

Aristotle thought that although various kinds of souls are different enough that no single definition of *soul* can cover them all, they are similar enough that we can still recognize a common nature in all their varieties.[13]

Aristotle taught that there are three kinds of soul, which constitute a hierarchy. Each higher level on the continuum of souls contains elements of the lower levels—but the lower levels do not contain the higher. This hierarchy is based on the capacities or *potentialities* possessed by each level of animal life. The more "potentiality" a thing has, the higher its place in the hierarchy.

The hierarchy of souls progresses from the simplest life functions to more complicated ones. Thus the lowest type of soul is called the *vegetative*, or *nutritive*, soul. This is the minimal level of life (animate matter). *The nutritive soul absorbs matter* from other things (as food is absorbed and transformed into blood or tissue). The second level of soul is the level of sensation; here we find the *sensitive*, or *sentient*, soul. *The sensitive*

"The meaning of our existence is not invented but detected."

What is called self-actualization is, and must remain, the unintended effect of self-transcendence; it is ruinous and self-defeating to make it the target of intention. And what is true of self-actualization also holds for identity and happiness. It is the very "pursuit of happiness" that obviates happiness. The more we make it a target, the more widely we miss.

It may now have become clear that a concept such as self-actualization, or self-realization, is not a sufficient ground for a motivational theory. This is mainly due to the fact that self-actualization, like power and pleasure, also belongs to the class of phenomena which can only be obtained as a side effect and are thwarted precisely to the degree to which they are made a matter of direct intention. Self-actualization is a good thing; however, I maintain that man can only actualize himself to the extent to which he fulfills meaning. Then self-actualization occurs spontaneously; it is contravened when it is made an end in itself. . . .

We have to beware of the tendency to deal with values in terms of the mere self-expression of man himself. . . . If the meaning that is waiting to be fulfilled by man were nothing but a mere expression of self, or no more than a projection of his wishful thinking, it would immediately lose its demanding and challenging character; it could no longer call man forth or summon him. . . . I think the meaning of our existence is not invented by ourselves, but rather detected.

Viktor E. Frankl
Man's Search for Meaning: An Introduction to Logotherapy (New York: Pocket Books, 1963), pp. 8, 35–36, 156–157.

soul registers information regarding the form of things, but does not absorb or become those things (as when we look at or touch something). Human souls include a third, higher level of entelechy called the *rational* soul, which includes the nutritive and sensitive souls, as well as capacities for analyzing things, understanding various forms of relationships, and making reasoned decisions (called *deliberation*).

Human beings—as human beings, not as specific individuals—have the potential for scientific and philosophical knowledge and insight. The lowest level of life has the most limited potential; think, for instance, of single cells or worms. At the top of the hierarchy of souls, we observe greater capacities for discriminating among various aspects of the environment, for overriding impulse and instinct with rational deliberation based on goals and ends. We note a capacity for understanding the essence (form) of what's going on, and a capacity for creative and self-conscious intelligence. These capacities are lacking in lower life-forms.

Aristotle's ethics is built on this concept of a hierarchy of souls. It is sometimes classified as an ethic of "self-realization," but a much better term would be "soul-realization." Although limited by the biases of classical Greek culture, the *Nicomachean Ethics* is still readable and instructive. More than a thousand years after Aristotle, the great scholar Thomas Aquinas recognized the value of Aristotle's classical virtues for medieval Christians (see Chapter 7). A case can be made today for another serious

May God grant me power
to struggle to become not
another but a better man.

*Samuel Taylor
Coleridge*

look at an ethics of *ensoulment*. (If you are already familiar with the concept of self-realization from psychology, New Age metaphysics, or Eastern religions, I think you may be surprised by Aristotle's concept of self-realization. It is more complete than many contemporary systems using similar labels.) A good way to get a basic sense of Aristotle's self-realization ethic is to take a look at the concept of happiness expressed in the *Nicomachean Ethics*.

Natural Happiness

They are blind who have
no clear standard.

Plato

For the classical Greeks, as has been noted, goodness or virtue was excellence of function. Happiness was also understood in terms of function: A thing was "happy" when it functioned fully and well according to its own nature. A virtuous thing was a happy thing. In Aristotelian terms, happiness is the state of actualizing or realizing a thing's function, its *entelechy*. *A good life is one that provides all the necessary conditions and opportunities for a person to become fully him- or herself—and one in which the person has the character to do so.*

For Aristotle, happiness is a quality of life here and now, not something for the hereafter. It is neither entirely material nor entirely spiritual (formal). His is a philosophy of moderation in the fullest sense, based on common experience, stripped of sentimentality: Wealth is not enough to give us happiness, but poverty makes happiness impossible. Mental attitude is important, but so is physical health. No one can be happy *in the fullest sense* who is chronically ill or mentally deficient. Unattractive people are not as happy as attractive ones. No matter how great our efforts, happiness always contains an element of luck. A person raised well from infancy is a happier person than one who is not. A good life can be marred by a bad death.

Count no man happy until
he is dead.

Solon

Philosophical Query

As an example of the importance of luck in the good life, think about this Aristotelian maxim (derived from Solon): "Count no man happy until he is dead." Aristotle taught that a good life can be marred by a bad death. Discuss this general idea and then tie it to our present attitudes toward death, dying, and euthanasia.

The Good

Whereas for Plato the Form of Good was the highest Form of Being, for Aristotle the good is "that at which all things aim." In other words, the good for anything is the realization of its own nature (essence): *the good at which all things aim is their own entelechy.* When we use the expressions "for your own good," or "that's not good for you," we may have something similar in mind. "The good," then, is what's good for something's full functioning. It encourages the development (realization) of its true nature.

Because human beings are complex, consisting of all three elements of soul, it is possible to develop physically or emotionally or intellectually and still fail to realize our entelechy. It is also possible to lack the ability to achieve it, either because the external circumstances of our lives inhibit our full development or because some imbalance in our own character prevents us from fully developing.

Before we go any further, it's important to be clear about the distinction between "aging" and "developing." We're probably all familiar with people who grow old without growing up. We must not confuse biological growth and maturation with personal development. Aristotle linked the two: A *fully* functioning, *completely* happy person will be mentally, physically, spiritually, financially, professionally, creatively, and socially healthy and well-rounded.

As noted above, Aristotle's classical values add an objective component to happiness. This means that entelechy is not determined by the individual. Aristotle's view differs from those self-realization or self-fulfillment theories that claim "you can be anything you want to be." Such a claim would have struck him as ridiculous. It is as irrational and "unworthy" for a human being to try to live like an animal, for example, as it is for an acorn to try to be an ear of corn—or for us to try to make a dog into a child.

Philosophical Query

Discuss some of the common obstacles to becoming a fully functioning, balanced individual.

Teleological Thinking

According to Aristotle, observation of the natural world (which includes human behavior) reveals:

> Every art and every scientific inquiry, and similarly every action and purpose, may be said to aim at some good. Hence the good has been well defined as that at which all things aim. . . .
>
> As there are various actions, arts, and sciences, it follows the ends are also various. Thus health is the end of medicine, a vessel of shipbuilding, victory [is the end] of strategy, and wealth [is the goal] of domestic economy. . . .
>
> . . . If it is true that in the sphere of action there is an end which we wish for its own sake, and for the sake of which we wish everything else . . . it is clear that this will be the good or the supreme good. Does

To be sure, the whirl of life and culture in contemporary America is such that we apparently feel little need of, and obviously pay no heed to, such things as the ethical and political observations of an Aristotle. For what is there to human existence, save getting ahead and having a good time?

But Aristotle did not see things this way.

Henry Veatch

The strongest principle of growth lies in human choice.

George Eliot

"Know thyself" has be-
come "Do whatever you
please."

Bruno Bettelheim

"Can Mommy borrow your baby-blue pinafore tonight, sweetie?"

Drawing by M. Stevens, © 1994 *The New Yorker Magazine*, Inc.

it not follow that the knowledge of this supreme good is of great importance for the conduct of life, and that, *if we know it*, we shall be
like archers who have a mark at which to aim, we shall have a better
chance of attaining what we want?[14]

The technical name for this kind of thinking is *teleological*, from the Greek
root *telos*, meaning end, purpose, or goal. (*Entelechy* comes from the same
root.) **Teleological thinking** is a way of explaining or understanding a
thing in terms of its ultimate goal, or final cause. For example, in teleological terms, infancy is understood as a stage on the way to mature adulthood. Adulthood is the *telos* of infancy. Teleological thinking also refers
to understanding things functionally in terms of the relationship of the
parts to a whole—for example, considering a vehicle's transmission in
terms of the vehicle's ultimate function: speed, traction, comfort. Both
Aristotle's ethic and conception of virtue are teleological.

TELEOLOGICAL
THINKING

Way of explaining things
in terms of their ultimate
goals; understanding things
functionally in terms of the
relationship of the parts to
the whole.

The Science of the Good

In the first book of the *Nicomachean Ethics* Aristotle makes a famous and
insightful proclamation:

Our statement of the case will be adequate if it be made with all such clearness as the subject-matter admits; for it would be wrong to expect the same degree of accuracy in all [subjects]. . . . [Due to the nature of our subject] we must be content to indicate the truth roughly and in outline; and as our subjects and premises are true generally *but not universally*, we must be content to arrive at conclusions which are generally true.[15]

Aristotle was aware that moral considerations involve practical judgments of particular circumstances. We might characterize his position as "formal relativism." That means that even though there is an underlying structure, or form, of happiness for human beings, the specific way in which a particular human being realizes that form varies with his or her circumstances.

Let's use Aristotle's example to see the point: A wrestler and a young child do not eat the same kinds of foods or the same amounts. But this does not mean that the laws of nutrition are relative in the Sophists' sense of being radically determined by the individual or society. Indeed, the same laws apply to wrestlers and babies: minimum protein, fat, carbohydrate, and fluid levels must be met for good health. Appropriate caloric intake should be based on actual energy output, not on a merely theoretical model, and so on. But since individual metabolisms vary, since local temperature affects metabolism, since the quality of food varies, and so forth, we must modify each person's actual diet: "We must be content to indicate the truth roughly and in outline," Aristotle reminds us.

We can identify the general outline of conduct that will lead to the best possible life, but we cannot give a precise prescription for any individual's good life. Still, Aristotle says, we can arrive at a valuable approximation of the "good life" based on human nature and the good we each seek.

According to the *Nicomachean Ethics*, the good to which all humans aspire is happiness:

> As [all] knowledge and moral purpose aspires to some good, what is in our view the good at which the political science aims, and what is the highest of all practical goods? As to its name there is, I may say, a general agreement. The masses and the cultured classes agree in calling it happiness, and conceive that "to live well" or "to do well" is the same thing as "to be happy." But as to the nature of happiness they do not agree, nor do the masses give the same account of it as the philosophers.[16]

The *Nicomachean Ethics* is a careful survey of a variety of opinions regarding what constitutes "living well" in the best, fullest sense. Although Aristotle concludes that the best life is the life of philosophical contemplation, the heart of his ethics is a philosophy of moderation, fulfillment, activity, and balance.

The knowledge of the soul admittedly contributes greatly to the advance of truth in general, and, above all, to our understanding of Nature, for the soul is in some sense the principle of animal life. Our aim is to grasp and understand, first its essential nature, and secondly its properties.

Aristotle

The general movement, we may say, was from other-worldliness towards an intense interest in the concrete facts both of nature and history, and a conviction that the "form" and meaning of the world is to be found not apart from but embedded in its "matter."

Sir David Ross

Eudaimonia

The word Aristotle used that is so often translated as "happiness" is **eudaimonia**. The English language does not have a good one-word equivalent for *eudaimonia*. *Happiness* is almost too bland, although it's probably the answer most of us would give if asked what we want from life (or the afterlife, in many conceptions of heaven).

Eudaimonia implies being really alive as opposed to just existing: fully aware, vital, alert. It is more than being free of cares or worries. Rather, eudaimonia implies exhilaration—great suffering and great joy, great passions. It implies a full life, not a pinched, restricted one.

A life devoted solely to pleasure, says Aristotle, is "a life fit only for cattle." Pleasure is not the *goal* of life; it's the natural companion of a full and vigorous life. If you have ever seen an athlete or scholar or artist working very hard at what she loves, you know what Aristotle meant: deep and satisfying pleasure *accompanies* doing what we are meant to do. But the pursuit of pleasure as an end is shallow:

> Ordinary or vulgar people conceive [the good] to be pleasure, and accordingly approve a life of enjoyment. . . . Now the mass of men present an absolutely slavish appearance, as choosing the life of brute beasts, but they meet with consideration because so many persons in authority share [such] tastes.[17]

> The intention that man should be "happy" is not contained in the plan of Creation.
>
> *Sigmund Freud*

According to Aristotle, a life devoted to acquiring wealth is also a limited one. Its focus is too narrow to nourish the natural soul's full complement of qualities and needs. Think of people who work long, stressful hours to get rich—and then think of how much life they miss in the process. They never "stop to smell the roses." Even with all the money in the world, a person still needs self-discipline and the knowledge to use his or her riches wisely. The unhappy rich person is common enough to be a stereotype. Aristotle says, "The life of money-making is in a sense a life of constraint, and it is clear that wealth is not the good of which we are in quest; for it is useful in part as a means to something else."[18]

Aristotle also rejected fame and public success as leading to eudaimonia because he believed that the more self-sufficient we are, the happier we are; and the famous are less self-sufficient than most: They need bodyguards, managers, financial advisers, public adulation, and so forth. There is greater peace of mind, security, and satisfaction in knowing that I can provide for my needs than there is in depending on others, as any adolescent or convalescent knows. If one's happiness depends on fame it depends on the whims of a fickle public:

> The hell to be endured hereafter, of which theology tells us, is no worse than the hell we make for ourselves in this world by habitually fashioning our characters in the wrong way.
>
> *William James*

> But [the love of fame] appears too superficial for our present purpose; for honor seems to depend more upon the people who pay it than upon the person to whom it is paid, and we have an intuitive feeling that the good is something which is proper to a man himself and cannot be easily taken away from him.[19]

Eudaimonia results when pleasure is the natural companion of a fully functioning life, rather than the goal of life. Artisans working at their true calling—such as this glassblower—combine hard work and happiness in a vital, rich way.

The Good Life Is a Process

The highest and fullest happiness, according to Aristotle, comes from a life of reason and contemplation—not a life of inactivity or imbalance, but a rationally ordered life in which intellectual, physical, and social needs are all met under the governance of reason and moderation. The "reasonable" person does not avoid life: he or she engages in it fully. A rich and full life is a social life. "No one," Aristotle says in the *Ethics*, "would choose to live without friends, and no one would choose to have every conceivable good thing on the condition that he remain solitary, for man is a political (social) creature designed by nature to live with others."

The rational person alone knows how to engage in life fully, since he or she alone has fully realized all three souls: the nutritive, sensitive, and rational—according to the basic form or entelechy of human beings.[20] *The good life must be lived fully; it is a process, an activity, a becoming, not a static condition.* Not even moral virtue is adequate for happiness by itself, because virtue, ". . . it appears, lacks completeness; for it seems that a man may possess virtue and yet be asleep or inactive throughout life, and, not only [that], but he may experience the greatest calamities and

Continued observations of this basic dynamic nature of happiness, especially in clinical psychological practice, leads almost inevitably to the conclusion that deeper and more fundamental than sexuality, deeper than the craving for social power, deeper even than the desire for possessions, there is a still more generalized and more universal craving in the human makeup. It is the craving for knowledge of the right direction—or orientation.

William H. Sheldon, M.D.

misfortunes. But nobody would call such a life a life of happiness unless he were maintaining a paradox."[21]

Practicing a philosophy of *fully functioning* moderation is quite difficult, for it often requires that we stretch beyond those talents and areas of life we are currently satisfied with. Aristotle understood this, and attempted to present practical advice that could help us come closer to living a richer, more virtuous life: "The purpose of this present study is not . . . the attainment of theoretical knowledge; we are not conducting this inquiry in order to know what virtue is, but in order to become good, else there is no advantage in studying it."[22]

Philosophical Query

Consider Aristotle's position carefully here. It may conform more closely to our true feelings about virtue than our sentimental and idealistic platitudes imply. We may be taught that "virtue is its own reward," but how many of us *really* think as highly of a "good" person who hides away from the world as we do of someone who has faults and makes mistakes, but gets out there and gets involved in life? Is being "good" really enough?

Hitting the Mark

There are, perhaps, two ways to avoid mediocrity. The first is probably the most common today: to excel or fail at something in a big way. The other, it seems, is rarer, probably because it is so difficult for many of us: to live the fullest life possible, developing and nurturing *all* good and necessary qualities while avoiding all character defects.

Now, clearly the second way constitutes an impossible goal for a human being to meet completely. No one seems likely to avoid all defects of character. That does not, however, rule out the desirability of trying to hit this difficult mark. It's one thing to say "I can't be expected to get perfect scores on all my assignments," and quite another to jump to the conclusion "So there's no point in studying at all." Such a reaction is already extreme.

We saw that temperance was one of the cardinal virtues in Plato's *Republic*, and that it was a key virtue for Socrates. Aristotle goes so far as to base his entire moral philosophy on moderation: "First of all, it must be observed that the nature of moral qualities is such that they are destroyed by defect and by excess."[23]

The Principle of the Mean

The concept of moderation, what the Greeks called **sophrosyne**, seems dull and depriving to many people. It implies a life of rigid rules, no fun, playing it safe and avoiding any risks. But, as we have seen, Aristotle did

---

To attain any assured knowledge of the soul is one of the most difficult things in the world . . . if there is no . . . single and general method of solving the question of essence, our task becomes still more difficult . . . with what facts shall we begin our inquiry?

Aristotle

SOPHROSYNE

Wisdom as moderation; hitting the mark; quality of finding the mean between excess and deficiency.

Compulsive dedication to something may result in excellence at that particular something. But Aristotle cautions that great effort in the service of anything less than the goal of well-balanced thriving results in imbalance and overall dysfunction. Do you think these bodybuilders would agree?

not regard a narrow, boring, play-it-safe life as good. Indeed, the idea that moderation is boring is itself the product of an extreme view! The attitude that only living on the edge, "going for the gusto," abandoning self-restraint, can make life interesting is one-sided.

Aristotelian moderation is based on the concept of wisdom as *hitting the mark* between too much and not enough. If you study a target, you will notice that only a small circle in the center is the bull's-eye. There is more room on the target to miss the mark than there is to hit it.

A life completely devoted to playing it safe would be off the mark. Living that way actually limits opportunities to grow and fully experience life. Living on the edge, going from extreme to extreme, will not produce a good, full life either. The great artist who lives only for her work is not living a good, full life, since she indulges her work at the expense of other vital parts of herself. The scholar who hides in research does likewise. So, too, the compulsive jogger or bodybuilder. People who spend all their time doing charity work, praying, and reading holy scriptures are not balanced human beings. (Moral virtue, remember, is not enough, according to Aristotle.)

The happy man lives well and does well; for we have practically defined happiness as a sort of good life and good action.

Aristotle

Assume the virtue, even if
you have it not,
For use almost can change
the stamp of nature.

Shakespeare

Aristotelian moderation is the crux of becoming a whole person—of actualizing our potentialities, realizing our form. Achieving it may require that we do more of the things that are difficult for us and less of those we presently enjoy. Just as a proper diet is relative (the overeater must eat less than he is used to or wants to, the anorexic must do the opposite), the goal for each is a bull's-eye.

Each person's prescription for self-realization must be determined by his or her own actual condition. Some of us must become more social, others less so. Some students need to study less to become balanced human beings, others need to study more. If we see the call to moderation in terms of *who we are right now* and what it would take to make us fuller, more balanced, more "alive" and vibrant people, it is anything but a call to boring mediocrity.

> But let us first agree that any discussion on matters of action cannot be more than an outline and is bound to lack precision. . . . And if this is true of our general discussion, our treatment of particular problems will be even less precise, since these do not come under the head of any art which can be transmitted by precept, but the agent must consider on each different occasion what the situation demands, just as in medicine and in navigation. But although this is the kind of discussion in which we are engaged, we must do our best.[24]

Character and Habit

CHARACTER

From the Greek *charakter*, a word derived from *charassein*, "to make sharp" or "to engrave," character refers to the sum total of a person's traits, including behavior, habits, likes and dislikes, capacities, potentials, and so on; a key element of Aristotelian ethics and psychology, meaning the overall (generally fixed) nature or tone of a person's habits.

Central to Aristotle's ethics is the notion of character. By **character** Aristotle referred to the overall nature or tone of a person's habits. My character is the habitual or predictable and usual way I behave: my characteristic way of acting in different circumstances. A courageous person is characteristically brave. A slothful one is characteristically lazy.

Moral virtues, according to Aristotle, must be ingrained in us by training. We are not born with them.

> Moral virtue comes to us as a result of habit. . . . The virtues we first get by exercising them, as also happens in the case of the arts as well. For the things we have to learn before we can do them, we learn by doing them, e.g., men become builders by building. . . . So too we become just by doing just acts, temperate by doing temperate acts, brave by doing brave acts. . . . If this were not so, there would have been no need of a teacher, but all men would be born good or bad at their craft. . . . Thus in one word, states of character arise out of like activities. That is why the activities we exhibit must be of a certain kind; it is because the states of character correspond to the difference between these. It makes no small difference, then, whether we form habits of one kind or another from our very youth; it makes a very great difference, or rather all the difference.[25]

The coward cannot wait for courage, or he will remain a coward. The coward must first act courageously if he wishes to become brave. The poor student cannot wait for motivation, but must first *act the way the disciplined student acts* in order to become a better student. Aristotle anticipated a number of contemporary psychological schools with this emphasis on behavior as the prime element in shaping the human character.

Aristotle distinguishes practical wisdom from theoretical understanding and other forms of knowledge. He links practical wisdom to deliberation. This means that practical wisdom involves choosing the right goals *and* acting on them. But he reminds us that "our ability to perform such actions is *in no way enhanced by knowing them*, since the virtues are characteristics [that is, fixed capacities for action, acquired by habit]" [emphasis added].[26]

This reminds me of a saying a friend uses as a rule of thumb: "You can act yourself into right thinking, but you can't think yourself into right acting." Like all such sayings, this one needs to be taken with the proverbial grain of salt, but it does emphasize an Aristotelian point: *Happiness requires action.*

Knowing what is good and healthy does not—by itself—usually lead to doing what is good and healthy, as most of us realize. Aristotle thought that good habits ingrained in childhood produced the happiest, best life. He said it was better to "overtighten the bow string" in youth, because aging would naturally loosen it. Practical wisdom can help those of us lacking good habits to develop them. "A man fulfills his proper function only by way of practical wisdom and moral excellence or virtue: virtue makes us aim at the right target, and practical wisdom makes us use the right means."[27] Here, too, however, individual cases vary. According to Aristotle, not everyone is salvageable. But on the assumption that you and I are not yet lost, let us examine one of the more important tools in the *Nicomachean Ethics*: the mean.

Application of the Mean

A **mean** is the midpoint between two other points. On a line, it is the exact middle. *Aristotle characterized moral virtue as a mean between too little and too much.* In his terms, the mean is located between deficiency and excess. We might visualize it like this:

vice ——————— virtue ——————— vice
deficiency ——————— mean ——————— excess

Practical wisdom helps us determine where a given action falls on this continuum. One advantage of a visual aid like this is that it shows us an action can be *more or less* virtuous or vicious (meaning that it's a vice, not that it's necessarily cruel). Depending on the area encompassed by the mean, there is a certain amount of room within the general area of virtue,

Character is fate.

Heraclitus

His own manners will be his punishment.

Cicero

MEAN

From the Latin *medius*, the midpoint between two other points; for Aristotle, moral virtue was characterized as a mean between too little (deficiency) and too much (excess).

Table 5.1

Aristotelian Virtues and Vices

Deficiency/Vice	Mean/Virtue	Excess/Vice
Cowardice	Courage	Foolhardiness
Anorexia	Moderation	Gluttony
Stinginess	Generosity	Profligacy
Standoffishness	Friendliness	Obsequiousness
Shyness	Pride	Vanity
Pessimism	Realism	Optimism
Celibacy	Monogamy	Promiscuity
Dullness	Well-roundedness	Wildness

So, as . . . Aristotle . . . insisted, wisdom is to be contrasted with cleverness because cleverness is the ability to take the right steps to any end, whereas wisdom is related only to good ends, and to human life in general rather than to the ends of particular arts.

Philippa Foot

but there is even more room in the range of the extremes. Thus it is easier to go wrong than right.

Aristotle realized that some actions are excessive by their very nature; they can have no mean. For instance, there is no moderate, appropriate way to commit adultery. Other kinds of actions admit of degree, and so can have a mean. Some examples are shown in Table 5.1. Aristotle illustrated his point with a lengthy analysis of courage, which he placed between the deficiency of cowardice and the excess of foolhardiness, both of which are vices.

Aristotle points out that some vices are closer to the mean than others, because they reflect more of the virtue. In this case, foolhardiness is closer to courage and so is less a vice than cowardice. But it is still a vice. This is why the coward—who is further from the mean—is more easily recognized as flawed than the foolhardy person who takes too many or the wrong kind of risks. Movie characters like Rambo and Dirty Harry are more foolhardy than they are courageous in Aristotle's value system. In real life, they are not the people to emulate. An army cannot tolerate a platoon of Rambos any more than a police force can tolerate a division of Dirty Harrys.

One possible benefit of reflecting on the mean is a broadened sense of virtue. Thinking only in terms of right *or* wrong can lead to a perception of virtues and vices as simple opposites, whereas Aristotle's system treats them as part of an organic whole, in which each element affects the others and the overall functioning of the organism.

The wealthiest person on earth is not truly happy with high blood pressure or anorexia nervosa. Sadly, the media regularly report the tragic lives of physically strong athletes who succumb to drugs, promiscuity, or financial mismanagement. A brilliant scholar whose professional life is full and rewarding will not be *living as well as possible*, according to Aristotle, if she is physically decrepit from lack of exercise or socially inept from years of being buried in books. Such examples show how great virtue or talent in one or two areas cannot outweigh significant deficiencies in other areas if we take an organic view of life.

We can easily find many examples of excess or deficiency being mistaken for valuable character traits. An Aristotelian analysis of human activity as an organic complex affected by our characteristic virtues and vices can enrich our sense of possibilities. It can also improve our moral perspective.

> It is moral virtue that is concerned with emotions and actions, and it is in emotions and actions that excess, deficiency, and the median are found. Thus we can experience fear, confidence, desire, anger, pity, and generally any kind of pleasure and pain either too much or too little, and in either case not properly. But to experience all this at the right time, toward the right objects, toward the right people, for the right reason, and in the right manner—that is the median and the best course, the course that is a mark of virtue.[28]

According to Aristotle, we become our best selves in the process of becoming fully functioning human beings. *Aristotelian self-realization, like happiness, is a by-product of living a well-balanced life.*

Philosophical Query

Study and discuss Table 5.1, Aristotelian Virtues and Vices, using principles from the *Nicomachean Ethics* and the concept of the mean. Then add and discuss your own examples.

Contemporary Self-Realization

Self-realization or self-actualization theories are enjoying considerable popularity today. In our society, psychologists and "spiritual metaphysicians" have embraced the concept of self-realization much more than philosophers. A major difference between many of these self-realization theories and Aristotle's version centers on exactly what it is that we are trying to "realize."[29] Aristotle's position is that our individuality will emerge in the process of actualizing our basic human essence. A number of contemporary self-realization theories assert the contrary: They claim that our basic humanness will emerge as we actualize our true individuality.

Abraham Maslow and Carl Rogers

Psychologists **Abraham Maslow (1908–1970)** and **Carl Rogers (1902–1987)** were among the most important contemporary advocates of individualistic self-realization. Whereas Aristotle said "Aim for greatness of

---

Liars when they speak the truth are not believed.

Aristotle

Under favorable conditions man's energies are put into the realization of his own potentialities. Such a development is far from uniform. . . . But whatever course it takes him, it will be his given potentialities which he develops.

Karen Horney

soul," they say "Be yourself." The difference in emphasis is not trivial, for by stressing our *freedom* to be whoever we choose, individualistic self-realization radically shifts our focus from moderation through self-restraint and rationality to self-expression. As Maslow put it:

> The key concepts in the newer dynamic psychology are spontaneity, release, naturalness, self-choice, self-acceptance, impulse-awareness, gratification of basic needs. They *used* to be control, inhibition, discipline, training, shaping, on the principle that the depths of human nature were dangerous, evil, predatory, and ravenous.[30]

Maslow's emphasis, then, is *away from the rule of reason*. But this part of his position rests on a common error, which confuses an irrational attempt to deny or bury unpleasant emotions with being rational in the fullest sense. The unfortunate consequence of this error is to view rational self-control and deliberate management of expression as being identical with neurotic repression and defensiveness. Aristotle did not advocate the rigid rule of reason *against* emotions and appetites, however. Nor did he view the "depths of human nature" as any more dangerous or evil than any other natural force. Rather, he saw the lower parts of the soul as part of the natural order.

What replaces rational, balanced self-discipline and training in the newer dynamic psychologies is trust of one's feelings and openness to experience. Carl Rogers speaks of the "fully functioning person" in terms that reflect this free-flowing openness and trust:

> The good life, from the point of view of my experience, is the process of movement in a direction which the human organism selects when it is inwardly free to move in any direction, and the general qualities of this selected direction appear to have a certain universality.[31]

The universal pattern of development Rogers has in mind can be summed up as from defensiveness to openness. The philosophical question, then, concerns whether or not openness per se is a virtue. As Rogers sees it, the more "actualized" we become, the less "judgmental and inhibited" we become. He says, "The process seems to involve an increasing openness to experience. This phrase has come to have more and more meaning for me. It is the polar opposite of defensiveness." He continues:

> Thus, one aspect of this process which I am naming "the good life" appears to be a movement away from the pole of defensiveness toward the pole of openness to experience. The individual is becoming more able to listen to himself, to experience what is going on within himself. He is more open to his feelings of fear and discouragement and pain. He is also more open to his feelings of courage, and tenderness, and awe. He is free to live his feelings subjectively, as they exist

The unforgivable sin is [to not] become all that you can as a human being, given the circumstances of life that we have to accept.

R. D. Laing

in him, and also free to be aware of these feelings. He is more able to fully live the experiences of his organism rather than shutting them out of awareness.[32]

Perhaps the greatest difference between self-realization as Aristotle saw it and as it is commonly understood today lies in the abandonment of reason as a reliable guide; this in turn results in the loss of a moral center. It also results in failure to actualize our full capacity for reasoning, a capacity that Aristotle claimed is *essential* for being human. Maslow and Rogers, for instance, have no clear criteria for rejecting or accepting different life choices. A killer may be as fully functioning as a saint. Reflecting the values of classical Greece, Aristotle would reject most of the newer dynamic psychologies as unfit for human beings because they degrade the *essentially human* part of the soul by replacing reason with feeling as the chief guide.

Philosophical Query

Is it possible that my "true self," the one I dare to become, is a liar or worse? What map shall I use when, in Rogers's words, I "launch myself fully into the stream of life"?

Thomas Merton

The Trappist monk and Roman Catholic philosopher **Thomas Merton (1915–1968)** expressed an interesting variation of a self-realization ethic in his book *New Seeds of Contemplation*. By tying individual entelechy to God's will, Merton avoided the problem of relativism. His position has some of the contemporary feel of Maslow and Rogers, but with the added moral limits of Roman Catholic Christian values. Merton's work is a blend of philosophy, religion, and psychology. The following passage is typical:

> Many poets are not artists for the same reason that many religious men are not saints: they never succeed in being the particular poet or the particular monk they are intended to be by God. They never become the man or the artist who is called for by all the circumstances of their individual lives.
>
> They waste their years in vain efforts to be some other poet, some other saint. For many absurd reasons, they are convinced that they are obliged to become somebody else who died two hundred years ago and who lived in circumstances utterly alien to their own.
>
> They wear out their minds and bodies in a hopeless endeavor to have somebody else's experiences or write somebody else's poems or express somebody else's spirituality.[33]

Why do people feel so crowded? Because each wants to occupy the place of the other.

Rabbi Abraham Yaakov of Sadagora

As long as you have to defend the imaginary self that you think is important, you will lose your peace of heart. As soon as you compare that shadow with the shadows of other people, you lose all joy, because you have begun to trade in unrealities, and there is no joy in things that do not exist.

Thomas Merton

Philosophical Query

Thomas Merton's basic point is worth thinking about. It may apply to the writer hoping to be "another Hemingway" or "another Alice Walker," as well as to children desperately trying to become their parents—or desperately trying not to be anything like them. On the other hand, having a model or hero can be inspiring, and even Aristotle used the "good man" as a model. Discuss.

Commentary

There is no greater misfortune that can befall you than to be stricken from the roster of the living while you are still living.

Seneca

For Aristotle, self-realization was part of a natural process which could be understood only in terms of the whole. It was not directed by a personal God, nor was it a function of free-flowing self-expression. Aristotle saw limits as set by nature, not the individual. He thought that he had identified a fixed, natural hierarchy within the human soul. The rational soul is "designed" to control and guide—but not crush—emotions and appetites. Just as some actions (adultery, for instance) cannot hit a mean because their very nature is imbalanced, so, too, some personalities cannot be actualized because their very essences are excessive or deficient. Some lives are such that self-actualization is impossible. An acorn that falls too close to the parent tree may lack sufficient sunlight to burgeon, or it may be carried to a hostile environment by a bird, or used by an artist in a collage. Corn infected with disease will lack the material necessary to complete its development. Human beings raised in seriously defective environments, or born with major genetic impairments, and such, will never fully realize their entelechies.

The simple call to "be yourself" may sound appealing, but it proves to be insubstantial without solid philosophical grounding. While it is possible to be too self-controlled, no substantial good can come from realizing whatever limited conception of a self we happen to feel like—and this includes a self based only on religious, moral, or personal feelings.

A great Hasidic rabbi by the name of Zusya once said: When I die, God will not ask me, "Why were you not Moses?" When I die, God will ask me, "Why were you not Zusya?"

Aristotle, like Plato, extended the range of philosophic inquiry beyond the *sophos'* earliest search for wisdom. Basing his philosophy on observation and experience, he added the scientist's acuity to the *sophos'* sense of wonder. Aristotle did not abandon the search for wisdom; he enriched it by bringing it down to earth. The *Nicomachean Ethics* remains one of the most complete expressions of practical wisdom in the tradition of philosophy in the original sense. The spirit of the *sophos* rings throughout the *Ethics*, no more forcefully than when Aristotle says: "The purpose of this present study is not . . . the attainment of theoretical knowledge; we are not conducting this inquiry in order to know what virtue is, but in order to become good, else there is no advantage in studying it."

It is difficult to judge Aristotle's conception of the self-realized, superior person today. Clearly, his classical model of "human excellence" is alien to a culture that encourages the expression of virtually every emotion as healthy. His basic values are alien to a culture that prizes youthful spontaneity and talent over mature self-mastery and self-discipline. The modern self, it seems, is set free without a clear direction. The Aristotelian self is crafted according to standards of excellence discovered through philosophical contemplation and careful observation.

Summary of Main Points

1. Aristotle was Plato's most illustrious pupil and tutor of Alexander the Great. His interests included philosophy, logic, natural and social science, poetry, and drama. Aristotle founded his school known as the Lyceum.

2. Aristotle saw dangers in Plato's failure to begin from a clear assessment of actual facts. In contrast to Plato's rationalistic approach, Aristotle brings to full maturity a second major approach to the study of the good life: collecting of facts and using factual information to make this a better world.

3. Aristotle is a philosophical naturalist. Naturalism is the belief that reality consists of the natural world and that the universe is ordered. Everything follows consistent and discoverable *laws* of nature, and can be described in terms of fundamental laws.

4. According to Aristotle, form can be abstracted from matter but cannot exist independently of matter; this kind of form is sometimes referred to as essence. Matter is the common material stuff found in a variety of things; it has no distinct characteristics until some form is imparted to it or until the form inherent in a thing becomes actualized. Individual things are "formed matter."

5. Aristotle claimed that complete understanding of a thing required identifying its "four causes." The Four Causes are the Material Cause (the material the thing is made of); the Formal Cause (the form the thing takes); the Efficient Cause (the "triggering" motion that begins the thing); and the Final Cause (the *telos*, or ultimate purpose for which the thing exists).

6. Aristotle identified what he called an "inner urge" in every living thing, a drive to become its unique self. He called this inner urge *entelechy*, meaning "having its end within itself." Things do not just happen—they develop according to natural design. Nature is ordered and guided "internally." The technical name for this kind of thinking is *teleological*, from the Greek root *telos*, meaning end, purpose, or goal.

7. Aristotle taught that there are three kinds of soul and that they constitute a hierarchy. Each higher level of soul contains elements of the lower levels—but the lower levels do not contain the higher. This hierarchy is based on the capacities or potentialities possessed by each level of animal life. The more potentiality a thing has, the higher its place in the hierarchy.

8. The lowest soul is called the vegetative, or nutritive, soul. This is the minimal level of life (animate matter). The second level is the sensitive, or sentient, soul. The sensitive soul registers information regarding the form of things, but does not absorb or become those things (as when we look at or touch some-

thing). Human souls include a third, higher level of entelechy called the rational soul, which includes the nutritive and sensitive souls plus capacities for analyzing things, understanding various forms of relationships, and making reasoned decisions.

9. According to Aristotle the good is "that at which all things aim." The good at which all things aim is their own entelechy. Because human beings are complex, consisting of all three elements of soul, it is possible to develop physically or emotionally or intellectually and still fail to realize our entelechy.

10. The word Aristotle used that is so often translated as "happiness" is *eudaimonia*. Happiness is almost too bland, however, for eudaimonia implies being really alive as opposed to just existing—being fully aware, vital, alert. Eudaimonia implies exhilaration—great suffering and great joy, great passions, a fully realized life.

11. Aristotelian moderation is based on the concept of wisdom as hitting the mark (*sophrosyne*) between too much and not enough. Virtue consists of hitting the mark of moderation, and vice consists of being off by too much (excess) or too little (deficiency). Virtue is the mean between either extreme.

12. Aristotle taught that happiness requires activity and the happy person must develop good habits and learn practical wisdom. Knowing what is good cannot make us happy unless we have the character (habit) of acting wisely and moderately.

13. Self-realization theories remain popular today. Influential contemporary psychologists advocate self-realization but differ from Aristotle in their emphasis on feelings rather than reason. However, Aristotle's concept of self-realization remains the most thoroughly developed.

Study Questions

1. What is unusual about the nature of the writings attributed to Aristotle?

2. What do scholars mean by saying that Aristotle brought philosophy down to earth? How does this relate to Plato?

3. What is naturalism?

4. Distinguish between form and matter, according to Aristotle.

5. Why does Aristotle characterize things as "formed matter"? Explain.

6. Identify and describe the Four Causes.

7. What is the point of the story about the bricklayers? Explain.

8. What is entelechy and how is it significant to Aristotle's ethics?

9. Describe teleological thinking. Give an example of a teleological explanation.

10. What, according to Aristotle, is the relationship between soul and body?

11. Describe the hierarchy of souls. How does the hierarchy of souls relate to self-realization?

12. What is "the good," according to Aristotle?

13. Discuss Aristotle's use of the term *happiness*. Contrast it with the most common contemporary notion of happiness. Evaluate both.

14. What is *eudaimonia*? Is it the same thing as happiness? Explain.

15. In what sense can Aristotle's position be termed "formal relativism"? Is Aristotle a relativist? Explain.

16. What did Aristotle identify as the highest kind of life? Explain fully.

17. Explain the importance of sophrosyne to happiness.

18. What is the "principle of the mean"? Give one or two examples of using it to evaluate a course of action or moral choice.

19. How do character and habit affect happiness and virtue, according to Aristotle?

20. Give several examples of activities for which there is no mean.

21. Analyze one or two ranges of activity to show how some vices are more virtuous than others.

22. Critics accuse Aristotle of circular reasoning when he attempts to identify goodness by first looking at the good man. How does he solve the problem of studying virtue objectively?

23. Discuss the relationships among action, practical wisdom, and happiness in Aristotle's philosophy.

24. Compare and contrast classical Aristotelian self-realization with contemporary self-realization theories.

25. Using your own educational experiences as a general basis, analyze public education from an Aristotelian perspective.

Epicurus

I have never searched for happiness. Who wants happiness? I have searched for pleasure.

Oscar Wilde

Make haste and enjoy life while you have it. Why care what happens when you are dead?

Lie Zi

Second Interlude

The Hedonist

Nothing is sufficient to someone for whom little is not enough.

Epicurus

What do you want most? If you're like most people, you probably want "to be happy." And what makes you happy? Good grades? Friends? A loving family? Sex? Food? Cars? Clothes? Beaches or mountains? Power? Success? Attention? Although each of us might compose a different list, our lists will all contain things that give us *pleasure*. If we each composed a second list, of things that make us unhappy, it would contain things that cause us *pain*.

An acquaintance of mine has a T-shirt that says "Live To Party!" A few years ago Cyndi Lauper sprang to fame singing "Girls just want to have fun!" Madonna once boasted, "I'm a material girl living in a material world." In commercials, the television camera lingers lovingly on beer in wet, frosty mugs, with thick foam running down the sides. And then there are all those other advertisements, songs, music videos, movies, and books with sensual or luxurious themes.

In 1988 President Ronald Reagan declared drug abuse "the number one problem" in America. Substance abuse remains such a serious problem that in 1993 President Clinton included treatment for it in his proposed plan for national health care. Obviously, most people do not start abusing alcohol or other drugs intending to become addicted. They begin for the promise of pleasure or to numb pain and worry. So even though substance abuse is a serious problem in our society, it is rooted in a common desire to have pleasure or to avoid pain.

Despite three decades of national attention to sex education, unwanted and unplanned pregnancies plague us; near-epidemic rates of chlamydia, hepatitis C, and other sexually transmitted diseases persist. Apparently, even the very real threat of deadly HIV and AIDS infections is not enough to stop whatever impulses and momentary desires cause people to risk so much for perhaps a few moments of pleasure. (And of course, we must not overlook the contributions of alcohol and drug abuse to unsafe sex practices.)

In 1996, in spite of nationwide concerns over the dangers of tobacco, smoking cigars emerged as one of "the" hot new trends as both male and female celebrities took it up, subscribing to glossy magazines devoted entirely to cigars, joining exclusive "smoking clubs" where they could sit comfortably in large leather chairs, puffing on fine cigars and sipping expensive liquors, wines, and "brand-name waters," while enjoying spectacular views of New York, Los Angeles, London, Rome, Paris, and other elegant locales. Today, "upscale" cigar shops are showing up in suburban malls across America, doing very well by selling not just cigars, but expensive cigar lighters, leather cases, hardwood humidors, and other *accöutrements* of the *connoisseûr*. Two of the "hottest" markets are the luxury and "near-luxury" markets for automobiles, sports-utility vehicles, and vans: Infiniti, Lexus, Mercedes, Acura, BMW, Jaguar, Range Rover, Humvee, Land Cruiser, Suburban, and more. Middle- and working-class college students cut corners on other things so they can enjoy three-dollar lattés and cappuccinos and two-dollar biscotti—and so do accountants, clerks, philosophy teachers, and nurses. Sometimes it seems as if everyone has a cellular phone (the slimmer and smaller the better). The increasing popularity of collecting expensive fountain pens has generated new life for shops and catalogues specializing in "fine writing implements": pens, inks, papers, accessories. (Note: Adding "s" to certain words appears to give them a "certain flair, style, or elegance" known as *panache*: coffees, teas, meats, cheeses. . . .)

Eastern Europe has been undergoing remarkable changes for nearly a decade. For many years, the most desired items on the Soviet black market have been Levi's, rock and roll recordings, and other luxury goods. Now as the former Soviet Union struggles to establish a new economy and open itself to greater freedoms, Pepsi Cola, Domino's Pizza, and McDonald's (among others) have established franchises there. A few years ago, former New York governor Mario Cuomo was quoted as saying: "They're running away from communism toward our way of life because of television and basketball. You play basketball in this country for a month, you go back, you're never going to be happy waiting in line for a potato."[1]

Today much of Asia, Mexico, Central and Latin America, and parts of other developing areas are looking more and more like the United States as we all pursue "the good life," the life of pleasure. And why not? America

That pleasure is the goal is proved by the fact that from our youth up we are instinctively attracted to it and when we obtain it seek for nothing more and shun nothing so much as its opposite, pain.

Bruno Bettelheim

Never before has the seductive market way of life held such sway in nearly every sphere of American life. This market way of life promotes addictions to stimulation and obsessions with comfort and convenience. Addictions and obsessions—centered primarily around bodily pleasures and status rankings—constitute market moralities of sorts. The common denominator is a rugged and ragged individualism and rapacious hedonism in quest of a perennial "high" in body and mind.

Cornel West

was founded on the pursuit of happiness. Our Declaration of Independence begins with the announcement that "life, liberty, and the pursuit of happiness" are among our most basic rights. So important was "the pursuit of happiness" to the founders of America that it is characterized as an "unalienable right." An *unalienable* right is the strongest kind there is: It flows from our very nature. Free speech, economic choice, religious liberty, private property, and equality of opportunity are guaranteed in the Constitution *because each is essential to the pursuit of happiness.*

The nature and conditions of happiness have concerned philosophers from all cultures, throughout history. Among the earliest and most persistent responses to the search for happiness is hedonism.

The Hedonistic Vision

HEDONISM

From the Greek root for "pleasure," the general term for any philosophy that says pleasure = good and pain = evil.

PSYCHOLOGICAL HEDONISM

The belief that all decisions are based on considerations of pleasure and pain because it is psychologically impossible for human beings to do otherwise.

ETHICAL HEDONISM

The belief that although it is possible to deliberately avoid pleasure or choose pain, it is morally wrong to do so.

Hedonism, from the Greek root for "pleasure," *hēdonē*, is the general term for any philosophy that says pleasure = good, and pain = evil. For a strict hedonist, nothing that provides pleasure can be bad. Some hedonists stress the pursuit of pleasure and others emphasize avoiding pain.

Philosophers distinguish two main forms of hedonism. **Psychological hedonism** is the belief that all decisions are based on considerations of pleasure and pain, that it is psychologically impossible for human beings to do otherwise. Even acts of self-sacrifice are hedonistic: The self-sacrificer either derives pleasure from being able to sacrifice something for a purpose or else fears the guilt, pain, or damnation that would accompany any other course of action. We may lose sight of the importance of pain and pleasure in our motivations because we use terms like *good* and *bad* or *right* and *wrong* to talk about pleasure and pain.

Ethical hedonism is the belief that although it is possible to deliberately avoid pleasure or choose pain, it is morally wrong to do so. We have a general moral obligation to seek pleasure and avoid pain. We *ought* to enjoy ourselves as much as possible.

Simply put, the hedonist sees the happy life as one possessing the most possible pleasure accompanied by the least possible pain. The pursuit of pleasure, says the hedonist, is our birthright. The baby in its cradle coos when it is cuddled, fed, or played with. It cries when it is uncomfortable. No baby has to be taught this; it "comes with the territory." We have to learn to be honest, to work hard, to delay gratification, but we do not have to be taught to seek pleasure and avoid pain. On the contrary, we have to be forced to go against our basic hedonistic natures.

Ironically, even when we are being discouraged from hedonistic living, we are trained and educated according to hedonistic principles! *Pain* (spanking, detention, no supper) and *pleasure* (hugs, allowances, gifts) are

Suicide and Soup

What would you think of the proposition that the pleasures of a good soup can overcome thoughts of suicide? That's the thrust of the following anecdote reported by one of the most elegant hedonistic writers of the early twentieth century, the Chinese-American scholar Lin Yutang.

Lin writes that one of the greatest of the ancient Chinese poets, Ch'u Yuan (343–290 B.C.), once went through a period of depression so deep that he had to struggle against suicide. He wrote a poem to persuade himself that it was good to be alive. In it he urged his soul to return and not leave his body. Among other things, he reviewed for his soul many of the good things of life:

food, wine, beautiful girls, and music. According to Lin Yutang, one of Ch'u's most convincing arguments is based on the infinite variety of food. Here's part of Arthur Waley's translation:

> Oh Soul, come back to joys
>   beyond telling!
> Where thirty cubits at harvest-
>   time
> The corn is stacked;
> Where pies are cooked of
>   millet and bearded-maize.
> Guests watch the steaming
>   bowls
> And sniff the pungency of
>   peppered herbs.
> The cunning cook adds slices
>   of bird-flesh,
> Pigeon and yellow heron and
>   black-crane.

> They taste the badger stew.
> O Soul, come back to feed on
>   foods you love!
> Next are brought
> Fresh turtle, and sweet
>   chicken cooked in cheese
> Pressed by the men of Ch'u.
> And pickled suckling-pig
> And flesh of whelps floating
>   in liver-sauce
> With salad of minced radishes
>   in brine;
> All served with that hot spice
>   of southernwood
> The land of Wu supplies.
> O Soul, come back and
>   choose the meats you love!

Arthur Waley, *Translations from the Chinese* (New York: Knopf, 1919, 1941).

used to control us. Psychological hedonists cite such patterns as evidence that no one escapes the rule of pain and pleasure. We just alter their sources.

Our hedonistic nature is even reflected in most concepts of heaven and hell. Hell is bad because it is associated with pain and suffering. Heaven is good because in heaven we no longer suffer: Our bodies are perfect; we never have to say good-bye to those we love; we don't have boring jobs. Some pictures of heaven even include golden streets, mansions, clear brooks, delightful food. All include the indescribable *pleasure* of being in God's presence. Many religions see God as a source of pleasure or protection from pain. And according to most religious beliefs, God uses hedonistic principles to reward the good with eternal happiness and punish the bad with eternal pain.

There is ample evidence of our hedonistic natures in other aspects of our lives. We want the pleasures of relationships—not the hassles. In books and magazines, on television, and in psychotherapy, we're counseled to leave our marriages or jobs if they don't make us happy. College courses are often chosen not on the basis of their substance and content, but on

Smoking cigars has become fashionable in recent years. Cigar smoking is so popular now that new, expensive private clubs cater to the well-to-do. In this picture, aficionados enjoy opening-night puffs at the elegant New York City Club Macanudo, described as a "private cigar bar." Do significant social success and wealth always encourage hedonism? What do you think accounts for our fascination with such accoutrements of success as ultra-slim cell phones, luxury vehicles, and, for cigar lovers, gold lighters, teakwood humidors, and twenty-dollar cigars?

Because we cannot relate to the sensuous and material present we are most happy when good things are expected to happen, not when they are happening. We get such a kick out of looking forward to pleasures and rushing to meet them that we can't slow down enough to enjoy them when they come. We are therefore a civilization which suffers from chronic disappointment—a formidable swarm of spoiled children smashing their toys.

Alan Watts

how easy or difficult they are. In poor neighborhoods throughout this country people wear designer jeans and jackets; they carry boom boxes and portable stereos, and wear Air Jordans or Nikes.

There are many ways to explain such a voracious appetite for entertainment, fashion, and luxury items. Hedonists see it as evidence that the pursuit of pleasure is natural and universal. After all, no matter how dismal our lives, we put enormous energies and whatever money we can into pleasure-producing activities. But if the pursuit of pleasure is "natural" and universal and unavoidable, what is there to philosophize about?

The difference between *philosophical* hedonism and the instinctive pursuit of immediate pleasure rests, among other things, on the possibility that while most people *think* they know what they need to be happy, a cursory look around makes it clear that many of us don't. We may be able to provide ourselves with *momentary distractions* or *isolated pleasures*; but that's not the same thing as *being happy*.

So powerful is the desire for happiness through seeking pleasure or avoiding pain that influential and able examples of the archetype of the hedonist can be found in virtually every historical period and culture. But experience suggests that for most people, life remains full of frustration and suffering despite their great efforts to be happy. Thus the hedonistic philosopher argues that the pursuit of pleasure and flight from pain may be universal, but the experience of genuine happiness is not. It does not occur naturally for most people, but is the result of intelligent reflection and careful selection based on practical wisdom. We may all want to be happy, but too few of us achieve our goal. We'll see why as we take a look at Epicurus, one of the most remarkable of the classical sages. But to fully appreciate his refined hedonism, we need to make a quick stop at a more popular expression of hedonism.

Cyrenaic Hedonism

Aristippus (c. 430–350 B.C.) lived in the town of Cyrene on the coast of North Africa in what is now Libya. Cyrene was founded by Greek colonists on the edge of a plateau near the Mediterranean coast. The soil and climate made the area rich in flowers, fruits, and lush vegetation. By the time Aristippus was born, Cyrene was a prosperous city, noted for its marble temples, its opulent public square, and the huge, luxurious homes of its wealthiest citizens. Like ancient Athens, Cyrene's strategic location helped make it a wealthy and exciting trading center.

Aristippus

Aristippus was born with all the advantages such a place had to offer, so perhaps it is not surprising that he was the first philosopher to make a direct statement of hedonism. In fact, from what we know of it, Aristippus's version is probably the purest, most uncompromising statement of the hedonistic vision.

Aristippus was a friendly and clever young man, fond of pleasures of all sorts. He heard about Socrates while attending the Olympic Games with a friend, and was so impressed that he rushed to Athens to meet Socrates. He quickly became a member of the closest, most involved group of his followers, and eventually did some teaching himself. He annoyed some of his Socratic friends, who thought he was behaving like a Sophist, when he began to travel about teaching and collecting higher and higher fees.

Ultimately, Aristippus returned home and opened a school of philosophy in Cyrene. His form of hedonism, called **Cyrenaic hedonism**, takes its name from his hometown. As you get a fuller picture of this philosophy, see if you don't recognize elements of the Cyrenaic archetype all around us.

The Meaning of Life Is Pleasure

As noted in Chapter 3, Socrates evaluated pleasures in terms of their relationship to goodness and truth, and their effect on the soul. Knowledge of goodness and truth was of the highest value for him. Aristippus, on the other hand, was utterly convinced that physical benefits are the highest possible good. As Aristippus observed life in lush Cyrene, he concluded that *pleasure is the principal motive for living and that pleasure is always good—regardless of its source.*

Aristippus thought it was obvious, to anybody who cared to see it, that all people seek pleasure (whether they are aware of it or not). He argued

CYRENAIC HEDONISM

Philosophy that advocates the unreflective pursuit of intense, immediate pleasure; makes no qualitative distinctions among pleasures.

The archetype of the Cyrenaic hedonist can be found in all historical periods—usually with disastrous results.

One of the worst sins Dante could think of was to sulk in the sunlight. To those who did he assigned the eternal punishment of wallowing in the mud.

Irwin Edman

It is a hard matter, my fellow citizens, to argue with the belly, since it has no ears.

Cato the Elder

that the meaning of life must be discerned by observing our *actual behavior*. Doing so reveals that the meaning of life is pleasure. The simple, healthy, proper course of life, according to Aristippus, is to follow our natural desires openly, without guilt or apology, and learn how to most enjoy ourselves. Since pleasure is the natural goal of all life, we should try to have as much intense, sensual pleasure as we can. The Chinese-American philosopher **Lin Yutang (1895–1976)** expresses the sensual quality of hedonism especially well:

> Just as it is impossible for me to say whether I love my children physically or spiritually when I hear their chattering voices or when I see their plump legs, so I am totally unable to distinguish between the joys of the flesh and the spirit. Does anybody ever love a woman spiritually without loving her physically? And is it so easy a matter for a man to analyze and separate the charms of the woman he loves—like laughter, smiles, a way of tossing one's head, a certain attitude toward these things?[2]

The Cyrenaics asserted that because sensory pleasures are more intense than mental or emotional ones, they are the best of all. Therefore, physical pleasure is superior to all other things. Only physical pleasures make life exciting, dynamic, worth living. Not only that, but actual pleasures of the moment are much more desirable than potential pleasures that may

"WHAT'S THE SENSE OF HAVING A GOOD TIME
IF YOU DON'T KNOW YOU HAD A GOOD TIME?"

Reprinted with special permission of King Features Syndicate, Inc.

There is no such thing as pure pleasure; some anxiety always goes with it.

Ovid

(or may not) occur in the future. In the first place, we are certain only of the present; the future may not even come. And besides, things may be different for us in the future. Today I may think that I would love to have a Porsche. Suppose I save my money, work extra hours—in short, suffer now for the pleasure of a Porsche later. I might die before I get my Porsche. Then what good was my suffering? My tastes might change while I struggle to save my money, so that by the time I can have my Porsche it no longer pleases me. Or the way Porsches are made might change so that I don't enjoy mine once I have it. Thus the wisest course is to choose the most pleasure right now, and buy the most enjoyable car I can today.

Men who are devoid of integrity and who live for food and nothing else . . . surely they are no better than beasts? If you are no better than a dog or chicken, others will not rely on you. Danger and disgrace will then befall you.

Lie Zi

Knowledge and Pleasure

Cyrenaic hedonists were not interested in anything that wasn't directly related to the pursuit of pleasure. Consequently, they were not interested in the study of nature or mathematics, and their only interest in logic was a very basic concern with the subjective nature of experience.

The Cyrenaics taught that our subjective sensations are knowable, but that a complete understanding of their objective causes is impossible. The belief that we can *know* what pleases or displeases us at the moment, but only *speculate* on their objective natures, is known as the problem of **subjectivism.** Perhaps the simplest way to understand the problem of subjectivism in relation to hedonism is in reference to tastes in food. Many people like licorice or chickory or grits or jalapeño peppers, for instance. Many others do not. Now, certain questions can be raised in regard to what any one of these foods *really* tastes like. I may find this jalapeño jelly mild. You

SUBJECTIVISM

Belief that we can know only our own sensations, not their objective causes.

may insist that it's hot. Are we both having the same taste experience but giving it different names? Or are we each actually tasting something quite different? Even if we both call the same thing "sweet," how can we be sure that "sweet" refers to the same sensation?

The consequence of such a view is that *whatever feels good is good*. Lacking any objective standard of comparison, the Cyrenaic hedonist concludes that the individual is the measure: of that which is pleasure, that it is pleasure; of that which is pain, that it is pain. And since any pleasure is by definition good, it follows that I ought to be doing whatever I enjoy doing. The principle of maximizing pleasure and minimizing pain is known as **hedonistic utility**.

The idea of deliberately maximizing pleasure and minimizing pain transforms psychological hedonism into ethical hedonism. Although we are, by nature, predisposed to seek pleasure and avoid pain, some of us become confused and our instincts and habits get corrupted. Hence we attempt to stifle the pursuit of pleasure because we see it as somehow sinful or immoral. We may actually add pain to our lives if we think that by suffering we become purified or ennobled. Our natural hedonism may be subdued by childhood training, religious indoctrination, or a puritanical culture. Thus, the ethical hedonist argues, it makes sense to advise people that they *ought* to do what they are by nature trying to do: enjoy themselves.

The Cyrenaics considered all pleasures to be of equal kind; they had no hierarchy of pleasures. Any distinction between "good" and "bad" pleasures was as absurd and contradictory as distinguishing between good and bad sins or good and bad virtues. The only difference among pleasures, then, is their intensity: *Whatever pleases me most at the moment is the highest good there can be.* Perhaps this is part of what's implied by the beer commercial that advises: "You only go around once, so grab all the gusto you can get." No pleasure can be "sick" in such a value system. Only being victimized and controlled by any pleasure is "sick." No enjoyment can be wrong. No passion is evil in itself. Only loss of self-control is wrong, for loss of self-control leads to less pleasure.

The Self Is Utterly Free

In *The Culture of Narcissism* (1979), history professor Christopher Lasch discusses what he calls the "new narcissists," individuals who live only for themselves and for the moment. The "new narcissists" feel free to walk away from social roles such as parent, student, or citizen whenever they become too confining or boring and pursue "self-fulfillment," "personal growth," and so forth, as they wish. Lasch writes:

> Having no hope of improving their lives in ways that matter, people have convinced themselves that what matters is psychic self-

---

HEDONISTIC UTILITY

Principle of maximizing pleasure and minimizing pain.

Do not craze yourself with thinking, but go about your business anywhere. Life is not intellectual or critical, but sturdy. Its chief good is for well-mixed people who can enjoy what they find, without question.

Ralph Waldo Emerson

improvement: getting in touch with their feelings, eating health food, taking lessons in ballet or belly-dancing, immersing themselves in the wisdom of the East, jogging, learning how to "relate," overcoming the "fear of pleasure." . . .

To live for the moment is the prevailing passion—to live for your-self, not for your predecessors or posterity. We are fast losing the sense of historical continuity [emphasis added].[3]

We can compare Lasch's observation with a conversation Xenophon reported in which he, Socrates, and Aristippus discussed the nature of the city-state. Socrates believed in an ordered city-state in which some command and others obey. Aristippus rejected both roles. He wanted no part of being in control, since political power and responsibility only create problems and obligations. He also rejected being controlled:

"No," replied Aristippus, "for my part I am no candidate for slavery; but there is, as I hold, a middle path in which I am desirous of walking. That way leads neither through control nor slavery, but through liberty, which is the royal road to happiness. . . . My plan for avoiding such treatment is this. I do not shut myself up within a city-state, but am a stranger in every land."[4]

In other words, participation in public life is a "hassle." Being a fully involved citizen usually interferes with the Cyrenaic's pursuit of enjoyment. The only reason for people to get into politics is if they derive pleasure from it. We have no social or civic obligations, according to Aristippus.

To be a "stranger in every land" is to be a free *individual.* By extension, the Cyrenaic can also claim to be "a stranger in every relationship." Why should I try to work through the difficult spots in marriage or parenting if my only purpose in life is to achieve as little pain and as much pleasure as possible, *now, for me*? *My only obligation is to enjoy every moment.*

Epicurus

Though **Epicurus** (341–270 B.C.) was born in the Asia Minor city of Samos, he was an Athenian citizen because his father had moved to Samos as an Athenian colonist. When he was eighteen years old, Epicurus went to Athens in order to complete the two years of military service required of Athenian males. The Macedonian king of Greece, Alexander the Great, had just died, and the Athenians, who had resented his rule, revolted against the regent Alexander had imposed on them. It took less than a year for this revolt to be crushed, but Epicurus drew an important lesson from it: Political activities and ambitions are pointless.

> The problem about appealing ultimately to human desires is that this appears to exclude rational criticism of ethical motivations at the most fundamental level.
>
> *Thomas Nagel*

> But myself, I classify with those who wish for a life of the greatest ease and pleasure that can be had.
>
> *Xenophon*

Epicurus

And so we speak of plea-
sure as the starting point
and the goal of the happy
life because we realize that
it is our primary native
good, because every act of
choice and aversion originates with it, and because
we come back to it when
we judge every good by
using the pleasure feeling as
our criterion.

Epicurus

Epicurus remained in Athens for a time, and studied with major followers of both Plato and Aristotle. He never accepted Plato's philosophy
and came to reject Aristotle's as well. He referred to himself as self-taught
and never acknowledged any philosophical teacher or master. He saw himself as a moral reformer who had discovered a brand-new message, one
that could save others from unhappiness:

> Vain is the word of a philosopher which does not heal any suffering
> of man. For just as there is no profit in medicine if it does not expel
> the diseases of the body, so there is no profit in philosophy either if
> it does not expel the suffering of the mind.[5]

Epicurus left Athens and for some years taught in outlying cities. But
Athens remained the cultural and intellectual center of the Greek-influenced
world. The two most important schools of the era were there: Plato's
Academy and Aristotle's Lyceum. They attracted the finest minds of the
time. It is not surprising, then, that Epicurus returned to Athens to establish his own school.[6]

Epicurus, then thirty-five years old, had refined and developed his philosophy and had already established an impressive reputation as a teacher.
By the mere fact of moving his school to Athens, he directly challenged
and provoked the philosophical establishment represented by Plato and
Aristotle. His move signaled the beginning of a genuine intellectual revolution.[7] Epicurus was convinced that he had something brand-new to present. He viewed Platonic and Aristotelian philosophies as outdated, overly
theoretical, and hence irrelevant to daily life and happiness. Epicurus's attack was aided by the internal quarreling and disagreements weakening
those schools.

The Garden

Epicurus called his school the Garden. A serene retreat from the social,
political, and even philosophical turmoil of Athens, Epicurus's Garden became as well known for good living and pleasant socializing as it was for
its philosophy.

One of the unusual features of the Garden was that it welcomed everyone. It was one of the very few places in Greece where women were allowed and encouraged to interact with men *as equals*. By taking as obvious
the essential equality and dignity of women, Epicurus's Garden provided
a truly unique experience for *both* men and women, since elsewhere men,
as well as women, were denied the opportunity to experience equality.
Epicurus also made no distinctions based on social status or race. He accepted all who came to learn: prostitutes, housewives, slaves, aristocrats.
His favorite pupil was his own slave, Mysis.[8] Epicurus took as his mistress
a courtesan (a kind of prostitute) named Leontium, and under his nurturing influence she wrote several books.

Guest, thou shalt be happy
here, for here happiness is
esteemed the highest good.

*Motto hung over the
entrance to the Garden*

As you might expect, rumors were rampant about exactly what went on in the Garden. We can lose sight of the truly radical nature of Epicurus's understanding and tolerance if we judge it only in light of today's more enlightened attitudes. But in his time, the mere acceptance of all races, sexes, and social classes would have been enough to brand Epicurus as a dangerous and ungrateful rebel, regardless of his philosophical ideas. Yet he went well beyond theoretical tolerance, actively welcoming and encouraging all comers. Even in our own time, such an attitude is often met with fear and criticism.

Epicurus the Sage

Epicurus was generous and friendly in other matters as well. He regularly contributed his own money to the group and had a reputation for being a sympathetic companion and reasonable adviser.[9] Epicurus himself lived a simple and moderate life. He took as his motto "Live unobtrusively" (*lathe biosas*). He sought peace of mind, called *ataraxia*. He avoided the commotion of political involvement and remained detached from the hubbub of the world. It was reported that his regular diet consisted of modest amounts of bread, cheese, a little wine, and water.

His enemies claimed that he overindulged when he could get away with it and lived modestly only when others were watching and for show, but Diogenes Läertius disputes this. Epicurus himself was quite eloquent in this regard: "My body exalts in living delicately on bread and water and it rejects the pleasures of luxury, not in themselves, but because of the trouble that follows upon them."[10]

More than just a thinker or teacher (though he did write many books), Epicurus was regarded as a sage by his friends and pupils. He taught in the Garden by example as well as by word for thirty-six years. His followers memorized his "golden maxims" and tried to model their lives after his. Many of them were inspired by his courage in the face of chronic ill health; he was apparently unable even to walk for many years because of gout. His disciples said that he continued to practice his philosophy and teach wisely right up to his death at the age of seventy-one. Even in his last, painful hours he thought of his friends, writing from his deathbed:

> I write to you on this happy day which is the last of my life. The obstruction of my bladder, and the internal pains, have reached the extreme point, but there is marshaled against them the delight of my mind in thinking over our talks together. Take care of Metrodorus' [his most famous pupil] children in a way worthy of your lifelong devotion to me and to philosophy.[11]

The Roman philosopher Seneca said that Epicurus's pupils saw him as a god among men, and that after his death their motto was "Live as though the eye of Epicurus were upon thee." He left his property to the Garden, in

Epicurus.—Yes, I am proud of the fact that I experience the character of Epicurus quite differently from perhaps everybody else. . . . Such happiness could be invented only by a man who was suffering continually.

Friedrich Nietzsche

How many things I can do without!

Socrates

the hope "that all those who study philosophy may never be in want . . . so far as our power to prevent it may extend."[12] All in all, he was a gentle, friendly philosopher, who practiced what he believed to be true and tried to share his wisdom with others.

Epicurean Philosophy

The idea of a Being who interferes in the world is absolutely impossible. . . . A God who rewards and punishes is unthinkable because man acts in accordance with an inner and outer necessity, and would, in the eyes of God, be as little responsible as an inanimate object for the movements it makes.

Albert Einstein

Epicurus had studied the ideas of the materialistic philosopher **Democritus (c. 460–370 B.C.)**, which were based on the principle "Nothing can come from nothing." Following Democritus, Epicurus reasoned along these lines: If it were possible for something to come from nothing, then there would be no order in nature. A shoe might come from a stone, a pig from a daffodil. Put another way, to say that something can come from nothing amounts to saying that things can just pop into existence out of nowhere for no reason. Further, Epicurus reasoned, "Nothing can be dissolved into nothing." If things could break down into nothing (no-thing whatsoever), the universe would disappear, since each dying and decaying thing would ultimately disappear.

Epicurus says:

The sum total of things was always such as it is now, and such as it will ever remain. For there is nothing into which it can change. For outside the sum of things there is nothing which could enter into it and bring about change.[13]

This means that all existence shares a common base: material atoms. Even gods and souls are made of matter. According to Epicurus, it is logically absurd to speak of existence without speaking of existing in some space. And it is equally absurd to speak of existing "immaterially," without a bodily component (no matter how submicroscopic):

Aristippus was only concerned with the body, as though we did not somehow have a soul.

Cicero

Hence those who maintain that the soul is incorporeal [spiritual or non-material] speak foolishly: if it were so, it could neither act nor be acted upon, while we can clearly see both these properties [the power to act and to be acted upon] in the soul.[14]

Epicurus was not an original thinker in this area. He agreed in essence with Democritus and used his materialistic doctrine to make philosophical and psychological points. (See the First Interlude.)

Democritus had claimed that if *everything*—including soul or spirit—is really material, then God is too. If nothing can exist outside of the sum totality of things, the whole, then God must be part of the natural order. According to this line of reasoning, it is unintelligible and self-contradictory to speak of God, or anything, existing apart from nature. Where could God

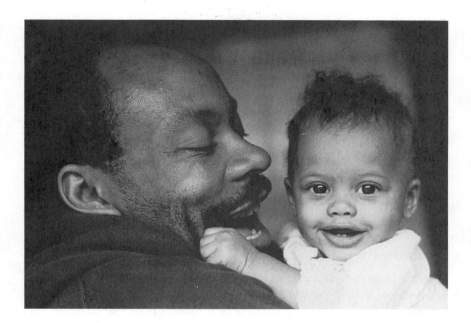

"I sometimes think what a terrible punishment it would be for a ghost or an angel to have no body . . . Terribly sad it would be if we should one day return to this earth as ghosts and move silently into our children's bedroom, to see a child lying there in bed and have no hands to fondle him and no arms to clasp him, no chest for his warmth to penetrate to, no round hollow between cheek and shoulder for him to nestle against, and no ears to hear his voice."

Lin Yutang

be? If the soul (or mind) is not physical, how, for example, can drinking beer (a physical act) intoxicate it?

Lin Yutang expresses this sense of the union of "spirit and flesh" exceptionally well:

> The most obvious fact which philosophers refuse to see is that we have got a body. Tired of seeing our moral imperfections and our savage instincts and impulses, sometimes our preachers wish that we were made like angels, and yet we are at a total loss to imagine what the angel's life would be like. We either give the angels a body and a shape like our own—except for a pair of wings—or we don't. . . . I sometimes think that it is an advantage even for angels to have a body with the five senses. If I were to be an angel, I should like to have a school-girl complexion, but how am I going to have a school-girl complexion without a skin? I still should like to drink a glass of tomato juice or iced orange juice, but how am I going to appreciate iced orange juice without having thirst? How would an angel paint without pigment, sing without the hearing of sounds, smell the fine morning air without a nose? How would he enjoy the immense satisfaction of scratching an itch, if his skin doesn't itch? And what a terrible loss in the capacity for happiness that would be! Either we have to have bodies and have all our bodily wants satisfied, or else we are pure spirits and have no satisfactions at all. All satisfactions imply want.

It is not what earnest people renounce that makes me pity them, it is what they work for. . . . So much tension is hysterical and degrading; nothing is ever gained by it worth half what it spoils. Wealth is dismal and poverty cruel unless both are festive. There is no cure for birth and death save to enjoy the interval.

George Santayana

No civilized man ever regrets a pleasure, and no uncivilized man ever knows what a pleasure is.

Oscar Wilde

I sometimes think what a terrible punishment it would be for a ghost or an angel to have no body, to look at a stream of cool water and have no feet to plunge into it and get a delightful cooling sensation from it, to see a dish of Peking or Long Island duck and have no tongue to taste it, to see crumpets and have no teeth to chew them, to see the beloved faces of our dear ones and have no emotions to feel toward them. Terribly sad it would be if we should one day return to this earth as ghosts and move silently into our children's bedroom, to see a child lying there in bed and have no hands to fondle him and no arms to clasp him, no chest for his warmth to penetrate to, no round hollow between cheek and shoulder for him to nestle against, and no ears to hear his voice.[15]

Freedom from Religion

Epicurus believed that happiness results from peace of mind, or tranquillity. As he studied the world around him, he concluded that perhaps nothing was more confusing and disturbing to others than fear of death and fear of the gods. Epicurus rejected both concerns on "scientific grounds." As a *strict materialist*, he rejected the possibility of a supernatural (nonmaterial) existence.

Apart from any logical difficulties with theories about the supernatural, just raising theological issues is frustrating and disturbing to most people. People have always argued with, lectured, tortured, and condemned one another over theological disagreements. If the purpose of life is the happiness that flows from a serene mind, then what could be more important than to free ourselves from this distressing quality of religion? Epicurus did not deny the existence of God (or gods). What he did, however, was just as upsetting to many: He rejected the most common conceptions of God.

Faith in immortality was born of the greed of unsatisfied people who make unwise use of the time that nature has allotted us. . . . For the wise man one human life is sufficient, and a stupid man will not know what to do with eternity.

Epicurus

From the time of Homer, the Greeks believed that good or bad circumstances resulted from the favor or disfavor of the gods. The gods of Olympus had to be worshiped, bribed, and flattered when they decided to meddle in human affairs. The struggle between moral skepticism and conventional morality that we saw in the chapters on the Sophists and Socrates continued during Epicurus's time.

One common reaction to political upheaval, social unrest, and intellectual doubt (such as that occurring in Greece at the time) is a renewal of religious fervor among some groups, often accompanied by an increase in superstitious beliefs and practices. Many Greeks attributed practically everything to divine punishments or rewards. Everything was "prophetic," every decision full of risk: If the soul is immortal, then any failure to appease the gods could result in horrible punishment now or after death. So the believer had to be very sure that his or her choice of belief and prac-

Since 1986, Sikh and Hindu extremists have clashed in India. In this 1987 picture, anti-Sikh rioters protest the killing of 34 Hindu bus passengers by Sikh terrorists. Today, religious disagreements exacerbate tensions in Eastern Europe, the Middle East, parts of Africa, and, of course, the United States. Such "holy wars" led Epicurus and Lucretius to seek to "free humankind from religion."

tice was correct. As Epicurus saw it, religion created disagreement, anxiety, and fear. And this is why he considered his first task to be freeing us from the tyranny of religion.

Epicurus argued that the qualities attributed to the gods—jealousy, favoritism, inconsistency, susceptibility to praise and flattery, and so on—are too much like the qualities attributed to human beings.

> The gods do indeed exist, since our knowledge of them is a matter of clear and distinct perception; but they are not like what the masses suppose them to be, because most people do not maintain a pure conception of the gods. The [sacrilegious] man is not the person who destroys the gods of the masses but the person who imposes the ideas of the masses on the gods. The opinions held by most people about the gods are not true conceptions of them but fallacious notions, according to which awful penalties are meted out to the evil and the greatest of blessings to the good. The masses, by assimilating the gods in every respect to their own moral qualities, accept deities similar to themselves and regard anything not of this sort as alien.[16]

If there are gods, Epicurus reasoned, surely they are happy. If they are incapable of being happy they cannot be gods. And if the gods are to be

Epicurus saved mankind from religion.

Lucretius

The blessed and indestructible being of the divine has no concerns of its own, nor does it take trouble for others.

Epicurus

happy, they cannot depend on human behavior or beliefs, which are unreliable and inconsistent. Further, the gods cannot be concerned with rewarding or punishing human beings, since that would add worry to their own lives and so detract from their peace of mind. So, Epicurus concluded, the gods must be indifferent to human affairs if they are to be happy. Therefore, the gods do not interfere in the daily affairs of human beings.

The very first of Epicurus's *Leading Doctrines* is:

> The blessed and indestructible being of the divine has no concerns of its own, nor does it make trouble for others. It is not affected by feelings of anger or benevolence, because these are found where there is lack of strength.[17]

In other words, the divine nature is not troubled of itself and it causes no trouble for others. The divine nature is not influenced by either anger or favoritism, since to be influenced by others is characteristic only of the weak and unhappy. It is easier for us to be happy when God is indifferent to us than when He takes an interest in us. Epicurus has kept his promise. Given his radical conception of God, he has indeed freed us from religion.

Quality versus Quantity

Neither life nor death is good or bad of itself, Epicurus said; only the quality of our pleasures or pains is important. This is a major departure from Cyrenaic hedonism's emphasis on intensity (quantity). Rather than seek to have the most of anything, including the longest possible life span, the wise and sophisticated person chooses to have the finest.

Being asked what was the difference between the wise man and the unwise, Aristippus said, "Strip them both and send them among strangers and you will know." To one who boasted that he could drink a great deal without getting drunk, his rejoinder was, "and so can a mule."

Diogenes Läertius

> Most people, however, recoil from death as though it were the greatest of evils; at other times they welcome it as the end-all of life's ills. The sophisticated person, on the other hand, neither begs off from living nor dreads not living. Life is not a stumbling block to him, nor does he regard not being alive as any sort of evil. As in the case of food he prefers the most savory dish to merely the larger portion, so in the case of time, he garners to himself the most agreeable moments rather than the longest span.[18]

Philosophers distinguish between what is desired and what is desirable. Practically anything can be desired by someone somewhere. But that does not mean that it is desirable. This distinction goes beyond Aristippus's "go for the gusto" to a much more disciplined and subtle concept. In Epicurus's words:

> Because of the very fact that pleasure is our primary and congenital good we do not select every pleasure; *there are times when we forgo certain pleasures, particularly when they are followed by too much unpleasantness. Furthermore, we regard certain states of pain as*

Truly Happy Moments

To me, for instance, the truly happy moments are: when I get up in the morning after a night of perfect sleep and sniff the morning air and there is an expansiveness in the lungs, when I feel inclined to inhale deeply and there is a fine sensation of movement around the skin and muscles of the chest, and when, therefore, I am fit for work; or when I hold a pipe in my hand and rest my legs on a chair, and the tobacco burns slowly and evenly; or when I am travelling on a summer day, my throat parched with thirst, and I see a beautiful clear spring, whose very sound makes me happy, and I take off my socks and shoes and dip my feet in the delightful, cool water; or when after a perfect dinner I lounge in an armchair, when there is no one I hate to look at in the company and conversation rambles off at a light pace with the world; or when on a summer afternoon I see black clouds gathering on the horizon and know for certain a July shower is coming in a quarter of an hour, but being ashamed to be seen going out in the rain without an umbrella, I hastily set out to meet the shower halfway across the fields and come home drenched through and through and tell my family that I was simply caught by the rain.

Lin Yutang
The Importance of Living (New York: John Day, 1937), p. 127.

preferable to pleasures, particularly when greater satisfaction results from our having submitted to discomforts for a long period of time. Thus every pleasure is a good by reason of its having a nature akin to our own, but not every pleasure is desirable. In like manner every state of pain is an evil, but not all pains are uniformly to be rejected. At any rate, it is our duty to judge all such cases by measuring pleasures against pains, with a view to their respective assets and liabilities, inasmuch as we do experience the good as being bad at times and, contrariwise, the bad as being good [emphasis added].[19]

Less Is More

A life of extremes almost always causes avoidable sufferings. Some are obvious: obesity or anorexia, sloth or stress, bankruptcy, unrelenting pressures to "keep up with the Joneses," and ultimately even boredom. A life of disciplined moderation avoids the excesses of overindulgence or asceticism (denying all pleasures). In the long run, according to Epicurus, the quiet pleasures of moderation produce the finest life.

> We consider limitation of the appetites a major good, and we recommend this practice not for the purpose of enjoying just a few things and no more but rather for the purpose of enjoying those few in case we do not have much. We are firmly convinced that those who need expensive fare least are the ones who relish it most keenly and that a natural way of life is easily procured, while trivialities are hard to

All bodily suffering is negligible; for that which causes intense pain has a brief duration, and that which endures long in the flesh causes mild pain.

Epicurus

No one was ever better for sexual indulgence, and it is well if he be no worse.

Epicurus

come by. Plain foods afford pleasure equivalent to that of a sumptuous diet, provided that the pains of [abject poverty] are wholly eliminated. Barley bread and water yield the peak of pleasure whenever a person who needs them sets them in front of himself. Hence becoming habituated to a simple rather than a lavish way of life provides us with the full complement of health; it makes a person ready for the necessary business of life; it puts us in a position of advantage when we happen upon sumptuous fare at intervals and prepares us to be fearless in facing fortune.[20]

Friendship

Epicurus founded the Garden to teach that only the wise, fully aware individual will be truly happy. Happiness cannot come from the gods, nor can it come from society or political action. The only truly useful and effective bond among individuals is friendship. Epicurean friendship is a free bond uniting individuals who share similar feelings, values, and lifestyles.[21] In true friendship, nothing can be imposed that is not natural and proper for each individual. In this way, nothing violates the essence of the individual. As Giovanni Reale notes, "Epicurus sees almost another self in the friend."[22] Epicurus transformed the notion of friendship into a way of bringing out the true self in each individual.

Even though everything Epicurus wrote fell under the law of hedonistic utility (maximize pleasure, minimize pain), he took care to treat friendship as something special:

Although no words are spoken, there can be tacit understanding of another. A friend after one's own heart is hard to find. If you have got such a friend, what more can be lacking?

Lie Zi

The virtuous man cultivates above all wisdom and friendship; and of these the one is a mortal good, the other is immortal.[23]

Every friendship is *desirable of itself* even if it has begun from utility.[24]

He is no friend who is continually asking for help, nor he who never associates help with friendship. For the one barters kindly feelings for a practical return and the other destroys the hope of every good for the future.[25]

Friendship can go around the earth, proclaiming to us all to wake up in order to give joy to each other.[26]

The Epicurean Fallacy

Perhaps you associate the term *Epicurean* with expensive tastes, exotic food and drink, elegant clothing, and a life devoted to the pursuit of such pleasures. If so, you are not alone. Even in Epicurus's time, many people mistakenly thought that Epicureanism was a philosophy of expensive self-indulgence. The **Epicurean fallacy** is the error of confusing the active pursuit of specialized pleasures with disciplined moderation and restraint. But for Epicurus, the highest pleasures are intellectual, and the greatest good is peace of mind, not intense or exquisite physical pleasure.

> Thus when I say that pleasure is the goal of living I do not mean the pleasures of libertines or the pleasures inherent in positive enjoyment, as is supposed by certain persons who are ignorant of our doctrine or who are not in agreement with it or who interpret it perversely. I mean, on the contrary, the pleasure that consists in freedom from bodily pain and mental agitation. The pleasant life is not the product of one drinking party after another or of sexual intercourse with women and boys or of the seafood and other delicacies afforded by a luxurious table. On the contrary, it is the result of sober thinking—namely, investigation of the reasons for every act of choice and aversion and elimination of those false ideas about the gods and death which are the chief source of mental disturbances.[27]

EPICUREAN FALLACY

Error of confusing the active pursuit of specialized pleasures with Epicurus's philosophy of disciplined moderation and restraint.

Commentary

There is a problem with Cyrenaic hedonism that you may already have identified: the unreflective pursuit of pleasure tends to backfire. Living for the moment sounds good, but more often than not, tomorrow tends to arrive with a hefty price tag. Partying students tend to flunk out of school

The Philosophical Entertainer

Alan Watts (1915–1973) was an interesting figure who rose to prominence in the 1960s. After becoming an Episcopal priest, he gradually turned to Eastern philosophy and religion, founding the American Academy of Asian Studies in San Francisco during the 1950s. After leaving the priesthood, Watts became a popularizer of Zen Buddhism and then Taoism. Referring to himself as a "philosophical entertainer," Watts lived an increasingly hedonistic life. He advocated free love and Asian attire, praising, for example, the sensuous joys of the kimono's freedom and its silky, colorful beauty. He contrasted this with the "uptight," "unnatural," restrictive nature of Western dress, comparing the comfort of sandals to the torture of oxfords and high heels.

Watts is at his best in "Murder in the Kitchen," in *Does It Matter?* An excerpt follows:

. . . For the perfect accomplishment of any art, you must get the feeling of the eternal present in your bones—for it is the secret of proper timing. No rush. No dawdle. Just the sense of flowing with the course of events in the same way that you dance to music, neither trying to outpace it nor lagging behind. Hurrying and delaying are alike ways of trying to resist the present. . . . To try to have time, that is, to move as quickly as possible into the future gives you abstract food instead of real food. Instant coffee, for example, is a well-deserved punishment for being in a hurry to reach the future. So are TV dinners. So are the warmed over nastinesses usually served on airplanes, which taste like the plastic trays and dishes on which they are served. So is the meat which is not roasted but heated through in thirty-second electronic ovens. So are mixtures of grape juice and alcohol, prepared in concrete vaults, pretending to be wine. . . .

Abstractionists would, if possible, save time by eating the menu instead of the dinner. . . .

or end up in dead-end jobs or are arrested for driving under the influence or become burned out and depressed. One day I turn off the football game and notice that my wife no longer loves me and my children are in trouble. Beer and pizza no longer cut it. What then?

Contemporary hedonists point out that most of us actually do a pretty poor job of pursuing pleasure. The drawbacks of unrefined Cyrenaicism are obvious. Such a life is little more than an animal existence, reduced to the indiscriminate satisfaction of urges as they arise. Who but a glutton would prefer lots of fast food to a smaller amount of gourmet fare? What kind of person would prefer hundreds of sexual partners to one fine friendship? More is not necessarily better; instant is often inferior; the pleasures of the moment often have some long-term negative consequence.

More significantly, the hedonist can point to the rather shabby quality of life we settle for. Crowded highways, noisy cities, and a polluted environment rob us of pleasurable experiences. Yet even when we consciously try to add pleasure to our lives, we may be overwhelmed by mediocrity. We can embark on a cross-country odyssey but repeat the limited experiences we have at home by staying at bland motel chains, eating at fran-

Another way of eating the menu is preferring money to wealth—a psychic disorder directly related to the hallucination that time is a physical reality. To be fair, there are still some substantial and excellent products for sale in our supermarkets, but if you are bewitched by money, what happens? You take your loaded cart to the cashier, who clicks out a long strip of paper and says, "Thirty dollars and twenty-five cents, please!" You are suddenly depressed at having to part with so much "wealth"—not realizing that your wealth is now in the shopping bags and that you are going to walk out with it. For the money was a future, a "promise to pay," an abstraction now converted into present and substantial reality—and you are unhappy because you have exchanged the expectation of good things to come for actual goods!

Thus I have promised myself that when I reach the age of seventy, I shall retire to a mountain slope near the ocean and raise a small garden of herbs—culinary, medicinal, and psychedelic. Beside the garden I shall build a redwood barn where bunches of drying plants will hang from the beams, and where long shelves will be lined with jars and bottles of dulcamara and spikenard, ginseng and aloes-wood, lobelia, mandragora, and cannabis, pennyroyal, horehound, and meadowsweet. There also I shall maintain an alchemist's laboratory-cum-kitchen with a library, and if the world presses too much in on me, my wife will respond to unwanted visitors in the words of Chia Tao's poem "Searching for the Hermit in Vain":

The Master's gone alone
Herb-picking, somewhere
    on the mount,
Cloud-hidden, where-
    abouts unknown.

Alan Watts
"Murder in the Kitchen," in *Does It Matter?* (New York: Vintage, 1970), pp. 33, 34, 35, 36, 55.

chised coffee shops and fast-food outlets, watching the same TV shows we do at home, listening to nearly identical radio stations, and shopping for the same brands in St. Louis that are available in Boise. Would a real hedonist prefer this safety, predictability, mediocrity?

Most of us choose our pleasures poorly. Lin and Watts (see boxes) were both convinced that America would be a much saner, healthier place if it were honestly and openly and wisely hedonistic. That is, rather than waste our time eating pap, listening to repetitive, copycat music, wearing the same clothes as everyone else, a gloriously, richly hedonistic society would reflect variety, quality, and joy—genuine diversity.

It is difficult to classify Lin Yutang or Alan Watts as strictly Epicurean or Cyrenaic hedonists, because both systems are probably inadequate guides to the good life. Epicureanism robs us of too much vigor and variety. It is a philosophy of retreat, one might even say of fear. The Epicurean's efforts to avoid pain can lead to a withdrawal from life, a leveling of emotion that extracts a high price for tranquillity.

Cyrenaicism, on the other hand, provides a balance against living vicariously. When we reduce our lives to a mad dash to save time, when most

Happiness, I have discovered, is nearly always a rebound from hard work. . . . For happiness must be tricked!

David Grayson

When someone brought his son as a pupil, [Aristippus] asked a fee of 500 drachmae. The father objected, "For that sum I can buy a slave." "Then do so," was [Aristippus's] reply, "and you will have two."

Diogenes Läertius

HEDONISTIC PARADOX

The harder we try to be happy, the harder it is to be happy.

of our experiences come from television, and we avoid the touch and taste and smell of life, we rob ourselves.

Why must we choose between safety and excess? If hedonism can be made into a viable philosophy, it will probably have to be as a balance between Cyrenaicism and Epicureanism. But there remain serious objections to hedonism in either form.

Aristippus was indifferent to social and political concerns, and Epicurus was perhaps too tempted by the Garden—tendencies that severely limit their philosophies. They also have the same problem the Sophists had: There is no criterion for condemning behavior that harms others. The only prohibition the hedonist can offer is trivial: We shouldn't harm others if doing so will cause us pain. But this position is amoral by most standards, since the moral dimension of life is usually thought to include duties and obligations to ourselves *and* others. And wisdom, as the *sophos* knew, always includes a moral dimension.

Why advocate hedonism if by nature we all seek pleasure and avoid pain? There is no more point to advising us to do this than there is to advising us to eat. The hedonist might respond that just because we are compelled by nature to eat, it does not follow that we eat wisely or well. Similarly, there is much to gain from learning how to pursue pleasure wisely. This leads to a last comment.

Moral philosophers talk about the **hedonistic paradox**: The harder we try to be happy, the harder it is to be happy. Put differently, if I make having a good time the most important thing in my life, it becomes more difficult to do than if I pursue a variety of interests and goals, and have a good time along the way. We have probably all had the experience of anticipating some special occasion to such a degree that once the event arrived we were somehow disappointed.

Philosophers and armchair psychologists have long known that the most fulfilling lives are rarely hedonistic. Happiness seems to be a by-product of other things. That is not to say that hedonism has no merit, for it is as easy to lose sight of what is genuinely pleasurable as it is to be hypnotized by the mindless pursuit of pleasure.

The Stoic

Epictetus and
Marcus Aurelius

You shame yourself, my soul, you shame yourself, and you will have no further opportunity to respect yourself; the life of every man is short and yours is almost finished while you do not respect yourself but allow your happiness to depend upon . . . others.

Marcus Aurelius, Emperor of Rome

STOICISM

Philosophy that counsels self-control, detachment, and acceptance of one's fate as identified by the objective use of reason.

STOIC

Individual who attempts to live according to Stoic doctrine.

I t's the Friday before a three-day weekend and you are looking forward to a romantic vacation on the beach with your special friend. You get off work a bit late and head for the bank to get some cash. Pulling onto the freeway, you're immediately locked into a bumper-to-bumper mass of vehicles, lurching along at fifteen miles per hour. Forty-five minutes later, still a couple of miles from the bank, you notice that you're low on fuel. You begin to steam. Someone tries to cut in front of you and you explode in a rage, shaking your fist and shouting obscenities. When you finally get to the bank, there's no place to park.

After circling the parking lot for twenty minutes, you manage to park. The line in the bank looks endless and there are only three tellers. The man in front of you has a bag of checks and cash from his business. You continue to steam. It seems like every customer chats with the tellers. And the tellers! It takes them forever to do anything. As you inch along in line you glare at various bank officers in order to let them know how angry you are at the inefficient way they run their bank.

By the time you get out of the bank, you're behind schedule and it's rush hour—pre-holiday, Friday-afternoon rush hour. You race out of the parking lot, squealing your tires as you cut into traffic. Rushing through an intersection at high speed, you catch the attention of a police officer. It's not enough that you get a ticket for reckless driving—the officer takes forever checking out your license and writing the ticket. When you finally get going again, you feel like a bomb about to go off.

If you have ever had an experience anything close to the one just described, you've shared the nearly universal sense of frustration, anger, and anxiety caused by "stupid people" and "events beyond our control." This kind of reaction to external events is so common that a school of philosophy sprang up to deal with just such experiences, among other things. Yet its basic tenets go against the grain for most people, at least initially. It is called **Stoicism,** and those who practice it are called **Stoics.**

Stoicism initially emerged as a reaction against hedonism. Whereas the hedonist seeks pleasure or avoids pain, the Stoic seeks serenity (peace of mind) through self-discipline. Stoicism asserts that seeking anything but self-control results in *avoidable* unhappiness. Happiness comes only through detachment from all "externals." Put another way: Everything is a matter of attitude. The disciplined, reasonable person can be happy under any and all conditions.

Stoics believe that *nothing can make you happy or unhappy without your consent*. All unhappiness is the result of bad thinking, poor character, and confusing what we can control with what we cannot control. Regarding the opening story, a Stoic would diagnose your frustration and anger as self-induced. Traffic jams, lines and crowds, little brothers, dumb sweethearts, and cars running out of gas are normal, common aspects of life. There is nothing new or surprising in anything that happens to you. In fact, nothing "happens to you." *You* are the problem.

> Your medicine is in you, and you do not observe it. Your ailment is from yourself, and you do not register it.
>
> *Hazrat Ali*

Philosophical Query

Stop for a moment and reflect on this: Is it possible to be calm under all circumstances? Or do certain circumstances *force* us to be distressed and agitated? How, then, can we explain the incredible feats of Hindu yogis who can control their blood pressure, heart rates, even whether they bleed?

Why do some people seem happy in horrible circumstances, while others suffer in the midst of being loved, healthy, and financially well-off?

Do you think happiness is all a matter of attitude or not? Discuss.

The Cynical Origins of Stoicism

The origins of Stoicism go back to the Cynics. **Cynicism** was a philosophic "school" only in the loosest sense. Founded by **Antisthenes (c. 455–360 B.C.),** its most famous proponent was **Diogenes (c. 412–323 B.C.).** As a philosophical school, Cynicism existed from the fourth century B.C. until the sixth century A.D., although by the first century A.D. its reputation had seriously diminished.

Although the Cynics revolted against the rigidly ordered philosophies of Plato and Aristotle, they admired Socrates. Socrates was the model on which Antisthenes built his philosophy, and, by extension, Socrates was a model for the Stoics. It is said that Antisthenes walked almost five miles every day to hear Socrates.

Antisthenes was apparently more impressed with Socrates' lifestyle and character than with his philosophical ideas, though he, too, sought to base his life on the rule of reason. Socrates' disdain for fashion, his ragged, functional clothing, lack of shoes, ability not to sleep or eat for long periods,

CYNICISM

Philosophy based on the belief that the very essence of civilization is corrupt and that civilization destroys individuals by making them soft and subject to the whims of fortune.

"A Socrates Gone Mad"

Diogenes studied under Antisthenes, who, by the way, hated students. Diogenes took his master's teachings to heart and went him one better. Being called a dog was not enough for him; he actually lived with a pack of stray dogs.

Alexander the Great (356–323 B.C.), having heard of Diogenes, made a point of meeting him. Diogenes was sitting on the seashore when the magnificent, handsome young king of Greece and conqueror of the known world rode up on his powerful charger. Looking down on the reclining Cynic, he said:

"I am Alexander the Great."
"I am Diogenes, the dog," replied the Cynic.
"The dog?"
"I nuzzle the kind, bark at the greedy, and bite louts."
"What can I do for you?" asked the Ruler of the World.

"Stand aside, you're blocking my light."

So impressed was Alexander with the uncompromising character of Diogenes that he later said, "If I were not Alexander, I would be Diogenes."

This sketch is based on material in Guy Davenport's *Herakleitos and Diogenes* (San Francisco: Grey Fox Press, 1979), pp. 35–37.

CYNIC

Individual who lives an austere, unconventional life based on Cynic doctrine.

I can see Antisthenes' vanity through the holes in his cloak.

Plato

his physical toughness and forthright honesty made a tremendous impression on the young Cynic.

After Socrates' death, Antisthenes founded a school called the Cynosarges (the Silver Dog). The word **Cynic** comes from the Greek word for "dog," and this label was later given to Diogenes because he "lived like a dog." That is, he was unwashed and rough-looking; he scrounged for food; and he refused to follow conventional standards of dress and behavior.

Because Antisthenes attended some lectures of Gorgias the Sophist, and because he stayed so close to Socrates, it is not surprising that he was especially affected by Socrates' stinging attacks on such sophistic values as power, celebrity, prestige, wealth, and clever deception. The Cynics despised the widespread hedonism and hypocrisy that they saw throughout Athens. They believed that the very essence of civilization is corrupt: manners are hypocritical and phony; material wealth weakens people, making them physically and morally soft; the desire for success and power produces dishonesty and dependency; flattery, fashion, and convention destroy the individual and make him or her vulnerable to the whims of fortune. And as the tragic death of Socrates underscored, not even the wisest person can control other people or external events.

So the less an individual needs to be happy, the less vulnerable he or she is. Diogenes, for example, lived in an abandoned wine barrel on the beach, and once said: "When I saw a child drinking from his hand, I threw away my cup." The Cynics lived austere, unconventional lives. They distrusted luxury as a "hook" that always brought complications and ultimately frustration into people's lives. What happiness was possible, according to the Cynics, came from self-discipline, rational control of all desires and appetites, and minimal contact with conventional society.

Diogenes preferred the free rent of an abandoned wine barrel and the company of dogs to the softening corruptions of sophisticated pleasures and the degradation of currying favor with so-called important people.

The hedonist Epicurus also emphasized a simple life and the avoidance of pain, rather than a mad rush to acquire pleasures and luxuries. For example, Epicurus said that "all bodily suffering is negligible; for that which causes intense pain has a brief duration, and that which endures long in the flesh causes mild pain."[1] But the Cynics still found Epicureanism too soft, too conventional, and too dependent to suit them. The Epicureans relied too much on their friends and certain "proper" pleasures. Cynicism was rough-and-tumble. Its most famous advocates were sarcastic and hostile toward conventions and institutions. They relied only on themselves.

Few Cynics exhibited the moral or intellectual virtues of Antisthenes or Diogenes, and eventually Cynicism fell into disrepute. The popular image of the Cynic was a hostile, arrogant individual who despised everyone else and hated the society in which he lived. Indiscriminate scorn and contempt for practically everything replaced penetrating social criticism.

Today the terms *cynic* and *cynical* are commonly used to refer to a general attitude of basic contempt for people, an excessively hostile or critical stance, or a tendency to distrust other people's motives.

The Stoics, however, agreed with the original Cynics' assessment of Socrates. They accepted the basic Cynic premise that excessive desires always

Discourse on virtue and they pass by in droves; whistle and dance the shimmy, and you've got an audience.

Diogenes

Do you think you could distinguish a contemporary Diogenes from a "street person"? To what extent might beliefs about the importance of money, status, material comfort, and the like blind us to accepting the possibility that at least some "street people" (and other social outcasts) are philosophical Cynics?

lead to unhappiness. Like the Cynics, the Stoics valued self-control, courage, and dignity. The Stoic Epictetus characterized the "true Cynic, the free open-air spirit," as one saying to himself:

> "Henceforth, my mind is the material I have to work on, as the carpenter has his timber and the shoemaker his leather: my business is to deal with my impressions aright. My wretched body is nothing to me, its parts are nothing to me. Death? Let it come when it will, whether to my whole body or part of it. Exile? Can one be sent into exile beyond the Universe? One cannot. Wherever I go, there is the sun, there is the moon, there are the stars, dreams . . . conversation with the gods." The true Cynic when he has ordered himself thus . . . must know that he is sent as a messenger from God to men concerning things good and evil, to show them that they have gone astray and are seeking the true nature of good and evil where it is not to be found.[2]

Let us see how the Stoics built on basic Cynic principles.

Plato winces when I track dust across his rugs: he knows that I'm walking on his vanity.

Diogenes

The Slave and the Emperor

Though the philosophical school known as Stoicism was founded in Greece by **Zeno (c. 334–262 B.C.)** around 300 B.C., it flourished in Rome. Zeno lectured at a place called the *stoa poikile*, or painted porch; the term *Stoic* comes from *stoa*—originally Stoics were "men of the porch."

Under Alexander the Great, Greece conquered the Persian empire (what is now Iran and Iraq) and established Greek rule over a large area of the Near East and Egypt. As a result, Greek culture became more sophisticated and cosmopolitan, absorbing ideas and customs from the cultures it conquered. As the Greek empire expanded, the importance of individual city-states such as Athens and Sparta diminished and people identified themselves as part of a larger, more international community.

Alexander's empire was unstable, however, and began to fall apart almost immediately after his death. For most of the third century B.C. no single dominant power emerged in the Mediterranean region. By the middle of the second century B.C., Rome had destroyed what was left of Alexander's kingdom and annexed Greece as a Roman province called Achaia. By 100 B.C., Rome essentially controlled the entire Mediterranean area.

The Romans were not particularly interested in abstract, speculative thinking. Pragmatic and religiously tolerant, they borrowed heavily from Greek culture, including philosophy. Given their interest in establishing social order, the Romans were especially attracted to the Stoics' emphasis on duty and self-control. It especially appealed to the Romans' sense of *virility*. To the Romans, virility meant manliness, courage, and moral strength. It did not, as it does today, refer to "macho" qualities or masculine sexuality. The English word *virtue* comes from the same root as *virile*.

The two most philosophically influential Stoics are a Roman slave and a Roman emperor: Epictetus and Marcus Aurelius. The Roman senator Seneca, although not a particularly original thinker, was one of the finest Stoic writers. We will be using some of his *Discourses* and *Moral Letters* to supplement our two main sources.

For many years, Stoic literature has been some of the most popular of all philosophical writings. Let us see why as we encounter the archetype of the Stoic in two radically different forms: a slave and an emperor.

> Lameness is an impediment to the leg, but not to the Will; and say this to yourself with regard to everything that happens. For you will find such things to be an impediment to something else, but not truly to yourself.
>
> *Epictetus*

Epictetus: From Slave to Sage

Stoicism appealed to Romans living in times of great uncertainty under emperors of widely differing abilities and virtues. It spread throughout the Roman world because it was advocated by three important public figures: **Cicero (106–43 B.C.)**, **Cato (95–46 B.C.)**, and **Seneca (c. 4 B.C.–A.D. 65)**. But, ironically, one of the most important Stoic philosophers was a former slave named **Epictetus (c. A.D. 50–130)**. Perhaps because a slave's life is not his own, Epictetus acquired special insight into the major issue of Stoicism: controlling what we can and accepting what is beyond our control.

We do not know much about Epictetus's early life. His mother was a slave living in Hierapolis, a city in the Asia Minor province of Phrygia. Epictetus was brought to Rome as the slave of a former slave named Epaphroditus, who seems to have been Nero's administrative secretary. Epictetus must have demonstrated unusual abilities, for Epaphroditus sent the youth

Epictetus

For we come into the world with no innate conception of a right-angled triangle or of a semi-tone, but we are taught what each of these means by systematic instruction. . . . On the other hand every one has come into the world with an innate conception as to good and bad, noble and shameful, becoming and unbecoming, happiness and unhappiness, fitting and inappropriate, what is right to do and what is wrong.

Epictetus

Epictetus to study with Musonius Rufus, the most powerful Stoic since the days of Zeno. Even so, Epictetus never lost sight of the fact that he could be bought or sold, pampered or tortured, at his owner's whim. As a slave, he was constantly reminded that what happened to him had no bearing on his own wishes or behavior. As a slave, the only absolute control Epictetus had was over his own reactions to what happened. His motto was *Anechou kai apechou*: Bear and forbear.

Epictetus was once so badly tortured—for another slave's mistake—that his broken leg did not heal properly, and he limped for the rest of his life. The story goes that as his leg was being twisted, Epictetus reminded his master that a person's leg was likely to break under such torture. Epaphroditus ignored this, and when his leg finally broke, Epictetus said, "See, it's just as I told you." He later said, "I was never more free than when I was on the rack." He had learned that he could control his attitude, but that fate controlled his life:

> If the captain calls, let all those things go and run to the boat without turning back; and if you are old, do not even go very far from the boat, so that when the call comes you are not left behind.[3]

Ultimately freed sometime after Nero's death in the year 68, Epictetus became a well-known teacher. Sometime around the year 90, all the philosophers were ordered out of Rome by the emperor Domitian, who was angry about the encouragement certain Stoics had given to those who opposed him. Epictetus fled to Nicopolis in northern Greece, where he taught until he was very old. He was a popular teacher, and his schools in both Rome and Nicopolis throve during his lifetime.

A modest man, famed for his sweetness and simplicity, Epictetus lived in a sparely furnished house, content with a straw mat and pallet for a bed and a clay lamp (after his iron one was stolen). He was especially loving toward children, and he was charitable toward all those who came to him for advice and guidance. Following the example of Socrates, he published nothing. His ideas have come down to us in the form of the class notes of his student Flavius Arrianus, called the *Discourses*, and a truly remarkable set of excerpts from them called the *Enchiridion*, also known as the *Manual* or *Handbook* (because it was made into hand-sized books that were carried into the field by Roman soldiers.)[4]

Marcus Aurelius: Philosopher-King

Marcus Aurelius Antoninus (A.D. 121–180) was bound by duty. By temperament a scholar and a recluse, he lived surrounded with commotion, deception, and crowds. Marcus so impressed the emperor Hadrian that he advised Marcus's uncle Aurelius Antoninus (commonly known as Antoninus Pius) to adopt Marcus. When Marcus was forty, Antoninus Pius, then

Marcus Aurelius

emperor, appointed him heir, over Pius's other adopted son, Lucius Verus. From the beginning of his reign, Marcus faced calamity and disruption.

When Pius died in 161, Marcus generously named his stepbrother Verus co-emperor—against the wishes of the senate—but got little help from him. All the serious work of governing was done by Marcus. As emperor, he was obliged to contend with flatterers, liars, and enemies. He was regularly dragged away from Rome to deal with uprisings and barbarian invasions along the frontiers. He was betrayed by a trusted general, and spent the last years of his life away from home on a difficult military campaign. He suffered through the deaths of four of his five sons, and even endured unsubstantiated rumors that his wife took many lovers in his absence and that his sole surviving son was not his own. To himself, he wrote:

> Everywhere and at all times it is in thy power piously to acquiesce in thy present condition, and to behave justly to those who are about thee, and to exert thy skill upon thy present thoughts, that nothing shall steal into them without being examined.[5]

Marcus was loved by many Romans for his kindness and mercy. He refused to turn away from his incompetent stepbrother, choosing instead to carry out both their duties until Verus died in 169, after which Marcus ruled alone. He convinced the senate to pardon the family of the traitorous general, when other emperors would have destroyed it. He stood by his wife as cruel rumors about her virtue spread everywhere and his own soldiers mocked his masculinity. He went so far as to promote those accused of being her lovers when doing so was good for Rome.

> Let it make no difference to thee whether thou art cold or warm, if thou art doing thy duty; and whether thou art drowsy or satisfied with sleep; and whether ill-spoken of or praised; and whether dying or doing something else. For it is one of the acts of life, the act by which we die: it is sufficient then in this act also to do well what we have in hand.[6]

Marcus Aurelius was the last truly great figure of Imperial Rome, combining classical philosophy with a spiritual quality that foreshadowed the Christian-influenced Scholasticism of the Middle Ages. He was also one of the kindest, wisest, and most virtuous philosophers.

> Only attend to thyself, [Marcus,] and resolve to be a good man in every act which thou doest; and remember. . . . Look within. Within is the fountain of good, and it will ever bubble up, if thou wilt ever dig.[7]

His last years were hard and lonely, spent on a military campaign along the Danube. Yet rather than succumb to bitterness or lash out at others, he sought solace in philosophy. Late at night, after his public duties were done, he did his duty to his soul, sitting alone in his tent writing what are

To pursue the unattainable is insanity, yet the thoughtless can never refrain from doing so.

Marcus Aurelius

People find no rest because of four pursuits—long life, reputation, office, possessions. Whoever has these four goals dreads spirits, fears other men, cowers before authority, and is terrified of punishment. I call him "a man in flight from things." He can be killed, he can be given life; the destiny which decides [his state of mind] is outside him.

Yang Zhu

For humans, a life of hardship is the norm and death is the end. Abiding by the norm, awaiting my end, what is there to be concerned about?

Rong Qiqi

Why Should Anywhere I Go Not Be All Right?

One of the great joys of learning is the discovery of common themes and threads. This is especially so in matters of wisdom. The great sages are at their most powerful when they speak of acceptance in the face of great hardship. Sometimes, it seems as if one spirit speaks with many voices and accents. Compare this passage from Chuang-tzu with the passage from Marcus Aurelius on page 226.

Tzu-lai fell ill, was gasping for breath and was about to die. His wife and children surrounded him and wept. . . . He said, "Don't disturb the transformation that is about to take place." Then, leaning against the door, he continued, "Great is the Creator! What will he make of you

now? Where will he take you? Will he make you into a rat's liver? Will he make you into an insect's leg?"

Tzu-lai said, "Wherever a parent tells a son to go, whether east, west, south, or north, he has to obey. The yin and yang are like a man's parents. If they pressed me to die and I disobeyed, I would be obstinate. What fault is theirs? For the universe gave me the body so I may be carried, my life so I may toil, my old age so I may repose, and my death so I may rest. Therefore, to regard life as good is the way to regard death as good.

"Suppose a master foundryman is casting his metal and the metal leaps up and

says, 'I must be made into the best sword. . . .' The master foundryman would certainly consider the metal as evil. And if simply because I possess a body by chance, I were to say, 'Nothing but a man! Nothing but a man!' the Creator will certainly regard me as evil. If I regard the universe as a great furnace and creation as a foundryman, why should anywhere I go not be all right?"

Chuang-tzu
In Wing-Tsit Chan, trans. and comp., *A Source Book in Chinese Philosophy* (Princeton, N.J.: Princeton University Press, 1963), p. 197.

popularly known as his *Meditations*, but which he addressed "To Myself." This journal is one of the finest, most widely read examples of both Stoic thought and personal reflection in Western literature.

On this last campaign, Marcus Aurelius, a man once described as "by nature a saint and sage, by profession a warrior and ruler," died at the age of fifty-nine, worn down by fatigue and toil.[8]

Misfortune is not fate but providence.

Sarvepalli Radhakrishnan

The Fated Life

Though fate is an important aspect of their philosophy, the Stoics were rather imprecise about what it meant in specific terms. In some mysterious way, the actual course of our lives is directed by the *Logos*, which the Stoics thought of as World Reason or Cosmic Mind (see the First Interlude). Sometimes the *Logos* is referred to as God, Zeus, Nature, Providence, Cosmic Meaning, or Fate. Seneca says:

Reflect on the precarious nature of the human condition by reading the box "Why Should Anywhere I Go Not Be All Right?" on p. 222 and study these two photographs of the actor-director Christopher Reeve. It is all-too-easy to think that science, good habits, and technology can give us control over our lives. Reeve's public courage and lack of self-pity remind us of Epictetus's doctrine that although the role we play in life's saga may not be up to us, how we play it is. The picture on the right shows Reeve at a dinner for the American Paralysis Association, one of a number of organizations and causes that he supports.

We are all chained to [fate]. . . . All of us are in custody, the binders as well as the bound . . . some are chained by office, some by wealth; some weighed down by high birth, some by low; some are subject to another's tyranny, some to their own; some are confined to one spot by banishment, some by a priesthood. All life is bondage.[9]

The Stoics learned, as many of us do, that our lives are not entirely our own. This discovery did not, at least in the cases of Epictetus and Marcus Aurelius, lead to despair or escapist indulgence, but to a shift in the focus of responsibility. Rather than complain about what they could not control,

Show me a man who though sick is happy, who though in danger is happy, and I'll show you a Stoic.

Epictetus

the Stoics chose to master what they could: their own minds. By mastering their thoughts, they believed, they could master their feelings. Serenity comes to that individual whose will is in accord with the World Reason, the *Logos*, for right thinking leads to a reduction of frustration and anxiety. In the words of Epictetus:

> Remember that thou art an actor in a play, of such a kind as the author may choose: if short, a short one; if long, a long one: if he wishes you to act the part of a poor man, see that you act the part naturally: if the part of a lame man, of a magistrate, of a private person (do the same). For this is your duty, to act well the part that was given to you; but to select the part belongs to another.[10]

The Stoic *Logos*

Under the guidance of the *Logos* the universe remains rational and ordered. Epictetus said, "Events do not just happen, but arrive by appointment." Everything that occurs is connected to everything else. Everything that exists is connected to the *Logos*. Our individual minds are "emanations" or "sparks" from the *Logos*, which is sometimes characterized as "fire." (The Stoics borrowed this idea from Heraclitus.) Our finite human reason is, thus, a small reflection of divine reason. Seneca puts it like this:

> We do not need to lift our hands to heaven . . . God is near you, with you, inside you. Yes . . . there is a holy spirit abiding within us. . . . No man is good without god.[11]

The ideas of a rationally ordered universe and our intimate relation to the *Logos* are central aspects of Stoicism. If the universe is divinely ordered, then there is a plan. Things happen to us for a reason—a divinely ordained reason.

If this is true, then nothing that happens can be "wrong" or "bad," since everything that happens is part of God's rational plan. When I truly grasp this, I will no longer fear for the future nor complain about the past or present, but can remain calm like Zeno when he heard that all his possessions were lost in a shipwreck and said, "Fortune bids me philosophize with a lighter pack."

What can I do, then, if the course of my life's events is beyond my control? The Stoic answers that I can concentrate on developing an attitude of courageous acceptance. My efforts should be directed toward that part of my life over which I exert absolute control: my attitudes, or my will.

Do to me what is worthy
  of Thee
And not what is worthy
  of me.
    Saadi

Philosophical Query

Do you agree that the test of faith is anxiety? Are the Stoics correct in insisting that one who truly realizes that *everything* is governed by a divine plan will lose all fear and anxiety? Justify your position.

Either belief in God is unconditional or it is not belief at all.

    Viktor E. Frankl

Of the 85,000 residents of Billings, Montana, approximately one hundred are Jews. In December of 1993, someone threw a cinder block through five-year-old Isaac Schnitzer's window. The reason: A Hanukkah menorah had been sitting in it. Thousands of Billings's residents showed their solidarity with the small Jewish community by placing pictures of menorahs in their own windows—and by posing for this powerful picture, a picture that reflects the cosmopolis.

The Disinterested Rational Will

If we are "bits" of the *Logos*, it follows that our virtue and happiness will consist in being as much like the *Logos* as possible. Being perfectly rational, the *Logos* is not partisan; that is, the *Logos* is objective. It is calm and serene, viewing events with "disinterest." Seneca says:

> Just as the rays of the sun do indeed warm the earth but remain at the source of their radiation, so a great and holy soul is lowered to earth to give us a nearer knowledge of the divine; but though it is in intercourse with us, it cleaves to its source . . . it looks toward it, it seeks to rejoin it, and its concern with our affairs is superior and detached.[12]

To be *disinterested* is to have no *personal* attachments or motives. For example, a judge or a teacher should be disinterested when she passes sentence or grades papers—she should not play favorites. Marcus Aurelius was disinterested when he promoted the men accused of being his wife's lovers.

The Stoics make an intriguing case that our best chance for happiness is to adopt a disinterested attitude toward our own lives, as well as toward all life. The Stoics thought such a perspective would result not in a world of self-centered isolationists, but in a sense of universal communion and duty. Turning to the *Logos* meant looking beyond the particular laws, customs, and prejudices of one's self and society and rejecting them if they deviate from Nature/*Logos*. Unlike the hedonist's evaluation of the welfare of others only in terms of one's own happiness, the Stoics viewed all humans as citizens of a "universal city," a *cosmopolis*. The hedonist is indifferent to others; the Stoic is indifferent to self. When our duties are

Glory be to that God
Who slays our wives and
destroys our children
And Whom withal we love.

Prayer of Attar

"Life passes by like a galloping horse"

From the point of view of Tao, what is noble and what is humble? They all merge into one. Never stick to one's own intention and thus handicap the operation of Tao. What is much and what is little? They replace and apply to each other. . . . Time cannot be arrested. The succession of decline, growth, fullness, and emptiness go in a cycle, each end becoming a new beginning. This is the way to talk about the workings of the great principle and to discuss the principle of all things. The life of things passes by like a galloping horse. With no activity is it not changing, and at no time is it not moving. What shall we do? What shall we not do? The thing to do is to leave it to self-transformation.

Chuang-tzu
The Chuang-Tzu, in Wing-Tsit Chan, *A Source Book in Chinese Philosophy* (Princeton, N.J.: Princeton University Press, 1963), p. 206.

---

dictated by disinterested reason, not custom or personal preference, we become members of a community, a human fellowship.

Marcus Aurelius alludes to universal fellowship in this beautiful passage:

> It is man's peculiar distinction to love even those who err and go astray. Such a love is born as soon as you realize that they are your brothers; that they are stumbling in ignorance, and not willfully; that in a short while both of you will be no more; and, above all, that you yourself have taken no hurt, for your master-reason has not been made a jot worse than it was before.
>
> Out of the universal substance, as out of wax, Nature fashions a colt, then breaks him up and uses the material to form a tree, and after that a man, and next some other thing: and not one of these endures for more than a brief span. As for the vessel itself, it is no greater hardship to be taken to pieces than to be put together. . . .
>
> Only a little while, and Nature, the universal disposer, will change everything you see, and out of their substance will make fresh things, and yet again others from theirs, to the perpetual renewing of the world's youthfulness.[13]

Which of you by worrying can add a moment to his life-span?

Jesus, Matthew 6:26

Philosophical Query

Discuss the advantages and disadvantages of disinterestedness. When is it a virtue? When is it not? Give some examples, and explain them.

Whereas other philosophies distinguished between good and bad emotions according to various criteria, the Stoics rejected emotion to the extent it was humanly possible. The best attitude, they claimed, was rational, detached acceptance.[14] Seneca says:

> Philosophers of our school reject the emotions; the [Aristotelian] Peripatetics keep them in check. I, however, do not understand how any half-way disease can be either wholesome or helpful. . . .

"What is the fruit of your Stoic doctrines?" someone once asked Epictetus. "Tranquility, fearlessness, and freedom," he answered.

"But," you object, "it is natural for me to suffer when I am be-
reaved of a friend; grant some privileges to tears which have the right
to flow! It is also natural to be affected by men's opinions and to be
cast down when they are unfavourable; so why should you not allow
me such an honorable aversion to bad opinion?"

There is no vice which lacks some plea. . . . we are in love with our
vices; we uphold them and prefer to make excuses for them rather
than shake them off. We mortals have been endowed with sufficient
strength by nature, if only we use this strength. . . . The real reason
for failure is unwillingness, the pretended reason, inability.[15]

> Controlling your emo-
> tions is difficult but can be
> *empowering.*
>
> *James Bond Stockdale*

Stoic Wisdom

By the time of Marcus Aurelius, Stoicism had a religious quality that made
it especially attractive to the growing Christian community in the Roman
world. As we have seen, classical philosophies were naturalistic: they placed
rational humanity at the center of things. By contrast, Christian values
place a personal God at the center. Though the Stoics were classical in
their emphasis on the impersonal *Logos* as being material, and on reason
and self-control of the human will as the means to salvation, they also
anticipated Christianity in their emphasis on the divine will and on our
submission to it. As you will see, many of the Stoics' specific lessons also
have a decidedly Judeo-Christian flavor to them. Thus Stoicism stands as
the most influential transitional philosophy between classical and Christian values.

> [T]he lecture-room of the
> philosopher is the hospital;
> students ought not to walk
> out of it in pleasure, but
> in pain.
>
> *Epictetus*

Control versus Influence

Given the Stoic position that our lives are fated but that our wills remain
free, our first task must be to distinguish what we can control from what
we cannot control. *Control* is a most important concept. Because Stoic literature is often imprecise and inconsistent, it will help the modern student
of Stoicism to consider the distinction between *control* and *influence*.

Even though the Stoics believed in destiny, or fate, they also talked about
choosing appropriate actions, in addition to just controlling our attitudes.
This suggests that a given individual's fate is painted in broad strokes: *X*
will not get into medical school; *Y* will marry *Z*. But *X* may have the freedom to apply to medical school, and *Y* may be free to break up with *Z*
two or three times. There appear to be gaps in our fate. For instance, in
the first section of the *Enchiridion* Epictetus says:

> Some things are up to us
> and some are not up to
> us. Our opinions are up to
> us, and our impulses, de-
> sires, aversions. . . . Our
> bodies are not up to us,
> nor are our possessions,
> our reputations, our public
> offices.
>
> *Epictetus*

> If then you desire . . . great things, remember that you must not
> (attempt to) lay hold of them with small effort; but you must leave
> alone some things entirely, and postpone others for the present.[16]

There's certainly nothing wrong with taking reasonable precautions to manage our lives and protect our property, but the Stoics remind us not to confuse exerting influence with having control. All the car alarms and Club®-style locks in the world won't give us control over even one car, if the Stoics are correct.

Later he says:

> When you are going to take in hand any act, remind yourself what kind of act it is. If you are going to bathe, [remind] yourself what happens in the [public] bath; some splashing the water, others pushing against one another, others abusing one another, and some stealing.[17]

Elsewhere, he talks about choosing to be a philosopher or deciding to train for the Olympics. Thus Epictetus implies that we have at least some degree of influence over our actions. We *must* have influence over more than just our attitudes; otherwise, such advice is illogical. Advice makes sense only where there is some choice.

Although the Stoics are theoretically inconsistent when they counsel accepting fate on the one hand and then advise us to live moderately and wisely on the other, their position contains merit because *it is consistent with common experience.* A careful survey of the human condition reveals that many of us expend a great deal of effort trying to control things that we cannot control while nearly ignoring those areas over which we do have control. This insight, I think, reflects the genius of Stoicism.

A common example will make the point. Technically speaking, you cannot *control* your grades in school, although you have considerable *influence* over them. No matter how carefully you listen to instructions, no matter how good your notes, how thorough your studying and grasp of the material, you cannot *guarantee* a passing grade in any course. Your professor may have a personal grudge against you or be depressed or ill while grading your work. A clerical error may alter your grade in a class,

"None strive to grasp what they already know"

There is often chaos in the world, and the love of knowledge is ever at the bottom of it. For all men strive to grasp what they do not know, while none strive to grasp what they already know. . . . Thus, above, the splendor of the heavenly bodies is dimmed; below, the power of land and water is burned up, while in between the influence of the four seasons is upset. There is not one tiny worm that moves on earth or an insect that flies in the air but has lost its original nature. Such indeed is the world chaos caused by the desire for knowledge!

Chuang-tzu
The Wisdom of Laotse, trans. and ed. Lin Yutang (New York: Modern Library, 1976), p. 287.

and the system may refuse to correct it. By the same token, you cannot even guarantee a failing grade. Another clerical error may result in an A for a class you haven't attended for weeks. The professor may confuse your name with that of another student, for example.

We are foolish when we exert no effort on our own behalf. We all know that. But, the Stoic reminds us, we are also foolish to believe that we *control* our GPAs. Rather than trying to control our grades, we should work wisely to *influence* them and should make sure to *control our attitudes* toward them.

This difference may be difficult to grasp in a culture that pronounces "You can be anything you want to be if you work hard enough." From the Stoic point of view it is misleading to talk about controlling our lives (or grades); we can only influence them up to a point. And we must remember this warning: *The results of our efforts are out of our hands.*

Off campus we see this as well. Jim Fixx, the running enthusiast, ate sensibly and exercised regularly, yet died in his forties of an inherited heart condition. The film genius Orson Welles ate what he wished, never exercised, smoked cigars, and weighed over four hundred pounds when he died—at age seventy. Such an example is not an excuse for self-indulgence, but a hard fact of life: *We do not control our destinies; we influence them just enough so that we should do our best to behave responsibly.*

This is the crux of Stoicism. The inconsistencies in Stoic writing are due, in part, to our ignorance of precisely when influence becomes control in a particular case. There are ways to learn what to try and what to avoid, but in all cases the Stoic remains aware that the *Logos* ultimately rules the universe. The individual's task is to identify the *Logos*'s will and then put his or her will in harmony with it. While we may not have control over the events in our lives, we do have control over our happiness. The wise person is easy to identify: He or she is the serene individual who lives courageously and responsibly, who graciously accepts everything that happens, be it good or bad, without becoming bitter or broken.

Begin the morning by saying to yourself, I shall meet with the busy-body, the ungrateful, arrogant, deceitful, envious, unsocial. All these things happen by reason of their ignorance of what is good and evil. But I who have seen the nature of the good that it is beautiful, and of the bad that it is ugly, and the nature of him who does wrong, that it is akin to me . . . I can neither be injured by any of them, for no one can fix on me what is ugly, nor can I be angry with my kinsman, nor hate him. For we are made for co-operation, like feet, like hands, like eyelids, like the rows of the upper and lower teeth. To act against one another then is contrary to nature; and it is acting against one another to be vexed and to turn away.

Marcus Aurelius

Some Things Are Not in Our Control

To achieve serenity and wisdom, we must remain clear about what is not in our control:

> Not in our power are the body, property, reputation, offices . . . and in a word, whatever are not our own acts . . . the things not in our power are weak, slavish, subject to restraint, in the power of others. Remember that if you think the things which are by nature slavish to be free, and the things which are in the power of others to be your own, you will be hindered, you will lament, you will be disturbed, you will blame both the gods and men.[18]

"Not in our power" means not under our control. If I realize that these things are not under my control, I can adopt a healthy attitude toward them. For instance, since my reputation is not totally up to me, I can quit trying so hard to make everyone like me. I cannot *make* anyone like me or dislike me. My family likes me even when I'm a fool, and some of my students don't like me no matter how hard I try to be likable. Instead of directing my efforts where they are ineffective, I can devote them to what I have more control over: myself. In practical terms, this means that I take appropriate action and then mentally let go of the results.

Once I realize that how long I live, who likes me or doesn't, and my social status are beyond my total control, I can quit being obsessively fearful. I can manage my health with moderation, but will not be bitter if after watching my diet and exercising daily I develop cancer. Bitterness will not get me well. Bitterness, or envy, or resentment are never my fate; they are always my choice.

Not getting into the university of my choice might be my fate. Resenting it for the rest of my life is not—it's my choice. I can ask you to marry me, and marry you if you say yes, but I cannot make you happy. I cannot make you stay with me. If you leave, my anger and despair are not my fate—they are my choice.

Philosophical Query

Reflect on letting go in the sense of doing what seems right and then relaxing. Provide a few of your own examples of how fear of consequences and an obsession with control can affect us. Discuss ways for identifying and striking a balance between letting go in a wise way and in an irresponsible way.

Some Things *Are* in Our Control

What is in our power is our free will. Epictetus insists, contrary to what we may believe, that we alone control our feelings. We control our feelings because we control our thinking. We can reason out that other people's

---

Do not be distressed, do not despond or give up in despair, if now and again practice falls short of precept. Return to the attack after each failure, and be thankful if on the whole you can acquit yourself in the majority of cases as a man should.

Marcus Aurelius

All wisdom can be stated in two lines:
   What is done for you—allow it to be done.
   What you must do yourself—make sure you do it.

Khawwas

Reason or a halter.

Diogenes

Addicted to Unhappiness

Let's face it: Reality often stinks. People don't always act the way we would like them to act. This doesn't seem to be the best of all possible worlds. . . . Moreover, society often gets worse: seems *more* polluted, economically unfair, burdened with ethnic prejudices, politically oppressive, violence-filled, superstitious, wasteful of natural resources, sexist, and ultraconformist.

But you *still* don't have to feel desperately unhappy. Unkind reality doesn't depress millions of humans. What does? Their unthinking addiction to . . . *the idea that people and things should turn out better than they do and that you must view it as awful and horrible if you do not find good solutions to life's grim realities.* An idiotic idea . . .

Albert Ellis and Robert A. Harper
A New Guide to Rational Living
(North Hollywood: Wilshire Book Co., 1978), p. 177.

These smokers are examples of the lengths we will go to in order to sustain an "addiction to unhappiness." Could being a smoker be part of a person's fate? Could being an alcoholic? Overweight? Lazy? How can we distinguish between defects of character and things not in our control?

likes and dislikes are beyond our total control. This should free us from depending on other people's opinions of us for self-esteem or happiness.

In our power are opinion, movement towards a thing, desire, aversion; and in a word, whatever are our own acts. And the things in our power are by nature free, not subject to restraint or hindrance . . . if you think that only which is your own to be your own, and if you think of what is another's, as it really is, belongs to another, no man will ever compel you, no man will hinder you, you will never blame any man, you will accuse no man, you will do nothing . . . against

That which happens to . . . every man is fixed in a manner for him suitable to his destiny. . . . For there is altogether one fitness and harmony. . . . And so accept everything which happens, even if it seems disagreeable, because it leads to this, to the health of the universe and to the prosperity . . . of the whole.

Marcus Aurelius

All that happens without us knowing why is destiny. For the man who trusts destiny, there is no difference between long life and short. For one who trusts his mind, there is nothing which is agreeable or offensive.

Lie Zi

Attachment is the great fabricator of illusions; reality can be attained only by someone who is detached.

Simone Weil

your will, no man will harm you, you will have no enemy, for you will not suffer any harm.[19]

I wonder how many hours of human suffering can be chalked up to trying to control how others feel about things. I also wonder how hard we try to control our own thoughts. For example: Mike suffers and worries every time Janet is annoyed with him. He buys her flowers, is distracted at work, agonizes until she likes him again. If he had control over how she felt, he would never let her be annoyed. Since she gets annoyed and he doesn't want her to be annoyed, it follows logically (and causally) that he *cannot* control her feelings. But—irrationally—he tries to, again and again.

Suppose that Mike reads Epictetus. Now, instead of trying to make Janet feel a certain way, he tries to control his own thoughts and behavior. When he starts to worry, he consciously, and with great effort at first, forces himself not to dwell on Janet. He may not be able to stop worries about her from popping into his mind, but he can stop himself from dwelling on them. He can exert his *will* over his own thinking. He is not responsible for his first thoughts, but he is responsible for his second thoughts.

This is a difficult lesson. It may be especially difficult to accept today, when we place so much importance on relationships, and when we have been told that inadequate parents and abusive spouses are often responsible for our unhappiness. Epictetus has something interesting to say about relationships.

Relationships

Relationships must be evaluated with the same disinterested detachment as everything else. *According to the Stoics, we suffer to the extent that we take our own lives personally.*

Duties are universally measured by relations. Is a man a father? The [duty] is to take care of him, to yield to him in all things, to submit when he is reproachful, when he inflicts blows. But suppose he is a bad father. Were you then by nature [guaranteed] a good father? No; [just] a father. Does a brother wrong you? Maintain then your own position towards him, and do not examine what he is doing, but what you must do [in order] that your will shall be [in accord with] nature. For another will not damage you, unless you choose; but you will be damaged when you shall think that you are damaged. In this way then you will discover your duty from the relation of a neighbor, from that of a citizen, from that of a general, if you are accustomed to contemplate [your relationships].[20]

This is an excellent example of applying disinterested reason to daily affairs. The Stoics believed that a disinterested study of life shows that no one is *entitled* to good, healthy parents, loving, supportive brothers and sisters, obedient children, or sexy, interesting, loyal boyfriends, girlfriends, or spouses. If the *Logos* provides *everything we need* to be happy, then it is clear that no one needs good parents, and so on. The reason is obvious: Not everyone gets them. They are not things to which we are entitled, or the *Logos* would have provided them.

The only way to grasp this point is to set our *feelings* aside and apply *disinterested reason* to relationships. For example, the traditional marriage vow commits each spouse to the other "for richer or poorer, in sickness and in health." This means that the essence of my relationship to my wife is simply that: She is my wife. As a husband—not as an individual—I have obligations, regardless of how my wife behaves, which stem from the nature of the marital relationship. They are not based on the personalities or preferences of the individuals involved. Similarly, as a son, I have duties toward my father whether or not I "like" him and whether or not he is a good father.

This interpretation of relationships seems overly simplistic given our sophisticated psychological knowledge of the damage that bad, abusive relationships can cause. So it will be necessary to modify Epictetus's strict position. But to give him his due, there is much to be learned from adopting a grown-up attitude toward relationships. What can I gain by resenting my childhood, for example? All my righteous indignation over some parental lack, all the suffering and bitterness in the world cannot make up for whatever I missed in childhood. That truly is beyond my power.

In Epictetus's time, social roles were less flexible than they are now. But even today, I can still be a Stoic without being a martyr. I can remind myself that so long as I am in this marriage or have this job, for instance, *I* have duties that are not contingent on other people fulfilling *their* duties. What kind of teacher would I be if I did not prepare my lessons carefully just because many of my students come to class unprepared? What kind of student would you be if you whispered and passed notes to your friend just because your teacher was not interesting?

As the Stoics remind us, our spouses, friends, teachers, and bosses are not the real causes of our happiness or unhappiness. When we look at relationships only in terms of how others behave toward us or whether they "make" us happy or unhappy, we fail to grasp one of the most fundamental aspects of life.

Philosophical **Query**

Discuss the preceding passage from Epictetus about relationships. What lessons might it have regarding our relationships and the things that make us unhappy?

Everything Has a Price

One reason we may be frustrated by events is that we tend to focus on the object of our desire while ignoring its cost. Yet everything has a clearly marked price tag. The athlete with a fine physique has paid the price of

> You cannot judge by annoyance.
>
> *Idries Shah*

> What you're supposed to do when you don't like a thing is change it. If you can't change it, change the way you think about it.
>
> *Maya Angelou*

> "These sons belong to me, and this wealth belongs to me"—with such thoughts a fool is tormented. He himself does not belong to himself; how much less sons and wealth?
>
> *The Buddha*

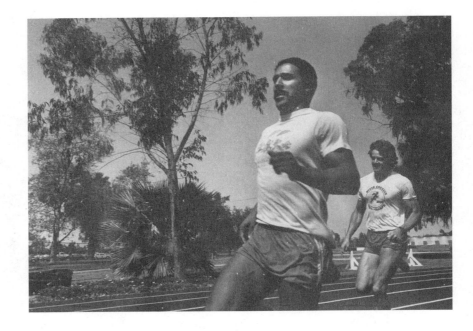

The athlete with the fine physique and the class valedictorian (facing page) have paid the price of training and discipline. As Epictetus said: "You will be unjust and insatiable, if you do not part with the price in return for which . . . things are sold." If we remember this Stoic principle, we will not envy or resent those who have paid the price when we have not.

Do not value either your children or your life or anything else more than goodness.

Socrates

Whether you like it or not, you'd better accept reality the way it occurs: as highly imperfect and filled with most fallible human beings. Your alternative? Continual anxiety and desperate disappointment.

*Albert Ellis and
Robert Harper*

training and discipline, perhaps giving up a broad education or full social life. The ambitious character at the office has paid the price of flattering the boss and working late while you did not have to "kiss up" and were home enjoying your family life. The A student has paid the price of missing many parties and other kinds of socializing.

We suffer unnecessarily when we try to have things without paying the price:

> You will be unjust then and insatiable, if you do not part with the price, in return for which . . . things are sold, and if you wish to obtain them for nothing. Well, what is the price of lettuces? An obulus perhaps. If then a man gives up the obulus and receives the lettuces, and if you do not give up the obulus and do not receive the lettuces, do not suppose that you receive less than he who has got the lettuces; for as he has the lettuces, so you have the obulus which you did not give . . . you have not been invited to a man's feast, for you did not give the host the price at which the supper is sold; but he sells it for praise (flattery), he sells it for personal attention. Give him the price, if it is for your interest, for which it is sold. But if you wish both not to give the price, and to obtain the things, you are insatiable and silly. Have you nothing then in place of the supper? You have indeed, you have the [satisfaction of] not flattering . . . him . . . whom you did not choose to flatter; you have [not had to put up with him].[21]

What would you think of someone who screamed and turned red with rage when asked to pay for a basket of groceries at the market? He or she would be "silly," to say the least. How is this different from the couple who once eagerly desired a baby and now resent the infant's demands? Or the married man who chafes at his obligations? Or the woman who has a job, a social life, and three children and is surprised that she feels tired and run-down? As obvious as the notion of a price seems, many of us seem to be stunned when we are expected to pay.

Suffering and Courage

Stoicism is a "mature" philosophy. Its appeal seems to increase with experience, that is, with frustration and disappointment. The process of growing up emotionally and philosophically involves adopting realistic expectations and accepting one's limits. The challenge of maturity is how to do this without becoming overly negative or giving in to inertia. How can I develop an attitude of Stoic detachment and acceptance and still have hopes and take action?

The key seems to involve seeing ourselves as part of the whole, in perspective—as opposed to seeing ourselves as a special part of the universe. If we can do this, we become members of the cosmopolis. We gain peace of mind from recognizing that illness, death, and disappointment are as much a part of everyone's life as are joy and delight. Shared suffering is diminished suffering.

The Stoics sometimes compared the *Logos* to a parent or teacher. They pointed out that suffering can be viewed as a gift, if we understand that the best teachers are strictest with those pupils in whom they see the most

Let others practice lawsuits, others study problems, others syllogisms; here you practice how to die, how to be enchained, how to be racked, how to be exiled.

Epictetus

Life Is Difficult

This is one of the greatest truths. It is a great truth because once we truly see this truth, we transcend it. Once we truly know that life is difficult—once we truly understand and accept it—it is no longer difficult. Because once it is accepted, the fact that life is difficult no longer matters.

Most do not fully see this truth that life is difficult. Instead they moan more or less incessantly, noisily or subtly, about the enormity of their problems, their burdens, and their difficulties as if life were generally easy, as if life *should* be easy. They voice their belief, noisily or subtly, that their difficulties represent a unique kind of affliction that should not be and that has somehow been especially visited upon them, or else upon their families, their tribe, their class, their nation, their race or even their species, and not upon others. I know about this moaning because I have done my share.

M. Scott Peck
The Road Less Traveled: A New Psychology of Love, Traditional Values and Spiritual Growth (New York: Simon & Schuster, 1978), p. 15.

Some in ten years, some in one hundred, we all die. Saints and sages die, the wicked and foolish die. In life they were Yao and Shun, in death they were rotten bones. In life they were Jie and Zhou, in death they were rotten bones. Rotten bones are all the same, who can tell them apart?

Yang Zhu

---

ability. They also noted that suffering cannot be bad by nature, or else good men like Socrates would not have suffered. In other words, who am I that I should escape the ordinary trials of life? The goal isn't to avoid them, but to use them to become a good person. Seneca said, "The greater the torment, the greater shall be the glory." He adds:

> Prosperity can come to the vulgar and to ordinary talents, but to triumph over the disasters and terrors of mortal life is the privilege of the great man. To be lucky always and to pass through life without gnawing of the mind is to be ignorant of the half of nature. You are a great man, but how can I know, if Fortune has never given you a chance to display your prowess? You have entered the Olympic games but have no rival; you gain the crown but not the victory . . . I can say . . . "I count you unfortunate because you have never been unfortunate. You have passed through life without an adversary; no man can know your potentiality, not even you." For self-knowledge, testing is necessary; no one can discover what he can do except by trying.[22]

What of the unfortunate soul who tries to get out of everything difficult, who takes only easy courses or ends relationships at the first sustained period of responsibility? What of the poor characters whose careers suffer because they change jobs as soon as they are challenged, and so never get promoted? Or the person who lingers in an inferior job or bad relationship out of fear and inertia? Since there is really no way to avoid pain, it is especially tragic to see those who try, for not only are they doomed to failure, they suffer additionally because they lack character. They live at the whim of circumstances. Seneca says:

> So god hardens and scrutinizes and exercises those he approves and loves; but those he appears to indulge and spare he is only keeping

tender for disasters to come. If you suppose anyone is immune you are mistaken. . . . Why does god afflict every good man with sickness or grief or misfortune? Because in the army, too, the most hazardous duties are assigned to the bravest soldiers. . . . In the case of good men, accordingly, the gods follow the plan that teachers follow with their pupils; they demand more effort from those in whom they have confident expectations. . . . What wonder, then, if god tries noble spirits with sternness? The demonstration of courage can never be gentle. Fortune scourges us; we must endure it. It is not cruelty but a contest.[23]

Thus, the Stoics say, our misfortune on this earth is not a result of God's disfavor, but possibly His respect or understanding of what we need to endure but would avoid if left to our own devices. Certainly faith in a divine will seems to obligate us to reach such a conclusion. Even without belief in God, we can still ask the Stoic's question: Which is more reasonable, to endure inescapable hardship and to suffer mental torment, or to endure inescapable hardship but accept it with courage and gratitude? As I have framed the question, it answers itself. Without trivializing it, we can say that Stoicism comes down to this: *While making reasonable efforts to get what we want, it is wise to learn to be happy with what we get.*

> If you regard yourself as a man and as a part of the whole, it is fitting for you now to be sick and now to make a voyage and run risks, and now to be in want, and on occasion to die before your time. Why, then, are you vexed? . . . For it is impossible in such a body as ours, that is, in this universe that envelops us, among these fellow-creatures of ours, that such things should not happen, some to one man, some to another.
>
> *Epictetus*

Stoicism Today

As we saw in the discussion of self-realization (Chapter 5), psychologists sometimes devise practical applications for wisdom philosophies. Stoicism forms the basis of certain cognitive (rationalistic) psychological therapies. Three of the most influential are William Glasser's *reality therapy*, Albert Ellis's *rational-emotive therapy*, and Viktor Frankl's *logotherapy*. All three systems are based on controlling emotions by controlling irrational thinking. Consequently, they deny the primacy of emotions, but do not condemn feelings as the Stoics did. Like Stoicism, these therapeutic approaches emphasize self-control; they stress clearly stating accurate observations of reality; and they call for maturity and courage from their clients.

> Sorrow is merely a state of mind and may not be warranted by the circumstance. Hence whether or not you feel sad over something is all in the mind.
>
> *Lie Zi*

Reality Therapy: William Glasser

In his book *Reality Therapy: A New Approach*, contemporary psychiatrist William Glasser presents a theory of psychotherapy that shares certain fundamental values with both Cynicism and Stoicism. Reality therapy attempts to make people more realistic and responsible. This requires self-control and a rational assessment of actual conditions that directly contradicts Cyrenaic hedonism.

If you want to protect yourself from "fear and guilt," and those are the crucial pincers, the real long-term destroyers of will, you have to get rid of all your instincts to compromise, to meet people halfway.

James Bond Stockdale

Do not seek to have events happen as you want them to, but instead want them to happen as they do happen, and your life will go well.

Epictetus

It may seem strange, but most people . . . elect not to continue with their life journeys—to stop short by some distance to avoid the pain of giving up parts of themselves. If it does not seem strange, it is because you do not understand the depth of the pain that may be involved. In its major forms, giving up is the most painful of human experiences.

M. Scott Peck

Glasser claims that cloudy thinking and poor character are the chief sources of suffering. He agrees with the Stoic emphasis on character:

> Very few of us realize how much we choose the misery in our lives. Even when we do, we still go ahead with the disastrous choice because we are convinced that we don't have the strength to choose better. A child doesn't give up in school, or a wife on her marriage, because each believes it's a good move. They give up because they no longer have the strength to keep up the struggle. . . . Weakness is the cause of almost all the unfortunate choices we make.[24]

Rational-Emotive Therapy: Albert Ellis

Although a Stoic thread in Glasser's reality therapy is clear, Albert Ellis's rational-emotive psychotherapy is even more directly stoically oriented. Ellis, executive director of both the Institute for Rational Living and the Institute for Advanced Study in Rational Psychotherapy, teaches that we are almost completely responsible for our fate. As a practicing psychologist, Ellis grew disenchanted with other therapies that, he thought, encouraged people "to focus upon great masses of irrelevant information" about themselves and engendered confusion, weakness, and dependency.[25] According to Ellis, nonrational forms of psychotherapy assume that

> . . . events and experiences are of paramount importance in a person's life, that he cannot help being traumatized by the unpleasant occurrences of his earliest years, and that if he truly understands the origins of these occurrences he will overcome their noxious influences. Actually, as Epictetus demonstrated some two thousand years ago, humans are not bothered by the things that happen to them but by their *view* of these things.[26]

Ellis's work shows a clear philosophical influence. In the following passage, Ellis and co-author Robert A. Harper cite examples of philosophers to illustrate their belief that correct use of reason can radically change our lives for the better:

> History gives us several outstanding instances of those who changed themselves and helped change others by hardheaded thinking. Zeno of Citium, for example, who flourished in the third century B.C., and founded the Greek Stoic school of philosophy. The Greek philosopher Epicurus; the Phrygian Epictetus; the Roman emperor Marcus Aurelius; the Dutch Jew Baruch Spinoza. These and other outstanding rational thinkers, after reading about the teaching of still earlier thinkers (Heraclitus and Democritus, among others), and doing some deep thinking of their own, enthusiastically adopted philosophies radically different from their original beliefs. More to the point for purposes of our present discussion, they actually began to *live* these philosophies, to *act* in accordance with them.

All this, mind you, without benefit of what we today would call formal psychotherapy. Granted, of course, these individuals performed outstandingly—and held rare places in human history. But they did see the light of another's reasoning and use it for their own saner living.[27]

In the following excerpt, note the strong influence of Epictetus:

Whether you like or not, you'd better accept reality the way it occurs: as highly imperfect and filled with most fallible human beings. Your alternative? Continual anxiety and desperate disappointment. . . .

We do have the power to change and control ourselves to a considerable degree (if we work hard and long enough at modifying our own beliefs and actions); we do not have a similar power to control the behavior of others. . . . If, therefore, you get unduly aroused over the way others act, instead of paying more attention to how you respond to their actions, you upset yourself over an outside event beyond your control. This seems akin to tearing out your hair because a jockey, a prizefighter, or an actor does not perform the way you would like. Very silly business indeed!

If you control your own destiny, by the proper cultivation of your own emotional garden, the most harrowing things that happen will not perturb you too much and you may even help change things and people for the better. But if you unduly upset yourself over outside happenings, you will inevitably consume so much time and energy that you will have little left for the proper cultivation of your own garden.[28]

Logotherapy: Viktor E. Frankl

Perhaps the most philosophical, and certainly the most Stoic, psychology today is Viktor E. Frankl's logotherapy. During World War II, Frankl, an Austrian Jew, was imprisoned for three years in the Nazi concentration camp at Auschwitz. In addition to the suffering and degradation he suffered there, upon his release he discovered that his whole family had been destroyed. Based on his personal and clinical experiences with suffering on a scale few of us can even imagine, he developed his own psychological school.

Logotherapy, as you might sense, means *Logos*-based healing. Frankl used the definition of *Logos* as "meaning" and felt that the individual's struggle to find a meaning in life is a primary motivation. He stated that the "will to meaning" is as strong as the will to pleasure or the will to power. Logotherapy combines the insights of Stoicism with contemporary psychology's more sophisticated understanding of the relationship of feeling to thinking. Frankl's firsthand experiences with utter loss—and the power of the will to give that loss meaning—make logotherapy especially interesting to the student of Stoicism.

It is the mind which moulds man's destiny, action being but precipitated thought. It follows that one's lightest thought has vast effects, not only on the thinker, but on all that lives.

Christmas Humphreys

We can only bow our heads in the presence of those broken beneath the burden of their destiny. The capacity of the human soul for suffering and isolation is immense.

Sarvepalli Radhakrishnan

His most famous book is *Man's Search for Meaning*. If you have not read it, I recommend it to you. Let's see how Frankl talks about Stoicism:

> Whenever one is confronted with an inescapable, unavoidable situation, whenever one has to face a fate that cannot be changed, e.g., an incurable disease, such as inoperable cancer, just then one is given a last chance to actualize the highest value, to fulfill the deepest meaning, the meaning of suffering. For what matters above all is the attitude we take toward suffering, the attitude in which we take our suffering upon ourselves.[29]

> Suffering ceases to be suffering in some way at the moment it finds a meaning, such as the meaning of a sacrifice. . . . It is one of the main tenets of logotherapy that man's main concern is not to gain pleasure or avoid pain, but rather to see a meaning in his life. That is why man is ready to suffer, on the condition, to be sure, that his suffering has a meaning.[30]

> What a man has done cannot be undone . . . [but] through the right attitude unchangeable suffering is transmuted into a heroic and virtuous achievement. In the same fashion a man who has failed by a deed cannot change what happened but by repentance he can change himself. Everything depends on the right attitude in the same way and manner as in the case of suffering. The difference lies in the fact that the right attitude is, then, a right attitude to himself.[31]

Epictetus in Vietnam

Perhaps the greatest testimonies to the merit of Stoicism come from those who have suffered greatly, as Frankl reminds us. One of the most interesting and compelling arguments for the practical value of a good philosophical education came from an unexpected source: a highly trained United States Navy fighter pilot.

What we know as the *Enchiridion* of Epictetus can be a powerful consolation and support to people undergoing the severest trials. In fact, James Bond Stockdale, a former vice admiral in the United States Navy, credits his education in the humanities—and Epictetus in particular—with helping him survive eight years as a prisoner of war in North Vietnam, four years in solitary confinement. Stockdale was awarded the Congressional Medal of Honor after his release.

In April 1978 the *Atlantic Monthly* published a remarkable article by this unusual soldier-philosopher called "The World of Epictetus." Stockdale describes the brutal conditions the POWs were kept in, and his own fear and despondency. As he reviewed his life from his solitary cell, Stockdale "picked the locks" to the doors of his past experiences. He recalled cocktail parties and phony social contacts with revulsion as empty and val-

*Sidebar quotes:*

To bear pain, to endure suffering, is the quality of the strong in spirit. It adds to the spiritual resources of humanity.

Sarvepalli Radhakrishnan

Love only that which happens to thee and is spun with the thread of thy destiny. For what is more suitable?

Marcus Aurelius

The judge will do some things to you which are thought to be terrifying; but how can he stop you from taking the punishment he threatened?

Epictetus

James Bond Stockdale credits the lessons he learned from Epictetus's Enchiridion *with helping him survive eight years in a North Vietnamese prison camp, confirming the Stoic belief that through great effort of will we can transform total loss into "heroic and virtuous achievement."*

ueless. "More often than not," he said, "the locks worth picking had been old schoolroom doors."

In this passage, Stockdale testifies to the real-life value of Epictetus's *Enchiridion*:

The messages of history and philosophy I used were simple.

The first one is the business about life not being fair. That was a very important lesson and I learned it from a wonderful man named Philip Rhinelander. . . . He said, "The course I'm teaching is my personal two-term favorite—The Problem of Good and Evil—and we're starting our second term." He said the message of his course was from the Book of Job. The number one problem in this world is that people are not able to accommodate the lesson in the book.

He recounted the story of Job. It starts out by establishing that Job was the most honorable of men. Then he lost all his goods. He also lost his reputation, which is what really hurt. His wife was badgering him to admit his sins, but he knew he had made no errors. He was not a patient man and demanded to speak to the Lord. When the Lord replied in the whirlwind, he said, "Now, Job, you have to shape up! Life is not fair." That's my interpretation and that's the way the book ended for hundreds of years. I agree with those of the opinion that the happy ending was spliced on many years later. . . . People couldn't live with the original message.

For wherever a man's place is, whether the place which he has chosen or that in which he has been placed by a commander, there he ought to remain in the hour of danger; he should not think of death or of anything but disgrace. And this, O men of Athens, is a true saying.

Socrates

What's important is not fame, nor glory, but the ability to endure, to be able to bear one's cross and have faith.

Anton Chekhov

For it is better to die of hunger, exempt from fear and guilt, than to live in affluence with perturbation.

Epictetus

Rhinelander also passed on to me another piece of classical information which I found of great value. On the day of our last session together he said, "You're a military man, let me give you a book to remember me by. It's a book of military ethics." He handed it to me, and I bade him goodbye with great emotion. I took the book home and that night started to read it. It was the *Enchiridion* of the philosopher Epictetus, his "manual" for the Roman field soldier.

As I began to read, I thought to myself in disbelief, "Does Rhinelander think I'm going to draw lessons for my life from this thing? I'm a fighter pilot. I'm a technical man. I'm a test pilot. I know how to get people to do technical work. I play golf; I drink martinis. I know how to get ahead in my profession. And what does he hand me? A book that says in part, 'It's better to die in hunger, exempt from guilt and fear, than to live in affluence and with perturbation.'" I remembered this later in prison because perturbation was what I was living with. When I ejected from the airplane on that September morn in 1965, I had left the land of technology. I had entered the world of Epictetus, and it's a world that few of us, whether we know it or not, are ever far away from.[32]

The lessons that the old Roman slave learned on the rack gave comfort and courage to a solitary prisoner of war two thousand years later in the rice paddies of Southeast Asia.

Commentary

I consider it a dangerous misconception of mental hygiene to assume that what man needs in the first place is equilibrium or . . . a tensionless state. What man actually needs is not a tensionless state but rather a striving and struggling for some goal worthy of him.

Viktor E. Frankl

This summary glance at Stoicism shows up inconsistencies and difficulties. The nature of fate remains ambiguous: How detailed is my life "script"? Has the *Logos* determined that I drop a pencil or make a typing mistake as I write this? Or is my fate painted in broader strokes? If so, in what sense is it fate? Are all emotions "bad"? Is it *reasonable* to be so detached, if it's even possible? Can a disinterested person have a motive, or are motives emotional?

Such immediately obvious problems result partly from the Stoics' near indifference to everything but the issue of how to live the least disturbed life possible. They were not concerned with providing a completely worked-out philosophical *system*. Even so, Stoicism retains an appeal that rests on genuine insights into the causes of much suffering and unhappiness. The Stoics were highly practical "moral psychologists," whose chief interests were ethics and psychology. As such, the most insightful of them offer sage counsel and inspiration that is as pertinent and helpful today as it was when first presented over two thousand years ago.

When I first encountered Stoicism as an undergraduate, I found it annoying. The ideal Stoic seemed to be a bland, emotionless vegetable—certainly not the kind of person I wanted to be. I needn't have worried. Stoic self-control and discipline were unlikely to stifle my great emotions. And so I spent too many years fuming over traffic, long lines, the way the world behaved, my teachers, my students, being alone, not being alone—life.

Today, I recognize the depth of passion behind the words of Marcus Aurelius and Epictetus. They certainly were not bland, unfeeling people. I understand how much of my own frustration has come from not looking carefully for the price tag before I rushed to the checkout.

Given the condition of our society and basic human nature, I see enough merit in Stoic wisdom to compensate for certain ambiguities and inconsistencies in its expression. If nothing else, it sometimes helps me go to the bank on Friday afternoon without fuming and complaining—or helps me stay home without fuming and complaining.

Stoicism provides a counterbalance of sorts to today's love affair with instant gratification and emotional expressiveness. In its lessons on relationships and suffering, it wisely reminds us that what cannot be changed must be accepted graciously if we are ever to be happy. We live in a time when people seek external solutions to nearly every sort of predicament. Many will be found. But no external solution can make us happy or unhappy, for, as a late friend used to remind me, "Happiness is an inside job."

After his 1973 release from prison, James Bond Stockdale served as president of the Naval War College in Newport, Rhode Island, and president of the Citadel, the military college of South Carolina. Since 1981, he has been a senior research fellow at the Hoover Institution, located at Stanford University. In 1992, third-party presidential candidate Ross Perot asked Stockdale to be his vice presidential running mate. During an election-year debate among the three vice presidential candidates, Stockdale began, as Socrates might have, with two timeless questions: "Who am I? Why am I here?" Though the philosophical thrust of the questions was missed by most people, Stockdale's philosophical vision attracted national attention to Stoicism in general and Epictetus in particular.

Stockdale remains one of our most remarkable contemporary philosophers in the original sense. The lessons of wisdom he has learned are particularly compelling because they come from as broad a spectrum as is humanly possible—the extremes of defeat, degradation, torture, and isolation, on the one hand, and the heights of influence, national prominence, and academic recognition, on the other. Few of us experience such extremes in either direction; fewer yet in both. Thus, Stockdale provides us with a rare contemporary example of the Stoic sage. Who better to have the last word in our survey of one of the most influential archetypes of wisdom? Stockdale says:

> Stoicism is certainly not for everybody, and it is not for me in every circumstance, but it is an expression in philosophical terms of how people find purpose in what they have every right to see as a purposeless world. . . . [Stoicism] speaks to people everywhere who persist in

We grow older. But it is by no means certain that we shall grow up.

Walter Lippmann

To live under the false pretense that you will forever have control of your station in life is to ride for a fall; you're asking for disappointment. So make sure in your heart of hearts, in your inner self, that you treat your station in life with *indifference*, not with contempt, only with *indifference*.

James Bond Stockdale

Giving up comforts and trying to carry out efforts. That is the practice of the Sufi.

Bayazid Bistami

> What is the result at which all virtue aims? *Serenity.*
>
> *Epictetus*

> In this day and age, the greatest devotion, greater than learning and praying, consists in accepting the world exactly as it happens to be.
>
> *Rabbi Moshe of Kobryn*

competing in what they see as a buzz-saw existence, their backs to the wall, their lives having meaning only so long as they fight for pride and comradeship and joy rather than capitulate to either tyranny or phoniness. . . .

. . . We who are in hierarchies—be they academic, business, military, or otherwise—are always in positions in which people are trying to manipulate us, to get moral leverage on us. The only defense is to keep yourself clean—never to do or say anything of which you can be made to feel ashamed. . . .

Am I personally still hooked on Epictetus's Principle of Life? Yes, but not in the sense of following a memorized doctrine. I sometimes become amused at how I have applied it and continue to apply it unconsciously. An example is the following story about myself.

As the months and years wear on in solitary confinement, it turns out each man goes crazy if he doesn't get some ritual into his life. I mean by that a self-imposed obligation to do certain things in a certain order each day. Like most prisoners, I prayed each day, month after month, continually altering and refining a long memorized monologue that probably ran to ten or fifteen minutes. At some point, my frame of mind became so pure that I started deleting any begging of God and any requests that would work specifically for my benefit. This didn't come out of any new Principle of Life that I had developed; it just suddenly started to seem unbecoming to beg. I knew the lesson of the book of Job: life is not fair. What claim had I for special consideration? And anyway, by then I had seen enough misery to know that He had enough to worry about without trying to appease a crybaby like me. And so it has been ever since.[33]

Summary of Main Points

1. Antisthenes was the founder of a philosophical school known as Cynicism and Diogenes was its most famous advocate. The Cynics believed that the very essence of civilization is corrupt, that manners are hypocritical, that material wealth weakens people, and that civilization destroys the individual and makes him or her vulnerable to the whims of fortune.

2. According to the Cynics, the death of Socrates showed that not even the wisest person can control other people or external events. They concluded that the less an individual needs to be happy, the less vulnerable he or she will be. Cynics live austere, unconventional lives.

3. Founded in Greece by Zeno, Stoicism grew out of Cynicism and achieved widespread influence in first-century Rome, ultimately spreading throughout Christianized Europe. The Roman slave Epictetus, the Emperor Marcus Aurelius, and the senator Seneca are the most influential Stoic writers.

4. Stoics advised learning to want whatever we get by willing ourselves to accept whatever circumstances we are in without resentment.

They believed that the cosmos is wisely governed by the *Logos* (World Reason) and that everything happens as part of a divine plan. The wise person anticipates and goes along with fate; the foolish one wishes things were otherwise.

5. According to the Stoics, human beings are bits of the *Logos* because we have rational souls. Happiness comes from the effective use of reason to alter the will. Based on their concept of a disinterested World Reason, the Stoics taught that it is wise to minimize personal attachments and motives. One way to do this is to evaluate things in terms of the goal of a universal harmony rather than from an individualistic view.

6. The Stoics rejected emotion to the extent it was humanly possible, favoring detached, rational acceptance over personal, emotional involvement.

7. Central to Stoicism is the distinction between control and influence. Though the Stoics believed that life is fated, they understood this in a loose sense. Because we cannot know precisely what our fate is, we must take reasonable action without pinning our happiness on a particular result.

8. According to the Stoics, we can control our ideas and attitudes but we cannot control "externals" such as reputation, social status, relationships, health, and wealth. A great deal of Stoic literature concerns learning how to identify what we cannot control and exercising control over our will.

9. Stoic virtues include strength of will, courage, dignity, and maturity.

10. According to Stoic doctrine, everything has a price that reason can reveal. The ultimate price of happiness is personal detachment from external conditions; peace of mind comes from indifference to everything except accepting the will of the *Logos*.

11. The Stoics looked upon suffering as a test of character and praised the ability to accept unavoidable suffering without bitterness or complaint. They taught that only great struggle could produce greatness of character.

12. Stoicism remains influential today in the form of various schools of cognitive psychotherapy. Three of the most important are William Glasser's reality therapy, Albert Ellis's rational-emotive therapy, and Viktor Frankl's logotherapy. The philosopher-warrior James Bond Stockdale continues to define Epictetus's Principle of Life and communicate it to a growing audience.

Study Questions

1. What is Cynicism?
2. Explain how Cynicism influenced Stoicism. Be specific.
3. What is the relationship of Socrates to Cynicism and Stoicism?
4. Compare and contrast hedonism, Cynicism, and Stoicism.
5. Discuss how the social climate of ancient Rome encouraged the emergence of Stoicism.
6. Discuss the relationship of the lives of Marcus Aurelius and Epictetus to their philosophies.
7. What is the *Logos*?
8. How are the *Logos* and fate related in Stoicism?
9. Identify and discuss possible problems with the Stoic notion of fate.
10. Stoicism was quickly absorbed into Christianity. Identify and comment on any similarities you are aware of.
11. What is the disinterested rational will, and why is it important to Stoic doctrine?
12. Explain and defend the Stoic view of emotions. Then analyze it.

13. What do the Stoics think falls under our control? What do the Stoics think does not fall under our control? Do you agree? Why or why not?

14. Analyze the relationship between influence and control.

15. Discuss the difference between avoidable and unavoidable suffering. How can we tell which is which? Why does it matter?

16. State the essence of Stoicism in twenty-five words or less.

17. Explain the Stoic attitude toward relationships. How does it differ from today's attitudes? Explain.

18. Using a not-too-embarrassing example from your own life, illustrate the principle of paying the price.

19. How do the Stoics interpret suffering? What do you think of their view?

20. What does Seneca mean when he says "I count you unfortunate because you have never been unfortunate"?

21. Can you find additional examples of Stoicism today?

22. Do you know any Stoics? If so, describe them.

23. What do you think of Stockdale's claim that a good philosophical education is highly practical? Give his position and then comment on it.

The Scholar

Thomas Aquinas

Now, among the inquiries that we must undertake concerning God in Himself, we must set down in the beginning that whereby His Existence is demonstrated, as the necessary foundation of the whole work. For, if we do not demonstrate that God exists, all consideration of divine things is necessarily suppressed.

Thomas Aquinas

I once watched a television news reporter interview a sobbing woman who sat on the pile of rubble that had once been her small mobile home. Everything she owned had been destroyed by a tornado. Through her tears, the victim expressed her gratitude to God for saving her life. As she explained it, she was preparing supper when she "mysteriously" had the urge to go to the corner market for a loaf of bread. She was gone for only a few minutes, but in those minutes the tornado struck. "If I hadn't gone for that bread," she said into the camera, "I would be dead now. God told me to go get that bread in order to save my life."

Does this mean that God *wanted* those people who were not warned to die? Suppose the woman's neighbor had been planning to go to the store but got a phone call just as he started for the door. Should we conclude that God arranged the timing of the call to make sure he didn't escape the tornado?

After all, if God is the cause of *everything* that happens, *everything* includes tornadoes and torture, as well as salvation and joy. If God knows *everything*, does He know your grade on your philosophy final right now? But if God knows things before they happen, how can *we* be held responsible for them? If God knew before you were born that you would get a C minus in philosophy, isn't *He* the cause of your grade, not you? And if there is even one thing that He does not know, even one thing, how can He be all-wise?

These and related questions are of more than just academic interest. They are vitally important to anyone who attempts to reconcile faith with reason. One "solution" to such problems has been to hold a *dual-truth point of view*. This is the position that there is one small-t truth on the finite, human level, and another, superior, capital-T Truth for God. Another strategy is to declare that these problems demonstrate that the ways of God are a "mystery" to human beings. In both cases, inconsistencies and ambiguities are not so much confronted as they are evaded.

Many believers and nonbelievers alike feel cheated when asked to accept inconsistent beliefs or simply to dismiss the most vital questions of faith. If you doubt this, wander through the sections of your college library's stacks dealing with theology and religious philosophy. You will find a large number of books and articles attempting to reconcile faith with reason. If you have ever seriously wrestled with the problem of evil (How can a good, loving, wise, powerful God allow evil?) or the problem of moral responsibility (If God gave Adam and Eve a corrupt nature, how can they—and we—justly be held responsible?), you have entered a timeless struggle.

Our culture has been heavily influenced by an ongoing clash between Christian values and the values established in classical Greece. In the classical view, human beings, despite our many faults, represent the most important life-form. The classical philosopher believed that objective knowledge and logic could unlock the keys to the universe, improving our lives in the process. The good life was seen as being a product of reason. Reason was valued over faith, because knowing was thought to be more useful than believing.

The Christian view presents a completely different picture. Human beings are seen as fallen and corrupt creatures, finite and ignorant. Christian theology teaches that we are incapable of avoiding sin and the punishment of hell through our own efforts. Only the undeserved grace and sacrifice of a loving God can save us. Obedience to the revealed word of God is also necessary for salvation. Faith is valued more highly than reason, because salvation is more important than worldly progress or success in a life that is relatively brief compared to the afterlife—where we will spend eternity in heaven (if we are saved) or hell (if we are not). As a result of its emphasis on the afterlife, Christian theology is sometimes characterized as *otherworldly*.

> God does not play dice with the universe.
>
> *Albert Einstein*

> I inquired, "Whence is evil?" and found no result. . . . What torments did my heart then endure!
>
> *St. Augustine*

The God-Centered Universe

Are faith and reason inevitable enemies? Can the human mind know God through reason? Does being a "good Christian" prohibit questioning and trying to understand certain things? Why did God give us the ability to reason if we are asked to ignore what reason reveals? When conflicting religious beliefs all claim to rely on divine authority and revelation, how can we choose among them? These are among the great questions of the Middle Ages.

Whereas the classical mind was predominantly secular, the medieval mind was chiefly theological. **Theology**, from the Greek *theos* (God) and *logos* (study of), means "talking about God" or "the study or science of God." The Middle Ages saw philosophers turn from the study of man and

> THEOLOGY
>
> From the Greek *theos* (God) and *logos* (study of); "talking about God" or "the study or science of God."

nature to "otherworldly" inquiries and the study of God. Rather than *discover* the truth through reason and science, the scholar studied church dogma and theology in order to *explain* what God chose to reveal.

The great transition from the classical to the medieval worldview occurred in a series of steps. Late Stoicism, especially in the *Meditations* and *Letters* of Marcus Aurelius, marks the beginning of the shift from pagan to Christian philosophy. Though pagan himself, Marcus in the *Meditations* expresses values and interests that were to become hallmarks of Christian philosophy: devaluing of this life and its temporary nature, a strong sense of duty, and the idea that human beings are related to the Logos (see Chapter 6). But Marcus differed from his medieval successors in his view of humans as social and political beings.[1]

The Seeds of Change

The Christian religion arose after the death of Jesus Christ, through the efforts of the early apostles and disciples, especially Paul. Christianity originally consisted of scattered groups of believers anticipating the Second Coming of Christ, which would signal the end of the world. Thinking that they would soon be in heaven, early Christians saw no need to develop political interests. Similarly, they were uninterested in science and philosophy and remained indifferent to much of what went on around them. Their chief concern was salvation through faith. Expecting that the risen Christ would return at any moment, they were understandably impatient with the affairs of this world. Thus they devoted themselves to converting non-Christians and to preparing their own souls for judgment. In a major contrast with the classical view of life, they saw no time or need to fashion philosophical, social, or moral theories.

When Christianity was new, its primary energies lay in survival and expansion. As time passed and the world did not end, Christians found it increasingly difficult to avoid dealing with problems of the here and now. Principles and rules for interpreting the basic teachings of Christ collected as the New Testament became necessary when it grew clear that the Second Coming might not occur until well into the future.

Interpreting revealed sacred dogma is always dangerous, however, for once the inevitability of interpretation is accepted, the door is open to competing interpretations. If *every* claimed interpretation is reliable, God's revealed will is going to appear chaotic, inconsistent, contradictory, and capricious. There must be criteria for distinguishing revelation from delusion and dogma from error. And there must be criteria for choosing criteria. And criteria for choosing criteria for choosing criteria. . . .

Some reinterpretation of Christian teachings was clearly called for, if the Second Coming might be generations away. Giving all our goods to the poor is one thing when we expect to be in heaven in the immediate future; practical considerations complicate matters if the final judgment may be

Can there be a future good so great as to render acceptable, in retrospect, the whole human experience, with all its wickedness and suffering as well as all its sanctity and happiness?
I think that perhaps there can, and indeed perhaps there is.

John Hick

The dominant theme of the Middle Ages was the God-centered universe. In this illustration, though God and Satan struggle over a dead man's soul, it is clear that God holds the supreme, central place.

years away. As the centuries passed and the Second Coming did not occur, Christianity continued to expand until Christians dominated Europe. As Christian doctrine increased in complexity, theological issues added to practical complications.

The Need to Reconcile Faith and Reason

The great paradoxes of faith are sometimes superficially dismissed by people who have never really grappled with them. Their religious training may have given them simple answers to the problems of free will, evil, predestination, God's nature, and others. Or they may have been taught to "exalt faith" by condemning reason. It is easy to *say* that faith surpasses understanding until you fully grasp the complex depths and significance of these problems. Whatever our individual religious beliefs, most of us are also rational creatures for whom it is somehow unsatisfying to accept contradictions and serious inconsistencies concerning something as important as our religious faith. Most of us are uncomfortable when we learn that we are violating rational principles.

The basic **principles of reason**—also called **rules of inference**—define the limits of rationality. That is, consistently violating them moves us to

PRINCIPLES OF REASON or RULES OF INFERENCE

Principles (such as the law of contradiction) that define the limits of rationality by their very structure and that cannot be rationally refuted since we rely on them in order to reason.

the realm of the irrational or illogical. They are true by their very structure (by definition). They cannot be rationally refuted, since we rely on them in order to reason. Contemporary logicians recognize several rules of inference. One of the most important is the law of contradiction.

The **law of contradiction** (sometimes known as the law of noncontradiction) says: *No statement can be both true and false at the same time and under the same conditions.* Or to use symbols (as philosophers who study logic often do), *p* cannot be both *p* and *not-p at the same time*. For example: Either this is a philosophy book or it is *not* a philosophy book. It cannot be both a philosophy book and not a philosophy book. It can, however, be a philosophy book *and* a doorstop at the same time. There is no contradiction involved in asserting that it is a philosophy book and more. The contradiction occurs in the mutually exclusive assertions: "This is a philosophy book" *and* "This is not a philosophy book."

Take a moment to reflect on the law of contradiction. See if you can get a sense of just how basic it is to rationality. Because it is a fundamental principle of reasoning, we are usually disturbed to discover that our ideas are contradictory, for such awareness commits us to resolving the contradiction or holding irrational ideas.

In matters of faith, trying to avoid the possibility of contradiction by claiming that the human mind is finite and unable to understand God and His ways is ultimately unsatisfying, for it removes us from meaningful communication with God. If we can never fully comprehend God, if we must trust that things *are not at all what they seem* (for instance, that evil only *appears to be evil* from our level but is *really* good from God's), then our "solution" may not be what it appears to be, either. The mere assertion of human limitations reduces all theology and religion to the realm of the unknowable, or it leaves us where we started: If we can know *some* things about God, *which* things, and how do we know? Like it or not, we are susceptible to principles of reason—and so are our most sacred beliefs.

Consequently, scrutinized according to logical principles, the most commonly accepted attributes of God—all-knowing, all-good, all-powerful—generated problems concerning the suffering of innocents, the existence of evil, and the possibility of free will. Efforts to resolve these contradictions resulted in such doctrines as Original Sin, the elect, and the sin of intellectual pride. Once the idea of a personal God replaced the impersonal Logos of the Greeks, new questions arose for those willing to face them.

LAW OF CONTRADICTION

(sometimes known as the law of noncontradiction) Rule of inference that says no statement can be both true and false at the same time and under the same conditions.

Philosophical Query

Have you ever felt that you had to choose between "hard" scientific and rational evidence and "soft" faith or intuitive religious belief? We also may encounter this tension in regard to our beliefs about psychic experiences, astrology, reincarnation, and other supernatural events. Why do people get so upset when someone points out inconsistencies or contradictions in their beliefs? If faith is higher than understanding, why do inconsistencies matter? What could count as evidence for such beliefs?

Does including religious beliefs with "psychic" or "New Age" beliefs in this Query offend you? Do you think it might offend others? Why do you think "linking" such beliefs might bother people? Do you think believers on one "side" or the other (religious or psychic) are more likely to be offended? Why or why not? (Note: You can analyze this Query regardless of your personal feelings and beliefs.)

The Life of Thomas Aquinas

Thomas Aquinas (c. 1225–1274) was born near Naples.[2] His father, who was related to the count of Aquino, planned for Thomas to achieve a position of importance in the Catholic church. To this end he enrolled Thomas in the Benedictine abbey school at Montecassino when Thomas was around five. The Benedictines are Roman Catholic monks famed for their modest lifestyle, which involves physical labor as well as spiritual discipline. As a general rule, Benedictines remain in one monastery for life. While under their care, Thomas was well grounded in basic religious knowledge, academic skills, and good study habits.

Thomas Aquinas

The monks of Montecassino taught by emphasizing close scrutiny of Scripture, careful reading and writing, and rote memory of long and complicated passages. Years later, when he was a famous scholar, Thomas drew upon what he had learned at Montecassino in answer to a request for advice on how to study:

> Make up your mind to start on small streams rather than to plunge into the sea; for one should progress from easier matters to those that are more difficult. . . .
>
> . . . Do not be concerned about what speaker you are listening to; instead, when something good is said, commit it to memory. Be sure that you understand whatever you read. Make sure you know the difficulties and store up whatever you can in the treasure-house of the mind; keep as busy as a person who seeks to fill a vessel.[3]

Every saint has a past and every sinner a future.

Oscar Wilde

The Dominican

The spiritual authority of the Benedictine monasteries of the time had begun to decline, in great part due to their wealth and prosperity. In 1239, Thomas was sent to study at the Imperial University of Naples, where he made friends with some Dominican monks. Dominicans were dedicated

You can say that you trust God anyway—that no arguments can undermine your faith. But that is just a statement describing how stubborn you are; it has no bearing whatsoever on the question of God's goodness.

B. C. Johnson

to education and to preaching to common people. They took vows of poverty, chastity, and obedience. Unlike the Benedictines, who tended to establish their monasteries in the country, the Dominicans established themselves in the towns. They quickly became the intellectual elite of the thirteenth century.[4] Thomas was so attracted to the Dominican way of life that he decided to join the order. This decision disturbed his family, who had been looking forward to enjoying the advantages of being related to a powerful priest or bishop. That Thomas would become a poor monk was not in their plans.

Nonetheless, Thomas entered the Order of Preachers, as the Dominicans are known, in 1243 or 1244. His mother was so unhappy about it that she sent a distress signal to his older brothers, who were soldiers at the time. Thomas was traveling with other Dominicans when the brothers tracked him down and ordered him to remove his Dominican habit. When he refused, they kidnapped him. His family held him captive for several months. They applied various arguments and pressures but did allow him to wear his Dominican habit and to study—though they kept him confined to his room. One biographer reports the interesting but unlikely story that his family sent a provocatively dressed girl into his room one night while Thomas slept: "She tempted him to sin, using all the devices at her disposal, glances, caresses and gestures."[5] The saint in Thomas proved stronger than temptation, and he prayed until the girl left. He even managed to write a treatise *On Fallacies* while in family captivity. Finally, convinced of Thomas's sincerity and strength, his family released him. Soon after, the Dominicans sent him first to Cologne to continue his studies with the acclaimed teacher Albertus Magnus and then to the University of Paris.

The University of Paris

What we know today as universities began as medieval cathedral schools, though cathedral schools lacked central libraries and clusters of special buildings. Cathedral schools were religious in nature, originally consisting of masters and students under the authority of the supporting cathedral. These independent schools were associated with cathedrals and monasteries in such cities as Cluny, Tours, Chartres, and Paris. Notre Dame eventually supported more than one school. They spread from France to England and throughout Europe.

It is clear from what has been said that there is a substance which is eternal and unmovable and separate from sensible things.

Aristotle

As the number of schools increased, they vied to possess the best libraries and faculty, as well as competed over the quality and drama of the great public debates (called disputations) they held. Associated with both the Dominicans and Franciscans, these individual schools, which were clustered about Paris, tended to specialize in copying and commenting on selected texts, in consolidating oral teachings into unified written form, or in subject areas such as rhetoric or theology. In time, the individual schools merged into the University of Paris, which was closely supervised by the bishop of Paris, the chancellor of Notre Dame, and the pope.

As they developed, universities became centers of medieval learning, based in part on the quality of their faculties and in part on the availability of important new translations of philosophical texts. Most notable among these was the work of Aristotle; also significant were the great commentaries on Aristotle made by Arabian scholars from Baghdad and Spain, and original Arabic and Jewish works of epistemology, metaphysics, and ethics by al-Farabi, ibn-Gabriol, Avicenna, and Averroîs.

Only the clergy were permitted to study and teach at the universities, and Latin was the universal language of church and school. It is not surprising, then, that for the first time the unification, organization, and synthesis of knowledge became major philosophic tasks, strengthened by the authority and firm hierarchy of the church. The fundamental philosophical and social movement of the thirteenth century was toward the synthesis and consolidation of a single spiritual truth.[6]

Much of the teaching was conducted in the great public debates, the disputations, so the universities sought great debaters who could enhance the school's reputation by the quality of their disputations. The Dominicans were renowned debaters, and by 1231 they held two faculty positions in theology at the University of Paris.[7]

On disputation days all other classes were suspended. One type of disputation was the *disputed question*, which consisted of two sessions. In the morning session bachelors in theology (the equivalent of graduate students today) carefully studied a set of problems (the question) and then, under the guidance of their teacher, publicly stated complications, ambiguities, and contradictions in the form of numbered objections. The student was required to demonstrate familiarity with important works bearing on the topic by citing various authorities and quoting their positions. Lastly, the student suggested the best solution he could to the original question. This was all done before a large audience of other students, faculty, and distinguished guests.

In the afternoon session, the master of the school of theology summarized the morning session and, going through the objections one by one, provided his own final answer to the questions, together with his reply to the objections. The master would eventually write and publish a summary known as a *disputed question*. The basic structure of these oral disputations—statement of the question, detailed list of objections and commentaries on the objections, and final resolution—is the basic model on which Aquinas constructed his *Summa Theologica*.

Medievalist Martin Grabmann characterizes these public debates as tournaments for the clergy. Priests of all ranks and any church officials who happened to be in town attended. The time, place, and topic of the dispute were announced in all the schools of the university. The bachelor

I maintain that all attempts to employ reason in theology in any merely speculative manner are altogether fruitless.

Immanuel Kant

Thomas Aquinas was a master of the "disputed question." Medieval disputations sometimes lasted for days and have been characterized as philosophical combat.

Theology is an effort to explain the unknowable in terms of the not worth knowing. . . . [It] is not only opposed to the scientific spirit; it is opposed to every other form of rational thinking.

H. L. Mencken

being tested responded to questions formulated by the masters present. If necessary, the student could be prompted by the teacher who had helped him prepare for the dispute. Grabmann says:

> These disputations exercised enormous attraction upon teacher and pupil alike. They provided a continuous coming together between the master and his scholars, they spurred the ambitions of the young, and stretched their intellectual capacities to the limit. In the disputation the personal capability of the student appeared most articulately and publicly. The disputations also exhibited a certain dramatic interest. They were a kind of tournament, a contest or duel with the weapons of the mind. The alternating movement of these duels, the gradual development and complication of problems, the blow for blow presentation of suggestions and solutions, questions and answers, distinctions and negations, the various sophisms and entrapments in which

one tried to entice the adversary—all these, and other moments too, were well calculated to keep the interest and expectation of both the participants in, and spectators of, such exercises of disputation at the highest tension and suspense.[8]

Albertus Magnus: The Universal Teacher

While at Cologne, Thomas was encouraged in the search for philosophical unity by his teacher **Albertus Magnus (Albert the Great) (c. 1200–1280)**, who was among the first scholars to realize the need to ground Christian faith in philosophy and science. If this were not done, the church would lose influence in the face of great advances in secular and pagan knowledge. Rather than ignore the huge quantity of learning made available by the Crusades, Albert chose to master it. He read most of the Christian, Arabian, and Jewish writers, and wrote continuously about what he read. Albert was called the "Universal Teacher" because of the breadth of his knowledge and because he tried to make Aristotle accessible by paraphrasing many of his works.

Although Albert has been criticized for not being creative and consistent, his efforts at synthesis laid a foundation for Thomas Aquinas. Albert quoted extensively and without alteration, and from this Thomas learned the value of broad knowledge and extensive documentation. In his own work, however, Thomas went beyond his teacher by using his sources to construct a coherent philosophy of his own. Still, his scholarly skills owe a great deal to Albert, who recognized his ability while Thomas was still a young man, as a famous anecdote reveals: When Thomas first arrived in Paris, his rural manners, his heavyset, farm-boy physique, and slow, quiet ways earned him the nickname of "the Dumb Ox," and his handwriting was so bad that others could barely read it. Yet he studied hard and remained good-natured as the other students laughed at him—until the day he answered one of Albert the Great's questions with such stunning brilliance that the master said to the others: "We call this man the Dumb Ox, but someday his bellow will be heard throughout the whole world."

> My father taught me that the question "Who made me?" cannot be answered, since it immediately suggests the further question "Who made God?"
>
> *John Stuart Mill*

The Task of the Scholar

Shortly before Thomas was born, the church had forbidden the teaching of Aristotle's natural science and *Metaphysics*. His Unmoved Mover was an impersonal, natural force, not a loving, personal God. Entelechy (soul) was part of nature, inseparable from the body that housed it, and so it seemed that Aristotle denied the possibility of personal immortality. Yet the thorough, systematic quality of Aristotle's work on scientific thinking, logic, and nature gradually won more and more medieval converts. As Aristotle's influence spread throughout the University of Paris, questions arose regarding both the relationship of Aristotle's classical naturalism to orthodox Christianity and the accuracy of newly arrived Arabian commentaries on Aristotle. The faculty realized that Aristotle would have to be integrated into Christian theology. This task became the great, courageous accomplishment of Tommaso d'Aquino, "the Dumb Ox of Sicily."

In 1252 Thomas received his master's degree from the University of Paris, where he was also lecturing. He taught theology at the papal court in Rome in 1259, and from 1268 to 1272 lectured in Paris once more. During the twenty years that he was an active teacher, Thomas wrote disputations on various theological questions, commentaries on books of the Bible, commentaries on twelve works of Aristotle and others, and nearly forty other miscellaneous notes, sermons, lectures, poems, and treatises. His crowning achievements are the multivolume summaries of arguments and theology known as the *Summa Theologica* and *Summa contra Gentiles*.

Thomas was sent to Naples to establish a Dominican school in 1272, and in 1274 he was commanded by Pope Gregory X to attend the Council of Lyons. He died on the trip to Lyons on March 7, 1274. As reported by Brother Peter of Montesangiovanni, his last hours reflected his submission to the authority of the church.

The Wisdom of the Scholar

SCHOLASTICISM

Christian philosophy that dominated medieval Europe from about A.D. 1000 to 1300, stressing logical and linguistic analysis of texts and arguments in order to produce a systematic statement and defense of Christian beliefs.

The term **Scholasticism** refers to the mainstream of Christian philosophy in medieval Europe from about 1000 to about 1300, just after the death of Aquinas. It comes from the Greek *scholastikos*, meaning "to enjoy leisure" or "to devote one's free time to learning."

Scholastic philosophy rested on a strong interest in logical and linguistic analysis of texts and arguments for the ultimate purpose of producing a systematic statement and defense of Christian beliefs. As the revealed word of God, the Bible was central to this project, but always was interpreted in accord with the authority of the church and the wisdom of selected earlier Christian writers.

A central effort of Scholastic philosophers was the attempt to reconstruct Greek philosophy in a form that not only was consistent with but supported and strengthened Christian doctrine. An important aspect of this effort was the imposition of a hierarchy of knowledge, in which the highest place was held by revelation, as interpreted by the church; next were faith and theology; philosophy came last, subordinated to both faith and revelation.[9]

Medieval scholars were the first *professors of philosophy*; their task was to teach, to expound on texts, to write about them, to debate in class and in public, and to publish great educational summations of official doctrine.[10] Generally viewed as the most complete realization of medieval Scholasticism, Thomas Aquinas is the archetype of the scholar. Unlike modern professional philosophers, Thomas was not free to *pursue* the truth wherever it led; he *started from the truth*—always ultimately supporting Christian doctrine.

In Scholastic philosophy, the *way* a case was made and analyzed became an integral part of what was being claimed. Method remains an important concern to today's scholars. Logic and linguistic analysis were vital elements in proving a case—as they are today. Scholarly, intellectual standards were developed for documenting an argument with citations from approved sources—standards that any student who has ever written a research paper will recognize. In fact, in the first twelve questions of the *Summa Theologica*, Thomas refers to other authors 160 times.

Scholastic philosophers had to present their arguments publicly and defend them against all comers—a precursor to the modern professor's obligation to publish and present and defend papers. Subject matter became specialized, and a universal impersonal, technical, scholarly style of writing was developed to communicate with a select audience of students and teachers devoted to mastering an elaborate professional technique.[11]

The emergence of the Scholastic *professor of philosophy* reflects a move away from the importance of a particular philosopher, away from the *sophos* whose work closely reflected his life, to a less personal view of the individual thinker as a part of a scholarly community. Thus, although Thomas's work reflected his life, the product of his work is scholarly and technical in ways unlike anything produced before. He says:

> That which a single man can bring, through his work and his genius, to the promotion of truth is little in comparison with the total of knowledge. However, from all these elements, *selected and co-ordinated and brought together*, there arises a marvelous thing, as is shown by the various departments of learning, which by the work and sagacity of many have come to a wonderful augmentation [emphasis added].[12]

Although many of the issues that troubled Thomas are closely tied to the medieval worldview, his arguments for the existence of God, and his discussions of fate, free will, evil, and God's nature transcend the Middle Ages, and speak to timeless questions about our relationship to God. Thomas's stature as a philosopher is independent of his importance as a medieval Catholic theologian, for he addresses eternal, truly catholic (universal) questions for anyone who takes seriously the existence of a loving, powerful, personal God—and polls consistently report that nearly 90 percent of all Americans do.[13]

But if most Americans take the existence of God "seriously," why do religious beliefs seem to provoke so much controversy and bitterness? Could it be because, too often, some of our most cherished beliefs are

The creationist, whether naive Bible-thumper or an educated bishop, simply *postulates* an already existing being of prodigious complexity. If we are going to allow ourselves the luxury of postulating organized complexity without offering an explanation, we might as well make a job of it and simply postulate the existence of life as we know it!

Richard Dawkins

A philosopher is a blind man in a dark room looking for a black cat that isn't there. A theologian is the man who finds it.

H. L. Mencken

"unanchored" by objective standards and mechanisms for testing and ranking them?

Why Do People Argue About Spiritual Matters?

If God did not exist it would be necessary to invent him.

Voltaire

Absent some sort of objective proof or rational argumentation, all we have to offer those who disagree with us about spiritual and religious matters are appeals to bald assertions of our sincerity, insistent claims that we are "saved" or happier than they, and other "bits of autobiography." The result is that, although we may believe that we are discussing the content of our beliefs, we are actually reporting information about ourselves (hence, "autobiography"). As a result, those who already believe what we do, continue to believe what we do. And while those who do not believe what we do may have learned something about *us*, we have provided them with no evidence demonstrating the actual merits of the beliefs themselves.

But, clearly, our great and persistent disagreements over matters of faith are not meant to be reduced to assertions of personal feelings (subjective states), but are intended to be about claimed realities, about *what is true*. Our timeless concerns are about whether or not God actually exists—objectively, really. Otherwise, there is nothing to dispute. Consider the hypothetical case of Ross, who believes that only God *X* exists; Dean, who believes that only God Not-*X* exists; and Joe, who believes that no god whatsoever exists. If Ross, Dean, and Joe were simply reporting subjective states, they would not need argumentation, because they would each be right. "Right" would be equivalent to "reporting present beliefs accurately."

But Ross, Dean, and Joe think that they are doing more than reporting products of thinking. And, hence, as reasoning creatures, as rational agents, they are "compelled" to apply "laws of reason" to their beliefs. If the phrase "laws of reason" seems too authoritarian or dated to you, try the more expansive and less imposing term "standards of evidence." The main point here is to note that, for the most part, we agree with Ross, Dean, and Joe: Our religious questions are about what is "real," what exists, what is true. They are not just about what people feel or think is true.

In Thomas's time, like our own, there were conflicting claims about what constituted proper "standards of evidence" for evaluating matters of theology, church authority, and religious faith in general. One view held that all truth claims must be tested against *revealed* truths. From this perspective, *revelation* was the chief and only reliable source of knowledge of God and God's ways. At the opposite extreme were those philosophers and scientists who argued that truth could only be *discovered through concrete experience and deductive reasoning*.

God and Natural Reason

Thomas approached this problem from an Aristotelian, "naturalistic" position. This is sometimes referred to as *natural theology* because it appeals to what Thomas calls *natural reason* or *natural intelligence*. By "natural" here, Thomas means "of this world," not sloppy or undisciplined. "Natural reason" is, thus, reason unaided by divine revelation, human reason; and natural theology is theology based on appeals to natural reason. Although Thomas had great respect for, and submitted to, church authority, his efforts to "prove" God's existence begin with appeals to concrete experience and empirical evidence, not revelations or dogma—an argument style favored by Aristotle. (You may wish to review the material concerning Aristotle's ideas regarding form, matter, change, and cause in Chapter 5.)

As we review selected passages from Thomas, keep in mind that no introductory survey can do justice to the complexity of Thomas's thought. So although what follows is a plausible interpretation of some of the most studied and disputed arguments in the history of philosophy, it cannot serve as a definitive account.

Please don't let the previous remarks intimidate you. Thomas's "Five Ways" are so influential and persuasive that I am sure you've already thought about some of them, at least in simplified form. You may even think of them as "your own" since popularized versions of them have become staples of Christian "apologetics," the offering of reasons to justify the divine origin of faith. And if you disagree with arguments attempting to prove that God exists, you've no doubt reflected on some version of one or more of Thomas's "Ways." Whatever your personal beliefs, here's a chance to test your thinking against perhaps the greatest Christian philosopher to date.

To get the most out of your efforts, I recommend approaching the Five Ways as a whole, focusing on what Thomas is arguing, and why it matters, before accepting or rejecting the individual arguments. That being accomplished, you'll be in a good position to assess not only this particular version of Thomas's arguments, but more general issues of faith and evidence.

As Thomas might inquire of us: What question could be more important than "Does God exist?"?

> Supposing science ever became complete so that it knew every single thing in the whole universe. Is it not plain that the questions, "Why is there a universe?" "Why does it go on as it does?" "Has it any meaning?" would remain just as they are?
>
> *C. S. Lewis*

Proving the Existence of God

While the believer may be content with faith, the philosopher is obligated to present rational and/or empirical evidence. Although Thomas believed in God, he also thought God's existence could be demonstrated by natural reason. To this end he offered his famous five proofs for the existence of God. Each proof follows a basic pattern, beginning with some natural effect that we are all familiar with, such as movement or growth. Thomas then tries to show that the only possible explanation for this effect is God. *The Five Ways are cause-effect arguments, beginning with our experience of effects and moving toward their cause, God.*

The Five Ways are most effective if viewed as part of a single argument. The first three ways deal with avoiding an infinite chain of causes in nature. Their conclusion is that an Unmoved Mover/Uncaused Cause must exist, that is, a being whose existence depends only on its own essence and not on anything external to itself. But Aristotle said much the same thing without concluding that a personal god exists; such an impersonal cause could just as easily be basic matter and energy. The fourth and fifth ways are thus crucial. They are needed to introduce some hierarchical quality into the overall description of causes and effects that can transform them into a personal God.

The First Way: Motion

The Five Ways begin with the argument Thomas thought was the easiest to understand, the **argument from motion**. Starting with the indisputable observation that things are moving, the argument points out that motion must be given to each object by some other object that is already moving. (By "motion," Thomas means both linear motion and more complex "life-motion," animating motion.) For instance, a rack of balls at rest on a billiard table is set in motion only after being struck by the *already moving* cue ball. In turn, the cue ball is set in motion after being struck by the tip of the *already moving* cue stick. But the cue stick cannot move unless something *already moving* moves it: a gust of wind, an earthquake, a cat, or Minnesota Fats. I am given life (ani-motion) by my *already* moving (alive) parents, who had to be given life by their *already* moving parents, who . . .

It *might* be possible to keep imagining an infinite chain of things already in motion moving other things. But no such infinite regress can account for the fact that things *are actually in motion*. Given that things are moving, we know that some *first already moving thing* had to move other not-yet-moving things. Thomas reasoned that some "first mover" had to exist outside the series of *becoming*—some force or being with the ability to move other things without itself needing to be moved by any outside force. God is just such an Unmoved Mover. Here is Thomas's argument:

> Therefore, whatever is moved must be moved by another. If that by which it is moved be itself moved, then this also must needs be moved by another, and that by another again. But this cannot go on to infinity, because then there would be no first mover, and, consequently, no other mover, seeing that subsequent movers move only inasmuch as they are moved by the first mover; as the staff moves only because it is moved by the hand. Therefore it is necessary to arrive at a first mover, moved by no other; and this everyone understands to be God.[14]

ARGUMENT
FROM MOTION

Attempt to prove the existence of God based on the reasoning that in order to avoid an infinite regress, there must be an Unmoved Mover capable of imparting motion to all other things; Aristotelian argument that forms the basis for the first of Thomas Aquinas's Five Ways.

Philosophical Query

Is there any other explanation for motion besides an "unmoved mover"? If so, what is it? If not, is Thomas's conclusion sound?

The Second Way: Cause

The explanation given above for the motions of billiard balls is incomplete. We can still ask what accounts for the very existence of billiard balls, cue sticks, Fats, and parents. Thomas answered with a second argument, similar in pattern to his first, but based on the Aristotelian concept of cause. Because the second argument concerns the initiating cause of the existence of the universe, it is called the **cosmological argument**, from the Greek word *kosmos*, meaning "world," "universe," or "orderly structure."

In a nutshell, the cosmological argument asserts that it is impossible for any natural thing to be the complete and sufficient source of its own existence. In order to cause itself, a thing would have to precede itself. Put another way, in order for me to be the source of my own existence, I would have to exist before I existed. This is as absurd as it is impossible.

In broad strokes, my existence is explained by my parents' existence, and theirs by my grandparents' existence, and so on. But if *every* set of parents had to have parents, there could never be any parents at all. At least one set of parents must not have had parents. In the Bible, this is Adam and Eve. But even Adam and Eve did not cause their own existence. They were created by God, who creates but is uncreated. This is why it is said that "God always was, is, and will be."

In Thomas's understanding of things, any series or system of causes and effects requires an originating cause. In order to avoid an infinite regress of causes, which he thought was impossible, there had to be an Uncaused Cause.

The cosmological argument is based on Aristotle's concept of *efficient cause*. Efficient cause is the force that initiates change or brings about some activity. The efficient cause in the development of a human fetus, for example, is the entire biochemical process of changes in the mother's womb that nurtures the growing fetus. In the case of an acorn, the efficient cause that produces an oak tree consists of rain, sun, soil, and temperature interacting to initiate growth and development. Thomas argues:

> In the world of sensible things we find there is an order of efficient causes. . . . Now in efficient causes it is not possible to go on to infinity, because in all efficient causes following in order, the first is the cause of the intermediate cause, and the intermediate is the cause of the ultimate cause, whether the intermediate cause be several, or one only. Now to take away the cause is to take away the effect. Therefore, if there be no first cause among efficient causes, there will be no ultimate, nor any intermediate, cause. . . . Therefore it is

COSMOLOGICAL ARGUMENT

From the Greek word *kosmos*, meaning "world," "universe," or "orderly structure"; argument for the existence of God that since it is impossible for any natural thing to be the complete and sufficient source of its own existence, there must be an Uncaused Cause capable of imparting existence to all other things; Aristotelian argument that forms the basis for the second of Aquinas's Five Ways.

necessary to admit a first efficient cause, to which everyone gives the name God.[15]

Philosophical Query

Discuss the cosmological argument. Is Thomas's reasoning sound or not? Are you comfortable with the possibility that there is no "first cause"? If there isn't, can we explain the existence of the universe at all? Discuss.

The Third Way: Necessity

Thomas's third proof, the **argument from necessity**, may seem odd to you. It is based on the difference between two classes of things: those whose existence is only contingent or *possible* and those whose existence is *necessary*. Contingent things might or might not exist, but they do not have to exist, and they all eventually cease to exist. You and I do not exist of necessity: We just happen to exist given the particular history of the world. Our existence is contingent, dependent on something else. This is true, in fact, of every created thing in the universe. It is even possible and imaginable that the universe itself never existed, or that it someday will cease to exist. In other words, the universe is also contingent.

But, Thomas pointed out, it is not possible to conceive of a time in which nothing whatsoever existed. There would be no space; time itself would not exist. There would be no place for something to come into existence from or to. There would be nowhere for anything to move, if there were anything to move, which there would not be. Without movement, there would be no passage of time. If no time passes, nothing happens. *Thus, if nothing had ever existed, nothing would always exist.* But all around us we see things in existence. Therefore, there was never no-thing. Getting rid of the double negatives, this becomes: There was always something—or there is something that always existed and always will. (See Democritus, First Interlude.)

The logic of Thomas's Third Way relies on the principle of sufficient reason and the principle of plenitude. According to the **principle of sufficient reason**, nothing happens without a reason. Consequently, no *adequate* theory or explanation can contain any brute, crude, unexplained facts. The **principle of plenitude** is the metaphysical principle that given infinity and the richness of the universe, any real possibility must occur—at least once. In other words, there must be something whose existence is necessary and not just possible. There needs to be some reason that what is possible actually happens. In short, God's existence is necessary. As Thomas puts it:

> We find in nature things that are possible to be and not to be, since they are found to be generated, and to be corrupted, and consequently, it is possible for them to be and not to be. But it is impossible for them always to exist, for that which can not-be at some time

---

ARGUMENT FROM NECESSITY

Argument for the existence of God based on the idea that if nothing had ever existed, nothing would always exist; therefore, there is something whose existence is necessary (an eternal something); Aristotelian argument that forms the basis for the third of Aquinas's Five Ways.

PRINCIPLE OF SUFFICIENT REASON

The principle that nothing happens without a reason; consequently, no adequate theory or explanation can contain any brute, crude, unexplained facts. First specifically encountered in the work of the medieval philosopher Peter Abelard (1079–1142), it is usually associated with the rationalist philosopher Gottfried Wilhelm Leibniz (1646–1716), who used it in his famous "best of all possible worlds" argument.

PRINCIPLE OF PLENITUDE

The name given by American historian of ideas Arthur O. Lovejoy (1873–1962) to the metaphysical principle that, given infinity, any real possibility must occur (at least once).

is not. Therefore, if everything can not-be, then at one time there was nothing in existence. Now if this were true, even now there would be nothing in existence, because that which does not exist begins to exist only through something already existing. . . . Therefore, we cannot but admit the existence of some being having of itself its own necessity, and not receiving it from another, but rather causing in others their necessity. This all men speak of as God.[16]

Philosophical Query

Scholastic arguments often hinged on whether or not something was conceivable (clearly imaginable). One cardinal principle held that no one could even conceive of absolute nothingness. Do you agree? Explain. Whether or not you agree, do you find the argument from necessity convincing? Discuss.

The Fourth Way: Degree

The first three arguments for the existence of God fail to establish the existence of a good and loving being. They only deny the possibility of an infinite series of causes and effects, an infinity of *becomings*. Even if some element or entity functions as an ever-existing Prime Mover or Uncaused Cause, these characteristics alone do not describe God. In the fourth and fifth arguments, Thomas makes a qualitative shift in his proofs.

The fourth way rests on the idea of qualitative differences among kinds of beings. Known as the **argument from gradation**, it is based on a metaphysical concept of a hierarchy of souls (see Chapter 5). In ascending order, being progresses from inanimate objects to increasingly complex animated creatures. (For instance, a dog has more being than a worm, and a person more than a dog.) Thomas believed that what contemporary philosopher Arthur O. Lovejoy called "the great chain of being" continued upward through angels to God.

This chain of being, Thomas thought, is reflected in the properties of individual things, as well as in the kinds of things that exist. For example, there are grades of goodness, going from the complete lack of goodness (evil) to pure goodness (God), from the complete lack of honesty to complete honesty, from utter ugliness to sublime beauty, and so forth. In very general terms, existence flows downward from perfection and completeness to varying lower stages, each descending level possessing less being.

Of the Five Ways, the significance of this argument can be especially difficult for contemporary thinkers to grasp because it rests on a metaphysical worldview that is alien to many of us today. Yet we cannot just dismiss it as a quirk of the medieval mind-set. The Five Ways form a cumulative argument. The first three arguments cannot establish the existence of *a qualitatively different kind of being*. The fifth argument, as we shall see,

[Religious ideas], which are given out as teachings, are not precipitates of experience or end-results of thinking; they are illusions, fulfillments of the oldest, strongest and most urgent wishes of mankind.

Sigmund Freud

ARGUMENT FROM GRADATION

Argument for the existence of God based on the idea that being progresses from inanimate objects to increasingly complex animated creatures, culminating in a qualitatively unique God; Aristotelian argument that forms the basis for the fourth of Aquinas's Five Ways.

According to the principle of gradation, the man in this photo has more "being" than the dog, which has more than the tree. Does such a view reflect reality or does it foster a kind of arrogance in which we see ourselves as superior to—rather than a part of— the natural world? Which attitude does the way the dog is looking at the man seem to support?

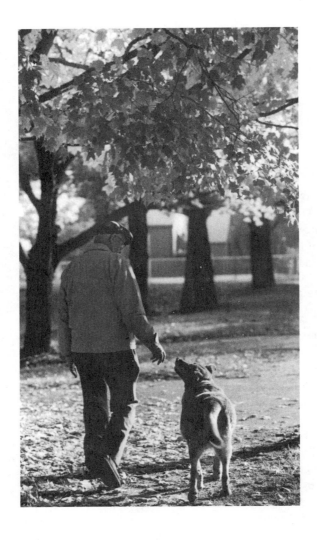

[T]here is no escape from the conclusion that it is unlikely that God is all good. Thus the problem of evil triumphs over traditional theism.

B. C. Johnson

only establishes that the universe is ordered. Without the argument from gradation, Thomas can make a case only for an eternal something that follows orderly patterns. But this "something" is almost a contemporary scientist's description of the universe; it is certainly not a description of God. Without the introduction of qualitatively different kinds of entities, Thomas cannot establish the existence of God by rational argument.

Here is Thomas's argument from gradation:

Among beings there are some more and some less good, true, noble, and the like. But *more* and *less* are predicated of different things according as they resemble in their different ways something which is the maximum, as a thing is said to be hotter according as it more nearly resembles that which is hottest; so that there is something which is truest, something best, something noblest, and, consequently, something which is most being, for those things that are greatest in truth are greatest in being. . . . Therefore there must also be something which is to all beings the cause of their being, goodness, and every other perfection; and this we call God.[17]

Philosophical Query

Do you have any sense of grades of being? Is there anything in your own experience that supports Thomas's argument? Discuss the argument from gradation.

The Fifth Way: Design

Thomas's **teleological argument**, also called the argument from design, is one of the most widely known and used arguments for the existence of God. Teleological thinking, as we learned in Chapter 5, is a way of understanding things in terms of their telos, or end. For example, infancy is understood in relationship to adulthood: The adult is the telos of the infant; the oak tree is the telos of the acorn. When archaeologists uncover some ancient artifact unlike anything ever seen before, they often "recognize" that it was made for a purpose, a telos, even if they do not know what specific purpose. In other words, they infer the existence of a designer who shaped the mysterious object.

Thomas asserts that the entire natural world exhibits order and design. Water behaves in orderly ways, as do rocks, crabs, clouds, reindeer, and people. Today, we are even more aware of the complex interrelatedness of the natural world than Thomas was: Rain forests in the Amazon basin scrub the atmosphere in ways that affect the whole earth; this is their telos. Cells and chromosomes, molecules, atoms, and subatomic particles exhibit order with each performing a specific function, a telos. On inspection, the universe reveals order; otherwise, we could not quantify scientific laws.

Order, Thomas argued, implies intelligence, purpose, a plan. Here again he follows the pattern of starting with common observations and searching for principles to explain them. In this case, Thomas held that the order we observe in inanimate nature cannot come from matter itself, since matter lacks consciousness and intelligence. Design, by its nature, implies conscious intent. Thus, if the world exhibits evidence of design, it follows logically that there must be a Designer:

We see that things which lack knowledge, such as natural bodies [matter and inanimate objects], act for an end, and this is evident from their acting always, or nearly always, in the same way, so as to obtain the best result. Hence it is plain that they achieve their end, not fortuitously, but designedly. Now whatever lacks knowledge cannot move towards an end, unless it is directed by some being endowed with knowledge and intelligence; as the arrow is directed by the

TELEOLOGICAL ARGUMENT
Also called the argument from design, this widely known argument for the existence of God claims that the universe manifests order and purpose that can only be the result of a conscious intelligence (God); Aristotelian argument that forms the basis for the fifth of Aquinas's Five Ways and the basis of William Paley's watchmaker argument.

Creation produces myriad forms. Whatever one's form, one should cherish and take care of it and use it to live well.

Lie Zi

archer. Therefore some intelligent being exists by whom all natural things are directed to their end; and this being we call God.[18]

Philosophical Query

Is order the same thing as design? Does the universe seem to be ordered and well designed? Discuss. (For more on this intriguing topic, see Chapter 9.)

Commentary on the Five Ways

Thomas's arguments begin with empirical observations and then attempt to show that the only logically consistent, adequate explanation for them requires the existence of God. If other equally plausible arguments can account for these observations, then Thomas has not conclusively proved the existence of God; he has at best shown that God's existence is possible or probable.

Underlying Thomas's first three arguments is his conviction that an infinite series of events (motions or causes) is impossible, even inconceivable. But is it? Not according to modern science and mathematics. The simplest example of an infinite series is the positive numbers. No matter what number you reach, you can always add $+1$. If one infinite series is possible—and it is—then another is possible. So to the extent that Thomas's arguments rely on the impossibility of any infinite series, they fail.

But *is* Thomas merely denying the impossibility of *any* infinite series? Probably not; it is more likely that he is denying the possibility of an infinite series of *qualitatively identical* finite series. Recall, Thomas is attempting to establish the metaphysical grounding for all natural existence, all contingent or dependent existence. Simply adding to the *same kind* does not account for the very existence of the kind.

It is certainly possible to argue that nature exhibits as much ugliness and disorder as it does design and purpose. What's the telos of starving children or freak accidents? Where is the hand of the most good, most noble designer in poverty and inequity? Perhaps Thomas only *projected* his own sense of order onto the world, rather than *observing* order in it. Many observers simply deny the presence of design; they fail to see the world as well ordered.

But don't be too quick to reject Thomas's proofs. Historian of philosophy W. T. Jones points out that the force of Thomas's arguments rests on whether or not they "account for" motion, cause, goodness, and design. He distinguishes between explanations *inside* a system and explanations that account for the system *as a whole*.[19] Ignorance of this difference is a chief source of conflict between science and religion. Scientific explanations are explanations within systems; Thomas, on the other hand, was attempting to account for the universe as a whole. Let us examine this difference.

Science has not killed God—quite the contrary. It is clearer now than ever that what we can learn from science is limited to what is abstract and quantifiable. Because of what science has achieved, the unresolved (and undoubtedly unresolvable) dilemmas of what Unamuno called the "man of flesh and bone; the man who is born, suffers, and dies—above all, who dies"—are more poignant, the mysteries deeper. God is needed now more than ever.

René J. Muller

In 1953, Stanley Miller, a biochemist at the University of Chicago, provided the first empirical evidence for the possibility that organic life could evolve from inorganic matter. Miller tried to replicate conditions as they could have been soon after the earth formed. He put methane, ammonia, and hydrogen—elements believed to have been present in the early atmosphere—into a glass container. As the chemicals were mixed with steam from boiling water, they passed through glass tubes and flowed across electrodes that were constantly emitting a spark. At the end of a week, a soupy liquid had formed in the container. This liquid contained organic compounds and amino acids—building blocks for organic matter and life-forms. In the decades since Miller's experiment, many of these building-block chemicals have been produced in laboratory conditions thought to mimic conditions during various stages of the earth's history.

Such experiments might explain the origins of life *within* the universe, understood as a system composed of basic matter and energy. But they cannot address certain kinds of questions regarding the universe *as a whole*. Where did the matter and energy come from? In his experiment, Miller *acquired* matter and energy, he did not *create* them from nothing. He "created" only in the sense that an artist creates—by transforming what is already there. Interestingly, experiments like Miller's can be used to support Thomas's arguments. Miller had to design his experiment, being careful in his selection of gases. Then he had to provide a fitting environment and introduce motion/cause in the form of electrical impulses. The existence of the experimenter and the need for carefully controlled conditions can be interpreted as demonstrating the need for the intervention of the Designer. If the analogy is carried further, the scientist represents the need for God to get the whole thing going.

Which interpretation is correct, the Thomistic or the scientific? The question cannot be answered without qualification. Scientific explanations enable us to understand and control events within the natural order. Even if scientists agree on the steps that produced the universe, such explanations cannot account for the existence of matter and energy themselves. All they can account for is the behavior of matter and energy, *given their existence and given how they exist*.

Thomas's arguments, though beginning with empirical observations, attempt something else. They address questions about the whole. For many people, science—with all its virtues—cannot satisfy a need to understand where we came from and why. Thomas the Scholar stands between science and religion, attempting to reconcile faith, reason, and experience.

Given Thomas's intentions, and taken together, the Five Ways are persuasive and suggestive, even if they are not conclusive. Some religions tend to dismiss or even mock attempts to prove God's existence as unworthy of the faith that "surpasses all understanding." Some scientists and philosophers tend to dismiss and even mock attempts to answer timeless "why" questions as naive or irrational. To the true believer, faith is enough. To the

Religions are the great fairytales of the conscience.

George Santayana

Take from your scientific work a serious and incorruptible method of thought, help to spread it, because no understanding is possible without it. Revere those things which go beyond science, which really matter, and about which it is so difficult to speak.

Werner Heisenberg

The Only Person Responsible Escaped

To proceed with the Biblical curiosities. Naturally you will think the threat to punish Adam and Eve for disobeying was of course not carried out, since they did not create themselves, nor their natures nor their impulses nor their weaknesses, and hence were not properly subject to anyone's commands, and not responsible to anybody for their acts. It will surprise you to know that the

threat *was* carried out. Adam and Eve were punished, and their crime finds apologists unto this day. . . .

As you perceive, the only person responsible for the couple's offense escaped; and not only escaped but became the executioner of the innocent.

In your country and mine we should have the privilege of making fun of this kind of morality,

but it would be unkind to do it here. Many of these people have the reasoning faculty, but no one uses it in religious matters.

Mark Twain
"Letters from Earth," in *What Is Man? And Other Philosophical Writings*, ed. Paul Baender (Los Angeles: University of California Press, 1973), Letter III.

pure scientist or analytic philosopher, the fact that the universe is here is enough. Both approaches, in their extreme forms, repress some of the most powerful, important aspects of the human experience.

Complications for Natural Theology

If Thomas's arguments are difficult and unconvincing to you, keep in mind, though, that he was applying what he called "natural reason" to a complex theology. Part of the difficulty he, or any philosopher who attempts such a task, faces is that various articles of faith seem to contradict each other and appear inconsistent with common experience. Had Thomas been able to follow either faith *or* reason, he could have avoided certain inconsistencies and confusions more easily. Instead, he struggled with the most difficult questions facing the Christian philosopher. (Similar difficulties face Jewish and Muslim philosophers as well.) To get a clearer sense of the complexities involved, we'll look at Thomas's analysis of the problem of reconciling free will and evil with God's omnipotence and foreknowledge.

If God is the wise and good First Cause, it follows that He wills everything that happens, including the existence of each individual. Nothing occurs by chance. Chance is merely the name we give to events that occur in a causal sequence unclear or unknown to us. Since *all* causal sequences lead back to the First Cause, everything happens "for a reason," or, more accurately, "nothing happens unless God causes it." It would seem to follow, then, that because of God's foreknowledge and the fact that He causes everything to happen, every event *must* occur exactly as it does.

If there were not a Devil, we would have to invent him.

Oscar Wilde

In Thomas's language, every event that occurs does so out of *necessity*—nothing that happens can be merely *possible*. If everything that happens must happen exactly as it does, how can humans be free? Yet free will—the freedom to choose our own actions—is a necessary condition for moral responsibility. We cannot *justly* be held responsible for events over which we have no control.

The Problem of Evil

I think the **problem of evil** is the most important theological question for any religion or philosophy that asserts the existence of an all-powerful, all-wise, all-good God. The problem in its basic form: *If God can prevent the destructive suffering of the innocent, yet chooses not to, He is not good. If God chooses to prevent the suffering, but cannot, He is not omnipotent. If God cannot recognize the suffering of the innocent, He is not wise.*

The problem of evil is a timeless question that confronts nearly every thinking person. It is often cited as a barrier to faith in the Judeo-Christian-Islamic God by agnostics and atheists. Quick answers to the problem of evil are usually worse than no answers because they involve obvious absurdities or suggest a callousness that's inconsistent with charity. If someone answers that suffering builds character, I offer you the starvation, molestation, or torture of children: Modern psychology has clearly shown that the damage caused by childhood suffering is often severe enough to last a lifetime. If someone answers that we are unable to understand the ways of God, I remind you that this gap of comprehension must apply to *everything else* about God if we are to be consistent. But these are distractions.

The real force of the problem of evil always comes back to justifying preventable evil and suffering. Given the qualities attributed to the Judeo-Christian God, how can He not be responsible for evil? Thomas himself deplored contradictions. Is it not contradictory to assert that God is the cause of everything, and then to say that He is not responsible for the existence of evil (just everything else)?

Thomas reasoned that God willed the universe in order to communicate His love of His own essence, in order to "multiply Himself." Now of course, this does not mean that God created other gods, for as we have seen, God must be a unique essence. It means that God created the universe as a reflection of His love.

Evil, in Thomas's view, is not a positive, created entity, however. Rather, it is a lack of goodness, which he calls a "privation," and as such, it is not "creatable." Instead, evil is a kind of necessary *by-product* of free will. But it is not a product of the informed human will: *No one can deliberately will evil who fully recognizes it as evil.* For example, Thomas points out that an adulterer is not *consciously willing a sin*, but is willing something that appears to be good, say, sensual pleasure. In this case, however,

---

PROBLEM OF EVIL

If God can prevent the suffering of the innocent, yet chooses not to, He is not good. If God chooses to prevent the suffering, but cannot, He is not omnipotent. If God cannot recognize the suffering of the innocent, He is not wise.

Even that which is called evil, when it is regulated and put in its own place, only enhances our admiration of the good; for we value and enjoy the good more when we compare it with the evil.

St. Augustine

Perhaps the greatest theological question of all is the problem of evil. Is there any way to reconcile the suffering of the innocent (especially children) with the existence of an all-wise, all-good, all-powerful God?

Has all this suffering, this dying around us, a meaning? For, if not, then ultimately there is no meaning to survival; for a life whose meaning depends upon such a happenstance—whether one escapes [suffering] or not—ultimately would not be worth living at all.

Viktor E. Frankl

Now, as we all know, good often proceeds from apparent evil, and the reverse.

Nasrudin

the pleasure is sought in a way that lacks goodness. To lack goodness is to be evil.

Even the most deliberate, diabolical willing of evil—the most blatant defiance of God—is not really *chosen as evil*. Even if the person uses the word *evil* to describe an action, it is misperceived as being something desirable, something good. In the last few years we've seen an increase in concern about satanism and the occult. Satanists seek power, *which they view as good*. If they use the word *evil* to shock the rest of us, that does not alter the fact that *to them "evil" is good*. Satan himself thought it was bad to be second to God and viewed his rebellion as *good for himself*. No one can choose evil as evil.

Philosophical Query

Do you agree that no one *can* choose evil as evil? Why or why not? Explain. Compare Thomas's position with Socrates' position in Chapter 3.

But God surely foresaw the evil that would occur in His creation. Is He not responsible for it, then, since He went ahead with the Creation? Thomas argued that God willed the creation of a universe in which His love could be multiplied. In His wisdom, He chose to do this through a rich natural order that allowed for the possibility of physical defect and suffering. Physical suffering is not the same as moral evil. God did not directly will suffering, He willed sensitive, rational creatures.

Now it is necessary that God's goodness, which in itself is one and simple, should be manifested in many ways in His creation; because

Would You Consent?

"Tell me yourself, I challenge you—answer. Imagine that you are creating a fabric of human destiny with the object of making men happy in the end, giving them peace and rest at last, but that it was essential and inevitable to torture to death only one tiny creature—the baby beating its breast with its fist, for instance—and to found that edifice on its unavenged tears, would you consent to be the architect of those conditions? Tell me, and tell me the truth."

"No, I wouldn't consent," said Alyosha softly.

Fyodor Dostoevsky
The Brothers Karamazov, trans. Constance Garnett (London: Heinemann, 1912).

creatures in themselves cannot attain the simplicity of God. Thus it is that for the completion of the universe there are required diverse grades of being, of which some hold a high and some a low place in the universe. That this multiformity of grades may be preserved in things, God allows some evils, lest many good things should be hindered.[20]

This is an interesting point. It means that the inescapable price for awareness and feeling is the possibility of pain. The eye that is exquisitely sensitive to beauty, for example, will be equally sensitive to ugliness. The only way we could suffer less is if we loved less. It is the nature of love to experience both happiness and sadness. To use Thomas's logic, to think of love without thinking of concern for our loved ones is contradictory. Can I love my family and friends and not miss them when they are away or dead? Is it love if I never let my children leave home, to spare myself missing them? Can I love others and not suffer when they suffer? We all realize that love without suffering is not possible. Feeling and awareness, Thomas argued, involve both pleasure and pain; they are inseparable.

According to Thomas, God could not have fully manifested His nature if He had created a universe of limited choices in which we were forced to love Him and do His will. God, Thomas says, is worthy of love freely given. If we had no choice but to love God, it would no longer be love. It would not be worthy of God. Besides, love under coercion is one of those contradictions Thomas said could not exist. Therefore, since God chose to create a universe in which we could love, He *had* to give us the freedom necessary for love. "Freedom" that prohibits certain choices is not freedom; it is another contradiction.

This, then, is Thomas's solution to the problem of evil: *Though God did not deliberately will evil, He willed the real possibility of evil: Evil must always be possible when love and goodness are free choices.* God wills the good of the whole universe. From the standpoint of the whole, a

The claim could be made that God has a "higher morality" by which his actions are to be judged. But it is a strange "higher morality" which claims that what we call "bad" is good and what we call "good" is bad. Such a morality can have no meaning to us. . . . God's "higher morality," being the opposite of ours, cannot offer any grounds for deciding that he is somehow good.

B. C. Johnson

universe containing free moral choices is better than a restricted universe without love and responsibility. We are more like God with freedom than without it.

According to Thomas, the overall perfection of the universe requires a range of beings, some of which get sick, decay, die, and so on. By virtue of being human, as a union of body and soul, we are subject to physical pain and suffering. God could have created beings that do not suffer physical death and pain (like angels), but they would not be human. He could not create *humans* who do not suffer.

God willed us freedom that we might love Him in this world, not so we could use it for moral evil. But He could not give us the freedom to choose good without also letting us choose evil. God wills our free choice of good by allowing us the free choice of good or evil. Mature parents understand this. At some point, the child's greatest good must be purchased at the risk of letting him or her make bad decisions. Some of these can have terrible consequences. But love of the child requires the risk.

> My life is still governed by a faith I no longer have.
>
> *Ernest Renan*

Philosophical Query

Reflect on the idea that God chose to allow evil in order to allow free will and love. Do you think freedom with the real possibility of abuse is better than forced limitation, no matter how "good" the reasons for limitations? What might this imply about forms of government? About censorship? About banning books or rock and roll or drugs? Which is more godlike, protecting people for their own sakes or letting them do harm? Has Thomas provided a satisfactory solution to the problem of evil? Discuss.

Commentary

Perhaps you find Thomas's arguments not quite convincing. Why doesn't God make His existence clearly indisputable to everyone? Why require proofs anyway? Why didn't God use His wisdom and omnipotence to create us so that we do not suffer or do wrong? These are always unanswerable questions, for they amount to asking why did God create *this* universe?

As a Christian philosopher, Thomas pursued his natural theology as far as he could, but he refused to speculate on God's ultimate motives. In the end, he accepted the limits of the human mind when it confronts the infinite. There's even a tradition that Thomas turned toward mysticism late in his life. He is supposed to have said that everything he had written was "as straw"—but he wouldn't say what he "saw" that taught him that.

Thomas's philosophy is alive today as a vital component of Roman Catholicism, but the impact of his great efforts extends beyond the church. He is the first philosopher to have actually produced a comprehensive, logically ordered synoptic (holistic) science, when science is understood as *organized knowledge*. That is, he fulfilled the promise of Aristotle and actually produced a cohesive *system* that included all the known sciences of his time.

Of course, the fragmentation and specialization of knowledge today make such an achievement virtually impossible. That does not reduce the desirability, and perhaps the need, for a cohesive, consistent, all-encompassing philosophy, even if it must be less grand. From Thomas we can learn more than the Scholastic method. In his great effort we see that faith need not be a substitute for philosophical rigor. We see that in spite of the confusions and problems in his arguments, it is still preferable to balance faith with reason rather than to believe, not in humility, but in ignorance.

The logical and theoretical questions Thomas faced still confront basic Christian doctrine. Questions about ultimate causes remain beyond the scope of science, but they do not disappear just because scientists cannot answer them. In Thomas Aquinas we encounter a rare, magnificent attempt to blend faith, reason, and experience into wisdom. If so comprehensive a system is no longer possible, it does not follow that no comprehensive vision is possible. The very effort to construct a consistent, coherent philosophy may be worth more than any risk to our faith in science or religion.

Thomas squarely faced the tension between reason and faith and, without abandoning either, gave faith his ultimate allegiance. The next major figure in the history of philosophy, René Descartes, faced the same tension, but gave himself to reason. In so doing, he ushered in the modern era.

> Of all the pursuits open to men, the search for wisdom is more perfect, more sublime, more profitable, and more full of joy.
>
> *Thomas Aquinas*

Summary of Main Points

1. Scholastic philosophy was a product of a hierarchical society based on a God-centered view of the universe.

2. Scholastic philosophy developed out of efforts to reconcile Aristotle's naturalism with the increasingly complex theological problems that developed when it became clear the Second Coming of Christ might not occur for generations.

3. The reconciliation of faith and reason was based, in part, on the law of contradiction: No statement can be both true and false at the same time and under the same conditions.

4. Scholastic philosophy rested on a strong interest in logical and linguistic analysis of texts and arguments for the ultimate purpose of producing a systematic statement and defense of Christian beliefs.

5. Thomas Aquinas introduced new levels of thoroughness, scholarship, and methodical rigor to philosophy in the form of his massive summaries known as summae.

6. Thomas's efforts to prove the existence of God using the Five Ways are among the most widely studied examples of Scholastic thinking.

7. The Five Ways are: the argument from motion; the cosmological argument; the argument from necessity; the argument from gradation; and the argument from design.

8. Thomas's logic relies on two principles: The principle of sufficient reason is the idea that

nothing happens without a reason, that no *adequate* theory or explanation can contain any brute, crude, unexplained facts. The principle of plenitude is the metaphysical principle that given infinity and the richness of the universe, any real possibility must occur—at least once.

9. In spite of their limits, the Five Ways recognize a common desire to account for the whole of existence. Though science may be able to identify and explain the causal patterns of the universe and the systems it contains, scientific thinking may not be able to account for the existence of the universe itself.

10. The problem of evil derives from the apparently inescapable conclusion either that God cannot prevent evil, and is therefore not all-powerful, or that God will not prevent evil, and is therefore not all-good.

11. Thomas answers the problem of evil from two directions: First, he argues that evil is not a positive thing, but a lack of goodness. Hence, it cannot come from God. Evil, like love, is a necessary by-product of free will.

12. Second, Thomas returns to the importance of love, asserting that God created the universe in order to multiply His love. Because it involves caring, love always involves suffering. Because love cannot be forced, it always requires freedom of choice.

13. Genuine freedom of choice includes the real possibility of evil. God does not will evil; He wills freedom and love.

Study Questions

1. Compare and contrast the classical worldview with the medieval.

2. What is theology? Distinguish between natural and revealed theology.

3. What basic conditions led to the development of Christian philosophy? Where did the need for interpretation come from?

4. What does it mean to say that human beings are susceptible to principles of reason?

5. What is the significance of Albertus Magnus to Thomas Aquinas?

6. State the law of contradiction. What is its connection to the origins of Scholastic philosophy?

7. In your own words, give a brief description of Scholasticism and describe the chief characteristics of scholarship.

8. In what ways is the medieval scholar the forerunner of the modern professor?

9. In summary—but thorough—form, state Thomas's Five Ways for proving the existence of God.

10. Which of the Five Ways do you think is the weakest? Explain why.

11. Discuss the influence of Aristotle in Thomas's philosophy.

12. Compare and contrast scientific attempts to explain the origin of the universe with theological or philosophical ones.

13. What is evil, according to Thomas?

14. State the problem of evil.

15. Explain how the traditional Judeo-Christian concept of God generates the problem of evil.

16. What is the relationship of free will to love?

17. How does Thomas solve the problem of evil? What do you think of his solution?

Overview of Modern Themes

Good sense is of all things in the world the most equally distributed . . . is by nature equal in all men.

René Descartes

'Tis not contrary to reason to prefer the destruction of the whole
world to the scratching of my finger.

David Hume

Sapere aude!—Dare to reason! Have the courage to use your own
minds!—is the motto of the enlightenment. . . . If I have a book
which understands for me, a pastor who has a conscience for me,
a doctor who decides my diet, I need not trouble myself. If I am
willing to pay, I need not think. Others will do it for me.

Immanuel Kant

It is generally agreed that the "modern era," also known as the *Enlightenment* or the *Age of Reason*, began in the first half of the seventeenth century with the publication of two seminal texts: Sir Francis Bacon's *Novum Organon*, published in 1620, and the 1637 publication of René Descartes' *Discourse on Method*. This does not mean that Bacon and Descartes—by themselves—created a new philosophical era. Their ideas were, of course, reactions and responses to the ideas of both earlier and contemporary writers and thinkers.

In the realm of philosophy, Descartes challenged and ultimately rejected the cumbersome and complex disputations and speculations of Scholastic philosophy in favor of his own simpler, more "natural" appeals to "common reason"—written in ordinary French rather than in scholarly and obscure Latin. Along with Descartes (Chapter 8), this unit focuses on two other seminal Enlightenment philosophers: David Hume (Chapter 9) and Immanuel Kant (Chapter 10).

To better grasp the significance of the Enlightenment philosophers' shattering revolt against Scholastic philosophy, we'll begin with a very general look at two famous and philosophically influential "revolutions," one in theology, the other in science.

Reason, Reformation, and Revolution

What we now refer to as the *Reformation* and the *Copernican Revolution* signaled a major shift away from the medieval worldview, with its organic emphasis on a God-centered, earth-centered universe in which everything had an allotted place in a fixed hierarchy. The modern worldview, in stark contrast to the medieval, removed the earth from the center of the universe, and put the reasoning "individual" at the forefront of philosophy, replacing faith as the path to truth with objective and methodical reason.

In the medieval worldview, everything was understood in terms of its place in the whole scheme of things. God ruled the universe, the pope ruled the church, the king ruled the state, and so on down through lords, merchants, craftsmen, and serfs. In such a worldview, natural order was transformed into a divine purpose that was reflected in a hierarchy of authority that permeated the entire universe. Throughout the Middle Ages, most Europeans accepted that this hierarchy came from God—and therefore accepted the authority of God's church and pope as legitimate.

The Reformation

By the fourteenth century, the authority of the Roman Catholic church and of the pope had eroded. The credibility of the papacy was severely damaged by a series of disputes and scandals, as popes began to keep church offerings for their own use, and to sell offices and ecclesiastical titles. These abuses led to cries for reform.

What is known today as the Protestant Reformation began in Germany on October 31, 1517, when **Martin Luther (1483–1546)**, a Roman Catholic Augustinian monk and professor at the University of Wittenberg, nailed 95 theses (criticisms of church teachings and practices) to the church door. The papacy viewed this as a gesture of rebellion rather than a call for debate, and labeled Luther a heretic. Luther persisted, and in 1520 he published three significant treatises: *An Open Letter to the Christian Nobility of the German Nation Concerning the Reform of the Christian Estate*, *The Babylonian Captivity of the Church*, and *A Treatise on Christian Liberty*.

On April 18, 1521, Luther stood before the Holy Roman Emperor Charles V and an assembly of German nobility at the Diet at Worms. Luther refused to recant unless he could be proven wrong by the Bible *or by clear reason*. Luther's bold words of refusal to bow to institutional or civic authority in matters of truth still ring: "Here I stand; I can do no other." Although Luther and his ideas generated popular support, he was formally excommunicated in 1521.

Church authorities realized Luther's ideas and actions constituted a public challenge to the entire medieval and Scholastic worldview. By asserting that the individual's channel to God was "justification by faith" rather than by "works" (that is, living a good life in accord with the teachings of the church), Luther made the individual believer his or her own "authority." In *A Treatise on Christian Liberty* he says:

> You ask, What then is this Word of God, and how shall it be used, since there are so many words of God? I answer, The Apostle explains . . . "The just shall live by faith." . . . Hence it is clear that, as the soul needs only the Word for its life and righteousness, so it is justified by faith alone and not by any works; for if it could be justified by anything else, it would not need the Word, and therefore it would not need faith. . . .
>
> It is clear then that a Christian man has in his faith all that he needs and needs no works to justify him.[1]

In rejecting "works," Luther included the sacraments and confession—two important Catholic practices that made the institutionalized church an essential part of salvation. Moreover, if, as Luther claimed, the institution and *authority* of a church are unnecessary, then "every believer is a priest." In spite of having been labeled a heretic, Luther had enough political support in Germany that the church was reluctant to use force against him. He went on to establish his own church—which, ironically, very quickly institutionalized its own rigid requirements and began ejecting heretics.

The philosophical significance of Luther's move lay in its implication that individual experience and interpretation are more truly Christian than unquestioning acceptance of an official, authoritative position. Luther's revolt against institutionalized authority is one of the major markers of the decline of the medieval worldview.

The Copernican Revolution began when Copernicus showed that the earth is not the center of the universe. As Kierkegaard put it, "Since Copernicus man has been rolling toward X." These sixteenth-century drawings represent pre-Copernican and Copernican (opposite page) views of the universe.

As doubts grew about the legitimacy or necessity of an authoritarian, institutionalized church hierarchy, reliance on individual reasoning and experience increased. And since the reach of the medieval church extended into the teachings and practices of science, challenges to authoritarian and archaic science paralleled challenges to theology.

The Copernican Revolution

As we're learning, in the Middle Ages, it was commonly believed that the universe was carefully created by a God of harmony and design, and that human beings were the centerpiece, the very purpose, of Creation. The heavens themselves, so it was believed, reflected this: God made the sun and moon to shine upon us, and placed the earth so that the rest of the universe revolved around us. As part of this divine harmony, the natural (physical) world was also thought to reflect spiritual order.

This *geocentric* worldview, with the earth at the center of the universe, can be both comforting and reassuring: If the universe physically manifests a sense of divine order and purpose, then each of us is assured that

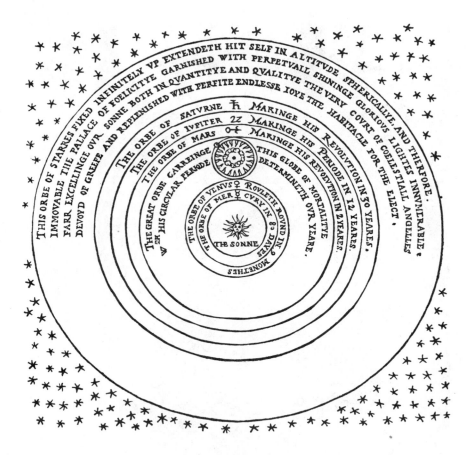

we "belong" where we are, socially and geographically. The universe is our neighborhood and earth is "home"—the universe is not a cosmic accident of such immensity that it lacks a fixed center and reduces the entire earth to less than a speck.

But as it became clearer and more widely known that the earth is a sphere, with no fixed "up" or "down," the old worldview began to totter. Once Luther's contemporary Nicolaus Copernicus mapped the heavens, it toppled.

Some ancient Greek astronomers—in particular, the philosopher Aristarchus of Samos (third century B.C.)—had concluded that the earth revolves around the sun. However, most of Aristarchus's writings were lost, and later astronomers rejected his ideas, in part because they seemed contrary to common experience and in part because they conflicted with Aristotle's teachings. Aristotle believed the earth was the unmoving center of the universe and that the sun, moon, and planets moved in semiregular "epicycles" around it. Ptolemy, an astronomer of the second century A.D., gave Aristotle's ideas even more weight by designing a mathematical model that seemed to predict planetary motions quite well.

This illustration from Martin Luther's Bible shows God as the orderer of the Ptolemaic universe. So convinced was Luther of the accuracy of this picture of the heavens, that he called Copernicus "that fool [who would] reverse the entire art of astronomy. . . . Joshua bade the sun and not the earth to stand still."

By the fifteenth century, however, calculations using the Ptolemaic model no longer matched the observed positions of the planets. This inspired **Nicolaus Copernicus (1473–1543)** to look for a more accurate model. His proposal that the sun is the center of the solar system set in motion a revolution in thinking. He made his case in such a way that knowledgeable astronomers realized the entire Ptolemaic model had to be revised.

Aristotle believed that the earth was the center of the universe, so Copernican astronomy directly refuted Aristotle. Because Thomas Aquinas and the church were so closely tied to Aristotelian philosophy and science, any major threat to Aristotle threatened church authority. If the church—guided by God—was in error here, where else might it be in error? Copernicus was sensitive enough to the church's attitude toward criticism and unofficial doctrines that he withheld publication of his discoveries until shortly before he died.

Once his work was known, the earth was cut loose from its central place of honor, both physically and psychologically, and became just one more planet revolving around the sun. If the earth was reduced in significance, what about us? This major change in perspective did not *feel right* to either Catholic or Protestant theologians. Thus Martin Luther called Copernicus "that fool [who would] reverse the entire art of astronomy.... Joshua bade *the sun* and not the earth to stand still."[2]

Luther's opinion notwithstanding, Copernicus was no fool. Although the details of his model were inaccurate (for instance, he thought the earth's path around the sun was a circle, but it really is an ellipse), his hypothesis that the earth is part of a sun-centered system was correct, and he achieved it by applying careful calculations to careful observations. The danger in his position can be clearly observed if we speak bluntly: Copernicus rendered both church authority and the consensus of unqualified nonastronomers irrelevant. His careful application of reason and observation began revolutions in both astronomy and philosophical thought.

Where Are We, Then?

The struggle for "authority," for the right to determine truth, between "the church" and "science," that began in the early Enlightenment continued until God was reduced to the role of spectator. Faith in God was replaced by faith in the orderly discovery of laws of nature, and in the power of human reason to ensure continuous progress and improvement of the human condition.

It was taken for granted that the scientific method could and would unlock all the mysteries of the universe. Given the wealth of scientific discoveries in physics, optics, astronomy, biology, and so on, it was but a simple step to conclude that God (if there is a God) has created a universe of such regularity and order that He no longer need bother running it. Further, having imbued us with reason, God has no need to govern or rescue us.

For almost three centuries, many "enlightened" thinkers remained convinced that, with the exception of "idiots," people possessed an innate, virtually equal capacity for rational thinking that could be nurtured, developed, and tapped to produce progressively better lives for each generation.

You might recognize this optimistic faith in science and reason as fundamental principles of American thinking. Indeed, the framers of our Constitution were children of the Enlightenment who believed that science and universal reason would combine to produce a rational, free, ever-progressing society.

A major task of the Enlightenment was to start anew—just like America, just like each new wave of immigrants—to use reason to accomplish a kind of individual and cultural *rebirth*, uncluttered by past superstitions and "unprovable" beliefs, to create a "new world" based on objective, universal knowledge.

Our contemporary culture remains heavily influenced by modern themes and ideas. Among the most significant are historically radical notions of the individual; democratic assertion of social and political equality based on a common human capacity to interact "objectively" and "reasonably"; faith in modern science to control nature and to discover "the truth" about "reality"; optimism that practical applications of science and reason can solve social, medical, political, and personal problems. As you study this unit, watch for these and related themes.

The Rationalist

René Descartes

But what then am I? A thing which thinks.
René Descartes

I t's a glorious Sunday morning and you go outside to watch the sun rise. Glancing at the paper, you happily note that your horoscope is favorable. Later you hurry on to church, where you teach Sunday school. The sermon is on Genesis 1:31–2:3:

. . . and God saw all that he had made, and it was very good. Evening came, and morning came, the sixth day.

Thus, the heavens and earth and everything in them were completed. On the sixth day God brought to an end all the work he had been doing; on the seventh day, having finished all his work, God blessed the day and made it holy, because it was the day he finished all his work of creation (Revised Standard Bible).

After a pleasant day, you watch a multicolored sunset, looking forward to tomorrow. It's the first day of the new term, and you've just been awarded tenure at the university. Your field is paleontology, your specialty is evolution. You are quite happy.

And yet your life is full of fundamental inconsistencies and superstitions. In your daily affairs, you forget that the sun neither rises nor sets—the rotation of the earth only makes it appear to move. Relying on your horoscope conflicts with both your religious beliefs and scientific education, but you continue "just for fun." As a paleontologist you teach that it took billions of years for the earth to form and life and consciousness to emerge, yet you also believe that the Bible is the unerring word of God.

You are not alone. Like many others, you have mastered the knack of compartmentalizing your beliefs so that possible inconsistencies are not so obvious. On the rare occasions when you acknowledge inconsistencies, you brush them aside with a variety of strategies: "The Bible is written in the language of faith. Science has its own language. They're both saying the same thing in different ways. The Bible says creation took 'six days,' and biblically that's true. Science says evolution took 'billions of years,' and that's true too—just from a different perspective. And there must be something to astrology. Millions of people believe in it. Besides, it's possible that God is the author of our horoscopes."

Although vaguely dissatisfied with the inconsistencies among your beliefs, you never get around to resolving them. Why should you? We live in an era that fosters rather than discourages such fundamental confusions. We turn to science for medical cures and environmental solutions, yet some of us also turn to crystals and trance channelers, psychics and astrologers. The same person who lobbies against abortion because "life is sacred" may also lobby against higher taxes for education, Medicare, and welfare.

What has come to be known as the modern era of philosophy began when a solitary French philosopher attempted to resolve similar difficulties and contradictions. Modern philosophy began with a new vision of the cosmos and our place in it.

> For many people it is, more than anything else, the appalling depth and extent of human suffering, together with selfishness and greed which produce so much of this, that makes the idea of a loving creator implausible.
>
> *John Hick*

René Descartes: The Solitary Intellect

René Descartes (1596–1650) was born into an old and respected family in the French province of Touraine. His mother died of tuberculosis a year after his birth, and Descartes believed he inherited a frail constitution from her. His father was a famous lawyer, whose career kept him away from home for months at a time.

When he was approximately nine or ten years old, Descartes was sent to the Jesuit college at La Flèche, where his physical weakness and mental strength were both acknowledged—he was allowed to sleep later than the other students (a lifelong habit). At La Flèche Descartes studied Greek, Latin, history, liberal arts, science, mathematics, and philosophy, in addition to music, dancing, and fencing.

Descartes spent the next few years living the life of the young gentleman he was. He practiced his fencing, rode horses, and—already in love with mathematics—briefly took up gambling to see if he could devise a system to break the bank. At the University of Poitiers he earned degrees in civil and canon law.

In 1618, when Descartes was twenty-two years old, the Thirty Years' War broke out. To the surprise of his friends, a strong, healthy Descartes first enlisted in the army of the Prince of Nassau, and later joined the army of the Duke of Bavaria. It is not clear whether he ever saw combat.

All the while, Descartes continued to study, being especially fond of mathematics. On November 10, 1619, he had a revelation that would transform him, and ultimately change entirely the direction of Western philosophy. As he later wrote, "I remained the whole day shut up alone in a stove-heated room, where I had complete leisure to occupy my thoughts."[1] There, Descartes says, he "discovered the foundations of a wonderful new science." The next night, full of excitement and anticipation over his discovery, he had three dreams, in one of which he heard a clap of thunder. He took it to be "the Spirit of Truth descending to take possession" of him.

René Descartes

> As soon as age permitted me to emerge from the control of my tutors, I quitted the study of letters . . . resolving to seek no other science than that which could be found in myself, or at least in the great book of the world.
>
> *René Descartes*

Descartes believed he had been divinely encouraged to establish a universal method of reasoning, based on mathematical principles, which, if followed carefully enough, would guarantee the absolutely certain truth of its results.

After this remarkable experience, Descartes' outward life seemed little changed. His inheritance, first from his mother and then from his father, had freed him from the need to make a living, so he traveled, studied, conversed, and wrote. He lived alone most of his life, except for his servants, and during a twenty-year period lived in twenty different houses.

Solitary and secretive, Descartes preferred to avoid the distractions and commotion of city life and social involvements. Most of his philosophical discourse took the form of letters. There were times when he didn't want his friends to know where he was; he even asked them not to write to him for a while. Descartes thought he worked better this way, completely free to devote all his energy, at his own pace, to his studies. In a letter to a friend, Descartes wrote from Amsterdam: "And thus in this large city where I now am, since I seem to be practically the only one here who is not a merchant or in trade; all are so bound up in their profitable business transactions that I could remain here my entire life without being noticed by anyone."[2] Living this way, Descartes was able to study philosophy, geometry, physics, optics, circulation, and other subjects. Conducting experiments and dissections, as well as making important discoveries in mathematics, he rejected the Scholastic model of science and philosophy, turning instead to firsthand observations and deductions.

In 1635 Descartes had an illegitimate daughter (who died at the age of five) with a servant girl. Later, he referred to the episode as "a dangerous commitment" from which he had "extricated" himself. He was not entirely immune to the charms of women, however. He had a close six-year correspondence with Princess Elizabeth, daughter of the dethroned queen of Bohemia. At nineteen the princess read his *Discourse on Method*, and was surprised and delighted to discover philosophy written in clear, everyday language.

Through a friend who had become the French ambassador to the court of Queen Christina of Sweden, Descartes was ultimately convinced in September 1649—against his better judgment—to join her court in Stockholm. He was not happy there. He had little time for his experiments, and the queen forced him to break his lifelong habits of sleeping late and working at leisure—she wanted to be tutored in philosophy at five in the morning! This forceful woman even managed to get Descartes to write a ballet. The cold weather and austere conditions had a weakening effect on his frail health. By the end of January 1650, he was ill with pneumonia. He died February 11, two months before his fifty-fourth birthday.

In his bold reliance on the disciplined use of his own reason; in his refusal to accept as true anything that did not square with what he had personally verified as true; in his exaltation of the thinking, conscious self as the foundation of all certainty, René Descartes stands not only as the "father of modern philosophy," but as the original archetype of the modern rationalist.

Descartes' metaphysics, as he so clearly sees himself, is the natural product of a precious ingredient of the past which today is in danger of rapid extinction—privacy—that marvelous compound of withdrawal, self-reliance, quiet, solitude, contemplation, and concentration which seems the exclusive possession of a bygone age.

A. W. Levi

He has lived well who has lived secretly.

Ovid (adopted by Descartes as a motto)

Above all, Descartes admired almost nothing and no one.

C. Adam

Descartes' Proposal

Most philosophers agree that modern philosophy began with Descartes. His remarkable revolution was not so much a shift in the content of philosophical problems as it was a radical new orientation toward the *method* by which philosophy is practiced. His rather uninteresting life is completely overshadowed by his work—just as today a scholar's work may be his or her life.

Modern philosophy emphasizes methodology, technique, and personal, social, and historical detachment. Its origins lie in the decline of a stable social order, the loss of central authority by the church, and the proliferation of scientific advances. More sophisticated mathematics and improved scientific instruments resulted in discoveries that challenged and contradicted Aristotelian naturalism. Scientists were able to move beyond metaphysical speculations to careful observations. No authority—church or political—could refute what the individual observer *saw* or the individual mind *calculated* for itself.

Descartes was a Catholic, but his argument that each individual possesses the "natural light of reason" and needs no intervening authority to interpret "the great book of the world" may remind you of Luther's claim that each person can go directly to God without the church as an intermediary. In other words, Descartes set aside the so-called accumulated wisdom of the past, insisting that each person must examine what is true and false afresh.

Descartes had been educated in the Scholastic tradition. As we saw in Chapter 7, Thomas Aquinas and the other Scholastic philosophers gave great weight to the authority of the church, Plato, Aristotle, and other classical and religious figures. Creative reasoning was possible—but always with an eye toward what was accepted as authoritative.

Reliance on authority is often appropriate and unavoidable in a complex world, but authority is always a secondary source of knowledge. Authoritative claims should always be accepted with caution, subject to rejection or modification in light of our own experiences.

We make an error in reasoning called the **fallacy of false authority** when we accept the word of experts who are speaking outside their proper fields, or when we uncritically rely on the testimony of others without checking it against our own experiences and reason. Some everyday examples would be letting your parents pick your spouse, turning to a pastor for medical advice, or giving uncritical acceptance to whatever the majority of a group decides.

Descartes' scientific interests led him to observe and experiment for himself, however, and he soon discovered that Aristotle's writings on nature contained many errors.

> But so soon as I had achieved the entire course of study at the close of which one is usually received into the ranks of the learned, . . .

Method consists entirely in the order and disposition of the objects toward which our mental vision must be directed if we would find out any truth. We shall comply with it exactly if we reduce involved and obscure propositions step by step to those that are simpler, and then starting with the intuitive apprehension of all those that are absolutely simple, attempt to ascend to the knowledge of all others by precisely similar steps.

René Descartes

FALLACY OF FALSE AUTHORITY

The error in reasoning that results from accepting the word of experts who are speaking outside their proper fields or uncritically relying on the testimony of others without checking it against our own experiences and reason.

I found myself embarrassed with so many doubts and errors that it seemed to me that the effort to instruct myself had no effect other than the increasing discovery of my own ignorance. And yet I was studying at one of the most celebrated schools in Europe.[3]

In Descartes' time, the distinction between science and philosophy was not clear. His interests and abilities in philosophy, mathematics, and science made this confusion especially intolerable to him. He expected scientific claims to be provable by appeals to observation and clear thinking. So he made a radical proposal: Let's start fresh, throwing out everything we think we know, and build a system of knowledge based entirely on ideas whose truth can be clearly and distinctly known—to us, firsthand.

Rationalism

Descartes' proposal puts him among the ranks of the rationalist philosophers. Chapter 4 defined rationalism as an epistemological position in which reason is the primary source of all knowledge. Reason is said to be superior to sense evidence. Reason alone can distinguish reality from illusion and give meaning to all other kinds of experience.

In general, rationalists believe that abstract reasoning can produce undeniable, absolutely certain truths about nature, existence, the whole of reality. Many of these important, ultimate truths can be discovered without observation, experiment, or even experience. These are called **a priori** or, sometimes, **innate ideas**. Thus, to the rationalists, reason—not empirical observation—is the ultimate test of truth.

According to this so-called **coherence theory of truth**, new or unclear ideas are evaluated in terms of rational or logical consistency and in relation to already established truths. The ultimate criteria for basic, originating truths are clarity and distinctness. Once fundamental truths are established, the rationalist uses a deductive, mathematical/logical method to test and establish other, more complex ideas. True ideas are coherent (rationally consistent) with each other, and the rationalist's aim is to achieve absolute certainty of the sort possible in mathematics. "My method," said Descartes, "contains everything which gives certainty to the rules of arithmetic."

The coherence theory of truth is in direct opposition to the correspondence theory of truth (in Chapter 9) and differs from the other major theory of truth, the pragmatic theory (in Chapter 13).

Against Authoritarian Thinking

Descartes' first philosophical work was *Rules for the Direction of the Mind*. The twenty-one principles contained in *Rules* reappear in Descartes' major philosophical works, *Discourse on Method* and *Meditations on First Philosophy*.

Descartes has transformed wisdom into a work, a project, a making, a determinate problem, for he denies that he can work with anything else.

Robert E. Meagher

A PRIORI IDEAS (or INNATE IDEAS)

Truths that are not derived from observation or experiment, characterized as being certain, deductive, universally true, and independent of all experience.

COHERENCE THEORY OF TRUTH

Truth test in which new or unclear ideas are evaluated in terms of rational or logical consistency and in relation to already established truths.

Rule 3 advises: *Once we have chosen a subject to study, we should confine ourselves to what we can clearly intuit and deduce with certainty for ourselves.* We must not rely on what others have thought or on our own as-yet-untested beliefs. We must look for ourselves, with new eyes and new understanding. Referring to the Scholastics, among others, Descartes cautions that "in a too absorbed study" of the works of earlier thinkers, we become "infected with their errors, guard against them as we may."

This is a general caution against authoritarian thinking, in which we give more weight to the opinions of others than to our own experience and clear thinking. When we accept views *solely* on the weight of the authority or prestige of those who hold them, or because of loyalty to a cause or belief structure, we become nonrational at best. We are memorizers, not thinkers. Loyalty becomes more important than honesty and truth.

Descartes points out that it is common to overlook clear, simple truths (intuitions) when we do encounter them. We quickly complicate them with cloudy but elaborate "explanations." He speculates that we surround the truth with ambiguities because we are afraid that the simplicity of our discoveries will make them seem unimportant. He adds:

> For we shall not, e.g., turn out to be mathematicians though we know by heart all the proofs others have elaborated, unless we have an intellectual talent that fits us to resolve difficulties of any kind. Neither, though we may have mastered all the arguments of Plato and Aristotle, if yet we have not the capacity for passing solid judgment on these matters, shall we become Philosophers; we should have acquired the knowledge not of a science, but of history.[4]

Philosophical Query

Use Descartes' distinction between memorizing ideas and understanding them to examine your own education. Give examples of both. Describe the distinction between learning to love psychology or literature and becoming a *historian* of psychology or literature in Descartes' terms. Speculate on ways this distinction might be used to reform education.

Addressing the fact that we are bombarded with conflicting knowledge claims, Rule 4 succinctly states: *There is need of a method for finding the truth.*

> So blind is the curiosity by which mortals are possessed, that they often conduct their minds along unexplored routes, having no reason to hope for success. . . . it were far better never to think of investigating truth at all, than to do so without a method. For it is very certain that unregulated inquiries and confused reflections of this kind only confound the natural light and blind our mental powers. . . . In [method] alone lies the sum of all human endeavour, and he who would approach the investigation of truth must hold to this rule. . . .[5]

I shall not say anything about Philosophy, but that, seeing that it has been cultivated for many centuries by the best minds that have ever lived, and that nevertheless no single thing is to be found in it which is not the subject of dispute, and in consequence which is not dubious, I had not enough presumption to hope to fare better there than other men had done. And also, considering how many conflicting opinions there may be regarding the self-same matter, all supported by learned people, while there can never be more than one which is true, I esteemed as wellnigh false all that only went as far as being probable.

René Descartes

More than 350 years after Descartes complained that we "investigate the most difficult questions with so little regard to order," many educated people consult astrologers, tarot card readers, palm readers, and such without taking the time to learn about scientific method as used in astronomy, physics, chemistry, psychology, and medicine.

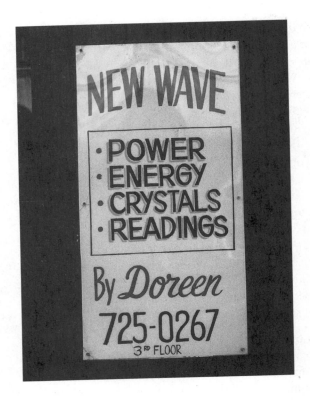

Descartes' success is indicated by the extent to which the central notions of his philosophy became the common conception of man and the universe for nearly three centuries.

Alexander Sesonske and Noel Fleming

Descartes' concern over lack of method remains relevant today. For example, in 1997 we knew about the cloning of mammals, highly sophisticated genetic modeling, an airplane that is almost invisible to radar, and computers that talk. Some years earlier we had discovered that the president of the United States scheduled important speeches and meetings on the advice of his wife's astrologer, and another president's wife conversed with the spirit of Eleanor Roosevelt. The scientific understanding of the general populace continues to decline, yet millions of people still read their horoscopes, consult psychics, and devote years of effort and thousands of dollars to what Descartes referred to as "blind curiosity." Some religious groups still evaluate scientific conclusions on theological grounds. Students are taught to memorize information and techniques, rather than to seek understanding. Perhaps we should be applying a more rational method to our present madness.

Philosophical Query

People who have little or no scientific education sometimes engage in fierce debates about evolution. Individuals who don't keep up with world events nonetheless express opinions about foreign affairs, balancing the federal budget, or the meaning of the First Amendment. Have you ever been guilty of investigating "the most difficult questions with so little regard for order"? Did your investigation pay off or not? Discuss the general advantages of "method," and identify one or two current areas of controversy that might benefit from "method."

The Method of Doubt

Descartes believed that a mathematically precise method was the only reliable way to discover the truth about the universe. He proposed to use the new spirit of scientific inquiry and mathematical rigor to reexamine—everything! His effort not only marks the beginning of an entirely new philosophical orientation, it is fascinating and relevant to our times.

Descartes attacked earlier philosophy on the grounds that it did not demand rational comprehension from the individual intellect. It did not rest *solely* on ideas known through "the clear light of natural reason."

> I thought that the sciences found in books—and those at least whose reasonings are only probable and which have no demonstrations, composed as they are of the gradually accumulated opinions of many different individuals—do not approach so near to the truth as the simple reasoning which a man of common sense can quite naturally carry out respecting the things which come immediately before him.[6]

"Common sense," which Descartes also referred to as *natural reason*, is the ability to think found in all normal human minds. It does not depend on divine revelation or special education—at least according to Descartes. Though not everyone has the talent or interest to do every kind of refined thinking, Descartes believed all reasoning individuals could apply his method to basic (timeless) questions concerning human nature, truth, the existence of God, and so forth.

> Good sense is of all things in the world the most equally distributed, for everybody thinks himself so abundantly provided with it, that even those most difficult to please in all other matters do not commonly desire more of it than they already possess. It is unlikely that this is an error on their part; it seems rather to be evidence in support of the view that the power of forming a good judgment and of distinguishing the true from the false, which is properly speaking what is called Good Sense or Reason, is by nature equal in all men. Hence too it will show that the diversity of our opinions does not proceed from some men being more rational than others, but solely from the fact that our thoughts pass through diverse channels and the same objects are not considered by all. For to be possessed of good mental powers is not sufficient; the principal matter is to apply them well.

If I write in French, which is the language of my country, rather than in Latin, which is that of my teachers, that is because I hope that those who avail themselves only of their natural reason in its purity may be better judges of my opinions than those who believe only in the writings of the ancients . . . those who unite good sense with study . . . alone I crave for my judges.

René Descartes

The greatest minds are capable of the greatest vices as well as of the greatest virtues, and those who proceed very slowly may, provided they always follow the straight road, really advance much faster than those who, though they run, forsake it.[7]

Philosophical Query

Comment on the preceding passage. Do you agree with Descartes? Why? Is common sense the same thing as good sense? Analyze the notion of common sense. Do you really think there is such a thing? What is your evidence either way?

The Cartesian "I"

Descartes did not write in Latin, the "universal language of scholars," but in everyday French. His aim was to reach beyond the confines of the university and church to a wider audience of European intellectuals. Descartes cast all his works in the first person to describe his own thinking, both his *conclusions* and his *thinking process*. He wanted to call our attention to the reasoning mind itself. Until Descartes, philosophers tended to focus on the content of ideas and on their logical relations to each other, not on the mind itself. Although "reason" was discussed and referred to, often cited as the guide by which we should live, the "reasoning thing" itself was not directly studied.

As we study Descartes' ideas, don't always interpret the "I" as referring to Descartes—allow it also to refer to you while you are reading (and, I hope, thinking along with) the words Descartes wrote. By occasionally becoming the "I" yourself, you can participate in the *conscious flow* of Descartes' reasoning in a way that will help you evaluate his arguments as if they were your own. You will be reflecting and meditating on your own conscious mind.

Methodic Doubt

Descartes was convinced that he could apply a mathematically oriented method to the most fundamental problem of all: How can I know that I know anything?

In geometry, Descartes pointed out, we begin with self-evident truths such as "A straight line is the shortest distance between two points." More complex theorems based on these truths are then called upon to prove less-evident truths. Descartes proposed to apply this basic method to philosophy. In his *Rules*, he stated that *we must not accept anything we can doubt at all*.

His first task, then, was to find a self-evident, independent truth from which to start. For instance, we *know* with *rational certainty* that *if A = B* and *if B = C*, then *A = C*. Can we know anything besides mathematics

---

There does seem to be, so far as science is concerned, nothing in the world but complex arrangements of physical constituents. All except for one place: consciousness.

J. J. C. Smart

and logic with such certainty? Can our grasp of any factual idea ever be as certain as our understanding of a deductive principle? Since Descartes had a mathematical model in mind, he could not settle for any lesser degree of certainty.

In his effort to base his philosophy on an absolutely certain foundation, Descartes had a brilliant, culture-altering insight. He discovered **methodic doubt**. Simply put, *methodic doubt involves deliberately doubting everything it is possible to doubt in the least degree. Whatever remains will be known with absolute certainty.* In order to apply methodic doubt, Descartes had to rely on a standard of truth that could tell him whether or not it was reasonable to doubt something.

Standard of Truth

No matter what method we employ in a search for truth, we must have some criterion for distinguishing truth from falsity. Descartes proposed that we "might assume as a general rule that the things which we conceive very clearly and distinctly are all true." He defined *clear* as "that which is present and apparent to an attentive mind," and *distinct* as "that which is so precise and different from all other objects that it contains within itself nothing but what is clear." We might say that for Descartes, knowledge requires precision and detail.

Throughout his philosophical writings Descartes appeals to clear and distinct knowing as the ultimate standard to be used in accepting or rejecting ideas. To produce the most certain conclusions possible, he rejected *anything* he did not know "clearly and distinctly." He also believed that certain very basic propositions *need only to be understood* to be recognized as true. To understand something clearly and distinctly, according to Descartes, is a matter of perceiving that there are no reasonable grounds on which it can be doubted. In other words, *to recognize something clearly and distinctly is to know that it is true.*

Some philosophers are troubled by Descartes' standard of truth. They claim that *the standard itself* is ambiguous and subjective and thus cannot be known with clarity and distinctness! Their point is that "clear and distinct" vary from individual to individual; I might be convinced I know something clearly and distinctly and still be wrong about it. In other words, they accuse Descartes of basing his rationalism on the subjective states of the perceiver; they interpret this to mean that, in spite of his talk about reason, Descartes actually bases his philosophy on his feelings and moods.

Philosophical Query

A common criticism of Descartes' standard of truth is that he failed to apply it to itself: *Do we know with clarity and distinctness that only what we know with clarity and distinctness is true?* Can we know it? Not if,

METHODIC DOUBT
Cartesian strategy of deliberately doubting everything it is possible to doubt in the least degree so that what remains will be known with absolute certainty.

It must always be recollected, however, that possibly I deceive myself, and that what I take to be gold and diamonds is perhaps no more than copper or glass.

René Descartes

as critics claim, Descartes' position is itself unclear and ambiguous. Do you have a clear and distinct idea of Descartes' criteria? How can we tell when an inability to perceive something clearly and distinctly is the fault of the individual or of the quality of the idea? Discuss carefully.

Innate Ideas

As you wrestle with these issues, keep in mind that getting started is the most difficult part of establishing a new or original philosophical orientation. We must begin with initially unquestioned assumptions and basic principles. To a certain extent, these must be known before we can know anything else. That is, they must be first or *prior* to knowing everything else. Such ideas are called *a priori*. A priori ideas are characterized as being certain, deductive, universally true, innate, or independent of all experience.

A priori knowledge is derived from reason without reference to sense experience. Truths of reason and laws of logic are usually thought to be a priori. Examples include: "All triangles contain 180°" and "Every event has a cause." A priori knowledge contrasts with **a posteriori knowledge**, that is, empirical knowledge derived from sense experience. This kind of knowing comes from the accumulation of experience. It is not regarded as certain or necessary, because the conditions under which it is acquired change, perceivers vary, and factual relationships change. For example, the statement "My shirt is white" can be true for a particular set of circumstances today and false tomorrow. It is not universally or eternally true in the way that "Every event has a cause" is. A posteriori truths are called factual truths or truths of fact, as opposed to rational truths. (Not all philosophers agree that a priori truths exist. The empiricists—whom we will meet in Chapter 9—insist that all knowledge comes from sense experience.)

As a brilliant geometer, Descartes was familiar with the axioms for geometric proofs, which he characterized as a priori ideas. He believed we are born with certain ideas "implanted" in us by God. For example, we are born with the idea of a triangle in our minds. When we see triangles or triangular-shaped objects, we are reminded of this innate idea. Descartes often appeals to the standard of clarity and distinctness as if its truth should be obvious to us with a bit of reflection. All we need is to be "reminded" of it to recognize its truth.

A PRIORI KNOWLEDGE

Derived from reason without reference to sense experience. Examples include: "All triangles contain 180°" and "Every event has a cause."

A POSTERIORI KNOWLEDGE

Empirical knowledge derived from sense experience and not regarded as universal because the conditions under which it is acquired change, perceivers vary, and factual relationships change.

Philosophical Query

Is Descartes correct? What about seemingly sincere, rational, and intelligent people who say they do not, perhaps cannot, see the truth of *this* idea about innate ideas? Compare Descartes' problem here with Plato's problem of accounting for levels of ignorance of the forms. Do you think forms are innate ideas? Are innate ideas forms? (See Chapter 4.)

The Cartesian Genesis

Descartes wanted to find an absolutely certain, indubitable starting point for his philosophy. He chose a form of deliberate, methodological skepticism that we have labeled *methodic doubt*. As we will see in Chapter 9 from the work of David Hume, there are levels of skepticism, progressing from total doubt about everything to temporary or particular doubt invoked just for the process of analysis. Descartes' skepticism is part of his method, and is, consequently, of the temporary—but still serious—sort. This means he does not really doubt everything he challenges in his *Meditations*; systematically doubting is the process of Cartesian inquiry, not the end result. Descartes hoped to use skepticism to establish complete certainty.

In the six *Meditations*, Descartes begins by seeing whether it is rationally possible to doubt everything. He reasons that by doing this, he will quickly discover if there is any certain, undoubtable truth. In the course of the *Meditations* Descartes tears down the old world of Scholastic philosophy, unquestioned beliefs, and ambiguous ideas, and attempts to create a brand-new, certain, clearly proved, rational order. He suggests that his readers reflect on one meditation a day, reading carefully and leisurely. After six days, Descartes, like God in the biblical book of Genesis, will have finished with his own creation. The attentive, rational reader, by becoming the Cartesian "I" in the manner noted earlier, will also have torn down and rebuilt his or her previously unquestioned house of beliefs on a solid, rational foundation. Let's look at some of the more interesting and important stages of this Cartesian Genesis.

The Doubting Self

Descartes begins the *Meditations* by giving his methodic doubt the widest possible scope. He calls Meditation I *Of the things which may be brought within the sphere of the doubtful*. In the first two paragraphs Descartes invokes the skeptical method and introduces the standard of clarity and distinctness. He quickly points out that it would be impossible to examine every belief he currently holds. Instead, he will examine the origins and foundations of basic kinds of beliefs. If there is *any* possibility, however remote, that they could be mistaken, Descartes will reject them and every idea that depends on them:

> It is now many years since I detected how many were the false beliefs that I had from my earliest youth admitted as true, and how doubtful was everything I had since constructed on this basis; and from that time I was convinced that I must once and for all seriously undertake to rid myself of all the opinions which I had formerly accepted, and

Descartes' *Meditations* probably rivals Plato's *Republic* as the work most frequently read or recommended as an introduction to philosophy.

Alexander Sesonske and Noel Fleming

After the guarantee of the criterion of clear and distinct ideas has been elaborated, however, it turns out that the relations apprehended by reason are but misleading representatives of the true relations whose basic nature must remain a mystery to us. There is a powerful and basic undercurrent of irrationalism in Descartes, the first of the modern rationalists.

Leonard G. Miller

Even if life and all of you and everything is like just a dream I'm having,
I still figure I'm going to need all the money I can lay my hands on.

Reprinted by permission of Chronicle Features, San Francisco, CA.

commence to build anew from the foundation if I wanted to establish
any firm and permanent structure in the sciences. . . .

Now for this object it is not necessary that I should show that all of
these are false—I shall perhaps never arrive at this end. But inasmuch
as reason already persuades me that I ought no less carefully to with-
hold my assent from matters which are not entirely certain and indubitable than from those which appear to be manifestly false, if I am
able to find in each some reason to doubt, this will suffice to justify
my rejecting the whole. And . . . owing to the fact that the destruction
of the foundations of necessity brings with it the downfall of the rest
of the edifice, I shall only in the first place attack those principles
upon which all my former opinions rested.[8]

Philosophical Query

How carefully have you examined your own fundamental beliefs? What—
if anything—is wrong with trusting beliefs handed down by others? Why
not rely on the testing of others, trusting their conclusions? Discuss. Also
comment on the opposite extreme from Descartes: the tendency to believe
something if it could possibly be correct. What is the relationship between
possible and *plausible*, and what might it have to do with this entire issue?
Explain.

Maybe It's All a Dream?

Like most of us, Descartes had uncritically assumed that the most true and certain things known come from the senses. For example, it is obviously true that my computer exists as I type this sentence, and it is obviously true that the book you are reading exists. What can be more certain than simple, direct sensations and perceptions of our immediate environment?

But our senses sometimes deceive us. For example, we may think we are looking at an airplane and later discover that it is a bird. Witnesses to crimes disagree over descriptions of perpetrators, and we think we recognize the figure coming down the sidewalk only to be wrong. Even so, aren't we always sure of immediate sensations? Though our senses may deceive us about distant events, there are many other things we know through our senses "as to which we cannot reasonably have any doubt." Descartes cites an example:

> At the same time I must remember that I am a man, and that consequently I am in the habit of sleeping, and in my dreams representing to myself the same things or sometimes even less probable things, than those who are insane do in their waking moments. How often has it happened to me that in the night I dreamt that I found myself in this particular place, that I was dressed and seated near the fire, whilst in reality I was lying undressed in bed! At this moment it does indeed seem to me that it is with eyes awake that I am looking at this paper; that this head which I move is not asleep, that it is deliberately and of set purpose that I extend my hand and perceive it; what happens in sleep does not appear so clear and distinct as does all this. But in thinking over this I remind myself that on many occasions I have in sleep been deceived by similar illusions, and in dwelling carefully on this reflection I see so manifestly that there are no certain indications by which we may clearly distinguish wakefulness from sleep that I am lost in astonishment. And my astonishment is such that it is almost capable of persuading me that I now dream.[9]

With this example, Descartes rejects sense knowledge as a sufficient foundation for certainty. In so doing, he also rejects the primacy of the external, physical world. It is *possible* that the whole so-called real world is nothing but an elaborate mental construct, a hallucination. Remember, in the interest of constructing a flawless philosophy, Descartes is being ultracautious. He has dispensed with considering degrees of probability. Whether or not you consider it *probable* that your world is a dream, it is *possible*, according to Descartes.

But even if the world is a dream, it still has regularity, predictability, and so on, doesn't it? Maybe the world is just a dream implanted in the mind by God.

In the interplay of reality and illusion, how can you be sure that you are now not dreaming and that events seen during a state of dream may be closer to the truth?

Lie Zi

All that is comes from the mind.

The Dhammapada

Beyond Intellect There Is Yet Another Stage

In 1091, the Persian philosopher **Abu Hamid Muhammad al-Ghazali** (1058–1111) was appointed professor of Islamic theology at the Nizamiyah College in Baghdad. In 1095, al-Ghazali, by then a man of great influence, suffered a spiritual crisis and nervous breakdown that resulted in a speech impediment that prevented him from lecturing. He left the college and ultimately embraced a mystical form of Islam known as *sufism*. Al-Ghazali briefly returned to teaching, but eventually quit for good and founded a monastic community in Tus, the city of his birth. The passage that follows is from his work *The Deliverance from Error*. Note how al-Ghazali's work anticipates Descartes' first Meditation by five hundred years. Whereas Descartes exalted reason over faith, al-Ghazali "transcended"

reason with the mystic's direct and immediate experience of God (Allah).

To thirst after a comprehension of things as they really are was my habit and custom from a very early age. . . . as I drew near the age of adolescence the bonds of mere authority . . . ceased to hold me and inherited beliefs lost their grip upon me, for I saw that Christian youths always grew up to be Christians, Jewish youths to be Jews and Muslim youths to be Muslim. . . .

I therefore said within myself: "To begin with, what I am looking for is knowledge of what things really are, so I must undoubtedly try to find what knowledge really is." It was plain to me that sure and certain knowledge is that

knowledge in which the object is disclosed in such a fashion that no doubt remains along with it, that no possibility of error or illusion accompanies it, and that the mind cannot even entertain such a supposition. Certain knowledge must also be infallible. . . . Thus, I know that ten is more than three. Let us suppose that someone says to me: "No, three is more than ten, and in proof of that I shall change this rod into a serpent": and let us suppose that he actually changes the rod into a serpent and that I witness him doing so. No doubts about what I know are raised in me because of this. The only result is that I wonder how he is able to produce this change. Of doubt about my knowledge there is no trace.

Philosophical Query

How can we know the difference between a dream or hallucination and reality? Seriously consider how a confused person might verify that he or she was or was not dreaming.

The Evil Genius

Perhaps, like Descartes, you are having some trouble seriously doubting your experiences of the real world. Descartes says, "These ancient and commonly held opinions [that I am not dreaming] still revert frequently to my mind." To test his beliefs, he decides to allow himself deliberately "to be deceived, and for a certain time pretend that all these opinions are entirely false and imaginary." Descartes is in no danger of losing his bearings; this is still methodic doubt, not real confusion or delusion. He even

After these reflections I knew that whatever I did not know in this fashion and with this mode of certainty is not reliable and infallible knowledge; and knowledge that is not infallible is not certain knowledge. . . .

Thereupon I investigated the various kinds of knowledge I had, and found myself destitute of all knowledge with this characteristic of infallibility except in the case of sense-perception and necessary truths. . . .

I proceeded therefore with extreme earnestness to reflect on sense-perception and on necessary truths, to see whether I could make myself doubt them. The outcome of this protracted effort was that I could no longer trust sense-perception either. . . .

. . . "Do you not see," [my ego] said, "how, when you are asleep, you believe things and imagine circumstances, holding them to be stable and enduring, and, so long as you are in that dream-condition, have no doubts about them? . . . Why then are you confident that all your waking beliefs, whether from sense or intellect, are genuine? They are true in respect of your present state; but it is possible that a state will come upon you whose relation to your waking consciousness is analogous to the relation of the latter to dreaming. In comparison with this state your waking consciousness would be like dreaming! When you are in this state, you will be certain that all the suppositions of your intellect are empty imaginings. . . ."

It became clear to me . . . that what is most distinctive about mysticism is something which cannot be apprehended by study, but only by immediate experience . . . by ecstasy and by a moral change. What difference between *knowing* the definition of health and satiety . . . and *being* healthy and satisfied! . . .

Beyond intellect there is yet another stage. In this another eye is opened, by which he beholds the unseen, what is to be the future, and other things which are beyond the ken of intellect.

Abu Hamid Muhammad al-Ghazali *The Deliverance from Error*, in *The Faith and Practice of Al-Ghazali*, trans. W. Montgomery Watt (London: George Allen and Unwin, 1953), pp. 21–68.

says not to worry about giving in to too much doubt and distrust, since he is "not considering the question of action, but only of knowledge."

At this point, Descartes introduces one of the most intriguing figures in the history of philosophy, the *evil genius*:

> I shall then suppose, not that God who is supremely good and the fountain of truth, but some evil genius not less powerful than deceitful, has employed his whole energies in deceiving me; I shall consider that the heavens, the earth, colours, figures, sound, and all other external things are nought but the illusions and dreams of which this genius has availed himself in order to lay traps for my credulity; I shall consider myself as having no hands, no eyes, no flesh, no blood, nor any senses, yet falsely believing myself to possess all these things; I shall remain obstinately attached to this idea, and if by this means it is not in my power to arrive at the knowledge of any truth, I may at least do

What is important is not liberation from the body but liberation from the mind. We are not entangled in our own body, but entangled in our own mind.

Thomas Merton

what is in my power [i.e., suspend my judgment], and with firm purpose avoid giving credence to any false thing, or being imposed upon by this arch deceiver, however powerful and deceptive he may be.[10]

This cold possibility of ultimate delusion concludes the first Meditation. Descartes has reduced his world to himself and one all-powerful, all-evil source of deception. He reasons that if he can find one anchor point of undoubtable certainty in the midst of the possibility of error in *all* quarters of his life, he will have found his unshakable foundation.

Philosophical Query

Before reading any further, stop for a moment and play with Descartes' idea of an evil genius. Try to get into the spirit of doubting as much as you can. Do not be limited by what you actually doubt; this is an intellectual exercise, not a personal confession. See if you can extend the range of what might on the remotest possibility be false or other than you think it is. Can you be *absolutely sure* that there is no evil genius?

Cogito, ergo sum

Could the evil genius so arrange things that nothing is as I think it is? In the physical realm he could. He could trick me into thinking that I have a body when I don't, that things have shapes, colors, and so on, when they really don't. Descartes says that—as difficult as it is to imagine—he might even be able to deceive me regarding certain innate, a priori ideas, so that maybe 7 + 5 does not really equal 12 or triangles don't have three sides. Is there anything the evil genius cannot trick me about? If I can be tricked into thinking things exist that do not exist, and if I can be fooled into thinking things do not exist when they really do, then maybe I am being deceived about my own existence. Maybe I don't exist at all. Is that possible?

> Not at all; of a surety I myself [must] exist since I persuaded myself of something [or merely because I thought of something]. But [what if] there is some deceiver or other, very powerful and very cunning, who ever employs his ingenuity in deceiving me. Then without doubt I exist also if he deceives me, and let him deceive me as much as he will, he can never cause me to be nothing so long as I think that I am something. So that after having reflected well and carefully examined all things, we must come to the definite conclusion that this proposition: I am, I exist, is necessarily true each time that I pronounce it, or that I mentally conceive it.[11]

COGITO, ERGO SUM

Latin version of Descartes'
famous sentence "I think,
therefore I am."

This is the famous "cogito," from the Latin sentence **Cogito, ergo sum,** meaning *I think, therefore I am.* In some ways, this Cartesian insight, more than anything else, marks the beginning of the modern worldview.

Note the difference between "Descartes thinks, therefore he exists" and "I think, therefore I exist," where the "I" refers to whomever speaks or thinks the sentence. The cogito must be understood in the first person. In that form, it meets Descartes' conditions for being utterly unshakable. No rational person can doubt his or her own existence as a conscious thinking entity—while being aware of thinking about anything.

Descartes interprets this to mean that while bodily existence may seem more solid and certain than ideas, mental existence is in actuality more certain. He goes on:

> I find here that thought is an attribute that belongs to me; it cannot be separated from me. I am, I exist, that is certain. But how often? . . . to speak accurately [at this stage of the Meditations] I am not more than a thing which thinks, that is to say a mind or soul, or an understanding, or a reason, which are terms whose significance was formerly unknown to me. I am . . . a real thing and really exist; but what thing? I have answered: a thing which thinks.
>
> . . . What is a thing which thinks? It is a thing which doubts, understands, [conceives], affirms, denies, wills, refuses, which also imagines and feels.[12]

Descartes argues that we identify and know everything—including bodily and material things—through the mind. He grounds all knowledge in mental states, in awareness. Thus the foundation of Descartes' philosophy and, to a considerable extent, of the modern worldview is the thinking self. Although Descartes was a rationalist, the thrust of the cogito is not *reasoning* but *self-awareness*. St. Augustine had a similar formula: "I doubt, therefore I am," and in *Nausea* (Chapter 12) Jean-Paul Sartre wrote, in effect, "I am nauseated, therefore I exist."

So far, Descartes has established that the thinking thing possesses absolute certainty of its own existence as a consciously thinking thing. So there is one rather limited fact I know with certainty. Do any other insights follow from this bedrock experience of self-consciousness? Can Descartes move from it to re-create the external world?

Philosophical Query

When I was a student I felt compelled to challenge anything presented to me as being *irrefutable*. As soon as I heard about the cogito I assumed I would be able to refute it, to show that it was not necessarily true. That proved easier said than done. Try for yourself; it is interesting, and it is the only way to grasp Descartes' point. Discuss your efforts.

For those who like a dramatic and specific date, the simple but far-reaching phrase of Descartes, "I think, therefore I am," will do very well for the beginning [of the Age of Reason]: 1657.

Crane Brinton

When a person is in any state of consciousness it logically follows that he is not sound asleep.

Norman Malcolm

The Innate Idea of God

Descartes begins the third Meditation still treating everything he thinks of as part of himself as merely "perceptions and imaginations" from his own mind. That being so, his next step is to survey his own thoughts, to see whether there might be something he has overlooked or been unaware of so far. He reasons that the most important issue is the existence of God: "I must inquire whether there is a God as soon as the occasion presents itself; and if I find that there is a God, I must also inquire whether He may be a deceiver; for without a knowledge of these two truths I do not see that I can ever be certain of anything."[13]

In other words, if Descartes can establish the existence of God, he will have a foundation for truth concerning other ideas. If God is not an evil deceiver, Descartes argues, He will have created the reasoning mind to seek and know the truth. Rationally verifying the existence of God will not only guarantee the possibility of knowledge with certainty, it will bridge the gaps between religion and science and between the imagination and reality. If God is the source of reason, then it follows that He wills the use of reason in pursuit of truth. If so, then God is the impetus behind science. If God is not a deceiver, then He will have given Descartes the ability to distinguish the real from the merely imagined. Thus the issue of God's existence and nature is crucial to Descartes' entire rationalistic enterprise.

The Perfect Idea of Perfection

Clearly, Descartes says, the *idea* of God exists. He notes the obvious: Such an idea does exist—he has it. But does it follow that an *object* corresponding to this idea exists?

> Hence there remains only the idea of God, concerning which we must consider whether it is something which cannot have proceeded from me myself. By the name of God I understand a substance that is infinite [eternal, unchangeable], independent, all-knowing, all-powerful, and by which I myself and everything else, if anything else does exist, has been created. Now all these characteristics are such that the more diligently I attend to them, the less do they appear capable of proceeding from me alone; hence, from what has been already said, we must conclude that God necessarily exists.[14]

Descartes' position amounts to this: I have in me the clear and distinct idea of a perfect being. Where could I, an imperfect creature, ever get the idea of perfection? A perfect being is not just a bigger, stronger, quantitatively improved Descartes. If my idea of God were merely of a kind of superhuman being, then I might have created it out of wishful thinking. But how could I even have a notion of perfection, or want to be more perfect myself, "unless I had within me some idea of a Being more perfect than myself, in comparison with which I should recognize the deficiencies of my nature?"[15] In other words, because of its very uniqueness, the idea of God must come from God. To clearly and distinctly understand the idea of God is—at the same instant—to know with certainty that God exists.

This line of reasoning is known as an ontological argument. The term *ontology* derives from the Greek roots *onta*, "truly real," and *logos*, "study of." An **ontological argument** is an attempt to prove the existence of God by referring either to the meaning of the word *God* when it is understood a certain way, or by referring to the purportedly unique quality of the concept of God.

The purest form of the ontological argument first occurs in the *Proslogion* of St. Anselm (1033–1109). A Benedictine monk who eventually became the archbishop of Canterbury, Anselm attempted to provide a rational basis for Christian doctrine. He asserted that the very idea of God "contains existence" because *by definition* God is "that than which nothing greater can be conceived." And of any two things, a real one is "greater" than an imaginary one. Hence, an existing God is greater than a merely imaginary God. Therefore, by definition, the term *God* refers to a real, existing being. When we use *God* to refer to a fantasy being, we have changed its meaning.

Descartes' similar argument says that no ordinary accumulation of knowledge can account for the idea of God as a perfect being. This issue hinges on whether or not the idea of God is qualitatively different from other ideas. For example, it is sometimes argued that God is nothing more than a bigger, smarter, tougher, more virtuous version of ourselves. What's so different about that? Since I know people can live to be ninety or a hundred years old, why can't I imagine one who lives forever? I can do some things. Why can't I fantasize about a being who can do all things?

Descartes, for all his dislike of Scholastic philosophy, follows a Scholastic line in his analysis of these matters. He seems to be saying that not only is God a perfect being, the idea of God is a "perfect idea." If it is, he reasons, where could it come from? Imperfect creatures such as ourselves can imagine only imperfect ideas; we could not come up with the idea of a *perfect* anything without help. Where could the idea of perfection come from? Only from a mind more perfect than ours.

Maybe the evil genius gave me the idea of perfection. But where would an imperfect, evil being get the idea? Only from a being more perfect yet. Ultimately, the existence of the *idea of perfection* can come only from an already perfect source: the perfect being.

> It is perfectly evident that there must be at least as much reality in the cause as in the effect; and thus since I am a thinking thing, and possess an idea of God within me, whatever in the end be the cause assigned to my existence, it must be allowed that it is likewise a thinking thing and that it possesses in itself the idea of all the perfections I attribute to God. . . . But if it derives its existence from some other cause than itself, we shall again ask, for the same reason, whether this second cause exists by itself or through another, until from one step to another, we finally arrive at an ultimate cause, which will be God.[16]

ONTOLOGICAL ARGUMENT

An attempt to prove the existence of God either by referring to the meaning of the word *God* when it is understood a certain way or by referring to the purportedly unique quality of the concept of God.

Cogito ergo non dormio. (I think, therefore I am not asleep.)

Descartes determines that he cannot have "received" the idea of God through the senses, nor has it suddenly burst upon his consciousness. He cannot have imagined it, for he lacks the ability to improve upon or to detract from it. Consequently, he says, "the only alternative is that it is innate in me, just as the idea of myself is innate in me."[17]

Descartes' argument is crucial to the Cartesian Genesis. His conception of God as a perfect being includes the qualities of all-knowing, all-powerful, all-loving, all-good. Descartes posits that such a God would not let him be constantly deceived by either himself or some evil genius. If, the argument goes, God gave us reason and faculties of perception, they must be basically accurate and reliable.

> And the whole strength of the argument which I have here made use of to prove the existence of God consists in this, that I recognize that it is not possible that my nature should be what it is, and indeed that I should have in myself the idea of a God, if God did not veritably exist—a God, I say, whose idea is in me, i.e., who possesses all those supreme perfections of which our mind may indeed have some idea but without understanding them all, who is liable to no errors or defect [and who has none of all those marks which denote imperfection]. From this it is manifest that He cannot be a deceiver, since the light of nature teaches us that fraud and deception necessarily proceed from some defect.[18]

Philosophical Query

Some philosophers insist that ontological arguments beg the whole question by defining God in terms of existing. In the case of Descartes' argument, there is also the question of whether or not we really do have a clear and distinct (precise) idea of God in the first place. Reflect on the idea of God. Is it clear and distinct? Do you have a clear and distinct idea of perfection—in beings or automobiles or marriages or anything? Does the ontological argument persuade you? Does Descartes' argument?

Reconstructing the World

Having shown that one mind and God exist, Descartes proceeds to reestablish knowledge of the objective existence of the rest of the world:

> Nothing further now remains but to inquire whether material things exist. . . . And certainly I at least know that these may exist. . . . For there is no doubt that God possesses the power to produce everything that I am capable of perceiving with distinctness.[19]

Descartes reasons that since he has a clear and distinct idea of himself *both as a mind and as having a body*, he must of necessity be both a mind and

Hamlet did think a great many things; does it follow that he existed?

Jaako Hintikka

There is no simple entity that you can point to and say: this entity is physical and not mental.

Bertrand Russell

a body. But the idea of being both mind and body is not innate or known to be true with deductive certainty. Thus the idea of the body must originate outside Descartes' mind.

> And . . . because I know that all things which I apprehend clearly and distinctly can be created by God as I apprehend them, it suffices that I am able to apprehend one thing apart from another clearly and distinctly in order to be certain that one is different from the other, since they may be made to exist in separation at least by the omnipotence of God. . . . On the one side, I have a clear and distinct idea of myself inasmuch as I am only a thinking and unextended thing, and as, on the other, I possess a distinct idea of body, inasmuch as it is only an extended and unthinking thing, it is certain that this I [that is to say, my soul by which I am what I am], is entirely and absolutely distinct from my body and can exist without it.
>
> . . . But, since God is no deceiver, it is very manifest that He does not communicate to me these ideas immediately and by Himself. . . . I do not see how He could be defended from the accusation of deceit if these ideas were produced by causes other than corporeal objects. Hence we must allow that corporeal things exist.[20]

Descartes reasoned that his own ideas of body and mind must be basically sound, since God allowed him to know clearly and distinctly that he is both.

At this point, the Cartesian Genesis is essentially complete. All that remains are the details of reconstructing knowledge of the world on a solid base by carefully following the rules of method.

The Cartesian Bridge

Descartes was a devout Catholic who took his religion seriously. He was aware of the challenge to religion posed by advances in physics and astronomy and the reemergence of **materialism** (also known as *behaviorism, mechanism,* or *reductionism*). Other philosophers, most notably **Thomas Hobbes (1588–1679)**, were arguing that everything is composed of matter (and energy) and can be explained by physical laws. This means all human activity can be understood as the natural behavior of matter according to mechanical laws. Thus, thinking is merely a complex form of behaving, and the body is a fleshy machine. The so-called mind can be reduced to the brain, and thinking and acting can be reduced to biochemical brain states and stimulus-response reactions. Since the laws of physics are universal, there can be no such thing as a free will. If everything is material, there can be no such thing as an immaterial soul. (This point of view, which is still held by many scientists and philosophers today, will be discussed more fully in Chapter 9 and the Fourth Interlude.)

> The relation between the body and the mind is so intimate that, if either of them got out of order, the whole system would suffer.
>
> *Mohandas Gandhi*

MATERIALISM

(also known as *behaviorism, mechanism,* or *reductionism*) Belief that everything is composed of matter (and energy), and can be explained by physical laws, that all human activity can be understood as the natural behavior of matter according to mechanical laws, and that thinking is merely a complex form of behaving: the body is a fleshy machine.

Darrow's Trip to Goofville

If I am told that next week I shall start on a trip to Goofville; that I shall not take my body with me; that I shall stay for all eternity: can I find a single fact connected with my journey—the way I shall go, the part of me that is to go, the time of the journey, the country I shall reach, its location in space, the way I shall live there—or anything that would lead to a rational belief that I shall really take the trip? Have I ever known anyone who has made the journey and returned? If I am really to believe, I must try to get some information about all these important facts.

Clarence Darrow
"The Myth of the Soul," *The Forum* 80 (October 1928).

Like the theologians, Descartes was alarmed by the amoral, secular nature of this particular view of the universe. Yet, as we have noted, he was a scientist himself, and his philosophy was designed to bridge the growing gap between the "new science" and religion. By showing that the mind is different in kind from the body, Descartes hoped to prove that the discoveries of the physicists posed no threat to free will or the existence of an incorporeal soul. The laws of physics apply only to matter, but the mind (soul) is an incorporeal thinking substance. Mind and body are two completely different kinds of substances. Thus science turns out to be the language of bodies; it cannot address minds or souls, so it is no threat to the church or basic Christian theology.

Cartesian Dualism

DUALISM

Any philosophical position that divides existence into two completely distinct, independent, unique substances.

MONISM

General name for the belief that everything consists of only one, ultimate, unique substance such as matter or spirit.

PLURALISM

The belief that there exist many realities or substances.

Any philosophical position that divides existence into two completely distinct, independent, unique substances or kinds of things is a form of **dualism**. The distinction may be between mind and body, natural and supernatural, spirit and matter, soul and body, good and evil, and so on. (**Monism** is the general name for the belief that everything consists of only one, ultimate, unique substance, such as matter; **pluralism** is the name for the belief in more than one substance.)

Cartesian dualism refers to Descartes' conviction that human beings are a mysterious union of mind (soul) and body, of incorporeal substance and corporeal substance, with each realm operating according to separate sets of laws. The mind follows the laws of reason, but otherwise is free. The body is governed by the laws of physics and falls under the rule of cause and effect: The human body is no freer than any other material thing. The soul is somehow dispersed to all parts of the body, but thinking enters the brain through the pineal gland.

And as a clock composed of wheels and counter-weights no less exactly observes the laws of nature . . . if I consider the body of a man as being a sort of machine so built up and composed of nerves, muscles, veins, blood, and skin, that though there were no mind in it at all, it would not cease to have made the same motions as at present, exception being made of those movements which are due to the direction of the will, and in consequence depend upon the mind.[21]

We can understand thinking without ever referring to the body, and we can understand the body without ever referring to the mind/soul. So, Descartes concluded, minds and bodies are essentially independent of each other. Science can study bodies and the natural world without ever treading in theology.

Initially, this rationale seems satisfactory. Indeed, it fits the "common-sense" view of Christian theology and ordinary experience. Cartesian dualism allows for the doctrine of the soul's continued existence after the body's death. Further, by defining himself as *thinking substance* rather than corporeal, Descartes reaffirms the primacy of the soul over the body. Human beings are essentially spiritual beings who happen to inhabit bodies. As a devout believer, Descartes has salvaged his faith from the threats of science. As a scientist, he has freed science to progress without church interference, since scientific discoveries are about the body and have no real bearing on the nature of the soul.

The Mind-Body Problem

Dualism generates one of the most tenacious timeless (and timely) questions: What is the relationship of the mind to the body?

So appealing is dualism to philosophers, preachers, psychologists, and most of the rest of us that in his influential and controversial book *The Concept of Mind*, contemporary philosopher Gilbert Ryle refers to it simply as "the official doctrine." Ryle says:

> The official doctrine, which hails chiefly from Descartes, is something like this. With the doubtful exceptions of idiots and infants in arms every human being has both a body and a mind. Some would prefer to say that every human being is both a body and a mind. His body and his mind are ordinarily harnessed together, but after the death of the body his mind may continue to exist and function.[22]

Versions of the "official doctrine" are obvious in beliefs about the immortality of the soul and reincarnation. It is implicit in psychological theories that view the mind as something other than the brain, and that differentiate mental states from bodily conditions and behavior. It is reflected in ordinary language when we talk about *having* a body, and in common experience when we feel as if "we" are somehow *in* our bodies. Religious and metaphysical versions of the official doctrine often compare the soul to a

Such a dualistic mode of perception not only impedes a holistic theory of liberation, but it is also substantially responsible for constructing the very world of alienation from which we seek liberation . . . operating on three levels: (1) alienation from oneself; one's own body; (2) alienation from one's fellow person in the "alien" community; (3) alienation from the "world": from the visible earth and sky.

Rosemary Radford Ruether

Here I confess that I have been suffering from a deception. For I believed that I was addressing a human soul, or that internal principle by which a man lives, feels, moves from place to place and understands, and after all I was only speaking to a mind.

Pierre Gassendi

driver and the body to a car. At death, we get out of the car or—if you believe in reincarnation—trade the old body in for a new one.

Descartes rejects the car-driver type of analogy and unites mind and body into "one whole."

Nature also teaches me by these sensations of pain, hunger, thirst, etc., that I am not only lodged in my body as a pilot in a vessel, but that I am very closely united to it, and so to speak so intermingled with it that I seem to compose with it one whole. For if that were not the case, when my body is hurt, I who am merely a thinking thing, should not feel pain, for I should perceive this wound by the understanding only, just as a sailor perceives by sight when something is damaged in his vessel; and when my body has need of drink or food, I should clearly understand the fact without being warned of it by confused feelings of hunger and thirst. For all these sensations of hunger, thirst, pain, etc., are in truth none other than certain confused modes of thought which are produced by the union and intermingling of mind and body.[23]

(The "union" or "intermingling" occurs, as noted earlier, in the pineal gland. Descartes apparently devoted some time to dissecting animal carcasses in order to study this mysterious gland.)

Dualism *feels consistent* with certain common experiences, but inconsistent with others: If I hit my thumb with a hammer, I experience no mind-body split. Yet there are serious consequences if we reject dualism in favor of a materialistic, behavioristic monism: When we reduce mental states to physical states, do we lose the possibility of free will, moral responsibility, and the possibility of survival after death? Such beliefs are important to the very meaning of life for many people, real enough and important enough so that any difficulties of *explaining* mind-body interaction pale beside the consequences of rejecting dualism.

But the fact that millions of people believe something does not make it true. Cartesian dualism—indeed, metaphysical speculation itself—stands in direct opposition to another major modern philosophical archetype: the skeptical questioner who turns to experience rather than to the mind for knowledge.

Philosophical Query

How plausible is this "official doctrine"? On Descartes' own terms, how "clearly and distinctly" do we understand the relationship of the mind to the body? How can a *completely* nonphysical thing interact with a *completely* physical thing? To ask Mark Twain's insightful question, How come the mind gets drunk when the body does the drinking? Why does my mind react to what happens to my body with such intensity if it's not part of my body?

The Epistemological Turn

As a general rule, allowing for the specialized concerns of individual philosophers, Western philosophy was dominated by metaphysical issues until the seventeenth century. These concerned the nature of ultimate reality, soul and substance, God, and levels of being. It was not until Descartes defined knowledge in terms of certainty and refined the use of methodic doubt that the importance of epistemology was fully recognized.

Prior to Descartes' inquiry into the foundations of knowledge, philosophers distinguished between good and bad reasons, and established standards of proof, but they did not directly study the *process of thinking* in the way Descartes did. He began what philosophers refer to as the *epistemological turn*. Philosophers point out that this major transformation in the character of philosophy took a century and a half to complete, culminating with Immanuel Kant's *Critique of Pure Reason* (Chapter 10).

To put it another way, we can say that whereas earlier philosophers sought knowledge about the good life, nature, the soul, God, the ideal society, and so forth, modern philosophers increasingly devoted themselves to acquiring knowledge about knowledge. This, we shall see, led them to emphasize the precise meaning of terms and standards of evidence. This important general principle seems obvious once it is expressed: *Before we can reasonably evaluate any beliefs about reality, we must inquire into the nature of the "instrument" we use to observe it.* Contemporary philosophy has followed this lead, and all major areas of the field have been dominated by epistemological concerns.

Commentary

Descartes' rationalism was inspired by a vision and three dreams, which he interpreted as a divine calling to establish his method of rational inquiry. Through the innovative use of methodic doubt, he established one irrefutable certainty, the cogito. Descartes claimed that God's existence was the foundation for all knowledge and the general reliability of the "natural light" of reason, yet for the contemporary observer the cogito is more solidly grounded than the proof for God.

Thus the modern era is grounded in Cartesian self-consciousness, self-reflection, and self-analysis. In its emphasis on an individual's inquiry after truth rather than official answers, Cartesian rationalism seems to pave the way for social and political democracy. The irony in this is that we note a kind of cool, analytic detachment as Descartes makes himself the subject of study in a new way. As the modern era develops, purity of method

It seems to me that the greatest lesson of adult life is that one's own consciousness is not enough.

Sir Fred Hoyle

From the "I conquer" applied to the Aztec and Inca world and all America, from the "I enslave" applied to Africans sold for gold and silver acquired at the cost of the death of the Amerindians working in the depths of the earth, from the "I vanquish" of the wars of India and China to the shameful "opium war"—from this "I" appears the Cartesian *ego cogito.* . . .

Enrique Dussel

Consciousness is a disease.

Miguel de Unamuno

ultimately takes precedence over the search for wisdom. This trend may be a consequence of the detached, depersonalized quality of rationalistic analysis that emerged in the work of Descartes.

The benefits of the Cartesian revolution include using clearer, simpler, ordinary language (an idea that significantly influenced subsequent philosophers). Descartes paved the way for psychological studies by showing that the "thinking thing" is not a neutral "window," but a dynamic entity whose very nature affects its observations and conclusions. He initiated the study of knowledge and the sources of knowledge that continues to this day. Even the rationalists' great epistemological opponents, the empiricists, found themselves in part responding to issues raised by rationalism.

Without intending to trivialize this most important philosophical question, our attitudes toward the mind-body problem and its solution seem to be greatly influenced by whether we focus on the wider or narrower view. By the wider view I mean the view that takes seriously both our (common?) *sense* of free will and cross-cultural reports of out-of-body experiences, belief in personal immortality in some form or other, and a recognizable difference between the spiritual and material realm. The narrower view is chiefly concerned with logical consistency, precise use of terminology, and demonstrable evidence, usually resting on an observable, empirical component.

I find myself drawn to the wider view for a number of reasons. Although I reject arguments based strictly and solely on the authority of custom, tradition, or numbers, I cannot ignore nearly universal, cross-cultural beliefs in a spiritual dimension of reality. Temperamentally preferring the certainty of observable evidence and the clarity of precise speaking, I am still not comfortable rejecting dualism just because it is difficult to express the exact nature of the mind-body relationship.

The mind-body problem remains. On the one hand, we have the problems of dualistic interaction. But a materialistic, reductionistic alternative renders as illusory and confused some of our most important, widely held beliefs. The average person has actually been rather receptive to bizarre-sounding scientific theories and discoveries, accepting without always understanding, for example, that the earth is a tiny sphere in a vast universe, that much of our behavior is inherited, that time and space are relative, and so on. This demonstrates a willingness to accept changing ideas of reality. What, then, accounts for the persistence of dualism, given the dominance of reductionistic materialism in the scientific and philosophic communities? I can only think that dualism speaks more accurately of reality as most of us experience it than reductionistic alternatives.

Unlike others of his time (and ours), Descartes refused to bow before religious authority, choosing to accept only what he knew for himself. Consider the alternative: believing—or trying to believe—and devoting your life to ideas you cannot really understand or that you know to be inconsistent and contradictory. The temporary victory of the Inquisition over the spirit of honest inquiry and rational rigor was merely the victory of force over reason. It is no more praiseworthy than contemporary efforts to legislate the appropriateness of ideas on religious, social, or political grounds.

Descartes was one of those dangerous philosophers mentioned in Chapter 1. He stands out as an archetype of the rationalist for his unwillingness to settle for inconsistencies and contradictions between his faith and his intellect. If his notion of "clear and distinct" is itself cloudy; if his introduction of God is suspicious; and if his attempt to account for mind-body interaction is unsatisfying, he is nonetheless remarkable for squarely facing up to the need to reassess his belief system for himself. He tried not to believe what he could not clearly understand. That in itself is a remarkable achievement.

Summary of Main Points

1. Descartes' scientific and mathematical interests demanded clear, provable evidence of a sort lacking in Scholasticism's cumbersome reliance on authority, and resulted in a radical proposal: Start fresh; throw out everything we think we know and build a system based entirely on ideas whose truth can be clearly and distinctly known to us firsthand.

2. Reliance on reason as the ultimate source of knowledge is a form of rationalism. In general, rationalists believe that abstract reasoning can produce absolutely certain truths about reality, and that some important ultimate truths can be discovered without observation, experiment, or experience. Such truths are known as innate ideas or a priori ideas. Ideas derived from experience are known as a posteriori ideas.

3. Rationalists rely on the coherence theory of truth: New or unclear ideas are evaluated in terms of rational or logical consistency and relation to already established truths.

4. Descartes replaced Scholastic authority with a rational method that restricts us to accepting as true only what we understand clearly and distinctly for ourselves.

5. Descartes' interest in the "thinking thing itself" was the first major step in a shift in emphasis in modern philosophy from metaphysics to epistemology.

6. Descartes recognized the need for orderly thinking, which he called *method*. This paved the way for the modern emphasis on technique (method) and marks a major shift from metaphysical, authoritarian medieval thinking to epistemological, technical modern thinking.

7. Descartes' method avoids the *fallacy of false authority*: an error in reasoning in which we accept the word of experts speaking outside their fields, or uncritically rely on the testimony of others without checking it against our own experiences and reason.

8. Descartes employed *methodic doubt* in his effort to find one absolutely certain and undoubtable idea. Methodic doubt is a form of skepticism that rejects any idea that could possibly be false, no matter how remote that possibility. Methodic doubt coupled with the concept of the evil genius led Descartes to raise questions about whether or not he was dreaming, and about the existence of his own body and of the entire external world.

9. Even an evil genius could not shake one fundamental idea: "I think, therefore I am." This is known as the cogito.

10. Having found an undoubtable truth, Descartes tried to build a reliable foundation for knowledge based on the innate idea of God. He did this by appealing to an ontological argument that attempts to prove the existence of God by showing that the idea "God" cannot be derived from human experience; it can only come from the existence of a perfect being.

11. Having established the existence of God to his satisfaction, Descartes believed he had clearly and distinctly demonstrated the reliability of reason and the possibility of certain knowledge, since if God is all-knowing, all-good, and all-powerful, He would not let us live in constant ignorance.

12. Descartes rejected the materialists' challenge to the notion of free will with Cartesian dualism, the belief that two completely different kinds of things exist, bodies and minds, and that human beings are a mysterious union of both. Dualism, however, generates the mind-body problem: What is the relationship of the mind to the body? How can a nonmaterial thing (mind) affect a material thing (body)?

Study Questions

1. What was Descartes' proposal, and how did his Scholastic education influence it?

2. What is the coherence theory of truth?

3. What is the method of doubt? Give a brief summary of its function in terms of Descartes' overall effort to discover certain knowledge.

4. Discuss Descartes' standard of truth. Do you think it is chiefly rational or psychological? Explain.

5. Descartes asserted that whatever we recognize "clearly and distinctly" is true. Explain the criticism that this formulation fails to meet its own standard. Do you agree that Descartes' rationalism is based on subjective states rather than on reasons understood "clearly and distinctly"? Discuss.

6. What are innate ideas? Give one or two examples.

7. What is skepticism? How is it important to Cartesian philosophy?

8. What is the cogito? Is it refutable? Discuss.

9. What is the evil genius, and what is its significance to the Cartesian Genesis? Explain.

10. Give Descartes' argument for the existence of God in your own words, then analyze it. Is it convincing? Why or why not?

11. What is Cartesian dualism?

12. What is the mind-body problem? How does Descartes deal with it? Is he successful? Why or why not?

Third Interlude

The Buddha

I call the motive to be the deed.

Buddha

The Buddha

So powerful was the person and vision of **Siddhārtha Gautama (c. 560–480 B.C.)** that he was recognized during his lifetime as an archetype unto himself. Today the archetype of the Buddha is a major source of meaning and purpose for over two billion people. The Buddha was a sage, yet more than a sage. He was fully human, yet more than human. Among his many names, perhaps the most enduring are the Awakened or Enlightened One (the original meaning of "the Buddha" in Sanskrit) and the Compassionate Buddha. Yet for all his influence, we have very little factual information about him; most of what we know comes from oral tradition and myth.[1]

Siddhārtha Gautama was born into wealth and power as the son of a prince (rajah) in what is today Nepal. Siddhārtha was intelligent and alert, a talented student and athlete. Legend says that he was a first-rate hunter and archer, and enjoyed a rich and active life. An only son, Siddhārtha was spoiled and indulged by his family; he became a hedonist and a womanizer. At sixteen he married his cousin, but this does not seem to have slowed his pleasure seeking.

The young prince lived in protected isolation, surrounded by servants who catered to his slightest whim. One version of his life claims that Siddhārtha's parents took great pains to shield him from the ugliness of life, even surrounding him with young, attractive servants to spare him the sight of the ravages of age. His parents protected him from the knowledge of

Siddhārtha Gautama

Indeed, the saving truth has never been preached by the Buddha, seeing that one has to realize it within oneself.

Sutralamakara

315

poverty and suffering by seducing him with every imaginable delight—within their palatial grounds. Hunger, sickness, and death were too crude for their precious son. He knew only luxury and pleasure; the outside world remained a mystery to him.

But Siddhārtha was not content. As with many young people, curiosity and rebelliousness led him away from home. During secret trips outside the palace to a nearby city he saw three of the now-famous Four Signs that altered his life forever. He saw a destitute and homeless beggar. He saw a dead man being prepared for cremation by weeping mourners. He saw a diseased and handicapped person. The seeds of the Buddha were planted when Siddhārtha encountered suffering.

Siddhārtha the Seeker

Before his forbidden excursions outside the family compound, Siddhārtha had no real idea of what sickness or old age could do to the body and spirit. He had no sense of the depths that poverty could reach. He was unaware of the power of grief. The price he had paid for living in a cocoon of soft pleasures and blindness to the suffering of others was a feeling of bored disease. Even ignorance failed to protect him, however. Driven by the restless boredom that almost always accompanies an unproductive, self-indulgent life, Siddhārtha felt compelled to stray outside. All the pleasures of his wealthy family could not quell his nagging sense of discomfort. He had to know more.

The young prince had no one to talk with about his troubling questions but his servant Channa, who was his hired companion and charioteer, his guardian and bodyguard. To every question Siddhārtha raised, Channa could only reply with great sadness and resignation, "Yes, master, there is no escape. Old age, sickness, death—such is the lot of all men."[2]

In today's language, we might say that Siddhārtha "had his eyes opened." His naive unawareness was spoiled forever. No longer were his pleasures as sweet. Try as he might, Siddhārtha could not shake the haunting images of old age, sickness, and death. His anxiety grew. How, he asked himself again and again, could anyone be happy, since—ultimately—there is absolutely no escape from suffering, disappointment, sadness, and loss? If no one escapes, why be born at all? How could any woman want to give birth knowing what awaited her child? None of his family or servants could answer him.

Walking outside the palace grounds one day, deep in despair, he saw a wandering monk, an ascetic. **Ascetics** turn away from pleasure and severely limit all sensual appetites in order to achieve salvation or peace of mind. Asceticism involves long hours of prayer and fasting, living on plain food, wearing simple clothes. Monks in many cultures live ascetic lives. In Western traditions Old Testament prophets were often ascetics. When John the

---

Cut out the love of self, like an autumn lotus with your hand! Cherish the road to peace. Nirvana has been shown by the Blessed One.

   The Buddha

If a fool is associated with a wise man even all his life, he will perceive the truth as little as a spoon perceives the taste of soup.

   The Buddha

ASCETIC

Individual who turns away from pleasure and severely limits all sensual appetites in order to achieve salvation or peace of mind.

In northwest Siberia's Khanty-Mansai National District, hunter and shaman Pyotor Yukhlymov unites his village in celebration of the sacred connection of all spirits by performing an ancient shamanic rite honoring a just-killed bear, reverently thought of as the Old Clawed One.

Baptist and Jesus went into the desert and lived on locusts, honey, and water and fasted, they were going through ascetic trials.

When Siddhārtha looked closely into the face of the wandering monk he was astonished to see serenity, purpose, and detachment. Here was the last of the Four Signs. Here, finally, was an answer. Siddhārtha knew that he must leave the security of his home and live as a monk, homeless, with only a simple robe and beggar's bowl. He would go to the wisest sages, no matter how far and difficult the journey. He would find someone to tell him the answers to life's most basic questions: Why live if suffering is inescapable? Is it possible to be happy in the face of inevitable sickness, old age, and death? What is the real meaning of life?

The adult has to break his attachment to persons and things.

Walter Lippmann

The Long Search

For years Siddhārtha wandered with his beggar's bowl, seeking one master or guru after another. Even though many of them were wise and deeply interested in helping Siddhārtha, he did not find his answer. He found only more teachers, and though he learned many clever philosophical notions, as well as techniques for meditating and disciplining the body, he found no satisfying answers to his basic, timeless questions.

Finally tiring of gurus and ordinary sages, he settled in a grove of trees on the outskirts of the village of Uruvela, India. There he formed a little

I once went a day without food and all night without sleep to enable me to think. I found no advantage in it; it's best to study.

Confucius

K'ung Fu-Tzu: "I Do Not Instruct the Uninterested"

The Latinized version of K'ung Fu-tzu (Grand Master Kung) is **Confucius** (551–479 B.C.). Confucius is the third of the three major Asian sages (along with Buddha and Lao-tzu). Master K'ung was born poor and had to educate himself—he studied under no particular teacher. He was the first great teacher in Chinese history. His goal was to make education available to everyone. He developed the doctrine of the *chun-tzu*, or "superior man"—a well-rounded gentleman of moderation. It is recorded that at one time Confucius had three thousand pupils. He began teaching in his twenties or thirties, and died at seventy-three.

Confucius creatively modified ancient concepts to produce a powerful code of conduct and an ideal to which Chinese citizens have looked for centuries. A collection of his doctrines known as the *Analects* may be the most influential book of Asian philos-

Confucius

ophy, with the close exception of the *Tao Te Ching*.

Confucius was a *humanist*, that is, he believed that "man can make the Way (Tao) great," not that "the Way can make man great." In this, he disagreed with his older contemporary, Lao-tzu. Both Lao-tzu and Confucius reacted to the corruption and social turmoil around them, but whereas Lao-tzu counseled "inaction" and psychological withdrawal, Confucius was chiefly interested in actively producing

a harmonious, well-ordered society. He believed that such a society requires rules and regulations and, most importantly, an elaborate bureaucracy of highly cultured and learned men. The term *chun-tzu* occurs 107 times in the *Analects*.

The *chun-tzu* possesses *jen*—general virtue. *Jen* is expressed in terms of *chung* (conscientiousness) and *shu* (altruism), which are the "one thread" of Confucianism.

With its emphasis on conformity, social order, and active life ("action"), Confucianism stands in direct contrast to Taoism, which stresses tranquility, individual life, and inaction. Here's a sampling of teachings from the *Analects*.

2:4 At fifteen I thought to study; at thirty I began playing my rôle; at forty I was sure of myself; at fifty I was conscious of my position in the universe; at sixty I

community with a few other seekers. For six years he meditated, fasted, and concentrated daily on his original questions. During this time, he is said to have conquered most physical appetites and weaknesses and learned how to control "the mad monkey of the mind."[3] But still he found no answers.

In his efforts to subdue his body, he nearly destroyed it. He is supposed to have said, "When I touched my stomach I felt my backbone." His extreme asceticism left him a wasted shell. In Buddhist art portraying him during this period, every bone and muscle pushes through his skin. Ultimately, Siddhārtha realized that his body was an important instrument in his search, and he realized that he must honor the spirit by honoring the body that houses it. This lesson was clear: The Way cannot be found by either indulgence or denial. We must walk a Middle Path.

was no longer argumentative; and now at seventy I can follow my heart's desire without violating custom.

2:13 Tuan-mu Tz'u asked about Great Man.

"First he sets the good example, then he invites others to follow it."

3:1 Confucius said of the Chis [clan] who used eight rows of eight singers and dancers at the celebrations in honor of their family—only the king should use so many—that if they could permit themselves this, they were capable of anything.

4:1 To live in the company of Men-at-their-best is the finest thing possible. How can a man be considered wise if, when he has the choice, he does not live in such surroundings?

4:2 I cannot discuss things with a gentleman who, while devoted to [the Way], is at the same time ashamed of poor clothes or bad food.

4:17 When you see a man of the highest caliber, give thought to attaining his stature. When you see one who is not, go home and conduct a self-examination.

4:23 When strict with oneself one rarely fails.

4:24 Great Man seeks to be slow of speech but quick of action.

6:20 Being fond of [the Way] is better than merely knowing it. Taking one's delight in it is better than merely being fond of it.

6:29 [Jen] according to the golden mean is indeed supreme. For a long time, however, few among the people have been capable of it.

7:8 I do not instruct the uninterested; I do not help those who fail to try. If I mention one corner of a subject and the pupil does not deduce therefrom the other three, I drop him.

7:20 I wasn't born knowing what to teach. Being fond of the ancients, I sought it through diligence.

9:18 I have yet to meet a man who is as fond of [jen] as he is of outward appearances.

14:23 Great Man reaches complete understanding of the main issues; Petty Man reaches complete understanding of the minute details.

14:24 Formerly men studied for self-improvement; today men study for the sake of appearances.

15:21 Great Man demands it of himself; Petty Man, of others.

From Wing-Tsit Chan, trans. and comp., *A Source Book in Chinese Philosophy* (Princeton, N.J.: Princeton University Press, 1963), Chapter 2: The Humanism of Confucius, and *The Sayings of Confucius: A New Translation*, trans. James R. Ware (New York: A Mentor Religious Classic, 1955).

Siddhārtha's fellow monks were disgusted when he began to take proper nourishment. They had been impressed with his ascetic ways as signs of strength and willpower. From this Siddhārtha learned another lesson: We must stop worrying about what others think of us and quit trying to impress people if we are ever to find wisdom. He realized that ascetic self-denial can be of value as a temporary corrective for indulgences or as a momentary cleansing, but it is not an adequate way of life. To subdue the appetites in order to show strength and willpower is a way of showing off, which prevents one from growing wise.

So Siddhārtha returned to his lonely wandering. One day when he was thirty, as he sat in meditation under a fig tree, he was given a special bowl of rice milk by a young woman because he reminded her of a figure she had

What ought to be done is neglected, what ought not to be done is done; the desires of unruly, thoughtless people are always increasing.

The Buddha

seen in a vision. In her vision, she had presented rice milk in a golden bowl to a single figure seated under a tree. She took this figure to be a god because of a special glow she saw around him. He was, of course, the Buddha.

Siddhārtha accepted the rice milk and, according to one legend, did not eat again for forty-nine days. Another legend says that he divided the milk into numerous portions, and these sustained him during his deepening meditation. After Siddhārtha had finished the rice milk, he threw the golden bowl into a nearby river, where it miraculously floated *upstream*. (This symbolizes the fact that the Buddha's teachings go against the currents of our ordinary, unenlightened thinking.) Siddhārtha then ceremoniously bathed in the river, and, taking the lotus position, once more sat under the fig tree and said: "Here I shall remain until I am answered or dead." The tree under which the Buddha sat became known as the Bodhi Tree—the Tree of Wisdom.

Finally, the awakening came. What Buddhist tradition refers to as the "greatest event in human history" occurred during the full moon of May, c. 524 B.C. Refusing to be swayed from his goal, heeding some inner call despite all costs, Siddhārtha Gautama had transformed himself from a spoiled, pampered young man into "the one who had awakened": the Buddha.

The Enlightened Vision

According to Buddhist teachings, it is impossible to "explain" the awakening. Nonetheless, we can get a rough idea of what the Buddha "saw." Siddhārtha saw himself and *all life* as part of an unending process of change, a great chain of being through which things come into and leave one form of existence for another. Everything is one. The whole universe is a system of interconnected, inseparable parts, rich and complex, composed of all varieties of life forever moving from one form to another.

The Buddha did not arrive at this perception intellectually. He *saw* it all at once, in what we in the West might call a mystical vision. The now-Buddha realized instantly how difficult it would be to teach a doctrine that could not be grasped by mere reasoning and that could not be realized by blind faith, but only by unswerving personal effort. Only by the greatest effort could an individual achieve release from suffering. The price of wisdom is love of the whole rather than love of any one part—including, especially, ourselves.[4]

The Bodhisattva

Siddhārtha had reached a state of bliss and utter detachment called nirvana. **Nirvana** is annihilation of the ego, a state of emptiness or "no-thingness." It is described as a state of bliss because there is only "pure con-

---

Though my skin, my nerves, and my bones should waste away and my lifeblood dry, I will not leave this seat until I have attained Supreme Enlightenment.

The Buddha

The intellect can understand any part of a thing as a part, but not as a whole.

R. H. Blyth

NIRVANA

Annihilation of the ego; a state of emptiness or "no-thing-ness"; a state of bliss; "pure consciousness" that leads to release from suffering while remaining conscious.

sciousness" with no sense of individuality, separateness, discrimination, or intellectualizing. It cannot be explained in words, since words are limiting and exist to identify similarities and differences. Nirvana is beyond even similarity. It can only be talked around or expressed in contradictions. It transcends all ordinary experience. Nirvana is release from suffering while conscious. (If you do not "understand" what nirvana is, don't feel inadequate. Nirvana can be experienced; it cannot be described or understood.) The experience of nirvana transforms us because it shifts our attention from timely concerns to timeless issues.

Siddhārtha now had to make another important choice: He could stay in nirvana, meditating and remaining uninvolved with the commotion and suffering of life. Or he could share his vision. Legend says that "the very earth trembled" while waiting for his decision. At last, the "Great Buddha Heart of Infinite Compassion prevailed."[5] Siddhārtha refused ultimate release and, because he chose to stay and help others, became the Buddha, "He Who Awoke," or "He Who Became Aware." This helpful part of him is sometimes referred to as "The Walking Buddha," the man who wandered about once more, only now as a teacher rather than as a seeker.

This Buddha who chose to remain among people giving help to other lost souls is known as the Bodhisattva in some branches of Buddhism. A **bodhisattva** is an enlightened being who voluntarily postpones his own nirvana in order to help all other conscious life-forms find "supreme release." A bodhisattva is *not* a savior. The Buddha did not intercede for others; he showed them a path. A bodhisattva is a wise and compassionate being who has gone beyond discrimination: there is no more "I," "mine," "yours." He no longer perceives separateness on any level. The bodhisattva no longer even perceives *a* self, *a* being, *a* person. His consciousness is forever altered. Siddhārtha, the Buddha, the great bodhisattva, was at last ready to teach personal transformation through compassion.

It did not take long for the Buddha to acquire many followers. As with other great sages, who the Buddha was became as significant as what he taught. In addition to his wife and son, Siddhārtha's disappointed ascetic companions became disciples of the Buddha. In order to "beat the drum of [truth] in the darkness of the world" and share his message with everyone, the Buddha sent groups of his earliest disciples out as teachers. The Buddha did not seek converts, and his monks were not missionaries. Their goal was to spread information that people could use to reduce suffering.

The Death of the Buddha

Legend teaches that the Buddha died from either poisonous mushrooms or tainted pork. His last meal was at the humble home of a blacksmith (significantly, a person of low status in ancient Asian culture). Soon after eating, the Buddha took sick. He asked his host to bury the rest of the food so

Do you know where to stop? Can you let unimportant things go? Can you learn not to depend on others but to seek it in yourself?

Chuang-tzu

BODHISATTVA

An enlightened being who voluntarily postpones his own nirvana in order to help all other conscious life-forms find "supreme release"; not a savior.

Surrounded on his death-bed, as in life, by sadness, wailing, and torment, Buddha remained serene, detached, and accepting.

A man who talks much of his teaching but does not practice it himself is like a cattleman counting another man's cattle. . . . Like beautiful flowers full of color, but without scent, are the well-chosen words of the man who does not act accordingly.

The Buddha

that no one else would eat it. Calling upon the discipline learned through years of meditation, he was able to control his pain well enough to travel to a certain river. He bathed in the river and then lay down in a mango grove "on his right side in the attitude of a lion with one foot on the other."[6]

As he lay dying, the Buddha made a special point to tell his closest disciple, Ananda, that the blacksmith was not to blame. The Buddha also sent special word to the blacksmith thanking him for his "alms." By this the Buddha meant that the blacksmith was blessed for having been the vehicle by which the Buddha would escape "the wheel of suffering" and attain nirvana. After sending this message, the Buddha crossed the river and resumed the lion's pose in a different grove.

The Buddha said, "Do not weep, do not mourn, oh ye monks." Like Socrates speaking to his disciples while the hemlock was being prepared (see Chapter 3), before his death the Buddha reassured his followers that change—including death and decay—is universal, natural, and inescapable.

As a mother, even at the risk of her own life, protects and loves her child, her only child, so let a man cultivate love without measure toward the whole world, above, below, and around, unstinted, unmixed with any feeling of differing or opposing interests. Let a man remain steadfastly in this state of mind, walking, sitting or lying down. This state of mind is the best in the world.[7]

After his death, the teachings of the Buddha were handed down in the form of an oral tradition, and it was not until the first century B.C. that monks began to transcribe these discourses onto ola leaves. They remained so until recent times, when the Pali Text Society took up the task of editing and printing them. They are now known collectively as the "three baskets": the *Vinaya Pitaka* (rules for monks), the *Sutta Pitaka* (basic teachings of the Buddha), and an organized later commentary known as the *Abhidhamma Pitaka*. Today, so many people produce books, journal articles, and video- and audiotaped lectures commenting on "Buddhism" that the diligent seeker will have trouble keeping up with a year's worth. Perhaps this is a tribute both to the profundity of the Buddha's pivotal insight and to a common human hunger for enlightenment.

Although this Interlude can be no more than a glimpse of the rich and profound legacy left by Buddha's great "experiment," even reflected wisdom casts valuable light. So let us tread tentatively and respectfully through this tiniest of corners in one of the world's greatest wisdom traditions.

> All humanity is sick. I come therefore to you as a physician who has diagnosed this universal disease and is prepared to cure it.
>
> *The Buddha*

Buddha's Philosophy Lab

In this light, contemporary Buddhists sometimes refer to the Buddha's teachings as "scientific." Considered this way, Buddhist teachings can be compared to the kind of coaching provided by a physical trainer who imparts knowledge of training techniques and nutrition based on firsthand experience with what works. For instance, you need not "believe in" the benefits of aerobic training for such training to benefit you—you need only to work out regularly and wisely.

As an archetypal sage, Buddha did not separate "understanding" from "action," "being" from "doing." His naturalistic "holism" reminds us of Aristotle's characterization of moral virtue as *habit*. Similarly, from a Buddhist perspective, a change of habit can trigger a change of mind (point of view), which in turn will trigger a change of heart (emotion or affect). Note, too, that given the organic nature of actions, thoughts, and feelings, alteration of one aspect of our lives always results in corresponding changes in the other two. It is common to "wait for enlightenment," or try to alter our thinking and wanting in order to change our behavior. But what happens until enlightenment sweeps us up? What happens if enlightenment does not come to us, but must be discovered or earned?

I am intrigued by one theme that runs through Buddhist literature and tradition, going back to the earliest stories of the Buddha himself. That is the theme of taking positive action *whether or not* we are enlightened and *whether or not* we are utterly convinced that such action will lead to enlightenment, peace of mind, or "salvation." In wisdom literature, this

> Your self-partiality is the root of all your illusions. There aren't any illusions when you don't have this preference for yourself.
>
> *Bankei*

One Day . . .

Some of the richest Buddhist literature consists of stories, which reveal the process of enlightenment indirectly. Though highly refined, these gemlike little tales leave the heart of the story unspoken. Thus they function like spiritual inkblots, drawing new insights from each listener's response. Here's a sampler of four.

One day a potential suicide was talking to a Buddhist monk, asking whether he had the right to commit suicide if he wanted to. The monk replied, "Anyone has the right to do anything. Everyone else has the right to resist it."

The student said, "Do you see suicide as a moral act?"

The monk answered, "Where there is no victim, every act is morally right, but I personally think suicide is a symptom of taking oneself too seriously."

One day the Buddhist monk Joshu fell down in the snow. He began wailing and crying for help. Seeing his distress, another monk lay down beside him and began thrashing about, crying and wailing as well. Joshu got up and left.

One day Chinso was up in a tower with some important people, and one of them saw a group of monks approaching. "Look," he said, "holy men." "No, they aren't," Chinso said, "and I'll prove it." When the monks were directly below, Chinso leaned out of the tower window and yelled, "Hey! Holy men!" When they all looked up in response to his call, he said to his companions, "See?"

One day a rich man asked Sengai to write something ensuring the continued prosperity of his family. Sengai wrote: "Father dies, son dies, grandson dies." This angered the rich man, who said, "I asked you to write something for the happiness of my family! Why do you make such a joke as this?" "This is no joke," Sengai explained. "If your son dies before you do, you would grieve greatly. If your grandson dies before your son, both of you would be brokenhearted. If your family, generation after generation, passes away in the order I have named, it will be the natural course of life. I call this real prosperity."

The first story is from Camden Benares, *Zen without Zen Masters* (Berkeley: And/Or Press, 1977), p. 37. The next three are paraphrased from Paul Reps, *Zen Flesh, Zen Bones: A Collection of Zen and Pre-Zen Writings* (Garden City, N.Y.: Anchor Books, 1973), p. 67.

---

approach is sometimes referred to as "changing the inner from outside," or by the formula, "As above, so below, as without, so within." Thus, the Buddha's early disciples were taught to repeat this simple formula:

> I take my refuge in the Buddha.
> I take my refuge in the *Dharma* [the teachings].
> I take my refuge in the *Sangha* [the community of believers].[8]

This three-part formula is still repeated daily by millions of Buddhists.

Can we, as philosophical seekers, do justice to Buddha's holistic approach without becoming Buddhists ourselves? After all, we can hardly be expected to "become" adherents of every kind of philosophy we study. Yet we do want to understand enough of the essence of each philosophy so that we can understand its appeal to sincere, intelligent persons. Fortunately, we do not need to "be" Buddhists to add a personal dimension to our philosophical considerations.

An effective way to get beyond simple intellectual assessment of this material is to combine our reading with regular moments of reflection. We can think of these reflective breaks as interludes within this Interlude, as experiments in "philosophy lab." Indeed, even at this cursory level, such a practice is in keeping with the Buddha's characterization of himself as an "experimentalist" who begins with and who "respects facts as they are *found* in the world."

"Respecting" facts begins, of course, with attempting to see them clearly—and then relating to them *as they are found*. The Buddhist scholar M. W. Padmasiri de Silva says that "facts to [Buddha] also have some significance in the light of his doctrine. That *significance* is something which emerges from the natures of things and is not imposed from the outside."[9]

A good place to begin our philosophical experiments is where Buddha began, with his insight that existence is unsatisfactory for sentient beings.

Unsatisfactoriness

Among the insights Buddha gained during his arduous search for enlightenment, three "realities" command our attention: impermanence, suffering, and egolessness. In simplistic contemporary terms, we can sum up this part of Buddha's teaching like this: "Although nothing lasts, suffering is everywhere, and the 'me' that suffers isn't even real."

If this seems alien to you, don't be too quick to dismiss Buddha's "insight" as negative or ridiculous. Although, as philosophers, we do not base our opinions on simple numbers, we must respect the fact that millions of human beings have found wisdom, solace, hope, and a way of life in the Buddhist tradition that sprang from Buddha's teachings. More significantly, as philosophers, we first need to approach Buddha's teachings in the spirit of Buddha's ultimate purpose: He offered therapeutic insights into the nature of human suffering, not merely theoretical explanations of it.

As we work through this section, then, let us reflect on the extent to which we experience "the fact of suffering" and whatever suffering brings with it. Moments of suffering seem to be surrounded by periods of ease, well-being, and happiness. But to what extent are these positive states lasting? Unmixed? That is, we also experience a sort of chronic, borderline consciousness of the inevitable return of suffering (or at least letdown and loss) even in the midst of our greatest happiness: the bittersweet feeling present at weddings, births, graduations, other ceremonies of recognition, and such everyday things as petting the dog (and fleetingly realizing that someday she'll die), watching a beautiful sunset (and reflecting on cycles

Men commonly believe that all things are known or perceived by God, because they believe the being of a God; whereas I, on the other side, immediately and necessarily conclude the being of a God, because all things must be perceived by him.

George Berkeley

As sure, therefore, as the sensible world really exists, so sure is there an infinite omnipresent Spirit, who contains and supports it.

George Berkeley

Unawareness of one's feet is the mark of shoes that fit; unawareness of the waist is the sign of a belt that fits; unawareness of right and wrong is the mark of a mind that is at ease. It does not change inside and is not affected by external events, and one feels at ease in all circumstances and situations. That is to be at ease through unawareness of being at ease.

Chuang-tzu

KARMA

From the Pali *kamma*; according to Buddhist tradition, the law of moral causation (moral cause and effect); it includes past and present actions and is not to be confused with fate or predestination; good or bad karma results from our own actions.

of life and death). You have the idea. A sense of "impermanence" or "fleetingness" surrounds the highest moments of human consciousness.

And so it is, that at the core of the Buddha's doctrine is the concept of the primal *unsatisfactoriness* (*dukkha*) generated by the perilousness of the human condition, and by the inescapability of physical suffering and sickness, psychological conflict, anxiety and anguish. As if this is not enough, Buddha reminds us that beneath our dissatisfaction lies a profounder insight: the *insubstantiality* of existence.[10]

Awareness of insubstantiality is related to the Buddhist doctrines of impermanence (ever-change) and egolessness. According to the Buddha, what we usually think of as "I" or "an individual" is a continuously changing combination of physical and psychological elements. Out of ignorance, we *project* a sense of "permanence" onto impermanent conditions. Because all is in flux, we are inevitably disappointed by change, destruction, and loss.[11]

Failing to see the true nature of the complex of conditions and reactions that we think of as "an individual," our "self" remains subject to suffering and perpetual dissatisfaction. We compound suffering whenever we insist on projecting (expecting and anticipating) the possibility of a continuous life of pleasure, joy, and stability for our individual selves. While in a state of projection, we find it difficult to truly accept that *we* are subject to sickness, grief, and suffering. We resist the deeper insight via repression, aggression, greed, lust (consumption), denial, anger, and so forth. So it is that a fundamental "human condition" or "predicament" is our heritage. As one translation of Buddha's First Noble Truth poetically puts it: "When we are born, suffering comes with us."

Is this vision of the fundamental human condition pessimistic? Perhaps it would be, if Buddha had nothing more to teach, but Buddha promised that through a discipline of meditation, we can learn to control unruly desires and projections, to pay attention to and to see clearly whatever is before us. Seeing what is before us, he believed, would show us the path to right living and thinking, through which we could realize what happiness is possible, given the facts—not the projections—of the human condition.

Thus, we see that central to Buddha's teachings is a notion of free will, a belief that we can control our thoughts, attitudes, and behavior, and that thoughts, attitudes, and behavior have consequences. These consequences, their causes, and their control are called *karma*.

Karma

The word *karma* comes from the Pali word *kamma*, a term referring to acts of the will that are expressed in thought, word, and deed. The concept of *karma* combines *kamma* (action-cause) with *vipaka* (reaction-effect). According to Buddhist tradition, **karma** is the *law of moral causation* (moral cause and effect); it includes past and present actions, and is not to be confused with fate or predestination. Good or bad karma results from our own actions.[12]

Buddha did not teach that everything that happens is due to *karma*. In the first place, different laws govern natural change, physical phenomena, certain psychological processes, and so forth. In the second place, if *karma* alone accounted for the human condition, a person with good *karma* would always be good, and a person with bad *karma* would always be bad. Yet such is not the case. Indeed, self-reliance and peace of mind come only from understanding *karma*, and living wisely in light of that understanding. "No one," said the Buddha, "can escape the wheel of suffering who does not understand the causes of suffering."

The Four Noble Truths

The Buddha's basic teachings rest on what are called the **Four Noble Truths**:

1. No one can deny that suffering is the condition of all existence.
2. Suffering and general dissatisfaction come to human beings because they are possessive, greedy, and, above all, self-centered.
3. Egocentrism, possessiveness, and greed can, however, be understood, overcome, rooted out.
4. This rooting out, this vanquishing, can be brought about by following a simple, reasonable Eightfold Path of behavior in thought, word, and deed. Change of viewpoint will manifest itself in a new outlook and new patterns of behavior.[13]

The Buddha taught that we suffer because we are partial to ourselves. For example, I cannot be bored listening to you complain about your philosophy class for the umpteenth time unless I am judging you or wishing you were talking about something interesting to *me*. It's the me that gets bored. I cannot be envious of the attention my parents give my brother without being greedy for more attention for me. If I were not greedy for my share, I would be delighted by his delight. The more self-conscious I am, the more selfish is the ego I have to place at the center of things.

Contemporary Buddhist commentators and philosophers use the term *ego* differently from psychologists; they use it to refer to various self-centered, immature, and selfish tendencies. A person with too much ego thinks of himself or herself as unique and special in ways that emphasize differences. The loss or annihilation of this false ego *projection* results in the emergence of the soul or true self, the *Buddha nature*. The awakened or reborn soul/self sees similarities rather than differences, acts from love rather than fear, helps rather than judges. The bliss of nirvana comes from the annihilation of the self-consciousness, judgmentalism, greed, and fear that characterize ego.

FOUR NOBLE TRUTHS

Foundation of Buddha's teachings: (1) to exist is to suffer; (2) self-centeredness is the chief cause of human suffering; (3) the cause of suffering can be understood and rooted out; (4) suffering can be alleviated by following the Eightfold Path.

'Tis impossible upon any system to defend either our understanding or senses; and we but expose them farther when we endeavour to justify them. . . . Carelessness and inattention alone afford us any remedy. For this reason I rely entirely upon them; and take it for granted, whatever may be the reader's opinion at this present moment, that an hour hence he will be persuaded there is both an external and internal world.

David Hume

EIGHTFOLD PATH

Buddha's prescription for rooting out suffering: (1) right understanding; (2) right purpose; (3) right speech; (4) right conduct; (5) right livelihood; (6) right effort; (7) right mindfulness; (8) right meditation.

The Buddha himself taught that the way to transcend the ego and see the interconnected hole of life is through *loving-kindness*. At the moment we feel love for others we cannot be bored or hostile with them. In moments of love, we take joy in a three-year-old's scribbles or Grandpa's poems. We listen to sister's problems with concern; we cannot be hostile or bored or defensive at the same time we feel compassion for her. As the Buddha promised, a change of viewpoint results in a new outlook and new patterns of behavior. But it is difficult to maintain our compassion even with those we already love. How can we alter our viewpoint to love every living thing?

The causes of suffering, as we know in moments of insight, are located in our thoughts, words, and deeds; thus, the cure for suffering must encompass how we live, how we think, and what we glean. Buddha's Eightfold Path addresses each of these in a way that—if practiced—replaces ego projections with a new, clear point of view.

The Eightfold Path

According to Buddha, understanding the Four Noble Truths and following the law of *karma* are keys to release from suffering, but only if combined as a new way of life that combines three vital components of Buddhist practice into an **"Eightfold Path"** of wisdom (*panna*), right conduct (*sila*), and right mental training (*samadhi*). The first two steps along the Eightfold Path are the steps of *panna*, steps three, four, and five are the steps of *sila*, and steps six, seven, and eight are the steps of *samadhi*:

1. Right understanding (or views).

2. Right purpose.

3. Right speech.

4. Right conduct.

5. Right livelihood.

6. Right effort.

7. Right mindfulness (or awareness).

8. Right meditation.[14]

Now let's look at a modified version. Gerald Heard, an Anglo-Irish historian and philosopher, phrased the Eightfold Path in an especially contemporary and insightful form:

1. First you must see clearly what is wrong.

2. Next you must decide that you want to be cured.

3. You must act and

4. speak so as to aim at being cured.

5. Your livelihood must not conflict with your therapy.

6. That therapy must go forward at the "staying speed," that is, the critical velocity that can be sustained.

7. You must think about it incessantly and

8. learn how to contemplate with the *deep mind*.[15]

It is probably quite an understatement to note that the wisdom expressed in the Eightfold Path sounds so obvious, almost trivially simple. But simple is not always easy, and we often overlook the obvious. Consider: In many schools of psychology, the most important therapeutic event is the moment of insight in which the client *sees for the first time* some important factor in his or her unhappiness. Something similar occurs in many religions, either at the moment of "rebirth" or during periods of atonement: The fallen soul *sees by the grace of God* his or her fallen nature and the way of salvation.

One of the most effective treatment programs for alcoholism is Alcoholics Anonymous (AA), which is based on a list of guidelines for living called the Twelve Steps. The very first step begins, "We admitted we were powerless over alcohol and that our lives were unmanageable." The key to the first step is to *see* fully *our own* actual condition, whatever it involves. This, of course, is the first step on the Eightfold Path.

As you reflect on the rest of the Eightfold Path, keep in mind that it was presented as a guideline for a way of life. Following this deceptively simple program takes years of dedication. It helps to remind ourselves that the Eightfold Path is designed to change *us* by changing our way of seeing things (consciousness), our behavior, and our emotions. It is designed to subdue our egocentric sense of identity, replacing the self-centered *me* with a compassionate heart. If I can change the way I view things, I have in effect changed the world.

The difficulty of the Eightfold Path is underscored by one poignant version of the Buddha's deathbed statement to his monks that ends, "Perhaps someone, somewhere will not misunderstand me." Buddha said:

> By one's self evil is done, by one's self one is purified. The pure and the impure stand and fall by themselves. No one can purify another. . . . Work with diligence. Be lamps unto yourselves. Betake yourselves to no external refuge. Look not for refuge to anyone beside yourself. Hold fast to the Truth as to a lamp.[16]

Although Buddha counseled his monks to be lamps unto themselves, and not to seek refuge from others, he did not counsel them to turn away from others. Rather, Buddhist social ethics combine altruistic humanism with the notion of a "righteous" social order. Indeed, Buddha's efforts to reconcile the personal and the social, the spiritual and the mundane, and the

These teachings are simple truth, and their power is that they can be applied immediately to our everyday life and the world we live in.

Jösel Tendzin

It should not be thought that the eight categories or divisions of the Path should be followed and practised one after the other in the numerical order given in the usual list . . . But they are to be developed more or less simultaneously, as far as possible according to the capacity of each individual. They are all linked together and each helps the cultivation of the others.

Wapola Rahula

Lao-tzu: Wisdom of the Old Boy

Legend says that Lao-tzu (c. 575 B.C.) was a bureaucrat in ancient China, known only by his nickname, Lao-tzu, variously translated as the Old Master, the Old Man, the Old Boy, or the Old Philosopher. According to legend, when Lao-tzu was 160 years old he grew so disgusted with the hypocrisy and decay of his time that he decided to resign from his bureaucratic position in order to pursue virtue in a more natural environment. Heading west, he reached the Han-ku Pass, where the keeper of the pass recognized the old sage, saying, "You are about to withdraw yourself from sight. I pray you compose a book for me." Lao-tzu honored the keeper's request by producing a little (five-thousand-word)

Lao-tzu

book known today as the *Tao Te Ching*.

Next to the *Analects* of Confucius, the *Tao Te Ching* is the most influential book in Chinese history. Nearly a thousand commentaries on it have been written in China and Japan. The *Tao Te Ching*, or *The Classic of the Way*

and the Power, is second only to the Bible in the number of translations available in English. Today, interpretations of Taoism are continuously emerging in popular philosophical and psychological literature.

Literally, Tao means "way" or "path" in the sense of "the way to go." Rather than present a *philosophic system*, Lao-tzu struggled to express a sense of the ultimate, underlying great principle, rule, or cause of "the way all things are." His vision is holistic: it encompasses the totality of the cosmos. When viewed holistically, the Old Boy suggests, the universe expresses harmony, purpose, order, majesty, and "calm power." Error, suffering, and unhappiness accompany all

intellect with the emotions are appealing to many contemporary philosophers and thinkers.

How can it be known that what I call knowing is not really not knowing and that what I call not knowing is not really knowing? . . . From my point of view, the principle of humanity and righteousness and the doctrine of right and wrong are mixed and confused. How do I know the difference among them?

Chuang-tzu

Buddha Now

In contemporary philosophical terms, Buddha's teachings reflect what contemporary psychologist Carol Gilligan labeled "the ethic of care" and "the ethic of justice." (See Chapter 15.) Much of what Buddha taught also seems to fit well with such major "liberation ethics" themes as respect for family, feminist concerns, respect for all life-forms, rejection of social castes, and such.

But Buddhist ethics are circumscribed in a way that most contemporary humanistic ethics are not: Buddha placed *dharma*, "the cosmic order of the universe," over the social and political order; our task, whether as citizens or leaders, is to do what we can to see to it that our lives, and those of all attempts to separate things, to understand the part without the whole.

So it is that Lao-tzu advises getting beyond judgments of good and bad, since good requires the bad for its very existence. The following selection from the *Tao Te Ching* expresses Lao-tzu's vision of "the union of opposites" and the impossibility of "dividing" Tao into words. (You might find it interesting to compare this material with the fragments of Heraclitus in the First Interlude.)

We look at it and do not see it;
    Its name is The Invisible.
We listen to it and do not
    hear it;
    Its name is The Inaudible.
We touch it and do not find it;
    Its name is The Subtle
    (formless).
These three cannot be further inquired into,
And hence merge into one.
Going up high, it is not bright, and coming down low, it is not dark.
Infinite and boundless, it cannot be given any name;
It reverts to nothingness. . . .
It is The Vague and Elusive.

When the people of the world all know beauty as beauty
    There arises the recognition
    of ugliness.
When they all know the good as good,
    There arises the recognition
    of evil.

Therefore:
    Being and non-being produce each other;
    Difficult and easy complete each other;
    Long and short contrast each other;
    High and low distinguish each other;
    Sound and voice harmonize with each other;
    Front and back follow each other.

Lao-tzu
Tao Te Ching, in Wing-Tsit Chan, trans. and comp., *A Source Book in Chinese Philosophy* (Princeton, N.J.: Princeton University Press, 1963), pp. 146 and 140.

creatures, reflect *dharma*. Although exactly what this means is beyond the scope of our Interlude, we can be confident that, for Buddha, social ethics center on organic human relationships, "where the ethic of responsibility and the recognition of differences in need" both play vital parts.[17]

This "holism" is especially appealing in our fragmented, specialized culture. In the following section, note how many of today's "hippest," "greenest," and "trendiest" popular moral values reflect Buddhist themes and teachings.

Buddha's Dharma Family

The family constitutes the central unit of Buddhist social ethics. Each member of the family is linked with each other member of the family through reciprocal duties. That is, each family member has a place (function) as part of a whole. From this, it follows that issues of status and "sexual equality" are treated "organically," rather than "formulaically." Buddhist discourses

When there is a motive to be virtuous, there is no virtue.

Lie Zi

ascribe to Buddha himself the foundations of a long tradition of initiating Buddhist nuns and recognizing that women could rise to the level of sainthood (*arahat*). Whether or not women could rise to the level of being Buddhas, however, became a source of contention among later traditions.[18]

Buddha rejected all distinctions based on social status (caste) and race. He taught that the only distinctions that matter are those of character. He accepted people from all social and racial groups into his spiritual order, making no distinctions based on caste or socioeconomic status. In this, he reminds us of other great teachers and sages, such as Socrates and Epicurus.

Buddha's concept of "society" or "family" was much deeper than we ordinarily expect. His concern for *all suffering* extended throughout the range of sentient life, from humans through animals, to lower life-forms as well. Thus, Buddhist ethical concerns guide our behavior in relation to *all* living beings.

The Buddha's Legacy

Buddha's concern with the moral development of human beings may remind you of Aristotle, Epicurus, or the Stoics, among others (Chapters 5 and 6 and the Second Interlude), but his particular emphasis on emotions and rejection of caste systems (to say nothing of his pacifism) reminds us that he is a paradigmatic Asian sage, and not a Western philosopher-sage.

Like all sages, the Buddha was a perceptive psychological observer. He realized that even though we all must actively work for our own enlightenment, most of us benefit from the support and guidance of regular, intimate association with others working toward a common goal.[19] What he envisioned was the free association of seekers on all levels of the path. What occurred was something else.

The Buddha himself never prescribed certain dress, such as shaved heads and saffron (yellow/orange) robes.

> If the mere wearing of a robe could banish greed, malice and other weaknesses, then as soon as a child was born his friends and kinfolk would make him wear the robe and would press him to wear it saying, "Come thou favored of fortune! Come wear the robe; for by the mere wearing of it the greedy will put from them their greed, the malicious their malice, and so on!"[20]

He did not think it mattered where one lived, what one ate, and so on. Any serious seeker following the Eightfold Path would avoid extremes and remain in the *Middle Way*. Awareness, compassion, and helpfulness were more important than the particular clothes we wear or food we eat or place we live: "Let those who wish to dwell in the forest, dwell in the forest, and let those who wish to live in the village, live in the village."[21]

We are all chained to Fortune. Some chains are golden and loose, some tight and of base metal; but what difference does it make? All of us are in custody, the binders as well as the bound—unless you suppose the left of the chain is lighter. Some of us are chained by office, some by wealth; some are weighed down by high birth, some by low; some are subject to another's tyranny, some to their own; some are confined to one spot by banishment, some by a priesthood. All life is bondage.

Seneca

"IN TODAY'S VIOLENT WORLD, FIGURING OUT THE SOUND OF ONE HAND CLAPPING SEEMS BESIDE THE POINT— WHAT, O WISE ONE, IS YOUR THOUGHT ON THE MATTER?"

© 1986, reprinted by permission of Richard Stine

Ironically, but probably unavoidably, in the centuries since the Buddha lived, his basic message has been transformed into "schools of Buddhism," as if there could be "schools of truth."

As happened among the followers of Socrates, Moses, Jesus, and Muhammad, sects and divisions arose. "Experts" in theory and ritual emerged, quarreling and competing for the title of true successor. The two main branches of Buddhism are Hīnayāna or Theravada, "the Way of the Elders," and Mahayana, after its founder Mahayana, "The Greater Vehicle of Salvation." Other Buddhist sects such as Tibetan Buddhism and Japanese Zen Buddhism are usually seen as branches of the many-sided Mahayana branch.

The quarrels among Buddhists are less hostile and more tolerant than those among other philosophies and religions. The power of the Buddha's original vision is perhaps nowhere more clearly felt than in this restraint. Buddhists of one school tend to accept Buddhists of another, for in all cases, "the individual disciple is seen as directly, personally involved in his own salvation, a point of view which allows exceptional latitude in matters of instruction and practice."[22]

> Nobody is normal, everybody is a little bit crazy or unbalanced, people's minds are running all the time. Their perceptions of the world are partial, incomplete. They are eaten alive by their egos. They think they see, but . . . all they do is project their madness upon the world. There is no clarity, no wisdom in that!
>
> *Taisen Deshimaru*

Five Precepts

Buddha's core values are reflected in the *Five Precepts* or "abstentions." Buddha forbade (1) killing or hurting any living creature; (2) stealing; (3) wrong indulgence in sexual pleasure; (4) lying; and (5) use of intoxicants.[23] These precepts are the fundamental conditions for living a good life and for establishing a good community.

Three in the Morning

Chuang-tzu (c. 399–295 B.C.) is the second great Taoist sage. Very little is known about his life, but the book bearing his name contains some of the richest stories in Taoist literature. Chuang-tzu sometimes referred to himself as "the Great Clod." The stories attributed to him reflect a generous soul, capable of great humor and great sadness. Here's an excellent example:

> On Knowing and Not Knowing the Oneness of Things. Only the truly intelligent understand this principle of the levelling of all things into One. . . . But to wear out one's intellect in an obstinate adherence to the individuality of things, not recognizing the fact that all things are One—this is called "Three in the Morning." What is "Three in the Morning"? A keeper of monkeys said that with regard to their rations of nuts each monkey was to have three in the morning and four at night. At this the monkeys were very angry. Then the keeper said they might have four in the morning and three at night, with which arrangement they were well pleased. The actual number of nuts remained the same, but there was a difference owing to (subjective evaluations of) likes and dislikes. It also derives from this (principle of subjectivity). Wherefore the true Sage brings all the contraries together and rests in the natural Balance of Heaven. This is called (the principle of following) two courses (at once).

Chuang-tzu
In *The Wisdom of Laotse*, trans. and ed. Lin Yutang (New York: Modern Library, 1976), p. 244.

Besides all the endless variety of ideas or objects of knowledge, there is likewise Something which knows or perceives them; and exercises divers operations, as willing, imagining, remembering about them. This perceiving, active being is what I call mind, spirit, soul, or myself.

George Berkeley

As you might imagine, questions arose almost immediately over exactly what Buddha meant and exactly how to follow these precepts. Such is always the case with the teachings of truly archetypal (paradigmatic) figures. And that is understandable—the power of paradigmatic "clarity" seems to admit of fewer "modifications" (excuses?) of the following popular categories: yes-but, you-don't-understand, my-case-is-special, and that-was-then-this-is-now. Consider just one timely topic: human relations with animals.

Buddha flatly condemned animal sacrifice and hunting, both widely practiced in his time. He forbade his monks to participate in warfare and from digging in the ground, lest they injure animals, birds, or insects (as well as people). "So, then," you may be thinking, "Buddha forbade meat eating." Here, things get murky.

Buddha seems to have taught that *if* one practiced compassion, one would be *inclined* toward vegetarianism. Also, Buddha taught his monks to follow his practice of silently carrying a begging bowl through the marketplaces and streets, accepting whatever food was offered. This included accepting meat *so long as the monk was convinced that the meat was not specially killed and prepared for the monk's meal.*[24] (Monks who were ill were allowed to request certain foods.) And although taught that the path

The Buddhist priest Chüjan's painting Seeking the Tao in the Autumn Mountains *(c. 940–1000) reflects his vision of Tao as the fundamental natural harmony of all things.*

of "right livelihood" prohibited selling and killing animals, he did not restrict his monks' food except to forbid what was poisonous.

Further, Buddha's adventures among the ascetics made him well aware of the temptation to make a fetish out of dress, diet, or other ritualistic behavior. He did not want to encourage his monks to become food fetishists, equivalent, perhaps, to those Jesus chided for losing sight of the spirit of the law by getting caught up in its letter. In any event, Buddha seemed to view vegetarianism as a positive practice that could, perhaps even would, emerge as a natural consequence of realizing compassion—but he did not require it.

In this case (vegetarianism), as in others such as acquiring wealth or practicing meditation, Buddha exhibited a blend of realism, pragmatism, and, I think, enlightened compassion when dealing with the inevitable conflicts between our "merely" human needs and our moral ideals. Is this an easier, softer way? I think not, for it seems relatively easy to reject the standards of sainthood as rigid, unrealistic, absolutes, genuinely beyond

Who knows why Heaven dislikes what it dislikes? Even the sage considers it a difficult question.

Lao-tzu

our moral capacities. Ironically, it may not be as easy to reject a call to simple decency, a call to manifest reasonable self-control and basic loving-kindness in all of our affairs.

What the Buddha Did Not Explain

To form monsters, and join incongruous shapes and appearances, costs the imagination no more trouble than to conceive the most natural and familiar objects. . . . What never was seen, or heard of, may yet be conceived; nor is any thing beyond the power of thought, except what implies an absolute contradiction.

David Hume

Whether you believe in God or not does not matter so much, whether you believe in Buddha or not does not matter so much; as a Buddhist, whether you believe in reincarnation or not does not matter so much. You must lead a good life.

The Dalai Lama

Ultimately, the Buddha calls us to adopt a way of life, not "a philosophy," as we in the West understand "having a philosophy." Buddha insists that in order to discover the truth, we must somehow "set aside" the kind of "analytic thinking" that leads to establishing schools of Buddhism or to quibbling over *the* correct interpretation of the Five Precepts. The Buddha says:

> If you will now and at all times, whether walking, standing, sitting, or lying, only concentrate on eliminating analytic thinking, at long last you will inevitably discover the truth. . . . [Relying on analytic thinking is] like using yellow leaves of gold to stop the crying of a child, and [is] decidedly not real. If you take it for something real, you are not one of our sect and, moreover, what relation can it [analytic thinking] have to your real self? . . . In reality, everything is pure and glistening, neither square nor round, big nor small, long nor short; it is beyond passion and phenomena, ignorance and Enlightenment. . . .[25]

As philosophers, we may feel tempted, even obligated, to analyze Buddha's call to set aside analytic thinking! This should not surprise or discourage us. We've already seen enough paradoxes and disagreements over fundamental values, the nature of reality, and so forth to know that among the timeless philosophical questions are: What is philosophy? What is philosophy good for? How is philosophy done?

We also, know, however, that the function of the sage is to engage us, to challenge us to ask deeper questions: Who am I? How am I to live? And it is to Buddha the sage that we shall turn as we take our leave of the Compassionate One. Perhaps we can experience a pale reflection of the power of the Buddha's transforming vision by considering one of his most famous and intriguing sermons, called "On Questions Not Tending Toward Edification." Another title might be, "What You Don't Need to Know to Live Wisely and Compassionately." This sermon touches on one of the most difficult things for most of us to accept: We need to find a way of living a meaningful life in the absence of absolute answers.

Western philosophers and theologians seem to find it especially difficult to accept the Buddha's refusal to present a theology or system of metaphysics. The Buddha was a pragmatic and insightful spiritual teacher who believed that questions of theology and complex philosophy only confuse and distract us from our search for wisdom. This underscores the irony in the existence of "schools" of Buddhism. The Buddha believed that we are better served by dealing with the here and now in helpful, honest ways than in fretting and quibbling over unanswerable metaphysical claims and theological doctrines. The insistence on absolute, ultimate explanations, answers, and proofs gets in the way of living fully in the moment. Here's a brief excerpt from one of the richest passages in Buddhist literature:

> It is as if . . . man had been wounded by an arrow thickly smeared with poison, and his friends and companions, his relatives and kinsfolk, were to procure for him a physician or surgeon; and the sick man were to say, "I will not have this arrow taken out until I have learnt . . . the name of the man who wounded me or whether the man who wounded me was . . . tall, or short, or of the middle height . . . whether the man who wounded me was black, or dusky, or of a yellow skin . . . whether the man who wounded me was from this or that village, or town, or city. . . .
>
> That man would die without ever having learnt this. . . .
>
> In exactly the same way . . . anyone who should say, "I will not lead the religious life under the Blessed One until the Blessed One shall explain to me that the world is eternal or that the world is not eternal . . . or that the saint either exists or does not exist after death";—that person would die . . . before [it was] ever explained to him.
>
> The religious life . . . does not depend on the dogma. . . .
>
> Accordingly, . . . bear always in mind what it is that I have not explained. . . .
>
> And what . . . have I explained? Misery . . . have I explained; the origin of misery have I explained; the cessation of misery have I explained. And why . . . have I explained this? Because . . . this does profit, has to do with the fundamentals of religion, and tends to . . . [tranquillity], knowledge, supreme wisdom, and Nirvana; therefore, I have explained it.[26]

The Buddha stands between the traditional Western models of a philosopher and a saint or prophet. Saints and prophets of the Judeo-Christian-Muslim religious traditions differ from the Buddha's conception of the sage in important ways. The most significant is in their relationship to "the one, true God," the Creator who is distinct from His creatures. For the Buddha, "all is one," and there is no equivalent to the god of the Bible.

For the Buddha, only those who actively work to achieve awareness deserve the title "sage"—and then only if they act on and live by what they have discovered to be *true for themselves*. No teachings, no scriptures, no theories take the place of experience. When we see clearly, we do not need teachers, scriptures, or theories. When we do not see clearly—for ourselves—nothing else matters.

The follower of the law, even if he can recite only a small portion of it but, having forsaken passion and hatred and foolishness, possesses true knowledge and serenity of mind; he is attached to nothing in this world or that to come, has indeed a share in the religious life.

The Buddha

The Logos is eternal, but men have not heard it, and men have heard it and not understood.

Heraclitus

Would a sick person
be helped
Merely by reading
a medical text?

Shantiveda

"All right," you may grant, "but what about when we do see clearly?" Then, too, it seems "nothing else matters," as this delightful story from the teachings of the ninth-century Ch'an (Zen) master Hsi Yun *almost* tells us:

Stepping into the public hall [His Reverence] said:

"The knowledge of many things cannot compare to giving up the search. The sage is one who puts himself outside the range of objectivity. There are not different kinds of mind, and there is no doctrine which can be taught."

As there was no more to be said, everybody went away.[27]

The Skeptic

David Hume

We declare at the outset that we do not make any positive assertion that anything we shall say is wholly as we affirm it to be. We
merely report accurately on each thing as our impressions of it
are at the moment.

Sextus Empiricus

A friend of mine once told me that her third cousin could move objects by psychokinesis, that is, by "mind power." She insisted that she had seen him send ashtrays and glasses across a room, without touching them or leaving his chair, merely by concentrating very deeply. I was intrigued, because I had known this woman for years, and she seemed intelligent and sane to me—yet I had never seen such a phenomenon for myself. I asked to be allowed to witness this amazing feat, but was told that, sadly, this remarkable individual had died some years before. This did not surprise me, and I may have been too blunt in saying so. "You don't believe me, do you?" my friend said, obviously annoyed with me. "You never believe anything! You're too skeptical."

A **skeptic** is a person who demands clear, observable, *undoubtable* evidence—based on experience—before accepting any knowledge claim as true. The word *skepticism* (from the Greek *skeptesthai*, "to consider or examine") refers to both a school of philosophy and a general attitude. Originally, a skeptic was a special kind of doubter, one who withheld judgment while waiting for better evidence. Sextus Empiricus (c. 200) even devised a *skeptical grammar*, which ends every proposition with "so it seems to me at the moment." There are variations of skepticism, progressing from total doubt about everything to temporary or particular doubt invoked just for the process of analysis—what Descartes called "methodic doubt" (Chapter 8).

My friend's reaction was common: She took my demand for firsthand evidence personally. That is, she interpreted it as an attack on her integrity. She would have preferred that I accept her claim as true simply because we were friends. I have experienced this reaction many times, and am even guilty of it myself. Yet anyone who is seriously interested in the pursuit of truth in general, or in the truth of a specific claim, must demand more than the personal testimony of others, no matter how sincerely they may give it or how much we may care for them.

Standards of evidence vary with the conditions. The more important the issue is, the stricter our standards must be. And the more important the issue is, the greater is our obligation to demand evidence.

A healthy dose of skepticism can save us from making big mistakes. Skepticism can be especially valuable when we really want to believe the claims made by those trying to sell us things (including ideas and beliefs).

Philosophical Query

Have you ever been angry or insulted when someone pressed you for evidence? Or has anyone ever gotten angry with you for asking for evidence? Why do you suppose that is? Is it rude to ask "How do you know that?" or "Can you prove that?" when people make claims about important, or even not so important, things? Analyze this question and see if you can justify *not* asking for evidence.

There is also the matter of expertise and training, as well as time, interest, and ability in the matter of justifying our beliefs. Often we must rely on the testimony of qualified experts, but this differs considerably from relying on unqualified (or at least unverified) testimony. Ideally, we should accept as true only what we can verify for ourselves. My friend was not qualified to determine the genuineness of psychic experience. Further, accepting her claim at face value would have been unreasonable; I would be discounting my own experience without ever having seen the phenomenon for myself or even having read about incontrovertible, repeatable, carefully controlled cases of similar powers.

Scepticism, while logically impeccable, is psychologically impossible, and there is an element of frivolous insincerity in any philosophy which pretends to accept it.

Bertrand Russell

Yet consider how rarely we seem to demand good evidence for beliefs and knowledge claims. We buy so-called health foods on the recommendation of neighbors and fellow students. In recent years, books describing their authors' experiences as "channels" for "ancient entities" have sold quite well. Many of these books also discuss out-of-body experiences, past lives, and other psychic feats. How can the reader determine whether such claims are true? What could count as proof?

Political candidates make claims about nuclear energy, education, the environment, even moral values. Automobile manufacturers make claims for the reliability and safety of their vehicles. Political action groups make claims concerning abortions, racial prejudice, toxic effects, crime rates, drugs, and so forth. How often have you asked for verification of such claims? When a salesperson makes claims about this refrigerator or that CD player, do you ask for supporting data?

All of these issues (and more) involve knowledge claims. In technical language, they are *epistemological issues*. The study of the theory of knowledge, **epistemology**, is the branch of philosophy concerned with the origins, quality, nature, and reliability of knowledge. Beginning with Descartes, philosophy has been dominated by epistemological issues, which concern us all. We want and need to *know* the truth about the sorts of claims noted above. The truth makes a difference to us in big and little matters. If nothing else, we need the truth in order to make informed choices.

EPISTEMOLOGY

Branch of philosophy that studies the nature and possibility of knowledge.

Philosophical Query

Who is a qualified expert in areas such as psychic phenomena, miracles, nutrition, or philosophy? What is the relationship between the reports of experts and your own experience? When the two conflict, which should you trust? Why? How do you know? Discuss.

John Locke

Attempts to answer fundamental epistemological questions gave rise to the two major orientations of modern philosophy. The first, as we learned in Chapter 8, is rationalism. The other dominant philosophical orientation rejected the primacy of reason and insisted that all knowledge comes from experience. It is known as **empiricism**, from the Greek root *empeiria*, meaning "experience."

Empiricists believe that all ideas can be traced back to *sense data*. Abstractions and complex beliefs are said to be combinations and mental alterations of original impressions and perceptions, as when, for example, we imagine a man with a horse's head. Reason is unable to provide knowledge of reality; that must be derived from experience. The strictest empiricists believe that even mathematical and logical principles are derived from experience.

EMPIRICISM

Belief that all knowledge is ultimately derived from the senses (experience) and that all ideas can be traced to sense data.

A potent form of empiricism emerged with the advent of modern philosophy. Because its three founding philosophers were all British, it has come to be called *British empiricism*.

The earliest of the three British empiricists, **John Locke (1632–1704)**, was disturbed by the confusion and uncertainty surrounding seventeenth-century philosophy and theology. Like Descartes, he was troubled by Scholastic philosophy (Chapter 7), which he had encountered as a student at Oxford. He was especially critical of its emphasis on formal disputations and debates, which he said were "invented for wrangling and ostentation, rather than to discover the truth." Locke's *An Essay Concerning Human Understanding*, published in 1690, established the groundwork for empiricism as it is generally understood today.

John Locke

Educated as a physician, Locke was aware of the great changes and progress being generated by science. He was trained to rely on his own powers of perception. He pointed out that as a physician you cannot "wait until you have reached mathematical certainty about the correct treatment" before helping a patient. You have to observe and act based on what you perceive. You must turn to the facts.[1]

In the winter of 1670, Locke had a series of philosophical discussions concerning morality and religion with some friends. It wasn't long before the friends found themselves confused and puzzled. Their inability to reach clearly right or wrong answers—in the way a chemist or baker often can—had a profound effect on Locke. He realized he had to take a step back and examine the nature and limits of knowledge before trying to sort out the truth or falsity of specific ideas:

> After we had awhile puzzled ourselves, without coming any nearer a resolution of those doubts which perplexed us, it came into my thoughts that we took a wrong course; and that before we set ourselves upon inquiries of that nature, it was necessary to examine my own abilities, and see what *objects* our understanding were, or were not, fitted to deal with.[2]

Without some clear idea of the ultimate source of knowledge, we have little hope for resolving philosophical agreements. If you have ever been involved in a nearly endless, unsettled disagreement over social, moral, political, or religious issues at some casual gathering, you know what Locke experienced. Each person seems to have an unstated set of rules and assumptions regarding what is "obviously" true and what is "ridiculous," which sources of information are reliable and which are not. Without a clearly stated and agreed-upon set of basic principles, such "discussions" often amount to nothing more than each person repeatedly affirming a set of favored beliefs and denouncing all others.

Locke proposed to study the origins of our ideas in order to better understand the nature and process of acquiring knowledge. He hoped he could thereby find a way to settle difficult issues. He eventually went on to develop the first modern empirical philosophy. Although his philosophy contains

Unless some things are certain, it is held, nothing can be even probable.

A. J. Ayer

its own inconsistencies, Locke introduced a stunning new philosophical emphasis on logical rigor and analytic precision that would shake the foundations of many of our most cherished beliefs. He began by calling for philosophers to refocus their attention "outward," on experience.

Experience Is the Origin of All Ideas

> There is indeed nothing more ridiculous than to imagine that any motion or modification of matter should produce thought.
>
> *Thomas Reid*

According to Locke, all *ideas* originate in *sensation* and *reflection*. Specifically, he says we can think about things only *after we have experienced them*. In other words, all ideas originate from sense data. For example, no one born blind can ever have an idea of color, according to this theory. Those of us who are sighted "abstract" the *idea of color* from specific sense data by reflecting on, say, red, green, yellow, and blue circles. In doing so, we note that they have two common qualities, circularity and color. Our blind friend can trace their shape, and thus acquire sensations of circularity, but color, which is only perceived through sight, will remain unknown.

As part of his empirical inquiry into the nature of human understanding, Locke attempted to explain and classify different kinds of ideas and the ways we combine and reorganize sense data from simple into increasingly complex and abstract ideas. He insisted that all ideas are copies of the things that caused the basic sensations on which they rest. Ideas, then, are less intense copies or images of sensations. Your idea, for example, of a baseball is a copy of the set of sensations and impressions you have received from seeing and handling actual baseballs. If your idea of a baseball includes the shape of a cube, it is a poor copy. It does not *correspond* to reality.

CORRESPONDENCE (OR "COPY") THEORY OF TRUTH

Truth test that holds that an idea (or belief or thought) is true if whatever it refers to actually exists (corresponds to a fact).

This position is known as the "copy theory" or "representation theory," or, most recently, **correspondence theory of truth**, a term attributed to contemporary philosopher Bertrand Russell. The correspondence theory of truth is a truth test that holds that an idea (or belief or thought) is true if whatever it refers to actually exists. In other words, an idea is defined as true if it corresponds to a fact. The procedure for checking the truth of an idea is called *confirmation* or *verification*.

Favored by empiricists, the correspondence theory of truth is in direct contrast with the *coherence theory of truth* favored by rationalists (see Chapter 8), and differs from the other major truth theory, the *pragmatic theory of truth* (see Chapter 13).

Let's see what happened when Locke applied his empirical truth test to one of the foundations of Continental rationalism, innate ideas—ideas that by their very nature are not "copies" of external experience.

INNATE IDEAS (OR *A PRIORI* IDEAS)

Truths that are not derived from observation or experiment; characterized as being certain, deductive, universally true, and independent of all experience.

Locke's Rejection of Innate Ideas

In Chapter 8, we learned that Descartes, as a rationalist, believed in a special class of ideas known as *a priori* or **innate ideas**. So-called innate ideas are truths that are not derived from observation or experiment; they are characterized as being certain, deductive, universally true, and independent of all experience. Examples of innate ideas include mathematical equivalences such as "2 + 3 = 5," and deductive principles of reason such as "Every event has a cause" and "All triangles contain 180°."

In the *Meditations*, Descartes based a major part of his case for the certainty of reason—as well as for general reliability of the senses and knowledge of the existence of an external world—on the clarity and distinctness of "the innate idea of God." (See pages 303–307.) Thus, if Locke's view proves to be the correct one, Descartes' entire project collapses. Whereas Descartes' prototype of "reason" was modeled after mathematical (deductive) reasoning, Locke's model was fashioned from his experiences as a physician.

In Locke's estimation, Cartesian-style speculation, abstract thinking modeled after geometric method, can at best "amuse our understanding with fine and useless speculations." It cannot, however, adequately deal with concrete problems. When used for more than amusement, Cartesian-type reasoning is dangerous because it distracts "our inquiries from the true and advantageous knowledge of things." All that can result from such "idle speculation," suggests Locke, is "to enlarge the art of talking and perhaps [lay] a foundation for endless disputes. . . ." It cannot provide useful knowledge, the way, say, Isaac Newton's new scientific reasoning can.[3]

Locke accused the rationalists of labeling their pet ideas "innate" in order to convince others to accept them second hand, without question:

> We may as rationally hope to see with other men's eyes, as to know by other men's understandings. So much as we ourselves consider and comprehend of truth and reason, so much we possess of real and true knowledge. The floating of other men's opinions in our brains, makes us not one jot the more knowing, though they happen to be true.

> When men have found some general propositions that could not be doubted of as soon as understood, it was, I know, a short and easy way to conclude them innate. This being once received, it eased the lazy from the pains of search, and stopped the inquiry of the doubtful concerning all that was once styled innate. And it was of no small advantage to those who affected to be masters and teachers, to make this the principle of principles,—*that principles must not be questioned*. . . . [This] put their followers upon . . . [a] posture of blind credulity. . . .[4]

In other words, from Locke's point of view, Descartes' attempt to introduce a method of inquiry that would free us from the dogmatic shackles of Scholasticism merely results in another dogmatism, a rationalistic one.

Locke argued that without appealing to the ultimate test of experience, reason has no "ground," or standard, for distinguishing truth from fantasy. Modifying a characterization used by some rationalistic philosophers, who compared the mind to a pantry well stocked with "innate

Suppose that a [plain] man meets a modern philosopher, and wants to be informed what smell in plants is. The philosopher tells him that there is no smell in plants, nor in anything but the mind; that it is impossible there can be smell but in a mind; and that all this hath been demonstrated by modern philosophy. The plain man will, no doubt, be apt to think him merry.

Thomas Reid

It is genius, and the want of
it, that adulterates philosophy, and fills it with error
and false theory.

Thomas Reid

ideas," Locke suggested that the mind is better compared to an empty
pantry, waiting to be stocked by experience.[5] But Locke's most famous
comparison was to describe the mind at birth as a completely blank tablet,
or clean slate, a **tabula rasa**, to use the Latin equivalent:

> *All ideas come from sensations or reflection*—Let us then suppose the
> mind to be, as we say, white paper, void of all characters, without any
> ideas:—How comes it to be furnished? . . . Whence has it all the *ma-
> terials* of reason and knowledge? To this I answer, in one word, from
> EXPERIENCE. In that all our knowledge is founded; and from that it
> ultimately derives itself.[6]

Locke's Dualism

Although Locke rejected Descartes' theory of innate ideas, he did agree with
Descartes that "something substantial" underlies and holds together the
sensible qualities of experience (color, taste, size, shape, location, sound,
motion, and such). This substantial something is *substance*, a complex
idea, according to Locke.

> The mind being, as I have declared, furnished with a great number
> of simple ideas, conveyed in by the senses as they are found in exte-
> rior things, or by reflection on its own operations, takes notice also
> that a certain number of these simple ideas go constantly together;
> which being presumed to belong to one thing, and words being suited
> to common apprehensions . . . are called, so united in one subject, by
> one name; which, by inadvertency, we are apt afterward to talk of
> and consider as one simple idea, which indeed is a complication of
> many ideas together: because . . . not imagining how these simple
> ideas *can* subsist by themselves, we accustom ourselves to suppose
> some *substratum* wherein they do subsist, and from which they do
> result, which therefore we call *substance*.[7]

Locke proceeds to argue that we have only an obscure idea of substance
"in general." He claims that upon analysis, we have no clear, distinct idea
of substance itself, but only a notion of "such qualities which are capable of producing simple ideas in us." Locke says that if pressed to explain "what is the subject wherein colour or weight inheres," all we can
offer is "the supposed, but unknown, support of those qualities we find
existing, which we imagine cannot subsist . . . without something to support them."[8]

Having affirmed the general idea of substance, Locke next inquires into
kinds of substances. He reports that observation and experience reveal
that certain sorts of simple ideas seem to cluster together. From these clusters of simple ideas, we form ideas of "a man, horse, gold, water," and so
on. According to Locke, while philosophers may have trouble describing
it, our everyday experiences confirm the existence of substance:

I appeal to every one's own experience. It is the ordinary qualities observable in iron, or a diamond, put together, that make the true complex idea of those substances, which a smith or a jeweler commonly knows better than a philosopher; who, whatever *substantial forms* he may talk of, has no other idea of those substances, than what is framed by a collection of those ideas which are found in them.[9]

According to Locke, the substance that holds "extended things" together, things known through sensible qualities, is *matter*. Locke claims that upon reflection, the "same thing happens concerning the operations of the mind, viz. thinking, reasoning, fearing, &c." That is, we identify a "thinking substance":

> . . . some other *substance*, which we call *spirit*; whereby . . . supposing a substance wherein thinking, knowing, doubting, and a power of moving, &c., do subsist, we have as clear a notion of the substance of spirit, as we have of body; the one being supposed to be (without knowing what it is) the *substratum* to those simple ideas we have from without; and the other supposed (with a like ignorance of what it is) to be the *substratum* to those operations we experiment in ourselves within.[10]

Thus, Locke affirms the existence of two substances: *matter* and *mind*. So, although Locke rejected Descartes' rationalism and theory of innate ideas, he accepted a Cartesian-type of *dualism*, in which mind and matter are viewed as different kinds of substance.

Primary and Secondary Qualities

In addition to distinguishing between two kinds of substance, Locke distinguished between two kinds of qualities. **Primary qualities** are sensible qualities that exist independently of any perceiver. Shape, size, location, and motion are examples of primary qualities. **Secondary qualities** are qualities whose existence depends on a perceiver. Examples of secondary qualities include color, sound, taste, and texture. Thus, we can say that primary qualities are *objective* properties of things; they exist in the *object*. Secondary qualities depend on—"exist in"—a knowing or perceiving *subject*; thus, they are said to be *subjective* properties.

We have seen the importance of this basic objective-subjective distinction many times. It is at the heart of the quarrels between the Sophists and Plato, as well as the earliest efforts of philosophers to identify reality and to distinguish it from appearance. Locke's distinction between primary qualities (located in independently existing material objects) and secondary qualities (located in subjective mental acts and perceptions) is important because so much is riding on it.

If primary qualities do not exist, then what of the possibility of objective knowledge? What can we know of the existence of an independent

The mind is a kind of theatre, where several perceptions successively make their appearance; pass, repass, glide away, and mingle in an infinite variety of postures and situations.

David Hume

PRIMARY QUALITIES

According to Locke, objective sensible qualities that exist independently of any perceiver; shape, size, location, and motion are examples of primary qualities.

SECONDARY QUALITIES

According to Locke, subjective qualities whose existence depends on a perceiver; color, sound, taste, and texture are examples of secondary qualities.

If Physics Is to Be Believed . . .

We think that the grass is green, the stones are hard, and the snow is cold. But physics assures us that the greenness of the grass, the hardness of the stones, and the coldness of snow are not the greenness, hardness, and cold- ness that we know in our own experience, but something very different. The observer, when he seems to himself to be observing a stone, is really, if physics is to be believed, observing the effects of the stone upon himself.

Bertrand Russell
Our Knowledge of the External World as a Field for the Scientific Method in Philosophy (Chicago: Open Court, 1915).

reality? In other words, some real distinction between primary and secondary qualities *seems* necessary for confirmation of the "world of common sense." The "world of common sense" is simply a term for the widely held view that an objective world exists independently of our perceptions, and that it exists "out there," and not simply as a figment of our imaginations or mental construct.

Locke's Egocentric Predicament

Locke holds a position known as **epistemological dualism**, the view that knowing contains two distinct aspects: the knower and the known. Given the basic empiricist premise that all knowledge comes from our own ideas, which in turn are based on our own sensations and perceptions, epistemological dualism presents us with a fundamental problem: If all knowledge comes in the form of my own ideas based on sense data, how can I verify the existence of anything external to the sensations that constitute sense data? That is, won't the very process of verification take place within the realm of my own ideas?

This problem has been termed Locke's **egocentric predicament** because Locke's copy theory seems to put us in the egocentric position of being able to know only a world of our own mental construction, a self-limited world. Indeed: If there is no "external world," can there be any mind other than my own? How could I know? How could I distinguish another mind from my own—if all I ever know are my own subjective perceptions?

And if, as Locke suggests, all true ideas are based on sense data that correspond to something else, how can we ever verify the objective, independent existence of an external reality? How can we ever apply Locke's own standards of verification to his notion of primary qualities?

At this point, it seems as if all I can know are my own perceptions (secondary qualities). As soon as I am *aware* of them, I have labeled and organized them. That is, even if external objects exist, the process of perceiving sense data is a process of becoming aware of *my ideas*. I don't ever seem to be able to actually experience things themselves. If, as Locke claims, my ideas are "messages" from my senses, how can I—or anyone—verify that the messages come from *independently existing things*? Locke himself asks, "How shall the mind, when it perceives nothing but its own ideas, know that they agree with things themselves?"

Locke tries to avoid the egocentric predicament by asserting that we "somehow know" that mental and physical substances—and an objective external reality—exist. We just don't have a clear idea of the *difference* between minds and bodies or other aspects of ultimate reality:

> Sensation convinces us that there are solid extended substances [matter and bodies]; and reflection that there are thinking ones [minds, souls]; experience assures us of the existence of such beings; and that one has the power to move body by impulse, the other by thought; this we cannot have any doubt of. Experience, I say, every moment furnishes us with clear ideas both of one and of the other. But beyond these ideas, as received from their proper sources, our faculties will not reach.[11]

In other words, Locke holds on to both a "commonsense" view of reality *and* his copy theory of truth, even though he cannot verify either by appealing to the copy theory. In spite of his major differences with Descartes, he draws surprisingly similar conclusions for similar reasons.

Both Locke and Descartes shied away from pursuing the logical consequences of their basic premises. Descartes was able to establish the momentary certainty of the cogito but had difficulty moving beyond his own mind when he attempted to provide a certain foundation for the external world and God's existence. Locke was able to demonstrate the importance of experience as an element of knowledge and show that many of our ideas are based on sensation and experience. He was also able to show the inadequacy of pure reason as a foundation for all knowledge. But, like Descartes, he was unable to move from direct knowledge of his own ideas to direct knowledge of external reality.

Pursued to its logical conclusion, Locke's empiricism does seem to end in the egocentric predicament. If it does, not only are we denied knowledge of an external, independent reality, we are denied the possibility of knowing God, for what simple sensations and experiences can there be on which the idea of God rests? Locke chose, in the end, to affirm certain beliefs at the expense of philosophical consistency. The second of the British empiricists tried to be more consistent.

> As sure, therefore, as the sensible world really exists, so sure is there an infinite omnipresent Spirit, who contains and supports it.
>
> *George Berkeley*

Philosophical Query

Reflect on the claim that ideas are copies of sensations by considering these ideas: love, God, perfection, wisdom. Can you identify the sensations to which they correspond?

George Berkeley

George Berkeley

Men commonly believe that all things are known or perceived by God, because they believe the being of a God; whereas I, on the other side, immediately and necessarily conclude the being of a God, because all things must be perceived by him.

George Berkeley

George Berkeley (1685–1753) was an Anglican bishop who posed one of the most quoted and least understood questions in the history of ideas: Does a tree falling in the forest make a sound if no one is there to hear it? Berkeley's answer is no, and it is based on a clear sense of the predicament Locke's empiricism generated.

From a "commonsense" point of view it may seem absurd to deny the existence of a material world, but Berkeley pointed out that on closer examination it makes more sense to deny the existence of matter than it does to affirm it. Don't pass over this point too quickly. Taking empiricism a logical step further than Locke, Berkeley argues that the material world does not exist. Only ideas exist, and ideas are mental states, not material objects. This makes Berkeley an **idealist** or **immaterialist**: The idea of matter existing without mental properties is self-contradictory, for there is no way to conceive of what an unperceived, unexperienced existence would consist of. We can conceive of things only in terms of the perceptions (ideas) we have of them.

Berkeley challenged Locke's copy theory of truth by pointing out that the so-called objects Locke thought our ideas correspond to lack any fixed nature. They are constantly changing. There is no "thing" to copy, Berkeley said, only a cluster of constantly changing perceptions:

> [Some hold that] real things, it is plain, have a fixed and real nature, which remains the same notwithstanding any change in our senses or in the posture and motion of our bodies; which indeed may affect the ideas in our minds, but it were absurd to think they had the same effect on things existing without the mind.
>
> . . . How then is it possible that things perpetually fleeting and variable as our ideas should be copies or images of anything fixed and constant? Or, in other words, since all sensible qualities, as figure, size, color, etc., that is, our ideas, are continually changing upon every alteration in the distance, medium, or instruments of sensation—how can any determinate, material objects be properly represented or painted forth by several distinct things each of which is so different from and unlike the rest? Or, if you say it resembles some one only of our ideas, how shall we be able to distinguish the true copy from all the false ones?[12]

According to Berkeley, all of the qualities we assign to material objects are relative to the perceiver, what Locke called "secondary" qualities. For example, the coffee I am drinking is hot or cold depending on my perception of it. It is absurd to ask if it is *really* hot or cold. But, you might point out, it has an objective temperature, say 120 degrees Fahrenheit. Only, however, when someone measures it, that is, only when someone perceives a thermometer registering 120 degrees Fahrenheit. Even so, you're probably tempted to respond, it *does have* a certain temperature regardless of whether or not someone is aware of it.

Does it? What kind of temperature is it if no one anywhere is aware of it? And how can we ever—*in fact* or *in theory*—verify the existence of a thing's temperature *when no one is aware of it*? If there is an "objective, real" temperature, we will never know it.

We can know things only in terms of some perception of them through the senses, or as ideas perceived by the mind. And this being so, Berkeley argued, we know only perceptions—not *things in themselves*, only *things as perceived*. What difference does it make to insist that things exist independently of perceptions? If they do, we have no awareness of them, and they have no effect on us, so they are of no importance to us. When they do affect us, we perceive them. Thus if no one or no thing were around to perceive the famous tree falling all alone in the forest, it would be absurd to say that it made a sound. In *Three Dialogues Between Hylas and Philonous*, written in 1713, Berkeley points out that there is no difference between sound as perceived by us and sound as it is in itself. We may define sound in terms of what is perceived: sensations, atmospheric disturbances, decibels, waves, marks on a graph, or whatever, but in all cases sound remains *something that is perceived*.

> *Philonous:* It should follow then, that, according to you, real sounds may . . . never [be] heard.
>
> *Hylas:* Look you, Philonous, you may, if you please, make a jest of my opinion, but that will not alter the truth of things . . . sounds too have no real being without the mind.[13]

Berkeley takes the radical—but logically correct—step of concluding that this is true of everything. We know things only as different kinds of ideas about them. Berkeleian ideas imply consciousness, perception. It is self-contradictory to discuss ideas we do not know we have.

Consider the implications of this position for psychological theories of the unconscious *mind*: If an unconscious mind exists, it can have nothing to do with us. Moods and emotional states like guilt or self-hate exist only as we perceive them; they, too, are ideas in Berkeley's sense. When we do not perceive them, they do not exist. The notion of an *unconscious mind* is self-contradictory, since by definition a mind is a thinking, perceiving, hence conscious, thing.

Philosophical Query

Think about the notion of mind as contrasted to the brain and brain states. It seems clear that our behavior, moods, and even thoughts can be influenced by factors we are unaware of. These might include fatigue, hunger, the effects of medication, allergies, neurological disorders, and

The refutation of skepticism is the whole business of philosophy.

Rush Rhees

One has no knowledge of the sun but only of an eye that sees a sun, and no knowledge of the earth but only of a hand that feels an earth.

Arthur Schopenhauer

so on. Could we also have ideas, motives, and emotions we are unaware of? That is, could we have an "unconscious *mind*"?

It is equally absurd to posit an independent, external reality, for if it exists, we cannot have anything to do with it. If we accept Locke's starting point that all knowledge derives from experience, Berkeley reasons, we must conclude that all knowledge is limited to ideas, because *we experience things only as ideas*. So-called material or physical *states* are perceptions, mental acts. Pain is a perception; sweet and sour are perceptions; the moon is a perception; my own body is known to me only as a series of perceptions. *Esse est percipi*: To be is to be perceived.

As Descartes pointed out, there can be no doubt about my existence while I am aware of it: To think is to exist. Berkeley adds that to exist is to be thought about: Nothing, not even an unthinking thing, can exist unless something perceives it:

> The table I write on I say exists; that is, I see and feel it: and if I were out of my study should say it existed; meaning thereby that if I was in my study I might perceive it, or that some other spirit actually does perceive it. . . . This is all that I can understand by these and the like expressions. For as to what is said of the *absolute* existence of unthinking things [matter], without any relation to their being perceived, that to me is perfectly unintelligible. Their *esse* is *percipi*; nor is it possible they should have any existence out of the minds or thinking things which perceive them.[14]

Had Berkeley continued working out the logical consequences of his position, he would have had to accept a disturbing picture of reality: Only particular, immediate perceptions can be known to exist.

Berkeley stopped short of the skeptical conclusions implied by his premises. He introduced God as a guarantee that he had a continuing self, that he existed during deepest sleep, and that there was indeed an external world, safely encapsulated in the never-resting, all-perceiving mind of God. His successor, David Hume, did not stop, but pursued skeptical logic to unsettling consequences.

ESSE EST PERCIPI

Latin for Berkeley's belief that "to be is to be perceived."

David Hume: The Scottish Skeptic

David Hume (1711–1776) stands out in the history of ideas for the fearless consistency of his reasoning. I am aware of no other philosopher who so relentlessly and thoroughly follows the premises and principles on which his or her philosophy rests to such chilling and disturbing conclusions. Many great thinkers ultimately shied away from the logical conclusions of their ideas for personal, social, or religious reasons. Hume refused to

David Hume

do so. So powerful is his analysis that it effectively destroyed many important philosophies that went before it, and much of the philosophy, science, and "commonsense" beliefs that follow it. Ironically, the wielder of perhaps the sharpest philosophical ax was one of the sweetest, most accessible figures in Western philosophy.

Hume was born in Edinburgh, Scotland, and raised by his mother under a strict Presbyterian regimen. He attended three-hour morning services, went back for an hour in the afternoon, and joined in family prayers every evening. His father died the year after he was born, leaving his son a small income. Hume enrolled in the University of Edinburgh when he was twelve years old, but after three years dropped out without a degree, planning to devote himself to philosophy and literature. A short time later, Hume admitted he had lost the faith of his childhood, writing that once he read Locke and other philosophers, he never again "entertained any belief in religion."[15]

The small income his father left allowed him only the barest existence, and Hume's family tried to persuade him to do something more practical and profitable than just study literature and philosophy. He studied law from 1726 to 1729, but the experience was so unpleasant that he had a breakdown and for a time lost interest in everything. In his own words, "The law appeared nauseous to me."[16]

Hume moved to London "to make a very feeble trial for entering into a more active scene of life," though he must have had a somewhat active social life in Scotland, for on March 5 and again on June 25 of 1734 he was accused of being the father of Agnes Galbraith's child. Hume escaped censure by the church because he was out of Scotland, but poor Agnes was required to wear sackcloth in front of the congregation and be put on public display in the pillory for three consecutive Sundays.

Meanwhile, Hume was working for a merchant in Bristol, but "in a few months I found that scene totally unsuitable to me." He moved to France, where living expenses were lower, finally settling near Descartes' old college at La Flèche. There the Jesuits allowed him full access to their first-rate library. Already his skeptical, questioning mind and discomfort in the face of any authority not supported by clear evidence stood out. One of the Jesuits described Hume as "too full of himself . . . his spirit more lively than solid, his imagination more luminous than profound, his heart too dissipated with material objects and spiritual self-idolatry to pierce into the sacred recesses of divine truths."[17]

The Skeptical Masterpiece

The Jesuits were correct in one aspect of their assessment of Hume, for they recognized a mind given to no allegiance but its own experiences interpreted in an unforgiving rational light. While in France, Hume had what contemporary philosopher Richard Watson calls a "skeptical crisis." In

Americans especially might take their cue today from their forebears in the eighteenth century in making an approach to Hume's philosophy. For in 1787, when the statesmen of the new American republic were discussing for many arduous months their design of a new constitution for the United States, they alluded almost daily to various writings of Hume.

Charles W. Hendel

This Moping Method of Study

Learning has been [a] great . . . loser by being shut up in colleges and cells, and secluded from the world and good company. By that means every part of what we call *belles lettres* became totally barbarous, being cultivated by men without any taste for life or manners, and without that liberty and facility of thought and expression which can only be acquired by conversation. Even philosophy went to wreck by this moping recluse method of study, and became chimerical in her conclusions, as she was unintelligible in her style and manner of delivery; and, indeed, what could be expected from men who never consulted experience in any of their reasonings, or who never searched for that experience, where alone it is to be found, in common life and conversation?

David Hume
"Of Essay Writing," in *Of the Standard Taste and Other Essays*, ed. John W. Lenz (Indianapolis: Bobbs-Merrill, 1965), p. 39.

six weeks he gained sixty pounds, and remained a "fat, jolly fellow for the rest of his life."[18] He also completed the first two books of his powerful and disturbing *Treatise of Human Nature*.

In 1737 he returned to England hoping to publish the *Treatise* and immediately ran into objections from publishers. In December 1737 he wrote, "I am at present castrating my work, that is, cutting out its noble parts, . . . endeavoring it shall give as little offense as possible."[19] Hume found most resistance to his analysis of miracles. He agreed to remove the most offensive passages, but did not destroy them. In this censored form, the two-volume *Treatise* was published anonymously in January 1739. Hume received fifty pounds and twelve copies as his total payment. At the age of twenty-seven he had written one of the major works of modern philosophy.

In the *Treatise* Hume makes compelling arguments *against* materialism, the possibility of a spiritual, supernatural reality and personal immortality—this in the watered-down version! Pushing beyond Locke and Berkeley, Hume argued that neither matter nor mind exists. (A standing joke at the time referred to Berkeley and Hume with the slogan "No matter; never mind.")

The uncensored *Treatise* does not stop there. Hume ultimately reduces reason to the "slave of the passions" and alters the conventional picture of the nature of science by denying cause and effect as they are generally understood. Thus Hume challenged established religious beliefs, moral judgments, reason and rationalism, earlier forms of empiricism, and the certainty of science. He denied the existence of a "fixed self," the possibility of personal immortality, and the questioned possibility of miracles. It would not be surprising if such a book provoked a great storm of controversy. Ultimately, it would, but not among the general public and not right

Never [a] literary attempt was more unfortunate than my *Treatise of Human Nature*. It fell dead-born from the press, without reaching such distinction as even to excite a murmur among the zealots.

David Hume

away. The second edition of the *Treatise* was not published until after Hume's death.

An Honest Man

Unable to earn his living as a writer, Hume applied for a professorship at the University of Edinburgh, but was rejected. He took a somewhat humiliating job as the tutor of a young nobleman, who shortly went insane. Hume was ultimately dismissed and had to sue for his salary. He eventually secured a position as secretary to a general on a mission to Turin, Italy. Hume, having apparently gained more weight, began wearing a scarlet uniform. His appearance unsettled the young Earl of Charlemont, who wrote as follows: "His face was broad and fat, his mouth wide, and without any other expression than that of imbecility. . . . The corpulence of his whole person was far better fitted to communicate the idea of a turtle-eating alderman than that of a refined philosopher."[20]

Hume returned to London in 1748 and published *An Enquiry Concerning Human Understanding*. In 1749 he went back to Edinburgh and in 1751 published *An Enquiry Concerning the Principles of Morals*. These works reach the same conclusions as the *Treatise*, but in a softer tone.

The softer tone was not to last, for in about 1751 Hume wrote the most devastating, direct, and irreverent of his works, the *Dialogues Concerning Natural Religion*. In it Hume mounts an unrelenting attack on the argument from design (see Chapter 7) and other attempts to demonstrate the existence of or understand the nature of God. At the urging of friends, Hume withheld the *Dialogues* from publication. They were finally published in 1779, three years after his death.

Hume wearied of the heated discussion his philosophical reasonings provoked, and turned to politics and history. He finally achieved some success as an author with *Political Discourses* (1751) and *Essays on Various Subjects* (1753). The theory of economics discussed in the *Essays* was substantial enough to influence the great economist Adam Smith.

In 1752 Hume was elected keeper of the library for the Faculty of Advocates in Edinburgh. The pay was low, but Hume was delighted with the job because it gave him control of thirty thousand volumes. Taking advantage of this opportunity, he researched and wrote a *History of England*. He was a competent enough historian that Edward Gibbon, the author of *The Decline and Fall of the Roman Empire* (1776), cited him as an influence.

Hume published his *History* in six volumes, in reverse order, beginning with the years 1603–1649 and ending with the period from Julius Caesar to Henry VII in 1485. His attitudes toward Parliament and Bonnie Prince Charlie were unorthodox, and the controversy aroused by the first volume was so intense that Hume grew depressed and planned to move back

Upon the whole, I have always considered [David Hume], both in his lifetime and since his death, as approaching as nearly to the idea of a perfectly wise and virtuous man as perhaps the nature of human frailty will permit.

Adam Smith

to France. But France and England were at war and the second volume was nearly done. So Hume revised the first volume and continued with the others. By the publication of the sixth volume Hume's popularity as a writer had soared. James Boswell referred to him as "the greatest writer in Britain," and Voltaire said Hume's work was "perhaps the best history ever written in any language."[21] (Today, hardly anyone reads Hume's *History of England*, but no truly educated person fails to read something of Hume's philosophy.)

In spite of his success, Hume remained troubled by the unrelenting attacks from ecclesiastical and other sources. Relief arrived in the form of an appointment as deputy secretary to the Earl of Hertford, ambassador to France. Hertford also arranged that Hume should receive a pension of two hundred pounds for life.

His writing was more popular in France than in England, and by the time he returned to France he was almost a cult figure. The aristocracy loved him (the ladies most of all) and he loved them (the ladies most of all). The Earl of Hertford found that Hume was more popular and respected than the earl was. Once at a party an envious French intellectual made fun of Hume's weight, quoting the Gospel verse "And the word was made flesh." One of Hume's many lady admirers quickly countered, "And the word was made lovable."

After Britain appointed a new ambassador to France in 1765, Hume worked for a time as undersecretary at the Foreign Office in London. He retired to Edinburgh in 1769, being, in his own words, "very opulent (for I possessed a revenue of £1,000 a year), healthy, and though somewhat stricken in years, with the prospect of enjoying long my ease, and of seeing the increase of my reputation."[22]

Hume's home (on, fittingly, St. David Street) became an intellectual salon for Scottish celebrities, including Adam Smith. Hume was a friendly, supportive, encouraging mentor, despite the rigor and iconoclasm of his intellect. He remained a popular guest, even if he occasionally broke a host's chair.[23] He once proposed a tax on obesity but thought its passage unlikely because it might put the church in danger, and he blessed Julius Caesar for preferring fat men.

Part of Hume's charm came from his personal modesty. These days rock stars and television "personalities" in their teens think nothing of writing a two or three hundred page autobiography, yet one of the finest minds to have ever lived considered it sufficient to write an eight-page one—and then only shortly before he died. In it he wrote:

> In the spring of 1775 I was struck with a disorder in my bowels, which at first gave me no alarm, but has since, as I apprehend it, become mortal and incurable. I now reckon upon a speedy dissolution. I have suffered very little pain from my disorder; and what is more strange, have, notwithstanding the great decline of my person, never

I salute you, I love you, I revere you.

Denis Diderot,
to David Hume

Hume was a wonderful man. He and Benjamin Franklin used to have grand times together in Paris, eating and drinking and playing whist, and pulling bluestocking ladies down to sit on their fat laps.

Richard Watson

suffered a moment's abatement of my spirits; insomuch that were I to name the period of my life which I should most choose to pass over again, I might be tempted to point to this later period. I possess the same ardor as ever in my study, and the same gaiety in company. I consider, besides, that a man of sixty-five, by dying, cuts off only a few years of infirmities.[24]

In 1775 Hume lost seventy pounds due to his illness. In 1776 he was prepared to die "as fast as my enemies, if I have any, could wish, and as easily and cheerfully as my best friends could desire."[25]

Even in his last hours, Hume was not spared the attentions of the devout. James Boswell was troubled that the agnostic Hume, whom many erroneously believed to be an atheist, could be so cheerful in the face of death. But Hume did not deny the existence of God, a position known as *atheism*; he adopted the agnostic view that we do not know enough to assert or deny the existence of God.

Happiness in the face of death was thought to be a virtue of the devout believer, not the skeptical agnostic. Unrelenting even at the end, Boswell asked the dying Hume if he did *now* finally believe in an afterlife. Hume answered, "It is a most unreasonable fancy that we should exist forever." Asked if he didn't at least think the possibility of another plane of existence was desirable, the dying skeptic answered, "Not at all; it is a very gloomy thought." A small parade of women visited Hume, begging him to believe, but he distracted them with humor.[26]

David Hume died free of much pain on August 25, 1776. The story goes that a large crowd attended his burial, despite heavy rain. Someone was heard to say, "He was an atheist." "No matter," a voice answered from the crowd. "He was an honest man."

> 'Tis impossible upon any system to defend either our understanding or senses; and we but expose them farther when we endeavour to justify them. . . . Carelessness and inattention alone afford us any remedy. For this reason I rely entirely upon them; and take it for granted, whatever may be the reader's opinion at this present moment, that an hour hence he will be persuaded there is both an external and internal world.
>
> *David Hume*

Hume's Skeptical Empiricism

Hume's philosophy rests on the rejection of overly abstract, obscure, bloated speculations. Hume found most metaphysical speculation irrelevant to the lives of ordinary people. Being poorly worded, unclear, and based on unverified assumptions, it was also, he observed, never-ending. No metaphysical issue was ever clearly and thoroughly settled. For each theory about the soul or nature or reality, there were opposing theories and modifications, apparently infinite in number.

Hume thought such "abstruse speculation" was useful only to individuals with some theological motive, who, "being unable to defend [their views] on fair grounds, raise these entangling brambles to cover and protect their weaknesses." The only way to rid ourselves of these pointless excursions, he claimed, is to inquire seriously and thoroughly into the nature of human understanding, "and show, from an exact analysis of its powers and capacity, that it is by no means fitted for such remote and abstruse subjects."

In other words, Hume continued the epistemological turn, moving further away from metaphysics than Locke and Berkeley. Although he said we must "cultivate true metaphysics with some care in order to destroy the false," Hume moved modern philosophy firmly into the realm of epistemology.

Impressions and Ideas

In *An Enquiry Concerning Human Understanding*, Hume set out to modify Locke's theory of ideas in a way that removed any metaphysical residue. He began by pointing out the very obvious difference between, say, the painful perception of excessive heat or the pleasure of comforting warmth, and the memory of such perceptions. There is also, he noted, a difference between anticipating a perception in the imagination and actually perceiving it. He says, "The most lively thought is still inferior to the dullest sensation." This kind of distinction also applies to "mental perceptions," such as anger and hate.

Hume thought Locke was correct in claiming that thought is a "faithful mirror, and copies objects truly." But he reminds us not to overlook a vital fact: The copies are always duller and fainter than the original perceptions they are based on.

Hume proposes that we distinguish "ideas" from "impressions":

> Here therefore we may divide all perceptions of the mind into two classes or species, which are distinguished by their different degrees of force and vivacity. The less forcible and lively are commonly denominated *Thoughts* or *Ideas*. The other species wants a name in our language, and most others. . . . Let us, therefore, use a little freedom, and call them *Impressions*; employing that word in a sense somewhat different from the usual. By the term *impression*, then, I mean all our more lively perceptions, when we hear, or see, or feel, or love, or hate, or desire, or will. And impressions are distinguished from ideas, which are the less lively perceptions, of which we are conscious, when we reflect on any of those sensations or movements above mentioned.[27]

More careful analysis of ideas, no matter how fanciful, creative, or original, reveals that "all this creative power of the mind amounts to no more than the faculty of compounding, transposing, augmenting, or diminishing the materials afforded us by the senses and experience." In other words, all ideas can be traced to impressions and thus are derived from experience, even if they become so abstracted and diluted that they no longer resemble any identifiable impressions. If you doubt this, Hume says the only way to refute him is to produce an idea not derived from impressions or from combining and altering the ideas that impressions generate.

No sooner do we depart from sense and instinct to follow . . . reason . . . but . . . we are insensibly drawn into uncouth paradoxes, difficulties, and inconsistencies, which multiply and grow upon us as we advance in speculation; till at length, having wandered through many intricate mazes, we find ourselves just where we were, or, which is worse, sit down in a forlorn Scepticism.

George Berkeley

From this basic position, which he took for granted, Hume proposed one of the most powerful, controversial, devastating ideas in modern philosophy: the empirical criterion of meaning.

The Empirical Criterion of Meaning

Modifying Locke's copy theory of ideas, Hume developed an empirical test of meaning:

> When we entertain, therefore, any suspicion that a philosophical term is employed without any meaning or idea (as is a bit too frequent), we need to enquire, *from what impression is that supposed idea derived?* And if it be impossible to assign any, this will serve to confirm our suspicion. By bringing ideas into so clear a light we may reasonably hope to remove all dispute, which may arise, concerning their nature and reality.[28]

The **empirical criterion of meaning** holds that all *meaningful* ideas can be traced to sense experience (impressions). Beliefs that cannot be reduced to sense experience are technically not "ideas" at all: they are *meaningless utterances.*

To understand how the empirical criterion works, imagine for a moment that we are with some fellow philosophers discussing the existence of God and related theological issues. We might argue all evening about whether or not Thomas Aquinas's proofs for the existence of God work. We might argue about whether or not we are born with the innate idea of God or acquire the idea of God from experience. Or we might argue about the problem of evil or whether God favors one religion over another. Whatever position we take on these issues, at least one thing seems clear: We have an idea of God. But do we?[29]

If, as Locke thought, all ideas are derived from experience and the mind begins as a clean slate, the idea of God must be empirically based; it cannot be innate. What *impressions* can justify an assertion like "God is eternal"? We never experience "eternity." At most we experience "long, long time." We say that God is *perfect.* Have we ever experienced absolute perfection in anything? I am not speaking metaphorically or poetically, but precisely and literally: Do we even have a clear *idea* of perfection?

With an idea as important and controversial as God, the empirical criterion of meaning is explosive. It causes us to look anew at the very *idea* of God before we can begin to discuss God's nature and existence. Experience alone cannot provide the idea of an all-perfect, eternal, all-powerful God, because nothing in our experience even remotely resembles perfection, eternity, or infinite power. Thus if we accept the empirical criterion of meaning, the idea of God is neither true nor false—it is *meaningless.* That is, talk about God conveys no information. It is simply a form of confusion resulting from not paying close enough attention to what we say.

EMPIRICAL CRITERION OF MEANING

Meaningful ideas are those that can be traced back to sense experience (impressions); beliefs that cannot be reduced to sense experience are not "ideas" at all, but meaningless utterances.

Nihil in intellectu quod prius non fuerit in sensu. (Nothing is in the intellect which was not in the senses first.)

Thomas Aquinas

Hume's precise, logically rigorous use of the empirical criterion of meaning led to other startling, uncomfortable conclusions about some of the most cherished, influential ideas in philosophy, theology, and science. Let's see what happens when strict empirical standards are applied to some of the ideas we have already studied.

Philosophical Query

Do you agree that "talk about God conveys no information"? Explain. Apply the empirical criterion of meaning to such concepts as love, creativity, and intelligence. What, in general, do you see as the strengths and weaknesses of this criterion?

The Self

As we have seen, Descartes based modern philosophy on the thinking thing, the self. We seem intimately acquainted with a self. What could be more certain than the existence of my self? But what exactly does the word *self* refer to?

Hume says that we do not have any idea of self as it is commonly understood:

> For from what impression cou'd this idea be deriv'd? This question 'tis impossible to answer without a manifest contradiction and absurdity; and 'tis a question, which necessarily must be answer'd, if we wou'd have the idea of self pass for clear and intelligible. But self or person is not any one impression, but that to which our several impressions and ideas are suppos'd to have a reference. If any impression gives rise to the idea of self, that impression must continue invariably the same, thro' the whole course of our lives; since self is suppos'd to exist after that manner. But there is no impression constant and invariable. Pain and pleasure, grief and joy, passions and sensations succeed each other, and never all exist at the same time. It cannot, therefore, be from any of these impressions, or from any other, that the idea of self is deriv'd; and consequently there is no such idea.[30]

But if we have no such *impression* of self, what are we? Hume gives one of the most intriguing yet elusive answers in modern philosophy:

> For my part, when I enter most intimately into what I call *myself*, I always stumble on some particular perception or other, of heat or cold, light or shade, love or hatred, pain or pleasure. I never can catch *myself* at any time without a perception, and never can observe any thing but the perception. When my perceptions are remov'd for any time, as by sound sleep; so long am I insensible of *myself*, and may truly be

The solution to the problem of identity is, get lost.

Norman O. Brown

said not to exist. And were all my perceptions remov'd by death, and cou'd I neither think, nor feel, nor see, nor love, nor hate after the dissolution of my body, I shou'd be entirely annihilated, nor do I conceive what is farther requisite to make me a perfect non-entity. If any one upon serious and unprejudic'd reflexion, thinks he has a different notion of *himself*, I must confess I can reason no longer with him. All I can allow him is, that he may be in the right as well as I, and that we are essentially different in this particular. He may, perhaps, perceive something simple and continu'd, which he calls *himself*; tho' I am certain there is no such principle in me.

But setting aside some metaphysicians of this kind, I may venture to affirm of the rest of mankind, that they are nothing but a bundle or collection of different perceptions, which succeed each other with an inconceivable rapidity, and are in a perpetual flux and movement.[31]

In such passages, Hume sounds very much like a Buddhist or Hindu (see the Third Interlude). He has dissolved the self into a flickering series of perceptions with no underlying, constant *thing* to unite them. What has come to be known as Hume's **bundle theory of the self** is difficult for most of us to accept. Yet Hume's position is more consistent than some that are more comforting and popular.

Philosophical Query

Where and what are "you" in the midst of some exciting experience that totally absorbs your consciousness? That is, what happens to your "self" when you are not aware of it? What exactly are you aware of when you are self-conscious? A "self" or sweaty palms, uncomfortable desks, boring lectures? Discuss.

Personal Immortality

If we cannot speak clearly about the self, what happens to the common belief that the self (or the soul) survives after bodily death? If an *identity* of some sort survives bodily decay, what exactly does that identity find in the afterlife? Is the afterlife a place? How do we know that? And what do we mean when we talk of the soul going somewhere? Does such a concept have any clear content? Can we describe the soul's journey with the same detail and clarity as we recount a physical journey? I don't think we can.

Hume says, in his straightforward fashion, that there can be no persistent identity for us. We speak of "the oak tree" in the backyard, but in fact, each time we see it, "the oak tree" is different. It has a different number of leaves, it has grown, even when we cannot yet discern these changes. Any change in a thing changes its identity. In what sense can a two-hundred-pound man who has been married twice and fathered children be the "same

BUNDLE THEORY OF THE SELF

Humean theory that there is no fixed "self," but that the "self" is merely a "bundle of perceptions"; a "self" is merely a habitual way of discussing certain perceptions.

Strictly speaking, nothing exists except sensations (and the minds which perceive them).

W. T. Stace

In what sense is the "self" negotiating the turbulent rapids of Lava Falls in the Grand Canyon the same "self" that sat on a couch reading a book the week before? What are "you" in the midst of some all-absorbing, intense experience? Is there a "you" at all during the peak moments of such experiences?

Shall we esteem it worthy the labour of a philosopher to give us a true system of the planets, and adjust the position and order of those remote bodies; while we affect to overlook those, who, with so much success, delineate the parts of the mind, in which we are so intimately concerned?

David Hume

person" who was once a fifty-pound third grader? In what sense are you the "same person" who began reading this book? Your mind has different ideas. Your body has different cells. As Heraclitus noted, "We cannot step twice into the same river, for the water into which we first stepped has flowed on."

In other words, identity is not a property of things, but a mental act. Our minds *confer* identity on things; we do not perceive it. A self is merely a habitual way of discussing certain perceptions.

> The whole of this doctrine leads us to a conclusion, which is of great importance in the present affair, *viz.* that all the nice and subtle questions concerning personal identity can never possibly be decided, and are to be regarded rather as grammatical than as philosophical difficulties. . . . We have no just standard, by which we can decide any dispute concerning the time, when [things] acquire or lose a title to the name of identity. All the disputes concerning the identity of connected objects are merely verbal, except so far as the relation of parts gives rise to some fiction or imaginary principle of union, as we have already observ'd.[32]

Strictly speaking, Hume is correct. We do not *perceive identity*. Yet something gives order and continuity to our experiences, and Hume does not deny that. Rather, he insists on clearer, more precise talking, reasoning, and thinking about this and other important matters. In the process, Hume reaches the limits of reason, and, perhaps, of knowledge.

The Limits of Reason

In a sense, Hume is simply stopping at the first part of Berkeley's position. Hume says, "The mind has never anything present to it but the perceptions, and cannot possibly reach any experience of their connexion with objects. The supposition of such a connexion . . . is, therefore, without any foundation in reasoning."[33] This means we have no way of empirically establishing the independent existence of an external world, or what many of us mean by "reality." The only world we can ever know is the world of our own perceptions, ideas, and experiences.

> As several impressions appear exterior to the body, we suppose them also exterior to ourselves. The paper, on which I write at present, is beyond my hand. The table is beyond the paper. The walls of the chamber beyond the table. And in casting my eye towards the window, I perceive a great extent of fields and buildings beyond my chamber. From all this it may be infer'd, that no other faculty is requir'd, besides the senses, to convince us of the external existence of body. But to prevent this inference, we need only weigh the three following considerations. *First*, That, properly speaking, 'tis not our body we perceive, when we regard our limbs and members, but certain impressions, which enter by the sense; so that in ascribing a real and corporeal existence to these impressions, or to their objects, is an act of the mind as difficult to explain, as that which we examine at present. *Secondly*, Sounds and tastes, and smells, tho' commonly regarded by the mind as continu'd independent qualities, appear not to have any existence in extension, and consequently cannot appear to the senses as situated externally to the body. . . . *Thirdly*, Even our sight informs us not of distance or outness (so to speak) immediately and without certain reasoning and experience, as is acknowledg'd by the most rational philosophers.[34]

If we were merely reasoning creatures, we could accept this conclusion. Yet belief in an external world is one of the strongest, most universal beliefs. If, as Hume thought, there is no rational evidence whatsoever for belief in an external reality, then why is the notion so popular?

Hume concludes that the very nature of imagination accounts for the universal notion of the independent existence of an external world. The imagination completes and fills in gaps between perceptions. If we regularly

Accurate and just reasoning is the only catholic remedy, fitted for all persons and all dispositions; and is alone able to subvert that abstruse philosophy and metaphysical jargon, which, being mixed up with popular superstition, renders it in a manner impenetrable to careless reasoners, and gives it the air of science and wisdom.

David Hume

experience very much the same perceptions, say of the oak tree in the yard or our own face, we overlook the gaps between different perceptions. Hume says we "feign" or fabricate continuity. I assume that because my face looks "the same" this morning as yesterday morning, it has existed continuously all night and at other times when I had no perception of it.

Further, our experiences tend to occur with a kind of pattern or regularity, which Hume refers to as *coherence*. That is, when I turn my head to the left, my view in the mirror is a particular perception. When I tilt forward, I have a completely different perception, and so on. When I turn around and use a hand mirror to examine the thinning hair on the back of my head, I have yet another perception. What I never have is an impression of my whole head. But because my various views always follow a pattern, my imagination feigns or fabricates an idea of my whole head.

According to Hume, this process explains our belief in an external world. But it points to a startling conclusion: that a natural quality of the mind exists that is much more powerful than logical reasoning, and that always reasserts itself after being challenged on logical grounds.

> There is a great difference betwixt such opinions as we form after a calm and profound reflection, and such as we embrace by a kind of instinct or natural impulse, on account of their suitableness and conformity to the mind. If these opinions become contrary, 'tis not difficult to foresee which of them will have the advantage. As long as our attention is bent upon the subject, the philosophical and study'd principle may prevail; but the moment we relax our thoughts, nature will display herself, and draw us back to our former opinion. . . .[35]

Reason is, and ought only to be the slave of passions, and can never pretend to any other office than to serve and obey them.

David Hume

If Hume is correct, nature and reason are adversaries: "Nature is obstinate, and will not quit the field, however strongly attack'd by reason; and at the same time reason is so clear in the point, that there is no possibility of disguising her." This explains why many people are indifferent to logical precision or rational evidence. It might also account for the ease with which we accept poorly justified beliefs. It might even explain why you can study only so much philosophy (or anything else) and then find yourself almost compelled to do something nonintellectual. Nature acts as a corrective and cure to reason.

By the same token, the human mind has a rational component. A completely nonrational life would be barely human. Even the most primitive, nontechnical, "natural" cultures depend on reason. What Hume suggests is a kind of fluctuating balance between reason and nature, or logic and emotion. We find such a position less disturbing today than philosophers did in the eighteenth century, for Hume's skepticism indicates that a completely rational view of reality is not possible, or at least not for more than brief, concentrated periods. It suggests that reason, the great ideal of so many philosophers, is, in fact, the slave of emotions, shaped by psychology and biology.

Philosophical Query

Have you been able to take Hume's claims seriously? That is, have you seriously considered the *possibility* that we lack *knowledge* of the external world? Discuss some factors that make taking this idea seriously so difficult. Can you spot any errors in Hume's reasoning? Discuss.

The Limits of Science

Scientific reasoning rests on a pattern of **inductive reasoning**, which results in generalized rules or principles. Simplistically, we can say that it reasons from the particular to the general or from some to all. Conclusions about atoms or the behavior of iron filings or causes of rain are never based on experience with *all* things of a certain kind. Newton did not have to observe the behavior of all bodies to conclude they are subject to gravity. He based his conclusion on the behavior of just some bodies.

Scientists assume that such inferences are reliable because they identify *causal patterns*. In Hume's time, cause and effect were defined in terms of a *necessary connection*. That is, *A* was said to cause *B* if the occurrence of *A always and without exception* was followed by the occurrence of *B*. But if Hume's epistemology is correct, how can we perceive the actual connection, the causal relationship? Strictly speaking, all we actually observe is *A* followed by *B*. We observe constant conjunction; that is, a perception of *A* is always (or so far) followed by a perception of *B*. But that is a temporal sequence, not a necessary connection. Ironically, the great empiricist demonstrates, *on strictly empirical grounds*, that the very foundation of the empirical sciences is nothing more than a product of the human mind. According to Hume, there is no empirical evidence for the existence of cause and effect:

> We have sought in vain for an idea of power or necessary connexion in all the sources from which we could suppose it to be derived. It appears that, in single instances of the operation of bodies, we never can, by our utmost scrutiny, discover anything but one event following another, without being able to comprehend any force or power by which the cause operates, or any connexion between it and its supposed effect. The same difficulty occurs in contemplating the operations of mind on body—where we observe the motion of the latter to follow upon the volition of the former, but are not able to observe or conceive the tie which binds together the motion and volition, or the energy by which the mind produces this effect. The authority of the will over its own faculties and ideas is not a whit more comprehensible: So that, upon the whole, there appears not, throughout all nature, any one instance of connexion which is conceivable by us. All

INDUCTIVE REASONING

Reasoning pattern that proceeds from the particular to the general or from some to all and results in generalized rules or principles established with degrees of probability.

It follows from this definition of cause, that night is
the cause of day, and day
the cause of night. For no
two things have more con-
stantly followed each other
since the beginning of the
world.

Thomas Reid

events seem entirely loose and separate. One event follows another;
but we can never observe any tie between them. They seem *conjoined*,
but never *connected*. And as we can have no idea of any thing which
[is not based on an impression], the necessary conclusion *seems* to be
that we have no idea of connexion or power at all, and that these
words are absolutely without any meaning, when employed either in
philosophical reasonings or common life.[36]

What *do* we observe that we call cause and effect? Hume answers that
we observe a series of recognizable impressions, and that we come to expect the first part of the series to be followed by the second part. When
we are correct, we assume the connection is causal. But we cannot observe that one event *must* follow the other. All we *know* is that one event
happens to follow another. We may have observed this pattern countless
times, but that does not logically justify inferring any sort of necessity.

In other words, the mind creates the ideas of causality and necessity;
we do not observe them. The best we can do is take for granted that the
future will resemble the past: there is no way to prove that it will or that
it must. We are psychologically constructed so that we have no choice but
to *believe in* cause and effect. For the most part, our inferences regarding
the predictability and uniformity of experience have been borne out. But,
Hume cautions us, we should not forget that the real origin of science lies
in the operation of the human mind. We believe in an independent, external reality because we cannot help it.

Science is included in Hume's consistent skeptical conclusion: All
knowledge is limited to our own impressions; everything else is a product
of the imagination.

The Limits of Theology

Given his radical view of cause and effect, it is not surprising that Hume
rejected all efforts to prove the existence of God based on cause. The cosmological argument and the argument from motion were meaningless for
him. The ontological argument was meaningless as well, because the very
qualities ascribed to God—perfection, omniscience, omnipotence, and so
forth—do not correspond to specific impressions. They are empty noises.

Besides rejecting these arguments, Hume wrote perhaps the most devastating and complete critique of the argument from design, also known as
the teleological argument (see Thomas Aquinas's fifth way in Chapter 7).
After taking the briefest look at this compelling bit of logical analysis, we
can understand why Hume withheld publication of his *Dialogues Concerning Natural Religion* during his lifetime.

Recall that the core of the argument from design is the belief that all
about us we see evidence of God's handiwork. We perceive order and har-

mony and beauty throughout the universe. We sense the divine in a beautiful sunset or an ocean breeze; we feel God's presence in the miracle of childbirth or the renewing of the seasons. But as Hume points out, that's not the whole picture.

In the first place, we need to remind ourselves that the argument from design is an analogy in which God and Creation are compared to a craftsman and a crafted object (the most famous example is a watchmaker and a watch). Let us grant the similarity for purposes of analysis. Careful reasoning produces a disquieting conclusion:

> But were this world ever so perfect a production, it must still remain uncertain, whether all the excellences of the work can justly be ascribed to the workman. If we survey a ship, what an exalted idea must we form of the ingenuity of the carpenter, who framed so complicated, useful, and beautiful a machine? And what surprise must we feel, when we find him a stupid mechanic, who imitated others, and copied an art, which, through a long succession of ages, after multiplied trials, mistakes, corrections, deliberations, and controversies, had gradually been improving? Many worlds might have been botched and bungled, throughout an eternity, ere this system was struck out: Much labor lost: Many fruitless trials made: And a slow, but continued improvement carried on during infinite ages in the art of world-making. . . .[37]

Moreover, we need to think carefully about the relationship between the designer and the finished product:

> Did I show you a house or palace, where there was not one apartment convenient or agreeable; where the windows, doors, fires, passages, stairs, and the whole economy of the building were the source of noise, confusion, fatigue, darkness, and extremes of heat and cold; you would certainly blame the contrivance, without any farther examination. . . . If you find many inconveniences and deformities in the building, you will always, without entering into any detail, condemn the architect. . . . Accurate and just reasoning is the only catholic remedy, fitted for all persons and all dispositions; and is alone able to subvert that abstruse philosophy and metaphysical jargon, which, being mixed up with popular superstition, renders it in a manner impenetrable to careless reasoners, and gives it the air of science and wisdom.[38]

The argument from design depends, in great part, on the nature of the universe (the designed thing). Why would God design a world such as ours, which contains disorder, ugliness, injustice, and cruelty? Nature at best is inefficient: one part of the world drowns in torrential rains and another burns under drought; some regions have plenty and others starve. If this is "the best of all possible worlds," the critics argue, it only shows that God could not create a first-rate world.

The whole conception of God is a conception derived from ancient Oriental despotisms. It is a conception quite unworthy of free men. . . . A good world needs knowledge, kindliness and courage; it does not need a regretful hankering after the past or a fettering of the free intelligence by the words uttered long ago by ignorant men.

Bertrand Russell

Christianity does not—and cannot—explain how a God who is infinitely powerful and infinitely loving came to create a universe which turned out to be not very good.

Arnold Toynbee

There is even less reason to infer the existence of a good god once one takes a thorough, objective look at life:

> But allowing you, what never will be believed; at least, what you never possibly can prove, that animal, or at least human happiness, in this life, exceeds its misery; you have yet done nothing: For this is not, by any means, what we expect from infinite power, infinite wisdom, infinite goodness. Why is there any misery at all in this world? Not by chance surely. From some cause then. Is it from the intention of the Deity? But he is perfectly benevolent. Is it contrary to his intention? But he is almighty. Nothing can shake the solidity of this reasoning, so short, so clear, so decisive. . . .
>
> Look round this universe. What an immense profusion of beings, animated and organized, sensible and active! You admire the prodigious variety and fecundity. But inspect a little more narrowly these living existences, the only beings worth regarding. How hostile and destructive to each other! How insufficient all of them for their own happiness! How contemptible or odious to the spectator! The whole presents nothing but the idea of a blind nature, impregnated by a great vivifying principle, and pouring forth from her lap, without discernment or parental care, her maimed and abortive children.[39]

Based solely on our observations of human experience, we find insufficient evidence to assume the existence of a good, all-wise, all-powerful god. Imagine what kind of argument Hume could have made had he known of the Holocaust.

Philosophical Query

Take a moment to reconsider the argument from design in light of such twentieth-century horrors as chemical warfare, environmental disasters, AIDS, crack babies, crime rates, world hunger, and homelessness amid plenty. Do such examples refute the notion of design or not? Discuss.

Hume also pointed out that we have no real reason to compare the universe to a machine or crafted object in the first place. It makes as much, if not more, sense to view the universe as an organism:

> The world plainly resembles more an animal or a vegetable, than it does a watch or knitting-loom. Its cause, therefore, it is more probable, resembles the cause of the former. The cause of the former is generation or vegetation. The cause, therefore, of the world, we may infer to be some thing similar or analogous to generation or vegetation.[40]

At this point in the dialogue, Hume has the person representing orthodox belief object, asking, "What *data* have you for such extraordinary conclu-

---

I said that I could not imagine being an atheist any time before 1859, when Darwin's *Origin of Species* was published. "What about Hume?" replied the philosopher. "How did Hume explain the organized complexity of the living world?" I asked. "He didn't," said the philosopher. "Why does it need any special explanation?"

Richard Dawkins

sions? And is the slight, imaginary resemblance of the world to a vegetable or an animal sufficient to establish [any] inference in regard to both?"

Hume replies with the most important and devastating point of all:

> Right. . . . This is the topic on which I have all along insisted. I have still asserted that we have no *data* to establish any system of cosmogony [theory of the origins of the universe]. Our experience, so imperfect in itself, and so limited both in extent and duration, can afford us no probable conjecture concerning the whole of things.[41]

Strictly speaking, our own little corner of the universe is too small to permit useful generalizations about the whole. To conclude yea or nay about God's existence and nature is beyond the limits of both reason and experience.

In a note added to the *Dialogues* just before his death, Hume stated that *"the cause or causes of order in the universe probably bear some remote analogy to human intelligence."* But he insisted that this analogy does not suggest that God exists, at least the god of Judeo-Christian-Islamic religions.

The Limits of Rationalistic Ethics

As we have seen, Plato argued that reason's function is to rule the appetites and emotions. The Stoics attempted to control their passions through reason. Descartes attempted to replace the authority of the church with the authority of reason. Descartes was not alone in his vision of reason as the ground of all knowledge, including moral knowledge. The seventeenth and eighteenth centuries are sometimes characterized as the Age of Reason. Attempts to ground morals in reason continue in the present. But when Hume applied his empirical ax to moral philosophy, he challenged the role of reason in morality in an unprecedented way and achieved results similar to his critiques of theology and metaphysics.

As we shall see, Hume insisted that morality is grounded in sentiment, not reason. His devastating attack on any "metaphysic of morals" has had an enormous influence on modern and postmodern conceptions of morality, value judgments, and the possibility of moral knowledge. Immanuel Kant (Chapter 10) would refer to Hume's work as a "scandal in philosophy."

In his *Treatise of Human Nature*, Hume asserts that "reason alone" can never provide a motive for any action:

> Nothing is more usual in philosophy, and even in common life, than to talk of the combat of passion and reason, to give the preference to reason, and to assert that men are only so far virtuous as they conform themselves to its dictates. Every rational creature, 'tis said, is oblig'd to regulate his actions by reason; and if any other motive or

I am uneasy to think I approve of one object, and disapprove of another; call one thing beautiful, and another deform'd; decide concerning truth and falsehood, reason and folly, without knowing upon what principles I proceed.

David Hume

principle challenge the direction of his conduct, he ought to oppose it, 'till it be entirely subdu'd, or at least brought to a conformity with this common principle. On this method of thinking the greatest part of moral philosophy, ancient and modern, seems to be founded; nor is there an ampler field, as well for metaphysical arguments, as popular declamations, than this suppos'd pre-eminence of reason above passion. . . .

In order to shew the fallacy of all this philosophy, I shall endeavour to prove *first*, that reason alone can never be a motive to any action of the will; and *secondly*, that it can never oppose passion in the direction of the will.[42]

Hume did not deny that reason plays a role in making moral judgments. Rather, he argued that reason's role is secondary to the role of moral feelings or *sentiments*, because reason can never provide ultimate ends:

It appears evident that the ultimate ends of human actions can never . . . be accounted for by *reason*, but recommend themselves entirely to the sentiments and affections of mankind, without any dependence on the intellectual faculties. Ask a man *why he uses exercise*; he will answer, *because he desires to keep his health*. If you then enquire, *why he desires health*, he will readily reply, *because sickness is painful*. If you push your enquiries farther, and desire a reason *why he hates pain*, it is impossible that he can ever give any. This is an ultimate end, and is never referred to any other object.[43]

According to Hume, although reason has a useful role to play in moral discernment, moral judgments themselves ultimately rest on

some internal sense or feeling which nature has made universal in the whole species. For what else can have an influence on this nature? But in order to pave the way for such a sentiment, and give it proper discernment of its object, it is often necessary, we find, that much reasoning should precede, that nice distinctions be made, just conclusions drawn, distant comparisons formed, complicated relations examined, and general facts fixed and ascertained.[44]

That is, reason helps us clarify experience. It helps us identify facts. It does not, however, evaluate them. Hume's most famous sentence summarizes this point: "Reason is, and ought only to be the slave of the passions, and can never pretend to any other office than to serve and obey them."[45]

Philosophical Query

Compare Hume's claim that reason is incapable of ruling the passions with Plato's belief that reason's very function is to rule over the appetites and spirit (will). Refer to your own experience, as well as to any psychological or scientific knowledge you have.

> I found a certain boldness of temper growing on me, which was not inclined to submit to any authority in these subjects [philosophy and literature]. . . . When I was about eighteen years of age there seemed to be opened up a new scheme of thought, which transported me beyond measure, and made me, with an ardor natural to young men, throw up every other pleasure or business to apply myself entirely to it.
>
> *David Hume*

The Facts, Just the Facts

Hume's analysis of moral judgments resembles his analysis of causality. Recall that, according to Hume, we do not perceive the fact of "necessary connection," but associate the feeling of necessity with certain related events (events constantly conjoined). Moral judgments are like causal judgments: they are mental associations or projections, not perceptions of facts. When we like a certain characteristic, we call it a virtue or label it "good" or "right." When we dislike something, we call it a vice or label it "wrong" or "bad." These evaluations are not derived from reason, but from experience. It is "just a fact" that a certain combination of conditions produces cold or heat; likewise, it is "just a fact" that we associate some experiences with good feelings (these are desired), and some with bad feelings (these are disliked). In other words, through experience, we learn to associate certain facts with positive sentiments (being good or desired) and other facts with negative sentiments (being bad or disliked). The facts themselves are value neutral.

In the important and influential Part I of Book III of his *Treatise*, Hume makes a crucial distinction between *facts* and *values* (evaluations of facts). According to Hume, *facts themselves are valueless.* Moral judgments (like all evaluations) are not judgments of facts but reports of moral sentiments or feelings. Hume's fact-value distinction has exerted tremendous influence on all moral philosophy since. In the *Treatise* he says:

> But can there be any difficulty in proving, that vice and virtue are not matters of fact, whose existence we can infer by reason? Take any action allow'd to be vicious: Willful murder, for instance. Examine it in all lights, and see if you can find the matter of fact, or real existence, which you call *vice.* In whichever way you take it, you find only certain passions, motives, volitions and thoughts. There is no matter of fact in the case. The vice entirely escapes you, as long as you consider the object. You can never find it, till you turn your reflexion into your own breast, and find a sentiment of disapprobation, which arise in you towards this action. Here is a matter of fact; but 'tis the object of feeling, not of reason. It lies in yourself, not in the object. So that when you pronounce any action or character to be vicious, you mean nothing, but that from the constitution of your nature you have a feeling or sentiment of blame from the contemplation of it. Vice and virtue, therefore, may be compar'd to sounds, colours, heat and cold, which according to modern philosophy, are not qualities in objects, but perceptions in the mind . . .[46]

To fully grasp what Hume is saying, it helps to distinguish between *descriptive language* and *normative language*. Descriptive language—as the name suggests—is devoid of all subjective, evaluative characterizations. Using Hume's example of "willful murder," we might expect to find

Doubt is the nerve of all fresh and durable thinking. If Aristotle was right in the first book of his *Metaphysics* when he said that philosophy began in wonder, philosophy could not have got very far if she had not doubted searchingly.

Phillip P. Hallie

descriptive language in a police report: "Dean Fetters shot J. Scott Vargas in the chest six times. Vargas fell to the floor. He lost three quarts of blood and died at 6:15 p.m." and so on. No matter how precise and elaborate a purely factual description of the circumstance is, it will contain no moral judgments. Indeed, the moral judgment of murder is like the legal judgment of murder. Although we base both judgments on our beliefs about the facts, murder (in either the moral or legal sense) is an interpretation of the facts—not a description or observation. No one sees murder. We see Fetters shoot Vargas, and so forth. We do not see murder. In a court of law, we *decide* murder (or not). In the moral case, we react subjectively to the facts and feel murder (or not). Moral judgments, according to Hume, are like judgments about art or food—matters of moral taste or sentiment.

Philosophical Query

Hume's point here is very important. Don't rush by it. Take a moment and try to write a purely factual description of something you believe is immoral. Do you agree with Hume that the facts are value neutral and that all moral judgments are reports of feelings associated with certain facts? Discuss.

Moral Sentiments

Hume believed that the task before him was a "question of fact, not of abstract science" and that success was possible only by "following the experimental method, and deducing general maxims from a comparison of particular instances." Using the fact-value distinction, he attempted a "reformation" of moral philosophy, announcing that it was time to "reject every system of ethics, however subtle or ingenious, which is not founded on fact and observation."

Hume's efforts did, indeed, launch a revolution in moral philosophy. He helped establish a method of "ordinary language analysis" that became especially influential in the early part of the twentieth century, and whose influence is still significant. Notice how the empirical criterion of meaning affects Hume's language analysis in the following passage. Also note the role he gives reason.

> The very nature of language guides us almost infallibly in forming a judgment of [matters of Personal Merit]; and as every tongue possesses one set of words which are taken in a good sense, and another in the opposite, the least acquaintance with the idiom suffices, without any reasoning, to direct us in collecting and arranging the estimable or blamable qualities of [people]. The only object of reasoning is to discover the circumstances on both sides, which are common to these qualities; to observe that particular in which the estimable qualities

The intercourse of sentiments, therefore, in society and conversation, makes us form some general inalterable standard, by which we may approve or disapprove of characters and manners. And tho' the *heart* does not take part with those general notions, or regulate its love and hatred by them, yet are they sufficient for discourse, and serve all our purposes in company, in the pulpit, in the theatre, and in the schools.

David Hume

agree on one hand, and the blamable on the other; and thence to reach the foundation of ethics, and find those universal principles, from which all censure or approbation is ultimately derived.[47]

In all cases of moral judgment, what we call virtues are traits we, in fact, find agreeable. The feeling of agreeableness is what makes them virtues to us. We do not find them agreeable because they are virtues. We call them virtues because we find them agreeable. That's an important distinction.

We sometimes lose sight of the fundamental nature of all value judgments because we use different terms to distinguish among variations of experience.

Put another way, different pleasures are like different flavors; all the good flavors are pleasing, yet we call some sweet, some sour, some chocolate, some lime, some fruity, some salty, and so forth. Similarly, all unpleasant sentiments are alike, yet we call some disgusting, some ugly, some evil, some bad, some cowardice, and so forth.[48]

What, then, is unique to that "peculiar kind" of sentiment that Hume calls moral? Hume says that *moral sentiment is a disinterested reaction to character (motive)*. Moral virtue is *disinterested approbation* (liking or approval) of character or motive. Moral vice is *disinterested disapprobation* (disliking or disapproval) of character or motive. According to Hume, careful language analysis reveals that, *as a matter of fact*, moral judgments are disinterested judgments of character.

The Limits of Egoism

By asserting that moral judgments are "disinterested," Hume rejected egoism. (See Chapters 2, 3, and 10 and the Fourth Interlude for more about the relationship of self-interest to morality.) In his forceful attack, he refers to egoism as "a principle . . . supposed to prevail among many." Hume characterizes egoism as the belief that

> . . . all *benevolence* is mere hypocrisy, friendship a cheat, public spirit a farce, fidelity a snare to procure trust and confidence, and that while all of us, at bottom, pursue only our private interest, we wear these fair disguises, in order to put others off their guard, and expose them the more to our wiles and machinations.[49]

Hume argues that egoism is utterly inadequate as an account of real life. A clear look at the facts makes it plain that we have other motives than these. He rejects egoism as factually inaccurate and overly simplistic, warning that the love of such contrived simplicity "has been the source of much false reasoning in philosophy." He says:

> The most obvious objection to the selfish hypothesis is that, as it is contrary to common feeling and our most unprejudiced notions,

The sceptic wishes, from considerations of humanity, to do all he can with the arguments at his disposal to cure the self-conceit and rashness of the dogmatists.

Sextus Empiricus

there is required the highest stretch of philosophy to establish so extraordinary a paradox. To the most careless observer there appear to be such dispositions as benevolence and generosity; such affections as love, friendship, compassion, gratitude. . . . As this is the most obvious appearance of things, it must be admitted, till [the selfish] hypothesis be . . . proved.[50]

Hume's attack on egoism is withering in its clarity and appeal to everyday experience. He rejects and ridicules the complications implicit in the belief that our "real" motives are always some form of narrow self-interest. He compares that kind of claim with the equally absurd claim that a horse-drawn wagon is "really" moved by "minute wheels and springs, like those of a watch."

Consider, Hume suggests, feelings of grief. Which is more absurd, to assume that all feelings of grief over the deaths of our loved ones are really disguised self-interest, or to accept them as we experience them? Are we, Hume asks, ready to believe that our loving pets are really motivated solely by self-interest? Obviously not. The most cursory glance at our actual experiences with animals shows that conditioning (or even instinct) does not adequately describe all acts of animal loyalty and affection. Does this mean that animals can express disinterested benevolence but human beings can't? Hume thought such an idea was preposterous.

According to Hume, pure self-love is another of the fictions that results from rationalistic thinking that loses touch with actual experience because it is not based on empirical facts. When we take our actual experience into account, self-love is not an adequate explanation of human motivation. Even the most common objects of so-called self-love—power, praise, revenge, and such—have no appeal without other sentiments. Hume claimed that if "there is no appetite of any kind antecedent to self-love, [self-love] could scarcely ever exert itself," because self-love by itself is too "slender" a sentiment. That is, motives to action always involve seeking or avoiding something according to some appetite (sentiment) that precedes the action. In simple terms, self-love is never the only motive to action.

Hume is at his best when he challenges the egoist's shriveled view of human motivation:

> Where is the difficulty in conceiving, that . . . from the original frame of our temper, we may feel a desire of another's happiness or good, which by means of that affection, becomes our own good, and is afterwards pursued, from the combined motives of benevolence and self-enjoyments? Who sees not that vengeance, from the force alone of passion, may be so eagerly pursued, as to make us knowingly neglect every consideration of ease, interest, or safety; and, like some vindictive animals, infuse our very souls into the wounds we give an enemy; and what a malignant philosophy it must be, that will not

Even an act performed out of love is supposed to be "unegoistic"? But you blockheads!

Friedrich Nietzsche

Soon or late, it is ideas, not vested interests which are dangerous for good or evil.

John Maynard Keynes

allow to humanity and friendship the same privileges which are indisputably granted to the darker passions of enmity and resentment.[51]

Commentary

In the end, Hume compared full-blown skepticism to doubting the existence of an external reality, pointing out that the issue cannot be settled logically and rationally. No one can actually live as a skeptic:

> To whatever length anyone may push his speculative principles of scepticism, he must act . . . and live, and converse like other men. . . . It is impossible for him to persevere in total scepticism, or make it appear in his conduct for a few hours.[52]

Having reasoned carefully and thoroughly, without shying away from what he discovered, no matter how alien to common sense or established knowledge and custom, no matter how foreign to his heart's desire, the great archetype of the skeptic expresses a timeless lament in his own fashion:

> Where am I, or what? From what causes do I derive my existence, and to what condition shall I return? Whose favour shall I court, and whose anger must I dread? What beings surround me? and on whom have I influence, or who have influence on me? I am confounded with all these questions, and begin to fancy myself in the most deplorable condition imaginable, inviron'd with the deepest darkness, and utterly depriv'd of the use of every member and faculty.
>
> Most fortunately it happens, that since reason is incapable of dispelling these clouds, nature herself suffices to that purpose, and cures me of this philosophical melancholy and delirium. . . . I dine, I play a game of backgammon, I converse, and am merry with my friends; and when after three or four hours' amusement, I wou'd return to these speculations, they appear so cold, and strain'd and ridiculous, that I cannot find in my heart to enter them any farther.[53]

What, then, is the point of these difficult and frustrating skeptical inquiries if, in the end, not even Hume takes them seriously? Ah, but he does take them seriously. Using careful observation and analysis, Hume raises important points about both the limits of reason and the needs of the human heart.

Hume exposes cloudy and meaningless language and bogus theorizing. He shows clearly the ultimate inadequacy of rational and empirical efforts to prove God's existence or infer His nature. In Hume's own time a great scientific revolution had already established the force and usefulness of the scientific method. His analysis of cause and effect, as he acknowledges,

Scepticism is . . . a form of belief. Dogma cannot be abandoned; it can only be revised in view of some more elementary dogma which it has not yet occurred to the sceptic to doubt; and he may be right in every point of his criticism, except in fancying that his criticism is radical and that he is altogether a sceptic.

George Santayana

According to Hume, what we call virtues are traits of character that we find "agreeable"; moral judgments are matters of taste, feeling, or "sentiment." Consider the current moral controversy surrounding gay marriages. To what extent do you think this controversy involves matters of moral "sentiment"? As you study the two couples in these photographs, reflect on the extent to which moral feelings shape our lives.

does not destroy science but modifies a bit of what some see as its arrogance. Neither science nor theology can explain the ultimate origins of life or the ultimate nature of reality.

Hume has shown us how little we actually *know* of the most important and most common aspects of existence: self, personal identity, cause and effect, reality, the external world, the universe, and God. Read correctly, I think, Hume reveals that the power of logic and reason are, nevertheless, not all-powerful. He shows that the great theological beliefs to which so many are devoted are barely intelligible. In other words, Hume teaches us that neither the scientist, nor the philosopher, nor the priest has *the* method and *the* answer to timeless questions.

Hume reminds us that there is no absolute certainty in life, only enough uniformity to live reasonably well, if we are lucky. He shows that belief without reason is often meaningless, but that a life based solely on reason is not possible. We live and act on what George Santayana calls *animal faith*: a force within us that *trusts something* in spite of the limits of our experience and reason.

Additionally, Hume's use of the empirical method took root and ushered in a new and powerful philosophical movement that demanded increasingly clear use of language, precision of thought, and observable evidence.

Hume also reminds us that though our search for absolute answers cannot be completely satisfied, our search for wisdom is not in vain. Hume sometimes makes progress the way Socrates sometimes makes progress: by exposing ignorance, by showing us what is not an adequate answer. Human

As a philosophical critic Hume has few peers. No one has challenged more sharply rationalism's central thesis that matters of fact can be known without recourse to experience; nor has anyone revealed more clearly the severe problems raised by insisting that all factual claims be empirically verified.

John W. Lenz

intelligence and human experience cannot answer timeless questions with certainty. Does this necessarily lead to despair? I think not, though some may be despondent upon first hearing this, and others may be unable to face it. There is another possibility: to treat skepticism as a warning—a warning to avoid arrogant dogmatism; a warning to be tolerant of the other person's beliefs, since, in many cases, we have no better basis for our beliefs than she does for hers. Most of all, Hume reminds us that it is better to end in honest doubt than in dishonest belief.

Hume, the archetypal skeptic, suggests that a person will always be more than philosophy, religion, or science can hope to know:

> Man is a reasonable being; and as such, receives from science his proper food and nourishment: But so narrow are the bounds of human understanding, that little satisfaction can be hoped for in this particular, either from the extent of security or his acquisitions. Man is a sociable, no less than a reasonable being: But neither can he always enjoy company agreeable and amusing, or preserve the proper relish for them. Man is also an active being; and from that disposition, as well as from the various necessities of human life, must submit to business and occupation: But the mind requires some relaxation, and cannot always support its bent to care and industry. It seems, then, that nature has pointed out a mixed kind of life as the most suitable to the human race, and secretly admonished them to allow none of these biases to *draw* too much, so as to incapacitate them for any other occupations and entertainments. Indulge your passion for science, says she, but let your science be human, and such as may have a direct reference to action and society. Abstruse thought and profound researches I prohibit, and will severely punish, by the pensive melancholy which they introduce, by the endless uncertainty in which they involve you, and by the cold reception which your pretended discoveries shall meet with, when communicated. Be a philosopher; but amidst all your philosophy, be still a [human being].[54]

When you reach the fork in the road, take it.

Yogi Berra

Summary of Main Points

1. Skepticism is both a school of philosophy and a general attitude. A skeptic is a person who demands clear, observable, undoubtable evidence based on experience before accepting any claim as true.

2. Empiricism is the belief that all knowledge is ultimately derived from the senses (experience). Empiricists believe that all ideas can be traced to sense data. There are no innate ideas. At birth the mind is a clean slate, or tabula rasa.

3. John Locke, the first of the three British empiricists, claimed that all ideas are copies of the things that caused the basic sensations they rest on. Today Locke's copy theory is known as the correspondence theory of truth: an idea

(or belief or thought) is true if whatever it refers to actually exists.

4. Although Locke rejected Descartes' rationalism and theory of innate ideas, he accepted a Cartesian type of *dualism*, in which mind and matter are viewed as different kinds of substance.

5. Locke distinguished between *primary qualities* and *secondary qualities*. Primary qualities are sensible qualities that exist independently of any perceiver (shape, size, location, motion, and such). Secondary qualities are qualities whose existence depends on a perceiver (color, sound, taste, texture, and such).

6. The correspondence theory generates what is called the egocentric predicament: If all knowledge comes in the form of my own ideas, how can I verify the existence of anything external to them?

7. Locke's successor, George Berkeley, rejected the copy theory, pointing out that ideas are constantly changing. There is no fixed "thing" to copy; we know only perceptions. Berkeley's formula is *esse est percipi*: to be is to be perceived. This view is known as idealism or immaterialism.

8. Perception, however, cannot account for ideas such as the self or the apparent continuity of experiences—for example, that a burning candle is shorter if we return to look at it after being away for a time. Berkeley shied away from the logical consequences of immaterialism and posited the existence of a universal perceiver (God) to account for the existence of the external world and regularity of nature.

9. The third British empiricist, David Hume, continued the epistemological turn by rejecting overly abstract, obscure, bloated metaphysical speculation as meaningless and irrelevant to the lives of ordinary people. He asserted that no metaphysical issue was ever clearly and thoroughly settled.

10. Hume modified Locke's theory of ideas by distinguishing between two kinds of perceptions: Ideas are faint copies of impressions, which are intense. All ideas can be traced to the impressions on which they are based. All ideas are derived from experience.

11. Hume established the empirical criterion of meaning: All meaningful ideas can be traced to sense experience (impressions). Beliefs that cannot be traced to sense experience are technically not ideas at all; they are meaningless utterances. Strict application of the empirical criterion of meaning led Hume to skeptical conclusions regarding some of our most fundamental beliefs. (Locke and Berkeley deviated from strict empiricism rather than accept skeptical conclusions.)

12. Applying the empirical criterion of meaning, Hume argued that we have no idea of the self; the self is only a bundle of impressions, and identity is a mental act, not a property of things. Therefore, personal immortality is a meaningless concept.

13. Hume thought that imagination, not reason or experience, accounts for the persistence of our belief in the independent existence of an external world. Imagination ultimately overrides reason, and we cannot help believing in an independent, ordered, external world. We can accept the strict limits of reason only temporarily; we cannot live by them alone.

14. Strictly considered, Hume argues, there are no empirical grounds for belief in cause and effect. We experience only constant conjunction. Cause and effect are products of imagination.

15. The empirical criterion of meaning renders the cosmological argument, the argument from motion, and the ontological argument meaningless. The argument from design (teleological argument) fails because human experience cannot provide sufficient evidence of order on earth, much less order in the uni-

verse. It also denies the possibility of rationalistic ethics and claims that all moral judgments are based on sentiments.

16. In the end, Hume claimed that no one can actually live as a skeptic: Reason is, and ought to be, the slave of the passions.

Study Questions

1. What is skepticism?

2. Explain what is meant by the "epistemological turn." Briefly outline the stages of the turn from Descartes through Locke and Berkeley to Hume.

3. What is empiricism?

4. In your own words, reconstruct the basic empirical critique of rationalism.

5. What is the tabula rasa? What is its significance to Locke's empiricism?

6. What was Locke's egocentric predicament?

7. What is epistemological dualism?

8. Explain the philosophical significance of the question "Does a tree falling in the forest make a sound if no one is there to hear it?"

9. What is immaterialism?

10. Was David Hume an atheist? Explain.

11. Explain how Hume distinguished between impressions and ideas. Why is the distinction important to his philosophy?

12. What is the empirical criterion of meaning? Explain by applying it to an example of your own choosing.

13. How does Hume explain the self?

14. In your own words, characterize Hume's position regarding personal identity and immortality.

15. How does Hume account for the external world?

16. Sketch Hume's analysis of cause and effect.

17. First summarize, then analyze Hume's critique of the argument from design.

18. Summarize Hume's critique of rationalistic ethics. Then construct a Humean analysis of some contemporary moral issue. What are the advantages of Hume's approach? The disadvantages?

19. What does Hume mean when he says, "I am ready to throw all my books and papers into the fire, and resolve never more to renounce the pleasures of life for the sake of reasoning and philosophy"?

The Universalist
Immanuel Kant

Two things fill the mind with ever new and increasing admiration
and awe . . . the starry heavens above and the moral law within.

Immanuel Kant

Moral issues confront us daily. We live in a time troubled by intense moral controversies concerning abortion, euthanasia, affirmative action, capital punishment, substance abuse, monetary fraud, governmental deception, the environment, aid to the homeless, welfare, the rights of disabled persons, parental influence in the schools, pornography, AIDS, smoking in public, and sexual conduct. Such issues have political, financial, legal, religious, and psychological aspects. But in their *moral dimensions* they touch upon our most fundamental values concerning good and bad, personal worth and character, respect for ourselves and others—in sum, what it means to be a human being.

The word **moral** comes from the Latin *moralis*, meaning "custom," "manner," or "conduct." Moral refers to what people consider good or bad, right or wrong. There are two contrasting words: **nonmoral (amoral)** and **immoral**. The *moral-nonmoral* distinction is *descriptive*. It makes no value judgment and only distinguishes moral concerns from such nonmoral ones as economic, mechanical, nutritional, and so on. The *moral-immoral* distinction is *prescriptive*; it makes a value judgment about what we ought to do. The distinction between moral and immoral is equivalent to that between right and wrong or good and bad.

The moral dimension confronts us in courtrooms, classrooms, at work, and at home, as we try to determine who is or is not *responsible* for this or that act. Moral responsibility is different from the factual issue of determining who did what. It has to do with punishment or forgiveness; it affects whether we see a sexual offender as bad or sick, whether we scold a child or hug her, whether a criminal defendant is imprisoned, hospitalized, or released. Morality seems to be inseparable from responsibility.

Responsibility, in turn, implies freedom of choice, the ability to decide on one course of action over another, to think and behave one way instead of another way. For example, a person unwillingly drugged is not held morally accountable for actions performed under the influence of the drug, but a person who willingly gets drunk and then drives probably is.

MORAL

From the Latin *moralis*, meaning "custom," "manner," or "conduct"; refers to what people consider good or bad, right or wrong; used descriptively as a contrast to amoral or nonmoral and prescriptively as a contrast to immoral.

NONMORAL (AMORAL)

Not pertaining to moral; a value-neutral descriptive claim or classification.

IMMORAL

Morally wrong, bad, or not right; a moral value judgment or prescriptive claim.

Lawyers, theologians, psychologists, and parents continually wrestle with issues of free, responsible choice. Yet scientific evidence of causal patterns suggests that more and more conduct once labeled immoral may be beyond our control. We learn that some children who are abused grow up to abuse. Alcoholism may have a genetic component or at least a family pattern. Children raised without stable parental supervision seem to turn to crime more often than children from other backgrounds. Children whose families own and read lots of books tend to be better students than those whose families don't. Bio-psychologists and geneticists continue to discover physical and chemical "causes" of behavior. Studies reveal that identical twins separated at very young ages and raised without contact often grow up to get the same kind of job, marry people with the same name, have the same kinds of cars and pets, even like the same brand of toothpaste!

We cannot doubt the progress science has made since the seventeenth century in understanding human behavior. We can hardly doubt that some factors in our lives *make* us who we are. But if all nature is *governed* by laws of chemistry and physics, laws that admit of no exceptions, then I can no more be held responsible for helping you across the street than you can be held responsible for striking me with an ax because you're bored. If even our tastes in toothpaste are determined by genetic influences, how can we ever hold anyone responsible for anything? And if we cannot, how do we justify moral sanctions? If life loses its moral dimension, is it worth living? Stripped of the possibility of moral choice, how different am I from any other animal? What is the purpose of morally praising or blaming behavior if it *cannot be otherwise*?

Philosophical Query

Think for a moment about a nonmoral world, a world in which no one is held morally accountable. In such a world, every action would be viewed as the inevitable result of genetic, social, and historical causes. What are the advantages of such a view? The disadvantages? Think about some time when you made an excuse for yourself, claiming that you "couldn't help" doing or not doing something. What is gained and lost by making such excuses?

Without responsibility, there is no goodness. So, at least, feared and reasoned one of the most important philosophers of all time. (And the science of his day was much less sophisticated than today's science. Imagine his fears if he lived now.) Immanuel Kant attempted to meet the challenge of science to human freedom and responsibility by completing the epistemological turn begun by René Descartes and David Hume (see Chapters 8 and 9). He attempted to refute Hume's critique of rationalistic ethics by showing that morality is based on reason, not sentiment.

> [T]he Enlightenment has not remained incomplete, but unenlightened.
>
> *H. Böhme and*
> *G. Böhme*

The Little Professor

Immanuel Kant (1724–1804) was born in Königsberg in what was then known as East Prussia (now Kaliningrad in the former Soviet Union). His parents were poor but devout members of a fundamentalist Protestant sect known as Pietism. Pietists rejected the idea of imposing a church and priests between the individual and God, preferring immediate personal appeal to God. They emphasized faith and repentance, and lived severe, puritanical lives.

When he was eight years old Kant was sent to a school founded by a local Pietist preacher. The regimen was exceptionally strict, beginning daily at five-thirty in the morning. Students received an hour's daily instruction in Pietism, and each class period concluded with a prayer. Sundays were devoted almost completely to religious activity. Later in life, Kant said that he resented the school's heavy emphasis on a theology of terror and piety—fear of hell and trembling before a vision of a wrathful God. Yet he never lost his regard for righteousness and moral severity. As an old man he spoke respectfully of his parents' faith, saying, "People may say what they will of Pietism. Those in whom it was sincere were worthy of honor. They possessed the highest thing that man can have—the quiet, the content, the inner peace, which no suffering can disturb."[1]

At the age of sixteen, Kant entered the University of Königsberg, where he studied for six years. Upon leaving the university, he refused a lucrative offer to become a Lutheran minister, choosing instead to continue his studies. For the next nine years he meagerly supported himself as a private tutor. In 1755, Kant received the equivalent of today's doctoral degree. This earned him the privilege of lecturing at the university as a *Privatdozent*, a private teacher whose salary was paid directly by his students. The more students he attracted and retained, the more money he earned. Kant became a popular lecturer, and in 1770, when he was forty-six, the university hired Kant as a professor of logic and metaphysics. Though the salary was small, Kant was pleased with his improved status.

The Solitary Scholar

For the most part, Kant's life is noteworthy for not being noteworthy. He probably never traveled more than sixty miles from his birthplace in his entire life. One biographer said, "Kant's life was like the most regular of regular verbs," to which another added, "But it was not a *conjugated* verb. For Kant never married."[2]

He lived most of his life on a rigid schedule. The poet Heinrich Heine described Kant's penchant for routine:

> I do not believe that the great cathedral clock of this city accomplished its day's work in a less passionate and more regular way than its

Immanuel Kant

It is precisely in knowing its limits that philosophy consists.

Immanuel Kant

When I could have used a wife, I could not support one; and when I could support one, I no longer needed any.

Immanuel Kant

countryman, Immanuel Kant. Rising from bed, coffee-drinking, writing, lecturing, eating, walking, everything had its fixed time: and the
neighbors knew that it must be exactly half past four when they saw
Professor Kant, in his gray coat, with his cane in his hand, step out
of his housedoor, and move toward the little lime tree avenue, which
is named after him, the Philosopher's Walk. Eight times he walked
up and down that walk at every season of the year, and when the
weather was bad, or the gray clouds threatened rain, his servant, old
Lampe, was seen anxiously following him with a large umbrella
under his arm like an image of providence.[3]

Kant is reported to have missed his walk only once, when he became so
absorbed in reading Rousseau's *Emile* that he forgot to take it.

Kant was always in frail health, but not apparently seriously ill for the
greater part of his life. A near obsession with living a long time, coupled
with physical frailty, seems to have inclined him to hypochondria. A biographical sketch suggests that this, added to the severity of his early Pietist
education, may account for Kant's famous need for order and regulation.[4]
He kept favorite objects in exactly the same location, and could become
severely upset if a pair of scissors or a coffee cup was not in its proper place.

Kant was physically and emotionally distant from his sisters and brother.
Although he helped them financially, he appears not to have exchanged a
single word with his sisters for some twenty-five years.[5] On the other hand,
Kant was friendly with younger scholars and other friends. As a younger
man he was a welcome guest and enjoyed a modest reputation as a con-
versationalist in the Königsberg social set. He dressed as well as he could
in carefully tailored, if inexpensive, clothes, and enjoyed playing cards
and billiards. He was also something of a gossip. This social activity did
not last very long, however.

Kant increasingly distanced himself from others, becoming more and
more reclusive. The German language has two forms of the second-person
pronoun (*you*). One is formal, the other is personal or intimate. Kant addressed only two or three friends in the personal way, and ultimately disliked using a personal tone even with them.[6] Yet he cared enough about his
servant Lampe to have said, "Old Lampe must have a God, or else the poor
man cannot be happy; and people really ought to be happy in this world.
Practical common sense *requires* it. Very well, then, let practical reason
guarantee it."[7]

The Writer

Kant was a prolific writer. His works include the difficult but revolutionary
Critique of Pure Reason (1781 and a second edition in 1787), *Prolegomena to Any Future Metaphysics* (1783), *Foundations of the Metaphysics*

A Beloved Teacher

I have had the good fortune to know a philosopher who was my teacher. In the prime of his life he possessed the joyous courage of youth, and this also, as I believe, attended him to extreme old age. His open, thoughtful brow was the seat of untroubled cheerfulness and joy, his conversation was full of ideas most suggestive. He had at his service jest, wittcism, and humorous fancy, and his lectures were at once instructive and most entertaining. . . . No cabal or sect, no prejudice or reverence for a name, had the slightest influence with him in opposition to the extension and promotion of truth. He encouraged and gently compelled his hearers to think for themselves. . . . This man, whom I name with the greatest gratitude and reverence, is Immanuel Kant; his image stands before me, and is dear to me.

Johann Gottfried Herder (1744–1803) Quoted by Will and Ariel Durant in *Rousseau and Revolution*, vol. 10 of *The Story of Civilization* (New York: Simon & Schuster, 1967), p. 532.

of Morals (1785), *Critique of Practical Reason* (1788), *Critique of Judgment* (1790), and *Religion Within the Limits of Reason Alone* (1793).

The *Critique of Pure Reason* is one of the most difficult books ever written. Philosophy majors approach it with dread and then forever after boast proudly if they manage to read the entire thing. Kant once said that he did not fear being refuted; he feared not being understood. He had good reason to fear. On August 16, 1783, he wrote that his work was

the result of reflection which occupied me for at least twelve years. I brought it to completion in the greatest haste within four or five months, giving the closest attention to its contents, but with little thought of the exposition, or of rendering it easy of comprehension by the reader—a decision which I have never regretted, since otherwise, had I longer delayed and sought to give a more popular form, the work would probably never have been completed at all.[8]

Kant admitted that he deliberately left out illustrative examples because they would just add length to an already massive work. Besides, he added, examples are only necessary for popular appeal "and this work can never be made suitable for popular consumption."[9] When he sent the metaphysician Marcus Herz the manuscript of the *Critique of Pure Reason*, Herz sent it back only half read, saying, "If I finish it I am afraid I shall go mad."[10]

Kant's work was made difficult by another factor: Because he was trying to express new concepts, he felt that he had to invent new meanings for Latin terms or coin new phrases in German; he also gave his own unusual meanings to common terms and sometimes used the same term to mean different things. All of that notwithstanding, the little professor's big, difficult books forever altered Western thinking.

One of the mistakes oftenest committed, and which are the sources of the greatest practical errors in human affairs, is that of supposing that the same name always stands for the same aggregation of ideas.

John Stuart Mill

Kant retired from public lecturing in 1797, and although he physically declined, he remained a prolific writer. Immanuel Kant died a lonely old man who had never seen a mountain or the sea. Yet he shook the foundations of Western philosophy to such an extent that it has been said that whether or not philosophers agree or disagree with Kant, they must face him. Above his grave in the Königsberg cathedral his own words are inscribed, "The starry heavens above me; the moral law within me."

The philosopher-poet Friedrich Schiller, referring to the richness, complexity, and importance of Kant's philosophy, as well as its impact on the many philosophers whose work is in one way or another a response to Kant's, said, "See how a single rich man has given a living to a number of beggars."[11]

Seeds of Revolution

Kant's work was important and troubling, for it included devastating critiques of the dominant philosophical schools of the day (rationalism and empiricism), as well as popular theology. It is said that some clergymen called Immanuel Kant a dog, while others called their dogs Immanuel Kant.

When Kant was over seventy, he was even threatened by Frederick William II, King of Prussia, with "unpleasant consequences for yourself" if Kant continued to "misuse your philosophy to undermine and debase many of the most important and fundamental doctrines of the Holy Scriptures and Christianity; how, namely, you have done this in your book, *Religion Within the Limits of Reason Alone.*"[12] Kant prudently informed the king that his work was meant for the scholarly community and not the general public but, nonetheless, promised to "refrain from all public statements on religion, both natural and revealed."[13] In the end, though, the Prussian state fell apart, whereas by 1800 Kant's work dominated German intellectual life.

It is indeed true that I think many things with the cleverest conviction, and to my great satisfaction, which I never have the courage to say, but I never say anything that I do not think.

Immanuel Kant

From Enlightenment to Despair

The Enlightenment, sometimes called the Age of Reason, began in 1637 with Descartes' cogito: "I think, therefore I am."[14] This was an age shaped by the scientific revolution and by a shift in emphasis in philosophy from metaphysics to epistemology. Historian of philosophy W. T. Jones says that *optimism* is the one word that best characterizes the Enlightenment of the seventeenth and eighteenth centuries.[15]

Enlightenment thinkers reduced God to the role of spectator, as they discovered more and more mechanical laws to explain the operations of nature. Their faith lay in the orderly, ultimately understandable workings

This illustration of a print shop from Denis Diederot's Encyclopédie *illustrates the Enlightenment's optimistic faith in the spread of knowledge through free exchange of ideas. Does today's interest in the Internet reflect similar faith in the spread of knowledge through free exchange of ideas? Is the spread of information through free exchange of ideas something different?*

of nature, and in human reason as the only tool necessary to ensure progress and improvement of the human condition. They assumed that the scientific method would unlock all the mysteries of the universe. Given the regularity of the heavens and the discovery of laws of physics and astronomy, it was a simple step to conclude that God (if there was a God) had created a universe of such regularity and order that He no longer bothered running it. Further, having imbued us with reason, God had no need to govern or rescue us.

Disagreeing over exactly what "reason" is, Enlightenment champions of reason were nonetheless convinced that all people (with the exception of "idiots") possessed an innate, virtually equal capacity for rational thinking. If this is true, they concluded, then a proper education will enable everyone to live well. You might recognize this optimistic faith in science, reason, and universal education as a fundamental principle of American thinking. Indeed, the framers of our Constitution were children of the Enlightenment who believed that science and universal education would combine to produce a rational, free, ever-progressing society.

In his essay *What Is Enlightenment?* Kant eloquently expresses the age's equation of rational enlightenment with human freedom:

> *Sapere aude!*—Dare to reason! Have the courage to use your own minds!—is the motto of the enlightenment.
>
> Laziness and cowardice explain why so many men . . . remain under a life-long tutelage and why it is so easy for some men to set themselves up as the guardians of all the rest. . . . If I have a book which understands for me, a pastor who has a conscience for me, a

The life of Immanuel Kant is hard to describe; he had neither life nor history in the proper sense of the words.

Heinrich Heine

A world without absolute, unchallengable norms, without epistemological certainty, is a world of ultimate Protestantism: every man becomes his own philosopher, his own arbiter of the true and the real.

Richard Ruland and Malcolm Bradbury

The products of reason are not uniformly beneficial. The French Revolution began with a universal declaration of human rights and ended in the Reign of Terror when the mob defeated reason.

doctor who decides my diet, I need not trouble myself. If I am willing to pay, I need not think. Others will do it for me.[16]

Kant's faith in rational intelligence was so great that he claimed a "race of devils" could produce a sound community if they were intelligent. All that was needed, he thought, was to apply reason to the problems of knowledge and conduct.

Philosophical Query

Reflect on what Kant is saying about "tutelage" and about paying others to think for us. What contemporary examples can you think of? Also, beginning with the Sophists' early efforts at selling success and happiness, what historical examples of this tendency come to mind?

Alas, the products of reason are not uniformly beneficial. Then, as now, the technology made possible by scientific discoveries caused harm as well as benefit. For example, former peasants and farm laborers were drawn to large urban centers by the promise of employment; once there, they were easily exploited. The dirty, crowded slums that resulted made a stark contrast to the orderly serenity of the astronomers' heavens and the physicists' belief that nature never does anything without a purpose. The French Revolution, which began as a reasoned call to universal rights and freedoms in support of human dignity, ended in an irrational bloodbath, reason defeated by the mob. It was so horrible that we now know it as the Reign of Terror. In France and other parts of Europe, notably Kant's Prus-

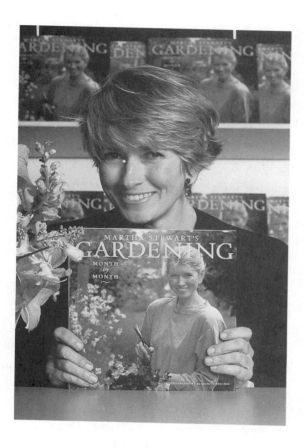

Kant hoped that the Enlightenment would free us from what he characterized as a kind of "self-imposed tutelage" that results from letting others think for us. What do you think is the difference between rational reliance on the expertise of others and "self-imposed tutelage"? Do you think that the enormous success of advice givers like Martha Stewart is due to self-imposed tutelage on the part of her customers?

sia, rulers and rigid absolutists reasserted control over "freethinkers, skeptics, and atheists," often lumping all scientific or philosophic thinkers into one dangerous group.

The optimism that lay behind Descartes' faith in reason to produce certainty and behind science's faith in experience to produce knowledge seemed to be leading only to confusion and despair. As Kant pointed out, philosophy—especially since Hume—was of little help in refuting the charges against it. It was, Kant said, "a scandal to philosophy and to human reason in general that the existence of things outside us . . . must be accepted merely on *faith*, and that if anyone thinks it good to doubt their existence, we are unable to counter his doubts by any satisfactory proof."[17]

A Scandal in Philosophy

In Chapter 9, we saw how radical Hume's skepticism was. Because Hume was one of the most logically consistent philosophers of his or any time, his critique of empiricism led him to such disturbing conclusions as we

But Hume suffered the usual misfortune of metaphysicians, of not being understood. It is positively painful to see how utterly his opponents . . . missed the point of the problem; for while they were ever taking for granted that which he doubted, and demonstrating with zeal and often with impudence that which he never thought of doubting, they so misconstrued his valuable suggestion that everything remained in its old condition, as if nothing happened.

Immanuel Kant

I freely admit it was David Hume's remark that first, many years ago, interrupted my dogmatic slumber and gave a completely different direction to my inquiries in the field of speculative philosophy.

Immanuel Kant

can never know cause and effect, the self, or the external world, and that moral judgments are somehow like matters of taste. Hume's withering *Dialogues Concerning Natural Religion* applied a strictly rational analysis to cherished arguments for the existence of God, and showed them to be illogical and unpersuasive. With his strict understanding of knowledge and reason, Hume concluded that reason is and ought to be "the slave of the passions." Hume's philosophy made the external world unknowable and rendered reason impotent to unlock the secrets of nature. His critique of rationalistic ethics seemed to show that reason was utterly incapable of motivating people. In other words, Hume undercut the very essence of Enlightenment thinking.

Kant was one of those rare thinkers who fully realized the consequences of Hume's relentless attack on the scope of reason. In the preface of his *Prolegomena to Any Future Metaphysics* he wrote:

> Since the origin of metaphysics so far as we know its history, nothing has ever happened which could have been more decisive to its fate than the attack made upon it by David Hume. He threw no light on this species of knowledge, but he certainly struck a spark by which light might have been kindled had it caught some inflammable substance and had its smouldering fire been carefully nursed and developed.
>
> . . . However hasty and mistaken Hume's inference may appear, it was at least founded upon investigation, and this investigation deserved the concentration of the brighter spirits of his day as well as determined efforts on their part to discover, if possible, a happier solution of the problem in the sense proposed by him. . . .
>
> But Hume suffered the usual misfortune of metaphysicians, of not being understood. It is positively painful to see how utterly his opponents . . . missed the point of the problem; for while they were ever taking for granted that which he doubted, and demonstrating with zeal and often with impudence that which he never thought of doubting, they so misconstrued his valuable suggestion that everything remained in its old condition, as if nothing happened.[18]

Kant knew he must somehow meet Hume's challenge and show that reason is potent, that our knowledge of causes and effects is real and not illusory, and that the external world and the self can be grounded in more than animal faith or wishful thinking.

The seeds of what Kant referred to as a "scandal" in philosophy actually were planted when Descartes doubted his own existence and divided everything into two completely distinct substances: minds and bodies. Descartes was never able to satisfactorily account for mind-body interaction or to establish with certainty the existence of an external, material world. Although Descartes refused to follow his rationalistic premises to their logical conclusions, the Continental rationalists who came after him did. Because their model of certainty was mathematical and geometric, they moved further and further away from experience. As a result, they established grand systems of logical relationships ungrounded in observation or perception.

The British empiricists chose another tack, viewing the human mind as the passive receiver of impressions and experiences. But this view leads to the unfortunate conclusion that all certain knowledge is confined to ideas. Ironically, beginning with experience, the empiricists were unable to get back to it. The result was Hume's admission that we must believe in an external world, in selves, and in causes and effects, without ever knowing them.

As it has so often in history, scientific progress challenged the dominant philosophies of the day. As Kant noted, something was drastically wrong with philosophy if between them the two major philosophical schools at the time denied the importance of perception, denied the possibility of knowledge of cause and effect, denied the verifiable existence of the external world, and rendered reason impotent as a motivator in human affairs, while science—not to mention common sense and everyday experience—clearly showed otherwise.

You might ask why Kant did not abandon philosophy, if it was so out of touch, so bizarre? Why not just accept the supremacy of science and let philosophy die of irrelevance? Kant found this course unsatisfying, for science was unveiling a mechanistic universe in which everything (at least once fully understood) would ultimately be shown to follow universal, unchanging laws of nature. If such a picture is complete and accurate, then God is unnecessary, free will is an illusion, and morality is impossible. If we have no choice but to follow "laws of nature," then values as they are usually understood disappear. Our behavior is only more complex than that of rocks or worms—it is not different in kind. The murderer and the saint are both following inescapable patterns of cause and effect.

How, Kant asked, could science, which clearly made progress, be headed for conclusions that reduced human life to blind mechanism? How could two radically different philosophies each reach such odd, unacceptable results? Was it possible to synthesize science with the good parts of rationalism and empiricism in a way that would give a rational account of the world without stripping us of moral worth and dignity? Surely there had to be better alternatives than the cold, unfree world of science or the unverifiable, impractical worlds of rationalistic and skeptical philosophy.

> [T]he demand for intellectual honesty is itself dishonest. . . . Rather, knowledge comes to us through a network of prejudices, opinions, innervations, self-corrections, presuppositions and exaggerations.
>
> *Theodor Adorno*

> If I am asked "What is good?" my answer is that good is good, and that is the end of the matter. Or if I am asked "How is good to be defined?" my answer is that it cannot be defined, and that is all I have to say about it.
>
> *G. E. Moore*

Philosophical Query

Do you think morality must disappear if everything we do can be explained according to scientific laws and patterns? Could there be another kind of morality based on laws of behavior and bio-psychology? Why or why not? What is lost in the purely "scientific" view? Anything important? Explain.

Kant's Copernican Revolution

In response to the "scandal in philosophy," Kant turned to an analysis (which he called a critique) of *how* knowledge is possible. In the process, he discovered an underlying *structure* imposed by the mind on the sensations and perceptions it encounters. We can think of this structure as the *formal* component of knowing. For this reason, Kant is known as a formalist. Kant theorized that neither reason by itself nor sensation by itself can give us knowledge of the external world. Knowledge is the result of the interaction between the mind and sensation. Knowledge and experience are shaped, structured, or formed by special regulative ideas called *categories*. This theory is known as **Kantian formalism,** or *Kantian idealism*, or *transcendental idealism*.

Kant noted that Descartes' principal error began with a failure to understand scientific method. Galileo had changed science by establishing a "common plan of procedure," a method for studying phenomena. Though Descartes had understood the importance of method, he had not fully understood that the *scientific* method is *both* empirical *and* rational. Kant realized that the empiricists were guilty of a similar error of incompleteness by discounting the importance of reason. Knowledge, as the scientific method shows, consists of both a rational and a perceptual (empirical) component. It requires both a subject (a knowing mind) and an object (that which is known).

The common belief during Kant's time, however, was that truth occurs when ideas in the mind agree with external conditions or objects, the "copy theory" (see Chapter 9). For example, if I think this book has a red cover, my idea is true if the cover actually is red. But as Kant realized, if all knowledge fits that model, we could never discover general laws of nature. We could discover only that *this* apple falls, not that all bodies are subject to gravity, because we never experience all bodies. Hume understood this but was willing to limit the domain of knowledge to particulars, in the end asserting that we could *only believe in* the most important aspects of our existence: the regularity of experience, the existence of an external world, the existence of a unified self, cause and effect, and a moral order.

If we accept Hume's initial premises, his conclusions follow. However, close inspection of the way science is actually done shows that scientists make precisely the kinds of generalizations Hume's *theory* says we cannot make. As Kant pointed out, *when a theory results in conclusions that are clearly inconsistent with experience, real-world evidence must outweigh theoretical consistency.* And everyday experience shows that knowledge of causes and effects, the external world, the self, and so on exists.

The scientific method is obviously more reliable and complete than Hume's philosophy. How do they differ? Kant pointed out that scientific thinking involves the *activity* of asking questions and framing hypotheses.

KANTIAN FORMALISM

(also known as *Kantian idealism* and *transcendental idealism*) Theory that knowledge is the result of the interaction between the mind and sensation, and structured by regulative ideas called categories.

There will always be metaphysics in the world, and what is more, in everyone, especially in every thinking man.

Immanuel Kant

It is not merely the passive recording of whatever happens; it requires the *active* setting up of controlled experimental conditions.[19] And this suggests that knowledge is a kind of *interaction*, a two-way street between the knower (the subject) and the known (the object).

Kant realized that he was proposing to change fundamental assumptions about the structure of knowledge, much as Copernicus had changed our assumptions about the structure of the universe. After astronomers had failed for centuries to make consistent sense of an earth-centered universe, Copernicus proposed the revolutionary hypothesis: that the sun is at the center, that the earth is part of a solar system. This assumption dissolved the great difficulties of the past and produced new, predictable knowledge. Kant was proposing a Copernican revolution in philosophy: Kant would reverse the course of his philosophical predecessors and assume that *instead of the mind having to conform to what can be known, what can be known must conform to the mind.*

Critical Philosophy

Kant proposed "a critical inquiry into the faculty of reason with reference to all the knowledge which it may strive to attain independently of reason." That is, he was proposing a critical reexamination of metaphysics. Metaphysics, as distinct from science, is an attempt to acquire and systematize knowledge derived by reason, not experience. Kant referred to earlier metaphysical philosophies as *dogmatic*, by which he meant, among other things, that they were *uncritical efforts* to understand the nature of whatever lies beyond immediate experience.

Kant asked a profoundly basic question: *Is metaphysics possible?* Can we know things beyond immediate experience? That is, does the human mind have the capacity for a priori knowledge, knowledge derived from reason without reference to sense experience (see Chapters 8 and 9)?

Kant called his attempt to discover whether a priori knowledge is possible *critical philosophy*. Hume had insisted that all knowledge begins in experience with sense impressions. But Hume confused knowledge that is *triggered by* experience with knowledge that is *based on* experience. Kant raised the possibility that our "faculty of knowledge" (mind, for short) might add something to the raw data of experience. Because experience *triggers* and hence *accompanies* all knowledge, we may fail to notice the effects the mind has on experience:

> But though all our knowledge begins with experience, it does not follow that it all arises out of experience. For it may well be that even our empirical knowledge is made up of what we receive through impressions and of what our own faculty of knowledge (sensible knowledge serving merely as the occasion) supplies from itself. If our faculty of knowledge makes any such addition, it may be that we are not in a

Hitherto it has been assumed that all our knowledge must conform to objects. But all attempts to extend our knowledge of objects by establishing something in regard to them by means of concepts have, on this assumption, ended in failure. We must, therefore, make trial whether we may not have more success if we suppose that objects must conform to our knowledge.

Immanuel Kant

position to distinguish it from the raw material, until with long practice of attention we have become skilled in separating it.

This, then, is a question which at least calls for closer examination, and does not allow of any offhand answer:—whether there is any knowledge that is thus independent of experience and even of all impressions of the senses. Such knowledge is entitled *a priori*, and distinguished from the *empirical*, which has its sources *a posteriori*, that is, in experience.[20]

CRITICAL PHILOSOPHY

Kant's term for his effort to assess the nature and limits of "pure reason," unadulterated by experience, in order to identify the actual relationship of the mind to knowledge.

Critical philosophy is an effort to assess the nature and limits of "pure reason," reason unadulterated by experience, in an effort to identify the actual relationship of the mind to knowledge. "Pure knowledge" is not morally pure, but refers, rather, to *independent reasoning* (a priori reasoning) to knowledge *not derived from* the senses.

Descartes began the epistemological turn by focusing on the mind as a rational substance. But by concentrating on the mind's rational function he ignored its *organizing function*, and so was unable to avoid generating conclusions that do not square with experience. The British empiricists, concluding with Hume, took the second step and demonstrated both the importance of experience and the limits of a priori reason. So strict was Hume's emphasis on experience as the sole source of knowledge that, coupled with the empiricists' view of the mind as a passive, neutral blank tablet, he was forced to conclude we cannot "know" that anything happens of necessity or even that we have a self.

Kant proposed a radical alternative, which we can think of as the third and final step of the epistemological turn: a critical analysis of what kind of knowledge we actually have based on a new view of the mind as actively interacting with impressions and perceptions.

Phenomena and Noumena

According to Kant, our knowledge is *formed* by two things: our actual experiences *and* the mind's faculties of judgment, called *categories of understanding*. This means we cannot know reality as it is. We can know reality only as it is organized by human understanding. **Phenomenal reality** is Kant's term for the world as we experience it. **Noumenal reality** is his term for reality as it is independent of our perceptions, what we commonly call "objective reality."

PHENOMENAL REALITY

Kant's term for the world as we experience it.

NOUMENAL REALITY

Kant's term for reality as it is, independent of our perceptions; what is commonly called "objective reality."

All we can *know*, Kant reminds us, is perceived reality. This is not the same thing as saying that we each have our own private, subjective reality. All other things being equal, Kant says, the human mind imposes uniform categories on reality. Because the faculty of understanding is uniform, all functioning minds impose the same basic order on experience. Thus we might think of Kant's distinction as between *human reality* and *pure reality*.

Although we never experience pure reality, we can know (understand) that our minds do not just invent the world. In Kant's language, the mind imposes order on a world of things-in-themselves. Things-in-themselves are *noumena*, things as they exist independently of us. We know they exist, but we can never know them, because in the act of imposing order, the mind changes things-in-themselves to a comprehensible form.

For example, the human ear cannot hear the noumena—the full spectrum of air vibrations known as sound. We cannot hear the highest-pitched sounds a dog hears or the lowest pitches an elephant hears. Human beings would not know that these other wavelengths of sound exist without the help of dog and elephant ears or sensitive instruments. In respect to knowledge, then, we can know only what our human faculty of understanding is capable of processing.

Why make such a distinction, since we will never experience noumena? Kant's response is twofold. First, the distinction shows us the limits of human understanding. Second, such a distinction is necessary in order to establish a foundation for a moral philosophy capable of preserving our moral autonomy and sentiments in light of the onslaught from science and Humean philosophy. But to accomplish this second goal, Kant must first somehow connect human reality to pure reality. To do that, he turns to what he labels "regulative ideas."

Transcendental Ideas

Kant argues that although we cannot directly experience noumena, a special class of *transcendental ideas* bridges the gap between the phenomenal and noumenal worlds. According to Kant's terminology, certain sorts of ideas are called transcendental because they are the products of reason alone, and not the result of the mind's interaction with sensation. That is, they are to be distinguished from empirical ideas, which are validated by sense data (experience). Although transcendental ideas are not "grounded in" experience, they are, nonetheless, triggered by experience when we rely on them to impose unity on the totality of our experiences. That is, they "unify" or "make possible" having experience in the first place. Without some sort of unifying structure, Kant argues, the mind could not "experience" raw sense data. It would be meaningless, undifferentiated—unexperienced. Thus, transcendental ideas do not correspond to any specific experience, but they "make experience possible."

Kant identified three such transcendental ideas: the ideas of *self*, *cosmos* (totality), and *God*. Kant referred to them as *regulative ideas* because they "regulate" and synthesize experience on a grand scale.

Everything that has its basis in the nature of our powers must be appropriate to, and consistent with, their right employment—if we can

Nowadays everyone in the world is deluded about right and wrong, and confused about benefit and harm. Because so many people share this sickness, no one perceives that it is a sickness.

Lao Zi

only guard against a certain misunderstanding and so discover the proper direction of these powers. We are entitled, therefore, to suppose that transcendental ideas . . . have an excellent, and indeed indispensably necessary, regulative employment, namely, that of directing the understanding towards a certain goal upon which the routes marked out by all its rules converge.[21]

And thus I conclude the analytical solution of the main question which I had proposed: "How is metaphysics in general possible?" by ascending from the data of its actual use, as shown in its consequences, to the grounds of its possibility.

Immanuel Kant

According to Kant, pure reason synthesizes all our psychological activities into a unity by positing the idea of *self*:

The first [regulative] idea is the "I" itself, viewed simply as thinking nature or soul . . . ; in a word, the idea of a simple self-sustaining intelligence. [Reason operates] to represent all determinations as existing in a single subject, all powers, so far as possible, as derived from a single fundamental power, all change as belonging to the states of one and the same permanent being.[22]

Philosophical Query

Have you ever met or heard of someone with no idea of self? What would such a person be like? What about people with multiple personality disorder? One woman claims to have ninety-four "personalities." Would such a person have ninety-four "selves" too? Discuss.

Pure reason also attempts to lend unity to experience by synthesizing all events into a single totality or *cosmos*. Although the idea of cosmos helps organize and frame our experience, we cannot establish its actual existence. The idea of cosmos remains, for Kant, a deep instinctive need that reason satisfies. But it remains a "mere idea"—though a most important one.

The second regulative idea of merely speculative reason is the concept of the world in general. . . . The absolute totality of the series of . . . conditions . . . is an idea which can never be completely realised in the empirical employment of reason, but which yet serves as a rule that prescribes how we ought to proceed in dealing with such series. . . . Cosmological ideas are nothing but simply regulative principles, and are very far from positing . . . an actual totality.[23]

Philosophical Query

Think carefully about your own sense of the universe. How real is it to you? Do you know or think of it as an actual, existing thing? Or does it, upon reflection, serve a function along the lines that Kant suggests? Does it help organize and support your understanding in a "regulative" way? What are the implications of Kant's position in regard to scientific attempts to discover the origin of the universe and in regard to religious beliefs in creation?

God, or "the highest intelligence," is Kant's third regulative idea. The idea of God cannot be dismissed, since it serves a necessary, regulative function.

> The third idea of pure reason, which contains a merely relative sup-position of a being that is the sole and sufficient cause of all cosmo-logical series, is the idea of *God.* We have not the slightest ground to assume in an absolute manner [the existence of] the object of this idea.[24]

Although Kant says God, too, is a necessary "mere idea," he sometimes talks as if God is an existing entity. By "mere" or "pure" idea, Kant means that God is not the kind of thing that can be verified by an appeal to experience. We know that some people don't believe in God and that others dismiss the idea of God as unimportant. Kant, however, claims that it is not possible to dismiss the *idea of God,* since it forms one of the organizing structures or categories of reason.

Philosophical Query

Do you think it's possible for a human to never, ever consider the idea of God? Do you know anyone who never has? Is Kant perhaps onto some-thing, at least regarding the importance of the idea of God? How impor-tant and necessary (unavoidable) do you think the idea of God is to the human mind? Explain.

Kant goes on to say that we must act as if self, cosmos, and God refer to existing things, but that, as in the case of all noumena, there is no way empirically to verify that they do. God, self, and cosmos are in an impor-tant sense real. They refer to universal ideas that regulate human under-standing. But if the rest of Kant's epistemology is correct, they remain, like other things-in-themselves, known through the operations of reason, not through experience.

The Objectivity of Experience

In very simple terms, Kant's complex project attempts to show that experi-ence is possible only under a certain general condition: objectivity. In other words, if there is to be any experience at all (if we can "experience any-thing"), then, Kant argues, the world must be objective relative to the per-ceiver. There must be a real distinction between how the world seems to me and how the world is *in order for me to have any experience at all.*[25]

Crudely put, if there were no difference between the world and me, I could not even have an idea of "having an experience." But I do have ex-perience. Indeed, the skeptical arguments of Hume only make sense if Hume (or any skeptic) understands that he has experience. But experience itself presupposes precisely what the skeptic doubts: his own independent

Words are used of God and creatures in an analogical way.

Thomas Aquinas

In this enquiry I have made completeness my chief aim, and I venture to assert that there is not one single metaphysical problem which has not been solved, or the solution of which the key at least has not been supplied.

Immanuel Kant

existence as a unified, continuing self that is part of an objective order, subject to causal laws.[26]

Although commentators on Kant understandably disagree over the precise nature of his *argument* here, the disagreement seems to center on the concept of the self, which Kant calls "the transcendental unity of apperception." This is the unity of self that allows me to say (and experience) that this thought or this sensation belongs to *me*, belongs to *one thing*, belongs to a unity that exists prior to *any* empirical verification. For Kant, such a transcendental unity of apperception is necessary in order for *me* to have any experience—and, of course, without "me" the whole world ceases to exist.

And this awareness of transcendental unity is possible because I *am aware of my own existence and identity through time*. And I can only be aware of my identity through time because I situate or locate myself in a world of actually existing things, things that endure through time. Thus, these things have the capacity to be other than I perceive them. That is, they are not merely my perceptions. Thus, they must exist objectively.

You may need to study the preceding passages more than once, and may wish to do additional reading to help get a better grasp of Kant's complicated, but influential, critical philosophy. And your philosophy instructor may have other interpretations of Kant. That's not surprising given both the complexity of Kant's subject matter and his complex treatment of it.

Kant himself is inconsistent in his treatment of the noumenal world and regulative ideas, sometimes talking about them as mental constructs and other times suggesting they are existing entities. That's not surprising either, since, if he is correct, the human need for unity and transcendence is very strong. One defense of Kant's inconsistencies might be the force and power of regulative ideas. They may not give us new empirical knowledge, but they allow us to meet our persistent metaphysical longings for an ordered, objective world.

One of the great weaknesses of the strictest empirical theories of knowledge is that by ruling out knowledge of the existence of God, mind (soul), and other transcendental metaphysical beliefs, they fail to satisfy deep, nearly universal needs. They are sometimes said to rob life of its specialness or mystery. Kant deserves credit for recognizing and respecting these needs, and for offering a rigorous and sustained explanation and defense of the kind of thinking that springs from them. (Of course, longing for something to be true does not mean that it is true. And as philosophers, we do not want to accept as true whatever we deeply long for just because we long for it. So the timeless questions remain.)

... [A]s soon as a philosophy begins to believe in itself ... [, it] always creates the world in its own image, it cannot do otherwise; philosophy is this tyrannical drive itself, the most spiritual will to power, to "creation of the world," to *causa prima*.

Friedrich Nietzsche

Having at least a rudimentary sense of Kant's critical project and methods, we are ready to turn to a more accessible, and equally influential, aspect of Kantian philosophy—his categorical imperative and the universalist moral philosophy upon which it rests.

The Metaphysics of Morals

You may have identified a basic strategy throughout Kant's philosophy so far. Kant shows great respect for powerful and persistent ways of thinking, even if they seem difficult to justify philosophically. I have in mind, for example, the persistence of belief in cause and effect, self-identity, the external world, and God. To establish his "metaphysics of morals," Kant starts with the hypothesis that somehow such ideas can be justified *because we keep relying on them.* They must have more than just the psychological value Hume assigned them, given how they work in our lives and their apparent universality. Kant thinks it is important to analyze the content of such beliefs, the form they take, and their possible sources. He uses this analysis to draw a picture of the active faculty of understanding.

Practical Reason

Although there is only one reason, one faculty of understanding, Kant distinguishes two functions of reason, which he called theoretical reason and practical reason. **Theoretical reason**, including scientific reasoning, is confined to the empirical, phenomenal world. Interaction with the world of experience produces laws of behavior that force reason to view everything mechanically. Theoretical reason thus concludes that human beings, like all phenomena, are governed by cause and effect in the form of inescapable laws of nature. Limited by the way the mind can understand the phenomenal world, we must accept that there is no freedom on that level. If freedom is necessary for morality, we must find our freedom elsewhere.

Using the distinction between the phenomenal world and the noumenal world, Kant asserts that it is possible to be both determined, or unfree (in the phenomenal world), and free (in the noumenal world). We have a phenomenal self that falls under the laws of nature and behavior and a noumenal self that is free. Thus, free will exists in the noumenal world. This means we are free and morally responsible even though from the empirical, scientific view of life, we cannot *experience* our freedom but only *think of it.* It is a mistake to attempt an empirical proof of human freedom. Science describes the phenomenal world, but it cannot deal with the noumenal world.

According to Kant, we use **practical reason** to move beyond the phenomenal world to the moral dimension. Practical reason begins with knowledge about moral conduct and produces religious feelings and intuitions. Practical reason helps us deal with the moral freedom provided by free will. In *Critique of Practical Reason,* Kant says that no matter how many natural causes and sensations might "drive" a person, "they cannot produce [a state of] *being under obligation,* they cannot account for moral duty."[27] The feeling of duty comes from within; it comes from being rational.

THEORETICAL REASON

According to Kant, a function of reason confined to the empirical, phenomenal world.

PRACTICAL REASON

According to Kant, moral function of reason that produces religious feelings and intuitions based on knowledge of moral conduct.

Metaphysical Moments

The name metaphysics is apt to suggest something difficult, unusual, and remote. Yet it has its familiar side. Most of us have times at which, in reflection, we seem to be confronted not with any particular isolated problem or any particular aspect of our experience, but with experience, or life, or existence, *as a whole*. These might be called our metaphysical moments. It is not easy to give a detailed description of them and for our purpose it is not necessary. Indirectly and roughly, however, it is possible to identify them by saying that if they did not occur there would be no point in religion and little in many works of art and philosophy.

S. Körner
Kant (Baltimore: Penguin, 1955), p. 13.

Kant uses the term *practical* reason to indicate that we do not act on impulses and desires alone. We also act from *conscious choice* based on our general principles. In direct opposition to Hume's claim that reason cannot be a motivator, Kant argues that we can consciously act when no desire is involved at all.[28] Consider, for example, the kind of inner conflict you might experience between a strong desire to buy a new CD and your awareness of your duty to repay a friend from whom you borrowed money. You can choose to repay your friend because you ought to, even though you do not want to. (This is not the same thing as doing something to avoid feeling guilty: that does involve desire.)

Philosophical Query

What would a person be like who could choose only what he or she desired? Do you think it is possible to choose to do something if no desire whatsoever is involved? Explain.

The Moral Law Within

Imagine a world in which *no one* had any moral obligations. Would any rational creature desire to live in it? Kant answers with a resounding no! Therefore, he reasoned, morality is absolutely necessary for human relationships. But a moral code can't be discovered by simply conducting anthropological studies, that is, by looking at people's cultural and individual habits and tastes.

Empirical studies can identify only what people *actually do*; they cannot identify what we *ought to do*. Whereas Hume dealt with the is/ought (fact/value) issue by denying that "ought" refers to any fact (Chapter 9), it seemed obvious to Kant that the very essence of moral judgments involves *duty*, or ideas of what we ought to do. Again, Kant begins his inquiry with awareness of and respect for the way we actually think. He

notes that very few people consistently think of their own moral judgments as mere matters of custom or taste. Whether we actually live up to
our moral principles or not, we think of moral judgments as concerned
with how people ought to behave.

Thus, if we begin with the *actual form* of moral judgments as they
occur in our lives, we see that they are judgments of universal duty. As an
example, Kant offered the moral judgment "We ought to tell the truth,"
which he said has the same status as "Every change must have a cause."
(Hume rejected the idea of cause.) Just as we cannot begin to think of or
even experience anything without already assuming the principle of cause
and effect, Kant thought that we cannot function without a sense of duty.
Practical reason imposes the notion of *ought* on us.

Morality and practical reason rely on concepts that transcend particular facts and immediate experience. Practical reason deals with human
behavior and relationships by continually monitoring how we ought to behave. Further, practical reason goes beyond merely addressing how we
should behave in particular circumstances and generates universal principles that apply to everyone's behavior at all times in similar circumstances.

Moral judgement belongs, as does religious judgement, to a level of ignorance at which even the concept of the real, the distinction between the real and the imaginary, is lacking.

Friedrich Nietzsche

Philosophical Query

Psychologists have identified a character disorder that is labeled as either
"sociopathic" or "antisocial personality disorder." One component of
this diagnosis is that such people are amoral, lacking any conscience. Do
you know people without any sense of moral duty? What are they like?
Does the existence of such people mean there is no such thing as a necessary, universal moral law? Discuss.

For Kant, morality is a function of reason. Specifically, morality is based
on our consciousness of necessary and universal moral laws (or rules, as
Kant calls them). Moral rules of behavior differ from other, pragmatic
rules because they alone have the quality of being thought of as universal
and necessary. And since only a priori judgments are universal and necessary, moral judgments must be a priori. This is why the empiricists could
not discover them.

Thus the moral law cannot be discovered in actual behavior. It is a function of reason, a component of how we think. From this it follows that
only rational creatures can be moral or held morally accountable. It also
follows that any and all rational creatures are moral beings. The capacity
for reason is the source of morality. Reason imposes moral obligation.

The Good Will

Kant thought that virtually everyone has the capacity to make sound moral
judgments. Valid moral principles will be the same for everyone, just as
the truths of geometry or logic are. Thus, for Kant, goodness depends not

on our behavior but on our will, on what we intend to do if circumstances do not prevent it. Though some erroneously evaluate morality on the basis of conduct and the results of our actions, Kant insisted that morality was entirely a matter of reason and good will.

It's important to note that Kant conceives of the good will as a component of rationality. He also believes that "ought implies can," by which he means it must be possible for human beings to live up to their moral obligations. Yet circumstances sometimes prevent us from doing the good we want to do. I may sincerely wish to minister to the sick, but be physically or financially unable. I may diligently try to love my neighbor, only to be rebuffed by him. Thus I must not be morally judged on the consequences of what I actually do. Put another way, morality is a matter of motives.

> A good will is good not because of what it performs or effects, not by its aptness for the attainment of some proposed end, but simply by virtue of the volition, that is, it is good in itself, and considered by itself is to be esteemed much higher than all that can be brought about by it in favour of any inclination, nay, even of the sum-total of all inclinations. Even if it should happen that, owing to special disfavour of fortune, or the niggardly provision of a step-motherly nature, this will should wholly lack power to accomplish its purpose, if with its greatest efforts it should yet achieve nothing, and there should remain only the good will (not, to be sure, a mere wish, but the summoning of all means in our power), then, like a jewel, it would still shine by its own light, as a thing which has its whole value in itself. Its usefulness or fruitlessness can neither add to nor take away anything from this value.[29]

We must not, of course, confuse a good will with rather halfhearted good wishes. After all, "The road to hell is paved with good intentions." I have the will to do something, in Kant's words, only when I "summon all the means within my power." This is much more than merely wishing to be good. It is certainly more than a cheerful expression of moral platitudes.

Philosophical Query

Does the idea of a good will help our analysis of the sociopath? Discuss.

Inclinations, Wishes, Acts of Will

In Kantian terminology, decisions and actions based on impulse or desire are known as *inclinations*, and Kant was convinced that morality could not be "reduced to" inclinations because inclinations are notoriously unreliable and inconstant. Inclinations are not products of practical reason; indeed, they are not products of reason at all. We can see this clearly when we consider the behavior and motivations of dogs, cats, and infants. Dogs, cats, and infants have very strong inclinations: to eat this but not that, now

---

Morality is not properly the doctrine of how we should make ourselves happy, but how we should become worthy of happiness.

Immanuel Kant

The altruism which in my view underlies ethics is not to be confused with generalized affection for the human race. It is not a feeling.

Thomas Nagel

but not later, and so on. But in Kant's sense of the term, they do not have "a will," they cannot *act from a will*.

Now it is important to be clear here. "Having a will" and "acting from a will" have a precise meaning for Kant, a meaning connected to acting from "internal commands" or maxims that are the result of rational deliberation. So, although we sometimes call infants or pets "willful," from a Kantian point of view, they are merely manifesting powerful inclinations, not a will. *Willing X* requires consciously and deliberately committing ourselves to bringing about X. There is something "wholehearted" and conscious about willing.

We can see that Kant's strong sense of willing is not so far from everyday language as it might first appear if we consider what we mean by "willpower." We often lament lacking the willpower to stop smoking, start exercising, stop overeating, study for philosophy class, and so on. We say, "She meant well" and "If wishes were horses, then beggars would ride." In other words, we distinguish between merely "wanting," "wishing," or "being inclined," and actually *willing* something, seriously committing ourselves wholeheartedly, consciously, and consistently—regardless of our inclinations and desires. We do not ordinarily talk about "wish power" or "want power."

In contrast to inclinations, acts of will reflect autonomy, the capacity to choose clearly and freely for ourselves, without "outside" coercion or interference. With inclinations, it is as if "one part of me wants to be healthy but another part of me wants to enjoy a smoke now," and so on. Rather than making a focused, unified, wholehearted commitment to not smoke, I make a "halfhearted gesture."

When we will something, we issue ourselves a kind of internal command, or order, of the type: "I refuse to eat meat" or "I will not lie." These *subjective intentions* can be framed as *maxims*, the reason or rule according to which an act is done (or not done). In these two examples, maxims might be framed as "Do not eat meat" and "Do not lie." In a sense, when I will something, I pass a law, framed as my maxim—and I obey my own law. I am both a lawgiver and a servant of the law.

Kant's moral philosophy is his attempt to distinguish morally proper maxims and motives from morally unacceptable ones. Ultimately, Kant thought that he was able to identify the "supreme moral principle," the moral motive that distinguishes the good will from all other motives: the will to do our moral *duty*.

Moral Duty

Kant thought it was crucially important to distinguish moral motives from others. I might tell the truth to impress you or to avoid going to jail for perjury. Obviously, such considerations are not moral. I may give money to charity in order to cut my tax bill. I might do what I think God

Consider any morality with this in mind: what there is in it of "nature" teaches hatred of . . . any all-too-great freedom, and implants the need for limited horizons . . . and thus in a certain sense stupidity, as a condition of life and growth.

Friedrich Nietzsche

Men are good in one way but bad in many.

Aristotle

commands in order to go to heaven or to escape hell, but then my motive is hedonistic. Only when I do a thing solely because it is my duty do I have a good will.

What, then, is duty? Kant says, *"Duty is the necessity of acting from respect for the [moral] law."*[30] He goes on to explain that duty does not serve our desires and preferences (he calls these "inclinations"), but rather *overpowers* them. Put another way, duty excludes considerations of personal preference or profit and loss from moral calculation. For example, suppose I have criticized my boss to others. When she asks me whether I've done this, I decide to tell her the truth because I am not sure what my co-workers have already told her. Even though I do my duty, I cannot get moral credit for it, according to Kant, because my decision is based on something other than moral duty—it's based on not getting fired.

> Thus the moral worth of an action does not lie in the effect expected from it, nor in any principle of action which requires to borrow its motive from its expected effect. For all these effects—agreeableness of one's condition, and even the promotion of the happiness of others—could have been also brought about by other causes so that for this there would have been no need of the will of a rational being; whereas it is in this alone that the supreme and unconditioned good can be found. The preeminent good which we call moral can therefore consist in nothing else than *the conception of law* in itself, which certainly is only possible in a rational being, in so far as this conception, and not the expected effect, determines the will.[31]

If this seems unduly strict (and it has to many philosophers), keep in mind that decisions based on "inclinations" are often inconsistent and always relative. My inclination might be to renege on a loan or to be rude to a dirty, smelly customer. How can anyone rely on me if I only follow my inclinations? My inclination on the day I asked you to dinner might have been to keep our date, but by Friday my inclination might be to stay home alone. And I might not be inclined to call and inform you of this, either. Imagine the chaos of a world in which our obligations were tied to our moods.

My moral obligations cannot be grounded in my whims and personal taste. Nor can yours. According to Kant, moral duty must be confined to considerations of the form: *What are the universal obligations of all persons in similar circumstances?* My duty cannot be based on what I want to do, what I like or don't like, whether or not the others involved are people I care about.

Having defined the good will in terms of acting only from duty, and having defined duty as acting from a conscious awareness of our obligations under rational, moral law, we now need a way to determine exactly what our duty is in this or that case. That is, we can at last ask, *What is the moral law?* Kant's answer is one of the most intriguing and widely debated principles in all moral philosophy. He calls it the *categorical imperative.*

Look at the means a man employs; consider his motives. A man simply cannot conceal himself!

Confucius

The way to appraise a "way of life" may well be by considering what's in it for you; the way to appraise the moral value of a course of action is by considering what's in it for everyone.

Jan Narveson

Philosophical Query

Do you think it is possible to have only one motive for an action? Is it common to have only one motive? Is it important to distinguish moral motives from pragmatic ones? Why? Compare Kant with Hume on this issue.

Hypothetical Imperatives

Kant's position is that the moral quality of an act is determined by the *principle* to which the will consciously assents. If, for instance, I resolve to feed the hungry and mistakenly serve tainted meat at a charity dinner, my intention is praiseworthy even though my action results in sickness or death. If, on the other hand, I intend to poison my sick wife in order to inherit her fortune and mistakenly give her a chemical that cures her, I am morally guilty of murder, for that was what I consciously willed.

Since they affect behavior, moral principles are always framed as commands, according to Kant. He refers to commands by their grammatical designation as *imperatives*. Examples of imperatives are "Shut the door," "Always brush your teeth after eating," "Love your neighbor as yourself," and "Double-space your term paper."

Imperatives that tell us what to do under specific, variable conditions are called **hypothetical imperatives**. In logic, a hypothetical proposition takes the form "*If* this, *then* that." These are also called *conditional* propositions, because they set up a conditional relationship: *If* it rains, *then* postpone the picnic. The imperative "Postpone the picnic" is binding only in the condition of rain. According to Kant, all empirical or factual imperatives are hypothetical, because they are binding only so long as certain conditions apply.

There are a variety of *kinds* of hypothetical imperatives. Some are technical, applying to chemists or surgeons or bakers. Others are social, telling us how to be popular or get dates. Some are legal, and so on. No hypothetical imperative is binding on everyone or even on one person all the time. When factual conditions change, so do hypothetical imperatives. No hypothetical imperative is a priori. All are relative.

In fact, Kant says, "the imperatives of prudence do not, strictly speaking, command at all."[32] No one has a necessary obligation to be practical, to make money, to eat wisely. Thus, though hypothetical imperatives can help us deal with life, they cannot be a basis for determining moral duty.

The Categorical Imperative

If moral duty must be universally—not conditionally—binding, how can we determine what to do? What principle can we follow that is not conditional? After considering the difference between telling the truth because

HYPOTHETICAL IMPERATIVES

Propositions that tell us what to do under specific, variable conditions.

it is a duty and telling it because of some payoff it might yield, Kant concludes that acting from duty is always based on the principle of a "conception of the law in general."

What Kant means can be characterized as *acting on the principle of acting on principle*. In the case of telling the truth, I tell the truth because I have a basic, general obligation to tell the truth—period. This obligation is general in the sense that I must not base it on particular considerations at all. I must not be partial to myself and my fears or my wants.

What is needed is a **categorical imperative**, a command that is universally binding on all rational creatures. This alone can guide the good will. Indeed, the good will is precisely that which summons all its powers in order to obey just such an imperative. Kant has stripped the good will of every Humean sentiment, every impulse, appetite, fear, preference, or other practical or person-specific consideration. What's left?

> There remains nothing but the universal conformity of [the will's] actions to law in general, which alone is to serve as its principle, *i.e.*, I am never to act otherwise than *so that I could also will that my maxim should become a universal law*. Here, now, it is the simple conformity to law in general, without assuming any particular applicability to certain actions, that serves the will as its principle, and must so serve it, if duty is not to be a vain delusion and a chimerical notion.[33]

Kant formulated the categorical imperative as *"Act as if the maxim of thy action were to become a universal law of nature."* In other words, we must act only according to principles we think should apply to everyone. Because a free will is a necessary condition of morality, Kant reminds us that the "universal law" in question comes from our own rational, willing assent—it is not imposed on us from the outside. Obeying God or nature or any other *overpowering force* out of fear or necessity is not moral. If we obey out of fear, our motive is partial and pragmatic; if we have no choice but to obey, we are not free. Moral law is obligatory because it springs from our own rational nature and becomes law only when we willingly assent to it.

By *maxim* Kant means the rule according to which an act is done. It is the principle behind my action, my rational motive. What happens if we try to apply the categorical imperative to a course of action? A survey conducted by the Carnegie Foundation for the Advancement of Teaching asserted that 40 to 90 percent of college students cheat on exams or papers.[34] Let us analyze college cheating.

Don't be in a hurry to conclude, "Yeah, yeah, we all know cheating is wrong. That's obvious. But just about everybody does it—the survey shows that. So it's not a big deal." By scrutinizing it along Kantian lines, we discover exactly why cheating is wrong and learn something about the nature of morality.

CATEGORICAL IMPERATIVE

According to Kant, a command that is universally binding on all rational creatures; the ultimate foundation of all moral law: "Act as if the maxim of thy action were to become a universal law of nature."

Even apart from the value of such claims as "there is a categorical imperative in us," one can still always ask: what does such a claim tell us about the man who makes it?

Friedrich Nietzsche

Calvin and Hobbes © Watterson. Dist. by Universal Press Syndicate. Reprinted with permission. All rights reserved.

We must begin by asking whether a rational person could universalize cheating. That is, would I be willing to cheat if by doing so I created a new law of nature that would *force* everyone to cheat in similar circumstances? Suppose the maxim under which I act is something like this: "Cheat only when necessary to get good grades in required classes outside your major that you think you'll never use in later life." Now suppose every college student *must* behave just as I do.

Reason reveals what such a world would be like. Here is an imaginative picture of a world in which my moral principle operates as a universal law of nature: One day, after I've graduated, I'm being prepped for surgery. Dozing under a mild sedative, I'm chatting with my nurse anesthetist as I'm waiting to be wheeled into the operating room. She casually mentions that she originally studied to be a pediatric nurse and decided to go into anesthesiology only when she couldn't get a job in pediatrics. As I'm wheeled into the operating room, it dawns on me that—having acted on *my* moral principle—she cheated in anesthesiology courses because when she took them they were not required in her major, and she thought she'd never use them!

Kant held that, as conscious, rational creatures, we each possess dignity that deserves universal respect and that is not contingent on how likable we are, how attractive, successful, and so forth. In this photo, the caregiver's sense of dignity is apparent in the way he is helping another man find clothes that fit. His posture reflects patience and concern—as well as his own dignity.

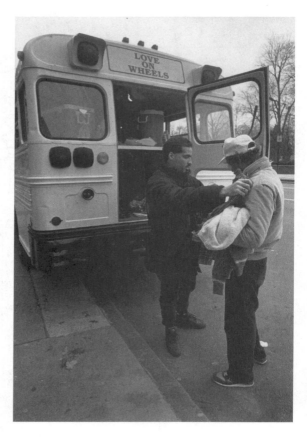

In more general terms, no rational person can universalize cheating in school because as cheating becomes widespread, the value of everyone's education becomes doubtful and diminished. Employers will not trust college degrees, since, according to my own law, they will have been acquired by cheating. No one will feel secure relying on anyone else's expertise. Cheating in school cannot be justified without making myself an exception to the *general rule* not to cheat.

But we already know that. What's the point of mentioning it? This kind of analysis shows one way of using the categorical imperative to bolster what we already know, to help us will and do what we ought. Rational analysis can do this by making clearer exactly what is wrong with a course of action.

We do not need science and philosophy to know what we should do to be honest and good, yea, even wise and virtuous.

Immanuel Kant

Philosophical Query

To get a clearer sense of the power of the categorical imperative to clarify the nature of various forms of behavior, formulate and then analyze the maxims that are required to justify: charging things on credit without being sure you can pay them off on time; enrolling in two different high-demand courses so that you can check them both out and drop the one you don't like; having sex without knowing if you are HIV positive; talking in the theater; forcing schools to teach the values of your religion.

The Kingdom of Ends

Kant held that as conscious, rational creatures, we each possess intrinsic worth. Because we are capable of reason and goodness, we possess dignity that deserves universal respect. We are more than mere objects to be used to further this or that end. We are persons competent to monitor and guide our own behavior according to principles. Our ability to reason carries with it an obligation to respect the rights of others to reason for themselves.

This intrinsic worth is not contingent on anything. It is not a function of how likable we are, how attractive, talented, clean, or even good we are. It is not contingent on how well we use our reason or on whether we use it at all. We possess worth because we *can* reason.

We have seen that, according to Kant, our basic obligations to one another cannot rest on inclinations or sentiments (desires), for that amounts to saying we have no moral obligations. Imagine a wedding in which the bride or groom promised to love, cherish, and respect the other "so long as I feel inclined to." The very concept of duty implies acting in an appropriate way regardless of our sentiments, regardless of convenience, comfort, or other personal factors. In Kant's terms this is an objective duty toward other rational beings—exactly what Hume denied:

> Man and generally any rational being *exists* as an end in himself, *not merely as a means* to be arbitrarily used . . . but in all his actions, whether they concern himself or other rational beings, must be always regarded at the same time as an end. All objects of inclination have only a conditional worth; for if the inclinations and the wants founded on them did not exist, then their object would be without value. . . . Rational beings . . . are called *persons*, because their very nature points them out as ends in themselves. . . . These, therefore, are not merely subjective ends whose existence has a worth *for us* as an effect of our action, but *objective ends*, that is, things whose existence is an end in itself: an end moreover for which no other can be substituted . . . for otherwise nothing whatever would possess *absolute worth*; but if all worth were conditional and therefore contingent, then there would be no supreme practical principle of reason whatever.

> If then there is a supreme practical principle or, in respect of the human will, a categorical imperative, it must be one which, being drawn from the conception of that which is necessarily an end for everyone because it is *an end in itself*, constitutes an *objective* principle of will, and can therefore serve as a universal practical law. The foundation of this principle is: *rational nature exists as an end in itself.*[35]

It is clear, then, that the idea of a fixed method, or of a fixed theory of rationality, rests on too naive a view of man and his social surroundings. To those who look at the rich material provided by history . . . it will become clear that there is only *one* principle that can be defended under *all* stages of human development. It is the principle: *anything goes.*

Paul Feyerabend

Man can never escape the ideal or absolute . . . man cannot be an animal; he can only be a philosopher or anthropologist who asserts that men are animals and ought to live like them.

Emil L. Fackenheim

PRACTICAL IMPERATIVE
(or PRINCIPLE OF
DIGNITY)

Kant's formulation of the
categorical imperative based
on the concept of dignity:
"Act in such a way that
you always treat humanity,
whether in your own per-
son or in the person of
another, never simply as a
means but always at the
same time as an end."

So sharply and clearly
marked are the boundaries
of morality and self-love
that even the commonest
eye cannot fail to distinguish whether a thing be-
longs to one or the other.

Immanuel Kant

Kant uses a beautiful expression to describe the moral universe, the universe of all moral beings, of all creatures possessing intrinsic worth. He
refers to it as the *kingdom of ends*, a kingdom in which everyone is an end
in him- or herself and no one is just a means to be used and tossed aside.

Kant formulates the categorical imperative around the concept of dignity in a way that is sometimes referred to as the **practical imperative** or
principle of dignity: *"Act in such a way that you always treat humanity,
whether in your own person or in the person of another, never simply as a
means but always at the same time as an end."*[36] I confess I'm partial to
this principle. It has, I believe, much to teach us.

If, for example, I view my students only as a way to make a living, or
only as a captive audience to indoctrinate with my views, I treat them as
means to an end without honoring their basic dignity as persons. We violate this principle of dignity when we hurl racial or gender insults at one
another, for then we are treating other persons as means of venting rage or
expressing feelings. No abusive parent or spouse treats the objects of his or
her abuse as *persons*. In the kingdom of ends there are no slaves, no sweat-
shops, no terrorists, no bullies, no rude clerks or surly customers, no unprepared teachers or students, only respectful and respected *persons*.

Yet in fact, my students *are* a *means* to an income for me. I *am* a *means*
to a degree or meeting a requirement for them. Bosses and employees are
means to each other, and so on. Note that the principle does not preclude
this. Rather, it adds a dimension of universal respect to all human relationships: We are means *and* ends. How often we seem to forget that others
are *persons* when we use them as status symbols or see only their outward
appearance or religious or political beliefs. Imagine a world in which clerks
and medical doctors and parents and children and spouses and students and
teachers and politicians and police officers and everyone else followed this
principle.

If I can remember that I live in a kingdom of ends, I can transform my
relationships from a sort of bartering for favors, or competing for power
and success. I can elevate my life to something beyond a contest in which
I and mine must struggle against a "different" and "inferior" them. In the
kingdom of ends, it is always *us*.

Philosophical Query

Consider the actual case of the parents who conceived a child for the
express purpose of producing a bone marrow donor for their nineteen-
year-old daughter who has leukemia. Doctors advised the parents that
a bone marrow transplant was the only hope of saving their daughter's
life. Unable to find a compatible donor match, the parents took the desperate step of having another child, and in 1991 bone marrow from the
specially conceived child, then just over one year old, was transplanted
to her nineteen-year-old sister. Can the parents' action be morally justified? Explain.

Commentary

Kant remains *the* major figure in modern philosophy. His effort to understand how the mind knows has shaped a significant portion of the field. Kant is also a major influence in modern psychology. In fact, many of the epistemological issues he raised are now being addressed by the cognitive sciences, which are devoted to unraveling the mysteries of perceiving, learning, knowing, and thinking.

In the field of ethics, three imposing visions dominate modern philosophy. One is Kantian formalism, the second is Humean subjectivism, and the third is utilitarianism (the subject of the Fourth Interlude). We will address some criticisms of Kantian ethics in the process of understanding the major alternative to it in the next chapter. Even so, some general remarks are in order.

In spite of the difficulty of his arguments and writing style, Kant's moral philosophy has proved to be influential beyond philosophical circles. Part of its power lies in a deep sense that it is wrong to make ourselves the exception in moral matters. If something is right (or wrong) for one person, it seems only fair that it be right (or wrong) for all persons in similar circumstances. We are offended when others make themselves or their loved ones exceptions. This may indeed stem from a sense of a "moral law within."

You may already have sensed that Kant's categorical imperative is a more refined and sophisticated version of the Golden Rule: "Do unto others as you would have them do unto you." Kant understood that a sloppy formulation of the Rule can be interpreted as saying "Treat others as you would *like* to be treated." Such a formulation generates what I call the Sadomasochistic Paradox, from an old joke in which a masochist says to a sadist, "Hurt me!" and the sadist replies, "No." The point, of course, is that how we *want* to be treated varies and is often determined by our individual tastes, background, personal beliefs, and temperament. It is certainly not a very reliable standard for treating others. If we have low self-esteem or some psychological quirk, we may want to be treated very poorly indeed. Kant's insistence that duty rise above inclination is meant to prohibit such individualistic interpretations of the Rule.

A common criticism of Kant's moral philosophy is that it promotes rash and irresponsible behavior by exempting us from responsibility for the consequences of our actions. After all, if the only truly good thing is a good will or motive, then all that matters morally is my intention—not the results of my behavior. Sophisticated Kantians point out, however, that any universalizable maxim must include concern for and consideration of the likely consequences of action. No defensible moral duty can condone indifference to what happens to others.

Another intriguing problem has to do with the conscience of a fanatic. By stressing the rational aspects of morality, Kant may have given too little

Deficiency in judgment is just what is ordinarily called stupidity, and for that there is no remedy.

Immanuel Kant

The majesty of duty has nothing to do with the enjoyment of life.

Immanuel Kant

Judaism would reject the Kantian axiom, "I ought, therefore I can": it would claim, instead, "Thou art commanded, therefore thou canst."

Abraham Joshua Heschel

weight to important psychological factors. A famous example involves a Nazi who is willing to universalize this maxim: "Always annihilate those whom you judge to be inferior and impediments to human progress." When it is pointed out that the Nazi may become the target of annihilation if he turns out to be an impediment to human progress, he is expected to see the "unreasonableness" of his maxim. If he still holds to it, knowing that it may result in his own destruction, he is said to be a "fanatic." But isn't this judgment based on our own inclinations (sentiments) and beliefs about what is reasonable? Yet how else can we determine what's rational? Did Kant merely use his own Western European Christian background to define "reasonable"? Is he, perhaps, guided by moral sentiment after all—as Hume thought? This is a complex and important problem, one the finest moral philosophers still struggle with.

The sociopath presents a dramatic example of the difficulties in determining what is rational. By most standards, sociopaths are intelligent and rational. Kant would not agree, because he sees the presence of a good will as a necessary condition of rationality. Thus, *by definition*, anyone lacking a good will is not rational. Kant's move *seems* arbitrary and circular, for it defines "reasonable" after the fact. In defense of Kant, we can offer the kinds of examples he uses in explaining the categorical imperative: repaying loans, keeping promises, telling the truth. It seems clear that social harmony, and perhaps civilized life itself, depend on such basic principles. But does that mean *everyone* must honor them? Sophists and egoists argue that it is perfectly "rational" to preach conformity to moral rules but to make myself the exception when it's to my self-identified advantage. As a *rational* egoist, all I need care about is that most people are conventionally moral most of the time.

Being "rational" is clearly not all that matters, as the harm caused by "rational" criminals, frauds, toxic polluters, and others clearly demonstrates. Experience offers countless examples of dangerous, immoral schemes hatched by rational individuals lacking good will. Equally dangerous is the well-intentioned but shortsighted or incompetent individual whose motives are unassailable, yet whose actions generate harm. The best will must be combined with a certain minimum of intelligence, insight, and ability. Just as being rational is not a sufficient condition for being moral, neither is having a good will.

The notion of happiness is so indefinite that although every man wishes to attain it yet he never can say definitely and consistently what it is that he really wishes and wills.

Immanuel Kant

Attempting to apply the categorical imperative results in seemingly irresolvable difficulties, because we lack the ability to frame moral rules so clearly that they do not generate problems. Suppose you promise a friend to repay borrowed money whenever he requests it. One evening your friend and a drug dealer show up. Your friend demands the money to buy an ounce of heroin. Should you repay it? Which is more important, keeping a promise or looking out for a friend's welfare when he or she is unable to? Can a drug user be rational when compelled by a powerful addiction? Does treating my friends as ends entail protecting them from themselves or letting them make their own choices no matter how harmful the consequences?

Imagine that a frightened man dashes into your office one day and hides behind your desk. Before you can ask him what's going on, a hysterical woman with a shotgun looks in your door and asks, "Is my cheating husband in here?" Should you tell the truth, because telling the truth is universalizable? Which value is higher, truth telling or life saving? Can I frame a moral maxim to guide me in choosing between conflicting moral rules in such a case? I could add qualifications to my rules, but then what is the purpose or benefit of having rules if they require so many qualifications that they cease to function as moral maxims? It is not clear there is *any* maxim that can be universalizable without qualification and still function as more than a very loose guideline.

In the end, however, I remain especially impressed by Kant's pattern of starting with commonly accepted ideas like causality, the unitary self, and free will and then trying to determine how the mind can know them. Some of the greatest philosophers have painted themselves into "scandalous" corners by either ignoring or trivializing commonly held ideas. Kant does not uncritically validate "common sense"; rather, he respects some nearly universal ideas of his own culture. He assumes that certain basic thinking patterns (as opposed to strongly held controversial beliefs) must have merit. They must serve some inherent, preconscious purpose. He then proceeds to subject them to his critical philosophy.

The result is certainly not a simplistic epistemology or moral philosophy. Kant presented a radically new picture of the mind as an active organizer and questioner of sensation. He identified important limits of empiricism and rationalism, and identified vital questions that wait to be answered. His insistence that "reason demands" a noumenal world beyond immediate experience and the reach of science remains a profound expression of a sense shared by many people.

To the extent that we worship scientific knowledge as the only secure kind, we remain somehow dissatisfied. Kant understood that we have within us more than the "moral law." We feel a need for fairness, a hunger to become good (or at least better), and an abiding sense of "something more," something just beyond the reach of science and theoretical reason.

> I have therefore found it necessary to deny *knowledge* in order to make room for *faith*.
>
> *Immanuel Kant*

> Kant can justly be called the father of modern philosophy, for out of him stem nearly all the still current and contending schools of philosophy. . . .
>
> *William Barrett*

Summary of Main Points

1. As Enlightenment thinkers discovered more and more laws of nature, they came to view human reason as the only tool necessary for progress. Faith in reason turned to frustration and despair, however, as reason was defeated by the mob during the Reign of Terror and technical progress was accompanied by slums and abusive working conditions.

2. Kant fully understood the serious implications of the "scandal in philosophy" that resulted from Hume's devastating use of the empirical criterion of meaning and the failure of rationalism and empiricism to adequately account for knowledge of the external world, cause and effect, and knowledge in general while science clearly showed otherwise. Yet Kant did not

want to abandon philosophy to science because science was unveiling a mechanistic universe without God and which, in its denial of free will, left no room for morality or human dignity.

3. Kant developed a special kind of analysis called a critique, which combined reason and experience in order to avoid the errors of rationalism and empiricism. Critical philosophy attempts to discover whether a priori knowledge and metaphysics are possible. Critical philosophy completes the epistemological turn in its efforts to assess the nature of "pure reason" and identify the actual relationship of the mind to knowledge.

4. Kant claimed that knowledge is formed by actual experience and faculties of judgment called categories of understanding. We know reality only as it is organized by human understanding (phenomenal reality), not reality as it is (noumenal reality).

5. Kant distinguished between theoretical reason and practical reason. Theoretical reason is confined to the phenomenal world; practical reason moves beyond the phenomenal world to the moral dimension. Practical reason helps us deal with the moral freedom provided by free will.

6. Practical reason reveals a moral dimension based on our consciousness of necessary and universal moral laws, which Kant calls rules or maxims. Moral rules cannot be discovered empirically; reason imposes moral obligation. Reason reveals that morality is a matter of moral duty (good will) rather than consequences, since circumstances sometimes prevent us from performing our moral duty.

7. Moral duty does not serve our sentiments and preferences, it overpowers them. Moral duty must be confined to considerations of the form: What are the universal obligations of all persons in similar circumstances? The moral quality of an act is determined by the principle to which the will consciously assents. Moral obligations are not hypothetical, dependent on individual circumstances, but categorical, universally binding on all rational beings.

8. Kant characterized moral duty as acting on the principle of acting on principle and identified the universal command that infuses all moral obligations, which he called the categorical imperative: Act as if the maxim of thy action were to become a universal law of nature.

9. As rational creatures capable of goodness, we belong to what Kant called the kingdom of ends. Because we can reason, we have intrinsic worth, we are ends in ourselves, not mere means to other ends. A special formulation of the categorical imperative acknowledges this worth: Act in such a way that you always treat humanity, whether in your own person or in the person of another, never simply as a means but always at the same time as an end.

Study Questions

1. Briefly explain how Kant completed the epistemological turn.
2. Identify and discuss one or two major Enlightenment themes and their relationship to Kant's philosophy.
3. What did Kant mean by "a scandal in philosophy"?
4. Briefly explain Hume's significance to Kant.
5. What was Kant's "Copernican revolution in philosophy"?
6. What is critical philosophy?
7. Distinguish between phenomena and noumena. Give examples of each.
8. Why did Kant think it necessary to posit the existence of the noumenal world?

9. How does Kant answer Hume's bundle theory of the self? Do you think he's successful? Explain.

10. What is practical reason?

11. Describe the moral dimension as Kant understood it.

12. Explain the reasoning behind Kant's efforts to make morality a matter of motives, not consequences.

13. Why does Kant claim that the only thing good in itself is a good will?

14. What does Kant mean by duty?

15. What is the categorical imperative? Apply it to one or two cases of your own choosing.

16. What is the practical imperative?

17. What is the kingdom of ends?

18. In what sense are Hume and Kant both Enlightenment thinkers? Compare and contrast their views of reason. Which view do you think is more realistic? Why?

11

The Materialist

Karl Marx

The philosophers have only *interpreted* the world in various
ways: the point is to *change* it.

Karl Marx

Have you ever really resented your job, or where you live, yet felt trapped by economic circumstances, unable to improve the basic conditions of your life? Or perhaps your education is uninspiring, something you feel pressured to do in order to get a good—or just an adequate—job? Most of us probably have felt such frustration occasionally. Sometimes, our lives seem to be controlled by our jobs and the need to earn a "decent living." It seems as if money determines everything.

During a discussion about youngsters selling cocaine, a twelve-year-old drug dealer explained that his father had long ago abandoned the family and left this boy, his mother, and two sisters to fend for themselves. The young dealer's economic logic was impressive: "I make four or five hundred dollars a day—tax free. Now my mother and sisters have nice clothes and food. We can go to a good doctor. How else could we do that? Nobody helped us before." How can we reasonably expect this boy to listen when we say "Go to school, study hard. Learn to delay gratification and someday you can get a decent job, and so on, and so on, and so on"? Economic reality is more powerful than such middle-class logic.

In the Fourth Interlude, we will learn how Jeremy Bentham and John Stuart Mill hoped to reform society by applying the greatest-happiness principle and an empirically based social hedonism. Mill, especially, hoped that providing decent living conditions and better education would mean a juster, more humane world.

Mill and Bentham were not the only social reformers inspired by the great inequities of the nineteenth century's fast-moving industrialization, however. Reform movements under the general banners of socialism and communism spread throughout France and Germany. English socialists whose views differed from Bentham's and Mill's also contributed to the overall climate of social analysis and criticism. What all these reformers had in common was a clear sense of injustice and increasing inequality. Where they differed, and often significantly, was on the exact causes of and hence the proper remedies to improve the dismal living conditions of the poor and the working class.

The very idea of distributive justice, or of any proportionality between success and merit, or between success and exertion, is in the present state of society so manifestly chimerical as to be relegated to the regions of romance.

John Stuart Mill

Besides utilitarianism, another, more influential theory emerged at roughly the same time. We know it today as Marxism. The most influential philosopher in history, if we judge influence by the numbers of people attempting to live by a philosophy, is its founder, Karl Marx. The sheer social and political impact of Marxism warrants a careful look at it. But, as you will discover, *philosophical Marxism* is not at all what we usually think of as Marxism or communism—and it is not what today's Marxists or Communists practice either. Let us see, then, what philosophical Marxism is, and what has made it so attractive to so many people.

The Prophet

Karl Marx

All I know is that I am not a Marxist.

Karl Marx

Karl Marx (1818–1883) was born in Trier, Germany. His father was a respected lawyer, and both parents were Jewish. Marx's father eventually distanced himself from the local Jewish community and changed the family name from Levi to Marx, most likely for social and business reasons.

From early on, Karl Marx proved to be highly intelligent and obsessively interested in nearly everything. He was also very independent and hard to control. At seventeen Marx entered the University of Bonn to study law. He enjoyed himself, writing romantic poems, socializing, spending more money than he had, even fighting in a duel—not to mention getting arrested once for disorderly conduct. His conventional father was not at all happy with his son's behavior and insisted that he transfer to the more serious and prestigious University of Berlin.

Marx's stay at Berlin proved to be crucial to his later philosophical growth. Big, busy, and ugly, Berlin epitomized the nineteenth-century idea of a modern city. It was a magnet for social agitators, radicals, and other intellectuals. Imagine the impact such an environment would have on a bright, curious, somewhat rebellious young man from a conservative small-town background.

Soaring with the Intellectual Spirit of the Age

One way or another, most philosophers have believed that truth exists, that it is knowable, and that whatever truth is, it is always the same for everyone. Yet, as we have seen, philosophers radically disagree about what can be known, about how to know it, and about the grand scheme of things. Sophists and skeptics even challenge whether there is any unchanging truth, questioning our ability to recognize it if there is.

Kant's effort to answer Hume's assault on reason was a direct influence on the idealist philosopher **Georg Wilhelm Friedrich Hegel (1770–1831)**, the dominant thinker being read in every major German university when Kant was a student. Though Hegel was primarily a philosopher, his influence spread across intellectual and artistic disciplines. One was either a

Hegelian or an anti-Hegelian, but no serious German intellectual could ignore Hegel. Hegel's works include *The Phenomenology of Mind (or Spirit)* (1807), *Science of Logic* (1812, 1816), *Encyclopedia of the Philosophical Sciences in Outline* (1817), and *Philosophy of Right* (1821).

Hegel pushed Kant's claim that the mind imposes categories (concepts) on experience to its ultimate conclusion. Rather than appeal to unknowable *noumena* to avoid slipping into Humean skepticism, Hegel argued that Kant's *categories of thought* are actually *categories of being*. According to Hegel, whatever exists is knowable. Therefore, it is contradictory to assert that noumena are unknowable because to do so we must somehow know that noumena exist.

For Hegel, Kant's categories exist independently of any specific individual's mind. They are both mental processes and objective realities. In Hegelian philosophy, capital-R Reality is referred to as Absolute Thought, Mind, Spirit, or Idea. Hegel believed that it is the unique task of philosophy to discover the relationships of various aspects of Reality to the Whole (Absolute Mind or Absolute Spirit). These relationships can be understood as part of a monistic system consisting of a single, evolving substance known as Absolute Spirit. History is the all-encompassing Absolute Spirit self-actualizing into perfection. Consequently, Hegel's philosophy is sometimes called **absolute idealism.**

Hegel insisted that Mind can only be recognized as "continuously developing consciousness." The pattern that all consciousness follows constitutes a "dialectical process." As Hegel uses the term, **dialectic** refers to a three-step pattern in which an original idea (thought or condition) known as a *thesis* is opposed by a contrary idea (thought or condition) known as the *antithesis*. The interaction or struggle between the thesis and antithesis produces a new idea (thought or condition) that combines elements from the others, known as the *synthesis*. Once established, the synthesis becomes the thesis for a new cycle until everything is realized in the infinite synthesis of Absolute Spirit. Each resulting level of consciousness includes its predecessors. The Hegelian Dialectic was supposed to represent the actual structure of reality, which for Hegel was the unfolding thought of the cosmic or absolute *Geist*, translated as Mind, or Spirit.

Hegel believed that it was possible to construct a complete picture of reality, a grand system that would incorporate all of philosophy, science, theology, art, history, and so on. In fact, he insisted that it is impossible to understand anything except as it relates to the Whole.

Thus, for Hegel, everything is always developing according to the dialectical process. Previous philosophers were unaware that they were working with a particular stage of the development of capital-R Reason as it unfolds in history. They were products of the *zeitgeist*, the "spirit of the age." By failing to recognize the *dialectical process* of which they were a part, these philosophers mistook something "abstracted" from the Whole for a fixed, independent entity. But nothing can be understood or even recognized this way. Things can only be understood when they are watched

ABSOLUTE IDEALISM (HEGELIAN)

Term used to identify Hegel's particular form of German idealism; a monistic philosophy which is based on an all-encompassing Absolute Spirit that is self-actualizing into perfection; Reality (Absolute Mind or Absolute Spirit) is independent of any individual's mind; not to be confused with Berkeleian idealism (immaterialism), in which objective reality is said to exist in the individual's mind.

DIALECTIC (HEGELIAN)

According to Hegel, a three-step pattern in which an original idea, known as a thesis, struggles with a contrary idea, known as the antithesis, to produce a new synthesis that combines elements of both.

phenomenologically as they develop in relationship to the Whole, the Ultimate Synthesis toward which history is unfolding. For Hegel, history does not "just happen." It is the rational development of progressively inclusive stages toward realization in Absolute Spirit. This Absolute Spirit is the ultimate synthesis of what Hegel saw as a tension between the subjective (Idea) and the objective (Nature).

Hegel was a grand systematizer—some would say *the* grand systematizer—who thought that history is the unfolding of the Absolute Idea of God (Absolute Spirit). He saw philosophy as the attempt to construct a comprehensive picture of everything as it relates to everything.

The young Marx was deeply influenced by Hegel, from whom he derived the crucial concept of alienation and the notion of historical evolution as an ongoing struggle.

Back Down to Earth

During this time, Marx became acquainted with a number of radical "freethinkers." These excited young people spent hours arguing the finer points of Hegelian philosophy. Marx thrived on the heady combination of intellectual stimulation and radicalism. Despite all the time spent in coffeehouses and beer halls, Marx completed his doctoral work in philosophy with a dissertation on the materialistic philosophy of Democritus and Epicurus. He planned to practice that noblest of all occupations, professor of philosophy.

Fate had other plans, however. Marx had been living on money from his father. When his father died about the time of Marx's graduation, he left only enough to support Marx's mother and younger siblings. This would have been no real problem if Marx had been able to secure an appointment as a professor. But by now the Prussian government had grown wary of the young, radical Hegelians and issued a decree prohibiting them from university employment.

Fortunately, Marx was offered a job by a liberal publisher named Moses Hess. Hess, himself a Hegelian, wanted Marx to help him edit a new, vocal "democratic journal" called *Rheinische Zeitung*. Even at this early age, Marx was an impressive figure. Writing about Marx to a friend, Hess said:

> He is the greatest, perhaps the one genuine philosopher now alive and will soon draw the eyes of all Germany. Dr. Marx is still very young (about twenty-five at most) and will give medieval religion and politics their *coup de grace*. He combines the deepest philosophical seriousness with the most biting wit. Imagine Rousseau, Voltaire, Holbach, Lessing, Heine, and Hegel fused into one person—I say fused, not thrown in a heap—you have Dr. Marx.[1]

Marx's admiration for Hegel was altered by an article called *Theses on the Hegelian Philosophy* by **Ludwig Feuerbach (1804–1872)**. Feuerbach was a materialist who challenged Hegel's notion that the driving force be-

History does nothing, it "possesses no colossal riches," it "fights no battles"! Rather it is man, actual and living man who does all this, who possesses and fights; "history" does not use man as a means for its purposes as though it were a person apart; it is nothing but the activity of pursuing his ends.

Friedrich Engels

hind historical eras was their *zeitgeist*, or unique spirit, the *spirit of the age*. Feuerbach argued that any given era was the accumulation of the actual, concrete material conditions of the time—not some abstract "spirit of the age." So important were material conditions, according to Feuerbach, that they controlled not just the way people behave, but *how they think* and *what they believe*. Different material conditions result in what we think of as different cultural eras. After reading Feuerbach, Marx retained Hegel's belief in the dialectics of history, and a single reality, but concluded that reality was material, not spiritual.

A chance combination of events in a thinker's life sometimes has a lasting and profound effect on his or her later theories. In Marx's case, a series of articles he had been doing for Hess on the exploitation of peasants in the wine-growing Moselle Valley crystallized his understanding of Feuerbach's thesis. Observing the way the landowners repressed the workers, actively inhibiting and even punishing their efforts at self-improvement, Marx concluded that material conditions did indeed dominate all others.

> All official and liberal science defends wage-slavery in one way or another, whereas Marxism has declared relentless war on that slavery. To expect science to be impartial in a society of wage-slavery is as silly and naive as to expect impartiality from employers on the question as to whether the workers' wages should be increased by decreasing the profits of capital.
>
> *V. I. Lenin*

The Wanderer

Like many social reformers and agitators, Marx paid a price for his outspoken concern for the downtrodden and his vehement attacks on those he saw as their oppressors. After Marx wrote a series of bitter editorials criticizing the Russian government, the rulers of Prussia—afraid of offending their powerful neighbor—shut down Hess's journal. This was April 1843, the same year Marx married Jenny von Westphalen.

Having a wife, no job, and no longer a Hegelian, Marx sought what he hoped would be a freer intellectual climate: He and Jenny moved to Paris. One of the social and political hubs of Europe at the time, Paris attracted thinkers and doers from around the world with its unique atmosphere of openness and encouragement. Naturally, such a climate attracted the most intense and talented freethinkers and radicals. It was not long before Marx felt right at home.

In Paris, Marx discovered another congenial group of radical thinkers, this time centered around the economic ideas of the **Comte de Saint-Simon (1760–1825)**. Saint-Simon was especially interested in the emergence of a powerful new middle class, known as the bourgeoisie. He concluded that *economic conditions determine history*. More specifically, Saint-Simon argued that historical change is the result of *class conflict*: Those who control the material necessary for production are in a perpetual struggle with those who do not. This idea, as we shall see, had a major impact on Marx's thinking.

Marx also befriended various revolutionary groups of exiled German workers. These workers were on the periphery of and were influenced by an organized group of French laborers who agitated for radical changes in the conditions of workers and in the relationship between workers and owners. Because they wanted property held in common and shared by all, they were known as communists. Marx developed a keen sense of the proletariat, or working class. He now possessed the seeds of his own philosophy.

Within a year of moving to Paris, Marx was expelled from the city, and from 1845 to 1848 he and his family lived in Brussels. While there, he helped organize the German Workers' Union, which became part of an international Communist League in 1847. Its first secretary was Marx's friend and collaborator Friedrich Engels. Marx and Engels wrote the official statement of beliefs and doctrines of the Communist League, which was published in 1848 as *The Manifesto of the Communist Party* (now known simply as *The Communist Manifesto*). It may be the most important and influential revolutionary tract ever written.

Marx next went to Cologne to help agitate for a revolt of the German people. His timing was poor, however, as a more conservative tide was sweeping across France and Germany. Marx was formally expelled from Germany by the government and returned to Paris. Not yet thirty-two years old, he was already perceived as a dangerous revolutionary. He had barely returned to Paris when the French government again made him leave.

In August 1849, Marx's friends gave him enough money to move to London. England, in spite of the flaws Marx and Engels would find in its class structure and capitalist economy, proved a haven of freedom of thought and expression. Thus, in one of the ironies of history, the great critic of capitalism found the freedom to criticize capitalism only in a capitalistic environment.

Marx never left London. For almost a decade he spent long days in the reading rooms of the British Museum, researching some, but mostly writing. After returning home, he often continued working late into the night. He and his family lived a hand-to-mouth existence, moving from one shabby apartment to another, unable to pay rent. Once, they were evicted without anything when the landlord confiscated their few possessions in lieu of rent. Food and medicine were always scarce. Their poverty was so dire that two sons and a daughter died in childhood.

Vindication

At forty-two, Marx was thought of as an old man. Poverty and exile had worn him down, and his influence over revolutionary thinkers had begun when he was so young that he was seen as a member of the old guard. His influence grew, however, with the emergence of the militant German Social Democracy party. After Marx became their authority on socialist theory, his financial condition improved. Then, in 1864, the International Workingmen's Association was established by revolutionaries in France and England. They, too, turned to Marx, and he came to dominate their general council. He tolerated no deviance from his views, and used any means necessary to defeat those who dared challenge him.

The teaching of Marx is all-powerful because it is true. It is complete and harmonious, providing men with a consistent view of the universe, which cannot be reconciled with any superstition, any reaction, any defence of bourgeois oppression. It is the lawful successor of the best that has been created by humanity in the nineteenth century—German philosophy, English political economy, and French socialism.

V. I. Lenin

During this time Marx began *Das Kapital*. The first of its three volumes appeared in 1867. This massive work established Marx's reputation as a philosopher. It eventually became what is sometimes referred to as "the Communist Bible," probably because of its nearly mythical status, and possibly because more people claim to give their allegiance to it than actually read it.

As his health and strength grew weaker, Marx was unable to devote the same care and attention to the two remaining volumes of *Das Kapital* that he had to the first. In fact, he never finished them. What we know as the second and third volumes were extensively edited by Engels in 1885 and 1894, after Marx's death. In many ways they are inferior to the first volume. (What is called the fourth volume was ultimately compiled later.)

In 1881, Jenny died after a long and painful bout with cancer. The death of the woman who had stood by the exiled, reviled philosopher through poverty and the loss of three children broke his spirit. He lived for fifteen more months in a state of grief and despair. Karl Marx died sleeping in a favorite armchair on March 14, 1883, two months after the death of his oldest daughter. His funeral was attended by his family and a few friends. At the funeral of his old friend, Engels said:

> Just as Darwin discovered the law of development of organic nature, so Marx discovered the law of the development of human history: the simple fact that man must first of all eat, drink, have shelter and clothing, before he can pursue politics, science, art, religion, etc.; that therefore the production of the immediate means of subsistence, and consequently the degree of economic development of a given epoch, form the foundation on which state institutions, legal conceptions, art and even religious ideas have evolved and in the light of which they must, therefore, be explained.
>
> Marx was before all else a revolutionist. His real mission in life was to contribute, in one way or another, to the overthrow of capitalistic society, and to the liberation of the proletariat, which he was the first to make conscious of its own position and needs. Fighting was his element. And he fought with a passion, a tenacity and a success few could rival.
>
> His name will live through the ages, and so also will his work.[2]

It is not the consciousness of men that determines their existence, but on the contrary, their social existence determines their consciousness.

Karl Marx

Friedrich Engels

Friedrich Engels (1820–1895), the son of a wealthy German textile manufacturer, came to Paris to meet Marx, after sending him some articles Engels had written criticizing English economists. The meeting changed forever the lives of both men and the shape of the world. They remained friends and collaborators until Marx's death.

Friedrich Engels

Engels was clearly a member of the bourgeoisie who enjoyed the pleasures and comforts provided by his father's money. He loved to hunt, write poems, and drink fine wines. Such a lifestyle did not please his strict Calvinist father, who sent young Friedrich off to learn the work ethic. Laboring on the docks of Bremen, Engels developed deep compassion for the condition of his less fortunate colleagues. He read radical literature, and was converted to communism by Marx's mentor, Moses Hess.

Engels tried a job in his father's Manchester, England, branch of the family business, but could not shake his interest in the working class. He spent more and more time studying slum conditions and noting the immense disparity between the conditions of the poor and the upper and middle classes. The utter degradation and despair he found in the slums squelched any lingering interest in becoming a businessman, and he began to write about what he saw.

In 1844, Engels published *The Condition of the Working Class in England*. His writing was strong, practical, and effective. He went on to write a series of attacks on the most important English economists of the day, accusing them of rationalizing and justifying the abuses the middle and upper classes heaped upon the poor. He saw their economic theories as capitalistic propaganda, not honest economic or historical research. As he and Marx discussed these essays, each realized that he had finally found someone who understood the power of economic and material conditions. It has been said that Marx was the deeper thinker and Engels added breadth and fire to his ideas.

Engels had a gift for acquiring the hard facts Marx needed to support his philosophical arguments, and for making Marx's often difficult and obscure thinking easier to follow. Thus he played a crucial role in the spread and acceptance of Marxist thinking. Engels and Marx worked together for over forty years, and Engels supported Marx and his family through the long years of poverty in London. When Marx died, Engels protected, advocated, and interpreted his philosophy for the rest of the world.

> The society of money and exploitation has never been charged, so far as I know, with assuring the triumph of freedom and justice.
>
> *Albert Camus*

Dialectical Materialism

DIALECTICAL PROCESS (HEGELIAN)

Internally governed evolutionary cycle in which progress occurs as the result of a struggle between two opposing conditions.

From Hegel, Marx took the ideas that there is only one uniform reality, and that history is an evolutionary cycle governed by an internal **dialectical process**, in which progress occurs as the result of a struggle between two opposing conditions. From Feuerbach, Marx concluded that reality is material, and that consequently the material conditions of life control it. And from Saint-Simon, he learned to observe the relationship between the owning/governing class and the producing/exploited class. Combining these elements with a deep concern for the conditions of workers and a keen awareness of the importance of economic conditions to other aspects of life, Marx constructed a social-political-economic philosophy known variously as Marxism, communism, historical materialism, Marxian dialectics, historical dialectics, or dialectical materialism. We must take care not to confuse Marx's philosophy with various kinds of governments that claim to be Marxist, for as we shall see, the gap between Marx's philosophy and Marxist regimes can be significant.

According to Marx's dialectical materialism, history is the ongoing result of a constant tension between two classes, an upper class of rulers/owners and a ruled and exploited underclass. From the struggle between different economic interests emerges a brand-new economic structure. Marx saw conflicting economic interests in terms of two classes, the **bourgeoisie,** or middle class, and the **proletariat,** or working class. The bourgeoisie consists of those who do not produce anything yet who own and control the means of production. The proletariat consists of all those whose labor produces goods and provides essential services, yet who do not own the means of production.

Marx took Hegel's concept of the dialectical process and applied it to historical stages, which he called "the five epochs of history." These epochs—(1) primitive/communal, (2) slave, (3) feudal, (4) capitalist, (5) socialist/communist—are named after their dominant economic system. Marx argued that as each epoch develops, its basic economic structure matures. In the process, the success of the economic structure alters the material conditions of people's lives. These altered conditions ultimately lead to the creation of a new social structure.

> At a certain stage in their development, the material productive forces of society come in conflict with the existing relations of production or—which is but a legal expression for the same thing—with the property relations within which they have been at work hitherto. . . . Then begins an epoch of social revolution. With the change of the economic foundations, the entire immense superstructure is more or less rapidly transformed. In considering such transformation a distinction should always be made between the material transformation of the economic conditions of production, which can be determined with the precision of natural science, and the legal, political, religious, esthetic, or philosophic—in short, the ideological forms, in which men become conscious of the social conflict and fight it out.
>
> No social order ever perishes before all the productive forces for which there is room in it have developed; and new higher relations of production never appear before the material conditions of their existence have nurtured in the womb of the old society itself. Therefore mankind always sets itself only such tasks as it can solve; since, looking at the matter more closely, it will always be found that the task itself arises only when the material conditions for its solution already exist, or are at least in the process of formation.[3]

In outline form, Marxian history looks like this: The original primitive stage of history developed because the discovery of increasingly

---

BOURGEOISIE

All those who do not produce anything, yet who own and control the means of production.

PROLETARIAT

All those whose labor produces goods and provides essential services, yet who do not own the means of production.

What else does the history of ideas prove than that intellectual production changes character in proportion as material production is changed? The ruling ideas of each age have ever been the ideas of its ruling class.

The Communist Manifesto

The German workers depicted grinding silverware in this 1887 engraving were typical of the alienated proletarians championed by Marx and Engels. Could they even afford to own the very utensils they worked so hard to produce?

sophisticated agricultural techniques, tools, and simple metals required more labor. Thus was born the slave economy (a thesis stage). Over time, the slave economy produced even more sophisticated skills and information. As a result, people began to cluster around towns, where craft guilds emerged. A crude form of specialization arose: As fewer people were needed to devote their time to meeting basic agricultural needs, craftsmen were free to develop specialized skills. These newer skills required more concentration of labor and a bit more freedom than slaves had. Thus a feudal system emerged in which great lords owned the land, and serfs in effect leased portions of it (an antithesis to the slave economy). As payment, the serfs owed the lord most of what they raised or produced. The serfs were allowed to keep only a small portion of the products of their labor. This was a period of semifreedom in which most people lived in semirural, semi-urban towns.

The crafts guilds, especially, resulted in specialized manufacturing techniques. Soon, more and more goods were available. The demand for goods gave rise to increased trading and bartering, and capitalism began to grow out of feudalism (a synthesis of slave and feudal economies and a new thesis stage). Money became increasingly important, and with the spread of money as the medium of barter, financial brokers emerged. The demand for goods, coupled with new steam-powered manufacturing techniques, ultimately meant the death of feudalism. Feudalism was too cumbersome and inefficient to meet the needs and desires of the emerging capitalist middle class.

What is competition from the point of view of the work man? It is work put up to auction.

M. Louis Blanc

The technology of industrialization pulled people to areas with sources of sufficient power and transportation, near rivers or coal mines. Great cities developed. Mass production created more, cheaper goods, and demand continued to accelerate. A new class of middlemen who neither owned nor produced grew in power. They invested and began to acquire capital. In Marx's view, the gap between the owners-investors and the workers will continue to grow as one class amasses more and more wealth at the expense of a larger, exploited class. This gap will eventually become intolerable, resulting in a violent revolution of the workers.

Philosophical Query

Do you think the gap between owners-investors and workers is closing or widening? Cite some contemporary examples to support your view.

Since the great injustices of capitalism (thesis) result from the private ownership of property, according to Marx, a new socialistic economy (antithesis) will eventually emerge in which private property is abolished. Society will ultimately be able to provide decent, meaningful lives to virtually everyone (synthesis). As a result, no one will need private property or wealth. Instead of having to compete for a good life, we will live harmoniously, doing creative, satisfying work that benefits us individually at the same time it benefits society collectively. There will be only one class, hence no class conflict. The economy will reach a state of balance, and history as such (not the world, just history as class struggle) will end.

Mystification and Materialism

Marx radically transformed Hegel's dialectic by confining it to the material world. He objected to excessively abstract philosophy, referring to it as **mystification**: the use of cloudy abstractions to create elaborate metaphysical systems that distract us from concrete material reality. Marx thought that instead of clarifying ideas, Hegel and other "abstractionists" and idealists make them "mysterious" and vague.

Mystifying logic, like money, does not *produce* anything, it merely alters relationships. Hegel's great error, and that of philosophers in general, according to Marx, is *abstraction*. Thus most philosophy lacks substance. Like Bentham and Mill, Marx believed sweeping metaphysical systems and grand-sounding statements about human dignity and virtue pale beside the actual, concrete, *existing conditions* under which the poor barely survive.

In the *Manifesto*, Marx asserts that "man's ideas, views and conceptions, in one word, man's *consciousness*, changes with every change in the conditions of his material existence, his social relations, and his social life." When Marx talks about "material conditions" he means more than just natural physical and biological conditions. He includes economic and social relationships.

MYSTIFICATION

Use of cloudy abstractions to create elaborate metaphysical systems that distract us from concrete material reality.

MARXIAN
MATERIALISM

Form of social determinism
based on a reciprocal re-
lationship between indi-
viduals and their environment; distinguished from
strict materialism and hard
determinism.

Thus Marxian materialism should not be confused with scientific materialism (Chapters 8 and 9), which leads to the conclusion that all behavior is governed by strict laws of cause and effect. Marx is a *social determinist*, not a *hard determinist*. Hard determinists deny the possibility of
free will or free action. **Marxian materialism**, by contrast, sees a reciprocal relationship between individuals and their environment.

Marx criticized other forms of materialism for failing to understand
just how important the role of human consciousness is in shaping society:

> The distinctive character of social development as opposed to the
> natural process of development lies in the fact that human conscious-
> ness is involved. . . . *Intelligent social action is creative action.* . . . By
> acting on the external world and changing it, man changes his own
> nature. . . . The material doctrine that men are products of circum-
> stances and a changed upbringing forgets that it is men that change
> circumstance, and that the educator himself needs educating.[4]

This reciprocity between individuals and their circumstances is a dialectical relationship. Marx's materialism avoids the futility and degradation
he saw in scientific materialism, while acknowledging the importance of
the material conditions of our lives.

Engels referred to Marx's philosophy as *dialectical materialism*, but
Marx himself referred to it as *naturalism*. Both characterizations are ex-
pressive of its overall thrust. Marx's emphasis, like that of his great utilitarian contemporary John Stuart Mill, is on the here and now. Like Mill,
Marx refers to what he is doing as "social science." He believed his unique
mixture of idealistic (Hegelian) and materialistic principles was the *only
way* to understand and predict the course of history:

> We see here how consistent naturalism or humanism is distinguished
> from both idealism and materialism, and at the same time constitutes
> their unifying truth. We see also that only *naturalism* is able to com-
> prehend the process of world history.[5]

According to Marx, the process of human history is shaped by inseparable social and economic conditions.

Economic Determinism

ECONOMIC
(as used by Marx)

The complete array of so-
cial relationships and arrangements that constitutes
a particular social order.

Philosophers and other intellectuals tend to attribute great power to ideas.
They talk of the transforming power of profound ideas such as democracy or truth. Marx, by contrast, proposes a radical view of ideas, namely,
that *the economic structure of a culture creates and forms its ideas.*

SUBSTRUCTURE OF
SOCIETY

In philosophical Marxism,
the material substructure or
base of society determines
the nature of all social
relationships, as well as
religions, art, philosophies,
literature, science, and
government.

Marx uses the term **economic** to refer to the complete array of social
relationships and arrangements that constitutes a particular social order.
He assigns a crucial role to the material **substructure** (or base) **of society**,

which consists of the means of production, the forces of production, and the relationships of production.

The **means of production** include natural resources such as water, coal, land, and so forth. The **forces of production** are factories, equipment, technology, knowledge, and skill. The phrase **relationships of production** refers to who does what, who owns what, and how this affects members of both groups. The relationships of production shape society.

The relationships of production constitute a complex system that shapes everything else. This material substructure determines the nature of all social relationships (parent-child, boss-employee, ruler-citizen, and so on), as well as religions, art, philosophies, literature, science, and government. According to Marx, the basic substructure of a society produces ideas and institutions that are compatible with it; these he referred to as the **superstructure of society**. The superstructure of a culture rests on and is determined by the substructure.

We can use a bit of what we have learned so far about the history of philosophy to see what Marx means. A sketchy Marxist survey of philosophy might go something like this:

Plato and Aristotle reflected the values of a slave economy. Plato's social hierarchy classified most people as warriors or artisans. Only an elite few, the guardians, were fit to rule. Aristotle's ethic of self-realization certainly did not apply to slaves and illiterate laborers and farmers. Both philosophies were shaped by the dominant social relationships of production at the time. The expanding Roman Empire needed strong, disciplined soldiers and citizens who could survive sometimes capricious emperors. Hence it nurtured just the right philosophy: Stoicism.

Thomas Aquinas's great summae reflect medieval Catholic theology, which justified the feudal order and excused the suffering of the exploited laboring classes as God's will. Such beliefs made the degradation of people acceptable, as it was part of our punishment for Original Sin, ordained by the will of God, and only "temporary" for those who would eventually escape servitude by going to heaven.

The more sophisticated methods of production whose arrival marked the beginning of capitalism required a less hierarchical, freer, more individualistic social structure. Technology began to replace human effort. The result of this economic shift was Descartes' emphasis on method, which is the philosophic version of technology, and his individualism, which followed the decline of the great feudal communities and guilds. This set the stage for the industrialization of Europe and the rise of capitalism. Further, Descartes' rationalism is clearly the product of an elitist gentleman.

The utilitarians' emphasis on universal education and praise of liberty is partly a justification of capitalism, which requires skilled, educated workers and entrepreneurs who are free from excessive government interference. (See the Fourth Interlude.) Both Bentham and Mill express the

MEANS OF PRODUCTION

In philosophical Marxism, the means of production include natural resources such as water, coal, land, and so forth; a part of the substructure of society.

FORCES OF PRODUCTION

In philosophical Marxism, the forces of production are factories, equipment, technology, knowledge, and skill; a part of the substructure of society.

RELATIONSHIPS OF PRODUCTION

In philosophical Marxism, relationships of production consist of who does what, who owns what, and how this affects members of both groups; a part of the substructure of society.

SUPERSTRUCTURE OF SOCIETY

According to philosophical Marxism, the superstructure of a culture consists of the ideas and institutions (religious beliefs, educational systems, philosophies, the arts, and such) compatible with and produced by the material substructure of the society.

growing tension and increasing inequality resulting from the Industrial Revolution. Their social policies reflect the changing nature of the relationships of production: Utilitarianism is a bourgeois philosophy that seeks to improve the conditions of the proletariat just enough to make them more efficient. It does nothing to significantly alter their basic state.

You may not agree with this Marxian analysis at all, but it does seem clear that social conditions affect art, literature, philosophy, and so on. Marx refined the notion of "social conditions" and insisted that the dominant, all-important social condition is the relationships of production.

> In the social production which men carry on they enter into definite relations that are indispensable and independent of their will; these relations of production correspond to a definite stage of development of their material powers of production. The sum total of these relations of production constitutes the economic structure of society—the real foundation on which rise legal and political superstructures and to which correspond definite forms of social consciousness. The mode of production in material life determines the general character of the social, political, and spiritual processes of life.[6]

The relationship between the economic structure of a society and the kinds of people, ideas, and institutions it produces will become clearer as we take an extended look at Marx's critique of capitalism.

Philosophical Query

Analyze your education from the standpoint of relationships of production. What values does public education really serve?

Critique of Capitalism

Given the importance Marx placed on the economic structure of society, it is not surprising that he developed a detailed critique of the prevailing nineteenth-century relationship of production, **capitalism**. Although many of Marx's ideas are clearly revolutionary, and although he did predict a violent overthrow of capitalism, Marx never actually made a moral judgment of capitalism. He thought of his analysis as "pure social science." His aim was to describe current social and economic conditions objectively, identifying their causes and predicting the next historical change.

In Marx's opinion, tension under capitalism is increased as *inequities of distribution* destroy any correlation between how much an individual contributes or produces, and how much he or she receives. There is a fundamental contradiction at the heart of capitalism: The law of supply and demand determines prices, yet the large pool of workers keeps wages low. Manufacturers keep prices higher than the actual cost of production, so

---

Communism is a society where each one works according to his ability and gets according to his needs.

Pierre-Joseph Proudhon

CAPITALISM

Economic system in which the means of production and distribution are all (or mostly) privately owned and operated for profit under fully competitive conditions; tends to be accompanied by concentration of wealth and growth of great corporations.

over time workers get less and less for their effort. The result is **surplus value**, which the owners accumulate in the form of capital. Those who contribute the least profit the most.

The bitter irony, Marx says, is that most of the people who suffer under capitalism have been conditioned by it to value it. They support a tax system that favors the rich, dreaming of the day when they, too, will be rich enough to benefit from it. Yet the laws determining who is allowed to own what, and who gets to keep what, are written by those who already own. Education is controlled by the same class, so the children of the most deprived grow up believing in free enterprise and "fair competition," only to be condemned to lives of poverty, or at least constant financial anxiety.

SURPLUS VALUE

Term Marx used to refer to the capital accumulated by owners; the result of keeping prices higher than the costs of production at the expense of workers.

Philosophical Query

Compare kinds of contribution: Who contributes more, the builders who construct houses or the developers who finance them? Who contributes more, the president of a corporation or the secretaries? Are ideas contributions? Discuss.

The Bourgeoisie and the Proletariat

Marx's critique of capitalism rests on an analysis of the two classes that have emerged under capitalism. In *The Communist Manifesto* he characterizes the bourgeoisie as disdainful of everything but capital. The government is nothing but "a committee for managing the common affairs of the whole bourgeoisie." In other words, the government is not "of, by, and for the people," but "of, by, and for the important people." The bourgeoisie reduces everything to crude calculations of self-interest and personal wealth:

> [The bourgeoisie] has left no other nexus between man and man than naked self-interest, than callous "cash payment." It has drowned the most heavenly ecstasies of religious fervour, of chivalrous enthusiasm, of Philistine sentimentalism, in the icy water of egotistical calculation. It has resolved personal worth into exchange value, and in place of the numberless indefeasible chartered freedoms, has set up that single, unconscionable freedom—Free Trade. In one word, for exploitation, veiled by religious and political illusions, it has substituted naked, shameless, direct, brutal exploitation.
>
> The bourgeoisie has stripped of its halo every occupation hitherto honoured and looked up to with reverent awe. It has converted the physician, the lawyer, the priest, the poet, the man of science, into its paid wage earners.
>
> The bourgeoisie has torn away from the family its sentimental veil, and has reduced the family relation into a mere money relation.[7]

I think that there is nothing, not even crime, more opposed to poetry, to philosophy, ay, to life itself than this incessant business.

Henry David Thoreau

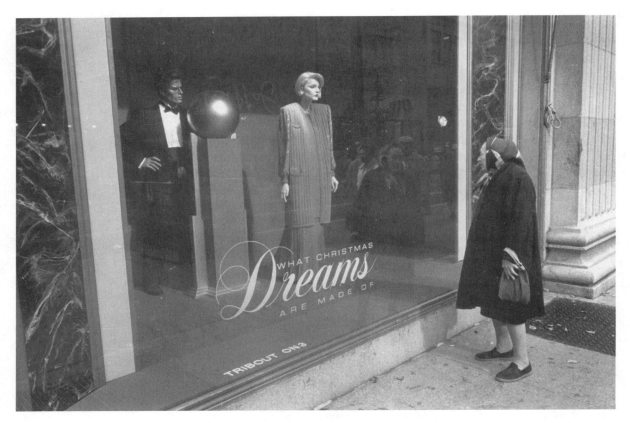

According to Marx, one of the bitterest ironies of capitalism is that those who suffer the most under capitalism have been conditioned to value it. The old woman in this picture may have worked very hard her entire life, yet remained unable to purchase expensive clothes like those in the store window. Would Marx find that appalling? What do you think?

Under capitalism man exploits man; under socialism the reverse is true.

Polish proverb

Expressions of frustration over the way doctors treat patients appear often in the media. We lament the demise of the family doctor who made house calls. We resent arriving on time for appointments only to be kept waiting and then having to pay high fees for a cursory examination, or a battery of tests whose chief purpose is to protect the doctor from a malpractice suit. Could this be an example of what Marx said happens when a profession is reduced to a means of making money?

Philosophical Query

We read that financial problems are perhaps the greatest cause of marital difficulties. If we marry after we have amassed some property, we are advised to protect ourselves by insisting on a carefully drawn-up prenuptial agreement. Is such thinking an example of reducing "the family rela-

Mill the Socialist?

Since the human race has no means . . . of existence at all but what it derives from its own labor and abstinence, there would be no ground for complaint against society if everyone who was willing to undergo a fair share of this labor and abstinence could attain a fair share of the fruits. But is this the case? Is it not the reverse of the fact? The reward, instead of being proportioned by the labor and abstinence of the individual, is almost in inverse ratio to it: those who receive the least, labor and abstain the most. Even . . . the inadequate self-control exercised by the indus- trious poor costs them more sacrifice and more effort than is almost ever required of the more favored members of society.

John Stuart Mill
On Socialism (1879; reprint, Buffalo: Prometheus, 1987), pp. 69–70.

tion into a mere money relation"? Is rewarding a child with money part of this pattern? Deciding not to have children because they are too expensive? Provide your own additional examples of reducing human relationships to "mere money relations." Can you find any evidence to refute Marx's basic contention that for the bourgeoisie, money matters most?

Marx and Engels claim that the bourgeoisie, with its hunger for more, cannot rest, cannot leave any corner of the world unexploited and unspoiled.

Constant revolutionising of production, uninterrupted disturbance of all social conditions, everlasting uncertainty and agitation distinguish the bourgeois epoch from all earlier ones. All fixed, fast-frozen relations . . . are swept away, all new-formed ones become antiquated before they can ossify. . . .

The bourgeoisie has through its exploitation of the world market given a cosmopolitan character to production and consumption in every country. . . . It compels all nations, on pain of extinction, to adopt the bourgeois mode of production; it compels them to introduce what it calls civilisation into their midst, i.e., to become bourgeois themselves. In one word, it creates a world after its own image.[8]

To be sure, labor produces marvels for the wealthy, but it produces deprivation for the worker. It produces palaces, but hovels for the worker. It displaces labor through machines, but it throws some workers back into barbarous labor and turns others into machines. It produces intelligence, but for the worker it produces imbecility and cretinism.

Karl Marx

The bourgeoisie cannot actually produce all that it needs and wants, Marx pointed out. Its enormous wealth and comfort have resulted from the exploitation of a great underclass, the proletariat. These are the people who actually provide the goods and services society requires to function. Controlled by the bourgeoisie, they are even compelled to produce frivolous luxuries whose real purpose is to generate ever-escalating production. Not only are the workers paid as little as the bourgeoisie can get away with in order to maximize profit, they are seduced by bourgeoisie-controlled education and media to consume these overpriced, useless products. Thus the proletarians are trapped in a never-ending cycle of debt,

Reprinted by permission: Tribune Media Services.

denied significant influence over their own work, and tricked and coerced into furthering the power and advantage of their own exploiters. As *The Communist Manifesto* explains it:

> In proportion as the bourgeoisie, i.e., capital, is developed, in the same proportion is the proletariat, the modern working class, developed—a class of labourers, who live only so long as they find work, and who find work only so long as their labour increases capital. These labourers, who must sell themselves piecemeal, are a commodity, like every other article of commerce, and are consequently exposed to all the vicissitudes of competition, to all the fluctuations of the market.
>
> Owing to the extensive use of machinery and to division of labour, the work of the proletarians has lost all individual character, and, consequently, all charm for the workman. He becomes an appendage of the machine, and it is only the most simple, the most monotonous, and most easily acquired knack, that is required of him. Hence, the cost of production of a workman is restricted, almost entirely, to the means of subsistence that he requires for his maintenance, and for the

propagation of his race. But the price of a commodity, and therefore, also of labour, is equal to the cost of production. In proportion, therefore, as the repulsiveness of the work increases, the wage decreases. . . . Not only are [the laborers] slaves of the bourgeois class, and of the bourgeois state; they are daily and hourly enslaved by the machine, by the overlooker, and above all, by the individual bourgeois himself. The more openly this despotism proclaims gain to be its end and aim, the more petty, the more hateful and the more embittering it is.[9]

If you have ever worked on an assembly line, or at picking fruits and vegetables, or in meat- or fish-packing plants, you will instantly understand the relationships of production that Marx and Engels are describing. Some of the most difficult and "repulsive" jobs are the most necessary to society, yet those who perform them are paid little and often respected less. Those who produce the least in Marxian terms work in air-conditioned offices, supported by hardworking staffs, and may receive salaries, bonuses, and stock options worth hundreds of thousands—if not millions—of dollars.

Marx and Engels were among the first modern philosophers to recognize the plight of women in modern society. When physical strength became less important, employment opportunities expanded for women and for men unable to do strenuous manual labor. But the work available and the pay offered were often substandard. Garment factories, for example, paid (and still pay) low piecework wages.

> The less skill and exertion of strength implied in manual labour, in other words, the more modern industry becomes developed, the more is the labour of men superseded by that of women. Differences of age and sex no longer have any distinctive social validity for the working class. All are instruments of labour, more or less expensive to use, according to their age and sex.[10]

According to philosophical Marxism, the corruption of the worker's judgment is a predictable effect of the capitalist substructure. The reality is that workers are exploited, even if *they* do not realize it. The fact that a powerless group submits to economic exploitation willingly does not alter the nature of the exploitative relationship.

Just as an abused spouse or child may lose the ability to perceive reality and hence mistakenly see herself or himself as somehow causing or deserving abuse, so too exploited workers, after generations of capitalistic conditioning through schools and the media, may fail to recognize their actual social condition.

We have already seen how working-class and middle-class people can come to identify with the *possibility* of acquiring wealth rather than with their *actual chances* of doing so. In other words, we may identify with the

The rushed existence into which industrialized, commercialized man has precipitated himself is actually a good example of an inexpedient development caused entirely by competition between members of the same species. Human beings of today are attacked by so-called manager diseases, high blood pressure, renal atrophy, gastric ulcers, and torturing neuroses: they succumb to barbarism because they have no more time for cultural interests.

Konrad Lorenz

CO-OPT

In Marxian social analysis, co-option occurs when workers identify with the economic system that oppresses them by confusing the remote possibility of accumulating wealth with their actual living and working conditions; being co-opted also refers to anyone who is somehow convinced to further interests that are to her or his ultimate disadvantage.

system rather than with our true role in it. Marxists refer to this as being **co-opted.** You are co-opted when you are tricked, seduced, or somehow convinced to further interests that are to your ultimate disadvantage—and think that you do so willingly.

In the past, when labor unions made their initial approach to various industries, exploited workers often resisted, identifying more with their bosses' values than with their own actual condition. If Marx is correct, we cannot base an assessment of the relationships of production just on the desires or beliefs of the workers, who often (perhaps usually) express the dominant values of the substructure, even when these values are contrary to their well-being.

Bourgeois education fosters competitiveness in the scramble for grades, scholarships, and athletic trophies; it preaches individuality and teaches the doctrine of free choice in the marketplace—all capitalistic values. Bourgeois religion helps suppress workers by teaching them that they are meant to suffer, that the love of money is the root of all evil, that hard work is a blessing and idle hands are the devil's workshop, that the meek shall inherit the earth. Capitalistic workers not only lose control of their time and the products of their work, since these belong to bosses and owners, they lose control of their beliefs. If Marx is correct, it is no wonder we find identifying with our true proletarian status so difficult.

Ultimately, Marx predicted, the proletariat expands; more and more of us join it. Whereas we once believed in "upward mobility," more and more citizens fear that the general direction will be "downward mobility" for increasing numbers—as Marx predicted.

> The lower strata of the middle class—the small tradespeople, shopkeepers, and retired tradesmen generally, the handicraftsmen and peasants—all these sink gradually into the proletariat, partly because their diminutive capital does not suffice for the scale on which modern industry is carried on, and is swamped in the competition with large capitalists, partly because their specialised skill is rendered worthless by new methods of production. Thus the proletariat is recruited from all classes of the population.[11]

As the ranks of the proletariat grow, the dialectical struggle with the bourgeoisie begins.

Philosophical Query

Economists are claiming that for the first time in decades, a generation of Americans is financially worse off than their parents. Many young adults have to live at home longer, have a more difficult time finding jobs, never become able to afford their own homes. Does this square with your experience? Does it support Marx's contention that more and more of us will slip into the proletariat? Is there another explanation? Discuss.

Differences of age and sex have no longer any distinctive social validity for the working class. All are instruments of labour, more or less expensive to use, according to their age and sex.

The Communist Manifesto

Class Struggle

All history, according to Marx and Engels, is the history of class struggle. In this struggle are the seeds of the next stage of history. The bourgeoisie has forged the instrument of its own destruction as it grows smaller but richer and more powerful. In our own time, social scientists are discussing the "shrinking middle class," the growing disparity between the haves and the have-nots. Escalating housing prices keep more and more young families from owning property. As the divorce rate remains high, working-class people suffer the economic (not to mention psychic) cost of supporting two separate households. Divorced mothers of young children face the dilemma of working and paying high child-care costs, or not working and living at or below the poverty level on state assistance or often inadequate child-support payments.

Medical insurance is now priced beyond the reach of so many working- and middle-class people that in 1993 President Bill Clinton began an unprecedented effort to fashion a federal health care program that would "guarantee" adequate care to all Americans. So far, Congress and the President have been unable to fashion a plan that can meet the needs of various groups. For the present, working- and middle-class people must use a continually increasing portion of their income to provide adequate health care for themselves and their families. This further diminishes their chances to save, invest, or buy a home. Yet the tax code remains full of breaks for those with business, investment, or real estate deductions. The wealthiest class in the country pays proportionally the smallest amount of taxes.

Marx and Engels said the overall situation cannot change until the proletariat becomes *fully aware* of itself. That is, so long as different segments of the population compete for raises and jobs, people whose class interests are identical will fail to see that they are.

> At this stage the labourers still form an incoherent mass scattered over the whole country, and broken up by their mutual competition. If anywhere they unite to form more compact bodies, this is not yet the consequence of their own active union, but of the union with the bourgeoisie, which class, in order to attain its own political ends, is compelled to set the whole proletariat in motion, and is moreover yet, for a time, able to do so. At this stage, therefore, the proletarians do not fight their enemies, but the enemies of their enemies . . . every victory so obtained is a victory for the bourgeoisie.[12]

Under this interpretation, it is in the bourgeoisie's short-term interest for different ethnic, gender, age, and religious groups to distrust and despise each other, Marx and Engels point out. If poor Anglos and poor Hispanics and poor people of color and poor Native Americans and poor Asian Americans and poor men and poor women spend their time blaming their own poverty on each other, they fail to see what they *all* have in common:

Socialism will never destroy poverty and the injustice and inequality of capacities.

Leo Tolstoy

The inherent vice of capitalism is the unequal sharing of blessings; the inherent virtue of socialism is the equal sharing of miseries.

Winston Churchill

exploitation by the bourgeoisie. So, for instance, a Marxist might argue that the bitter debate over affirmative action serves the bourgeoisie by obscuring the fact that *most people of all backgrounds are being kept out of the wealthy classes.* Indeed, for the bourgeoisie as a class, nothing could be better than for "token" members of all disadvantaged groups to become publicly successful through education and hard work. This will coopt others in those groups to "behave" and work hard while dreaming of "making it."

Change will come only when the exploited identify with each other and not with their race, religion, gender, or age, says *The Communist Manifesto.*

> But whatever form they may have taken, one fact is common to all past ages, viz., the exploitation of one part of society by the other. No wonder, then, that the social consciousness of past ages, despite all the multiplicity and variety it displays, moves within certain common forms, or general ideas, which cannot completely vanish except with the total disappearance of class antagonisms.
>
> The Communist Manifesto

This union is helped on by the improved means of communication that are created by modern industry, and that place the workers of different localities in contact with one another. It was just this contact that was needed to centralise the numerous local struggles, all of the same character, into one national struggle between classes. But every class struggle is a political struggle. . . .

This organisation of the proletarians into a class, and consequently into a political party, is continually being upset again by the competition between the workers themselves. But it ever rises up again, stronger, firmer, mightier. It compels legislative recognition of particular interests of the workers, by taking advantage of the divisions among the bourgeoisie itself. . . . The bourgeoisie itself, therefore, supplies the proletariat with its own elements of political and general education, in other words, it furnishes the proletariat with weapons for fighting the bourgeoisie.[13]

Philosophical Query

Discuss the possibility that affirmative action and similar social reform efforts actually serve the interests of an exploitative class by creating increased consciousness of difference and division. Are efforts to "honor diversity" aiding or hindering class consciousness? Is there a better solution to social inequality? Discuss.

As capitalism becomes increasingly efficient, it produces more than it can consume, and its technological progress renders large numbers of workers obsolete. Marxists say the result is an overburdened welfare state that provides barely enough sustenance—and no dignity—to its displaced workers.

The modern labourer, on the contrary, instead of rising with the progress of industry, sinks deeper and deeper below the conditions of existence of his own class. He becomes a pauper, and pauperism develops more rapidly than population or wealth. And here it becomes evident that the bourgeoisie . . . is unfit to rule because it is incompetent to assure an existence to its slave within his slavery, because it cannot help letting him sink into such a state, that it has to feed him, instead of being fed by him. Society can no longer live under the bourgeoisie; in other words, its existence is no longer compatible with society. . . . The development of modern industry, therefore, cuts from under its feet the very foundation on which the bourgeoisie produces and appropriates products.[14]

Marx and Engels predicted that more and more workers would suffer as the bourgeoisie acquired capital at their expense, and that the workers' unhappiness, frustration, and indignation would erupt in violent revolution. After the revolution a new social order would emerge, from which all class distinctions, private ownership of the means of production, and exploitation would disappear forever.

What happened? Is the revolution behind schedule or is it not going to come at all? To address this issue, we need to look at one of the most important aspects of Marxist theory, one that is often overlooked by capitalistic critics of Marxism.

> What the bourgeoisie therefore produces, above all, are its own gravediggers. Its fall and the victory of the proletariat are equally inevitable.
>
> The Communist Manifesto

Alienation

One of Marx's most interesting and compelling insights centers on the concept of **alienation**, a term he derived from Hegel. Marx thought of alienation as the most destructive feature of capitalism. Indeed, he thought it revealed an inherent irrationality, an inherent evil in the very basis of capitalism. Alienation occurs when the worker no longer feels at one with the product of his or her labor. An alienated individual rarely feels at home with him- or herself, or with others. Alienation is a state of powerlessness, frustration, repressed resentment, and despair. It results from the transformation of a human being into a commodity.

Marx was convinced we are happiest not when we are idle but when we are engaged in meaningful work. Meaningful work can be work of virtually any kind so long as the worker has control over its products. This is necessary psychologically, not just morally. Imagine the suffering of a designer whose boss controls what brushes, pens, and colors the designer can use; how much time can be devoted to each project; what is good enough (or not); what happens to the designs. No matter how much such a designer produces, he or she will suffer. Being detached from the work, prevented from exercising personal judgment and applying personal standards, the artist is alienated from his or her own work.

Large bureaucracies can also be alienating: we expect to get unclear answers to questions, wait in a long line at one window only to discover that it's the wrong window, and, worst of all, be greeted by hostile or indifferent employees. We feel alienated as they dehumanize us, but they are themselves dehumanized. Performing repetitive tasks without having any

ALIENATION

According to Marx, condition of workers separated from the products of their labor; primarily an objective state, but can also refer to not feeling "at one" with the product of labor.

To be alienated is to feel separated from the world as we experience it daily, from the "center" of ourselves, and from others who are having the same problem. Alienation is what a man feels when he has lost his sense of belonging to the world.

René J. Muller

say in how things are done, boxed into a rigid hierarchy of rules, these workers become commodities, the human equivalent of data processors. The "existing individual" is lost. Marx would say their behavior is the result of alienation.

Anyone who takes a job *solely* on the basis of what it pays becomes alienated in Marx's sense by reducing himself or herself to a money-making machine. Alienation pervades education as teachers are compelled to teach outside their areas of interest and genuine competence or be fired. Even teachers lucky enough to teach in their own fields can become alienated as school districts base course loads on financial, not educational, considerations. Taxpayers who resist paying for adequate education help reduce *their own children* to commodities, because they make a "mere money relationship" the basis of their decision.

The common value system behind such examples is that possessions and money to buy them become more important than time to do things right, than the experience itself, and than the people involved. Soon the alienated worker sees those he or she works for or provides services to as the means to a paycheck, not full human beings. This is what Marx meant when he said, "The *increase in value* of the world of things is directly proportional to the *decrease in value* of the human world." And, of course, full functioning and eudaimonia are impossible in such conditions; this is a "kingdom of means," not a "kingdom of ends."

According to Marx, alienation even extends to our relationship with nature (as environmentalists remind us today). Nature provides the material basis for all work. Yet unchecked capitalism uses up nature, because the capitalist does not feel part of nature.

> The more the worker *appropriates* the external world and sensuous nature through his labor, the more he deprives himself of the *means of life* in two respects; first, that the sensuous world gradually ceases to be an object belonging to his labor, a *means of life* of his work; secondly, that it gradually ceases to be a *means of life* in the immediate sense, a means of physical subsistence of the worker.[15]

The alienated worker sees money as the means of life, not the natural world that provides bread and milk and fruit and wood. Alienated from nature, we cannot see what we really depend on. Today we know the consequences of alienation from nature on a scale Marx could not have imagined.

Because so many of us must work to live, most of us spend the majority of our lives at our jobs. If we are alienated there, we are likely to be alienated elsewhere, for we cannot avoid being shaped by all those hours at work.

Philosophical Query

Discuss some examples of ways alienation spreads from the workplace into society at large, and the home in particular. Has it spread to your life? To school? Discuss.

Psychic Alienation

Marx describes alienation as *externalization*: Work is seen as something I *do*, not as an expression of who I *am*. When I am in a state of alienation, I develop a habit of separating myself from nature and other people. I lose touch with myself, becoming alienated from who I really am, or at least from who I *ought to be*.

What constitutes the externalization of labor?

First is the fact that labor is *external* to the laborer—that is, it is not part of his nature—and that the worker does not affirm himself in his work but denies himself, feels miserable and unhappy, develops no free physical and mental energy but mortifies his flesh and ruins his mind. The worker, therefore, feels at ease only outside work, and during work he is outside himself. He is at home when he is not working and when he is working he is not at home. . . . External labor, labor in which man is externalized, is labor of self-sacrifice, of penance. Finally, the external nature of work for the worker appears in the fact that it is not his own but another person's, that in work he does not belong to himself but to someone else . . . the activity of the worker is not his own spontaneous activity. It belongs to another. It is the loss of his own self.

The result, therefore, is that . . . the worker . . . feels that he is acting freely only in his animal functions—eating, drinking, and procreating, or at most in his shelter and finery—while in his human functions he feels only like an animal. The animalistic becomes human and the human becomes animalistic.[16]

To the extent that Marx is correct, it is no wonder we are so interested in our weekends and vacations, in our leisure: Only there do we feel fully free to be ourselves. Most of the week we sell our bodies and souls out of necessity: the capitalist machine demands that we work. Marx did not believe humans are by nature lazy. Quite the contrary; he believed we *want* and *need* meaningful work. Our obsessions with leisure, our absenteeism, our efforts to strike it rich or retire as early as possible only testify to the deep degree of alienation we must be experiencing in our work.

Marx distinguishes alienated life from species-life. **Species-life** is fully human life, life lived productively and consciously. **Alienated life**, in contrast, creates a sense of distance from nature and renders people unconscious of precisely how unhappy, unspontaneous, and unfulfilled they really are. In other words, alienation prevents us from being fully human. Thus alienation is anti-species or anti-human.

Marx, we see at last, is propounding not just an economic theory, but a sophisticated philosophy of *self-actualization*. He thinks that in the next historical stage, people will work to fulfill themselves, for the creative, self-actualizing joy of it. If that is difficult to believe, Marx says, it is because we are so alienated from human nature (our species) that we can conceive of work only in distorted, alienated terms.

> The less you are and the less you express of your life—the more you have and the greater is your alienated life.
>
> *Karl Marx*

SPECIES-LIFE

Fully human life lived productively and consciously; not alienated.

ALIENATED LIFE

Unconscious, unspontaneous, and unfulfilled life; deprived of fundamental conditions necessary for self-actualization.

Yet think of people with hobbies. Maybe you know a dentist who does woodworking in her spare time, or maybe you garden every chance you get. Other people write books or sew or knit or repair things around the house in their spare time or after they retire. These tasks take concentration and effort, yet we do not think of them as work. Students sometimes get distracted by interesting books they stumble onto in the library and read them instead of their assignments. Yet they do not think of that reading as work. Why not?

What makes something "work" is not whether it is difficult or easy, but *how we relate to it*. If we are involved in and care about it, if, in Marx's expression, we are "at home," we do not look upon a task as work. If we have significant say over how we do something and do it for reasons we understand and for values we hold, we may not like what we do, but we are not alienated from it. If we act from love when we cut the grass for our parents or help a friend move furniture, we are not alienated.

Whenever we feel that what we do matters, we feel productive. We come alive. The more alive and conscious we are, the more fully we participate in species-life.

> The animal is immediately one with *its life activity*, not distinct from it. The animal is its life activity. Man makes his life activity itself into an object of will and consciousness. He has conscious life activity. It is not a determination with which he immediately identifies. Conscious life activity distinguishes man immediately from the life activity of the animal. Only thereby is he a species-being. Or rather, he is only a conscious being—that is, his own life is an object for him—since he is a species-being. Only on that account is his activity free activity. Alienated labor reverses the relationship in that man, since he is a conscious being, makes his life activity, his *essence*, only a means for his *existence*.[17]

Philosophical Query

Discuss activities in which you participate in "species-life." Contrast such experiences with alienated activity. What can you do to decrease periods of alienation and increase your own "species-life"?

If capitalism were destroyed, Marx thought, we would revert to species-life. Once freed from the irrational, destructive pressure to survive only at the expense of others, we would be free to develop as human beings, to actualize ourselves as productive workers who find joy and fulfillment in personally meaningful work. If we are unable to accept that vision of ourselves right now, Marx would say it is because we are living alienated lives to one degree or another. Our distrust of Marx's utopia becomes a symptom of our distorted view of human nature. What we think of as human nature—people hustling for a buck, scheming to strike it rich, and look-

The business of America is business.

Calvin Coolidge

The philosopher, who is himself an abstract form of alienated man, takes himself as the yardstick of the alienated world. The whole history of alienation . . . is . . . nothing but the history of the production of abstract thought.

Karl Marx

ing forward to the day they can quit working—is not *human* nature at all: It is alienation.

One-Dimensional Man

Marxist and non-Marxist observers alike note that the violent overthrow of capitalism by the proletariat that Marx predicted has not occurred and seems less and less likely as we survey the world scene. Does this mean Marx was wrong in his critique of capitalism and alienation? It may not, for much of Marx's analysis remains persuasive and perceptive.

Marx's prediction was based on his belief that increased industrialization would lead to a greater and greater gap between the bourgeoisie and proletariat. The living conditions of the proletariat would become intolerable, and having "nothing to lose but their chains," they would revolt and destroy the system. An intriguing explanation of Marx's miscalculation on this score can be found in the book *One-Dimensional Man* by **Herbert Marcuse (1898–1979)**.

Marcuse, born and educated in Germany, came to America in 1934 to escape the Nazis. He taught philosophy at Brandeis University and the University of California at San Diego. In *One-Dimensional Man*, Marcuse argued that Marx was unable to anticipate the adaptive powers of capitalism. Specifically, he claimed that capitalist leaders have learned to manage the economy well enough to prevent the major disruptions (famines, shortages, depressions) Marx expected. Further, no one, Marx included, could have predicted the rapid, qualitative changes in technology that have altered the very nature of work for most people. Physical conditions of employment continue to improve for virtually all workers.

More importantly, many of us have been co-opted by a taste of the pie in the form of color television sets, stereos, nice cars, and so on. In other words, we are distracted from our true condition by being in a position to buy (or charge) technologically sophisticated, comforting goods. Yet we remain slave laborers, paying inflated prices for what we get, and still doing meaningless work. Marcuse thought our "economic prosperity" has been purchased by an irrationally large defense industry that is used to drive the economy, to keep it expanding.

Trapped in a cycle of consume-borrow-pay, we become one-dimensional people, not fully realized human beings consciously participating in our own species-life. Subtly conditioned by the media, we settle for immediate gratification and fail to notice or care about the gross and immoral inequities in the system—or, if we notice them, we are too tired, too frustrated, or too distracted by our own self-interest to attempt improving them.

> This society is irrational as a whole. Its productivity is destructive of the free development of human needs and faculties, its peace maintained by the constant threat of war, its growth dependent on the

We proceed from a *present* fact of political economy.

The worker becomes poorer the more wealth he produces, the more his production increases in power and extent. The worker becomes a cheaper commodity the more commodities he produces. The *increase in value* of the world of things is directly proportional to the *decrease in value* of the human world. Labor not only produces commodities. It produces itself and the worker as a *commodity*, and indeed in the same proportion as it produces commodities in general.

Karl Marx

All previous historical movements were movements of minorities, or in the interest of minorities. The proletarian movement is the self-conscious, independent movement of the immense majority, in the interest of the immense majority.

The Communist Manifesto

repression of the real possibilities for pacifying the struggle for existence—individual, national, international. This repression, so different from that which characterized the preceding, less developed stages of our society, operates today not from a position of natural and technical immaturity but rather from a position of strength. The capabilities (intellectual and material) of contemporary society are immeasurably greater than ever before—which means that the scope of society's domination over the individual is immeasurably greater than ever before. Our society distinguishes itself by conquering the centrifugal social forces with Technology rather than Terror, on the dual basis of an overwhelming efficiency and an increasing standard of living. . . .

The fact that the vast majority of the population accepts, and is made to accept, this society does not render it less irrational and less reprehensible. The distinction between true and false consciousness, real and immediate interest still is meaningful. But this distinction itself must be validated. Men must come to see it and to find their way from false to true consciousness, from their immediate to their real interest. They can do so only if they live in need of changing their way of life, of denying the positive, of refusing. It is precisely this need which the established society manages to repress to the degree to which it is capable of "delivering the goods" on an increasingly large scale, and using the scientific conquest of nature for the scientific conquest of man.[18]

A maxim of revolutionists is that the group most likely to revolt is the group with the least to lose. Thus one way to keep people in submission is to give them just enough that their desire for change is tempered by fear of losing what they already have. Marcuse argues that contemporary capitalism has co-opted the proletariat and bought us off with possessions. Our moral sense is eroded. We tolerate gross inequities in income distribution and subhuman living and working conditions for some people, because our gadgets and toys mean more to us than a saner, more just society.

Gross misdistribution of the work force is a product of the inherent irrationality of society, Marcuse suggests: People gravitate toward high-paying, high-status jobs rather than toward personally and socially fulfilling work. The result is too many lawyers and too few grade school teachers, too many stockbrokers and not enough nurses.

Complete renunciation of one's possessions is a thing which very few . . . are capable of. All that can legitimately be expected of the wealthy class is that they hold their riches and talents in trust and use them for the service of society. To insist on more would be to kill the goose that laid the golden egg.

Mohandas Gandhi

Philosophical Query

Consider the possibility that in some areas, at least, society might actually benefit from less technology. For example, at some point it becomes irrational to continue to improve agricultural productivity through the use of chemicals and planting procedures that deplete topsoil when there are able-bodied, willing people looking for work. We could have healthier crops, preserve nature, and provide the satisfaction and dignity of meaningful work to those who seek it by making agriculture more "human," more labor-intensive. Discuss. Provide additional supporting examples if you can.

Alienated Love

Psychologist and "socialist humanist" philosopher **Erich Fromm (1900–1980)** wrote in a Marxian vein about self-actualization and love in his book *The Art of Loving*. Specifically, Fromm attempted to show how the structure of capitalistic society shapes our personal relationships. Of special interest to us is the way he characterized love as a form of commodity transfer in which we "exchange personality packages." This thesis rests on a Marxian conception of alienation. In sum, Fromm argued that alienated people cannot really love—themselves, one another, or God. Along the way he raised some disturbing questions about our society. See what you think of this contemporary Marxist analysis.

Modern capitalism needs men who co-operate smoothly and in large numbers; who want to consume more and more; and whose tastes are standardized and can be easily influenced and anticipated. It needs men who feel free and independent, not subject to any authority or principle or conscience—yet willing to be commanded, to do what is expected of them, to fit into the social machine without friction; who can be guided without force, led without leaders, prompted without aim—except the one to make good, to be on the move, to go ahead.

What is the outcome? Modern man is alienated from himself, from his fellow man, from nature. He has been transformed into a commodity, experiences his life forces as an investment which must bring him the maximum profit obtainable under existing market conditions. Human relations are essentially those of alienated automatons. . . . Our civilization offers many palliatives which help people to be consciously unaware of this aloneness: first of all the strict routine of bureaucratized, mechanical work, which helps people remain unaware of their most fundamental human desires, of the longing for transcendence and unity. Inasmuch as the routine does not succeed in this, man overcomes his unconscious despair by the routine of amusement, the passive consumption of sounds and sights offered by the amusement industry; furthermore by the satisfaction of buying ever more things, and soon exchanging them for others. Modern man is actually close to the picture Huxley describes in his *Brave New World*, well fed, well clad, satisfied sexually, yet without self, without any except the most superficial contact with his fellow men, guided by slogans. . . .

The situation as far as love is concerned corresponds, as it has to by necessity, to this social character of modern man. Automatons

Not only has the bourgeoisie forged the weapons that bring death to itself; it has called into existence the men who are to wield those weapons—the modern working class—the proletarians.

The Communist Manifesto

The oppressed are allowed once every few years to decide which particular representatives of the oppressing class are to represent and repress them.

Karl Marx

Communism, like any other revealed religion, is largely made up of prophecies.

H. L. Mencken

cannot love; they can exchange their "personality packages" and hope for a fair bargain. . . .

Just as automatons cannot love each other, they cannot love God. The *disintegration of the love of God* has reached the same proportions as the disintegration of the love of man. This fact is in blatant contradiction to the idea that we are witnessing a religious renaissance in this epoch. Nothing could be further from the truth. What we witness (even though there are exceptions) is a regression to an idolatric concept of God, and a transformation of the love of God into a relationship fitting an alienated character structure. The regression to an idolatric concept of God is easy to see. People are anxious, without principles or faith, they find themselves without an aim except the one to move ahead; hence they continue to remain children, to hope for father or mother to come to their help when help is needed. . . .

. . . belief in God and prayer is recommended as a means to increase one's ability to be successful. Just as modern psychiatrists recommend happiness of the employee in order to be more appealing to the customers, some ministers recommend love of God in order to be more successful. "Make God your partner" means to make God a partner in business, rather than to become one with him in love, justice and truth. Just as brotherly love has been replaced by impersonal fairness, God has been transformed into a remote General Director of the Universe, Inc.; you know that he is there, he runs the show (although it would probably run without him too), you never see him, but you acknowledge his leadership while you are "doing your part."[19]

Philosophical Query

Go through the Fromm passage carefully. What is the relationship between alienation and the transformation of human beings into commodities? What do you think of Fromm's notion that capitalism shapes personal relationships? Does it apply to your family, to your relationships with your teachers? What do you think of his assessment of love? Of capitalistic religion? Explain.

Commentary

Here in the non-Communist world, many of us still confuse the crude, degrading, dehumanizing efforts of the large, formerly Communist states, which once composed the USSR, with philosophical Marxism. Marx's vision of self-actualized people living species-life to its fullest cannot be realized in bread lines; secret police are certainly not elements of species-life. The revolt Marx predicted may not have to be violent. Perhaps we are seeing something very much like it in the ongoing struggles occurring in the former Soviet Union, where people are saying, "We have had enough. We want meaningful work, personal freedom, and bread," and in the growing dissatisfaction among people of other Eastern Bloc countries.

Marx seems to have confused the evils of industrialization with capitalism. His critique of capitalism has much to teach us about the relationship of the material conditions of people's lives to the ideas and beliefs they hold. His assessment of the evils of the bourgeoisie reminds us of the dangers of class disparity and the separation of reward from performance. His overall critique raises important questions about the meaning of work and human dignity.

But we must not overlook the fact that Marx's philosophy itself is—by his own criteria—a product of *his* material condition. He acknowledged this possibility but insisted he could overcome this limit and produce an objective analysis of history. Yet it is clear that his sense of class consciousness is tied to nineteenth-century social and economic conditions.

I find it difficult to overlook the strong strain of resentment and bitterness that runs through the work of Marx and Engels. This may be a reflection of their identification with the abused workers of the postindustrial state. It may also help account for the fact that Marxism's greatest appeal is to people in underdeveloped countries. Contemporary political Marxism seems to derive much of its momentum from similar anger. That may be appropriate as an early reaction against exploiters, but anger alone cannot construct a healthy society. So far, Marxism has failed to appeal to the masses of workers in advanced capitalistic countries—precisely those it is aimed at.

Marx has been compared to an Old Testament prophet, and like a prophet he has taken us to task for our sins. These sins are indifference to gross inequities and injustice, the diminishment of the worth of people (ourselves included) for the exaltation of property and capital, alienation from nature and each other, and the sin of not being all that we can, of failing to live our species-life. He has shown us society in a new way, and called our attention to the importance of its substructure.

But he has assigned too little importance to the role of ideas as causes of change. He has romanticized the proletariat and oversimplified the relations between classes. Marx did not allow for the possibility of societal self-correction and consciously guided change, nor did he fully anticipate the shape of the modern economy. He did not, as no one could, imagine the effects of the great technological revolution we are living through. Lastly, in spite of his concern for the alienated, degraded worker, Marx's emphasis on classes and class struggle does not pay enough respect to the individual. One of the major problems with political Marxism is its tendency to sacrifice the individual for the good of the collective.

Still, Marx's vision of a fuller, better life adds him to the list of champions of the oppressed and exploited. Like a prophet, he called us to account for our errors and, like a prophet, he indicated a general direction, though he was not able to provide a detailed map. Perhaps that is enough.

The Communists disdain to conceal their views and aims. They openly declare that their ends can be attained by the forcible overthrow of all existing social conditions. Let the ruling classes tremble at a Communist revolution. The proletarians have nothing to lose but their chains. They have a world to win. Working men of all countries unite!

The Communist
Manifesto

The state is not abolished, it withers away.

Friedrich Engels

Summary of Main Points

1. Marx combined Hegel's dialectical view of history with Feuerbach's concept of a materialist *zeitgeist* (spirit of the age) to produce historical materialism, the view that history is the ongoing result of constant tension between two classes: the exploiters and the exploited. Engels helped Marx write *The Communist Manifesto* and spread historical materialism.

2. The dialectical process consists of an interaction between an original condition (thesis) and a contrary condition (antithesis) that produces a new condition containing elements of the thesis and antithesis (synthesis). The synthesis becomes the thesis for a new dialectical cycle.

3. Marx identified five "epochs of history" that comprise the dialectical development of history: (1) primitive/communal, (2) slave, (3) feudal, (4) capitalist, (5) socialist/communist. As each epoch develops, its basic economic structure matures and the material conditions under which people live change. According to Marx, ideas, values, and thinking itself are shaped by material conditions and social relations.

4. Marx argued that the economic structure of a culture creates and forms its own ideas. Most important is the material substructure, which consists of three components: (1) the means of production (natural resources); (2) the forces of production (factories, equipment, technology, and knowledge); (3) the relationships of production, which constitute a complex system that shapes everything else.

5. The material substructure produces ideas and institutions compatible with it. These constitute the culture's superstructure and include art, science, philosophy, religion, and government.

6. Marx was sharply critical of capitalism, which he saw as a stage on the way to a classless socialistic economy. In his view, the capitalist substructure contains a fundamental contradiction in the tension between the owners' desire to keep wages low while prices fluctuate according to the law of supply and demand. Marx predicted that as owners accumulated capital (surplus value), the condition of workers would decline.

7. Under capitalism, the two struggling classes are the bourgeoisie and the proletariat. The bourgeoisie consists of those who own the means of production but do not produce anything; it views everything in terms of money and self-interest. The proletariat consists of those who produce things but do not own the means of production (including their own time and labor).

8. Marx predicted that the demands of the bourgeoisie would result in an ever-growing proletariat whose living conditions would continue to decline until the proletariat would rise up in violent revolt and destroy the bourgeoisie and capitalism, leading to the next historical epoch, socialism.

9. The most destructive feature of capitalism, according to Marx, is alienation, which occurs when the worker no longer feels at one with the product of his or her labor; it is a state of powerlessness, frustration, and despair. Capitalism alienates people from one another, from nature, and from work.

10. Marx distinguished alienated life from species-life, which is lived productively and consciously. Species-life is fully human life, a product of self-actualization (which capitalism inhibits).

11. Herbert Marcuse argues that Marx failed to predict the adaptive powers of capitalism to make the expanding proletariat comfortable enough to prevent violent disruption of the entire economy. According to Marcuse,

the modern capitalist economy creates one-dimensional people who do not fully participate in species-life.

12. Erich Fromm used the concept of alienated love to explain how the structure of capitalis-tic society shapes personal relationships. According to Fromm, alienated people cannot really love, so under capitalistic conditions love becomes an exchange of "personality packages."

Study Questions

1. Describe the social conditions that led Marx and Engels to write *The Communist Manifesto*.

2. What was Feuerbach's influence on Marx?

3. What was Hegel's influence on Marx?

4. Explain why Marx's philosophy is sometimes called *historical materialism*.

5. What is the dialectical process of history? Explain in terms of the five epochs of history.

6. What does Marx mean by *mystification*? Give one or two examples.

7. Briefly explain the notion of economic determinism.

8. Identify the three components of the material base of society. Which is the most important, according to Marx? Why?

9. Distinguish between the superstructure and sub-structure of society.

10. Describe capitalism in terms of the relationships of production.

11. What is the bourgeoisie? Describe it; then discuss its significance to philosophical Marxism.

12. What is the proletariat? Describe it; then discuss its significance to philosophical Marxism.

13. Explain the significance of class consciousness and class struggle to Marxism.

14. What did Marx see as the inherent contradiction in capitalism? How is the contradiction related to his prophecy of violent revolution?

15. Thoroughly explain Marx's concept of alienation.

16. What is alienated labor? What is unalienated labor?

17. What is species-life? What roles do consciousness and alienation play in it?

18. What does Marcuse mean by the expression "one-dimensional man"?

19. How does Marcuse account for the failure of violent economic revolution?

20. In your own words, present Fromm's case that we are alienated from love of others and God.

Fourth Interlude

The Utilitarians

If all mankind minus one were of one opinion, and only one person were of the contrary opinion, mankind would be no more justified in silencing that one person than he, if he had the power, would be justified in silencing mankind.

John Stuart Mill

Life requires choices. The more complex a society, the larger and more diverse its population, the more difficult those choices become. Two competing tendencies struggle to control the general direction of any society: a desire for change and progress, and a desire for security and order. To do justice to both tendencies, a free society must try to balance individual rights and freedoms with the general social welfare.

You may have driven or ridden to work or school today on a roadway carved through what used to be a family farm. Let's call this family the Malones. When the community decided to build a highway across that land, it probably first offered to buy the land. Such an offer is technically only a courtesy, for virtually every community in this country can appropriate private land—at a "fair market price"—under what is called the right of eminent domain. If the Malones refused to sell, perhaps because three generations of Malones had lived and died on that land, the community could simply force them to leave (and pay them the price it determined was fair).

It's easy to sympathize with the Malones. We can all imagine how we would feel in similar circumstances. Such a use of government power seems almost un-American. In fact, however, it represents an application of one of the basic philosophical principles on which our society rests. The principle is that individual rights and desires should be protected, but that ultimately the good of the majority must take precedence over the good of any individual. This is a tricky, difficult balance to reach. Granting our sympathy for the Malones, how can the desires of one family outweigh so much good for so many others? Whether the Malones like it or not, their displeasure is a small price to pay for so much happiness for so many people.

The same kind of reasoning, stated or not, is the foundation of laws restricting what you can do with your property. The "greatest-happiness principle" limits when your neighbors can run their loud leaf blowers. It prevents you from refusing to rent apartments in a building you own to people of races, sexes, or ages you don't like. In certain cases, we easily understand, accept, and favor this reasoning.

The greatest-happiness principle is a more sophisticated, modern version of hedonism (Second Interlude). First presented in its new form by the British philosopher Jeremy Bentham, it was modified and refined by John Stuart Mill as *utilitarianism*. From the moment Bentham's work became known, utilitarianism has been an influential moral and social philosophy.

Jeremy Bentham

Philosophy and Social Reform

Modern utilitarianism developed as a response to social conditions created by a number of factors associated with what is called the Industrial Revolution—the period of time running roughly from 1780 to approximately 1835. As the term implies, this was an era characterized by massive social change and upheaval generated by applications of new scientific manufacturing techniques that, in turn, produced geographic, familial, spiritual, and economic disruption as a newly created class of "workers" competed for jobs that were often repetitious, dangerous, poorly paid—degrading and dehumanizing.

The advent of efficient steam and water power made large factories practical. Cloth weaving, for example, had once been a cottage industry, but the textile mills rendered handwoven fabrics too expensive. Hordes of workers sought jobs in the mill towns, creating large urban slums. Between 1800 and 1831, Leeds, Sheffield, Manchester, and Liverpool nearly doubled in population. Shabbily constructed buildings rented at such high prices that they paid for themselves in five years. Of course, such high rents resulted in overcrowding, as poorly paid workers lived two and three families to an apartment. In Manchester in 1845, for example, twenty-seven cases were documented of up to seven people trying to sleep in one bed.[1]

In 1798, **Thomas Malthus (1766–1834)**, an Anglican minister, published a work titled *An Essay on the Principle of Population as It Affects*

Have I a genius for anything? What can I produce? . . . What, of all earthly pursuits, is the most important? Legislation. Have I a genius for legislation? I gave myself the answer, fearfully and tremblingly: "Yes."

Jeremy Bentham

the Future Improvement of Society. In it, Malthus expressed grave doubts about the feasibility of social reform:

> I have read some . . . speculations, on the perfectibility of men and society, with great pleasure. I have been warmed and delighted with the enchanting picture which they hold forth. I ardently wish for such happy improvements. But I see great and, to my understanding, unconquerable difficulties in the way to them.[2]

The "great difficulties" Malthus feared were overpopulation and underproduction of food. He argued that although food production increases arithmetically (1 to 2 to 3 to 4 to 5 to 6, etc.), unchecked population growth progresses geometrically (1 to 2 to 4 to 8 to 16 to 32, etc.). Thus, according to Malthus, unchecked population inevitably outgrows the food supply.

Troubled both by the growing slums in the cities and by efforts to improve living conditions for the poor, Malthus concluded that there could be no justification for helping the disadvantaged. Raising wages would only enable the poor to marry younger and have even more children; population would outgrow food supply and poverty would return anyway. Welfare programs would only result in increased "idleness" and encourage large families—with the same result.

Malthus argued that the only way to avoid such harsh natural cures as epidemics and the historical cure of war or rebellion was to stop helping the poor and remove all restraints on the free enterprise system. Buyers, sellers, bosses, workers, and owners must be left to their own struggle. The law of supply and demand would make it more difficult for the poor to afford to marry early or support very many children, thereby checking the geometrical rise of population.

The conservative British ruling class eagerly embraced Malthusian principles. Factory owners and businessmen were able to justify low wages as their "duty." The evils of the Industrial Revolution could be rationalized away by blaming the miserable living and working conditions of the poor on the poor themselves. And certainly these conditions were discouraging.

In this context, Jeremy Bentham's insistence that legislators take into account the greatest happiness of the greatest number of people can be seen as the radical philosophy it was. It directly threatened and challenged the owners, bosses, and ruling classes: If "each counts as one and none more," privileges of class, wealth, and title lose their force. Bentham blasted those in power for pursuing their own narrow, socially destructive goals instead of wanting the greatest happiness for the greatest number. (Once again, we see how philosophy can be dangerous.)

Bentham's solution was to broaden the base of those in power—to establish democratic rule by the whole people, not a select class. If "the rulers are the people," the greatest-happiness principle will be followed almost naturally, Bentham reasoned. He believed "all government is in itself evil"; the only justification for government is to prevent worse evils.

It is clear that any society where the means of subsistence increase less rapidly than the numbers of the population is a society on the brink of an abyss. . . . Destitution is fearfully prolific.

M. Louis Blanc

Judgment is given to men that they may use it. Because it may be used erroneously, are men to be told that they ought not to use it at all?

John Stuart Mill

Thus the functions of government were social reform and establishment of the conditions most conducive to promoting the greatest happiness for the greatest number of people. This proved to be a nearly irresistible philosophy for many.

Simple Utilitarianism

Much of nineteenth-century philosophy was a response to Kant's work, but with the notable exceptions of G. W. F. Hegel and Arthur Schopenhauer, most philosophers rejected both Kant's elaborate systems and his transcendental metaphysics. They viewed metaphysics as cumbersome, irrelevant, and meaningless, unverifiable by science and unclear according to the empirical criterion of meaning (see Chapter 9). Philosophers' interest shifted from the search for transcendental truth or systemic coherence to practical remedies for the pressing problems of society. They explored social and political philosophy, empirically based ethics, and the application of scientific knowledge and thinking to immediate problems of human happiness.

Predictably, this secular, fact-oriented approach revived belief in the cultural relativity of values and beliefs. Philosophers no longer felt obliged to produce elaborate theories or systems, since they thought even their own theories had to be culturally limited. By contrast, particular strategies and factual information were thought to be reliable, provided they were "scientific" and "objective."

Moreover, the new scientific view of an evolving universe made elaborate metaphysical theories seem irrelevant. If the universe and everything in it is slowly changing, then any fixed "grand theory" would apply for only a brief time at best. Growing belief in evolution resulted in efforts to identify an evolutionary view of ideas, as opposed to a search for *the* static truth.

Lastly, the social change and turmoil generated by the Industrial Revolution, the French Revolution, and the Napoleonic Wars cast serious doubts on the adequacy of Kant's ethic of *good will*. Looking about them, philosophers noted that *what actually happens to people* is of supreme importance. A clear need for fact-based, humanistic reform emerged.

Science became the new hope, replacing Enlightenment conceptions of reason. Empirical awareness of the social, physical, and emotional factors of acting and deciding created a desire to identify and alter the actual causes of poverty, crime, ignorance, and other sources of widespread misery. Social and political issues eventually dominated metaphysical concerns. Epistemology was important only to the extent that it related to verifiable, immediate improvements in society. If the Enlightenment was the Age of Reason, the nineteenth century began as the Age of Reform. (How it ended is another story.)

Morality, the science of human happiness, [is] the principle which binds the individual to the species, and the inducements which are calculated to persuade us to model our conduct on the way most conducive to the advantage of all.

William Godwin

The Principle of Utility

Bentham attempted to base his philosophy on careful consideration and observation of social conditions and actual human behavior. In other words, he looked in exactly the opposite direction from Kant, who would have dismissed Bentham's work as "anthropology," not moral philosophy. This is not likely to have distressed Bentham, since he was deliberately trying to avoid the errors of ungrounded metaphysics and construct a scientific system.

Bentham declared that careful observation of actual behavior makes it crystal clear that pain and pleasure shape all human activity. As he says in the famous opening passage of *An Introduction to Principles of Morals and Legislation*:

> I. Nature has placed mankind under the governance of two sovereign masters, *pain* and *pleasure*. It is for them alone to point out what we ought to do, as well as determine what we shall do. On the one hand the standard of right and wrong, on the other the chain of causes and effects, are fastened to their throne. They govern us in all we do, in all we say, in all we think: every effort we can make to throw off our subjection will serve but to demonstrate and confirm it. In words man pretends to abjure their empire; but in reality he will remain subject to it all the while. The *principle of utility* recognizes this subjection and assumes it for the foundation of that system, the object of which is to rear the fabric of felicity by the hands of reason and of law. Systems which attempt to question it deal in sounds instead of sense, in caprice instead of reason, in darkness instead of light.[3]

Bentham is both a psychological hedonist (pain and pleasure "determine what we shall do") and an ethical hedonist (pain and pleasure "alone . . . point out what we ought to do"). Thus the principle of utility is also referred to as the *pleasure principle*.

The term *utility* has two related meanings. A thing's utility refers to its usefulness, to how well it performs its specific function. In this sense, a utilitarian automobile would have blackwall tires and only the most practical accessories like rear window defrosters or anti-lock brakes. Although this no-frills notion of utility enters into Bentham's meaning, he uses the term to mean *pleasure-producing or pain-avoiding*. We might simplify that to *pleasure-maximizing*—if we keep in mind that sometimes the best we can do to maximize pleasure is minimize pain.

Having asserted both ethical and psychological hedonism, and having described what he meant by utility, Bentham made a move that revolutionized the concept of hedonism: He enlarged the ethical interests of the hedonist. And since he thought we are all hedonists whether we know it or not, this amounted to enlarging everyone's general ethical obligation by transforming personal hedonism into a potent social and ethical philoso-

It is vain to talk of the interest of the community, without understanding what is in the interest of the individual. A thing is said to promote the interest, or to be for the interest, of an individual when it tends to add to the sum total of his pleasures; or, what comes to the same thing, to diminish the sum total of his pains.

Jeremy Bentham

phy, guided by the **principle of utility**: *Act always to promote the greatest happiness for the greatest number.*

Although John Stuart Mill coined the term *utilitarianism*, philosophers sometimes refer to Bentham's philosophy as utilitarianism, also. To avoid confusion, we'll refer to Bentham's as *simple utilitarianism*, to distinguish it from Mill's more refined and elaborate version, which we'll refer to as *utilitarianism*.

The Hedonic Calculus

Bentham wanted to make ethics a science. To that end, he tried to base his philosophy on observations of actual conditions and to derive principles of behavior from facts. Bentham thought he had found a scientific way to calculate the precisely proper course of action for any circumstance. He called his technique the *hedonic calculus*. Mill sometimes referred to the calculus as Bentham's "method of detail," because it took a detailed look at various factors.

To introduce mathematical precision to the difficult task of weighing alternative courses of action, Bentham proposed the notion of "units" of pleasure or pain, which he called *hedons* or *lots*. (Some contemporary philosophers use the term *utiles*.) Thus, when contemplating an action, we add units of pleasure or subtract units of pain.

But actions are complex, and Bentham identified four elements that affect pleasure or pain themselves, two that affect action related to pleasure or pain, and one based on the number of people affected. The seven elements are:

1. *Intensity.* How strong is the pleasure?

2. *Duration.* How long will the pleasure last?

3. *Propinquity.* How soon will the pleasure occur?

4. *Certainty.* How likely or unlikely is it that the pleasure will occur?

5. *Fecundity.* How likely is it that the proposed action will produce more pleasure?

6. *Purity.* Will there be any pain accompanying the action?

7. *Extent.* How many other people will be affected?

Positive units of pleasure or negative units of pain can be attached to each of these seven elements. The resulting totals can then be compared, and if the balance is on the positive (pleasure) side, the proposed choice is good; if the balance is on the negative (pain) side, the choice is bad. If a hedonic calculation results in more units of pleasure, we should perform the contemplated action; if more units of pain, we should not.

Bentham believed each of us already uses hedonic calculation on a commonsense, intuitive level; in his view, he was simply adding scientific rigor to our various informal methods of choosing pleasure and avoiding pain.

PRINCIPLE OF UTILITY

Always act to promote the greatest happiness for the greatest number.

This, then, is our Bentham. He was a man both of remarkable endowments for philosophy, and of remarkable deficiencies for it: fitted, beyond almost any man, for drawing from his premises conclusions not only correct, but sufficiently precise and specific to be practical: but whose general conception of human nature and life furnished him with an unusually slender stock of premises.

John Stuart Mill

Do scenes like the one in
this picture support an
egoistic interpretation of
human behavior? Is ignor-
ing street people a form of
selfishness? Are street people any less egoistic than
those who walk by them?

Overcome, you higher men,
the petty virtues, the petty
prudences, the sand-grain
discretion, the ant-swarm
inanity, the miserable ease,
the "happiness of the greatest number!"

Friedrich Nietzsche

The Egoistic Foundation of Social Concern

Bentham claimed that psychological egoism is natural and universal. Psychological egoism asserts that it is human nature for each of us to be interested chiefly in our own welfare. All decisions are made in terms of furthering or hindering what we want or need. In hedonistic terms, my chief
concern is my own pleasure or pain. That's not to say I don't care about
anyone or anything else, but my caring is defined by how those things affect my feelings. Those I love give me pleasure, which is in my interest.
Those I hate cause me pain, which is not in my interest. To those who cause
me neither pain nor pleasure, I am indifferent.

From this perspective, all values and value systems are pleasure/pain
based because by our psychological makeup we *must* always seek pleasure
or avoid pain. Thus, regardless of their terminology, all ethical systems attempt to produce pleasure. They may speak of right and wrong, good and
bad, and so forth, but these terms all reduce to pleasure and pain. Reason
is simply a tool whose function is to help determine the most likely consequences of our actions in terms of pain and pleasure. (Note how significantly this pragmatic, calculating concept of reason contrasts with Kant's
concept of the good will.)

Building on his egoistic foundation, Bentham thought that if people
could be shown how a better society for others would result in less pain
and more pleasure for *them*, genuine social reform would occur. Our natural self-interest provides an *egoistic hook* to show how our individual
welfare is inseparable from social welfare. Thus the proper role of gov-

ernment must be to ensure that the *enlightened self-interest* of each individual is allowed to develop. Further, to promote the greatest possible happiness for the greatest number, laws and regulations must be fair and effective, and designed to motivate people to consider others' welfare as well as their own.

Bentham and other liberal, *laissez-faire* reformers made a stunning connection between the welfare of the individual and the welfare of the community. They attempted to *show* how clear-thinking "selfishness" could produce a better world. Rather than chastise us for being self-interested, Bentham sought to take advantage of it.

Let's examine Bentham's egoistic hook by considering an actual issue. During a heated debate over a severe cut in tax money available for schools, a number of letters to the editor of a local newspaper made this basic point: "I have paid my dues. My children are grown and I've paid taxes for years. Why should I pay to send someone else's children to school? Let their families pay." Such letters reflect a disappointing lack of enlightened self-interest. It is in every individual's self-interest—even individuals who don't have children themselves—to see that all children get a good education. Poorly educated people are much more likely to be unemployed or dependent on government assistance for survival than adequately educated ones. Moreover, if poorly educated people turn to crime for survival, the rest of us will have to live in fear and to pay for more judges, district attorneys, police officers, and jails; we'll see a general decline in our own social services. Thus it is clearly in every individual's interest for as many children as possible to grow up to be well-educated, productive members of society.

Bentham's move was motivationally brilliant. In one fell swoop he found a way to link individual self-interest and the good of the community. Egoistic utilitarian logic is concrete and practical, based on everyday concerns and foreseeable consequences. We need not be able to reason abstractly to understand the basic wisdom of the greatest-happiness principle.

But such reasoning, though effective, remains egoistic and potentially destructive, for whatever sense of community it creates is based chiefly on selfish concerns, not compassion or empathy. The full force of utilitarianism did not emerge until Mill went beyond Bentham to produce a more refined altruistic utilitarianism.

> The utilitarian standard . . . is not the agent's own greatest happiness, but the greatest amount of happiness altogether, and if it may possibly be doubted whether a noble character is always the happier for its nobleness, there can be no doubt that it makes other people happier, and that the world in general is immensely a gainer by it. Utilitarianism, therefore, could only attain its end by the general cultivation of nobleness of character.
>
> *John Stuart Mill*

John Stuart Mill

John Stuart Mill (1806–1873), one of the most brilliant, interesting figures in philosophy, and in effect, the "son of utilitarianism," began life with nearly equal doses of favor and misfortune. A lucid defender of individual

John Stuart Mill

liberty, his childhood was severely restricted, his emotional needs virtually ignored.

Mill's parents were estranged—in his words, living "as far apart, under the same roof, as the north pole from the south." Mill's contemporary biographer, A. Bain, described John Stuart Mill's father, James Mill, as unfeeling:

> Even in his most amiable moods, he was not a man to be trifled with. His entering the room where the family was assembled was observed by strangers to operate as an immediate damper. This was not the worst. The one really disagreeable trait in [James] Mill's character, and the thing that has left the most painful memories, was the way he allowed himself to speak and behave to his wife and children before visitors.[4]

James Mill believed that the best way to love his children was by identifying and prohibiting their "vices."[5]

John Stuart Mill's destiny was sealed when Jeremy Bentham befriended his father, who was one of Bentham's younger disciples. John Stuart later said his father was influential in shaping Bentham's version of utilitarianism.

From Bentham, James Mill came to believe that all minds are the same at birth. Thus proper education—begun early enough—would produce a healthy, rational child. The two of them decided to use little John Stuart to show just how effective Bentham's ideas were. They gave him a rigorous education, carefully planned to produce a champion of utilitarianism.

Basing their program in part on Bentham's own experiences as a child prodigy, the experimenters saw to it that John Stuart learned Greek and arithmetic at three; Latin, geometry, and algebra at eleven; and logic and philosophy at twelve. Though not everything went smoothly (young John Stuart had some trouble with Plato's *Theaetetus*), he was such a whiz at math that he had to teach himself once he had surpassed his father's abilities.[6] In an effort to refine John Stuart's thinking and to prevent "the mere cramming of the memory," James Mill forced him to try to learn everything for himself before James would even consider explaining it. In his touching *Autobiography*, John Stuart Mill characterized his education:

> Most boys or youths who have had much knowledge drilled into them have their mental capacities not strengthened, but overlaid by it. They are crammed with mere facts, with the opinions and phrases of other people, and these are accepted as a substitute for the power to form opinions of their own; and thus the sons of eminent fathers, who have spared no pains in their education, so often grow up mere parroters of what they have learnt, incapable of using their minds except in the furrows traced for them. Mine . . . was not an education of cram. My father never permitted anything that I had learnt to degenerate into a

Few but those whose mind is a moral blank, could bear to lay out their course of life on the plan of paying no regard to others except so far as their own private interest compels.

John Stuart Mill

mere exercise of memory. He strove to make the understanding not only go along with every step of teaching, but, if possible, precede it. Anything which could be found out by thinking, I never was told, until I had exhausted my efforts to find it out for myself.[7]

Because of his ultimate brilliance, John Stuart Mill's education has been viewed as a testimony to the power of education itself. Bentham and James Mill produced not just a champion of utilitarianism, but a true genius. John Stuart Mill said his education gave him a quarter of a century advantage over others his age—but added that any average, healthy boy or girl could achieve the same results with the same training.[8] The personal cost, however, was high: Mill's education robbed him of his childhood. His father's strict control, though typical of the time, nonetheless stifled any expression of emotion or spontaneity.

I was so much accustomed to expect to be told what to do, either in the form of direct command or of rebuke for not doing it, that I acquired a habit of leaving my responsibility as a moral agent to rest on my father, my conscience never speaking to me except by his voice.[9]

Later, a friend would say of Mill, "He had never played with boys; in his life he never knew any."[10]

In an early version of his *Autobiography*, Mill said: "Mine was not an education of love but of fear. . . . My father's children neither loved him, nor, with any warmth of affection, anyone else."[11] This is not true of Mill himself, for as we'll see, Mill dearly loved one woman his entire adult life.

Mill's Crisis

When he was twenty, Mill began to pay the high price of his hothouse education in earnest with a depression or breakdown he described as a "dry heavy dejection."

I was in a dull state of nerves, such as everybody is occasionally liable to, one of those moods when what is pleasure at other times becomes insipid or indifferent; the state, I should think, in which converts to Methodism usually are when smitten by their first "conviction of sin." I seemed to have nothing left to live for. At first I hoped that the cloud would pass away of itself; but it did not. A night's sleep, the sovereign remedy for the smaller vexations of life, had no effect upon it. In vain I sought relief from my favourite books, those memorials of past nobleness and greatness from which I had always hitherto drawn strength and animation. I read them now without feeling, or with the accustomed feeling *minus* all its charm; and I became persuaded that my love of mankind, and of excellence for its own sake, had worn itself out.[12]

In the golden rule of Jesus of Nazareth, we read the complete spirit of the ethics of utility.

John Stuart Mill

Mill blamed the strict, critical, analytic environment he was raised in for robbing him of his feelings by insisting that only facts and reasons, only the objective, mattered. But a finely honed analytic mind, unaided by emotion, cannot provide life with meaning:

> I was . . . left stranded at the commencement of my voyage, with a well equipped ship and rudder, but no sail; without any real desire for the ends which I had been so carefully fitted out to work for; no delight in virtue or the general good, but also just as little in anything else.[13]

Mill was eventually able to pull himself out of his depression and begin the process of becoming a more integrated person by studying music and Romantic poetry. After reading a passage about the way a father's death affected his son in the memoirs of a French writer, Mill had an emotional catharsis:

> A vivid conception of the scene and its feelings came over me, and I was moved to tears. From this moment my burthen grew lighter. The oppression of the thought that all feeling was dead within me was gone. I was no longer hopeless: I was not stock or stone.[14]

The catharsis broke the stranglehold Bentham and his father had maintained for so long. Finally open to a wider range of experience, aided by his superior intellect, Mill developed an insight into the human condition fuller and deeper than his two teachers knew. Although he had bouts of depression for the rest of his life, and although he is reported to have remained rather serious, John Stuart Mill became a compassionate champion of the oppressed and a brilliant defender of classical liberal principles.

Redemption and Balance

Mill's rigid training was also balanced and softened by his remarkable relationship with Harriet Taylor. The couple fell in love when Mill was twenty-four. Harriet was married to a merchant quite a bit older than she and much more conservative in his interests. The relationship began with discussions of Mill's writings and Harriet's plans (she wanted to be a writer also). As Mill began to spend all his free time at the Taylors' house, it eventually became obvious to Harriet's husband that the relationship was more than simple friendship.

Harriet's husband and some of Mill's friends advised the couple to end their relationship. Instead, they became more discreet about appearing in public. Ultimately an arrangement was worked out so that Mill could stay with Mrs. Taylor when her husband was away, and she could stay with him during the summer and on weekends. This arrangement lasted over fifteen years. Two years after Harriet's husband died, she and Mill were finally married. After seven years of marriage, Harriet Taylor Mill died suddenly,

We should seek the general happiness because it will make us happier. No doubt Mill, like many others, thought that this was true as it may well be. But this is not relevant. For utilitarianism is out to show that we ought to have regard for the interests of other people on moral grounds.

Jan Narveson

Mill on Women's Rights

As I have already said more than once, I consider it presumption in anyone to pretend to decide [what] women are or are not, can or cannot be, by natural constitution. They have always hitherto been kept, as far as regards spontaneous development, in so unnatural a state that their nature cannot but have been greatly distorted and disguised; and no one can safely pronounce that if women's nature were left to choose its direction as freely as men's, and if no artificial bent were attempted to be given to it except that required by the conditions of human society, and given to both sexes alike, there would be any material difference, or perhaps any difference at all, in the character and capacities which would unfold themselves.

John Stuart Mill
"The Subjection of Women," in *Human Worth*, eds. Richard Paul Janaro and Darwin E. Gearhart (New York: Holt, Rinehart & Winston, 1972), p. 53.

while the couple were in Avignon. A grieving Mill said, "The spring of my life is broken."

Mill credited his wife with influencing his work for the better, saying:

What was abstract and purely scientific was generally mine; the properly human element came from her: in all that concerned the application of philosophy to the exigencies of human society and progress, I was her pupil. . . . Her mind invested all ideas in a concrete shape, and formed to itself a conception of how they would actually work: and her knowledge of the existing feelings and conduct of mankind was so seldom at fault that the weak point of any unworkable suggestion seldom escaped her.[15]

Others who knew them both suggested that Mill's vision of Harriet was more loving than it was objective. There may be some truth to that, but there can be no doubt that her relationship with Mill was beneficial and encouraging. Mill insisted that Harriet gave him a better sense of what truly mattered—and what did not—than he had on his own.

Mill's richer, fuller, and therefore *more useful* expression of utilitarianism clearly owes a major debt to his crisis and to his relationship with Harriet, to poetry, and to music. The emotional restrictions imposed by both Bentham and James Mill limited simple utilitarianism in much the same way that John Stuart Mill was emotionally blocked until his life opened up. Even so, Mill saw Bentham as a positive force for good. Mill stood, as it were, on the shoulders of Bentham, and so saw much deeper into life. He acknowledged his debt to Bentham, and to his father, and paid it with interest by producing a philosophy more solid, more fully human than they could ever have imagined.

Mill's writing shows the breadth and balance he worked so hard to develop: *System of Logic* (1843), *Principles of Political Economy* (1848),

Altruism itself depends on a recognition of the reality of other persons, and on the equivalent capacity to regard oneself as merely one individual among many.

Thomas Nagel

On Liberty (1859), Representative Government (1861), Utilitarianism (1863), the posthumous Autobiography (1873), and Three Essays on Religion (1874). His "On the Logic of the Moral Sciences" has been described as "the most enduring essay on the method of the social sciences which has ever been written."[16]

In 1873, a fatigued Mill and Harriet Taylor's daughter Helen, who cared for Mill after Harriet's death, went to Avignon, where Harriet had died so suddenly in 1858. After an especially strenuous day, Mill developed a high fever and died at sixty-seven on May 7, 1873. He was buried in Avignon beside his beloved Harriet. So ended the remarkable life of this most competent, archetypal utilitarian, John Stuart Mill, a lover of liberty and equality, reason and feeling, who worked tirelessly to improve the lot of all people.

Refined Utilitarianism

It is better to be a human being dissatisfied than a pig satisfied; better to be Socrates dissatisfied than a fool satisfied. And if the fool, or the pig, is of a different opinion, it is because they only know their own side of the question. The other party to the comparison knows both sides.

John Stuart Mill

Mill could not accept Bentham's simple version of hedonism, for Bentham leveled all pleasures. He did not assign higher importance to moral, intellectual, or emotional pleasures. His only criteria are those included in the hedonic calculus. All other factors being equal, for Bentham, the crucial difference between two pleasures is merely intensity. "Prejudice apart, the [child's] game of push-pin is of equal value with the arts and sciences of music and poetry. If the game of push-pin furnish more pleasure, it is more valuable than either."[17]

Bentham even referred to a "moral thermometer," implying that the only difference among various kinds of behavior was the "degree" of pleasure they produced. John Stuart Mill, who had been salvaged and made whole by music and poetry, knew better. He knew from personal experience that pleasures differ in *kind* as well as in *degree* and identified with the Epicurean hedonists: "There is no known Epicurean theory of life which does not assign the pleasures of the intellect, of the feelings and imagination, and of the moral sentiments, a much higher value as pleasure than those of mere sensation."[18] Thus Mill modified and interpreted the simple Benthamite utilitarianism he started with until it had become a much richer moral doctrine.

By introducing the notion of *quality* into utilitarianism, Mill refuted the orthodoxy he had been raised to defend. He dismissed Bentham's hedonic calculus as crude and unworkable, and appealed instead to a wider vision of human happiness based on a broader range of values. Most significant was Mill's declaration that all pleasures are not, in fact, equal.

In his analysis of this crucial issue, Mill offers a most persuasive solution to a timeless question we have encountered before: *Is there any way to prove that supposedly "enlightened" opinions and judgments are more than mere opinions?* Mill doesn't address the issue directly in terms of wisdom and enlightenment, but he does address the heart of this timeless question: *Is there an objective way to settle disagreements involving "levels" of knowledge and value disputes?*

Having inherited a dislike of abstract theories and systems, and having been trained as a social empiricist, Mill approached this ancient problem in a straightforward way. He included an objective component in the assessment of pleasure. His argument begins:

> If I am asked what I mean by difference of quality in pleasures, or what makes one pleasure more valuable than another merely as a pleasure, except its being greater in amount, there is but one possible answer. Of two pleasures, if there be one which all or almost all who have experience of both give a decided preference, irrespective of any feeling of moral obligation to prefer it, even though knowing it to be attended with a greater amount of discontent, and would not resign it for any quantity of the other pleasures which their nature is capable of, we are justified in ascribing to the preferred enjoyment a superiority in quality, so far outweighing quantity as to render it, in comparison, of small account.[19]

In other words, only those fully acquainted with two pleasures can decide which, if either, is better. If there is no consensus among them, then there is no objective difference in quality, only difference in taste or preference.

For example, only people well enough versed in two (or more) kinds of music actually know if one is qualitatively better than another. This is a necessary, *empirical criterion*. Many of us can only (honestly) say, "I don't like such and such, but then I've never really tried to understand it." If we really want to compare various kinds of music, we must either listen widely and carefully or ask those who know a great deal about music. If a consensus exists among those familiar with the types being compared, then on Mill's criterion, we have discovered a qualitative difference. Of course, the same pattern applies to comparing the competing pleasures/values of reading Shakespeare or romance novels, playing basketball or playing checkers, and so on.

Higher Pleasures

Mill argued that there are *empirical grounds* for asserting that what we might call "refined pleasures" are preferable to and hence better than the "cruder pleasures."

> Now it is an unquestionable fact that those who are equally acquainted with, and equally capable of appreciating and enjoying, both, do give a most marked preference to the manner of existence which employs their higher faculties. Few human creatures would consent to be changed into any of the lower animals, for a promise of the fullest allowance of a beast's pleasures; no intelligent human being would

Man does not strive for pleasure, only the Englishman does.

Friedrich Nietzsche

Mill claimed that some pleasures are qualitatively better than others. Is there any objective way to compare the qualities of playing the cello with playing video games?

consent to be a fool, no instructed person would be an ignoramus, no person of feeling and conscience would be selfish and base, even though they should be persuaded that the fool, the dunce, or the rascal is better satisfied with his lot than they are with theirs. They would not resign what they possess more than he for the most complete satisfaction of all the desires which they have in common with him. If they ever fancy they would, it is only in cases of unhappiness so extreme that to escape from it they would exchange their lot for almost any other, however undesirable in their own eyes. A being of higher faculties requires more to make him happy, is capable probably of more acute suffering, and certainly accessible to it at more points, than one of an inferior type; but in spite of these liabilities, he can never really wish to sink into what he feels to be a lower grade of existence.[20]

This is an interesting argument. Consider typical reactions to individuals with diminished mental or emotional capacities. We love and, perhaps, pity the mentally retarded, but we do not wish to join them. Techniques to control emotional disturbances by removing the possibility for emotion are properly seen as a last resort. Though we may jokingly claim that ignorance is bliss, few of us would consciously choose bliss if the price is ignorance.

Not everyone agrees with Mill that the "higher" faculties and their pleasures are superior, however. Many people live as if their values regarding pleasures are just the opposite from Mill's. Not only are their lives not devoted to the use and development of their higher faculties, they seem actively to discourage them. Why are the "higher" pleasures unpopular if they are objectively superior?

Lower Pleasures

Mill argues that there is no inconsistency between an appreciation of the superiority of the higher pleasures and succumbing to the temptation of more easily secured lesser pleasures. He recognizes that character and experiences are major components of our judgment and behavior:

> Men often, from infirmity of character, make their election for the nearer good, though they know it to be the less valuable; and this no less when the choice is between two bodily pleasures than when it is between bodily and mental. They pursue sensual indulgences to the injury of health, though perfectly aware that health is the greater good. It may be further objected that many who begin with youthful enthusiasm for everything noble, as they advance in years sink into indolence and selfishness. But I do not believe that those who undergo this very common change voluntarily choose the lower description of pleasures in preference to the higher. I believe that before they devote themselves exclusively to the one, they have already become incapable of the other. Capacity for the nobler feelings is in most natures a very tender plant, easily killed, not only by hostile influences, but by mere want of sustenance; and in the majority of young persons it speedily dies away if the occupations to which their position in life has devoted them, and the society into which it has thrown them, are not favorable to keeping that higher capacity in exercise. Men lose their high aspirations as they lose their intellectual tastes, because they have not time or opportunity for indulging them; and they addict themselves to inferior pleasures not because they deliberately prefer them, but because they are either the only ones to which they have access or the only ones which they are any longer capable of enjoying. It may be questioned whether anyone who has remained equally susceptible to both classes of pleasures ever knowingly and calmly preferred the lower; though many, in all ages, have broken down in an ineffectual attempt to combine both.[21]

When Mill speaks of character, he refers to socially conditioned habits. Though there are always exceptions, consider the enormous social pressures that can interfere with nurturing "higher" sentiments: Can we

The joy of understanding is a sad joy, yet those who have once tasted it would not exchange it for all the frivolous gaieties and empty hopes of the vulgar herd.

Anatole France

To Be Logical Men Should Not Be Selfish

It seems to me that we are driven to this, that logicality inexorably requires that our interests shall not be limited. They must not stop at our own fate, but must embrace the whole community. This community, again, must not be limited, but must extend to all races of beings with whom we can come into immediate or me- diate intellectual relation. It must reach, however vaguely, beyond this geological epoch, beyond all bounds. He who would not sacrifice his own soul to save the whole world is, as it seems to me, illogical in all his inferences, collectively. Logic is rooted in the social principle.

To be logical men should not be selfish.

Charles Sanders Peirce
Collected Papers of Charles Sanders Peirce, vol. 2, eds. Charles Hartshorne and Paul Weiss (Cambridge, Mass.: Harvard University Press, 1931–1935), p. 398.

The bad part of [Bentham's] writings is his resolute de- nial of all that he does not see, of all truths but those which he recognizes.

John Stuart Mill

reasonably expect children raised in extreme poverty, violence, turmoil, and instability to develop their higher faculties in school, if every after- noon they return to an empty apartment or social jungle? Can we reason- ably expect working parents to find time to work extra hours, raise healthy children, maintain their homes, and *then* develop and nurture their own higher faculties? It often seems as if our lives and culture conspire against the full, continuing development of the nobler faculties. Check any major bookstore and discover the dwindling proportion of fine literature and nonfiction as compared to pulp fiction and tabloid, self-help nonfiction. Compare the numbers of people flocking to inane but easily understood movies with those trickling into museums or art houses. Bombarded on all sides by seductive chemicals and toys, fatigued from self-imposed and inescapable pressures, we find that the lure of philosophy or literature or poetry can pale beside the temptations of a new mountain bike, Spielberg movie, relationship, or basketball game.

If we grant, at least for now, that there are "nobler sentiments" and that many factors conspire to crush them, must we just accept things as they are? Mill answers with a hearty no. Having added the notion of quality to utilitarianism, he expands Bentham's appeal to enlightened self-interest into a full-fledged altruistic social philosophy.

Altruism and Happiness

We have seen the general utilitarian connection between our own happi- ness and the happiness of others expressed in Bentham's conception of en- lightened self-interest. Mill's argument is less problematic than Bentham's, because it is based on a more solid relationship between the individual and the group. Mill asserts that, ultimately, utilitarianism rests on "the social feelings of mankind; the desire to be in unity with our fellow creatures." **Altruism**, from the Latin *alter*, "other," is the capacity to promote the welfare of others; altruism stands in clear contrast to egoism. According to Mill's altruistic utilitarianism, no individual's self-interest is *more* or *less* important than any other's.

> I must again repeat, what the assailants of utilitarianism seldom have the justice to acknowledge, that the happiness which forms the utilitarian standard of what is right in conduct is not the agent's own happiness, but that of all concerned. As between his own happiness and that of others, utilitarianism requires him to be as strictly impartial as a disinterested and benevolent spectator.[22]

ALTRUISM

From Latin for "other"; the capacity to promote the welfare of others; opposed to egoism.

Mill wanted to show that as civilization advances, the social spirit grows. In the effort, he made an eloquent defense of the importance of universal education to general happiness.

For Mill, the function of education is twofold: to instill the skills and knowledge necessary for an individual to live well and productively, and to create healthy, altruistic citizens. But to fulfill the second mandate, education must become a lifelong activity. People must be given opportunities to grow as part of their daily lives. They must be given fulfilling work and sufficient leisure to nurture more than their belly or bank account. The heart of such reform efforts must be widespread, good education.

An excellent example of utilitarian reasoning can be found in a brief examination of the rationale behind school desegregation and busing, which caused so much controversy beginning with the civil rights movement of

What Mill obviously thought needed advocating is that people have regard for other people's happiness, i.e., the general happiness.

Jan Narveson

the 1950s and lasting into the 1970s. At the time, some people argued for "separate but equal" schooling for black and white children. Close analysis of actual conditions showed that "separate but equal" was not possible, because most entirely black schools were in communities with inadequate tax bases to support good schools. Wealthier communities attracted the best teachers because they could offer better salaries, facilities, equipment, and teaching conditions.

Mill had pointed out that we must act from solid knowledge, not idealistic hopes. How could modern education reformers use empirical information to improve education for all children? The answer was surprisingly simple, though difficult for many to accept; it has yet to be fully implemented. The utilitarian solution was to take advantage of the self-interest of those parents with the most social and political influence. How could this be done? By sending *their children* to schools in other neighborhoods. The corollary to this, of course, involved busing black children to white schools.

What is utilitarian about this? Mill argued that we must be dispassionate, impartial spectators to everyone's interest, our own included. When I am not thinking exclusively of my own child, for example, it's clear that everyone is better off if all children go to good schools. But if I cannot or will not think dispassionately and objectively, I must be given *a personally effective motive*, an egoistic hook. One way to hook me is to send my child to an inferior school, so that my self-centered interest *in my own child* can be tapped to improve the school's quality, which would benefit other people's children as well. Even if many families resent integration, in the long run their unhappiness will be balanced against a greater good for society as a whole.

Until we all possess "nobler sentiments," we must perhaps be moved to act for the general good by such appeals to self-interest. Believing that *consequences* matter at least as much as motives, the utilitarian can be satisfied with getting me to help improve the school system even if I am coerced to do so by law. This kind of forced stretching of my concerns also falls under the heading of education.

Each person possesses an inviolability founded on justice that even the welfare of the society as a whole cannot override.

John Rawls

Selfishness and Contentment

Mill distinguished between what he called happiness and "mere contentment." Contentment, as Mill meant it, is the condition of animals and those unfortunate people limited to enjoying lower pleasures. A major purpose of Mill's utilitarianism is to make as many people as possible as *happy* as possible, not as *content* as possible. What, then, is happiness?

The ultimate end, with reference to and for the sake of which all other things are desirable (whether we are considering our own good or that of other people), is an existence exempt as far as possible from pain, and as rich as possible in enjoyments, both in point of quantity and quality . . . secured to all mankind; and not to them only, but so far as the nature of things admits, to the whole sentient creation.[23]

Mill argued that the principal cause of unhappiness is selfishness. He believed that happiness requires a balance between tranquillity and excitement, and selfishness robs us of both. It robs us of tranquillity because it is never satisfied, and it diminishes our possibilities for excitement (or stimulation) by narrowing our range of interests. Could that be why so many people seem to need artificial or extravagantly orchestrated excitement?

> When people who are tolerably fortunate in their outward lot do not find in life sufficient enjoyment to make it valuable to them, the cause generally is, caring for nobody but themselves. To those who have neither public nor private affections, the excitements of life are much curtailed, and in any case dwindle in value as the time approaches when all selfish interests must be terminated by death; while those who leave after them objects of personal affection, and especially those who have also cultivated a fellow-feeling with the collective interests of mankind, retain as lively an interest in life on the eve of death as in the vigor of youth and health.[24]

"A Mind Is a Terrible Thing to Waste"

Mill says that next to selfishness, the principal cause of an inability to be happy for an extended period is a lack of mental cultivation.

> A cultivated mind (and I do not mean that of a philosopher, but any mind to which fountains of knowledge have been opened, and which has been taught, in any tolerable degree, to exercise its faculties) finds sources of inexhaustible interest in all that surrounds it; in the objects of nature, the achievements of art, the imaginations of poetry, the incidents of history, the ways of mankind, past and present, and their prospects in the future. It is possible, indeed, to become indifferent to all this, and that too without having exhausted a thousandth part of it; but only when one has had from the beginning no moral or human interests in these things, and has sought in them only the gratification of curiosity.[25]

What a powerful, beautifully written description of one of the greatest of all tragedies: a wasted mind. A mind that has not been sparked to life and taught to wonder is condemned to shallow, limited satisfactions, dependent on the world to entertain it, since it has no momentum of its own.

Besides reducing life to ceaseless attempts at short-lived stimulation, a chronically bored mind at its worst can undertake a self-destructive quest for thrills. This restless searching for "something to do" deprives us of

One of the great drawbacks to the self-centered passions is that they afford so little variety. The man who loves only himself cannot, it is true, be accused of promiscuity in his affections, but he is bound in the end to suffer intolerable boredom from the invariable sameness of the object of his devotion.

Bertrand Russell

A Diminishing Preoccupation with Myself

Perhaps the best introduction to the philosophy which I wish to advocate will be a few words of autobiography. I was not born happy. As a child, my favorite hymn was: "Weary of earth and laden with sin." At the age of five, I reflected that, if I should live to be seventy, I had only endured, so far, a fourteenth part of my whole life, and I felt the long-spread-out boredom ahead of me to be almost unendurable.

In adolescence, I hated life and was continually on the verge of suicide, from which, however, I was restrained by the desire to know more mathematics. Now, on the contrary, I enjoy life; I might almost say that with every year that passes, I enjoy it more. This is due partly to having discovered what were the things that I most desired, and having gradually acquired many of these things. Partly it is due to having

successfully dismissed certain objects of desire—such as the acquisition of indubitable knowledge about something or other—as essentially unattainable. But very largely it is due to a diminishing preoccupation with myself.

Bertrand Russell
The Conquest of Happiness (New York: Liveright, 1958), quoted in Robert F. Davidson, *The Search for Meaning in Life* (New York: Holt, Rinehart & Winston, 1962), p. 86.

opportunities to synthesize our experiences, to reflect on ourselves, our relationships, our values, and our goals. Hence chronic boredom interferes with personal growth and may even prevent it.

Mill was convinced that science and clear utilitarian thinking could produce a better environment, one conducive to altruism as well as the mental, emotional, and physical development and well-being of individuals.

Mill's Vision

Mill thought that no insurmountable reasons or conditions existed that would prevent the emergence of a truly healthy society.

> Genuine private affections, and a sincere interest in the public good, are possible, though in unequal degrees, to every rightly brought up human being. In a world in which there is so much to interest, so much to enjoy, and so much also to correct and improve, everyone who has this moderate amount of moral and intellectual requisites is capable of an existence which may be called enviable; and unless such a person, through bad laws, or subjection to the will of others, is denied the liberty to use the sources of happiness within his reach, he will not fail to find this enviable existence, if he escape the positive evils of life, the great sources of physical and mental suffering—such as indigence, disease, and the unkindness, worthlessness, or premature loss of objects of affection.[26]

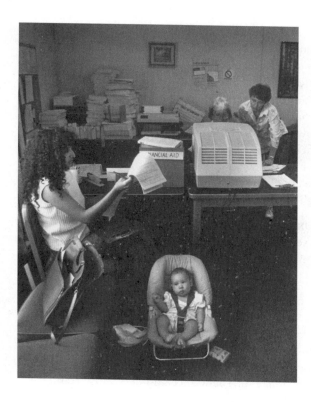

Mill argued that, for our own peace of mind, we need to provide social support for those in need—because we never know when we will need help. The quality of life without general assistance would diminish for all of us, Mill insisted.

The chief task, then, of all right-thinking, well-intentioned people is to address those causes of misfortune that can be avoided or altered.

From Mill's (and Bentham's) great concern for society, we have acquired the concept of public *utilities*, welfare and other forms of assistance for the poor, mandatory minimum education standards, and laws that are more humane. Mill showed how necessary liberty of thought and speech is for the general happiness, since we can determine the truth only by an ongoing clash of opinions. He worried about "the tyranny of the majority," and warned against the very great, and often ignored, dangers of assigning too much weight to majority beliefs.

In the end, Mill remained an optimist who believed that by applying reason and good will, the vast majority of humankind could live with dignity, political and moral freedom, and harmonious happiness. He believed that "the wisdom of society, combined with the good sense and providence of individuals," could extinguish poverty completely, and that scientific progress along with "good physical and moral education" could alleviate the scourge of disease.

As for the vicissitudes of fortune, and other disappointments connected with worldly circumstances, these are principally the effect of

The only part of the conduct of anyone for which he is amenable to society is that which concerns others. Over himself, over his own body and mind, the individual is sovereign.

John Stuart Mill

Dissent and dissenters have no monopoly on freedom. They must tolerate opposition. They must accept dissent from their dissent.

Abe Fortas

either gross imprudence, of ill-regulated desires, or of bad or imperfect social institutions. All these grand sources, in short, of human suffering are in a great degree, many of them almost entirely, conquerable by human care and effort; and though their removal is grievously slow—though a long succession of generations will perish in the breach before the conquest is completed, and this world becomes all that, if will and knowledge were not wanting, it might easily be made—yet every mind sufficiently intelligent and generous to bear a part, however small and inconspicuous, in the endeavor will draw a noble enjoyment from the contest itself, which he would not for any bribe in the form of selfish indulgence consent to be without.[27]

Mill's optimism is based on his view of a social human nature and a deep, nearly universal, sense of connectedness. It is a vision that sees no inevitable competition between my needs and yours, between ours and everyone else's:

> The deeply rooted conception which every individual even now has of himself as a social being tends to make him feel it is one of his natural wants that there should be harmony between his feeling and aims and those of his fellow creatures. If differences of opinion and mental culture make it impossible for him to share many of their actual feelings—perhaps make him denounce and defy those feelings—he still needs to be conscious that his real aim and theirs do not conflict; that he is not opposing himself to what they really wish for, namely, their own good, but is contrary, promoting it. . . . This conviction is the ultimate sanction of the greatest happiness morality.[28]

In so many ways, our lives, and those of people in many other countries, have directly benefited from the seed Jeremy Bentham and James Mill planted in John Stuart Mill, clearly the finest archetype of a utilitarian social reformer so far.

Consider, in closing, the following passage from Mill's *Autobiography*. Referring to the time of his crisis, it reveals that early on, Mill's wisdom was deeper than his utilitarianism could accommodate. His monumental effort to remain true to the philosophical orthodoxy of his father and Bentham hampered his philosophical expression, yet his great intellect and deeply compassionate moral sense found a voice anyway. As philosophers, we are obligated to note Mill's inconsistencies. As human beings, we can acknowledge and honor his great struggle for—and ultimately brilliant statement of—a most compelling case for the virtues of education, community, liberty, women's rights, concern for the disadvantaged, and freedom of speech.

Among the great social thinkers of the nineteenth century, Mill was the only one who failed to write a system encompassing the evolution of humanity. . . . Mill alone tried to do justice to all the competing drives and motives of human nature; he would never banish from his consciousness the many-sidedness and many-levelledness of social reality.

Lewis S. Feuer

> I never, indeed, wavered in the conviction that happiness is the test of all rules of conduct, and the end of life. But now I thought that this end was only to be attained by not making it the direct end. *Those*

The "Saint of Rationalism"

When we look for intellectual guidance today with respect to the problems of freedom in communist societies, the exhaustion of the environment, and the pressure of population, Mill is the only sociologist of the nineteenth century whose pages are not discolored with the acid of bias. Others claiming to prefigure the law of history were obsessed by the demon of making history; Mill held to the more modest ethic of acting as circumstances allowed on behalf of human happiness. In so doing, the "saint of rationalism" held to the conception of scientific truth with an integrity which the prophet-ideologists never approached.

Lewis S. Feuer
"John Stuart Mill as a Sociologist: The Unwritten Ethology," in Mill, *On Socialism* (Buffalo: Prometheus Books, 1987), p. 43.

only are happy (I thought) who have their minds fixed on some object other than their own happiness; on the *happiness of others*, on the *improvement of mankind*, even on some art or pursuit, followed not as a means, but as itself an ideal end. *Aiming thus at something else, they find happiness by the way.* The enjoyments of life (such was now my theory) are sufficient to make it a pleasant thing, when they are taken *en passant*, without being made a principal object. Once make them so, and they are immediately felt to be insufficient. They will not bear a scrutinizing examination. Ask yourself whether you are happy, and you cease to be so. The only chance is to treat, not happiness, but some end external to it, as the purpose of life.[29]

12

The Existentialist

Søren Kierkegaard
and
Jean-Paul Sartre

The question is not what am I to believe, but what am I to *do*?
Søren Kierkegaard

H as it perhaps occurred to you that something fundamentally important seems to be missing from most (or all) of the philosophies we have studied so far? Has the ancient challenge to philosophy been answered for *you*: "Philosophy, what practical difference do you make to *me*?" Perhaps you've wondered what, if any, bearing the categorical imperative has on your actual, day-to-day moral *living*. Do "proofs" for the existence of God, such as those offered by Thomas Aquinas, provide you with a living faith? Do they enhance your relationship with a living God? What do the rigorous inquiries of Hume or Descartes have to do with the concrete and immediate choices facing you as an "existing individual"? As a seeker of wisdom, do you wonder whether a utilitarian calculus or Marxian assessment of history makes any "real difference" to the daily sufferings of "real people"? If it sometimes seems to you that philosophy has passed over the genuine ("real-life") concerns of individuals, you are not alone. These are the sorts of questions that troubled one of the most fascinating, exasperating, engaging, and annoying philosophical writers of the modern era, Søren Kierkegaard.

Kierkegaard was one of a number of nineteenth-century philosophers and writers whose work is still widely—and heatedly—discussed outside of as well as within scholarly circles. The issues he struggles with, combined with his efforts to engage us personally, as "existing individuals," reach across time in much the same way that, say, Socrates' questions seem "alive" and personally engaging to contemporary readers. Like Socrates, Kierkegaard directly challenges us to reassess our lives, to ask, "How, then, shall *I live*? How shall I exist as a specific *individual*?"

Technological progress creates more problems than it solves. Efficiency experts or social engineering will not redeem humanity. Important as their contributions may be, they do not reach the heart of the problem.

Abraham Joshua Heschel

Virtual Existence, Virtual Identity

The power and poignancy of this kind of inquiry are amplified because, from a certain perspective, our entire culture seems to be at odds with the genuine concerns of "existing individuals." Modern institutions become increasingly massive, objectified, dehumanized, and impersonal. Science continues to reduce human suffering—and human achievement—to the effects of genetics and environmental conditioning. Bureaucracies reduce their employees to "fleshy automatons" whose every decision is guided by "company policy." Computerized assembly lines replace human workers. Mass production and prefabricated materials replace handmade goods and craftsmanship.

Even the so-called "democratic promise" of universal Internet access can be viewed as a form of depersonalization since our "embodied concreteness" is reduced to digitized bytes and blips. Can a "chat room" conversation or a "virtual relationship" possess the richness of actual conversations, of actual relationships? Will the promise of increased freedom be borne out as more and more of us join the so-called Information Age's "electronic global village," "chatting," "commuting," shopping, voting, and "going" to school via fiber-optic cables? Will the *human dimension* of our lives expand or wither?

Though we profess to value individuality, we more often reward conformity. Our politicians look and talk alike. Our celebrities are insipid and unoriginal. Even the most outrageous of them, such as Dennis Rodman or Madonna, can seem suspiciously like contrived types rather than authentic individuals: the thumb-your-nose-at-convention type, richer, famous versions of the "characters" we see sauntering through shopping malls and hanging out on corners everywhere.

We seem to be consumed by one craze after another, as we strive to belong to this group or that. Yuppies conform; gangsters conform; rappers and rockers conform; Christians, Muslims, and Jews conform; even children, whom we might expect to be free spirits, succumb to fads and fashions, mimicking music stars and athletes.

Instead of seeing ourselves as individuals, we may think of ourselves as "types," as "hyphenated Americans" (Italian Americans, Native Americans, African Americans), or we may identify with our sexual preference (gay Americans) or with our age (senior citizens) or with our gender (National Organization for Women) or with our religion. Our identity may come from membership in a group, gang, or club.

As we try to juggle a variety of roles—student, worker, spouse, parent, child, philosophy textbook writer—we learn, without always being conscious of it, to move from one discrete, disconnected experience to another. We become oblivious, perhaps, to the emptiness in our lives.

What if the key elements of our "identities" are only abstractions, lifeless concepts that do not encompass the real qualities of actual human existence? What, for instance, does it mean to be a woman? A Christian? A student? Can any objective description capture existence? We are understandably frustrated when a doctor sees only "the liver case" or "the pregnant diabetic" and does not see us as individuals. We feel deprived when we learn that we were chosen because "the company was looking for an Hispanic male."

More profound and subtle—and far more dangerous—is the peril of men in such numbers that each is induced to become a number himself and is steadily losing the vital differences on which his integrity as an individual depends, and substituting a kind of common denomination of the spirit in areas which were once his own and highly differentiated, enabling him to exorcise conformity and make a contribution uniquely his own to the life of his time.

Laurens Van der Post

We cope, it sometimes seems, only by a kind of self-deception through which we attempt to convince ourselves that we are living the way we *choose* to, that we are living reasonably, "all things considered." But are we—really?

Existentialism Was Bound to Happen

One of the most influential, intriguing, and arresting responses to the massing of society and the loss of respect for the individual goes under the name **existentialism**. Existentialism refers to any philosophy that says the most important philosophical matters involve fundamental questions of meaning and choice as they affect individuals. Existential themes include choice, freedom, identity, alienation, inauthenticity, despair, and awareness of our own mortality. Existentialists point out that objective science and rationalistic philosophy do not come to grips with the real problems of human existence: "What am *I* to do?" "To what can *I* commit myself?" "What does *my life* mean?" Existentialists believe that general answers, grand metaphysical systems, and supposedly objective and rational theories cannot address the existential (living, concrete) concerns of individuals.

The early existentialists were among the first to identify major issues unique to postindustrial, highly specialized, technical, "sophisticated" societies: increased loss of individuality; increased pressure to conform; the threat to human freedom and dignity from science and bureaucracy. Philosopher of history Samuel Enoch Stumpf says:

> Existentialism was bound to happen. The individual had over the centuries been pushed into the background by systems of thought, historical events, and technological forces. The major systems of philosophy had rarely paid attention to the uniquely personal concerns of individuals. Although Aristotle, for example, wrote a major treatise on ethics, Montaigne could say that "I can't recognize most of my daily doings when they appear in Aristotle." Nietzsche [Chapter 14] also wrote that "to our scholars, strangely enough, the most pressing question does not occur: to what end is their work . . . useful?" . . . [Traditional] philosophy for the most part dealt with technical problems of metaphysics, ethics, and the theory of knowledge in a general and objective manner, which bypassed the intimate concerns of [people] about their personal destiny. Historical events, particularly wars, showed a similar disregard for the feelings and aspirations of individuals. And technology . . . soon gathered a momentum of its own, forcing [people] to fit their lives into the rhythm of machines. Everywhere [people] were losing their peculiarly human qualities. They were being converted from "persons" into "pronouns," from "subjects" into "objects," from an "I" into an "it."[1]

EXISTENTIALISM

Term used to refer to any philosophy that emphasizes fundamental questions of meaning and choice as they affect existing individuals; existential themes include choice, freedom, identity, alienation, inauthenticity, despair, and awareness of our own mortality.

Though we profess to value individuality, our most successful politicians and celebrities are surprisingly unoriginal and uninspiring. Sometimes, they even look very much alike—as this photo of CBS This Morning anchor Paula Zahn interviewing Tipper Gore and Hillary Rodham Clinton shows, or the rock group Spinal Tap (facing page).

Unfortunately, many scholars and authors talk about existentialism as if it were a clearly defined school of philosophy. It is not. Let us resist reducing the existentialists to an abstraction, to a category, by acknowledging that there is no such thing as an existentialist school of philosophy. Individual philosophers, poets, novelists, dramatists, and artists address the nature and quality of daily human existence in their work. When they do, they are "existentialists."

In this chapter, we take a look at two of the most important thinkers first associated with that label, Søren Kierkegaard and Jean-Paul Sartre. Although Kierkegaard was a Christian and Sartre was an atheist, both were fierce champions of the real, the concrete, the existing individual.

Philosophical Query

Reflect back over your philosophical studies so far. Can you "recognize yourself" in the philosophies you've studied? In which ones? Discuss.

Had I to carve an inscription on my grave I would ask for none other than "the individual."

Søren Kierkegaard

Søren Kierkegaard

Søren Kierkegaard

The most important work of **Søren Kierkegaard** (1813–1855) was virtually ignored during his lifetime, in part because he wrote in Danish, in part because of what he wrote, in part because of his brilliant use of sarcasm and irony. Yet some 142 years later, Kierkegaard's journals and essays have a contemporary, living quality that still engages and disturbs many a reader. His work is not easy to fathom, but it is well worth the struggle.

Because he rebelled against the system and against objectivity, Kierkegaard's work confounds easy classification (which would delight him). His "unscientific" and "unsystematic" attacks on conventional Christian theology and dogma, on science, and on professional philosophy took the form of satirical essays, parables, anecdotes, real and fictional journals. Even after his works were translated into other languages and became widely known, Kierkegaard's reputation has remained mixed: Was he a philosopher? A writer of fiction? A theologian? A superficial wit?

What are scholars and philosophers to make of a writer who asserted that "truth is subjectivity" and "the System is a lie"? Can we criticize the inconsistencies and lack of a coherent philosophy in a writer who boldly denounced both systematic consistency and coherence? As we shall see, Kierkegaard's attack represented a radical shift in orientation from objectivity to subjectivity, from efforts to impose rational consistency to a search for authentic existence. Kierkegaard said, "The question is not what am I to *believe* [think, understand], but what am I to *do*?"

Kierkegaard saw himself as a disciple of Socrates. And like Socrates, his life and work make a seamless whole. We cannot know Kierkegaard the existentialist without meeting Kierkegaard the individual.

The Family Curse

Born in Copenhagen, Denmark, the youngest of seven children, Søren Kierkegaard was deeply and permanently influenced by his father Michael, a strict and devout Lutheran. One day, while herding sheep, young Michael cursed God over the conditions of his life. Until his death, he never forgot

Suppose, for instance, that you are climbing a mountain, and have worked yourself into a position from which the only escape is by a terrible leap. Have faith that you can successfully make it, and your feet are nerved to its accomplishment. But mistrust yourself, and think of all the sweet things you have heard the scientists say of *maybes*, and you will hesitate so long that, at last, all unstrung and trembling, and launching yourself in a moment of despair, you roll into the abyss.

William James

The real action is not the external act, but an internal decision in which the individual puts an end to mere possibility and identifies himself with the content of his thought in order to exist in it.

Søren Kierkegaard

what he had done and never forgave himself for his youthful outburst. Though he grew up to become a successful merchant, Michael Kierkegaard remained consumed by what he saw as his unforgivable blasphemy. Years later, weakened by grief and loneliness, he had sexual relations with a housemaid immediately after his first wife died. Overwhelmed with guilt and sadness, consumed by his two "great sins," Michael lived without peace of mind or genuine hope, seeing himself only as a sinner.

The youngest son of an elderly father, Søren was his father's favorite. To him went Michael's legacy: a sense of despair and melancholy, an obsession with the nature and possibility of a finite individual's relationship with an infinite God. Unusually intelligent and sensitive, Søren had few close friends as a child and spent most of his formative years in the company of his father.

In 1830, Kierkegaard enrolled in the University of Copenhagen to study theology. The "unforgiven" father wanted his son to become a minister. Kierkegaard soon discovered, however, that theology did not interest him as much as philosophy and literature. He spent the next ten years living a collegiate life devoted primarily to drinking and attending the theater. He became known for his good taste in food, clothes, and other Epicurean delights. During this time, he lost interest in religion and became estranged from his father.

Father and son made peace before Michael died in 1838, and Michael confessed the two great sins of his past to his son. Kierkegaard referred to the confession as "a great earthquake," and became consumed by its implications. He returned to the study of theology, passing his exams with honors in 1840. The next year he preached his first sermon and submitted a master's thesis on Socratic irony.

The Universal Formula

I owe everything I am to the wisdom of an old man and the simplicity of a young girl.

Søren Kierkegaard

At the same time, at age twenty-seven, Kierkegaard fell in love with Regina Olsen, the attractive fourteen-year-old daughter of an important government official. When Regina turned seventeen, the couple became formally engaged, but almost immediately Kierkegaard broke the engagement. For the rest of his life, he struggled to understand, explain, and justify this action. In his *Journals* he wrote, "It was a time of terrible suffering to have to be so cruel and at the same time to love her as I did. She fought like a tigress. If I had not believed that God had lodged a veto, she would have been victorious."[2]

Kierkegaard may have had more than one motive for breaking up with Regina Olsen. He may have been afraid of committed marriage. He may have found her cheery temperament incompatible with his somber melancholy. He may have feared that his depressions would harm her. He may have been a cad, as the popular opinion in Copenhagen had it. Perhaps all these motives played a part.

But of special interest to us is Kierkegaard's later interpretation of his "sacrifice" of Regina Olsen. Two weeks after he broke the engagement, Kierkegaard fled to Berlin, where he wrote *Either/Or, A Fragment of Life* (1843), his first important work, and *Repetition: An Essay in Experimental Psychology* (1843), through which he hoped to reestablish his relationship with Regina. But before he could publish *Repetition*, Kierkegaard learned of Regina's engagement to a former boyfriend. Stunned, hurt, and despairing, Kierkegaard destroyed the last ten pages of his original manuscript, which addressed his hope of a reconciliation with Regina.

For the rest of his short life, Kierkegaard claimed he had "offered up" his love for Regina Olsen as a sacrifice to God, just as Abraham offered Isaac in the Old Testament story (Genesis 22). Kierkegaard had thought he had to choose *either* God *or* "the world," and that choosing one excluded the other entirely. Torn between a career as a minister and a comfortable, middle-class life with Regina, Kierkegaard thought he had discovered a way to have both. His solution was what he interpreted as the "universal formula" revealed in the story of Abraham and Isaac: Having finally blessed Abraham and Sarah with a son in their old age, God then tested Abraham's faith by sending an angel to him, demanding the blood sacrifice of Isaac. Abraham submitted to God's will in a supreme act of faith, resisting the pull of his love for Isaac and resisting the moral code of his time which forbade such human sacrifice. At the last moment God stopped Abraham, and returned Isaac to him. Kierkegaard interpreted this story to mean: If you give something up for God, you get it back *plus* the love and salvation of God. In other words, by giving something up, you get to keep it! Applying this "formula" to his predicament of "*Either* devote my life to God *or* live in comfort with Regina," Kierkegaard "reasoned" a way to have both. He was stunned when he lost her. What went wrong? Didn't Kierkegaard do just what Abraham had done? Was his reasoning somehow flawed?

In his later works, Kierkegaard wrestled with the basic existential problems exemplified in this episode from one individual's life: What am I to *do* when confronted with the awesome finality of any choice? Can I objectively and scientifically model my relationship with God after Abraham's? Or Paul's? Or Christ's? How can I know what God wants *me* to do? Can I *reason* it out? What do *universal principles* have to do with *this choice*? Kierkegaard learned that he was not Abraham. He concluded that universal principles must give way to individual predicaments.

The Christian

Struggling with the existential predicament of choice and commitment, Kierkegaard grew increasingly interested in what it means to be a Christian. He became convinced that institutionalized Christianity suffers from the same inauthenticity as other institutions. **Inauthenticity** results when

What I really lack is to be clear in my own mind what I am to do. The thing is to understand myself, to see what God really wants me to do; the thing is to find a truth that is true for me, to find the idea for which I can live and die.

Søren Kierkegaard

INAUTHENTICITY

Condition that results when the nature and needs of the individual are ignored, denied, and obscured or sacrificed for institutions, abstractions, or groups.

AUTHENTICITY

Subjective condition of an individual living honestly and courageously in the moment, refusing to make excuses, and not relying on groups or institutions for meaning and purpose.

the nature and needs of the individual are ignored, denied, obscured, or made less important than institutions, abstractions, or groups. **Authenticity** is the subjective condition of an individual living honestly and courageously in the moment without refuge in excuses, and without reliance on groups or institutions for meaning and purpose. Given the stakes—salvation or damnation—Kierkegaard turned his penetrating wit and scathing criticism to the task of distinguishing "institutionalized Christianity" from authentic Christianity. He published three important attacks on the Danish church, *The Sickness Unto Death* (1849), *Training in Christianity* (1850), and *For Self-Examination* (1851).

When his "attacks on Christendom" were largely ignored, Kierkegaard decided to make a clear, dramatic existential step: He had to break officially with the church. At the time of this decision, the head of the Danish church was Bishop J. P. Mynster, who had been a close friend of Michael Kierkegaard. Because Søren himself respected and cared for the old man, he delayed his attack until Mynster died. Upon the bishop's death, however, he published his vehement attack on "false Christianity" in an article called "Was Bishop Mynster a Witness for the Truth?" Kierkegaard's answer was an unequivocal "No!" He argued that the bishop was a witness to an error, a witness to false Christianity.

Both the clergy and the general public rose to the defense of their beloved bishop as a symbol of a way of life. Kierkegaard continued to hammer away at what he saw as false Christianity, hypocrisy, inauthenticity, and "mere living." To these he countered with his famous "leap of faith," a complete commitment to God made each instant, made without guarantees, made alone, made in fear and trembling. He rejected an institutionalized religion of formulas, guarantees, security, and "group salvation."

On October 2, 1855, Kierkegaard was nearly broke. He visited his banker brother-in-law to withdraw the last of his money. On his way home, he fell to the street, paralyzed from the waist down. Destitute, helpless, and weak, Søren Kierkegaard died quietly November 11, 1855. He was only forty-two years old.

That Individual

Kierkegaard was buried in the huge Cathedral Church of Copenhagen. His eulogy was delivered to a crowd of both friends and enemies by his brother Peter, a respected member of the Danish church. Upset with the way the institution had violated the spirit of its great critic, his nephew caused a scene at the graveside. The irony of such a funeral would not have been lost on Kierkegaard.

The most interesting epitaph for Kierkegaard, however, is found in his own bitterly ironic words:

> The Martyrdom this author suffered may be briefly described thus:
> He suffered from being a genius in a provincial town. The standard

If you are always profoundly occupied, you are beyond all embarrassment.

Friedrich Nietzsche

he applied . . . was on the average far too great for his contemporaries; it raised the price on them too terribly; it almost made it seem as if the provincial town and the majority in it did not possess [absolute authority], but that there was a God in existence.

Yet it is true that he found also here on earth what he sought. He himself was *that individual* if no one else was, and he became that more and more. It was the cause of Christianity he served, his life from childhood on being marvelously fitted for such a service. Thus he carried to completion the task of translating completely into terms of reflection what Christianity is, what it means to be a Christian. . . .

. . . he could not ascribe [the grand enterprise he undertook] to any man, least of all would he ascribe it to himself; if he were to ascribe it to anyone, it would be to Providence, to whom it was in fact ascribed, day after day and year after year, by the author, who historically died of a mortal disease but poetically died of longing for eternity, where uninterruptedly he would have nothing else to do but to thank God.[3]

> It is not so much a question of choosing the right as the energy, the earnestness, the pathos with which one chooses. Thereby the personality announces its inner infinity, and thereby, in turn, the personality is consolidated.
>
> *Søren Kierkegaard*

Truth as Subjectivity

Perhaps the major existential issue is "What am *I* to *do*?" Not "How is an individual to live?" but "How am *I* to *exist*?" As Kierkegaard pointed out, any choice, once made, rules out *all* other possibilities. To be fully conscious of this is to experience what Nietzsche called *fatefulness*, the fact that our actions and choices create our individual destiny. Deciding to take a philosophy class—or deciding not to take one; deciding to marry that person—or not to marry that person; checking the air in a car's tires—or not checking it: on such inescapable daily choices hang the quality and shape of individual lives. The basic fact of Kierkegaard's *project*, as he referred to his existentialism, is the dilemma of lived choices:

> All our norms are nothing but desires in disguise.
>
> *Abraham Joshua Heschel*

What I really lack is to be clear in my mind *what I am to do*, not what I am to know, except in so far as a certain understanding must precede every action. The thing is to understand myself, to see what God really wishes *me* to do; the thing is to find a truth which is true *for me*, to find *the idea for which I can live and die*. What would be the use of discovering so-called objective truth, of working through all the systems of philosophy and of being able, if required, to review them all and show up the inconsistencies within each system;—what good would it do me to be able to explain the meaning of Christianity if it had *no* deeper significance *for me and for my life*;—what good would it do me if the truth stood before me, cold and naked, not caring whether I recognised her or not, producing in me a shudder of fear rather than a trusting devotion? I certainly do not deny that I still recognise an *imperative of understanding* and that through it one can

> For one thing is needful: that a human being should *attain* satisfaction with himself, whether it be by means of this or that poetry and art; only then is a human being at all tolerable to behold. Whoever is dissatisfied with himself is continually ready for revenge, and we others will be his victims.
>
> *Friedrich Nietzsche*

work upon men, *but it must be taken up into my life*, and *that is* what I now recognise as the most important thing. That is what my soul longs after, as the African desert thirsts for water. That is what I lack, and that is why I am left standing like a man who has rented a house and gathered all the furniture and household things together, but has not yet found the beloved with whom to share the joys and sorrows of his life.[4]

Philosophical Query

How do you make life choices? Do you make them clearly and consciously, or do things just somehow happen? Does your religion or philosophy help you make concrete choices? Does a psychological theory?

Kierkegaard realized that no amount of objective, systematic, abstract knowledge could ever provide a meaning for life. He did not deny the value of objective knowledge, which he refers to as an *imperative of understanding*, but he pointed out that the "objective facts" of a life cannot account for its existential quality. In *Either/Or*, he tells the story of a man who decides to scientifically and objectively study a Christian, in order to understand what it is to "be a Christian." Following his subject about, the observer notes what he eats, where he goes, when he reads the paper, what paper he reads, what brand of tobacco he smokes, and so on. After amassing quite a quantity of factual, objective data, the observer laments, "But he does just what I do!"

Kierkegaard's point, made ironically, is that objective information reveals facts or truths, not truth. What makes one individual a Christian and another a non-Christian, Kierkegaard claims, is not the objective conditions of their lives but their *inner condition: Truth is a subjective condition, not an objective one.*

The implications of this claim—that scientific, or objective, impersonal, understanding can never pass beyond factual description—are radical. Objective understanding cannot reveal truth; it cannot give Kierkegaard—or any existing individual—reasons to live; it cannot answer the most important question: What am I to do? Objective, scientific, philosophical, and theological systems and arguments cannot provide *"the idea for which I can live and die."* In an era seduced by faith that science inevitably leads to "progress," Kierkegaard's existential critique challenges "science" ("the system" or "the establishment") to answer: What am I to do? Give *me* a reason for which *I* can live and die.

Kierkegaard wanted to pass from fragmentation to integration. In his terms, he wanted to alter his life from a "chance assemblage of mere details" into an existence with a "focus and center." The modern age, with its drive toward massive institutions, infatuation with objectivity, and reliance on the scientific understanding of human behavior, inhibits personal integration. Neither scientific, objective understanding nor elaborate, ab-

The story is told (by Kierkegaard) of the absent-minded man so abstracted from his own life that he hardly knows he exists until, one fine morning, he wakes up to find himself dead.

William Barrett

For all their power and attraction, how can scientific discoveries, Pentium™ chips, and Internet access provide our lives with meaning, with Kierkegaard's idea for which I can live and die?

stract philosophical systems can deal with *"that individual."* Systems and theories only identify patterns and abstractions. They never even see "the existing individual."

Objectivity as Untruth

Philosophers have traditionally agreed that arguments and evidence should be evaluated rationally and objectively; evidence of partiality or bias is usually considered a serious weakness in a philosopher's arguments. Scientists, too, see impartial, impersonal, objective evidence as a praiseworthy goal.

Kierkegaard vehemently disagreed. He considered objectivity, impersonality, and impartiality as dangerous, insulting, and ugly delusions. That is, not only is impartiality impossible, but claims of objectivity and disinterest

We Are Being Destroyed by Our Knowledge

Our culture is superficial today, and our knowledge dangerous, because we are rich in mechanisms and poor in purposes. The balance of mind which once came of a warm religious faith is gone; science has taken from us the supernatural bases of our morality, and all the world seems consumed in a disorderly individualism that reflects the chaotic fragmentation of our character. . . . We move about the earth with unprecedented speed, but we do not know, and have not thought, where we are going, or whether we shall find any happiness there for our harassed souls. We are being destroyed by our knowledge, which has made us drunk with our power. And we shall not be saved without wisdom.

Will Durant
The Mansions of Philosophy: A Survey of Human Life and Destiny (New York: Simon & Schuster, 1929), pp. vii, viii, xff.

All logical thinking employs the language of abstraction. . . . It is easier to indulge in abstract thought than it is to exist.

Søren Kierkegaard

We do not err because truth is difficult to see. It is visible at a glance. We err because this is more comfortable.

Alexander Solzhenitsyn

are always lies. In the first place, preferring objectivity and impartiality to subjective involvement is itself a bias: *Favoring objectivity is a form of partiality.* Worse, our desire for objectivity deceives us by obscuring our individual (subjective) responsibility for our evaluations. The philosopher who says, "Reason demands that we must reject X because it is inconsistent" has herself *subjectively chosen* certain values: objectivity and consistency. Moreover, "reason" is a mere abstraction, a noble-sounding term that conceals an individual, subjective choice. But anything that obscures the existing individual interferes with authenticity, honesty, and passionate commitment.

The impersonal quality of objective language reduces the uniqueness of individual existence to generalizations, abstractions, and features in common. But the vital issues of existence confront the complex, individually existing self, not the general self of psychologists and philosophers, or Descartes' "thing which thinks," or Kant's "rational being," or Hume's "bundle of perceptions." Objectivity, by its very nature, is cool, detached, impersonal. Existence is not, according to Kierkegaard:

> The difficulty that inheres in existence, with which the existing individual is confronted, is one that never really comes to expression in the language of abstract thought, much less receives an explanation. . . . Abstract thought . . . ignores the concrete and the temporal, the existential process, the predicament of the existing individual arising from his being a synthesis of the temporal and the eternal situated in existence. . . .
>
> . . . Existing is ordinarily regarded as no very complex matter, much less an art, since we all exist; but abstract thinking takes rank as an accomplishment. But to really exist . . . that is truly difficult.[5]

Descartes, and all those who followed his lead, reduced existence to believing: "I *think*, therefore I am." Abstract, rationalistic philosophies ignore the real predicament of actual existence: deciding what to do. Actual decisions are not the neat, reasonable calculations of philosophers, nor are they the products of systematic scientific thinking. Abstract philosophies and all metaphysical systems merely observe life from a distance; they do not take part in it.

The Present Age

Kierkegaard viewed the mid–nineteenth century as an era of passionless mediocrity and conformity. He lamented the *massing of society*, by which he meant both the diminution of the individual's role in the face of mass production and the press (mass media), and the loss of truth in the face of objectivity and abstraction. He included what he saw as the inflated reputation of science and technological solutions to human problems in the massing of society. In *Either/Or*, Kierkegaard began a profound and eloquent analysis of conformism and mediocrity:

> Let others complain that the age is wicked; my complaint is that it is wretched, for it lacks passion. Men's thoughts are thin and flimsy like lace, they are themselves pitiable like lacemakers. The thoughts of their hearts are too paltry to be sinful. For a worm it might be regarded as a sin to harbor such thoughts, but not for a being made in the image of God. Their lusts are dull and sluggish, their passions sleepy. They do their duty, these shopkeeping souls, but they clip the coin a trifle . . . ; they think that even if the Lord keeps ever so careful a set of books, they may still cheat Him a little. Out upon them! This is the reason my soul always turns back to the Old Testament and to Shakespeare. I feel that those who speak there are at least human beings: they hate, they love, they murder their enemies, and curse their descendants throughout all generations, they sin.[6]

In an essay called *The Present Age* (1846), which, according to philosopher William Barrett, "has become the source of nearly all the Existentialist criticisms of modern society," Kierkegaard continued his attack on conformity.[7] "The crowd," he points out, overwhelms the individual, yet the individual feels frightened and lost without "the crowd." The mediocre, alienated individual needs a group to identify with, to provide "peer approval." Yet, Kierkegaard insists, a collective identity is always somehow false; in order to belong, to fit in, we must betray some part of ourselves, must cease living our own lives and begin living "a kind of life."

Philosophical Query

During the 1993 trial of four men for allegedly attacking truck driver Reginald Denny during the Los Angeles riots triggered by the verdict in the first Rodney King beating trial, a sociologist testifying for the defense

Because the contemporary individual has no comprehensive picture of the social universe within which he lives and of the structure of modern society, he pays the price of meaninglessness and insignificance in his daily work and even a spiritual isolation from his fellows.

A. W. Levi

The intelligence of any group of people who are thinking as a "herd" rather than individually is no higher than the intelligence of the stupidest members.

Mary Day Winn

argued that the accused were not responsible for their actions because they were caught up in the "crowd contagion" of the moment. What do you think of such a defense? Analyze your own behavior as part of a group or crowd. Do you find that it is always "somehow false"? Is it possible to be more yourself in a crowd than when alone? Discuss.

An Age of Virtual Equality

[B]ecause man is always inclined to cling to isms, instead of seeking independent strength in himself, the danger arises that one makes father or mother out of the group and remains as infantile and insecure as before.

Marie-Louise von Franz

According to Kierkegaard's view of "the crowd," modern people are anonymous creatures dependent on experts to point the way to salvation or personal growth. Think about Kierkegaard's analysis in light of the many coalitions, committees, and other groups that continue to spring up in our own times as you read this passage:

> The present age tends toward a mathematical equality in which it takes so and so many to make one individual. Formerly the outstanding individual could allow himself everything and the individual in the masses nothing at all. Now everyone knows that so and so many make an individual, and quite consistently people add themselves together (it is called joining together, but that is only a polite euphemism) for the most trivial purposes. Simply in order to put a passing whim into practice a few people add themselves together, and the thing is done—they dare to do it. . . .
>
> The individual no longer belongs to God, to himself, to his beloved, to his art or to his science; he is conscious of belonging in all things to an abstraction to which he is subjected by reflection.[8]

In short, rather than being themselves, people conform to an image or idea associated with being a certain *type* of person. That's what Kierkegaard means by belonging to an "abstraction" (an image or idea) created by "reflection" (self-conscious thinking). Thus, for example, a woman tries to be "a Christian" or "a lawyer" based on some collective abstraction, some image or idea. She attempts to conform to a pattern. Today, many of us govern our lives by abstractions based on age, race, and gender.

Let us labor under no illusions. There are no easy solutions for problems that are at the same time intensely personal and universal, urgent and eternal.

Abraham Joshua Heschel

To the extent that we see ourselves and others as *abstract types*, we deal with generalizations rather than with concrete specifics; we overlook individual qualities. Certainly no one disputes the usefulness of generalizations. They provide us with the ability to identify patterns, to recognize principles of behavior, and so forth. What they do not—and cannot—do is recognize *existing individuals*. From an existentialist perspective, all acts of generalizing and abstracting require *leveling*. And for Kierkegaard, leveling, as the word itself suggests, is not a process of exaltation, but of reduction to mediocrity, reduction to numerical equality at the expense of authenticity:

> The abstract principle of leveling . . . like the biting east wind, has no personal relation to any individual, but has only an abstract relation-

ship which is the same for everyone. There no hero suffers for others, or helps them; the taskmaster of all alike is the leveling process, which itself takes on their education. And the man who learns most from the leveling and himself becomes greatest does not become an outstanding man or hero—that would only impede the leveling process, which is rigidly consistent to the end; he himself prevents that from happening because he has understood the meaning of leveling: he becomes a man and nothing else, in the complete equalitarian sense.[9]

Philosophical Query

Identify some current examples of leveling, and discuss the general notion of leveling. Must efforts at furthering equality result in leveling? Is leveling possibly desirable?

In courtrooms and classrooms, we use "abstractions" to level ourselves so that "everyone is treated the same." The press levels presidents and celebrities through exposés of their personal lives. The underlying message is "They're no different from us." Indeed, they are not, but the leveling nature of these exposés, coupled with the sameness and mediocrity of the people we elect to office and turn into celebrities, seems to support a Kierkegaardian conclusion that the modern age remains an era of increasing dullness, conformity, and lack of genuine individuals.

The poet and social critic Robert Bly uses the metaphor of "siblings" to characterize what he describes as a leveling trend away from a "vertical" culture with a hierarchy of social levels and corresponding rights and responsibilities. In its place, Bly sees the emergence of a worldwide "horizontal" culture, which he refers to as a culture of "siblings" who substitute "busiedness" for depth, passion, and commitment. Bly writes:

> . . . [W]e human beings limp along, running after our own fantasy. We can never catch up, and so we defeat ourselves by the simplest possible means: speed. Everywhere we go there's a crowd, and the people all look alike.
>
> We begin to live a lateral life, catch glimpses out of the corners of our eyes, keep the TV set at eye level, watch the scores move horizontally across the screen.
>
> We see what's coming out of the sideview mirror. It seems like intimacy; maybe not intimacy as much as proximity; maybe not proximity as much as sameness. Americans who are twenty years old see others who look like them in Czechoslovakia, Greece, China, France, Brazil, Germany, and Russia, wearing the same jeans, listening to the same music, speaking a universal language that computer-literacy demands. Sometimes they feel more vitally connected to siblings elsewhere than to family members in the next room.
>
> When we see the millions like ourselves all over the world, our eyes meet in conformity, resemblance, likeness, rather than distinction and

> . . . [I]n a universe suddenly divested of illusions and lights, man feels an alien, a stranger. His exile is without remedy since he is deprived of the memory of a lost home or the hope of a promised land. This divorce between man and his life, the actor and his setting, is properly the feeling of absurdity.
>
> *Albert Camus*

> Mass society, with its demand for work without responsibility, creates a gigantic army of rival siblings.
>
> *Alexander Misterlich*

Just as desert travellers combine into great caravans from fear of robbers and wild beasts, so the individuals of the contemporary generation are fearful of existence, because it is God-forsaken; only in great masses do they dare to live, and they cluster together en masse in order to feel that they amount to something.

Søren Kierkegaard

differences. Hope rises immediately for the long-desired possibility of community. And yet it would be foolish to overlook the serious implications of this glance to the side, this tilt of the head. . . .

Adults regress toward adolescence; and adolescents—seeing that—have no desire to become adults. . . . Perhaps one-third of our society has developed these new sibling qualities. The rest of us are walking in that direction. When we all arrive, there may be no . . . past paradigms, because only people one's own age will be worth listening to.[10]

Philosophical Query

Does your experience conform with Bly's assertion that more and more of us don't want to be adults? What do you think Bly might mean by "adult"? What do you mean by "adult"? Do you think Bly might be onto something, or is he probably just being fearful? Would a "sibling society" be a good thing? Discuss and explain.

Philosophers and critics offer a variety of interpretations of Kierkegaard's writings. This is not surprising given Kierkegaard's penchant for irony, "indirection," and Socratic engagement. I suspect that he would be delighted with the *fact* of these myriad interpretations, even if he should object to their content. One point seems clear, however: Kierkegaard identified and addressed one of the crucial issues of our time: How can we be our "true selves" in an age dominated by ever more sophisticated ways of influencing our thoughts, feelings, and actions? How can we find sufficient passion and clarity of focus to become ourselves in a world seduced by objectivity and conformity, and run by ever more massive institutions?

Yet for all his great wit and capacity for prescient social analysis, it is unlikely that even Kierkegaard at his most fanciful could have imagined some of the monstrous effects of the twentieth-century "crowd." Not so, however, for perhaps the most famous twentieth-century existentialist, Jean-Paul Sartre, whose atheistic existentialism is rooted in his experiences during World War II.

Sartre and the Age of Forlornness

The winners write history.

Sir Ross Delbert-Fetters

The century that elapsed after Kierkegaard's death witnessed two monstrous world wars, two of the most awful—in the full, original meaning of that word—examples of insult to the individual in the face of massive social forces in human history. World War I revealed the ugly underside of "technological progress" as technical knowledge was converted to superefficient mechanisms of destruction: mustard gas, heavy artillery delivered with near pinpoint accuracy, bombs dropped from airplanes. Human beings were destroyed *en masse*, on a scale of "efficiency" hitherto unimaginable.

The instability, primitive anger, and irrational behavior that triggered the contemporary existential reaction in philosophy, art, and literature continue today. What solace can more traditional philosophers offer these children playing in ruins of the old library in central Sarajevo? Is it possible to deny that life is absurd after seeing so many scenes like this?

Yet as horrible as World War I was, those early engines of destruction paled in comparison to the monolithic, impassive, massive assault on humanity that occurred in World War II. By the time that war was officially over, tens of millions of Jews, Gypsies, Russians, Ukrainians, Poles, "cripples," "criminal types," "degenerates," and others had been systematically, impersonally, and efficiently "eliminated" by Hitler's Nazi regime. By the war's conclusion, America had dropped atomic bombs on the Japanese cities of Hiroshima and Nagasaki, and whatever veil of innocence remained was stripped away forever.

Jean-Paul Sartre

Jean-Paul-Charles-Aymard Sartre (1905–1980) was born in Paris. When his father died while Sartre was still an infant, his mother, Ann-Marie, moved in with her parents. Jean-Paul was raised in the home of his grandfather,

Jean-Paul Sartre

Charles Schweitzer, an uncle of Albert Schweitzer, the famous Christian missionary doctor. In a passage from the autobiographical *The Words*, Sartre suggested that his ultimate view of life was shaped by "a deep childish revulsion against the sham façade of noble rectitude behind which his [Sartre's grandfather's] bourgeois family hid from itself, and from him, its real dereliction."[11] Sartre added that until the age of ten he "remained alone between an old man and two women."[12]

Whatever Sartre the man thought of his grandfather, Charles Schweitzer introduced Sartre the boy to the world of words and literature. Withdrawn and isolated, disturbed by his mother's Catholicism and his grandparents' Lutheranism, young Sartre discovered the magical world of writing and ideas in his grandfather's impressive library. Before his tenth birthday he knew he would be a writer: "By writing, I was existing, I was escaping from grown-ups, but I existed only in order to write, and if I said 'I' that meant 'I who write.'"[13]

In 1929, Sartre graduated from the Ecole Normale Supérieure, which accepted only the finest students who had passed a series of competitive examinations. Sartre taught philosophy at various schools for the next ten years. During this time, he realized an enormous gap existed between his "living, breathing" life and the values he had learned in his grandfather's home and taught to others at school. Conventional, academic philosophy disappointed him; its abstractions and elaborate metaphysical systems bore little or no relevance to his actual existence. Life, Sartre noted, is made up of difficult decisions and concrete experiences, but traditional philosophy, on the whole, fails to address these living issues and choices.

Nausea

Sartre's philosophical disillusionment ended when he discovered the phenomenology of **Edmund Husserl (1859–1938)**. **Phenomenology** sees consciousness as the basis of reality and aims to provide a descriptive analysis of consciousness in all its forms. Stressing the concrete rather than the abstract, experienced facts rather than theory, phenomenology attempts to reveal the "essence" of human consciousness using purely descriptive statements. It aims at making no conceptual presuppositions, hoping to get beyond them to consciousness itself.

Sartre studied with Husserl in Berlin during the 1933–1934 school year. Revitalized, he turned to writing as a way to discover who he was and to find a philosophical approach that worked. Much as Søren Kierkegaard studied himself, even "created himself," through reflexive (self-conscious) writing, Sartre began a series of projects aimed at helping him discover a way to live "alone, without God." Building on his newfound phenomenological approach, Sartre attempted to see and describe experience in its basic "uninterpreted" state. In his first novel, *Nausea*, he tried to get beyond words, theories, and assumptions in order to see life raw.

PHENOMENOLOGY

Philosophical method of analysis developed by Edmund Husserl; using purely descriptive statements, phenomenology tries to provide a "descriptive analysis" of consciousness in all its forms, stressing the concrete rather than the abstract and experienced facts rather than theory, in order to reveal the "essence" of human consciousness.

Calvin and Hobbes, © Watterson. Dist. by Universal Press Syndicate. Reprinted with permission. All rights reserved.

Unlike Descartes' methodical meditations, Sartre's phenomenological introspection yields no rational, permanent entity known as the self. Instead of order and permanence, Sartre found nausea—a pulsating, everflowing monstrous nothingness. The more Sartre contemplated existence, the less he found. Sitting in a garden, contemplating the roots of an old chestnut tree, Roquentin, the protagonist of *Nausea*, says:

> Never until these last few days have I understood the meaning of existence. . . . And then all of a sudden, there it was, clear as day: existence had suddenly unveiled itself. It had lost the harmless look of an abstract category: it was the very paste of things, this root was kneaded into existence. Or rather the root, the park gates, the bench, the sparse grass, all that had vanished: the diversity of things, their individuality, were only an appearance, a veneer. This veneer had melted, leaving soft monstrous masses, all in disorder—naked, in a frightful, obscene nakedness.[14]

Existence Is Absurd

Having peered into himself and found nothing permanent; having peered beyond words and abstractions to glimpse the world as it is and found only "melted . . . soft monstrous masses, all in disorder—naked, in a frightful, obscene nakedness," Sartre concludes that existence is absurd:

> The word absurdity is coming to life under my pen; a little while ago . . . I couldn't find it, but neither was I looking for it, I didn't need it: I thought without words. . . . Without formulating anything clearly, I understood that I had found the key to Existence, the key to my Nausea, to my own life. In fact, all that I could grasp beyond that returns to this fundamental absurdity. Absurdity: another word; I struggle against words; down there I touched the thing.[15]

A man is involved in life, leaves his impress on it, outside of that there is nothing.

Jean-Paul Sartre

The world of explanations and reasons is not the world of existence.

Jean-Paul Sartre

Oh, the Pure Innocent Child!

Oh, tell me who was it first announced, who was it first proclaimed, that man only does nasty things because he does not know his own interests; and that if he were enlightened, if his eyes were opened to his real normal interests, man would at once cease to do nasty things, would at once become good and noble because, being enlightened and understanding his real advantage, he would see his own advantage in the good and nothing else, and we all know that not one man can, consciously, act against his own interests, consequently, so to say, through necessity, he would begin doing good? Oh, the babe! Oh, the pure innocent child!

Fyodor Dostoevsky
Notes from the Underground, trans. Constance Garnett, in *Existentialism from Dostoevsky to Sartre*, ed. Walter Kaufmann (New York: New American Library, 1975), p. 67.

Sartre's sense of the absurd was shaped by his experiences during World War II. He was drafted into the French army in 1939, and in 1940 was captured by the Germans. Sartre spent nine months as a prisoner of war before being released because of poor health. He returned to Paris and soon became an influential member of the French Resistance movement. During this time he met Albert Camus, his only near-rival in modern existential influence, and the brilliant **Simone de Beauvoir (1908–1986)**, who became Sartre's mistress and lifelong friend.

The German occupation of France drove home to Sartre the fact that evil is not a mere abstraction; it is real and concrete. He concluded that civilization and order are a thin veneer: at any moment "the beast" can break loose and reveal "the absurd," which most of us try to deny through rationalizations in the form of abstractions and philosophical and religious beliefs. Failure to face the absurd is always accompanied by excessive denial, which prevents us from recognizing evil for what it is. Sartre wrote that during the occupation he had been taught "to take evil seriously."

> It is neither to our fault nor our merit if we lived in a time when torture was a daily fact. Chateaubriand, Oradour, the Rue des Saussaies, Dachau, and Auschwitz have all demonstrated to us that Evil is not an appearance, that knowing its cause does not dispel it, that it is not opposed to Good as a confused idea is to a clear one, that it is not the effect of passions that might be cured, of an ignorance that might be enlightened, that it can in no way be incorporated into idealistic humanism.[16]

After the horrors of the Holocaust and the terrors wrought by the Nazis' use of science and advanced technology, a whole generation shared a nauseating vision of the absurd. "It was the war," Sartre stated, "which made the obsolete frames of our thought explode, the war, occupation, resistance, the years that followed."[17]

The essential predicament of man has assumed a peculiar urgency in our time, living as we do in a civilization where factories were established in order to exterminate millions of men, women, and children; where soap was made of human flesh. What have we done to make such crimes possible? What are we doing to make such crimes impossible?

Abraham Joshua Heschel

Sartre's philosophy was shaped by the Holocaust, which made it difficult to simply dismiss the Death of God and the Nietzschean abyss (Chapter 14). Perhaps "forlornness" is too tame a term for the human condition following such atrocities. How could God let something like this happen? How could "decent, average" people let it happen?

The Celebrity Philosopher

After the war, Sartre devoted his life to reading, writing, and speaking out on various topics relating to social injustice and personal responsibility. Throughout this time, he maintained a rich and rewarding friendship with Simone de Beauvoir. She challenged and stimulated him as a man and as a thinker, greatly influencing both his ideas and their written expression, as he did hers. Sartre and Beauvoir were a unique couple whose influence extended beyond their individual works to their lives, as they became role models for postwar intellectuals.

In 1960, Sartre published *The Critique of Dialectical Reason*, in which he advocated "existential Marxism." Recognizing that political Marxism had lost its original respect for the individual, Sartre nonetheless saw the contemporary era as the "age of Marx":

> There was the period of Descartes and Locke, then the period of Kant and Hegel, and since then there has been the period of Marx. Each of these three philosophies has been in turn the soil from which all individual ideas sprang and has formed the cultural horizon.[18]

Sartre accepted Marx's emphasis on economic and class-based determinism. He agreed that the individual is a product of his or her class. But Sartre

What good three thousand years of so-called civilization, of religion, philosophy, and education, when right up to the 1980s, as this was being written, men go on torturing, killing, repressing their fellowmen? In fact, was there not a retrogression here? In my own brief time we have vastly multiplied our capacity to kill and destroy. With the advent of the bomber, we not only slaughtered soldiers but also innocent women and children far behind the lines of battle.

William L. Shirer

thought Marxism lost sight of the individual in its emphasis on class struggle and economics. Marxian materialism objectifies the individual, Sartre argued, and consequently loses touch with his or her subjective consciousness. In other words, Marxism, like other nonexistential philosophies, abstracts the actual, living individual out of existence. Sartre's efforts to construct an existential Marxism were designed to place the existing individual once again at the focal point of Marxist criticism of bourgeois values.

Sartre and the Marxists were uneasy allies. Sartre's existentialism was not scientific enough, according to orthodox Marxism. Even more significant is the fact that Sartre's emphasis on the individual cannot be reconciled with Marxism's emphasis on classes, on the collective. Further, Sartre grew disillusioned with Soviet communism. "The way I understand it," Sartre said, "I am a Communist, but I believe the USSR is destroying Communism."

Buoyed by the popularity of Sartre's and other existential plays and novels, existentialism became the "in" philosophy of hipsters, beats, hippies, artists, students, and avant-garde thinkers. Sartre became a kind of philosophical godfather to radical French students and remained a well-known public figure throughout his life. He flirted with Maoism, a form of Communism practiced in China. In 1968, Sartre spoke out on behalf of a student revolt and two years later edited a Maoist newspaper called *The People's Cause*. During the Vietnam War, Sartre spoke out vehemently against American "war crimes."

Yet Sartre remained an enigma. He never joined the Communist party. Though he has been described as arrogant and snobbish, he also enjoyed the company of younger thinkers. His affair with Simone de Beauvoir grew into a complex friendship in which each party remained fiercely loyal to the other, while remaining free to have affairs with others. When he was awarded the 1964 Nobel Prize in Literature, Sartre refused it because he did not want to be "turned into an institution."

After years of failing health and eyesight, Jean-Paul Sartre died April 15, 1980.

> I was prepared at an early age to regard teaching as a priesthood and literature as a passion.
>
> *Jean-Paul Sartre*

Freedom and Anguish

> We are left alone, without excuse. That is what I mean when I say that man is condemned to be free.
>
> *Jean-Paul Sartre*

Sartre concluded that to merely *be* an authentic self is not possible. There is no fixed "essence" lingering behind the roles we play. We are whatever we do, the totality of our actions. Thus, *an authentic self exists as and through the choices it makes for itself, uncontrolled by the values of others*. Put another way, we do not *have* a given nature; we *become* a certain kind of person. We are existentially free. There is no fixed self on which we build.

Authenticity is possible only when we realize the emptiness at the heart of the social self. So long as he tries to *think* himself into authenticity,

Sartre remains nauseated, alienated, paralyzed. He must find a way to bridge the gap between merely observing life by acting out a social role (even the role of criminal or rebel), and full, passionate involvement in life. Sartre's term for this passionate involvement is *engagement*.

Unlike those philosophers who seek to *understand* life, or to fit it into systems of thought governed by abstract principles, Sartre asked Kierkegaard's timeless question: "What am *I* to *do*?" Having seen beyond the façade of the social self to the reality of absolute freedom, Sartre had to decide what to do with such terrible freedom. The "social self" is an abstraction, a verbal portrait of what we *are* (our being), constructed from bits and pieces of past moments of self-consciousness. But at any given moment, through this or that choice, *we are whatever we do*. And no one can predict with anything approaching certainty what he or she will or will not do.

Philosophical Query

Describe yourself in terms of your mental concept of who you are (your social self), and give an objective description of what you do. Contrast how you live with how you think of yourself. Is there a difference? Why or why not?

Inauthenticity

For Sartre and countless others, living with the horror and irrationality of the Nazi occupation shattered any hope for an ordered universe governed by a wise, powerful, and loving God. Science provides no certainty; indeed, the Nazi concentration camps were "scientific" and "rationally ordered."

For Sartre, nature is only another bourgeois delusion, a mental construct designed to cover up the hideous absurdity of existence. By deceiving themselves into believing in either the certainty of science or the order of nature, individuals attempt to evade the awesomeness of choice. By pretending that facts dictate choices or that certain choices are "natural," we obscure our own responsibility. We are free to choose "the facts" or to reject them; free to "follow nature" or not, because we are free to define the facts and to define what is natural.

The characters in Sartre's most famous play, *No Exit*, are dead persons who never lived authentically, who identified themselves according to others' opinions of them. As a result, they became caricatures, mere sketches of living, real human beings. They meet in a hell fashioned by their own superficial choices. They have no exit from the consequences of their choices: They now *are* what they once only pretended to be: merely what others think of them. There is no real person behind the social mask.

In *No Exit* Sartre attacked the hypocrisy, inauthenticity, and cowardice of living for others rather than for oneself, of acting against one's "authentic self" to curry favor, to avoid rejection, and so on. While we do

By . . . getting in all sorts of worldly affairs, by becoming wise about how things go in this world, [the foolish] man forgets himself, forgets what his name is . . . does not dare to believe in himself, finds it too venturesome a thing to be himself, far easier and safer to be like the others, to become an imitation, a number, a cipher in the crowd.

Søren Kierkegaard

this, we never become authentic, *living individuals*; we remain mere "social types." Our duties—as social types—are defined by the group. In Kierkegaard's terms, we live through the crowd.

For instance, a young woman might try to live up to some currently faddish image of a successful type, say a businesswoman wearing stylish suits, driving a certain brand of car, and working for a Fortune 500 company. She might have constructed a plan for herself based on movies, magazine articles, and the popular image of this type. The qualities that make up this type are external to the individual, however. They are controlled by a social group. To succeed, the young woman will have to sacrifice until she becomes nothing more than a type of person. Her "success" will rest on other people's opinions of her. She may live under the delusion that she will be herself when she gets powerful enough or rich enough or when she retires. This delusion protects her from the truth: There is no real self waiting.

There is no exit from choice, no escape from freedom in a God-forsaken universe.

Philosophical Query

Identify some common social types from your own experience. What social type are you? Is it possible to be both a social type and an authentic self?

Forlornness

According to Sartre, since nothing limits our choices, we are not psychologically required to be this or that person. We are not chained to the past through heredity or environmental conditioning. Science and nature cannot tell us what to do, Sartre thought, and neither can God. God is truly dead: He does not answer us, but remains silent in the face of absurdity and horror. Thus we face life alone, without God, without certainty—we experience Sartrean **forlornness**—with only absolute freedom and the chilling responsibility that accompanies it.

> When we speak of forlornness . . . we mean only that God does not exist and that we have to face all the consequences of this. The existentialist is strongly opposed to a certain kind of secular ethics which would like to abolish God with the least popular expense. . . .
>
> The existentialist, on the contrary, thinks it very distressing that God does not exist, because all possibility of finding values in a heaven of ideas disappears along with Him; there can no longer be an *a priori* Good, since there is no infinite and perfect consciousness to think it. Nowhere is it written that the Good exists, that we must be honest, that we must not lie; because the fact is we are on a plane where there are only men. Dostoievsky said, "If God didn't

FORLORNNESS

Jean-Paul Sartre's term for his belief that we face life alone, without God, without certainty, with only absolute freedom and the responsibility that accompanies it.

After World War II, "existential themes" were popular with poets, writers, painters, musicians, and "beatniks." Alberto Giacometti's 1960 sculpture Walking Man *evokes a Sartrean sense of "existential angst" and "lonely toughness."*

exist, everything would be possible." That is the very starting point of existentialism. Indeed, everything is permissible if God does not exist, and as a result man is forlorn, because neither within him nor without does he find anything to cling to. He can't start making excuses for himself.[19]

Atheistic existentialism refuses to compensate for the silence of God by substituting a glib scientific or philosophic idol. Sartre denounced secular ethics that attempt to take ethical values seriously in such a way that "nothing will be changed if God does not exist." But if God does not exist, and if science cannot provide certainty, and if "nature" is a middle-class invention, *then everything has changed radically.*

Most significant, in Sartre's view, is that without God there is no fixed human nature, no "essence" that infuses us. *We* are not governed by fixed laws: We are free, not determined. First we exist; then we choose; then we act. We fashion our essence by how we actually live our lives—without God to guide and console us.

> If existence really does precede essence, there is no explaining things away by reference to a fixed and given human nature. In other words, there is no determinism, man is free, man is freedom. On the other hand, if God does not exist, we find no values or commands to turn to which legitimise our conduct. So, in the bright realm of values, we have no excuse behind us, nor justification before us. We are alone with no excuses.[20]

The universe was always insecure.

Herbert Butterfield

Philosophical Query

Given the horrors of our age—the threat of nuclear annihilation, chemical weapons, the Holocaust, child abuse, rampant pollution, AIDS and cancer, homelessness, and famine—which do you see as more horrible: the absence of God or the silence of God? Is God silent?

Condemned to Be Free

What a man actually needs is not the discharge of a tensionless state but rather the striving and struggling for some goal worthy of him. What he needs is not the discharge of tension at any cost, but the call of a potential meaning waiting to be fulfilled by him.

Viktor E. Frankl

A strong case can be made that our age is indeed forlorn, at least psychologically. Though science continues to explain human conduct in biochemical terms and according to behavioristic models, we cannot fail to see signs of forlornness in desperate attempts to find guidelines, guarantees, certainty: We look to science to "cure" everything from warts to character defects. We seek to absolve ourselves with excuses: "I come from a disadvantaged background." "I couldn't help it." "I was drunk." "I was overcome by my emotions."

Sartre insisted that in one aspect we are indeed not free: *We are not free not to be free.* In his famous phrase, *we are condemned to be free.* No divine commandments, no prophecies or omens, limit or lead us; no powerful, "irresistible" feeling excuses us.

> This is the idea I shall try to convey when I say that man is condemned to be free. Condemned, because he did not create himself, yet, in other respects is free; because, once thrown into the world, he is responsible for everything he does. The existentialist does not believe in the power of passion. He will never agree that a sweeping passion is a ravaging torrent which fatally leads a man to certain acts and is therefore an excuse. He thinks that man is responsible for his passion.
>
> The existentialist does not think that man is going to help himself by finding in the world some omen by which to orient himself. Because he thinks that man will interpret that omen to suit himself. Therefore, he thinks that man, with no support and no aid, is condemned every moment to invent man. . . . Whatever a man may be, there is a future to be forged, a virgin future before him. . . . But then we are forlorn.[21]

Sartre illustrated the freedom of forlornness with a story about one of his students. The young man's father had collaborated with the Nazis during the occupation of France, but his older brother had been killed fighting the Germans, and the young man wanted to avenge him. The boy and his mother lived alone, and the mother was upset by the father's betrayal of his country and dead son. Sartre's student was her sole consolation and reason for living. He faced the choice of leaving for England in order to fight, or staying in France to support his mother. What should the student do, and how could he know?

Who could help him choose? Christian doctrine? No. Christian doctrine says, "Be charitable, love your neighbor, take the more rugged path, etc., etc." But which is the more rugged path? Whom should he love as a brother? The fighting man or his mother? Which does the greater good, the vague act of fighting in a group or the concrete one of helping a particular human being to go on living? Who can decide *a priori*? Nobody. No book of ethics can tell him. The Kantian ethic says, "Never treat any person as a means, but as an end." Very well, if I stay with my mother, I'll treat her as an end and not as a means; but by virtue of this very fact, I'm running the risk of treating the people around me who are fighting, as means; and, conversely, if I go to join those who are fighting, I'll be treating them as an end, and, by doing that, I run the risk of treating my mother as a means.

If values are vague, and if they are always too broad for the concrete and specific case that we are considering, the only thing left is for us to trust our instincts. That's what this young man tried to do. . . .

But how is the value of a feeling determined? What gives his feeling for his mother value? Precisely the fact that he remained with her. I may say that I like so-and-so well enough to sacrifice a certain amount of money for him, but I may say so only if I've done it. I may say "I love my mother well enough to remain with her" if I have remained with her. The only way to determine the value of this affection is, precisely, to perform an act which confirms and defines it. But since I require this affection to justify my act, I am caught in a vicious circle.[22]

No system of ethics, no philosophy, could tell the student what choice to make, and if feelings "are formed by the act one performs," he could not seek the answer within himself. And so he turned to Sartre for advice.

But if you seek advice from a priest, for example, you have chosen this priest; you already knew, more or less, just about what advice he was going to give you. In other words, choosing your adviser is choosing yourself. . . . Which to choose? If the young man chooses a priest who is resisting or collaborating, he has already decided on the kind of advice he's going to get. Therefore, in coming to see me he knew the answer I was going to give: "You're free, choose, that is, invent." No general ethics can show you what is to be done; there are no omens in the world. The Catholics will reply, "But there are." Granted—but, in any case, I myself choose the meaning they have.
. . . Therefore, he is fully responsible for the interpretation. Forlornness implies that we ourselves choose our being.[23]

Philosophical Query

If valuing depends on choosing, and not the other way around, what do you value? Assess your values with a Sartrean analysis of your actions.

> There are those who sense the ultimate question in moments of wonder, in moments of joy; there are those who sense the ultimate question in moments of horror, in moments of despair. It is both the grandeur and the misery of living that makes [us] sensitive to the ultimate question.
>
> *Abraham Joshua Heschel*

> Man is always the same. The situation confronting him varies. Choice always remains choice in a situation. The problem has not changed.
>
> *Jean-Paul Sartre*

The question of the meaning of life is, as the Buddha taught, not edifying. One must immerse oneself in the river of life and let the question drift away.

Irvin D. Yalom

At this moment, when each of us must fit an arrow to his bow and enter the lists anew, to reconquer, within history and in spite of it, that which he owns already, the thin yields of his fields, the brief love of this earth, at this moment when at last man is born, it is time to forsake our age and its adolescent furies. The bow bends; the wood complains. At the moment of supreme tension, there will leap into flight an unswerving arrow, a shaft that is flexible and free.

Albert Camus

For instance, do you love your job more than school? To find out, see which receives most of your time, thoughts, and actions. Test other aspects of your life. What are the strengths and weaknesses of such a view of valuing and choosing?

The Self as Project

Sartre was concerned not with mere behavior, but with deliberate *action*. Action involves conscious choice. Unlike Mill, for Sartre it is not the consequences of our actions that matter but *whether or not we act at all*. By undertaking some freely and consciously chosen "project," we create the world in our own image. Acting cowardly, we create a craven world. Acting heroically, we create a heroic world. When we merely conform to social reality or attempt to live according to others' ideas and values, we "annihilate" our selves in order to maintain the world as we find it. Sartre called us to a more active, more heroic challenge: *Nihilate (re-create) the world as we find it in order to become an authentic self.*[24]

Sartre's call to a strenuous, courageous heroism is reminiscent of William James's (Chapter 13)—but with a tone of anguish and absurdity that was missing from James's more robust position. Sartre rejected the notion of a *given* world that forces one person to be cowardly, another lazy, a third an atheist. He insisted that we can "nihilate" the world that is given to us by taking action. Our actions, as opposed to our mere "behaviors," announce our intentions regarding "a result yet to be obtained." This "result yet to be obtained" is a *project*. We can overcome "the given" and thus nihilate it in the process of dedicating ourselves to a project.

> A first glance at human reality informs us that for it being is reduced to doing. . . . Thus we find no *given* in human reality in the sense that temperament, character, passions, principles of reason would be acquired or innate *data* existing in the manner of things. . . . Thus human reality does not exist first in order to act out later; but for human reality, to be is to act, and to cease to act is to cease to be. . . .
>
> . . . We shall never apprehend ourselves except as a choice in the making. But freedom is simply the fact that this choice is always unconditioned.[25]

For instance, in this view, a man is not born with the inescapable essence of "sufferer because of emotional abuse during childhood." He inherits that social self through the ideas and interpretations of others. That is his "given world." He can choose (intend) to overcome this interpretation by living a robust, heroic life; he can form his own "essence" by the way he acts.

This way of looking at things completely inverts the common understanding of human behavior. Instead of saying a man refuses to stand up to abuse because he is a coward, Sartre said that refusing to stand up to abuse makes him a coward. He lives in a coward's world. In Sartrean terms, a coward chooses to live in a particular world and that becomes his project. He could, according to Sartre, adopt a new project at any time.

A *free* project is not the same thing as an *easy* project. Lifelong habits, genetic disposition, social climate, and other factors may make it difficult for the coward to choose heroism, but they need not make it impossible.

Anguish

Sartre argued that even the most seemingly private and individual choices involve all people. By choosing to be this or that type of person, we create an image of the way others ought to be.

> If . . . existence precedes essence, and if we grant that we exist and fashion our image at one and the same time, the image is valid for everybody and for our whole age. Thus, our responsibility is much greater than we might have supposed because it involves all mankind. If I am a workingman and choose to join a Christian trade-union rather than be a communist . . . my action has involved all humanity. To take a more individual matter, if I want to marry, to have children; even if this marriage depends solely on my own passion or circum-stances or wish, I am involving all humanity in monogamy and not merely myself. Therefore, I am responsible for myself and for every-one else. I am creating a certain image of man of my own choosing. In choosing myself, I choose man.[26]

Don't confuse Sartre's point with Kant's categorical imperative (Chap-ter 10). Kant attempted to prove that what is right (or wrong) is always right (or wrong). Sartre did not agree. Sartre thought, rather, that we are each free to choose and create our own world. Cowards choose and cre-ate a certain world, lovers create their own world, and so on. What is uni-versal is not a specific act or kind of act, but the fact of human freedom. We cannot escape or evade freedom and, therefore, we cannot escape or evade responsibility. With awareness of freedom and responsibility comes **anguish**:

> The existentialists say at once that man is anguish. What that means is this: the man who involves himself and who realizes that he is not only the person he chooses to be, but also a lawmaker who is, at the same time, choosing all mankind as well as himself, cannot help escape the feeling of total and deep responsibility. Of course, there are many people who are not anxious, but we claim that they are hiding their anxiety, that they are fleeing from it. Certainly, many people believe that when they do something, they themselves are the only ones involved, and when someone says to them, "What if everyone acted that way?" they shrug their shoulders and answer,

Man is nothing else but what he makes of himself. Such is the first principle of existentialism.

Jean-Paul Sartre

ANGUISH

Term Sartre uses to de-scribe the awareness that even our most seemingly private and individual choices involve all people; by choosing to be this or that type of person, we create an image of the way others ought to be; not to be confused with Kant's categorical imperative.

"Everyone doesn't act that way." But really, one should always ask himself, "What would happen if everybody looked at things that way?" There is no escaping this disturbing thought except by a kind of double dealing. A man who lies and makes excuses for himself by saying "not everybody does that," is someone with an uneasy conscience, because the act of lying implies that a universal value is conferred upon the lie.[27]

Here, Sartre is concerned both with motives, which he often refers to as intentions, and their consequences. Sartre's early phenomenological interests taught him the significance of consciousness as a component of temperament. We might sum up his point this way: *Consciousness has incalculable consequences.* Consider Sartre's example of the person who does something questionable and makes the excuse that not everybody does it. By attempting to become the exceptional case, such a person creates a sense of being apart from the rest of humanity. This alienated sense of being apart manifests itself as arrogance (being above others), inferiority (being below others), indifference (not identifying with others), or severe inwardness (not noticing others).

Perhaps more important than precisely what we choose deliberately and with anguish is that we choose with eyes open and with a full sense of our responsibility to choose in good faith. Kant was concerned chiefly with a rational ground for universal rules; Sartre is concerned with the character and choices of existing individuals, as they affect the individual and humanity. Among other things, existentialism is a philosophy of individuals, not of rules or problems of theoretical consistency.

The existentialist calls on us to conceal as little as possible, to see clearly and fully the horrible range of our freedom and the inescapable weight of our responsibility. There is no escape from having to choose for myself:

> Anguish is evident even when it conceals itself. This is the anguish Kierkegaard called the anguish of Abraham. You know the story: an angel has ordered Abraham to sacrifice his son; if it really were an angel who has come and said, "You are Abraham, you shall sacrifice your son," everything would be all right. But everyone might first wonder, "Is it really an angel, and am I really Abraham? What proof do I have?"
>
> There was a madwoman who had hallucinations; someone used to speak to her on the phone and give her orders. Her doctor asked her, "Who is it who talks to you?" She answered, "He says it's God." What proof did she really have that it was God? If an angel comes to me, what proof is there it's an angel? And if I hear voices, what proof is there that they come from heaven and not from hell, or from the subconscious, or a pathological condition? What proves that they are addressed to me? What proof is there that I have been appointed to impose my choice and my conception of man on humanity? I'll never

Be careful with your words, for someone will agree with them. Be careful with your conduct, for someone will imitate it.

Lie Zi

find any proof or sign to convince me of that. If a voice addresses me, it is always for me to decide that this is the angel's voice; if I consider that such an act is a good one, it is I who will choose to say it is good rather than bad.

Now, I'm not being singled out as an Abraham, and yet every moment I'm obliged to perform exemplary acts. For every man, everything happens as if all mankind has its eyes fixed on him and were guiding itself by what he does. And every man ought to say to himself, "Am I really the kind of man who has the right to act in such a way that humanity might guide itself by my actions?" And if he does not say that himself, he is masking his anguish.

. . . [The] kind of anguish . . . that existentialism describes is explained, in addition, by a direct responsibility to the other men whom it involves. It is not a curtain separating us from action, but is part of action itself.[28]

Philosophical Query

Parents contemplating divorce experience the anguish Sartre speaks of when they consider the incalculable consequences of their action. Staying married "for the sake of the children" implies one kind of world. Getting divorced because "everyone makes mistakes and there's no reason to pay for them forever" implies another kind. Analyze the different worlds "created" by these two interpretations. Are there other possible interpretations? What do you think of Sartre's claim that freedom involves responsibility and anguish?

Despair

If we adopt a rigorous Sartrean philosophy, then we must confine our planning and our efforts to what is under our immediate influence or control. We must stick to what falls under the domain of our will and ability. But this realistic, responsible approach, Sartre says, leads to **despair**. We are stripped of hoping that God, or society, or luck, or the general good of others will come to our aid or rescue.

As for despair, the term has a very simple meaning. It means that we shall confine ourselves to reckoning only with what depends upon our will, or on the ensemble of probabilities which make our action possible. . . . The moment the possibilities I am considering are not rigorously involved in my action, I ought to disengage myself from them, because no God, no scheme, can adapt the world and its possibilities to my will. When Descartes said, "Conquer yourself rather than the world," he meant essentially the same thing.

. . . given that man is free and that there is no human nature for me to depend on, I cannot count on men whom I do not know by relying

Because, during times of personal stress and cultural breakdown, people flock to the churches does not mean they are deriving genuine satisfaction from this religious activity . . . it is the therapist and not the priest who is looked to for the final word now.

René J. Muller

DESPAIR

Sartrean term referring to the refusal to base choices and actions on possibilities; the condition of confining ourselves to what directly falls under our present influence and control.

Man is but a foundling in the cosmos, abandoned by the forces that created him. Unparented, unassisted, and undirected by omniscient or benevolent authority, he must fend for himself, and with the aid of his own limited intelligence find his way about in an indifferent universe.

Carl Becker

on human goodness or man's concern for the good of society. . . . I've got to limit myself to what I see.[29]

We must not confuse *possibilities* with *probabilities*. Many improbable things are possible. Someone might possibly walk up to you on the street and hand you a million dollars. But it would be foolish and irresponsible in the extreme for you to run up thousands of dollars on a credit card based on that possibility. It is possible that your philosophy final exam will be canceled and your professor will give you an A on it anyway. But . . .

When we consider only probabilities that are "rigorously involved" in our action, we not only live more authentically, we encounter despair. We are cut off from false optimism based on being saved from the outside. We can no longer "depend on the kindness of strangers" like Blanche DuBois in Tennessee Williams's play *A Streetcar Named Desire*. We must step forward and take what action we can. Sartre says:

> The doctrine I am presenting . . . declares, "There is no reality except in action." Moreover, it goes further, since it adds, "Man is nothing else than his plan; he exists only to the extent that he fulfills himself; he is therefore nothing else than the ensemble of his acts, nothing else than his life."
>
> According to this, we can understand why our doctrine horrifies certain people. Because often the only way they can bear their wretchedness is to think, "Circumstances have been against me. What I've been and done doesn't show my true worth. To be sure, I've had no great love, no great friendship, but that's because I haven't met a man or woman who was worthy. The books I've written haven't been very good because I haven't had the proper leisure. I haven't had children to devote myself to because I didn't find a man with whom I could have spent my life. So there remains within me, unused and quite viable, a host of propensities, inclinations, possibilities, that one wouldn't guess from the mere series of things I've done."[30]

Philosophical Query

Discuss this passage, especially the last part. Have you ever felt that circumstances are against you? To what extent do circumstances matter? To what extent do they excuse and explain our life? Our self? Our character?

Optimistic Toughness

For Sartre, value is expressed through action and choice. Thus "there is really no love other than one which manifests itself in a person's being in love. There is no genius other than one which is expressed in works of art."[31] In other words, there is no sense in excusing ourselves by talking about hidden, untapped genius or potential. Sartre's is a philosophy of the actual, not the potential.

Despair is a reminder of our limits and responsibilities. But by reminding us of our limits—probabilities "rigorously involved" in our action—Sartre also reminds us of our power. The other side of this coin is that once we stop waiting for God or others or fate to take action, we may be more inclined to begin to act for ourselves. From existential forlornness, anguish, and despair comes authentic optimism, based not on wishful thinking and vague possibilities, but on tough truths and clear vision.

To those who object to Sartre's apparently harsh doctrine, he replies that existentialism actually calls us to "optimistic toughness." Though it seeks to strip us of our dreams, hopes, and expectations, it does so for the purpose of turning our attention, and hence our lives, to the reality of here and now—not the fantasy of maybe there later.

> To be sure, this may seem a harsh thought to someone whose life hasn't been a success. But, on the other hand, it prompts people to understand that reality alone is what counts, that dreams, expectations, and hopes warrant no more than to define a man as a disappointed dream, as miscarried hopes, as vain expectations. In other words, to define him negatively and not positively. . . .
>
> When all is said and done, what we are accused of, at bottom, is not our pessimism, but an optimistic toughness. . . . When the existentialist writes about a coward, he says that this coward is responsible for his cowardice. He's not like that because he has a cowardly heart or lung or brain; he's not like that on account of his physiological make-up; but he's like that because he has made himself a coward by his acts. There is no such thing as a cowardly constitution; there are nervous constitutions; there is poor blood, as the common people say, or strong constitutions. But the man whose blood is poor is not a coward on that account, for what makes cowardice is the act of renouncing or yielding. A constitution is not an act; the coward is defined on the basis of the acts he performs. People feel, in a vague sort of way, that this coward we're talking about is guilty of being a coward, and the thought frightens them. What people would like is that a coward or a hero be born that way.
>
> . . . That's what people really want to think. If you're born cowardly, you may set your mind perfectly at rest; there's nothing you can do about it; you'll be cowardly all your life, whatever you may do. If you're born a hero, you may set your mind just as much at rest; you'll be a hero all your life; you'll drink like a hero and eat like a hero. What the existentialist says is that the coward makes himself cowardly, that the hero makes himself heroic. There's always a possibility for the coward not to be cowardly any more and for the hero to stop being heroic. What counts is total involvement; some one particular action or set of circumstances is not total involvement.[32]

Sartrean existentialism does not offer hope in the common understanding of that word. That is, it does not offer a comforting possibility that maybe

My matured conclusion has been that no system is to be trusted, not even that of science in any literal or pictorial sense; but all systems may be used and, up to a point, trusted as symbols.

George Santayana

A first glance at human reality informs us that for it being is reduced to doing.

Jean-Paul Sartre

someday the coward will cease being cowardly. It does, however, offer us a basic formula for transformation. In that, it is optimistic or hopeful, rather than pessimistic and negative.

Ironically, from a Sartrean perspective, excuses and explanations, though superficially comforting and compassionate, are ultimately pessimistic: They reduce us to the effects of uncontrollable forces (genes, childhood, culture). Our choices, if we believe such scientifically sophisticated explanations, are severely restricted. Our dignity is reduced to coping with the rough deal we've been dealt. "I've done pretty well considering the way I was treated as a child." "It's not my fault I went to inferior schools. I'm doing pretty well considering that my reading skills are weak."

We can understand how Sartre's position still "horrifies certain people." Determinism absolves us of complete responsibility. Perhaps the loss of free will is a small price to pay for being able to blame luck, heredity, and my past for the present condition of my life. Perhaps the comforts provided by wishes, dreams, and expectations are worth the price of losing sight of opportunities to act differently right now. Sartre, clearly, does not think so. For inevitably, with the loss of freedom comes the loss of human dignity:

> [Existentialism] defines man in terms of action; . . . there is no doctrine more optimistic, since man's destiny is within himself; . . . it tells him that his only hope is in his acting and that action is the only thing that enables a man to live. Consequently, we are dealing here with an ethics of action and involvement.
>
> . . . This theory is the only one which gives man dignity, the only one which does not reduce him to an object. The effect of materialism is to treat all men, including the one philosophizing, as objects, that is, as an ensemble of determined reactions in no way distinguished from the ensemble of qualities and phenomena which constitute a table or a chair or a stone.[33]

Commentary

Kierkegaard and Sartre are two of the very few philosophers sure to be found in virtually any popular bookstore. Other philosophers write as well or better. Other philosophers address important issues. But few speak to certain important problems of our time as pointedly as Kierkegaard and Sartre do. They understand the dangers of deferring choices to outsiders, to experts. Their strong attacks on using philosophy, religion, science, or anything else as mechanisms of denial and escapism strike a chord with scholars and nonscholars alike.

Contemporary social scientists attest to the power of "the crowd," and we all experience the pressures caused by the massing of society. De-

---

Take flight each day! At least for a moment, however brief, as long as it is intense. Every day a "spiritual exercise" alone or in the company of [men or women] who also wish . . . to better [themselves]. . . . Leave ordinary time behind. Make an effort to rid yourself of your own passions. . . . Become eternal by surpassing yourself. This inner effort is necessary, this ambition, just. Many are those who are entirely absorbed in militant politics, in the preparation for the social revolution. Rare, very rare, are those who, in order to prepare for the revolution, wish to become worthy of it.

Georges Friedmann

spite our many freedoms, increased leisure, and psychological sophistication, authenticity seems rare. Kierkegaard's great virtue is his reclamation
of the existing individual. We can easily lose sight of the fact that individuals construct philosophies, individuals interpret revelations, individuals
draw scientific conclusions. We run the risk of a kind of moral and intellectual psychosis if we fail to recognize the subjective element in all truth
claims and decisions.

Yet Kierkegaard may swing too much in the direction of subjectivity
and individuality. For all his insight and prophetic power, he was unable
to overcome his own alienation from science and objectivity. Surely, not
even the leap of faith can completely ignore objective reality. The problem
here is to modify Kierkegaard without transforming his philosophy into
just what he loathed: an abstract, rationalistic, objective "system."

Also, even though a lack of passion is deadly, the presence of passion
is no guarantee of authenticity. Blind, uncontrollable passion can destroy
individuality as surely as excessive abstraction. Anyone who has been
"consumed" or "swept away" by passion knows that it is possible to lose
ourselves in passion as well as in crowds.

On balance, Kierkegaard's critique of inauthentic faith, mass societies,
and the dangers of blindly sterile objectivity stands as a beacon in our per-
ilous times. Our danger today seems to be not too much passion, but too
much sentimentality masquerading as passion; not the risky leap of faith,
but the pseudosafety of mass-movement religion; not too much subjectivity, but too much self-centeredness. One might even say that in spite (or
because?) of our knowledge of the human psyche, we still encounter few
authentic individuals.

Sartre reminds us that with or without God, life remains the same: We
must choose this or choose that. Not choosing is not an option. He reminds us of the dangers of excuse-making and fatalism. In a time when
science threatens to explain and excuse away the individual, we need such
reminders.

Since we do not know exactly where the line between freedom and
determinism is, we cannot easily escape into excuses, no matter how
tempting they may be or how hard we try to convince ourselves that we're
pawns of the past, of DNA, of our "conditioning." Although we may be
born with tendencies and limits, Sartre reminds us that we are not born
cowards or heroes. We become what we do. And until science explains all
facets of the human condition, freedom will remain for us to use wisely or
to squander.

Because so much of our world seems so absurd, the need for optimistic
toughness, for courageous, self-defining action, is as great as it has ever
been. It is impossible not to glimpse the absurd today. We see around us a
world of obscene inequality: Some nations cannot find places for their
mountains of garbage, while others cannot feed their children. We possess
enough nuclear weapons to destroy the world many times, yet research

Man is never driven to
moral behavior; in each
instance he decides to behave morally. Man does
not do so to satisfy a moral
drive and to have a good
conscience; he does so for
the sake of a cause to which
he commits himself, or for
a person whom he loves, or
for the sake of his God. If
he actually did it for the
sake of a good conscience,
he would become a Phar-
isee and cease to be a truly
moral person.

Viktor E. Frankl

into chemical weapons continues. Many of us insist that life is sacred, yet older and "imperfect" children by the thousands await adoption. We have more laws than any nation in history—and more crime. We say that we value "life, liberty, and the pursuit of happiness," then go to war in courtrooms across America to prevent mortally ill fellow human beings from dying with self-defined dignity at self-chosen places of comfort and privacy. More than thirty years after the civil rights movement and twenty years after the beginning of the modern women's movement, racism and sexism seem to be unchecked, if not on the rise. The more we try to fix things, the more convoluted and complex they appear to become.

It is easy to dismiss existentialism as "romanticized pessimism" or "adolescent philosophizing." Understandably, we remain tempted by the hope that knowledge will save us, that clearer thinking, better science, and managed social reform will make our world a better, decent place. Perhaps they will. But history suggests that when we make progress, it always comes at some price. Improving the lot of one group results in real or perceived losses for another group. As soon as one disease is cured, a newer, more complex one emerges. Each incremental increase in specialization makes it more difficult to communicate across and within disciplines, and we risk losing sight of the whole in our frenzy to master the parts.

Sometimes I am tempted to take solace in sophisticated explanations of why we are who we are, but reflection suggests that no one knows for sure. Modern science continues to discover knowledge of many things; nonexistentialist philosophy continues to refine and clarify our capacities for understanding. So I do not dismiss or turn my back on science, nonexistentialist philosophy, or social progress. But should they achieve every one of their goals this minute, they would still have no answer to the profoundest existential questions: What is it to be a human being? Is our suffering and struggling worth living for? Has it a meaning? Has *my life* a meaning?

It's all right if you're tempted to laugh and ask: "What do you expect, that some philosophy book or scientific theory is going to answer your personal identity questions?" *That's the whole point:* With or without God; with or without loving families; with or without wise advisers; with or without children; with or without jobs; with or without formal education; of whatever age, race, gender—Kierkegaard's question haunts all of us, tracks us like a Socratic hound: What are we—you and I and they—to *do*?

Modern man may be characterized as a being who is callous to catastrophes. A victim of enforced brutalization, his sensibility is being increasingly reduced; his sense of horror is on the wane. The distinction between right and wrong is being blurred. All that is left to us is our being horrified at the loss of our sense of horror.

Abraham Joshua Heschel

Summary of Main Points

1. Existentialism addresses fundamental questions of meaning and choice as they affect individuals. Existential themes include choice, freedom, identity, alienation, inauthenticity, despair, and awareness of our own mortality.

2. Søren Kierkegaard claimed that truth is subjectivity and the crowd is untruth. He rejected the view that science and objective truth could provide meaning for the individual. He criticized conformity and the degradation that he

claimed results when theories and systems are used to explain and define individuals.

3. For Kierkegaard, the most important issue facing any individual is how to relate to God. He criticized efforts to reduce that relationship to a performance contract, and rejected as "false Christianity" all efforts to objectify faith or base belief on facts (science).

4. Kierkegaard criticized what he saw as the inflated reputation of science and the massing of society, which he thought combined to alienate individuals from themselves by leveling everyone "toward a mathematical equality." People are pressured to conform to types, becoming abstractions rather than authentic individuals. Both mass movements and objective knowledge fail to address the individual.

5. Jean-Paul Sartre's experiences during World War II convinced him that the veneer of civilization barely and only temporarily obscures awareness of the absurdity of the human condition. Philosophical abstractions and clichéd religious beliefs cannot account for such things as the Holocaust. "It was the war," Sartre said, "which made the obsolete frames of our thought explode." Sartre concluded that evil is real and concrete.

6. Sartre believed that existence precedes essence, that there is no fixed essence behind the roles we play. An authentic self exists only through the choices it makes uncontrolled by the values of others. We create our essence by how we live. We are condemned to be free, since no

essence determines our choices. Inauthenticity results from refusing to choose responsibly and courageously; it is a product of hiding behind abstractions in the form of social duties and roles defined by the group, not the individual.

7. Full awareness of our freedom to choose makes us anxious. God's silence as we face our choices makes us forlorn. Sartre's solution is that we create a heroic world by acting heroically. We refuse to deny our authentic self by conforming to social roles, and we re-create (or nihilate) the world that is given to us by taking heroic action. The authentic self becomes a freely chosen project.

8. According to Sartre, even the most individual and seemingly private choices involve all people, because by choosing to be this or that type of person we create an image of how others ought to be. We cannot evade or escape the responsibility that accompanies all choice. Anguish accompanies all authentic choice because we can never calculate all the consequences of our actions—yet we cannot escape choosing.

9. Authentic choice must be confined to what is under our immediate influence or control. This limit strips us of relying on God, society, luck, or the good will of others. Sartre says that when we confine ourselves to considering only what depends on our will, we experience despair. Ultimately, though, passionate engagement and heroic action lead to optimistic toughness: life lived fully and authentically.

Study Questions

1. Give a general characterization of existentialism, identifying some of its key concerns.

2. What was Kierkegaard's "universal formula"? How did it influence his thinking? What did he learn from the episode with Regina Olsen?

3. Sketch Kierkegaard's critique of "false Christianity." What is "false Christianity"?

4. Compare and contrast Kierkegaard's idea of faith with the more common conception of faith as belief.

5. Explain what Kierkegaard meant when he said that "truth is subjectivity." Is this the same as "truth is relative"? Explain.

6. Explain what Kierkegaard means by "passion," referring to his analysis of the "present age."

7. How did Sartre's experiences during World War II influence his philosophy?

8. What is the absurd and what is its significance to Sartre's view of human freedom?

9. What did Sartre mean by the phrase "existence precedes essence"? What does "essence precedes existence" mean? Why is the issue important?

10. Distinguish between an authentic and an inauthentic self. What is the relationship between social roles and authenticity, according to Sartre?

11. What is forlornness and what causes it?

12. Explain what Sartre meant when he said we are condemned to be free. What kind of freedom did he have in mind?

13. What is a Sartrean "project"?

14. What does it mean to "nihilate the world as we find it"? Is it possible? Why does Sartre think we should try?

15. What is anguish? Can it be avoided? Explain.

16. What is despair? What is its relationship to probabilities?

17. Explain what Sartre meant by "optimistic toughness."

18. What is meant by the phrase "sibling society"?

The Pragmatist

William James

As a rule we disbelieve all facts and theories for which we have no use.

William James

William James

All our scientific and philosophic ideals are altars to unknown gods.

William James

PRAGMATISM

From the Greek for "deed"; belief that ideas have meaning or truth value to the extent that they produce practical results and effectively further our aims; empirically based philosophy that defines knowledge and truth in terms of practical consequences.

In Chapter 1 we saw that philosophy has a reputation for being dangerous and subversive, for destroying people's beliefs without replacing them. We also noted that it has the almost contradictory reputation of being irrelevant, of making no real difference in our lives. "Philosophy bakes no bread," it is said. We have seen very powerful minds disagree about the most fundamental things: Does the "mind" exist? Do we have free will? Do the consequences of our actions matter if the motives are good? What is knowledge? Is reason more reliable than experience, or is it the other way around? Is there only one reality? Is there a God? Is God good? Can we know anything? Is history a process? What is virtue?

What can a reasonable person, a person of genuine common sense, make of all this? It seems as if each of the great philosophers builds a whole system around one or two insights. These systems can appear far-fetched and bizarre compared to life as most of us experience it; though intellectually stimulating and interesting, they hardly seem *useful*. Isn't life too short to waste on building grand philosophical systems full of abstract terms, which have no practical use except perhaps to provide philosophers with jobs?

The first truly great *American* philosopher demanded that philosophy answer these kinds of questions. **William James (1842–1910)** was the most original and influential advocate of **pragmatism**, an empirically based philosophy that defines knowledge and truth in terms of practical consequences. He believed philosophy must be more than a mere intellectual enterprise, that its true purpose is to help us live by showing us how to discover and adopt beliefs that fit our individual needs and temperaments. He thus shifted the focus of inquiry from the search for objectively true absolute beliefs to the search for *beliefs that work for us*. His philosophy is provocative, enthusiastic, optimistic, and vigorous; it speaks to the nearly universal need for ideas and truths that matter to individuals. Voicing the lament of the common person—"What difference does this or that philosophy make to my life?"—James offers an uncommonly rich answer.

The late nineteenth century teetered between pessimistic despair and optimistic faith in scientific progress. Thomas Eakins's painting The Agnew Clinic *depicts the kind of medical theater William James might have attended as a medical student.*

An American Original

William James was both a product and shaper of his time. The last half of the nineteenth century was a period of great confidence in science. People believed in continuous progress, influenced in part by a social interpretation of Darwin's theory of evolution that promised never-ending growth and improvement. This was also an age of bold action, as the Rockefellers and Carnegies and Vanderbilts carved up the land and established great industrial empires. People were impatient, wanting to move on, to get things done. In America, especially, it was an era of expansion, of strength. James captured this spirit so well and expressed himself in such a clear, powerful, anti-intellectual way that he became the best-known, most popular, and most influential *American* philosopher so far.

The Education of a Philosopher

William James's father was a restless man, so William spent a considerable part of his childhood moving about. In 1855, when his father lost faith in American education, he moved the entire family to Europe. They left America in June; in August, James's father sent William and his younger brother Henry (the famous novelist) to school in Geneva; by October the entire family had moved to England. Later they moved to France. In Boulogne, sixteen-year-old William started college and for the first time managed to attend the same school for an entire year.

There are some people, and I am one of them, who think that the most important and most practical thing about a man is still his view of the universe. We think that for a landlady considering a lodger it is important to know his income, but still more important to know his philosophy.

G. K. Chesterton

If we take the whole history of philosophy, the systems reduce themselves to a few main types which, under all the technical verbiage in which the ingenious intellect of man envelops them, are just so many visions, modes of feeling the whole push, and seeing the whole drift of life, forced on one by one's total character and experience, and on the whole preferred—there is no other truthful word—as one's best working attitude.

William James

My first act of freedom will be to believe in free will.

William James

That spring, however, the Jameses moved to Rhode Island. William wanted to continue his college studies, but his father was unimpressed with American colleges and so prevented him. A year and a half later the family moved back to Switzerland. By this time, William's early interest in science was replaced by a desire to be an artist, but after a year of art study, he turned back to science.

In 1861, William James entered Harvard as a chemistry major. His interests shifted to biology, anatomy, and ultimately physiology. James was so impressed by Jean Louis Agassiz, one of Harvard's most influential faculty members, that he accompanied him on an expedition to the Amazon. After eight months, James had had enough. He said, "When I get home I'm going to study philosophy all my days," but what he actually did was return to Harvard Medical School, where he had already taken some classes.

During his years as a student, James suffered mentally and physically. He described himself as being "on the continual verge of suicide." Unable to continue his medical studies because his hospital work put too much strain on his back, he went to Germany for the mineral baths. His letters home were funny and lighthearted, but elsewhere he noted that "thoughts of the pistol, the dagger and the bowl" were never far from him.[1] When he felt up to it, he returned to medical school and ultimately passed his licensing exam at age twenty-six. Later in the same year, though, he went into a severe depression, writing in his diary, "Nature & life have unfitted me for any affectionate relations with other individuals."[2] He was in a constant state of anxiety and dreaded being alone.

James was saved by an idea from the French philosopher Charles Renouvier, who had characterized free will as the ability to hold on to one idea among a number of possibilities. Willing himself to hold on to the idea of health and well-being, James effectively *decided* to get well: He *willed* himself well, by concentrating all his mental energy to produce "the self-governing resistance of the ego to the world."[3] James announced: "My first act of freedom will be to believe in free will." His depression lifted like a veil, and he was at last free to follow the restless intellect he had inherited from his father. As a result of his lingering sickness and unhappiness, he developed an interest in the relationship between mind and body. Speaking of James, a friend said:

> "Active tension," uncertainty, unpredictability, extemporized adaptation, risk, change, anarchy, unpretentiousness, naturalness—these are the qualities of life which James finds most palatable, and which give him the deepest sense of well-being. They are at the same time the qualities which he deems most authentic, the accents in which the existent world speaks to him most directly. . . .[4]

In 1872, James completed his education and took a job teaching physiology at Harvard. Within three years he was made assistant professor and remained affiliated with Harvard for nearly thirty-six years—the rest of his professional life.

In 1876, James's father announced to William, "I have met your future wife." And indeed he had. Alice Gibbens was a bright, vibrant, strikingly honest young woman. Though they fell in love, William declared himself unfit to marry her, and sent her a series of self-critical, suffering letters designed to discourage any thoughts of marriage. Alice understood William well, and so went to Quebec, saying she did so "to remove temptation from his path." The distance apparently diminished James's fears, however, and made Alice even more appealing. His letters became ardent efforts at courtship. Two years after his father's announcement, William and Alice were married.[5]

Though William James had found the support and care he needed to help steady his restless temperament and tendency to depression, for the rest of his life he struggled to remain healthy, using his particular good humor, aggressive intellect, and psychological insights—but he gave credit for what success he achieved to his wife for saving him.

The Philosopher as Hero

James's interest in medicine and physiology developed into curiosity about psychology, and in 1878 the Henry Holt Company signed him to write a psychology textbook. It took him twelve years to finish *Principles of Psychology* (1890), but the wait was worth it, and the book's wide appeal established James as an important figure in the early history of modern psychology.

About this time, his focus began to shift once more. He became increasingly interested in philosophy, but because of his broad interests, his bouts with depression, and his experience in science, medicine, and psychology, he saw philosophy in a different light from most professional philosophers of his time. James regarded philosophy as a matter of personal involvement, as a function of the will, and as a means to overcome despair and futility. He developed the kind of philosophy *he needed* to cope with his life and presented it in an appealing and powerful series of lectures that made it accessible to others.

Much of James's work is couched in heroic, often masculine terms, which were more fashionable and common then than they are now. But we would be doing a serious disservice to James if we reject his philosophy for that reason. Pragmatism is not a *male* philosophy but a philosophy that includes an element of heroic struggle; a philosophy of courage and action; a philosophy of vitality. A product of his times, James expressed these values in typically masculine terms. James was trying to resist inertia, to resist giving in to self-pity and self-defeat—and he used a vocabulary of heroic action. He called on us to become consciously responsible for our lives by strenuous exertion of will. In our contemporary era, which seems so often to reduce us to the helpless products of environment and heredity, a philosophy like James's is a refreshing vote of confidence in the individual human spirit.

We are all ready to be savage in some cause. The difference between a good man and a bad one is the choice of the cause.

William James

Pragmatic Study Habits

It is your relaxed and easy worker, who is in no hurry, and quite thoughtless most of the while of consequences, who is your efficient worker; and tension and anxiety, and present and future, all mixed up together in our mind at once, are the surest drags upon steady progress and hindrances to our success. . . .

My advice to students . . . would be somewhat similar. Just as a bicycle chain may be too tight, so may one's carefulness and conscientiousness be so tense as to hinder the running of one's mind. Take, for example, periods when there are many successive days of examination impending. One ounce of good nervous tone in an examination is worth many pounds of anxious study for it in advance. If you really want to do your best in an examination, fling away the book the day before, say to yourself, "I won't waste another minute on this miserable thing, and I don't care one iota whether I succeed or not." Say this sincerely, and feel it; and go out and play, or go to bed and sleep, and I am sure the results next day will encourage you to use the method permanently.

William James
"The Gospel of Relaxation," in *Talks to Teachers of Psychology*, quoted in Lin Yutang, *The Wisdom of America* (New York: John Day, 1950), p. 243.

Philosophical Query

Discuss the concept of "the hero." Identify heroic values and character traits as you understand them. Do you think people today have a clear understanding of heroism?

James himself did not actually live the kind of life he described as ideal. But he wanted to. He recognized the dangers and limits of too much sentimentality, too much "tender-mindedness," and offered what he saw as a healthier, more useful alternative. He understood, from his own weaknesses, the frustration of being unable to stick to anything, the frustration of not knowing what we want, the frustration of trying to make up our minds and choose one important thing. James's own experiences convinced him that life was too important, too complex, too rich to reduce to any of the philosophical systems that had gone before. And so he refused to offer a system; instead, he offered a *method*, a way of marshaling the will. But his method was grounded in philosophy, as Guy W. Stroh points out in *American Philosophy from Edwards to Dewey*:

Here is where a philosophy is required that will see the *whole puzzle*, face it squarely, and not deny any of the concrete facts. Such a philosophy will certainly need to borrow from psychology, since the problem is based in part at least on the facts of man's actual experience. But such a philosophy will have to go beyond psychology and address itself to the moral, human, and even metaphysical side of the problem. Only a philosophy, according to James, takes in the full sweep of man's ultimate problems, since only a philosophy expresses one's basic orientation to the meaning of things. Philosophy has the patience and courage to work continually at a problem when common sense and even science have long since set it aside or given it up.[6]

The Philosopher as Advocate

William James published his first philosophy book, *The Will to Believe and Other Essays in Popular Philosophy*, in 1896. In 1898, he was invited to give the Gifford Lectures in Edinburgh, Scotland, a truly rare honor for an American. These lectures were published in 1902 as *The Varieties of Religious Experience*. A classic of contemporary philosophy, this superb book still sells widely, its popularity extending far beyond academic circles.

After returning to Harvard, James delivered a series of lectures on pragmatism, and repeated these lectures at Columbia University to an audience of more than one thousand people. They were published as *Pragmatism* in 1907. *Pragmatism* also sold well and attracted the interest of both scholars and the general public. James was cheered up by its reception, to the point of announcing to his brother:

> I shouldn't be surprised if ten years hence it should be rated as "epoch-making," for of the definitive triumph of that general way of thinking I can entertain no doubt whatever—I believe it to be something quite like the protestant reformation.[7]

James's work became so influential that he effectively altered the shape of what has come to be known as American philosophy. He taught, among others, Supreme Court Justice Oliver Wendell Holmes, Teddy Roosevelt, and philosopher George Santayana. (Of all his students, he particularly disliked Roosevelt and Santayana.)

In 1907, the same year *Pragmatism* appeared, James retired from Harvard at the age of sixty-five. Responding at last to the criticism that he had failed to present a sustained, systematic explanation of his ideas, James resolved to craft a fuller expression of pragmatism in his remaining years. To his brother he wrote, "I live in apprehension lest the Avenger should cut me off before I get my message out. I hesitate to leave the volumes I have already published without their logical complement."[8]

James compiled a volume of essays, *The Meaning of Truth*, and one of lectures, *A Pluralistic Universe*. He hoped these books would be considered more "scholarly" and systematic than his others, but they were not the "logical complement" he sought. Alas, the Avenger did cut off the old rebel, the anti-intellectual champion of living philosophy, and these final books were published one year after his death, in 1911. Ironically, perhaps, William James remained truer to his philosophy than if he *had* written a more scholarly, systematic version of it, for then he would have been required to present an appeal to the abstract and logical "niceties" he had spent his whole life denouncing.

> Materialism fails on the side of incompleteness. Idealism always presents a systematic totality, but it must always have some vagueness and this leads to error. . . . But if materialism without idealism is blind, idealism without materialism is void.
>
> *Charles Sanders Peirce*

The very last words of James's very last essay reflect the spirit of pragmatism better than any scholarly system: "There is no conclusion. What has concluded that we might conclude regarding it? There are no fortunes to be told and there is no advice to be given. Farewell."[9]

Charles Sanders Peirce

Charles Sanders Peirce

The first expression of pragmatism actually appears in the work of **Charles Sanders Peirce (1839–1914)**. The son of a Harvard mathematics professor, Peirce studied philosophy, science, and mathematics, receiving a master's degree in mathematics and chemistry from Harvard. After working at the Harvard astronomical observatory for three years, he went to work for the United States Coastal and Geodetic Survey, where he remained for thirty years. He also lectured briefly at Johns Hopkins University. A brilliant but eccentric man, Peirce was never able to secure a full-time university position. As a result, he had a difficult time publishing his work. The last years of his life were clouded by physical infirmity, poverty, and social isolation and rejection. Through it all, William James remained his friend, supporting him and presenting his ideas to a wide audience. After Peirce's death his writings were collected and published. Although massive and difficult, his works have achieved a measure of success and are experiencing renewed interest among philosophers.

I regard Logic as the Ethics of the Intellect—that is, in the sense in which Ethics is the science of the methods of bringing Self-Control to bear to gain our Satisfactions.

Charles Sanders Peirce

Peirce's "Pragmaticism"

Peirce first presented what he referred to as "pragmatism" in an 1878 article titled "How to Make Our Ideas Clear," written for a popular magazine. This essay was ignored by philosophers until James devoted a series of lectures to it. James had intended only to present Peirce's ideas to a wider audience, but Peirce so strenuously objected to James's version of pragmatism that he "gave" him the term and coined yet another one for himself, *pragmaticism*:

> [The] word "pragmatism" has gained general recognition in a generalized sense that seems to argue power of growth and vitality. The famed psychologist, James, first took it up. . . . So then, the writer, finding his bantling "pragmatism" so promoted, feels that it is time to kiss his child good-by and relinquish it to a higher destiny; while to serve the precise purpose of expressing the original definition, he begs to announce the birth of the word "pragmaticism," which is ugly enough to be safe from kidnappers.[10]

Peirce was not just being cranky in insisting on clear and precise use of his term. His philosophy rested on a new theory of meaning. He coined the term *pragmaticism* from the Greek word *pragma*, which means "an act" or "a consequence." He wanted to show that the meanings of words depend on some kind of action. Peirce argued that ideas are meaningful only when they translate into actions and predict experiences associated with actions.

Pragmatic Theory of Meaning

Peirce argued that the only differences between the meanings of words such as *hard* and *soft* or *heavy* and *light* are how they *test out* in experience. He thus equated meaning with the effects related to words, saying, "Our idea of anything *is* our idea of its sensible effects." Meaningful statements must refer to predictable, observable, practical effects or consequences. "Consequently, the sum of experimental phenomena that a proposition implies makes up its entire bearing upon human conduct."[11] If a word cannot be tied to any observable practical results, it is meaningless, for its meaning is the sum total of its practical consequences:

> Now this sort of consideration, namely, that certain lines of conduct will entail certain kinds of inevitable experiences is what is called a "practical consideration." Hence is justified the maxim, belief in which constitutes [pragmaticism]; namely, *In order to ascertain the meaning of an intellectual conception one should consider what practical consequences might conceivably result by necessity from the truth of that conception; and the sum of these consequences will constitute the entire meaning of the conception.*[12]

Peirce's scientific background and interests influenced his strong dislike for the kind of vague, abstract rationalism found in Descartes and other "impractical" system spinners. Descartes had separated the mind and thinking from any necessary connection with experience. Peirce pointed out, however, that all thinking and all meaning are *context dependent*. Context includes material, social, and emotional components, as well as an intellectual one.

Agreeing with the empiricists, Peirce argued that meaning is based on experience and determined by experiment. He did not mean just formal, scientific experiment, but also the kind of informal testing we do every day, as when, say, we test a recently varnished tabletop to see whether it is hard yet. We "test" to see whether it is appropriate to apply the word *hard* to this surface, we "experiment" by looking to see whether it looks damp, by touching it lightly, and so on. Things are not just hard in some abstract, ideal, constant sense but in the real world of causal and material relationships.

> Let us illustrate this rule by examples; and, to begin with the simplest one possible, let us ask what we mean by calling a thing *hard*. Evidently that it will not be scratched by many other substances. The whole conception of this quality, as of every other, lies in its conceived

The rational purport of a word or other expression lies exclusively in its conceivable bearing upon conduct; if one can define accurately all the conceivable experimental phenomena which the affirmation or denial of a concept implies, one will have therein a complete definition of the concept, and *there is absolutely nothing more in it. . . .*

Charles Sanders Peirce

effects. There is absolutely no difference between a hard thing and a soft thing so long as they are not brought to the test.[13]

If there is no way of testing the effects of words (and ideas), no way of verifying their public consequences, they are meaningless. *Meaningful ideas always make a practical difference.*

Pragmatism

Like Peirce, James yearned for a philosophy free of "meaningless abstractions," a philosophy that stretched far beyond the merely technical and rationally coherent to embrace the whole of life. Building on Peirce's foundation, James advocated a new vision of a philosophical approach he claimed others had recognized before, but only in parts. In the process, James went beyond Peirce's intentions, and used pragmatism to present a moral theory and to make a case for religious belief. We might even say he made pragmatism into a kind of philosophical religion. That is, James attempted to present a philosophy that could provide values and ideals worth striving for, and that could satisfy our need to believe without appealing to metaphysical abstractions. Let us see how.

Pragmatic Method and Philosophy

James reflected a growing trend among philosophers to resist the abstract, to demand relevance and immediacy, and to deal with the "living issues" that face us. As he put it, "The whole function of philosophy ought to be to find out what definite difference it will make to you and me, at definite instants of our life, if this world-formula or that world-formula be the true one." There is a strong moral tone implicit in this position: It is not enough for philosophers to tackle questions of consistency or spin out grand theories. People are struggling through their lives, suffering, rejoicing, searching, and dying. We have a right—indeed, an obligation—to ask: "What difference does the theory of forms make to me, *now*? How is my life different if a tree falling in the forest does or does not make a sound? What practical difference does it make to me if the mind and body are two different substances?"

James often talked about feeling "at home" in the universe. Pragmatism was meant to be a *method* for solving those problems that interfere with feeling at home. Thus James looked for the *cash value* of statements, the practical payoff, and he rejected any philosophy that lacked it. This includes virtually all metaphysics.

The pragmatic method is primarily a method of settling metaphysical disputes that otherwise might be interminable. Is the world one or many?—fated or free?—material or spiritual?—here are notions either of which may or may not hold good of the world; and disputes over

Many of you are students of philosophy, and have already felt in your own persons the scepticism and unreality that too much grubbing in the abstract roots of things will breed. This is, indeed, one of the regular fruits of the over-studious career. Too much questioning and too little active responsibility lead, almost as often as too much sensualism does, to the edge of the slope, at the bottom of which lie pessimism and the nightmare or suicidal view of life. But to the diseases which reflection breeds, still further reflection can oppose effective remedies.

William James

such notions are unending. The pragmatic method in such cases is to try to interpret each notion by tracing its respective practical consequences. What difference would it practically make to anyone if this notion rather than that notion were true? If no practical difference whatever can be traced, then the alternatives mean practically the same thing, and all dispute is idle. Whenever a dispute is serious, we ought to be able to show some practical difference that must follow from one side or the other's being right. . . .

A pragmatist turns his back resolutely and once and for all upon a lot of inveterate habits dear to professional philosophers. He turns away from abstraction and insufficiency, from verbal solutions, from bad *a priori* reasons, from fixed principles, closed systems, and pretended absolutes and origins. He turns toward concreteness and adequacy, toward facts, toward action and toward power.[14]

James referred to theories as "only man-made language, a conceptual shorthand . . . in which we write our reports of nature; and languages, as is well known, tolerate much choice of expression and many dialects."[15]

If any theory with a practical payoff is true, does it not follow that one theory is as good as another to those who believe it? It would if James were advocating strict relativism, but for the most part, he did not see pragmatism that way. He saw it as a *method*, not a collection of beliefs. Thus he saw a use for various theories of verification and meaning so long as they are ultimately used to determine the "cash value" of beliefs. We may benefit from using both empirical and rational criteria, for instance.

> Pragmatism . . . asks its usual question, "Grant an idea or belief to be true," it says, "what concrete difference will its being true make in any one's actual life? How will the truth be realized? What experiences will be different from those which would obtain if the belief were false? What, in short, is the truth's cash-value in experiential terms?"
>
> The moment pragmatism asks this question, it sees the answer: *True ideas are those that we can assimilate, validate, corroborate and verify. False ideas are those that we cannot.* That is the practical difference it makes to us to have true ideas; that, therefore, is the meaning of truth, for it is all that truth is known as. . . .
>
> Our account of truth is an account of truths in the plural, of processes. . . . Truth for us is simply a collective name for verification-processes.[16]

From a strictly logical perspective, James's position seems to contradict itself, much as strict relativism contradicts itself: He asserts the truth of his theory, which in turn seems to deny the possibility of "a truth." If a theory is merely a "man-made language," then why should we speak James's language?

A possible answer is to view James as an *advocate*, whose chief purpose isn't to present a strict *argument* but rather to make a broad enough

We all, scientists and nonscientists, live on some inclined plane of credulity. The plane tips one way in one man, another way in another; and may he whose plane tips in no way be the first to cast a stone.

William James

case to convert and convince a wide audience. If we accept at face value James's insistence that he was offering us a *method* to live by, then we have to approach him differently than if he were offering philosophy as such. Indeed, James himself sometimes refers to pragmatism as a *creed*. A philosophical creed is a body of beliefs we can devote our lives to, whereas a philosophical *argument* is an attempt to make a rational case; the former appeals primarily to our hearts, the latter to our minds.

Pragmatism has been called "philosophically crude" because of its apparent indifference to theoretical precision and consistency. Yet it can be argued that precision and consistency *pay* in some areas—science and medicine, for instance—but *cost* in others—for example, when we demand rigor and precision that are inappropriate for the issue before us.

For James, our lives are shaped by our beliefs. And we *need to believe more than we can ever "prove" by overly strict, objective, neutral standards*, which he calls "agnostic rules for truth-seeking." He says, "If one should assume that pure reason is what settles our opinions, he would fly in the teeth of the facts." What does settle our opinions, then? James answers, *the will to believe*. And what we believe is a function of whether we are tough- or tender-minded.

The Temper of Belief

> The philosophy which is so important in each of us is not a technical matter, it is our more or less dumb sense of what life honestly and deeply means.
>
> *William James*

Because James was a brilliant, innovative, groundbreaking psychologist, he refused to confine philosophy to the intellectual realm. For him, the function of philosophy shifted from revealing "the truth" to learning how to live in the world. In psychological terms, pragmatic philosophy is meant to provide a way of becoming better adjusted to the world. This helps account for the inconsistency that troubles more traditional philosophers: Living "at home in the universe" does *not*, at least according to James, depend on knowing and believing what is true, but on believing things that suit *us*.

We can classify people, James thought, into two temperamental types.

Now the particular difference of temperament that I have in mind in making these remarks is one that has counted in literature, art, government, and manners as well as in philosophy. In manners we find formalists and free-and-easy persons. In government, authoritarians and anarchists. In literature, purists or academicals, and realists. In art, classics and romantics. You recognize these contrasts as familiar; well, in philosophy we have a very similar contrast expressed in the pair of terms "rationalist" and "empiricist," "empiricist" meaning your lover of facts in all their crude variety, "rationalist" meaning your devotee to abstract and eternal principles. . . .

I will write these traits down in two columns. I think you will practically recognize the two types of mental make-up that I mean if I head the columns by the titles "tender-minded" and "tough-minded" respectively.

THE TENDER-MINDED	THE TOUGH-MINDED
Rationalistic (going by "Principles"),	Empiricist (going by "facts"),
Intellectualistic,	Sensationalistic,
Idealistic,	Materialistic,
Optimistic,	Pessimistic,
Religious,	Irreligious,
Free-willist,	Fatalistic,
Monistic,	Pluralistic,
Dogmatical.	Sceptical.

Each of you probably knows some well-marked example of each type, and you know what each example thinks of the example on the other side of the line. They have a low opinion of each other. Their antagonism, whenever as individuals their temperaments have been intense, has formed in all ages a part of the philosophic atmosphere of the time. It forms a part of the philosophic atmosphere today. The tough think of the tender as sentimentalists and soft-heads. The tender feel the tough to be unrefined, callous, or brutal. Their mutual reaction is very much like that that takes place when Bostonian tourists mingle with a population like that of Cripple Creek. . . . [But] few of us are tender-footed Bostonians pure and simple, and few are typical Rocky Mountain toughs, in philosophy. Most of us have a hankering for the good things on both sides of the line.[17]

James thought philosophy had been dominated historically by extremists, so that most philosophies are unbalanced in either the tough or tender direction. The same might be said of contemporary philosophy. Today's tough-minded philosophies view scientific knowledge as the only secure kind; they include the strictest forms of behavioristic psychology and analytically oriented philosophies that apply such rigid standards of meaning that most basic, timeless questions are dismissed as meaningless. The extremes of tender-minded philosophy are anti-intellectual theology, pop psychologies, and "New Age metaphysics." Such extremism has rendered philosophy inappropriate for the vast majority of us, who are a mixture of tough and tender. But because we are easily persuaded, we end up trying to follow "fashion" or what James called the "most impressive philosopher in the neighborhood"—or the most impressive theologian, politician, or psychologist.

James believed that when we succumb to the "most impressive philosopher in the neighborhood," we do psychic violence to our unexpressed,

Man is not to blame for what he is. He didn't make himself. He has no control over himself. All the control is vested in his temperament—which he did not create—and in the circumstances which hedge him round from the cradle to the grave and which he did not devise. . . . He is as purely a piece of automatic mechanism as is a watch. . . . He is a subject for pity, and not blame.

Mark Twain

preconscious sense of the world. We deny important parts of ourselves and exaggerate others. When we try to live according to beliefs that do not suit us, we become dissatisfied and unhappy. The issue, then, for James is how to find a *cause*, how to find beliefs worth living for, worth fighting and dying for—how to find a philosophical religion.

Philosophical Query

If James is correct, those who criticize his free-floating style and apparently inconsistent views may be expressing their tough-minded temperaments. Do you agree with his distinction between tough- and tender-mindedness? Does it account for philosophical differences? Is it possible to evaluate this distinction without falling into one camp or the other? Which side are you on? Discuss the distinction.

> My strongest moral and intellectual craving is for some stable reality to lean upon, and as a professed philosopher pledges himself publicly never to have done with doubt on these subjects, but every day to be ready to criticize afresh and call in question the grounds of his faith the day before, I fear the constant sense of instability generated by this attitude would be more than the voluntary faith I can keep going is sufficient to neutralize.
>
> *William James*

The Will to Believe

We live according to beliefs that are products of our own temperaments and experience; they are not, according to James, the products of abstract reasoning; rather, we manage to find reasons to believe what we want and need to believe. And we have the right to do that, according to James, who once said he would have been better off titling his famous lecture *The Right to Believe* rather than *The Will to Believe*.

Because life *demands* a response, *demands* action, we have no choice but to believe *something*. Life presents us with what James calls *forced options*. We must make decisions whether we want to or not (even "not deciding" is a decision). We *cannot* remain detached and disinterested; life simply does not allow it. We are compelled to decide and to act, and reason is not a sufficient force for action. We do not act on what we understand, but on what we believe. The rationalist's and skeptic's demands for certainty cannot be met, yet we continue to live and act—without intellectual certainty.

> I, therefore, for one cannot see my way to accept the agnostic rules for truth-seeking, or willfully agree to keep my willing nature out of the game. I cannot do so for the plain reason that *a rule of thinking which would absolutely prevent me from acknowledging certain kinds of truth if those kinds of truth were really there, would be an irrational rule.* . . . If we had an infallible intellect with its objective certitudes, we might feel ourselves disloyal to such a perfect organ of knowledge in not trusting to it exclusively. But if we are empiricists, if we believe that no bell in us tolls to let us know for certain when truth is in our grasp, then it seems a piece of idle fantasticality to preach so solemnly our duty of waiting for the bell. Indeed we *may* wait if we will—I hope you do not think I am denying that—(we ought, on the contrary, delicately and profoundly to respect one an-

other's mental freedom) but if we do wait, we do so at our own peril as much as if we believed.[18]

The intellect does not discover the truths in which we believe; the will creates truth.

Truth Happens to an Idea

The rationalists' model of truth was taken from logic and mathematics. They said truth is universal, which amounts to saying it is *contextless*. The sum $2 + 2 = 4$ is true at all times, in all languages, for all creeds, for all ages, races, and genders of people, in all conditions of health or sickness. Indeed, because it is true for all "rational entities," it is true throughout the universe.

James rejected this simplistic, universalist notion of truth. He said experience makes it clear that ideas *become* true. Elsewhere, he said "truth *happens* to an idea." We *decide* whether or not an idea is true by "testing" it, as Peirce pointed out. James extended Peirce's pragmaticist theory of truth:

> Any idea upon which we can ride, so to speak; any idea that will carry us prosperously from any one part of our experience to any other part, linking things satisfactorily, working securely, simplifying, saving labor, is true for just so much, true in so far forth, true instrumentally.[19]

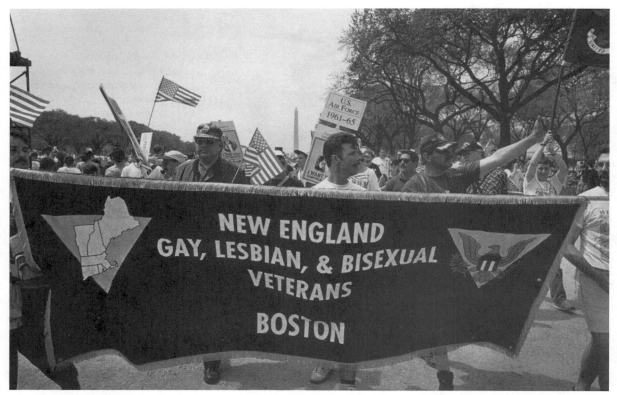

The truth happens to an idea: The issue of gays serving in the military achieved national prominence in the presidential election campaign of 1992 and consumed much of newly elected President Bill Clinton's first months in office. The Clinton administration modified its original policy as it discovered that a major change had little "cash value" early in its tenure. Do controversies over issues like lesbian and gay priests, euthanasia, and abortion support the pragmatic theory of truth, since it seems as if ideas are rejected or modified when they stop "working"?

Individual action is a means and not our end. Individual pleasure is not our end; we are all putting our shoulders to the wheel for an end that none of us can catch more than a glimpse at—that which the generations are working out.

Charles Sanders Peirce

If James is correct, we accept ideas as true only after we test them against our past experiences. Though a common tendency may be to reject new ideas, the public, communitywide aspect of truth-seeking, which Peirce emphasized, forces us—or most of us—to test and reevaluate ideas, keeping some and discarding others as we and the world change.

We have all witnessed this process. It is especially clear in the areas of moral and religious belief (areas James thought vital to human happiness). For example, looking back over history, we see that ideas about vice have changed. Few contemporary Americans believe that it is wrong for women to appear in public with bare ankles, but many people used to. Churches regularly convene councils to modify basic articles of faith, and entirely new religions emerge when old ones no longer *pay*.

Individuals and groups may simply refuse to accept changes, but on the whole, our beliefs do change, and thus our notion of what is true about

Peirce and James thought that the process of testing and reevaluating ideas is vital to human happiness. As our beliefs change, our notions of what is desirable change. But these changes can be slow. For example, some people are still uncomfortable with the idea of a male teaching preschool. As more men do, however, our ideas on this matter will be reevaluated.

the world changes—though, as James observed, we try to hang on to as many of our old ideas as possible until

> The individual . . . meets a new experience that puts them to a strain. Somebody contradicts them; or in a reflective moment he discovers that they contradict each other; or he hears of facts with which they are incompatible; or desires arise in him which they cease to satisfy. The result is an inward trouble to which his mind till then had been a stranger, and from which he seeks to escape by modifying his previous mass of opinions. . . . until at last some new idea comes up which he can graft upon the ancient stock . . .
>
> This new idea is then adopted as the true one. It preserves the older stock of truths with a minimum of modification, stretching them enough to make them admit the novelty, but conceiving them in ways as familiar as the case leaves possible. [A radical] explanation, violating all our preconceptions, would never pass as a true account. . . . We would scratch around industriously till we found something less eccentric. The most violent revolutions in an individual's beliefs leave most of his old order standing.[20]

Ideas are tested and accepted or rejected based on how well they work for us. Sometimes we see the virtue in a new idea; other times, we can no longer live with the stress and energy it takes to hold on to an old one.

So there is no such thing as disinterested truth. *Pragmatic truth is human truth.* "Purely objective truth," James asserts, "plays no role whatsoever,

This life is worth living, we can say, since it is what we make it, from the moral point of view; and we are determined to make it from that point of view so far as we have anything to do with it, a success.

William James

is nowhere to be found." He adds that the most absolute-seeming truths "also once were plastic. They were also called true for human reasons. They also mediate between still earlier truths and what in those days were novel observations."[21]

Useful, human truth is alive; rationalistic, abstract, dogmatic truth is "the dead heart of the living tree." Truth grows.

Philosophical Query

Can you think of recent examples supporting the claim that "truth happens to an idea"? Some Protestant churches, for example, have begun revising their policies regarding birth control, abortion, and gay marriages because older beliefs lack "cash value" for many of today's churchgoers. These churches usually experience a period of soul-searching turmoil, wrestling with the dilemma of holding on to old beliefs or losing touch with their congregations. Can you cite one or two recent examples of truth happening to an idea from current events or from your own situation?

The Dilemma of Determinism

James agreed with most moral philosophers that free will is a necessary condition for moral responsibility. He offered a unique and intriguing argument for believing in free will in a famous essay titled "The Dilemma of Determinism." He begins with a novel admission: "I disclaim openly on the threshold all pretension to prove to you that freedom of the will is true. The most I hope is to induce some of you to follow my own example in assuming it true, and acting as if it were true." Having warned us not to expect an airtight argument, James goes on to present a compelling case nonetheless. Let's see how.

Determinism is the belief that everything that happens must happen exactly the way it does. Some materialistic philosophers and scientists say determinism is inevitable since all matter is governed by cause and effect and follows laws of nature. James asks:

DETERMINISM

Belief that everything that happens must happen exactly the way it does because all matter is governed by cause and effect and follows laws of nature.

> What does determinism profess? It professes that those parts of the universe already laid down absolutely appoint and decree what the other parts shall be. . . . Indeterminism, on the contrary, says that the parts have a certain amount of loose play on one another, so that the laying down of one of them does not necessarily determine what the others shall be. It admits that possibilities may be in excess of actualities, and that things not yet revealed to our knowledge may really in themselves be ambiguous.[22]

Determinism asserts that possibilities are identical to actualities, that the future is already contained in the present. We cannot influence the future; it lacks ambiguity, having been sealed in the distant past. Clearly, this is a chilling, unsatisfying vision for most of us—at least James thought so.

Does determinism square with our actual feelings? James suggests that we answer this question by considering a newspaper article about the brutal murder of a woman by her husband. Ignoring his wife's screams for mercy, the husband chopped her to pieces. James asks whether any sane person can read such an account and not feel deep regret. But if the determinists are right, what is the point of regret? Determinists have no reasonable grounds for regretting anything.

> The judgment of regret calls the murder bad. Calling a thing bad means, if it means anything at all, that the thing ought not to be, that something else ought to be in its stead. Determinism, in denying that anything else can be in its stead, virtually defines the universe as a place in which what ought to be is impossible—in other words, as an organism whose constitution is afflicted with an incurable taint, an irremediable flaw. . . .
>
> It is absurd to regret the murder alone. It could not be different. . . . But how then about the judgments of regret themselves? If they are wrong, other judgments, judgments of approval, ought to be in their place. But as they are necessitated, nothing else could be in their place; and [for the determinist] the universe is just what it was before—namely, a place in which what ought to be appears impossible.[23]

Is it virtually impossible to think that such a murder "ought" to have occurred? Is it virtually impossible to be glad that it occurred? If James is correct, no sane person can help feeling some degree of sadness and regret when confronted by such horrors. Yet if the determinists are correct, such feelings are utterly pointless. *There is no rational ground for moral feelings, because "ought" can have no meaning.* If the determinists are correct, we are caused to have senseless, absurd, utterly false feelings and ideas.

James acknowledged that there is no scientific and objective way to refute such a possibility. But he insisted that our deep, unshakable moral sense of right and wrong, combined with our feelings of regret, make a *compelling* case for our need and right to believe in free will. We have to believe at least in the possibility, however remote, that some children will not be abused because some adults choose to help them; we have to believe that some bad will be avoided and some good done by our actions.

The Inner Sense of Freedom

James believed that change, surprise, and chance are regular parts of our experience.

> There is history. There are novelties, struggles, losses, gains . . . some things at least are decided here and now . . . the passing moment may contain some novelty, be an original starting-point of events, and not merely a push from elsewhere.[24]

The problem of human freedom is confused somewhat by the distinction between the self and the will. The will is only the self in its active side and freedom of the will really means freedom of the self. It is determination by the self.

Sarvepalli Radhakrishnan

The concept of responsibility offers little help. The issue is controllability. . . . What must be changed is not the responsibility of autonomous man but the conditions, environmental or genetic, of which a person's behavior is a function.

B. F. Skinner

The Problem Is Not a Real One

It must be observed that those learned professors of philosophy or psychology who deny the existence of free will do so only in their professional moments and in their studies and lecture rooms. For when it comes to doing anything practical, even of the most trivial kind, they invariably behave as if they and others were free. They inquire from you at dinner whether you will choose this or that dish. They will ask a child why he told a lie, and will punish him for not having chosen the way of truthfulness. All of which is consistent with a belief in free will. This should cause us to suspect that the problem is not a real one; and this I believe is the case. The dispute is merely verbal, and is due to nothing but a confusion about the meanings of words.

W. T. Stace
Religion and the Modern Mind (New York: HarperCollins, 1952), p. 279.

James appealed directly to our *inner sense of freedom* to verify this, a sense shared by most people (the exceptions, perhaps, being the philosophical and psychological extremists). In fact, he thought most of us have a deep "spiritual need" to believe that we are active agents who exert control over significant aspects of our lives, that we affect events, that we make a difference. We *need* this belief for our spiritual and mental well-being, and we have a right to believe what we need to believe.

James was convinced that belief in determinism is incompatible with our spiritual need for freedom. He thought the prestige and influence of science make people try to believe in determinism, but he did not believe that the evidence supporting determinism is conclusive. Echoing Hume, he claimed that we need to believe in a "more rational shape" for nature than our individual experience reveals. Consequently, we *believe in* the uniformity of laws of nature. But this uniformity of nature cannot be conclusively proved true, as Hume showed. Belief in free will cannot be conclusively proved to be correct either, James noted, but this does not make it inferior to belief in determinism. The basic status of both beliefs is similar.

All the magnificent achievements of mathematical and physical science—our doctrines of evolution, of uniformity to law, and the rest—proceed from our indomitable desire to cast the world into a more rational shape in our minds than the shape into which it is thrown there by the crude order of our experience. . . . I, for one, feel as free to try conceptions of moral as of mechanical or logical rationality. If a certain formula for expressing the nature of the world violates my moral demand, I shall feel as free to throw it overboard, or at least doubt it, as if it disappointed my demand for uniformity of sequence, for example; the one demand being, so far as I can see, quite as subjective and emotional as the other is. The principle of causality, for example—what is it but a postulate, an empty name covering simply a demand that the sequence of events shall one day manifest a deeper kind of belonging of one thing with another than the mere arbitrary juxtaposition which now phenomenally appears? It is as much an altar to an unknown god as the one Saint Paul found at Athens. All our scientific and philosophic ideals are altars to unknown gods. Uniformity is as much so as is free will.[25]

In the absence of conclusive proof, we must decide which belief better suits our needs. Believing as he did in the primacy of morality, James asserted that belief in free will better serves our need for "moral rationality." And since neither belief can be conclusively rejected, he argued that we have the right to test belief in free will against our regular experiences. If it "pays" more than believing that we have no control over our lives, then clearly it is the superior belief.

Perhaps the strongest "argument" against determinism is the fact that almost no one really believes absolutely everything he or she thinks, hopes, and does was determined from the first moments of the existence of the universe. Life presents us with inescapable moments of choice. How we respond is what matters most.

> Each man must act as he thinks best; and, if he is wrong, so much the worse for him. We stand on a mountain pass in the midst of whirling snow and blinding mist, through which we get glimpses now and then of paths which may be deceptive. If we stand still we shall be frozen to death. If we take the wrong road we shall be dashed to pieces. We do not certainly know whether there is any right one. What must we do? "Be strong and of a good courage." Act for the best, hope for the best, and take what comes.[26]

How can we know what is best? James says that we must discover the essence of the good.

Philosophical Query

Do you find it impossible to doubt that you possess free will—at least sometimes? Is belief in the possibility of free will necessary for your happiness?

Morality and the Good

James rejected metaphysical attempts to define the good. He argued that the only way to understand the good life was to study what people actually want and strive for. He surveyed and rejected strictly Aristotelian, hedonistic, Christian, Kantian, and utilitarian ethics, though he borrowed from each.

> Various essences of good have thus been . . . proposed as bases of the ethical system. . . .

I suppose life has made him like that, and he can't help it. None of us can help the things life has done to us. They're done before you realize it, and once they're done they make you do other things until at last everything comes between you and what you'd like to be.

Eugene O'Neill

If . . . man's nature . . . makes him do what he does, how does his action differ from that of a stone or a tree? Have we not parted with any ground for responsibility? . . . Holding men to responsibility may make a decided difference in their future behavior; holding a stone or tree to responsibility is a meaningless performance.

John Dewey

Choosing a Philosophy Is a Test of Character

It is simply our total character and personal genius that are on trial; and if we invoke any so-called philosophy, our choice and use of that also are but revelations of our personal aptitude or incapacity for moral life. From this unsparing practical ordeal no professor's lectures and no array of books can save us. The solving word, for the learned and the unlearned man alike, lies in the last resort in the dumb willingnesses and unwillingnesses of their interior characters, and nowhere else. It is not in heaven, neither is it beyond the sea; but the word is very nigh unto thee, in thy mouth and in thy heart, that thou mayst do it.

William James
"The Moral Philosopher and Moral Life," in *The Will to Believe and Other Essays in Popular Philosophy* (1897; reprinted in *Human Immortality*, New York: Dover, 1956), pp. 214–215.

Please remember that optimism and pessimism are definitions of the world, and that your own reactions to the world, small as they are in bulk, are integral parts of the whole thing, and necessarily help to determine the definition.

William James

No one of the measures that have actually been proposed has, however, given general satisfaction. . . . The best, on the whole, of these marks and measures of goodness seems to be the capacity to bring happiness. But in order not to break down fatally, this test must be taken to cover innumerable acts and impulses that never *aim* at happiness; so that, after all, in seeking for a universal principle we inevitably are carried onward to the *most* universal principle—that *the essence of good is simply to satisfy demand.* The demand may be for anything under the sun. There is really no more ground for supposing that all our demands can be accounted for by one universal underlying kind of motive than there is ground for supposing that all physical phenomena are cases of a single law.[27]

We have a basic obligation to "maximize satisfactions" and minimize frustrations, not just for ourselves but for others, according to James. Such a course is most likely to lead to happiness and increase the world's stock of goodness. Yet this must remain a fundamental, general obligation. The sheer number of people, coupled with the sheer number of demands we each have, makes being more specific impossible. All we can do is try our best to increase the general level of satisfaction and goodness, while remaining aware of our fallibility.

James did not offer an ethical *theory* as such, though he suggested moral "guidelines." He proposed a form of altruistic utilitarianism based on an optimistic vision of social progress. He believed modern civilization is better than past eras—he cited examples of slavery and torture—because the constant give-and-take, the "push and pull," of history results in continual refinement of satisfactions. The radical's forward drive is compensated for by the conservative's inertia; the dreamer's whimsy balances and is balanced by the scientist's objective eye, and so on.

It is important not to lose sight of the fact that James was also a psychologist and scientist. He gave more credence to observation and experience than to systematic argument. Further, he did not believe in universal moral principles or in the possibility of any finite, closed expression of morality. Thus, from his perspective, the kind of argument and system that would satisfy most philosophers would also falsify the reality of moral experience.

The Heroic Life

William James believed that life without heroic struggle is dull, mediocre, and empty. He was thinking of two approaches to life. In one, we choose (will) safety, security, and compliance. We try to avoid risks, try to avoid "hassles." The other kind of life deliberately includes danger, courage, risk; it is based on a will to excitement and passion.

James was not advising us to take up hang gliding and shooting the rapids. He was talking about a "real fight" for something important, about the struggle between good and evil. He said evil is "out there," to be resisted and fought. We might find it in the form of discrimination or toxic dumping. When we do, we can ignore it, make a token effort at resisting it by voicing our objections, or actually do something. If we confront it, we may lose our jobs, money, time, or solid A grade point average. We may fail. We may even be wrong: What we perceived as evil may not be evil. But at least we fought for or against something.

> For my own part, I do not know what the sweat and blood of this life mean, if they mean anything short of this. If this life be not a real fight, in which something is eternally gained for the universe by success, it is no better than a game of private theatricals from which we may withdraw at will. But it *feels* like a real fight—as if there were something really wild in the universe which we, with all our idealities and faithfulnesses, are needed to redeem: and first of all to redeem our own hearts from atheisms and fears. For such is a half-wild, half-saved universe adapted. The deepest thing in our nature is . . . this dumb region of the heart in which we dwell alone with our willingness and unwillingness, our faiths and fears.[28]

According to James, struggle and effort are vital elements of the good life. He believed that the "strenuous mood" is superior to sitting back and drifting along. Thus he did not think much of the Epicurean ideal of the retreat to the Garden or of Stoic detachment, when either meant reduced involvement in life and diminished passions (though he did admire the Stoic emphasis on strength of will).

James thought he had identified a natural fact of life: An active, strenuous approach is healthier and more satisfying than a passive, easygoing one.

What sort of thing would life really be, with your qualities ready for a tussle with it, if it only brought fair weather and gave those higher faculties of yours no scope?

William James

When we reason about the liberty of the will, or about the free will, we do not ask if the man can do what he wills, but if there is enough independence in his will itself.

Gottfried Wilhelm Leibniz

The deepest difference, practically, in the moral life of man is the difference between the easy-going and the strenuous mood. When in the easy-going mood, the shrinking from present ill is our ruling consideration. The strenuous mood, on the contrary, makes us quite indifferent to present ill, if only the great ideal is to be attained. The capacity for the strenuous mood probably lies slumbering in every man, but it has more difficulty in some than in others in waking up. It needs wilder passions to arouse it, the big fears, loves, and indignations; or else the deeply penetrating appeal of some of the higher fidelities, like justice, truth, or freedom. Strong belief is a necessity of its vision; and a world where all the mountains are brought down and all the valleys are exalted is no congenial place for its habitation.[29]

Philosophical Query

Discuss your formal and informal education in terms of the preceding passage. Have you been encouraged to adopt a strenuous mood or an easygoing one? Give some specific examples. Do you think James is on the right track? Why or why not?

Pragmatic Religion

James had deep respect for a religion that enriches our lives, that has "cash value." He noted that people in all cultures turn to a god (or gods) who *gets things done*, an active god, a god of the "strenuous mood," not a passive, ineffective god. This led James to offer an intriguing suggestion: If people do not believe in God, it may be because God is not *doing anything* in their lives. In *The Varieties of Religious Experience*, he attempted to discover how God *works* in people's lives. Combining an empirical, psychological study of a number of cases with a keen philosophical analysis, *Varieties* is one of James's most influential, popular, and still widely read works.

God is real since he produces real effects.

William James

James asserted that we judge the truth of religious ideas by what he calls their "immediate luminousness," adding, "in short, *philosophical reasonableness and moral helpfulness* are the only available criteria." He concluded that religious faith is important and meaningful on pragmatic grounds: Its presence or absence makes a clearly observable, practical, and concrete difference in our lives.

The practical needs and experiences of religion seem to me sufficiently met by the belief that beyond man and in a fashion continuous with him there exists a larger power which is friendly to him and his ideals. All that the facts require is that the power shall be other and larger than our conscious selves.

God is the natural appellation, for us Christians at least, for the supreme reality, so I will call this higher part of the universe by the name of God. We and God have business with each other; and in opening ourselves to his influence our deepest destiny is fulfilled.[30]

James thought that a religious orientation is more effective than a nonreligious one because it encompasses more. It addresses and derives from a wider range of experiences, including a wider, more expansive consciousness than a purely secular point of view. Besides the obvious psychological benefits of having God as a support and comfort, religious conversion can open us up and make us more responsive to all of life, according to James.

A Religious Dilemma

In his study of religious experience, James distinguished between two basic personalities, the "healthy-minded" and the "morbid-minded." Healthy-minded people "look on all things and see that they are good." Such people are vital, enthusiastic, and exuberant.

> In these states, the ordinary contrast of good and ill seems to be swallowed up in a higher denomination, an omnipotent excitement which engulfs the evil, and which the human being welcomes as the crowning experience of his life. This, he says, is truly to live, and I exult in the heroic opportunity and adventure. . . . [31]

In contrast, the attitude of the morbid-minded person is "based on the persuasion that the evil aspects of our life are its very essence, and that the world's meaning most comes home to us when we lay them most to heart."[32] In other words, morbid souls are negativistic and pessimistic. They see mostly (or only) evil, nastiness, untrustworthiness, and trouble.

> But there are others for whom evil is no mere relation of the subject to particular outer things, but something more radical and general, a wrongness or vice in his essential nature, which no alteration of the environment, or any superficial rearrangement of the inner self, can cure, and which requires a supernatural remedy.[33]

Interestingly, James the optimist says morbid-minded persons have a clearer, more realistic perspective than healthy-minded ones because they recognize a wider range of experience.

> It seems to me that we are bound to say that morbid-mindedness ranges over the wider scale of experience. . . . The method of averting one's attention from evil, and living simply in the light of good is splendid as long as it will work. It will work with many persons; it will work far more generally than most of us are ready to suppose; and within the sphere of its successful operation there is nothing to be

The healthy-minded . . . need to be born only once . . . sick souls . . . must be born twice—born in order to be happy. The result is two different conceptions of the universe of our experience.

William James

said against it as a religious solution. But it breaks down impotently as soon as melancholy comes. . . .

The normal process of life contains moments as bad as any of those which insane melancholy is filled with, moments in which radical evil gets its innings and takes its solid turn. The lunatic's visions of horror are all drawn from the material of daily fact. Our civilization is founded on the shambles, and every individual existence goes out in a lonely spasm of helpless agony. If you protest, my friend, wait till you arrive there yourself! . . . The completest religions would therefore seem to be those in which the pessimistic elements are best developed.[34]

To better grasp this point, think of what it means to be *always* joyful and enthusiastic in a world such as ours. This lopsided kind of "healthy-mindedness" might result from a lack of true empathy with the condition of other people. A shallow enough view of things can result in a childish (not childlike) view of life in which nothing is really bad. Or, if it is bad, it is not *that* bad. Or, if it is *that* bad, then it is somehow deserved.

In his analysis of healthy- and morbid-mindedness, James is interested in identifying the most practical spiritual balance. A soul that is blocked off from a major portion of experience, which, for want of a better word, we may refer to simply as evil, will be less effective, less "alive," than one that is not.

> Truth is made, just as health, wealth, and strength are made, in the course of experience.
>
> *William James*

Philosophical Query

What do you think of James's claim that morbid-minded people have a fuller, more realistic view of things than healthy-minded ones? How would you classify yourself? Discuss some of the strengths and weaknesses of both orientations.

Ultramarginal Life

According to James, the experience of being *reborn* makes happiness possible in a complex world, without resorting to the limited perspective of the healthy-minded. *Rebirth* in James's sense refers to a profound alteration of consciousness, and though this change results in a "religious" outlook, it is not confined to religion as such. Rebirth offers a solution to the dilemma of achieving a morally decent measure of happiness while acknowledging the pervasive presence of evil in the world. Put another way: Are healthy-minded ignorance or despondent pessimism the only options? James says profound spiritual experience—a "third possibility"—can avoid the extremes of ignorance or pessimism.

James identified two kinds of conversion experience, "instantaneous" conversion and a slower, gradual process of conversion he labeled "natural." He claimed the fruits of both kinds are comparable: an expansion of ordinary consciousness. According to James, our "field of consciousness" is always in a state of flux, with a changing border he called the *margin of consciousness*. Arguing from a strictly psychological perspective, James concluded that religious experience evokes responses from an "ultramarginal life." In contemporary terms, genuine religious experience flows from and opens channels to otherwise inaccessible realms of experience.

> I cannot but think that the most important step forward that has occurred in psychology since I have been a student of that science is the discovery, first made in 1886, that, in certain subjects at least, there is not only the consciousness of the ordinary field, with its usual centre and margin, but an addition thereto in the shape of a set of memories, thoughts, and feelings which are extra-marginal and outside the primary consciousness altogether, but yet must be classed as conscious facts of some sort, able to reveal their presence by unmistakable signs.[35]

Saintliness and Mysticism

James divided the fruits of spiritual experience—the unmistakable signs of the ultramarginal life—into two areas, conduct and thinking. The fruit of reborn conduct is **saintliness**, a way of life devoted exclusively to a heightened religious consciousness; the fruit of reborn thinking is **mysticism**, a way of thinking that views everything in terms of a powerful religious experience.

James proposed to "test saintliness by common sense, to use human standards to help us decide how far the religious life commends itself as an ideal kind of human activity." He noted that some saints are fanatics and others are naive. The fanatics are "masterful and aggressive," whereas the naive saints are "a genuinely creative social force." He reminded us that "the fruits of religion are like all human products, liable to corruption by excess. Common sense must judge them."[36]

In this beautiful discussion of the naive saint, James is at his best.

> If things are ever to move upward, someone must be ready to take the first step, and assume the risk of it. No one who is not willing to try charity, to try non-resistance as the saint is willing, can tell whether these methods will or will not succeed. When they do succeed, they are far more powerfully successful than force or worldly prudence. Force destroys enemies; and the best that can be said of prudence is that it keeps what we already have in safety. But non-resistance, when successful, turns enemies into friends; and charity regenerates its objects. These saintly methods are, as I said, creative energies; and genuine saints find in the elevated excitement with which their faith endows them an authority and impressiveness which makes them irresistible in situations where men of shallower nature cannot get on at all without the use of worldly prudence. This practical proof that worldly wisdom may be safely transcended is the saint's magic gift to mankind.[37]

There can be no final truth in ethics any more than in physics until the last man has had his experience and said his say.

William James

SAINTLINESS

According to James, a way of life devoted exclusively to a heightened religious consciousness; behavioral result of being reborn.

MYSTICISM (JAMESEAN)

According to James, a way of thinking that views everything in terms of a powerful religious experience; cognitive result of being reborn.

Mother Teresa is perhaps the best-known contemporary example of a holy person. Does she fit James's description of a saint or a mystic (or both)?

Those of us who have not experienced the "ultramarginal life" have only our practical wisdom to guide us. No wonder we are afraid to help the dirty stranger at the door, afraid to let him into our house. He might hurt us, soil the carpet, steal something. Our fears are *prudent*. Despite the parable of the Good Samaritan, it is not prudent to stop and help stranded motorists—it is "smarter" to call for help. It is prudent to defend ourselves.

Mahatma Gandhi, Martin Luther King, Jr., and Mother Teresa were (and are) not prudent. Though they may not be saints, these three individuals reflect the saint's magic gift. Gandhi's passive resistance altered forever the plight of India's poor and untouchables. King's courageous passive resistance did more than inspire millions around the world: It triggered a long, difficult move toward social and civil equality in America (Chapter 15). Mother Teresa's work with the poor and sick brings comfort to them and inspiration to a beleaguered world.

Like the saint, the mystic has practical value, according to James.

Looking back on my own experiences, they all converge towards a kind of insight to which I cannot help ascribing some metaphysical significance. The keynote of it is invariably reconciliation. It is as if the opposites of the world, whose contradictoriness and conflict make all our difficulties, were melted into unity. Not only do they, as contrasted species, belong to one and the same genus, but *one of the species*, the nobler and better one, *is itself the genus, and so soaks up and absorbs its opposite into itself*. This is a dark saying, I know, when thus expressed in terms of common logic, but I cannot wholly escape from its authority. I feel as if it must mean something, something like what the Hegelian philosophy means, if one could only lay hold of it more clearly. Those who have ears to hear, let them hear; to me the living sense of its reality only comes in the artificial mystic state of the mind.[38]

The mystic state is not artificial in the sense of being phony or less real, but "unnatural" in the sense of being rare and short-lived: "Except in rare instances, half an hour, or at most an hour or two, seems to be the limit beyond which they fade in the light of common day," James said.

Since there can never be conclusive, absolute proof that God does or does not exist, that mystical experience is or is not an insight into a higher wisdom, we each have a *right* to believe as we see fit. We have no *duty* to believe. We have no duty not to believe. We have no duty to accept the authority of another's religious experience, nor have we any duty to accept another's rejection of our own. Our only duty is to that belief that works for *us*.

Truth Is Always Personal

By the end of his life, James increasingly equated "true" with "useful." In "Is Life Worth Living?" he uses an analogy of a trapped mountain climber to illustrate his claim that sometimes psychological survival rests on the *will to believe whatever is necessary*:

> Suppose, for instance, that you are climbing a mountain, and have worked yourself into a position from which the only escape is by a terrible leap. Have faith that you can successfully make it, and your feet are nerved to its accomplishment. But mistrust yourself, and think of all the sweet things you have heard the scientists say of *maybes*, and you will hesitate so long that, at last, all unstrung and trembling, and launching yourself in a moment of despair, you roll into the abyss.
>
> In such a case (and it belongs to an enormous class), the part of wisdom as well as of courage is to *believe in the line of your needs*, for only by such belief is the need fulfilled.[39]

Thus, we see in James, as in Kierkegaard (Chapter 12), a turning of the tables as it were, so that subjectivity takes precedent over objectivity: Truth is always personal. In the end then, is James merely another Sophist advocating radical relativism borne of inability or unwillingness to understand and accept objective reality and the universal truths that flow from it? Is James manifesting "weakness" in his unwillingness to accept the world as it really is, in his refusal to face the hard fact that the world does not conform to our wishes?

The power to excel is not the same as the desire to excel. You know, a west Texas jackrabbit has a habit of running on three feet until pressed by the hounds, then he puts down his fourth foot and runs off and leaves them.

Senator Albert Gore, in a letter to his grandson Gore Vidal

James's ultimate position is that beliefs are "adaptations." As such, they can only be justified when they help us navigate our way through life. He did not think that encouraging wholehearted faith in *necessary* beliefs is the same thing as asserting that any belief that one holds is necessary *simply because one holds it.*

James's basic goal was to free us from enslavement to the notion that we must believe whatever science asserts—regardless of the consequences to our spiritual health and general well-being. Specifically, James argued that science should be evaluated in terms of the extent to which scientific beliefs are conducive to human happiness. Accordingly, if belief in scientific determinism and materialistic reductionism are inimical to human happiness, then disbelief is necessary for psychic survival and vitality.

For example, in testimony before the Massachusetts legislature, James spoke against a bill that would have prohibited Christian Scientists from practicing what were called "mind cures." "You are not to ask yourselves," James told the legislators, "whether these mind-curers really achieve the successes that are claimed. It is enough for you as legislators to ascertain that a large number of your citizens . . . are persuaded that a valuable new department of medical experience is by them opening up."[40]

As we have learned, for James, "the truth" is not the chief value. Usefulness is, but usefulness in the moral sense of producing healthy results. We can turn to James's personal life for an example of the kind of "necessary belief" James considered preferable to the truth. James considered Charles Sanders Peirce his friend and mentor, in spite of Peirce's rejection of James's pragmatism. Unlike James, Peirce was unable to support himself as a philosopher, and James wanted to help his friend. Knowing that Peirce would not welcome charity, James supported and protected Peirce with money that James told him came from Peirce's many "anonymous admirers." In fact, the money came from James. In this kind of case, James practiced his own principle: Better a *necessary lie* than a destructive—and unnecessary—truth.

Danger Signs

Viewed from a modern or Enlightenment perspective, William James, like Kierkegaard (Chapter 12), is seen as an advocate of a potentially explosive, "anti-intellectual," "unscientific," subjectivistic philosophical doctrine. Like Kierkegaard, James believed that there are no neutral observers of the human condition. Everything is a "point of view." According to James, moral absolutes are impossible, and attempts to impose them are especially bad. At best, we can have moral "rules of thumb," flexible guidelines. James says:

> There is hardly a good which we can imagine except as competing
> for the possession of the same bit of space and time with some other

---

Certain of our positivists keep chiming to us that, amid the wreck of every other god and idol, one divinity still stands upright,—that his name is Scientific Truth, and that he has but one commandment, but that one supreme, saying, *Thou shalt not be a theist.*

William James

What the hell, reality is a nice place to visit but you wouldn't want to live there.

John Barth

imagined good. . . . Shall a man drink and smoke, or keep his nerves in condition?—he cannot do both. Shall he follow his fancy for Amelia or for Henrietta?—both cannot be the choice of his heart. Shall he have the dear old Republican party, or a spirit of unsophistication in public affairs?—he cannot have both, etc. So that the ethical [or materialistic] philosopher's demand for the right scale of subordination in ideals is the fruit of an altogether practical need. Some part of the ideal must be butchered, and he needs to know which part. It is a tragic situation, and no mere speculative conundrum, with which he has to deal.[41]

Ultimately, James came to the "inconclusive conclusion that since nothing can be proved one way or the other, each of us is entitled to believe whatever he wants to believe."[42] He writes that:

We all, scientists, and non-scientists, live on some inclined plane of credulity. The plane tips one way in one [person], another way in another; and may [the person] whose plane tips in no way be the first to cast a stone.[43]

And since, James argued, belief in scientific method is *one belief* competing among many possible beliefs, belief in scientific method is no more sacrosanct than any other belief. Science, like various philosophies and religions, must compete for our allegiance against other visions and belief systems. And the vision that best suits our individual natures will win out. Note that, according to James, faith in science can be as powerful and effective as faith in religion or philosophy. He is not advocating committing ourselves to whatever whim or fancy strikes us. Rather, James argues, every person is entitled to commit himself or herself to those beliefs that best express our deepest selves, the fundamental quality of our "passional life."

James was less worried about being "duped" by a false belief than he was about being unhappy:

He who says, "Better go without belief forever than believe a lie!" merely shows his own preponderant private horror of becoming a dupe. He may be critical of many of his desires and fears, but this fear he slavishly obeys. He cannot imagine any one questioning its binding force. For my own part, I have also a horror of being duped; but I can believe that worse things than being duped may happen to a [person] of this world . . .[44]

We might say that for James, it is better to truly believe a personally useful lie than to pretend to believe a personally incompatible truth.

Like Kierkegaard before him (Chapter 12) and Nietzsche, his great German contemporary (Chapter 14), James was a foe of the passionless life, the "uncommitted" life. Like Kierkegaard and Nietzsche, James challenged

Our own universe, of which we see only a small part today, may not be unique. Its beginning is not the beginning of everything. Other universes may exist at an earlier stage.

Victor Weisskopf

science's claim to ultimate, objective, universal, and absolute authority. For James, it is far better to believe passionately in a "lie" than it is to half-heartedly accept a "truth."

Like Kierkegaard before him and Nietzsche beside him, James reacted to the modern world's assault on the existing individual. James did not see the neatly ordered universe of the optimistic Enlightenment philosophers. The Jamesian universe is pluralistic, expansive, incomplete, and unpredictable. It is *wide open*. To survive and thrive in such a universe, James thought, we need resourcefulness, good humor, stamina, and the willingness to risk living according to convictions that cannot be objectively, universally, and scientifically established beyond doubt. James's plane tips away from theoretical completeness and purity toward the concrete, existing individual. James writes:

> Probably a crab would be filled with a sense of personal outrage
> if it could hear us classify it without ado or apology as a crustacean,
> and thus dispose of it. "I am no such thing," it would say: "I am
> MYSELF, MYSELF alone."[45]

William James's vigorous pragmatism straddled two philosophical worlds, the modern and the postmodern. He is said to have "anticipated" many contemporary and postmodern philosophical questions. Whatever we make of his philosophy, James reminds us, will *not* be based on "pure," objective criteria. It will—and can only—be based on what we passionately and deeply need to believe.

We are a long way from the Enlightenment's faith in rationality, objectivity, and universality, practiced in the form of the scientific method.

One cannot criticize the vision of a mystic—one can but pass it by, or else accept it as having some amount of evidential weight.

William James

Yet it is essential to realize that our way of perceiving the world in everyday life is not radically affected by scientific conceptions. For all of us—even for the astronomer, when he goes home at night—the sun rises and sets, and the earth is immobile.

Pierre Hadot

Commentary

The most significant weakness in James's pragmatism is so much a part of what he saw as his mission that we must consider it from two perspectives. By tying truth to "what works" *for us*, James cuts himself off from any possibility of objective verification. Yet most philosophers still hold that the truth must refer to something beyond and not entirely determined by the individual. James seems to blur the distinction between truth and how we discover it. While we do test ideas by acting on them and by comparing them with our more established beliefs, their *truth* is independent of this process. Penicillin remains an effective antibiotic whether or not I believe that it is, for example.

There are two different issues here. If we are looking at factual matters, this criticism of pragmatism is persuasive. But if we consider beliefs about moral and spiritual concerns, as well as some social and psychological beliefs, pragmatism has something important to say. We can become confused about James's position if we lump both general categories of belief statements together.

Consider, on James's behalf, the pattern that social scientists refer to as a **self-fulfilling prophecy**. This is a belief that so affects events, it causes itself to be true. For example, a man who believes his date will not like him may project a mood of surly defensiveness and hostility, or passive, defeatist self-pity. Either mood may alienate his companion, who otherwise would have found him quite pleasant. If so, his prophecy of "She won't like me" has fulfilled itself. Similarly, students who expect to do poorly in a given course may not retain information because they are frightened or depressed by their expectations of failure; they may unconsciously devote less energy to their studies than they would have if they had believed more in themselves. Conversely, students who expect to do well may be more open and pleasant in class, which can inspire the professor to be a better teacher; they may ask more questions, pay more attention, and so on, thereby fulfilling their own beliefs.

Ironically, in recent years, certain work emerging from the *scientific* study of belief has been interpreted as supporting James's sense that the "best" beliefs are not always the "truest" ones.[46] Lyn Abramson, of the University of Wisconsin, and Lauren Alloy, of Temple University, report that "normal, healthy" people are subject to a variety of "cognitive illusions." Among these are mild, factually unwarranted optimism and insensitivity to failure. Combined, these two "illusions" result in tendencies to make "straightforwardly false" judgments. Ironically, because they often do not suffer from such illusions, clinically depressed individuals are "Sadder But Wiser," to use the subtitle from one of Abramson and Alloy's better known papers. In other research, social psychologist Shelley Taylor has found that victims of trauma and illness who are "unjustifiably optimistic" tend to be better adjusted and happier than more "realistic" victims of similar circumstances. Lastly, Daniel Goleman is one of a number of neo-Freudians who argue that forgetting unpleasant events (repression) is an important component of mental health.[47]

This raises the basic **pragmatic paradox**: *Pragmatism works only if we believe our ideas are true according to nonpragmatic criteria.* For instance, can I really be "reborn" if I believe there is no more evidence for than against the existence of a benevolent God? Can I really just say to myself, "Well, belief in God makes people feel secure and gives their lives meaning. I would like to feel secure and find a purpose for my life. Therefore, I shall believe in God"? Does not such belief work only when I sincerely believe it to be true—really and factually true, not just true because I believe it is true? Paradoxically, it seems as if only by believing in a nonpragmatic view of truth can pragmatism work.

James's version of pragmatism, after its initial success, is rejected by those philosophers who insist on standards of rigor that James labeled "extremist." Yet his influence cannot be overlooked. His insistence that

These, then, are my last words to you: Be not afraid of life. Believe that life is worth living, and your belief will help create the fact. The "scientific proof" that you are right may not be clear before the day of judgment (or some stage of being which that expression may serve to symbolize) is reached. But the faithful fighters of this hour, or the beings that then and there will represent them, may then turn to the faint-hearted, who here decline to go on, with words like those with which Henry IV greeted tardy Crillon after a great victory had been gained: "Hang yourself, brave Crillon! we fought at Arques, and you were not there."

William James

philosophy return to its "original sense" and address the practical issues facing us came at a time when the world was ready to listen. I am not sure how well "professional philosophers" have answered this vital challenge, but it lingers: branches of applied philosophy such as medical ethics, business ethics, computer ethics, the study of philosophers from other cultures, feminist and womanist analyses of modes of biased thinking share the pragmatic spirit of battling evil and fighting for the good.

Whether we wholeheartedly try to make philosophy "work" again or believe that practical social and moral reform are not the philosopher's concern, many professional philosophers are acutely aware of the challenge to do something that "matters" to a circle wider than that of their academic peers.

James's background in psychology led him to recognize how important belief and the will are to our basic sense of well-being. He demonstrated what other nineteenth-century philosophers and writers had begun to suspect, namely, that extreme rationalist and empiricist philosophies distort as much as (if not more than) they reveal. James was one of the great, early defenders of the individual, free will, and human complexity against the crushing forces of rationalistic abstraction and scientific determinism. He spoke eloquently for the person of "moderate" convictions and temperament and for the virtues of the active, vigorous struggle for good.

James offered a persuasive and unique defense of our right to believe. He showed that faith in a higher power cannot be dismissed as a form of psychological infantilism, and that its grounding in personal conviction is as solid as faith in science. Further, he showed that religious faith has restorative and unifying powers often missing from faith in science. James defended the "common sense" of the average person without pandering to it and called on us to test the higher life of the "strenuous mood." All in all, these are impressive accomplishments.

From his own early crisis and recurring periods of despair, William James fashioned a philosophy of salvation. He anticipated, because he felt, the deep despair that a cold, deterministic vision of life engenders. We saw in Chapter 12 how much this pervasive view of life still affects all of us, how we pay for the comforts and cures of science with a picture of ourselves as puppets of cause and effect. James reminds us:

> Now I wish to make you feel, if I can . . . that we have a right to believe the physical order to be only a partial order; that we have a right to supplement it by an unseen spiritual order which we assume on trust, if only thereby life may seem to us better worth living again. But . . . such a trust will seem to some of you sadly mystical and execrably unscientific. . . . In this very University . . . I have heard more than one teacher say that all the fundamental conceptions of truth have already been found by science, and that the future has only the details of the picture to fill in. But the slightest reflection on the real

conditions will suffice to show how barbaric such notions are. . . . No! our science is but a drop, our ignorance a sea. Whatever else be certain, this at least is certain—that the world of our present natural knowledge is enveloped in a larger world of some sort of whose residual properties we at present can frame no positive idea.[48]

William James said "No!" to deterministic reductionism. If he answered with too much exuberance and subjectivity for some of today's philosophers, that does not diminish his genius or foresight. If his analysis of faith is too soft, too inconsistent for the philosophers and scientists, and too naturalistic, too philosophic for the preachers, it remains compelling nonetheless. Although I am not particularly fond of the expression "cash value," I wholeheartedly agree with James's insistence that philosophy—especially—must make a difference, must *pay*. Otherwise, the spirit of the old *sophos* will have faded from us forever.

Summary of Main Points

1. William James's pragmatism is based on Charles Sanders Peirce's pragmatic theory of meaning: Ideas are meaningful only when they translate into actions and predict experiences associated with actions.

2. James reflected a late-nineteenth-century trend among thinkers who resisted excessive abstraction and demanded relevance from philosophy. He argued that philosophy should make a "definite difference" in people's lives, and attempted to construct a philosophical religion that could provide beliefs worth living and dying for. Pragmatism was meant to be a method for helping us feel "at home" in the universe.

3. Pragmatism rejects any philosophy that lacks "cash value." James believed that virtually no metaphysical theory has any practical payoff (cash value). "True ideas," he said, "are those that we can assimilate, validate, corroborate and verify. False ideas are those we cannot." Pragmatic truth is human truth.

4. James expanded the realm of philosophy beyond "revealing the truth" to providing a way to become better adjusted to the world. Thus his interest was not so much rigorous philosophical argument as advocacy of pragmatic beliefs that could give life meaning and vitality.

5. James divided people into tough-minded or tender-minded types, claiming that historically philosophy has been dominated by extremists of one type or the other, and thus remained unbalanced. He advocated what he saw as a more useful combination of these two extremes.

6. Pragmatism holds that reason serves the will and we live according to our beliefs. James said because life demands an active response, we have no choice but to believe something. We face "forced options." The intellect does not discover the truths in which we believe; the will to believe creates truths.

7. The pragmatic life rejects determinism as incompatible with our immediate sense of freedom. According to James, determinism, the idea that everything must happen exactly the way it does, is incompatible with our spiritual need for freedom. Determinism has

less cash value than belief in freedom, and since neither belief can be proved conclusively, the pragmatic thing to do is believe in what we need to be happy—freedom. Feelings of regret reflect our deep belief in free will.

8. Since we cannot escape choice, James advocated what he called the "heroic life," rejecting life without struggle as dull, mediocre, and empty. The heroic life is characterized by a "real fight" for something important; it is about the struggle between good and evil.

9. James valued religion that has cash value because, in his view, belief in a god of "the strenuous mood" helps people get things done. Religious faith is important on pragmatic grounds: Its presence or absence makes an observable, practical difference in people's lives. James believed a religious orientation is more effective than a nonreligious one because it encompasses more.

10. James distinguished between two basic personalities: The healthy-minded personality looks at all things as good; healthy-minded people are exuberant, vital, and enthusiastic. The morbid-minded personality sees the very essence of life as evil, untrustworthy, and troublesome; morbid-minded people are negativistic and pessimistic. James thought the morbid view is the clearer and more realistic, because it recognizes a wider range of experience than does the healthy view.

11. Profound religious experience makes it possible to be both morally decent (without descending into the pessimism of morbid-mindedness) and happy (without resorting to the limited perspective of healthy-mindedness). James refers to the expansion of consciousness that results from religious experience as being reborn.

12. Rebirth (profound religious experience) evokes experiences from an "ultramarginal life," a state of awareness that flows from and opens channels to otherwise inaccessible realms of experience. Ultramarginal life is expressed in conduct as saintliness and in thinking as mysticism. According to James, saints and mystics have practical value because they challenge us to expand our own range of beliefs and consciousness.

Study Questions

1. Discuss how James's personal life influenced some of his major pragmatic beliefs.

2. What is the pragmatic theory of meaning? Illustrate with an example.

3. What is the pragmatic method? What is it used for?

4. Explain what pragmatists mean by the "cash value" of an idea.

5. Compare and contrast tough-mindedness with tender-mindedness. What is the significance of this distinction?

6. Discuss James's notion of the "will to believe." In what sense do "reasons serve the will" according to James? Do you agree with him? Why or why not?

7. Explain what it means to assert that "truth happens." Give an example, then evaluate.

8. What is the dilemma of determinism? How does James deal with it? What do you think of his approach?

9. Discuss the pragmatic conception of the good.

10. Explain what James meant by the "heroic life."

11. Explain what James meant when he claimed that a religious orientation is more effective than a nonreligious one. Do you agree? Why or why not?

12. State, then discuss, James's opinion of optimism.

13. What are the fruits of spiritual experience, according to James? What do they have to do with the "ultramarginal life"? What does James see as their "cash value"? Do you agree? Discuss.

Overview of Postmodern Themes

Reality is not a matter of fact, it is an achievement.

William H. Gass

. . . [I]t is extremely difficult today for the Cartesian philosopher to sit comfortably on the throne of the cultural overseer, "neutrally" legislating "how rational agreement can be reached" and where others have gone astray. The ideal of absolute intellectual purity and the belief in a clear and distinct universe are passing. . . .

Susan Bordo

The Enlightenment notion of reason needs to be reformulated. . . . Reason is not innocent. . . . we reject claims to objectivity in favor of partial epistemologies that recognize the historical and socially constructed nature of their own knowledge claims and methodologies.

Henry A. Giroux

[I]f I have guessed any riddles, I wish that *this* proposition might show it!—They are far from being *free* spirits: *for they still have faith in truth.*

Friedrich Nietzsche

In the last part of our survey of Western philosophy we'll consider *post-modern* challenges to key *modern* (Enlightenment) ideas. Indeed, on many campuses it is fashionable to reject all modern (Enlightenment) philosophy as "elitist," "racist," "sexist," "imperialistic," or "oppressive" because of its insistence that rationality is *the* basis for all truth testing.

Some of the most fertile and interesting work in contemporary philosophy springs from issues raised by writers that contemporary philosopher Lawrence Cahoone identifies as "members of the postmodern family." For our purposes, we will use the term *postmodern* to refer to thinkers and ideas that question modern or Enlightenment efforts to be bias free. As a rule, postmodern thinkers reject the idea that a single, "objective" reality warrants belief in "universal" or "absolute" truth.

Although widely used, "postmodern" is a label that covers a great deal of territory, in much the same way that "existentialism" does. Both terms refer to philosophers, poets, novelists, dramatists, critics, and artists who share what might be thought of as a loose "family resemblance." Cahoone says:

> The term "postmodern" has in the last decade become an increasingly popular label for something about the end of the twentieth century. It also refers to a contemporary intellectual movement, or rather, a not very happy family of intellectual movements. But as it so often happens, dysfunctional families are the most interesting ones. The members of the postmodern family not only express conflicting views, but are interested in barely overlapping subject matters: art, communications, media, history, economics, politics, ethics, cosmology, theology, methodology, literature, education. Some of the most important members of the family refuse to be called by the family name. . . .[1]

What Is Philosophy? *(continued)*

What philosophy really and truly is remains one of the most argued-about topics in Western philosophy. This is an issue at least as old as Plato's assaults on sophistry, and probably much older than that. Let's retain our generous and inclusive attitude of inquiry as we approach the thorny matter of what philosophy is and can be. Doing so will prevent us from choosing sides or making rigid judgments before we've given alternative voices a fair hearing.

Of course, recommending any policy implies values and preferences, what existentialists and postmodern philosophers call a *point of view* or *vested interest*. Having a generous or inclusive "point of view" regarding philosophy is not without problems: If our inclusive description of philosophy is viewed as lacking the level of philosophical rigor and clear boundaries demanded by modern philosophers, then we are already in the post-

Do you think that the enormous range of scale reflected in these two pictures of a dust mite and the universe supports a "postmodern" challenge to Enlightenment faith in "perspectiveless" truth, objectivity, and unitary reality?

modern branch of the philosophical family. Yet if we begin with dogmatic insistence that all "real" or "true" philosophy must be rationally based, objective, and universal, are we not firmly positioned in the modern branch of the philosophical family? What to do?

Without evading our responsibilities as seekers of truth and wisdom, we can nonetheless suspend final judgment and consider ourselves *philosophical explorers* who are not ready to settle down at any specific site but are on a voyage of discovery. At this point, we are philosophical mapmakers. And, of course, we are always free to linger for a while in an especially intriguing or enriching locale, to move on quickly, to return to our starting point, or to relocate permanently.

Of Metaphors and Margins

The preceding paragraph consists of a metaphor. Some postmodern critics and philosophers see *all* writing and speaking as metaphorical; for them everything is interpretation. Thinking—even perceiving—are characterized as being "creative linguistic acts." Postmodern philosophizing emphasizes modes of communication, language structures, and subtexts—*hidden* meanings that are *revealed* in the very processes of trying to hide them. We might say that the postmodern attitude is one of hypercriticism—criticism of criticism, and criticism of criticisms of criticism, and so on—in which texts are "deconstructed" to reveal their hidden meanings, assumptions, and political agendas.

Thus, some postmodern critics argue that the "margins define the text." That is, what's not said, what's left out and excluded, reveal the text. From

This picture depicts a Nazi-supported "scientific" system of race determination applied to a German man. Considering some of the horrific uses of "rationality" and "technology" in this century, is optimism justified? Is the notion of "progress" intelligible on any broad scale? Yet, what better alternative is there to scientific rationality? (Is this issue framed fairly?)

such a perspective, the focus shifts from what a *writing* (book, article, essay, and such) includes to what's been overlooked and left out. Borrowing from the psychological concepts of repression and denial, postmodern critics claim that *because* the significance of an author's "decisions of exclusion" are made unconsciously, they reveal political values; socioeconomic loyalties; racist, sexist, or imperialistic motivations; and any other biases the author is unaware of or wants to conceal. In other words, the author's true values and motives are always hidden from her consciousness. She is unaware that "the truth is what is unsaid."

To some critics of postmodern thinking, such critiques reduce all utterance to "Freudian slips" through which we *inadvertently* reveal ourselves because we are always trying—and failing—to completely repress negative feelings and threatening emotions. And if *all* utterances are coded "slips," the concept of repression loses all meaning: If the "real meaning" of every statement is hidden from its maker, then so is the meaning of *this* statement. In other words, the assertion that all meaning is coded, repressed, and hidden is self-contradictory (as are assertions of unqualified relativism).

From a strictly postmodern point of view, however, such logically rigid criticism is itself the product of a vested interest in the myths of Enlightenment philosophy and overreliance on logical principles. In other words, it is unfair to hold the rejection of rational discourse to the standards of rational discourse.

Is Objectivity Possible?

According to one type of influential postmodern criticism, no fixed, absolute, timeless, or universal meaning is possible for any *writing*. (*Writing* and *writings* are terms that are increasingly used instead of *book*, *essay*, or *article*.) Nor can "the correct meaning" be assigned to any "linguistic act," including "theories" and "beliefs," because *meaning is always an interpretation*. Secularizing Martin Luther's claim that "every believer is a priest," this radical view asserts that "every reader is an author," because reading is a "creative act." "Reader response" *creates* the "text."

For example, every time "you" read the "writing" labeled Plato's *Apology*, "you" are different: "You" are older (if only by minutes). "You" have unique experiences between readings. Thus, each "reading-responding" is a *linguistic act* because "you" are in constant flux. So there can be no fixed identity, no unitary "I." Therefore, there can be no fixed, once-and-for-all meaning. And in no case can "you" (or anyone other than Plato) read **Plato's** *Apology* because "you" don't live in Plato's world—or anyone else's, for that matter. And, of course, even Plato couldn't read **the** *Apology*; he could only read one of myriad "Apologies-of-the-moment."

If this point of view is "correct" (if "correct" now means anything at all), then problems of subjectivism, raised by early Sophists (Chapter 2) and hedonists (Second Interlude), among others, are back. So, obviously, are problems of personal identity and knowledge of the external world raised by Cartesian dualists (Chapter 8) and skeptical empiricists (Chapter 9). Postmodern questions revolving around relationships between the thinker and the thought, the mind and body, and perception and reality harken back to the three major modern philosophers we've studied: Descartes, Hume, and Kant (Chapters 8–10).

Postmodern questioning of biases inherent in socioeconomic class distinctions echoes Marxian assertions concerning the relationship between the material and economic conditions under which we live (Chapter 11). Postmodern questions concerning the radical nature of human freedom ("Man is condemned to be free") and the place of the individual in massing societies ("The crowd is the untruth") also reflect concerns of Marx, as well as Kierkegaard and Sartre (Chapter 12). But the *grandfather* of postmodern philosophy is the enigmatic anti-philosopher Friedrich Nietzsche, whose explosive cultural critique is the subject of Chapter 14.

Is Objectivity Desirable?

Among the more significant contemporary critiques of modern philosophy is a growing body of philosophical work challenging modern philosophers' (and scientists') efforts to be "objective" and impersonal, to stay detached

George Tooker's 1956 painting Government Bureau *evokes the depersonalized, fragmenting "existential vacuum" identified by Viktor Frankl. We can almost hear the fragmented bureaucrats' litany: "Nothing personal. Take a number. Fill out these forms. It's company policy. Have a nice day. Next!"*

from their work—and from the social, political, and cultural consequences of their work. Some of the most intriguing work currently being done in this area raises questions about the philosopher's relation to her (or his) work and to the community itself. A key question concerns the desirability of personal detachment. In other words, in addition to questioning the possibility of objectivity, some contemporary philosophers question the goal of refusing to take a personal stand on philosophical issues.

In academic circles, a line is often drawn between *professing* scholarly knowledge and *advocating* personal beliefs and policies. In actual cases, the line between professing and advocating is notoriously slippery. This is especially true in subject areas of great social interest and consequence: Domestic abuse, affirmative action, welfare, sexual harassment, race, homosexuality, and religion are typical areas in which issues of "professionalism vs. advocacy" recur today. Some of the most disturbing and significant postmodern criticisms of Enlightenment thinking center on the issue of advocacy.

Rather than shun or repress their personal qualities, activist-oriented philosophers see all philosophers as *embodied advocates* of specific points of view, whether or not we acknowledge it. By this they mean that philosophers are not Cartesian "ghosts in the machine." That is, philosophers are male or female; gay or straight; black, white, Hispanic, Native American, or Asian; poor, middle class, or rich; liberal or conservative; Christian, Buddhist, or agnostic; and so on. In other words, philosophers exist in particular bodies located in very particular cultural contexts, and these will always affect their philosophizing.

From a postmodern worldview, embodiment and personal point of view are seen as inescapable, and neither "bad" nor "good." If personal points of view are the foundation of all philosophizing, then, it is argued, disembodied, "objective" philosophy is impossible. Impersonal philosophizing is seen as undesirable because emotions and personal points of view are considered valuable sources of knowledge that have been overlooked and misunderstood throughout the history of Western philosophy. In contrast to the modern philosopher's attempt to produce a *perspectiveless* philosophy expressed in an objective voice, postmodern philosophers write in *different voices*, voices of social advocacy, personal experience, care, relationship, and emotion.

Issues of objectivity, point of view, and advocacy are serious matters for all philosophers, whether postmodern or not. They raise questions about the foundations of Western philosophy, harkening back to the Presocratics' attempts to make sustained rational discourse the foundational mechanism for identifying reality, distinguishing between knowledge and opinion, and managing the world through science and reason. Whether postmodernism signals a shift in philosophical direction comparable to the transition from Scholastic to modern philosophy, or turns out to be one more burst of sophistic deflation, postmodern philosophers are to be commended for demanding—once again—that philosophy make a difference beyond the academy.

Since a comprehensive treatment of such complex matters is beyond the scope and purposes of this introductory philosophy text, we shall confine ourselves to a selective look at the "anti-philosophy" of Friedrich Nietzsche and an examination of issues of philosophical advocacy, an area that seems to be fertile ground for the emergence of new philosophical archetypes. Finally, we will part company after an informal discussion about the need for wisdom *today*.

14

The Anti-Philosopher

Friedrich Nietzsche

Who is most influential.—When a human being resists his whole age and stops it at the gate to demand an accounting, this must have influence. Whether that is what he desires is immaterial; that he can do it is what matters.

Friedrich Nietzsche

erhaps no philosopher of modern times has provoked as much controversy as **Friedrich Nietzsche (1844–1900)**. Of small physical stature, so nearsighted he was nearly blind, plagued by headaches, nausea, loneliness, and depression, Nietzsche voiced an explosive philosophy that attracts and offends people nearly a century after his death. One of a handful of philosophers who can be called "bestselling" authors, Nietzsche's work has a poetic, confrontational style that is both exhilarating and disturbing.

Although he died in 1900, Nietzsche thought of himself as a cultural prophet. In *The Will to Power* he says:

> What I relate is the history of the next two centuries. I describe what is coming, what can no longer come differently. . . . This future speaks even now in a hundred signs, this destiny announces itself everywhere; for this music of the future all ears are cocked even now. For some time now, our whole European culture has been moving as toward a catastrophe, with a tortured tension that is growing from decade to decade: restlessly, violently, headlong, like a river that wants to reach the end, that no longer reflects, that is afraid to reflect.[1]

Nietzsche saw himself as the first to recognize the symptoms of a profound sickness at the core of *modernity*. **Modernity** refers to the historical period of nineteenth- and twentieth-century nation-states and to a corresponding set of cultural conditions and beliefs dominated by Enlightenment ideals. Modernity includes: faith in science, objective truth, and rationality; expectations of inevitable progress; capitalism, urbanization, and large-scale industrial enterprise; mass literacy, media, and culture; political democracy; and anti-traditionalism, individualism, and secularization.

Nietzsche's most famous (or infamous) pronouncement that "God is dead" is part of a generalized assessment of modernity that consists of integrated negative and positive stages. The negative stage may be the most recognized because of Nietzsche's uniquely engaging and confrontational style of writing. Perhaps less well known—at least by the general public—is Nietzsche's life-affirming call to those who recognize the *great opportunity* for self-creation present in the death of God and all that flows from it.

Friedrich Nietzsche

MODERNITY

The historical period of nineteenth- and twentieth-century nation-states and a corresponding set of cultural conditions and beliefs dominated by Enlightenment ideals including: faith in science, objective truth, and rationality, expectations of inevitable progress, political democracy, capitalism, urbanization, mass literacy, mass media, mass culture, anti-traditionalism, large-scale industrial enterprise, individualism, and secularization.

Nietzsche has seldom been treated as a philosopher at all. . . . His language would have been less colorful had he known what he was trying to say, but then he would not have been the original thinker he was, working through a set of problems which had hardly ever been charted before. Small wonder his maps are illustrated, so to speak, with all sorts of monsters and fearful indications and boastful cartographic embellishment.

Arthur C. Danto

Although Nietzsche is popularly credited with being the first truly post-modern philosopher, with Nietzsche nothing is that simple; or perhaps as many philosophers insist, with Nietzsche nothing is clear. Depending on one's perspective, Nietzsche's work is either enriched or weakened by the use of cryptic utterances, biting irony, hyperbole, deliberate contradiction, and phrases and assertions that are carefully crafted to provoke the reader. Contemporary philosophers and critics disagree about whether Nietzsche was a philosopher of sustained brilliance, sporadic insight, raving irrationality—or even a philosopher at all. What is beyond dispute, however, is his enormous influence and significance on twentieth-century thought. Love him or hate him, Nietzsche remains an aesthetic, literary, psychological, and philosophical force to be reckoned with. He is, at the very least, a worthy adversary.

Friedrich Nietzsche, the iconoclastic son of a preacher and deeply spiritual atheist, who lived and died in lonely obscurity, stands outside of the common categories of philosophy. He is *sui generis*—of his own kind. I have tried to express something of this uniqueness by treating him as an *anti-philosopher*. He became that over the course of his life; but he was always an outsider.

The Outsider

I shall be asked why I have really narrated all these little things which according to the traditional judgement are matters of indifference . . . Answer: . . . It is precisely here that one has to begin to *learn anew*.

Friedrich Nietzsche

Nietzsche was born in the Prussian village of Röcken. When he was four years old, his father, a Lutheran minister, died, leaving the pious little boy to the care of his mother, grandmother, two aunts, and sister. As the only male in the household, young "Fritz" became the center of attention, coddled and protected. Nietzsche's studious demeanor and religious piety earned him the nickname "the little pastor."

Nietzsche originally planned to follow in his father's footsteps and become a Lutheran minister, but in his late teens, something changed. The "good boy" lost interest in his studies. He questioned the existence of God and even sneaked away and got drunk—on a Sunday.

At twenty, Nietzsche enrolled in the University of Bonn. Freed from the pampering and domination of five women, faced with uncertainties about his faith and childhood plans for the future, Nietzsche, like Kierkegaard, went through a period of rebellious high living.

He tried his best to fit into the raucous life of late-nineteenth-century German students: drinking, boisterous singing, romantic pursuits, duels. Nietzsche joined a student club, caroused, and even fought a halfhearted duel. Yet, for all his efforts, Nietzsche was not "one of the guys." He was personally disgusted with drunken excess, smoky beer halls, and the "coarse, Philistine spirit" of his fellows. The little pastor found that kind of student life intolerable and ultimately suffered a nervous collapse.

Nietzsche left Bonn and enrolled in the University of Leipzig. There he had the good fortune to meet Professor Friedrich Ritschl, who kindled in him a passion for philology, the study of classical philosophy and literature. Ritschl recognized that Nietzsche was a brilliant scholar, and encouraged and stimulated his genius.

Despite his academic brilliance, however, Nietzsche was already a lonely man, basically an outsider. When he first moved to Leipzig, he was still shaken by his disillusionment with Bonn and by the emptiness he felt having lost his religious faith. He went through the motions of being actively interested in his life, but found himself torn by doubts. Hedonistic pursuits left him disgusted and depressed, yet the way of the church remained closed off to him.

While in this state, Nietzsche came across the work of **Arthur Schopenhauer (1788–1860)**. Schopenhauer's philosophy is known as **pessimism,** the belief that life is disappointing and that for every satisfied desire, ten new unsatisfied ones emerge; our only hope is detachment and withdrawal. In his book *The World as Will and Idea*, Schopenhauer argued that life is nothing more than a constant will to survive. We are pawns of a life force, and our best hope is to detach our individual will from the cycle of wanting–getting–wanting more. Life, in Schopenhauer's vision, is an irrational, purposeless striving for a pointless existence. According to Schopenhauer, what little salvation there is comes only from resisting the blind will to *live at all costs* and curtailing our desires.

Given his mental turmoil and deep dissatisfaction, Nietzsche responded enthusiastically to Schopenhauer. He craved some kind of meaning but was unable to find it in either pleasure or religion. At a precarious time in his life, Schopenhauer gave him something to hold on to:

> It seemed as if Schopenhauer were addressing me personally. I felt his enthusiasm, and seemed to see him before me. Every line cried aloud for renunciation, denial, resignation. Here I saw a mirror in which the world, life, my own mind were reflected in fearful grandeur. Here the wholly disinterested and heavenly eye of art looked at me; here I saw illness and salvation, banishment and refuge, hell and heaven.[2]

From Schopenhauer, Nietzsche concluded that life makes no objective, absolute sense. Life is not the result of a divine plan, nor is nature orderly in any way that we can discern. Rather, life is the expression of *will*. Schopenhauer characterized the ultimate will as the will to live; Nietzsche disagreed. He insisted that life is governed by the **will to power,** a universal desire to control others and impose our values on them.

Beyond the Academy

Schopenhauer's pessimism, paradoxically, invigorated Nietzsche, and in 1868 Ritschl recommended him for a chair in classical philology. Ritschl

---

PESSIMISM

Schopenhauer's theory that life is disappointing and that for every satisfied desire, new desires emerge; our only hope is detachment and withdrawal.

WILL TO POWER

Nietzsche's term for what he thought is a universal desire to control others and impose our values on them.

By the second half of the nineteenth century, art and literature, as well as philosophy, began to reflect a romanticized vision of Schopenhauer's pessimism. Caspar David Friedrich's painting The Polar Sea *depicts glaciers destroying a ship: a symbol of over-civilized, industrialized man's inevitable defeat by the primal forces of irrational nature.*

The Greek philosophers went through life feeling secretly that there were far more slaves than one might think—meaning that everybody who was not a philosopher was a slave. Their pride overflowed at the thought that even the most powerful men on earth belong among their slaves.

Friedrich Nietzsche

was especially conservative, not given to excessive praise or hasty conclusions regarding the area of study to which he had devoted his life, so the recommendation he wrote for Nietzsche is all the more significant:

> However many young talents I have seen develop under my eyes for thirty-nine years . . . Nietzsche . . . is the first from whom I have ever accepted any contribution [to the philological journal *Museum*] at all while he was still a student. . . . He is the idol, and without wishing it, the leader of the whole younger generation of philologists here in Leipzig who—and they are rather numerous—cannot wait to hear him as a lecturer. You will say, I describe a phenomenon. Well, that is just what he is—and at the same time pleasant and modest. . . .
> . . . He will simply be able to do anything he wants to do.[3]

Though Nietzsche lacked his doctorate, his brilliance and Ritschl's strong advocacy combined to secure the position for him. "In *Germany*," Ritschl wrote, "that sort of thing happens absolutely never."

Nietzsche was only twenty-four when he was appointed professor. The university hurriedly conferred the doctorate on him—without requiring an examination—and Nietzsche plunged into a heavy academic routine. But his heart and mind could not be confined to the limits of philology or philosophy—or any other academic area as then defined.

In spite of noble intentions, Nietzsche was not a particularly effective professor. His lectures were often complex and difficult to follow, and fewer and fewer students attended them. He did not socialize well, and found his colleagues difficult. Academic routine drained him. His sole comforts came from his own writing and a few close friends.

Tragic Optimism

In 1870, the Franco-Prussian War broke out. Nietzsche volunteered as a medic and served for a short time before returning to Leipzig in poor health. Germany humbled both Austria and France in the war. Under the powerful vision of **Otto von Bismarck (1815–1898)**, small German principalities were unified into a single, powerful state dominated by Prussia. Nietzsche saw Bismarck as an example of a "higher morality" based on strength, power, and the will to dominate. He was impressed that Bismarck ruled by "blood and iron."

About this time, Nietzsche became intrigued with Darwinism. Combining Bismarck's will to power and domination with Darwin's idea of evolution, Nietzsche transformed Schopenhauer's pessimism into his own utterly unique doctrine of overcoming. Schopenhauer was right, Nietzsche thought, in recognizing that life consists of continual struggle and hardship. But Schopenhauer's reaction—retreat and renunciation—struck Nietzsche as weak-willed and decadent. He concluded that Schopenhauer's pessimism was unhealthy and life-denying.

Yet because struggle is in fact the essence of life, optimism is a shallow, false response. Things do not always go well. There is no grand design in which everything turns out for the best at the end of the story: *No meaning is revealed.*

Nietzsche's solution was **tragic optimism**, the sense of joy and vitality that accompanies the superior individual's clear-sighted imposition of his own freely chosen values on a meaningless world. The superior person is the person who neither shrinks from struggle nor struggles blindly, controlled by a pessimistic instinct to survive at any cost. The superior person *wills* to live deliberately and consciously. The superior person *overcomes* pessimism without retreating into lies about ultimate meaning or purpose. In Nietzsche's view, Schopenhauer failed to recognize that the struggle to survive aims at the dominance of the strongest and the fittest. The tragic optimist imposes meaning on a meaningless universe and overcomes his or her own innate fears and weaknesses.

Zarathustra Speaks

Citing ill health, Nietzsche resigned from the university in 1879, when he was thirty-four. He was granted a pension. Nietzsche knew he needed to break free from the confines of academic scholarship and carve out his own

. . . Schopenhauer, though a pessimist. . . . played the flute. Every day, after dinner: one should read his biography on that. And incidentally: a pessimist, one who denies God and the world but *comes to a stop* before morality—who affirms morality and plays the flute—what? is that really—a pessimist?

Friedrich Nietzsche

TRAGIC OPTIMISM

According to Nietzsche, the sense of joy and vitality that accompanies the superior individual's clear-sighted imposition of his own freely chosen values on a meaningless world.

Will the true Nietzsche please stand up? In an ironic fashion sure to delight the iconoclast, some philosophers have great difficulties taking Nietzsche seriously in light of his many personae, his romantic and ambiguous language, in short, his "slipperiness." So what, if anything, are we to make of this May 13, 1882 photograph of the young prophet of the overman, with his best friend Paul Reé and the woman he once professed to love, Lou Salome?

Life is no argument. The conditions of life might include error.

Friedrich Nietzsche

path. He came to see himself as the prophet of a higher, healthier morality, a morality so far beyond conventional values that it required the revaluation of all values. He took to referring to himself as an *immoralist* and an *iconoclast*. He spoke of "doing philosophy with a hammer"—tapping on the statues of great idols to see which are hollow and then smashing them to bits.

Freed from the demands of the university, Nietzsche polished and refined both his thinking and his writing. His greatest work was accomplished in the ten-year period following his retirement from teaching. For a time, he lost some of his ferocity, mellowed, perhaps, by the physical and cultural climates of Switzerland and Italy, where he spent most of his time.

His most "cheerful" books, *The Dawn of Day* (1881) and *The Gay Science* (1882), were written while he was friends with Lou Salome, a witty, appealing young Jewish intellectual. Nietzsche was quite taken with her. In their walks and talks together he found a special kind of companionship. He seems to have found in her both a disciple and a lover. We do not know whether he ever proposed to her, as she later claimed. In any case, Lou Salome ultimately left Nietzsche for another man. (Years later, when Nietzsche was famous, Lou Salome capitalized on her relationship with him.)

Devastated by her abandonment, Nietzsche retreated to the Swiss Alps. In this agonizingly lonely, hurt, and bitter mood, he produced his most famous work, *Thus Spake Zarathustra* (1885). The title comes from the Sanskrit phrase *Iti vuttakam*, meaning "Thus spoke the Holy One."[4] Nietzsche used the name of the ancient Persian prophet Zoroaster, but created his own Zarathustra. *Zarathustra* was a call to rise above decadence and mediocrity. Nietzsche later described *Zarathustra* as a revelation:

> "One hears—one does not seek; one takes—one does not ask who gives; a thought suddenly flashes up like lightning, it comes with necessity, unhesitatingly—I have never had any choice in the matter."[5]

Nietzsche's Zarathustra is at once a great destroyer of false values and in the same instant a creator of new, higher, healthier values. Nietzsche said that Zarathustra "as a type . . . *overtook* me."[6] Zarathustra the destroyer-creator announces the arrival of the next evolutionary type, the *Übermensch*, or the overman.

Nietzsche followed *Zarathustra* with what many consider the two most coherent statements of his philosophy, *Beyond Good and Evil* (1886) and *Toward a Genealogy of Morals* (1887). Consisting mostly of aphorisms and short essays, both books are essentially commentaries on the gospel of the overman espoused in *Zarathustra*. Nietzsche's purpose is clear: to destroy conventional morality and replace it with a higher "immoral" ideal. *Zarathustra* announces the death of God and of merely-human beings. It heralds the arrival of the next evolutionary step: overman.

Both Nietzsche and Socrates are intensely personal thinkers, actively engaged in changing, in one way or another, the moral quality of the life of the people around them, though they pursue their goals in radically different ways. . . . Both desperately need their audience's attention.

Alexander Nehamas

[Nietzsche] never hesitated to change his attitudes according to the needs of life rather than those of mere logic.

Janko Lavrin

The Last Philosopher

During this period of his life Nietzsche lived modestly, in rooming houses, refusing to succumb to pessimism. Writer Stefan Zweig's touching description of Nietzsche reminds us that there are many kinds of courage, many ways to be strong:

> Carefully the myopic man sits down to a table; carefully, the man with the sensitive stomach considers every item on the menu: whether the tea is not too strong, the food not spiced too much, for every

For me, then, nobility is synonymous with a life of effort, ever set on excelling oneself, in passing beyond what one is [at a given moment] to what one sets up as a duty and an obligation. In this way the noble life stands opposed to the common or inert life, which reclines statically upon itself, condemned to perpetual immobility, unless external force compels it to come out of itself.

José Ortega y Gasset

[Nietzsche] had more penetrating knowledge of himself than any other man who ever lived or ever was likely to live.

Sigmund Freud

mistake in his diet upsets his sensitive digestion, and every transgression in his nourishment wreaks havoc with his quivering nerves for days. No glass of wine, no beer, no alcohol, no coffee at his place, no cigar and no cigarette after his meal, nothing that stimulates, refreshes, or rests him; only the short, meager meal and a little urbane, unprofound conversation in a soft voice with an occasional neighbor (as a man speaks who for years has been unused to talking and is afraid of being asked too much).

And upon entering again into the small, narrow, modest, coldly furnished *chambre garnie*, where innumerable notes, pages, writings, and proofs are piled up on the table, but no flower, no decoration, scarcely a book and rarely a letter. Back in a corner, a heavy and graceless wooden trunk, his only possession, with the two shirts and the other worn suit. Otherwise only . . . manuscripts, and on a tray innumerable bottles and jars and potions; against the migraines, which often render him all but senseless for hours, against his stomach cramps, against spasmodic vomiting, against the slothful intestines, and above all the dreadful sedatives against his insomnia, chloral hydrate and Veronal. A frightful arsenal of poisons and drugs, yet the only helpers in the empty silence of this strange room in which he never rests except in brief artificially conquered sleep. Wrapped in his overcoat and a woolen scarf (for the wretched stove smokes and does not give warmth), his fingers freezing, his double glasses pressed close to the paper, his hurried hand writes for hours—words the dim eyes can hardly decipher. For hours he sits like this and writes until his eyes burn.[7]

Overwhelmed by disappointment and loneliness, disturbed by what he saw as rampant mediocrity and hypocrisy, Nietzsche struggled on with his writing. Less than three years before his final collapse, he wrote:

What found expression [in even my earliest work] was . . . a *strange* voice . . . one who concealed himself for the time being under the scholar's hood. . . . Here was a spirit with strange, nameless needs. . . . What spoke here was a mystical, almost maenadic [frenzied] soul that stammered with difficulty, a feat of the will, as in a strange tongue, almost undecided whether it should communicate or conceal itself. It should have *sung*, this "new soul"—and not spoken![8]

The last years of Nietzsche's life were tragic. His health deteriorated even further, and he became increasingly, bitterly isolated and lonely.

I call myself the last philosopher because I am the last man. Nobody talks to me but myself, and my voice comes to me like that of a dying person. . . . Though I try to conceal my loneliness from myself—the terrible loneliness of the last philosopher!—and make my way into the multitude and into love by lies, for my heart cannot

To a friend Nietzsche wrote: "If I could give you an idea of my feeling of loneliness! I have nobody among the living or among the dead, to whom I feel related. This is indescribably horrible!" (This photograph was taken at Villa Silberblick in Weimar, shortly before Nietzsche's death.)

bear the terror of the loneliest loneliness and compels me to talk as if I were two.[9]

As his disappointments mounted, Nietzsche quarreled with practically everyone, his human contact reduced to innkeepers, shop clerks, and others with whom he had superficial interactions. To a friend he wrote, "For the lonely one, even noise is a consolation. If I could give you an idea of my feeling of loneliness! I have nobody among the living or among the dead, to whom I feel related. This is indescribably horrible!"[10] For a soul with so much to *sing*, this must have been among the worst rebuffs of all.

In January 1889 in Turin, Italy, Nietzsche had another breakdown. His mother brought him home to Germany, and his life ended much as it had begun, in the care of his mother and sister. After their mother's death, Nietzsche's sister moved him to Weimar, where the prophet of struggle and overcoming spent the rest of his life half-paralyzed, slipping in and out of sanity. The "loneliest philosopher" died about midday, August 25, 1900.

I think of myself as the scrawl which an unknown power scribbles across a sheet of paper, to try out a new pen.

Friedrich Nietzsche

Philosophical Query

Some contemporary philosophers claim that all philosophy is a form of *autobiography*. By that they mean that all philosophy—and indeed all thinking and perceiving—expresses and reflects uniquely personal qualities of the philosopher. In your opinion, do the *life circumstances* of philosophers help us evaluate their philosophical writings? Do you think *autobiographical* considerations are significant? Insignificant? Discuss and explain.

Truth Is a Matter of Perspective

To choose what is harmful to *oneself*, to be *attracted* by "disinterested" motives almost always constitutes the formula for *décadence*.

Friedrich Nietzsche

When Nietzsche says, "I call myself the last philosopher because I am the last man," he may be referring to his doctrine of the more-than-human overman. (See pages 578–579.) If so, then by referring to himself as the last philosopher, Nietzsche is signaling that he is the last merely human philosopher. This may have been what he had in mind, since he thought that the next stage of cultural and human evolution would necessitate the destruction of all present value systems, including modern philosophical ones based on the possibility of objectivity.

According to Nietzsche, aesthetic vision (art or taste) is the basis of meaning, not science, not religion, not morality, not rationality. And for Nietzsche, like his Irish contemporary Oscar Wilde, art is a matter of *semblance*, a *pose*, "technically" a matter of *masks* and *lies*. Nietzsche wrote:

> I never failed to sense a *hostility to life*—a furious, vengeful antipathy to life itself [behind faith in absolutes]: for all of life is based on semblance, art, deception, points of view, and the necessity of perspectives and error.[11]

Nietzsche's controversial status as a philosopher is due, at least in part, to assertions of a form of relativism known as *perspectivism*. **Nietzschean perspectivism** is the contention that every view is only one among many possible interpretations, including, especially, Nietzschean perspectivism, which itself is just one interpretation among many interpretations. But, as the critic Alexander Nehamas reminds us:

> If every view is only an interpretation, and if, as perspectivism holds, there are no independent facts against which various interpretations can be compared, what is the object at which the many interpretations that we consider interpretations *of* Nietzsche are directed? . . . If perspectivism is correct, and, as it seems to claim, every interpretation creates its own facts, then it may seem impossible to decide whether any interpretation is or is not correct. And if there is nothing of which all these are interpretations, then the very idea of interpretation, which seems to require at least that there be something there to be interpreted, begins to appear suspect itself.[12]

We have already encountered this issue of the apparent self-contradiction at the heart of radically relativistic doctrines. (See Chapters 1, 2, and 3, for example.) There is, however, a characteristically postmodern quality to Nietzsche's perspectivist assertions: By repeatedly calling attention to his own aesthetic perspectivism, Nietzsche models what he asserts in a flagrantly self-referential way. He exuberantly adopts *points of view*, which he also refers to as *experiments*, thereby preventing his readers from forgetting that they, too, have points of view—from forgetting that they, too, conduct moral, philosophical, and spiritual *experiments*.

NIETZSCHEAN
PERSPECTIVISM

The contention that every view is only one among many possible interpretations, including, especially, Nietzschean perspectivism, which itself is just one interpretation among many interpretations.

Thus, whatever positive position Nietzsche takes is also a negative position—experimentally, from one point of view. In "Attempt at a Self-Criticism," Nietzsche refers to what he labels a deep *antimoral propensity* in his writing. As we will see later, this does not mean that Nietzsche himself has no moral code whatsoever; it means that Nietzsche's value system is anti-moral *from the perspective* of conventional (Christian) morality. Similarly, from the standpoint of most modern philosophy, Nietzsche can be considered an *anti-philosopher*.

An **anti-philosopher** is a radical critic of certain techniques and foundational doctrines of modern science and philosophy who disputes the possibility of objectivity and universality, and who rejects the absolute authority of reason. In other words, the anti-philosopher rejects the possibility of a *neutral stance* or *perspectiveless perspective*.

Philosophical Query

Do you think that the presence of a perspective makes a neutral stance impossible? What do you think *neutral* means in this kind of case? Does it mean *perspectiveless*? If it means something else, what else? Are perspectives the same things as biases? Discuss and explain.

Attack on Objectivity

What criteria for truth can Nietzsche, as an anti-philosopher, offer in place of objectivity and universality, and what standard of interpretation can he offer *in lieu* of rationality? Instead of recognizable philosophical *arguments*, Nietzsche offers a twofold *appeal*. The first component of this appeal, directed at our aesthetic sensibilities (taste), calls on us to "justify life as an aesthetic phenomenon." The second component of Nietzsche's anti-philosophical appeal rests on what he calls the *will to power*. Neither component *depends on* reason or scientific inquiry for justification.

In "On Truth and Lie in an Extra-Moral Sense," Nietzsche says that knowledge itself is an invention and goes so far as to doubt even our capacity for self-knowledge:

> What, indeed, does man know of himself! Can he even perceive himself completely . . . ? Does not nature keep much the most from him, even about his body, to spellbind and confine him in a proud, deceptive consciousness, far from the coils of his intestines, the quick current of his bloodstream . . . ? . . .
> In view of this, whence the urge for truth?[13]

The clear implication is that if nature keeps "much the most" from us concerning our very own selves, we have no chance of *discovering* the objective truth about anything. We can only *invent truths* according to our individual needs. Truths are aesthetic creations that serve the will to power.

ANTI-PHILOSOPHER

A radical critic of the techniques and doctrines of modern science and philosophy. The anti-philosopher disputes the possibility of objectivity and universality and rejects the absolute authority of reason; anti-philosophers also reject the possibility of a *neutral stance* or *perspectiveless perspective*.

The highest and strongest drives, when they break out passionately and drive the individual far above the average and the flats of the herd conscience, wreck the self-confidence of the community, its faith in itself, and it is as if its spine snapped.

Friedrich Nietzsche

Truth is seen as a function of the *physiology* and *pathology* of the individual, not some absolute, unchanging—objective—fact of nature or proposition derived from reason.

We have seen, in Chapters 12 and 13, how Enlightenment faith in reason and science produced sharp existential and pragmatic counterreactions. Among the nineteenth-century criticisms raised against faith in "scientific" rationality and objectivity (*scientism*), Nietzsche's cultural critique stands out for its intensity and scope.

Nietzsche's assault on objectivity includes rejecting the Cartesian notion of a unitary, fixed, rational self. Adopting a view similar to Hume's, Nietzsche insisted that the idea of a self that persists throughout a person's lifetime is a *fiction* or *metaphor*, not a fact. Metaphysicians, Christians, and scientists, Nietzsche said, are all prone to the same error: They believe that terms such as "substance," "God," and "gravity" refer to things as they objectively exist; consequently, they fail to grasp their metaphorical or fictive nature.

Moreover, according to Nietzsche, *a single hidden agenda* lurks behind science, philosophy, and religion: Scientists, philosophers, and the faithful all seek power over the world, over other people, even over themselves. This natural impulse to dominate and control is often disguised as *influencing, controlling, managing, understanding,* or *improving* life, nature, the environment, society, and human behavior. Whatever we call them, Nietzsche insists, these desires are manifestations of the *will to power*.

Philosophical Query

What can we make of Nietzsche's anti-philosophical, nonrational, nonscientific positions? Is it fair to demand systematic writings from one who rejects all systematizing? Is there any point to demanding rational consistency from a writer who mocks rationalism? What can be gained by applying Christian standards to a rejection of Christianity? (These are just the sorts of questions with which contemporary philosophers still struggle, with their Nietzsche studies and elsewhere.)

The Will to Power

Call it what we wish—objectivity, truth, or wisdom—Nietzsche says the single goal of science, religion, and philosophy is the exertion of power. Thus, it is *mendacious* for scientists (or priests or philosophers) to think of themselves as disinterested, detached, rational spectators capable of neutral, objective judgment. In this passage from *Toward a Genealogy of Morals*, Nietzsche expresses his disgust at the pretense of objectivity:

I know of nothing that excites such disgust as this kind of "objective" armchair scholar, this kind of scented voluptuary of history, half parson, half satyr . . . who betrays immediately with the falsetto of his applause what he lacks, *where* he lacks it, *where* in this case the Fates have applied their cruel shears with, alas, such surgical skill! This offends my taste. . . .

    . . . I do not like these whited sepulchers who impersonate life; I do not like these weary and played-out people who wrap themselves in wisdom and look "objective"; I do not like these agitators dressed up as heroes who wear the magic cap of ideals on their straw heads; but who are at bottom only tragic buffoons; and I also do not like these latest speculators in idealism . . . (that *no* kind of swindle fails to succeed . . . today is connected with the undeniable and palpable stagnation of the . . . spirit; and the cause of that I seek in a too exclusive diet of newspapers, politics, beer, . . . music . . . and then the *paralysis agitans* [Parkinson's disease] of "modern ideas").[14]

Nietzsche equates the will to truth with the will to power, and asserts that power is the basis of the distinction between good and evil:

> What urges you on and arouses your ardour, you wisest of men, do you call it "will to truth"? . . .
>
>   [I]t is a will to power; and that is so even when you talk of good and evil and of the assessment of values. . . .
>
>   Where I found a living creature, there I found will to power; and even in the will of the servant I found the will to be master. . . .
>
>   And life itself told me this secret: "Behold," it said, "I am that *which must overcome itself again and again.*"[15]

From Nietzsche's perspective, *all life and all happiness are governed by the will to power*:

> *Effect of happiness.*—The first effect of happiness is the *feeling of power*: this wants to *express itself*, either to us ourselves, or to other men, or to ideas or imaginary beings. The most common modes of expression are: to bestow, to mock, to destroy—all three out of a common basic drive.[16]

The positive force of Nietzsche's concept is captured in contemporary philosopher Philip Novack's characterization of the will to power:

> What, then, is the will to power? It is life's intrinsic and inexorable ache for *more*. Living processes incessantly seek the enjoyment of their own sensorium, the unblocked expression of their vitality, the radiance of their health, the overcoming of resistances, and the amplification of their self-feeling. Life in each and every one of its infinite manifestations carries within it a will to fulfillment, a will to expansion, a will to deeper, fuller being. . . . The will to power, Nietzsche tells us, includes but exceeds the will to self-preservation. For it seeks not only the continuance of life, but *more* life, an *intensification* of life.[17]

High and independent spirituality, the will to stand alone, even a powerful reason are experienced as dangers; everything that elevates an individual above the herd and intimidates the neighbor is henceforth called *evil*; and the fair, modest, submissive, conforming mentality, the *mediocrity* of desires attains moral designations and honors.

    Friedrich Nietzsche

One does not kill by anger but by laughter. Come, let us kill the Spirit of Gravity!

    Friedrich Nietzsche

The means employed by the lust for power have changed, but the same volcano continues to glow, the impatience and the immoderate love demand their sacrifice: and what one formerly did "for the sake of God" one now does for the sake of money, that is to say of that which *now* gives the highest feeling of power and good conscience.

Friedrich Nietzsche

From a Nietzschean point of view, modernity—with its mass movements, reliance on technology, science, educated *reasonableness*, and Christianized emphasis on altruism—devolves away from the *intensification* of life toward the mere extension and preservation of it.

The World as the Will to Power

In contrast to the seemingly intelligible, manageable, tamable world of the scientist and modern philosopher, and in contrast to the God-centered, created world of the theistic believer, Nietzsche offers another perspective:

> And do you know what "the world" is to me? Shall I show it to you in my mirror? This world: a monster of energy, without beginning, without end; a firm, iron magnitude of force that does not grow bigger or smaller, that does not expend itself but only transforms itself; as a whole, of unalterable size, a household without expenses or losses, but likewise without increase or income; enclosed by "nothingness" as by a boundary; not something blurry or wasted, not something endlessly extended, but set in a definite space as a definite force, and not a space that might be "empty" here or there, but rather as force throughout . . .
>
> [This is] my . . . world of the eternally self-creating, the eternally self-destroying, this mystery world of the twofold voluptuous delight, my "beyond good and evil," without goal, unless the joy of the circle is itself a goal; without will, unless a ring feels good-will toward itself—do you want a *name* for this world? A *solution* for all its riddles? . . . *This world is the will to power—and nothing besides!* And you yourselves are also this will to power—and nothing besides![18]

The twentieth century is the age of Nietzsche, as he predicted it would be: the age of dictators unmoved by any moral tradition, of wars made more deadly and devastating by the progress of science; the age of the "death of God" for those who lead the parade in thought and power.

Will and Ariel Durant

Nietzsche claimed that late nineteenth-century European culture was dominated by a superficially optimistic belief that scientific progress and Christian morality could subdue the will to power and thereby make life safe and meaningful for the masses. But just under the surface, Nietzsche said, lay a fatal, festering cultural sickness: modernity.

The Diseases of Modernity

As we have noted, the cultural sickness that Nietzsche describes rests on unabashed, unwarranted faith: in science, in philosophy, and in Christianity. Each of these "decaying" belief systems is, Nietzsche asserts, hostile to the will to power, the will to exalt ourselves, the will to *live*.

Science, for instance, reduces us to inevitable helpless effects, limited by the myth of objective reality, to whatever causal accounts of our world, our origins, and our selves science deigns to pronounce. Science cannot recognize *gods*, *lawgivers*, *overcomers*, and *creators*; science sees only *cases*, *conditions*, *types*, and *effects*. Thus, prolonged dominance of scientism results in self-contempt:

> *All* science . . . has at present the object of dissuading man from his former respect for himself, as if this has been nothing but a piece of bizarre conceit. One might even say that its [science's] own pride, its own austere form of stoical ataraxy [tranquillity], consists in sustaining this hard-won *self-contempt* of man as his ultimate and most serious claim to self-respect.[19]

According to Nietzsche, to the extent that faith in science dominates a culture, that culture must degrade the true individual.

The Problem of Morality

In Nietzsche's view, the same desires that attract us to science's false promise of control and objectivity attract us to such products of modern philosophy as utilitarian and Kantian ethics. (See Fourth Interlude and Chapter 10.) Like science, these modernist ethical schemes reduce the great passions of *living* to thin utilitarian calculations or pinched Kantian formulae. And just as the scientist is mendacious for failing to reveal her own will to power, so too is the modern moral philosopher mendacious for being blinded to the brute fact that his philosophizing is always philosophizing from a perspective, for a *purpose*:

> With a stiff seriousness that inspires laughter, all our philosophers demanded something . . . exalted, presumptuous, and solemn from themselves as soon as they approached the study of morality: they wanted to supply a *rational foundation* for morality—and every philosopher so far has believed that he has provided such a foundation. Morality itself, however, was accepted as "given." How remote from their clumsy pride was that task which they considered insignificant and left in dust and must—the task of description—although the subtlest fingers and senses can scarcely be subtle enough for it.
>
> Just because our moral philosophers knew the facts of morality only very approximately in arbitrary extracts or in accidental epitomes—for example, as the morality of *their* environment, *their* class, *their* church, the spirit of *their* time, *their* climate and part of the world—just because they were poorly informed and not even very curious about different peoples, times, and past ages—they never laid eyes on the real problems of morality; for these emerge only when we compare *many* moralities. In all "science of morals" so far one thing was *lacking*, strange as it may sound: the problem of morality itself; what was lacking was any suspicion that there was something problematic here. What the philosophers called "a rational foundation for

. . . I have chosen for myself the word *immoralist* as a mark of distinction and badge of honour.

Friedrich Nietzsche

One knows my demand of philosophers that they place themselves *beyond* good and evil . . . that they have the illusion of moral judgement *beneath* them.

Friedrich Nietzsche

morality" and tried to supply was, seen in the right light, merely a scholarly variation of the common *faith* in the prevalent morality; a new means of *expression* for this faith; and thus just another fact within a particular morality; indeed, in the last analysis a kind of denial that this morality might ever be considered problematic—certainly the very opposite of an examination, analysis, questioning, and vivisection of this very faith. . . .[20]

Of every morality, Nietzsche says, "one can still always ask: what does such a claim tell us about the man who makes it? . . . In short, moralities are also merely a *sign language of the affects*."[21] Far from expressing objective or universal truths, or even scientific facts, moral codes reflect the desires and perspectives of those who create them:

> . . . [M]an has ascribed to all that exists a connection with morality and laid an *ethical significance* on the world's back. One day this will have as much value, and no more, as the belief in the masculinity or femininity of the sun.[22]

The Problem of Being Moralistic

MORALISTIC, BEING

Being moralistic consists of expressing commonplace moral sentiments that conflict with one's behavior, and equating moral sentimentality with virtuous living; a form of hypocrisy that resembles a reaction formation.

REACTION FORMATION

Freudian ego-defense mechanism that attempts to prevent "dangerous" desires from being exposed and expressed by endorsing opposite attitudes and types of behavior as "barriers" against them.

Nietzsche accuses modern Western culture of *being moralistic*. To be **moralistic** is to express commonplace moral sentiments that conflict with one's behavior, and to equate moral sentimentality with virtuous living. Being moralistic is a form of hypocrisy that resembles what Freudian psychologists refer to as a *reaction formation*. **Reaction formation** is the name of the ego defense mechanism that attempts to prevent "dangerous" desires from being exposed and expressed by endorsing opposite attitudes and types of behavior as "barriers" against them. In the following passage, Nietzsche goes so far as to say that *the most distinctive feature of modern souls and modern books is moralistic mendaciousness*:

> For if a psychologist today has *good taste* (others might say, integrity) it consists in resistance to the shamefully *moralized* way of speaking which has gradually made all modern judgments of men and things slimy. One should not deceive oneself in this manner: the most distinctive feature of modern souls and modern books is not lying but their inveterate *innocence* in moralistic mendaciousness. To have to rediscover this "innocence" everywhere—this constitutes perhaps the most disgusting job among all the precarious tasks a psychologist has to tackle today; . . .[23]

From the perspective of modern Christian morality—and for Nietzsche all modern morality has a Christian basis—Nietzsche is an anti-moralist, or to use his more provocative term, he is "the first immoralist."[24]

At its base, in Nietzsche's view, modernity is anti-life and anti-nature, and modern, Christianized, moralities are symptoms of this *décadence*, this decay. In the following passage, Nietzsche ascribes the "error of modernity" to all of mankind (with an oblique reference to Kantianism):

> It is *not* error as error which horrifies me . . . it is the lack of nature, it is the utterly ghastly fact that *antinature* itself has received the highest honours as morality, and has hung over mankind as law, as categorical imperative! . . . To blunder to this extent, *not* as an individual, *not* as a people, but as mankind![25]

One might assume, given what Nietzsche says above, that modernist humanistic ethics such as utilitarianism would be more in keeping with Nietzsche's anti-Christian values. But that is not the case.

The Problem of Utilitarianism

At first glance, utilitarian ethics would seem to avoid the Nietzschean charge of being *anti-life*. After all, as we learned in the Fourth Interlude, utilitarians accept an egoistic basis for their philosophy; Jeremy Bentham even hangs the principle of utility on an *egoistic hook*. But according to Nietzsche, the great Mill notwithstanding, the utilitarians sublimate the individual to the group (which Nietzsche sometimes refers to as the *herd*). They also manifest unwarranted faith in reason and, in Mill's case, preach altruism.

Further, according to Nietzsche, the mendacious belief that bad actions stem from curable ignorance—not evil—is as old as Socrates. In *Beyond Good and Evil* Nietzsche links this optimistic faith in the capacity of reason to produce good behavior with utilitarian faith in science as the vehicle of social reform. He is particularly harsh on the modern notion that through proper education and the application of scientific empiricism, society can be reformed. In the following passage, Nietzsche's contempt for this perspective is clear:

> "Nobody wants to do harm to himself, therefore all that is bad is done involuntarily. For the bad do harm to themselves: this they would not do if they knew that the bad is bad. Hence the bad are bad only because of an error; if one removes the error, one necessarily makes them—good."
>
> This type of inference smells of the *rabble* that sees nothing in bad actions but the unpleasant consequences and really judges, "it is *stupid* to do what is bad," while "good" is taken without further ado to be identical with "useful and agreeable." In the case of every moral utilitarianism one may immediately infer the same origin and follow one's nose: one will rarely go astray.[26]

For Nietzsche, the equation of "bad" with "stupid" and "ignorant" is both a result of and a contributor toward the modern decline of culture, the reduction of the threatening—but vital—passions to mere "errors." And, of

In the last analysis, "love of the neighbor" is always something secondary, partly conventional and arbitrary-illusory in relation to *fear of the neighbor*.

Friedrich Nietzsche

How much or how little is dangerous to the community, dangerous to equality, in an opinion, in a state or affect, in a will, in a talent—that now constitutes the moral perspective: here, too, fear is again the mother of morals.

Friedrich Nietzsche

Among helpful and charitable people one almost regularly encounters that clumsy ruse which first doctors the person to be helped—as if, for example, he "deserved" help, required just *their* help, and would prove to be profoundly grateful for all help, faithful and submissive. With these fancies they dispose of the needy as of possessions. . . . One finds them jealous if one crosses or anticipates them when they want to help.

Friedrich Nietzsche

course, errors are correctable. But, Nietzsche says, what modern society sees as progress—gained by adopting a "scientific" attitude toward badness—is in fact a loss of grandeur.

The Problem of Altruism

Altruism in all forms, says Nietzsche—even the desire for altruism—is toxic. Thus, Kantian, Millian, and Christian moralities are *décadence moralities*, moralities that weaken the human spirit by trying to subdue and tame its most creative and selfish passions. The ideal modern citizen is tame, democratic, sheeplike, and compassionate. This view, however, is merely one *fashion in morality*:

> *Fashions in morality.*—How the overall moral judgements have shifted! The great men of antique morality, Epictetus for instance, knew nothing of the now normal glorification of thinking of others, of living for others; in the light of our moral fashion they would have to be called downright immoral, for they strove with all their might *for* their *ego* and *against* feeling with others (that is to say, with the sufferings and moral frailties of others). Perhaps they would reply to us: "If you are so boring or ugly an object to yourself, by all means think of others more than yourself! It is right you should!"[27]

Ironically—perhaps—the dominance of reason in the history of Western culture is also a symptom of decay, as Nietzsche sees things.

The Problem of Generalized Accounts

Insofar as we believe in morality we pass sentence on existence.

Friedrich Nietzsche

Nietzsche's critique of culture centers on his deep and abiding suspicion of all attempts to generalize or universalize a code for living. Nietzsche insisted that science, modern philosophy, and all transcendental schemes turn away from life itself, from vitality, joy, depth, and moral health to the degree that they speak of and to *all*. They sow cultural and spiritual disease *because they generalize where one must not generalize*:

> All these moralities that address themselves to the individual, for the sake of his "happiness," as one says—what are they but counsels for behavior in relation to the degree of *dangerousness* in which the individual lives with himself; recipes against his passions, his good and bad inclinations insofar as they have the will to power and want to play the master; little and great prudences and artifices that exude the nook odor of old nostrums and of the wisdom of old women; all of them baroque and unreasonable in form—because they address themselves to "all," because they generalize where one must not generalize. All of them speak unconditionally, take themselves for unconditional, all of them flavored with more than one grain of salt

and tolerable only—at times even seductive—when they begin to smell over-spiced and dangerous, especially "of the other world." All of it is, measured intellectually, worth very little and not by a long shot "science" much less "wisdom," but rather, to say it once more, three times more, prudence, prudence, prudence, mixed with stupidity, stupidity, stupidity. . . . "Morality as Timidity."[28]

Nietzsche thought that the anti-life nature of modernity accounted for the prevalence of the kind of softness that is the inevitable outcome of the rationalist's airy abstractions, the scientist's sterile generalizations, and the believer's timid, pity-evoking suppression of passion—all corrupted manifestations of what can be twisted but never stopped: the will to power.

So intense, Nietzsche said, is modernity's assault on individual expressions of the will to power that Western society is as soft as the consciences of its inhabitants:

> There is a point in the history of society when it becomes so pathologically soft and tender that among other things it sides even with those who harm it, criminals, and does this quite seriously and honestly. Punishing somehow seems unfair to it, and it is certain that imagining "punishment" and "being supposed to punish" hurts it, arouses fear in it. "Is it not enough to render him *undangerous*? Why still punish? Punishing itself is terrible." With this question, herd morality, the morality of timidity, draws its ultimate consequence. Supposing that one could altogether abolish danger, the reason for fear, this morality would be abolished, too, *eo ipso*: it would no longer be needed, it would no longer *consider itself* necessary.
>
> Whoever examines the conscience of the [citizen] today will have to pull the same imperative out of a thousand moral folds and hideouts— the imperative of herd timidity: "we want that some day there should be *nothing any more to be afraid of*!" Some day—throughout [the world], the will and way to . . . [someday] is now called "progress."[29]

In Nietzsche's view, all of modernity's efforts to make scientific and moral *progress* are pointing toward a great cultural shift that heralds the next level of evolution, the end of human history and the beginning of the age of the overman. Like it or not, Nietzsche says, science and philosophy do not provide us with meaning; we create it. And like it or not, religion does not provide us with salvation: God is dead.

God Is Dead

Nietzsche claimed he was the first to have "discovered" the death of God. In part, he meant that the *idea of God* has lost its full creative force, its full power. Science and technology are usurping God's place in people's

Inasmuch as at all times, as long as there have been human beings, there have also been herds of men (clans, communities, tribes, peoples, states, churches) and always a great many people who obeyed, compared with the small number of those commanding . . . it may fairly be assumed that the need for [herding together] is now innate in the average man. . . .

Friedrich Nietzsche

Those who claim to be hurt by words must be led to expect nothing as compensation. Otherwise, once they learn they can get something by claiming to be hurt, they will go into the business of being offended.

Jonathan Rauch

Almost two thousand years,
and no new god!

   Friedrich Nietzsche

"Faith" means not *wanting*
to know.

   Friedrich Nietzsche

lives. The full extent of the dethronement of God is not yet felt by the great masses, who still *believe that they believe* in God. Yet if we dig deep into our own psyches, Nietzsche prophesied, we will discover that we no longer have ultimate faith in God: Our true faith is in scientific and technological progress.

Moreover, Nietzsche thought there is no turning back; authentic faith in God is not possible in the modern world. God is dead and we have killed him, with "progress," with "optimism," with faith in this world. Yet so deeply ingrained is the language of God, the idea of God, that we are unaware of the great spiritual shift. The news of God's death has not reached us—that is, it has not penetrated to our very bones. We worship, but falsely. Our faith is empty at bottom. And even though some of us may sense that the old religions are dead and dying, we remain unable to face the consequences of life without God.

And terrible those consequences can be. If there is no God, Nietzsche said, then all values must be revalued. In one of the most famous passages in Western philosophy, Nietzsche, the prophet of the death of God, delivered his message in the form of a parable:

> *The madman.*—Have you not heard of the madman who lit a lantern in the bright morning hours, ran to the market place, and cried incessantly: "I seek God! I seek God!"—As many of those who did not believe in God were standing around just then, he provoked much laughter. Has he got lost? asked one. Did he lose his way like a child? asked another. Or is he hiding? Is he afraid of us? Has he gone on a voyage? emigrated?—Thus they yelled and laughed.
>
>   The madman jumped into their midst and pierced them with his eyes. "Whither is God?" he cried; "I will tell you. *We have killed him*—you and I. All of us are his murderers. But how did we do this? How could we drink up the sea? Who gave us the sponge to wipe away the entire horizon? What were we doing when we unchained the earth from its sun? Whither is it moving now? Whither are we moving? Away from all suns? Are we not plunging continually? Backward, sideward, forward, in all directions? Is there still any up or down? Are we not straying as through an infinite nothing? Do we not feel the breath of empty space? Has it not become colder? Is not night continually closing in on us? Do we not need to light lanterns in the morning? Do we hear nothing as yet of the noise of the gravediggers who are burying God? Do we smell nothing yet of the divine decomposition? Gods, too, decompose. God is dead. God remains dead. And we have killed him."[30]

This parable must be understood in light of Nietzsche's overall cultural critique, in which he predicted the decline of Christianity. That is, he saw the world as no longer innocent. Copernicus and Galileo had forever changed our sense of scale: The earth is a tiny, virtually invisible speck in a massive, purposeless universe. "What were we doing when we unchained the earth from its sun?" This new universe has no fixed center: "Is there still any up or down? Are we not straying as through an infinite nothing?" Darwin had forever altered our sense of ourselves as God's special creation. The new image of merely-human beings is ignoble: We are but one species among thousands struggling to survive, descendants of some primordial ooze.

What the masses think of as "progress" has come at a great price: the price of a way of life, the price of our vision of ourselves. It is difficult to comprehend the enormous scale of this change, this death of a worldview, Nietzsche insisted. Indeed, some of us may lack the intelligence, the courage, and the will to comprehend it.

> How shall we comfort ourselves, the murderers of all murderers? What was holiest and mightiest of all that the world has yet owned has bled to death under our knives: who will wipe this blood off us? What water is there for us to clean ourselves? What festivals of atonement, what sacred games shall we have to invent? Is not the greatness of this deed too great for us? Must we not ourselves become gods simply to appear worthy of it? There has never been a greater deed; and whoever is born after us—for the sake of this deed he will belong to a higher history than all history hitherto.[31]

Nihilism

According to Nietzsche, the death of God leads to nihilism. From the Latin word for "nothing," **nihilism** refers to the belief that the universe lacks objective meaning and purpose. Consequently, moral, social, and political values are *creative interpretations*; they reflect their subjective origins. Without God, there can be no objective base for values.

According to Nietzsche, nihilism was the wave of the future (our present). He predicted that as more and more people perceive religious values to be empty and science as having no meaning or purpose to offer us, a sense of emptiness will initially prevail: "It all amounts to nothing. Life is a cosmic accident. There is no supernatural order; no divinely or rationally ordained goal." Without God, without *the* goal, what is left? Only many goals; only *this* momentary goal. Without God, we can turn only to ourselves.

Since there is no objective meaning, Zarathustra's new "law tablet" (which replaces the Ten Commandments of the dead God) rests on the will to power:

> For one should make no mistake about the meaning of the title that this gospel of the future wants to bear. "*The Will to Power*: Attempt at a Revaluation of All Values"—in this formulation a countermovement finds expression . . . a movement that in some future will take

Holding on to opinions is like holding a live fish; a little wiggling and they slip away. Once the fish is dead, one holds it more securely—it has become a conviction.

George Linville

NIHILISM

From Latin for "nothing"; belief that the universe lacks meaning and purpose.

Nihilism as the wave of the future: The Nazis claimed Nietzsche as one of their philosophical fathers. While their doctrine of power and the master race often echoes Nietzschean language, no mass movement could ever reflect Nietzsche's philosophy of self-overcoming. How many overmen can you spot in this crowd?

the place of this perfect nihilism . . . and certainly can come only after and out of it. For why has the advent of nihilism become *necessary*? Because the values we have had hitherto thus draw their final consequence; because nihilism represents the ultimate logical conclusion of our great values and ideals—because we must experience nihilism before we can find out what these "values" really had.—We require, sometime, *new values*.[32]

In a nihilistic universe, what determines what counts? What determines which physique is beautiful? What determines whether it is better to be meek or arrogant? According to Nietzsche, the answers are always found in the particular, subjective interests of individuals and groups. We *choose* value systems and philosophies based on our sense of power: Which interpretation gives me and my kind advantage over others?

Overman

OVERMAN

Nietzsche's "higher type," a more-than-human being that will emerge only by overcoming the false idols of conventional morality and religion; announced in *Thus Spake Zarathustra*.

The death of God signals both a great calamity and a great opportunity—depending on the individual's perspective. It is a calamity to those inferior types who cannot bear to stand on their own. It is a glorious opportunity for the fearless, the brave, the overman.

The **overman** is a new "higher type" that will emerge out of the weakness and hypocrisies of the common herd. He is more than a merely-human being. Zarathustra says the overman cannot emerge except through struggle and by abolishing the false idols of conventional morality and decadent religion.

> But my fervent will to create impels me ever again toward man; thus is the hammer impelled toward the stone, O men, in the stone there sleeps an image, the image of my images. Alas, that it must sleep in the hardest, the ugliest stone! Now my hammer rages cruelly against its prison. Pieces of rock rain from the stone; what is that to me? I want to perfect it; for a shadow came to me—the stillest and lightest of all things once came to me. The beauty of the overman came to me as a shadow. O my brothers, what are the gods to me now?
>
> Thus spoke Zarathustra.[33]

Without God to limit us, to define us, to smother us, we can finally grow "beyond man." In Nietzsche's philosophy, "man," meaning the merely-human being, is defined in terms of God. We are created in "the image of God" and remain perpetual "children of God." When God dies, we are left without identity or purpose, in a vast universe that "just is." The same science that has given us so much has robbed us of purpose. The deeper science looks, the less it finds: molecules, atoms, electrons, quarks, energy . . . the abyss.

Nietzsche, the prophet of the next stage in human evolution, predicts that the next order is virtually a new species in terms of its psychological and spiritual differences from mere man. Having no permanent, absolute, universal identity without God, we must create one. The overman is Nietzsche's answer to the pessimism and nihilism that follow in the wake of God's death:

> The greatest recent event—that "God is dead," that the belief in the Christian god has become unbelievable—is already beginning to cast its first shadows. . . . The event itself is far too great, too distant, too remote for the multitude's capacity for comprehension even for the tidings of it to be thought of as having *arrived* as yet. Much less may one suppose that many people know as yet *what* this event really means—and how much must collapse now that [the possibility of] faith has been undermined because it was built upon this faith [in God's existence], propped up by it, grown into it; for example, the whole of our . . . morality.[34]

Nietzsche never fully developed a picture of the overman. Of course, given that the overman is farther from mere man than we are from an ape, no merely-human being can comprehend the overman. Nietzsche readily admitted that he is only the prophet of the higher type, adding, "But from time to time I may be granted a glance—only one glance—at something perfect, something that has attained its end, something happy, powerful, triumphant."[35]

We should be mindful of everything, for we can interpret everything.

Hermann Hesse

If we have our own why of life, we shall get along with almost any how.

Friedrich Nietzsche

I mistrust all systematizers and I avoid them. The will to a system is a lack of integrity.

Friedrich Nietzsche

An Iconoclast Looks at Education

I have never tired of calling attention to the *despiritualizing* influence of our current science-industry. The hard [servitude] to which the tremendous range of the sciences condemns every scholar today is a main reason why those with a fuller, richer, *profounder* disposition no longer find a congenial education and congenial *educators*. There is nothing of which our culture suffers more than of the super-abundance of pretentious jobbers and fragments of humanity; our universities are, *against* their will, the real hothouses for this kind of withering of the instincts of the spirit. And the whole of Europe already has some idea of this—power politics deceives nobody. . . .

To call the taming of an animal its "improvement" sounds almost like a joke to our ears. Whoever knows what goes on in menageries doubts that the beasts are "improved" there. They are weakened, they are made less harmful, and through the depressive effect of fear, through pain, through wounds, and through hunger they become sickly beasts. . . .

. . . What the "higher schools" . . . really achieve is a brutal training, designed to prepare huge numbers of young men, with as little loss of time as possible, to become usable, abusable. . . . "Higher education" and huge numbers—that is a contradiction to start with. All higher education belongs

only to the exception: one must be privileged to have the right to such a privilege. All great, all beautiful things can never be common property . . . What conditions the decline of German culture? That "higher education" is no longer a privilege. . . .

. . . No one is any longer free to give his children a noble education: our "higher schools" are all set up for the most ambiguous mediocrity, with their teachers, curricula, and teaching aims. And everywhere an indecent haste prevails, as if something would be lost if the young man of twenty-three were not yet "finished," or if he did not yet know the answer to the "main question": *which* calling? A higher kind of human being,

Slave Morality

Though we may never fully grasp exactly what or who the overman is, we can perhaps glimpse its shadow indirectly by taking a look at the actions and beliefs of what amounts to its opposite: the slave or underman.

Underman, from the German *untermensch*, is one of the terms Nietzsche uses for the "merely human" type of person who cannot face being alone in a godless universe. Underman refuses to be an individual, does not even exist as an individual. Underman turns to the group or herd (Kierkegaard's "the crowd") for power, identity, and purpose. The inferior individual's awareness of his or her own inferiority produces envy and resentment of all "higher types" and "elitist" value systems.

In an effort to control their superiors, members of the herd create **slave morality**, a value system based on guilt, fear, and a distortion of the will to power in which the characteristics of the inferior type—humility, passivity, dependency—are praised as virtues, while the characteristics of the superior type—love of domination, delight in one's own talents, fearlessness—are condemned as arrogance and coldheartedness. Slave morality

UNDERMAN

Nietzsche's term for the type of person who cannot face being alone in a godless universe, an inferior individual seeking safety and identity in a group or from another; characterized by resentment and hypocrisy.

if I may say so, does not like "callings," precisely because he knows himself to be called. He has time, he takes time, he does not even think of "finishing": at thirty one is, in the sense of high culture, a beginner, a child. Our overcrowded secondary schools, our overworked, stupefied secondary-school teachers, are a scandal: for one to defend such conditions . . . there may perhaps be *causes*—reasons there are none.

Friedrich Nietzsche
Twilight of the Idols, in *The Portable Nietzsche*, trans. Walter Kaufmann (New York: Penguin, 1968), pp. 502, 508, 510–511.

In Twilight of the Idols, *Nietzsche says: "'Higher education' and huge numbers—that is a contradiction to start with. All higher education belongs only to the exception: one must be privileged to have the right to such a privilege. All great and beautiful things can never be common property . . . What conditions the decline of . . . culture? That 'higher education' is no longer a privilege. . . . our 'higher schools' are all set up for the most ambiguous mediocrity, with their teachers, curricula, and teaching aims. And everywhere an indecent haste prevails . . ." Have modern technology and egalitarianism made it possible for all, or most, of us to be "well educated"?*

creates inhibitions, false ideals of equality, restrictive duties "owed" to our inferiors, and weakening of strong instincts by "bad conscience." The herd is always hostile to the individual.

In other words, slave morality tries to convince the powerful that they should protect the weak. According to Nietzsche, slave morality arose when rules conquered instincts in ancient Greece. Today, rationalistic Greek and Christian ethics are the two chief sources of slave morality in modern culture. Fairness, equality, moderation, "stepping aside," refusing to claim the full rights accompanying superior ability and talent, and fear of confrontation are all characteristics of slave morality.

History up to the present is a record of the withering away of a noble *master morality*, as century by century the virtues of the herd weakened Western culture, Nietzsche says, until today, we resist even talk about higher types. We claim that all people are fundamentally equal. Zarathustra speaks:

You higher men learn this from me: in the market place nobody believes in higher men. And if you want to speak there, very well! But the mob blinks: "We are all equal."

SLAVE MORALITY

In Nietzschean philosophy, a distortion of the will to power in which the characteristics of the inferior type (underman) are praised as virtues, and the characteristics of the superior type (overman) are condemned as arrogance and cold-heartedness; a morality of inhibitions, equality, restrictive duties, and "bad conscience."

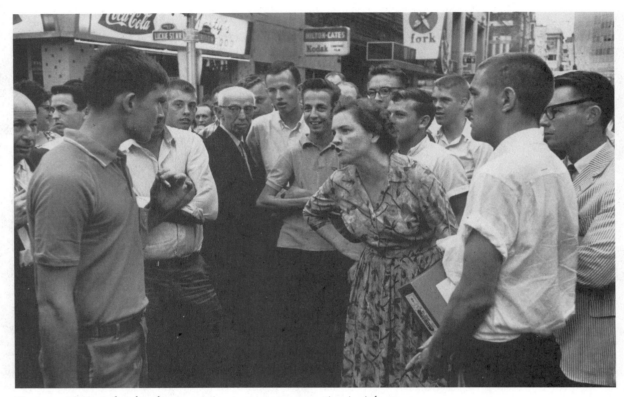

During a 1963 civil rights demonstration to protest segregation in Atlanta, an angry mob abused the demonstrators with kicks, punches, and burning cigarettes. This anonymous woman passerby confronted the mob for its crude, herd-like behavior. According to Nietzsche, "the herd" is always hostile to the genuine individual.

"You higher men"—thus blinks the mob—"there are no higher men, we are all equal, man is man; before God we are all equal."

Before God! But now this God has died. And before the mob we do not want to be equal. You higher men, go away from the market place![36]

Philosophical Query

Do you think today's "marketplace" mentality discourages excellence in individuals? Using specific examples, discuss why or why not.

Ressentiment

Slave morality originates from a deep form of psychically polluting resentment that Nietzsche always referred to with the French word *ressentiment*. In the following passage from *Toward a Genealogy of Morals*, Nietzsche distinguishes between the slave morality of the underman and the master morality of the overman:

> The slaves' revolt in morals begins with this, that *ressentiment* itself becomes creative and gives birth to values: the *ressentiment* of those who are denied the real reaction, that of the deed, and who compensate with an imaginary revenge. Whereas all noble morality begins out of a triumphant affirmation of oneself, slave morality immediately says No to what comes from outside, to what is different, to what is not oneself: and *this* No is its creative deed. This reversal of the value-positing glance—this *necessary* direction outward instead of back to oneself—is of the nature of *ressentiment*: to come into being, slave morality requires an outside world, a counterworld; physiologically speaking, it requires external stimuli in order to react at all: its action is always at bottom a reaction.[37]

In other words, slave morality is alien to true individuality. It is so opposed to the authentic individual, that his or her own self-creating urges and impulses are stifled in favor of "external stimuli" that function as guidelines from others and from the herd. Slave morality is inauthentic (phony and uncreative) because it is "always a reaction," never an originating impulse. (See Chapter 12 for more on authenticity.) Slave morality settles for the "imaginary revenge" of the afterlife: "God will punish the bad people since we are too weak to do so."

The underman fears "the other" whether in the form of the authentic individual or in the merely different. Thus, slave morality encourages conformity; national, racial, gender, and religious bigotry; and unthinking patriotism: "slave morality immediately says No to what comes from outside, to what is different, to what is not oneself." The underman lacks the god-like confidence necessary for "the value-positing glance," the ability to impose one's own values without reference to "external stimuli" for guidance and security.

From a healthy aesthetic perspective, underman is repulsive, characterized by weakness, evasion, hypocrisy, and so forth. Slave morality is a morality of resignation, deferment, withdrawal from the full range of life, and prohibition. In reality, the underman does not reject the lusty, fateful, self-affirming, creative aspects of the human psyche because they are bad, but because the underman is too weak, sick, and corrupt to live up to them—and out of *ressentiment* wants to prevent others from living up to them, as well.

Philosophical Query

As you might expect, Nietzsche's characterization of slave morality was and remains controversial. Do you think it is dangerous? Is it unfair to expect people not to have some *ressentiment*? Is today's tendency to see many people as "victims" a reflection of slave morality? Discuss.

Another century of readers—and the mind itself will stink.

Friedrich Nietzsche

That everyone can learn to read will ruin in the long run not only writing, but thinking too.

Friedrich Nietzsche

If society consisted of highly valuable individuals, it would be worthwhile to adapt to it, but generally it is dominated by weak and stupid people and thus suffocates all higher individual values.

Marie-Louise von Franz

Nietzsche and the Nazis

Nietzsche's characterization of the overman in terms of a "master race" and "master morality" led to the misguided and unfortunate appropriation of his name by Adolf Hitler's Nazi party. Hitler was encouraged by Nietzsche's sister, Elisabeth Förster-Nietzsche. Like the Nazis, she and her husband, Bernard Förster, were indeed Aryan supremacist racists who failed to understand that by "master race" Nietzsche meant "psychological type," not biological, racial, ethnic, or national group. In her hunger for approval and resentful will to power, Nietzsche's sister destroyed much of his work and encouraged Hitler's public adoration of her brother as a philosophical support for Nazism.

Yet it is clear that no anti-Semite wrote the following, produced more than two generations before the Nazis even existed:

Incidentally, the whole problem of the *Jews* exists only in nation states, for here their energy and higher intelligence, their accumulated capital of spirit and will, gathered through a long school of suffering, must become so preponderant as to arouse mass envy and hatred. In almost all contemporary nations, therefore—in direct proportion to the degree to which they act up nationalistically—the literary obscenity is spreading of leading the Jews to slaughter

Master Morality

MASTER MORALITY

In Nietzschean philosophy, the *aesthetic* honor code of the overman; morality that looks only to the authentic individual (overman) for values that transcend the slave's good–evil dichotomy with: glorious–degrading; honorable–dishonorable; refined–vulgar, and so on; "good" equals "noble" and "evil" equals "vulgar."

If there are two fundamentally different types of people (underman and overman), then there must be two radically different types of morality. One universal standard cannot apply equally to the "common herd" and the superior, perfected overman.

Although both types possess the *will to power*, they differ significantly in their approaches to power. For the overman, the will to power is expressed openly, honestly, and nobly through exuberant, life-affirming self-creation and self-imposition. That is, the overman creates—experiments with—a "new law tablet," a code of values that is the opposite of the weak underman's slave morality. Because the underman lacks courage and nobility, he or she must resort to appeals to a "father God," to neurotic guilt, and demands for pity (dressed up as an "obligation" to show compassion). In the herd, the will to individual power is perverted through manipulation, *ressentiment*, and indirection shaped by feelings of gross inadequacy—it is not expressed honestly and openly.

Master morality, in contrast to slave morality, is an *aesthetic-heroic* code of honor. That is, the overman looks only to him- or herself for value. And value is defined in aesthetic terms: noble–ignoble (shameful); glorious–degrading; honorable–dishonorable; refined–vulgar; and so on. In simple terms, for the overman, "good" equals "noble" and "evil" equals "vulgar."

According to Nietzsche:

To be unable to take one's own enemies, accidents, and misdeeds seriously for long—that is the sign of strong and rich natures. . . .

as scapegoats of every conceivable public and internal misfortune. . . . I should like to know how much one must forgive a people in a total accounting when they have had the most painful history of all peoples, not without the fault of all of us, and when they have produced the noblest man (Christ), the purest sage (Spinoza), the most powerful book, and the most effective moral law in the world.*

The following selections from *Human, All-Too-Human* reflect Nietzsche's great, unwavering distaste for "true believers," "groupthink," and mass movements:

And to say it once more. Public opinions—private lazinesses.

Enemies of truth. Convictions are more dangerous enemies of truth than lies.

Not suitable as a party member. Whoever thinks much is not suitable as a party member: he soon thinks himself right through the party.**

*Friedrich Nietzsche
Human, All-Too-Human, in *The Portable Nietzsche,* trans. Walter Kaufmann (New York: Penguin, 1968), section 475.

**Ibid., sections 482, 483, 579.

Although Adolf Hitler, with the help of Nietzsche's sister, Elisabeth Förster-Nietzsche, tried to take advantage of Nietzsche's growing reputation by claiming that the Nazi doctrine of "Aryan supremacy" had roots in Nietzschean philosophy, there is no evidence that Hitler ever read a word of Nietzsche's philosophy. In this publicity photo, Hitler gazes "admiringly" at a bust of Nietzsche.

Such a man simply shakes off with one shrug much vermin that would have buried itself deep in others; here alone is it also possible—assuming that is possible at all on earth—that there be real "*love* of one's enemies." How much respect has a noble person for his enemies! . . . Conversely, imagine "the enemy" as conceived by a man of *ressentiment*—and here precisely is his deed, his creation: he has conceived "the evil enemy," "*the evil one*"—and indeed as the fundamental concept from which he then derives, as an after-image and counterinstance, a "good one"—himself.[38]

There are no evil thoughts except one: the refusal to think.

Ayn Rand

It is better to be envied
than pitied.

   Herodotus

Since each morality originates as a reflection of those it serves, it is not surprising that slave morality reflects envy, *ressentiment*, authoritarian conformity, collectivism, and obligations to all others, who are defined as "equals." Master morality, in stark contrast, reflects the overman: proud, fierce, courageous, self-sufficient, glorious, bold, and so forth.

Whereas the overman's morality begins with her affirmation of her own beloved self, the underman's morality begins with the invention of the "evil other," the *evil one*. For the overman, "bad" is the afterimage. For the underman, "good" is the afterimage. Thus, master morality is positive in its orientation; slave morality is negative.

Whereas the overman shrugs off the "vermin" of guilt, regret, self-pity, envy, and *ressentiment*, the underman's entire moral code clings to them as safety checks on such "evil" impulses as self-love, joy in the midst of mistakes, and happiness here and now.

If Nietzsche is correct, we live in the twilight of a culture. The "horizon is free" because no new value system and vision have replaced the old dying one. Those who live through the twilight of the old beliefs will experience confusion, fear, a strong desire to hold on to idols; but they will also experience unlimited opportunities for growth. In the twilight of our idols, we are handed the opportunity to fashion our own way. It is up to us to define—to actually create—our very selves.

Zarathustra says:

No victor believes in
chance.

   Friedrich Nietzsche

"*I teach you the overman.* Man is something that shall be overcome. What have you done to overcome him?

"All beings so far have created something beyond themselves; and do you want to be the ebb of this great flood and even go back to the beasts rather than overcome man? What is the ape to man? A laughingstock or a painful embarrassment. And man shall be just that for the overman: a laughingstock or a painful embarrassment. You have made your way from worm to man, and much in you is still worm. Once you were apes, and even now, too, man is more ape than any ape. . . .

"Man is a rope, tied between beast and overman—a rope over an abyss. A dangerous across, a dangerous on-the-way, a dangerous looking-back, a dangerous shuddering and stopping. . . .

"I love all those who are as heavy drops, falling one by one out of the dark cloud that hangs over men; they herald the advent of lightning, and, as heralds, they perish.

"Behold, I am the herald of the lightning and a heavy drop from the cloud; but this lightning is called *overman*."[39]

The very same conditions of nihilism and value annihilation that despirit, discourage, and frighten the underman exhilarate and inspire the overman. Having overcome merely human resentment and self-loathing, overman *looks forward to being precisely what and who he (or she) is.*

The Eternal Recurrence

In *The Gay Science*, Nietzsche articulates his doctrine of the **eternal recurrence**, the idea that everything that is happening now will one day happen again—in exactly the same way. Based on principles of Newtonian physics and Darwinian evolution, the doctrine holds that: 1) Given the laws of thermodynamics that neither matter nor energy are created or destroyed; and 2) given that the past reaches backward to infinity; and 3) given that natural selection—not divinely ordained creation—accounts for human evolution; 4) it follows that every possible configuration of the universe must have already occurred an infinite number of times.[40]

This means that the future—our future, yours and mine—has already been. Everything that has yet to happen in our lives has already happened! That is, every possible history (configuration of matter, energy, and evolution) will occur and recur infinitely: Since the basic stuff of existence will never increase or decrease, it must continually and continuously recombine in every possible way.

Of course, experientially and psychologically, we experience each occurrence of this history as if it were the first and only occurrence. And—most significantly for Nietzsche—some occurrence is the first occurrence, so how we fashion ourselves the first time is how we will be again and again, forever and ever.

Nietzsche expressed great delight in his "discovery" that the infinity of recurrence revealed that not only are we the creators of ourselves and our lives *this time*, but: *Every act, thought, and feeling recurs eternally, exactly as it occurs the first time.* That fact (as Nietzsche saw it) is both our heaviest burden and the key to joyful wisdom.

Zarathustra says that his teaching "despises all woeful wisdom," the wisdom "which is always sighing: 'All is vain.'"[41] But all is vain only to the inferior type, the merely human. To the higher type, the heaviest burden is also the greatest good news. The *curse* of the underman is the *gospel* of the overman:

> *The heaviest burden.*—What if a demon crept after you one day or night in your loneliest solitude and said to you: "This life, as you live it now and have lived it, you will have to live again and again, times without number; and there will be nothing new in it, but every pain and every joy and every thought and sigh and all the unspeakably small and great in your life must return to you, and everything in the same series and same sequence—and in the same way this spider and this moonlight among the trees, and in the same way this moment and I myself. The eternal hourglass of existence will be turned again and again—and you with it, you dust of dust!"—Would you not throw yourself down and gnash your teeth and curse the demon who thus spoke?[42]

ETERNAL RECURRENCE
Nietzschean idea that everything that is happening now will one day happen again—in exactly the same way. Based on principles of Newtonian physics and Darwinian evolution, the doctrine holds that every possible configuration of the universe must have already occurred an infinite number of times.

. . . [I]f you ever wanted one moment twice, if ever you said: "You please me, happiness, instant, moment!" then you wanted *everything* to return!

Friedrich Nietzsche

Did you ever say Yes to joy? O my friends, then you said Yes to *all* woe as well. All things are chained and entwined together, all things are in love. . . .

Friedrich Nietzsche

The idea of eternal recurrence is depressing, overwhelming, crushing to those consumed by envy and resentment, to those exhausted by self-pity, to those fixated on *what life has done to them*. But to healthier types the idea of eternal recurrence brings the exhilarating realization that: *Whatever I do this time, I commit myself to for eternity; whoever I make myself into this time, I make myself into for eternity*. Once more, we see the effects of Nietzschean perspectivism. What crushes the underman nourishes the overman:

> Or have you experienced a tremendous moment in which you would have answered him: "You are a god and never did I hear anything more divine!" If this thought gained power over you it would, as you are now, transform and perhaps crush you; the question in all and everything: "do you want this again and again, times without number?" would lie as the heaviest burden upon all your actions. Or how well disposed towards yourself and towards life would you have to become to have *no greater desire* than for this ultimate eternal sanction and seal?[43]

Thus, for Nietzsche, how we react to the possibility of eternal recurrence reveals who we are, exposes our judgment of ourselves, and hence of life itself. The die, once cast, cannot be called back. It is up to us to live—from this moment on—in such a way that we will shout "Yes!" with joy and delight, with seriousness and exuberance, to living just this life forever. If we can do that, we will not fear our fate; we will love it.

Philosophical Query

Reflect on the possibility of eternal recurrence. What difference do you think belief in eternal recurrence could make in your life? Considering the possibility of "eternal" glory, should you live heroically? Think also about eternally repeating low or shameful episodes. Do you think there might be merit in using the doctrine of eternal recurrence as kind of a moral tune-up, a way of reorienting ourselves from time to time? Can you think of any negative consequences to using the doctrine that way? Discuss and explain.

Amor Fati

In the absence of God, Nietzsche says, we must redeem ourselves with the *sacred Yes to life* expressed through **amor fati**, the love of our specific fate expressed as joyous affirmation of the eternal recurrence. Nihilism teaches us that there is no divine purpose or design that gives meaning and quality to our lives. Science shows us that matter follows inexorable laws. God is dead. What is left?

. . . I see many people die because they judge that life is not worth living. I see others paradoxically getting killed for the ideas and illusions that give them a reason for living (what is called a reason for living is also an excellent reason for dying). I therefore conclude that the meaning of life is the most urgent of questions.

Albert Camus

AMOR FATI

Nietzsche's term meaning "the love of fate"; expressed as joyous affirmation of the eternal recurrence and delight that everything is exactly as and what it is.

What alone can *our* teaching be?—That no one *gives* a human being his qualities: not God, not society, not his parents or ancestors, not *he himself*. . . . *No one* is accountable for existing at all, or for being constituted as he is, or for living in the circumstances and surroundings in which he lives. The fatality of nature cannot be disentangled from the fatality of all that which has been and will be. He is *not* the result of special design, a will, a purpose . . . it is absurd to want to *hand over* his nature to some purpose or other. *We* invented the concept of "purpose": in reality purpose is *lacking*. . . . One is necessary, one is a piece of fate . . . there exists nothing which could judge, measure, compare, condemn the whole. . . . *nothing exists apart from the whole*. . . . We deny God; in denying God, we deny accountability: only by doing *that* do we redeem the world.[44]

Amor fati blesses everything exactly as it is. Through *amor fati*, we realize that we exist as parts of a complex whole that can be only precisely what it is and cannot be otherwise. *Amor fati* cures us of the corruption imposed by modernity and slave morality; it restores us to innocence by redeeming us from the ancient concepts of sin and guilt before others and before God. Nietzsche says:

My formula for greatness in a human being is *amor fati*: that one wants nothing to be other than it is, not in the future, not in the past, not in all eternity. Not merely to endure that which happens of necessity, still less to dissemble it . . . but to *love* it. . . .[45]

> He who is afraid to look back, alas, has already done so in his own heart.
>
> *George Linville*

Commentary

Nietzsche was nothing if not authentic. And as disturbing as much of his philosophy can be, there is no escaping its power to provoke a response—often a passionate response. His assertive denial of objective meaning has influenced a whole generation of scholars and literary critics (called *new critics* and *deconstructionists*). Nietzsche's influence on postmodern scholarship cannot be overestimated. Nietzschean influences on current critical theories are found in the rejection of the possibility of unbiased (objective) interpretation, the view that all scholarship is autobiography, and unapologetic self-reference on the part of academic authors.

In the postmodern world, a world without objective value, without God, without "the truth," all that is left seems to be "my truth"—or more precisely, "my truths." Ironically, however, when nihilistic self-promotion becomes the trend and "being an individual" becomes a consciously contrived goal, Nietzschean originality and authenticity disappear. Being "a Nietzschean" is no more possible than following someone else's orders to be free! After all, it was Nietzsche himself who insisted that "Those who

> I *want* no "believers"; I think I am too sarcastic to believe in myself.
>
> *Friedrich Nietzsche*

understand me, understand that I can have no disciples." There is bitter (but not unexpected) irony in the notion of being "a Nietzschean."

Nietzsche's critique of contemporary culture is subtle and profound. On the whole, our culture does seem to have lost faith in the very idea of a single true religion and a common, shared value system that asserts more than sweeping generalities. Education seems to have lost any central focus and seems increasingly reduced to training without purpose or to efforts by various groups (herds?) to enforce their individual points of view (today we call them agendas). Even the current national debate over school curricula has postmodern Nietzschean roots: If there is no objective meaning, then everything is a "point of view," an expression of "diversity." If everything is a point of view, why should I have to accept your point of view or you mine? If everything is a point of view, there is no true history, no true interpretation of literature, no clear hierarchy of values.

Though it is not currently *politically correct* to suggest that we are not all equal, that some of us are entitled to more than the rest, we do not appear to believe the doctrine of equality that we preach: each new wave of immigrants ("the evil other") generates hostility, fear, and resentment. We certainly seem to be a culture searching for something, some clear, unifying set of values.

So it is, that for us, Nietzschean questions remain: Is God dead? If so, what next? If not, whence our widespread resentments, confusions, and fears? Are we all equal in any significant sense? If not, what then? Can we bear to ask these questions? Dare we not ask them?

Clearly, Nietzsche was more effective at attacking ideas than he was at articulating a positive philosophy (at least in the traditional sense of articulating a philosophy). His rhetoric is often histrionic, and his attitudes toward "inferior types" offend our modern sensibilities. But there are times when I find the *idea* of the idea of eternal recurrence useful as a moral and psychological thermometer. Can I, dare I, say *Yes!* to every moment of my life? Should I? Am I presently living in a way such that the idea of reliving today invigorates me, rather than leaves me flat, or worse, leaves me despondent? And if I cannot say *Yes!*—why not? If I resent anything, why do I not rise to the occasion and change it—or rise to the occasion and embrace (accept) it?

Perhaps there is power in sometimes *acting as if God is dead*, acting as if only you and I can *redeem the world* by courageous, responsible, and decent action. For those of us who believe in God, such an *acting-as-if* can remind us to live as friends and helpers of God, not merely onlookers or children in the childish sense.

Perhaps those of us who do not believe in God and who are tempted to worship at the twin altars of science and technology might benefit from a healthy form of skepticism as we face the seductive promises of salvation via science, the Internet, medical breakthroughs, new "learning technologies," and so forth.

To dream here perhaps of equal rights, equal training, equal claims and obligations: that is a typical sign of shallow-mindedness.

Friedrich Nietzsche

Great Man is always at ease; Petty Man is always on edge.

Confucius

Perhaps we might all benefit from the occasional bracing call to grow up and own up to our own lives.

I leave the last word to Nietzsche, a hopeful word, expressed in 1882 as a comment "For the New Year," but which speaks to the psychological possibility of renewal and affirmation of life at any moment:

> Today everyone is permitted to express his desire and dearest thoughts: so I too would like to say what I have desired of myself today and what thought was the first to cross my heart this year—what thought shall be the basis and guarantee and sweetness of all my future life! I want to learn more and more to see what is necessary in things as the beautiful in them—thus I shall become one of those who make things beautiful. *Amor fati*: may that be my love from now on! I want to wage no war against the ugly. I do not want to accuse, I do not want even to accuse the accusers. May *looking away* be my only form of negation! And, all in all: I want to be at all times hereafter only an affirmer.[46]

> I wonder how far Moses would have got if he'd taken a poll in Egypt? What would Jesus Christ have preached if he'd taken a poll in Israel?
>
> *Harry S Truman*

Summary of Main Points

1. Nietzsche saw himself as the first to recognize a profound sickness at the core of modernity. Modernity refers to the historical period of the nineteenth and twentieth centuries and a corresponding set of cultural conditions and beliefs dominated by Enlightenment ideals, including faith in science, objective truth, and rationality.

2. Influenced by Schopenhauer's pessimism, Nietzsche concluded that life itself is an irrational, purposeless striving for a pointless existence. Nietzsche disagreed with Schopenhauer in a fundamental way, however, insisting that life is governed by the will to power, a universal desire to control others and impose our values on them. Nietzsche's response to pessimism was tragic optimism, the sense of joy and vitality that accompanies the superior individual's clear-sighted imposition of his own freely chosen values on a meaningless world.

3. Nietzschean perspectivism, the contention that every view is only one among many possible interpretations, rejects the possibility of a neutral stance or perspectiveless perspective. According to Nietzsche, art or aesthetic vision (taste) is the basis of meaning, not science, not religion, not morality, not rationality.

4. According to Nietzsche, all life is governed by the will to power. This will to power is often disguised as influencing, controlling, managing, understanding, or improving life, nature, the environment, society, and human behavior. The will to power is also the basis of the distinction between good and evil.

5. Nietzsche accuses modern Western culture of being moralistic, a form of hypocrisy that resembles what Freudian psychologists refer to as a reaction formation, the name of the ego defense mechanism that attempts to prevent "dangerous" desires from being exposed and expressed by endorsing opposite attitudes and types of behavior as "barriers" against them.

6. Nietzsche claimed that he "discovered" the death of God: The idea of God had lost its

full creative force, its full power, because science and technology have usurped God's place in people's lives. Nietzsche thought that authentic faith in God is no longer possible.

7. According to Nietzsche, the death of God leads to nihilism, the belief that the universe lacks meaning and purpose, and that moral, social, and political values are creative interpretations; they reflect their subjective origins, because without God, there is no objective base for values.

8. Slave morality is a distortion of the will to power in which the characteristics of the inferior type are praised as virtues, while the characteristics of the superior type are condemned as arrogance and coldheartedness. Slave morality creates inhibitions, false ideals of equality, restrictive duties "owed" to our inferiors, and weakening of strong instincts by "bad conscience."

9. Master morality is an aesthetic-heroic code of honor. The overman looks only to him- or herself for value defined in aesthetic terms: noble–ignoble (shameful); glorious–degrading;

honorable–dishonorable; refined–vulgar; and so on; "good" equals "noble" and "evil" equals "vulgar."

10. According to Nietzsche, the death of God provides a glorious opportunity for the fearless "perfect type," the more-than-human overman. The overman is a "higher type" that will emerge out of the weakness and hypocrisies of the common herd. The overman will abolish the false idols of conventional morality and decadent religion, replacing them with master morality.

11. Eternal recurrence is the Nietzschean idea that everything that is happening now will one day happen again—in exactly the same way. Based on principles of Newtonian physics and Darwinian evolution, the doctrine holds that every possible configuration of the universe must have already occurred an infinite number of times. Through *amor fati* (the love of fate), the overman approaches the eternal recurrence with delight that everything is and eternally will be exactly as and what it is.

Study Questions

1. What is modernity? What is the disease of modernity? Explain.

2. What is pessimism and how did it influence Nietzsche's philosophy?

3. What is meant by referring to Nietzsche as an anti-philosopher? Explain.

4. What is the will to power? What role does it play in Nietzsche's philosophy?

5. What is tragic optimism? What is tragic about it? Optimistic? Why did Nietzsche reject ordinary optimism?

6. What does Nietzsche mean when he accuses modern Western culture of being moralistic? What is a reaction formation? How are the concept of being moralistic and the concept of reaction formation related?

7. Explain what is meant by characterizing master morality as an aesthetic-heroic honor code.

8. What is the eternal recurrence? In what sense is it a glorious opportunity for the overman? Is it also an opportunity for the underman?

9. What is *amor fati*? How does it relate to the eternal recurrence? Explain.

10. Who was Zarathustra? What is his relationship to the overman?

11. What did Nietzsche mean by the death of God?

12. What is nihilism and how is it related to the death of God?

13. What is the overman? How do the death of God and nihilism relate to the overman?

14. Characterize, contrast, and evaluate master morality and slave morality.

15. What is *ressentiment*, and what is its importance to Nietzsche's philosophy?

Emerging Archetypes

It is the age of Socrates again: our moral life is threatened, and our intellectual life is quickened and enlarged by the disintegration of ancient customs and beliefs. Everything is new and experimental in our ideas and our actions; nothing is established or certain any more. The rate, complexity, and variety of change in our time are without precedent . . . all forms about us are altered, from the tools that complicate our toil, to the wheels that whirl us restlessly about the earth, to the innovations in our sexual relationships, and to the hard disillusionment of our souls.

Will Durant

W hat is the role of the philosopher in contemporary society? Do philosophers have a role to play beyond that of philosophy teachers and scholars? Traditionally, the philosopher has been viewed as a detached observer, someone outside the mainstream of society. Beginning with the apocryphal story of Thales falling into a well, one still popular stereotype of the philosopher is of the befuddled, impractical critic, the character who gives advice and asks silly riddles about God making rocks too large to lift and trees falling in empty forests—but who bakes no bread. Less benign philosophical stereotypes include that of the icy, impersonal *logic chopper*, the individual who has mastered the art of exposing contradictions and ambiguities in other people's arguments and beliefs, but who has no positive, practical skills to offer. A more charitable picture of the contemporary philosopher is of the well-intentioned intellectual who asks "good questions" but who, nonetheless, fails to understand and come to grips with "practical matters."

The popular notion of the philosopher as somehow irrelevant to modern life probably owes a great deal to the importance of objectivity and rationality for most modern philosophers. With the notable exceptions of such philosophers as Kierkegaard, James, and Nietzsche (Chapters 12, 13, and 14), most modern philosophers write in a detached, impersonal voice. Even Marx (Chapter 11) wrote in an impersonal voice when he said that the time had come for philosophers to change the world.

In this last chapter, we will take a selective look at some contemporary philosophers who see the role of the philosopher as something more than impersonal observer and commentator. These philosophers do not separate themselves from their philosophical practices, nor do they think that philosophy must be impersonal and uninvolved with politics and social policy. I have chosen to refer to such philosophers under the broad heading of *philosophical advocates*. A **philosophical advocate** is a philosopher whose work identifies, clarifies, and actively opposes a perceived injustice; philosophical advocates give philosophical credence to personal experience based on gender, ethnic background, or social status.

Contemporary philosophers disagree among themselves over whether or not it is proper for philosophers—as philosophers—to base philosophical views on *autobiography* (the philosopher's specific life circumstances) or *advocacy* ("taking sides" by promoting specific social and political positions based on the philosopher's gender, race, social, ethnic, or economic circumstances). The more traditional philosophical camp argues that philosophers should strive for detached (objective) rationality—not become personally attached to their philosophical conclusions. The other camp argues that philosophers have both *rights* and *obligations* to take personal stands on timely issues—as philosophers.

Philosophical advocates refuse to remain on the sidelines of the major social controversies of our time. These include, but are not limited to, issues of racial and ethnic equality, women's rights and gender influences. I believe that new philosophical archetypes are likely to emerge from some form of philosophical advocacy as more and more contemporary philosophers refuse to separate themselves from their philosophical work. I also believe that it is unwise to predict precisely who the chief exemplars of these new archetypes will be, since that determination must be made over time. Consequently, I recommend treating this last chapter as a kind of *philosophical preview of coming attractions* indicating some (but not all) fertile and important areas of contemporary philosophical activity.

It has been suggested that the public-private distinction is the single most important issue for feminism, and indeed that it is, in the end, what feminism is all about.

Susan Mendus

Public and Private Philosophy

In simplified terms, we can characterize the current critique of modern philosophy as follows: With rare exceptions, Western philosophers have failed to recognize that they have personal, social, gendered, and ethnic perspectives. Consequently, some modern and contemporary philosophers remain blind to the fact that their philosophy reflects the interests of only a small portion of the human community.

Too often, this blindness results in a separation of professional philosophy from the "real-life" concerns of women and all persons not of the typical (privileged) philosophical classes: highly educated white males. The result, it is argued, is a tradition that has systematically excluded or marginalized the voices of philosophers concerned with family matters, children's interests, and other traditionally "unphilosophical" and "private" matters.

According to feminist philosophers, one source of this blindness is the masculinization of philosophy. We will use material from the feminist philosopher Susan Bordo's critique of the "Cartesian masculinization" of philosophy to get a representative view of a feminist critique of "masculinizing" principles that were established at the very beginning of the

idiot: originally from the Greek *idiotes*, a disparaging term for private person; one who does not participate in community affairs; one who shuns the body politic; sometimes translated as "good for nothing."

Henry David Thoreau (1817–1862)

Martin Luther King, Jr.'s philosophy was greatly influenced by Henry David Thoreau. Perhaps the most famous expression of civil disobedience in this country is a lecture Thoreau gave before the Concord, Massachusetts, Lyceum in January 1848.

At the heart of Thoreau's civil disobedience was the relationship between civil law and the so-called higher moral law, the relationship between individual conscience and statute law. Thoreau pointed out that majorities rule not because they are always right, but because they are strong. Here are some excerpts from the lecture that so greatly affected Martin Luther King, Jr.:

> Can there not be a government in which majorities do not virtually decide right and wrong, but conscience? . . . Must the citizen ever for a moment, or in the least degree, resign his conscience to the legislator? Why has every man a conscience, then? I think that we should be men first, and subjects afterward. It is not desirable to cultivate respect for the law so much as for the right.
>
> If I have unjustly wrested a plank from a drowning man, I must restore it to him though I drown myself. . . . This people must cease to hold slaves . . . though it cost them their existence as people. . . .
>
> . . . Practically speaking, the opponents to a reform in Massachusetts are not a hundred thousand politicians of the South, but a hundred thousand merchants and farmers here, who are more interested in commerce and agriculture than they are in humanity, and are not prepared to do justice to the slave. . . . There are thousands who are in opinion opposed to slavery . . . who yet in effect do nothing to put an end to [it]; who, esteeming themselves children of Washington and Franklin, sit down with their hands in their pockets, and say that they know not what to do, and do nothing; who even postpone the question of freedom to the question of free-trade, and quietly read the prices-current . . . What is the price-current of an honest man and patriot to-day? They hesitate, and they regret, and sometimes they petition; but they

Enlightenment. Next, we will see how Susan Moller Okin challenges an important contemporary attempt to realize the Enlightenment promise of Kantian universality in her influential book *Justice, Gender, and the Family*.

One of the most interesting and controversial claims from the area of moral psychology is the notion that women approach practical reasoning from a different perspective from that of men and communicate their reasoning "in a different voice." *In A Different Voice* is, in fact, the title of a very significant book by the Harvard psychologist Carol Gilligan. We will examine some of her ideas. Next, we will look at some epistemological questions concerning whether different emphases on rationality, imagination, emotion, and intuition characterize *different ways of knowing*—distinctly different male and female ways of knowing the world.

In the last section of this chapter, we will consider the life and work of Martin Luther King, Jr. as an example of philosophical advocacy, and note the reemergence of the prophet as a contemporary philosophical archetype.

do nothing in earnest and with effect. . . . There are nine hundred and ninety-nine patrons of virtue to one virtuous man.

All voting is a sort of gaming, like checkers or backgammon, with a slight moral tinge to it, a playing with right and wrong, with moral questions; and betting naturally accompanies it. The character of the voters is not staked. I cast my vote, perchance, as I think right; but I am not vitally concerned that the right should prevail. I am willing to leave it to the majority. Its obligation, therefore, never exceeds that of expediency. Even voting for the right is doing nothing for it. It is only expressing to men feebly your desire that it should prevail. A wise man will not leave the right to the mercy of chance.

If the injustice is part of the necessary friction of the machine of government, let it go, let it go . . . but if it is of such a nature that it requires you be the agent of injustice to another, then, I say, break the law. Let your life be a counter friction to stop the machine. What I have to do is to see, at any rate, that I do not lend myself to the wrong which I condemn.

As for adopting the ways which the State has provided for remedying the evil, I know not of such ways. They take too much time, and a man's life will be gone. . . .

. . . I know this well, that if one thousand, if one hundred, if ten men whom I could name—if ten honest men only—ay, if one HONEST man, in this State of Massachusetts, ceasing to hold slaves, were actually to withdraw from this copartnership [with the state], and be locked up in the county jail therefor, it would be the abolition of slavery in America. For it matters not how small the beginning may seem to be: what is once well done is done forever.

Henry David Thoreau
"On the Duty of Civil Disobedience," in *Walden; or Life in the Woods and On the Duty of Civil Disobedience* (New York: Holt, Rinehart and Winston, 1964), pp. 282, 285–286, 286–287, 290–291.

Can Experiences of Oppression Be Generalized?

The extent to which philosophers must have particular experiences in order to philosophize about them is a difficult and controversial issue. In the case of feminism, for instance, the question arises of whether or not one must be a woman in order to philosophize about the oppression of women. Is it possible, for example, for oppressed men to transfer their particular experiences of oppression to women's experiences?

Of course, the problem of necessary experience extends beyond the simple male-female biological dichotomy. Must one be gay to philosophize about homophobia and gay rights? Must one be black to philosophize about racial oppression in America? Can the experiences of oppressed African Americans provide a common foundation for a social policy that will be fair to oppressed Native Americans? Can victims of anti-Semitism use their own experiences to philosophize about prejudice on a more general scale?

An appreciation of the *historical* nature of the masculine model of knowledge to which the feminine "different voice" is often contrasted helps to underscore that the embodiment of these gender-related perspectives in actual men and women is a cultural, not a biological phenomenon.

Susan Bordo

Who Qualifies the Qualifiers?

The problem of qualification is a common one. We often hear statements such as: "Well, you just won't understand until you have children of your own." "Things are different now, Dad. You can't understand what it's like not to have a tattoo." "I resent Professor Pacheco criticizing affirmative action. His parents are wealthy. He has no right to talk about something he has never experienced."

Spoken in a simplistic way, such comments may be nothing more or less than variants of personal attack fallacies (*ad hominem* arguments) that confuse criticisms of the arguer with refuting her argument. On a deeper level,

they raise significant questions about wisdom if wisdom is defined (at least in part) as generalized knowledge about life. If we are not qualified to speak about things that we have not experienced directly, is wisdom possible? Is knowledge? Is communication? Discuss this sensitive and important problem carefully. Do not overlook the importance of letting persons and groups speak for themselves, particularly regarding social and legal policy. Do you have any suggestions for accommodating both the particular and the general, the private and the public, in our search for wisdom?

Are we always unqualified to speak about social conditions we have not experienced directly? Are the views of members of a group always more reliable than those of nonmembers? Does it follow that if objectivity and impersonal analysis do not guarantee truthfulness then personal advocacy will?

("Judging among judges" is an ancient, perhaps timeless issue. See, for example, the Allegory of the Cave on pp. 135–138, Chuang-tzu on p. 640, and John Stuart Mill's approach to ranking quality of experience on p. 462.)

Sed quis custodiet ipsos custodes? (Who will reform the reformers?)

Juvenal

Such questions are difficult to answer for many reasons. In the first place, there is the problem of who can judge between competing claims of insight and uniqueness. Consider, for instance, a basic issue such as whether or not men can be feminists. If we argue that women should be the ones to determine who gets to speak out on "women's issues," must we then also argue that women cannot speak out on "men's issues"? Are we committed to a principle such that only those who suffer a particular form of oppression are qualified to address its identification and remedy? If we are, then does it also follow that only African-American working-class women can speak to the oppression of African-American working-class women—but not to the oppression of African-American middle-class women or Laotian-American professional women or Haitian-American working-class women? Should philosophers who have not given birth and raised children philosophize about motherhood?

These are not frivolous questions; they raise controversial issues that extend beyond feminist philosophy. The issue of qualifications reaches into campus politics; for instance: Must teachers of African-American philosophy be African Americans? Can males teach Women's Studies courses? The issue of qualifications reaches into local and federal politics: Will female politicians represent women better than they represent men?

© Mike Ramirez/Copley News Service.

Asking and answering such questions is fraught with peril, since any answer must appeal to some foundational principle of justification. Because contemporary feminist philosophers are among the most significant and active philosophers and scientists working on fundamental questions of justification, qualification, and generalization of experience, one of the issues they raise concerns the extent to which modern philosophy reflects a masculine bias. We will look at this issue, but first, let me propose an inclusive definition of feminism.

Toward an Inclusive Feminism

Feminist and *feminism* are terms with many shades of meaning. In the narrowest sense, **feminism**, from the French *féminisme*, refers to attempts to attain equal legal and political rights for women. In the broadest sense, feminism refers to any theory that sees the relationship between the sexes as unequal due to the subordination or oppression of women and the disparagement of women's particular experience, and that aims to identify and remedy the sources of that inequality and oppression.

Some female feminists insist that only women can be feminists. They sometimes refer to men who otherwise satisfy their criteria for being a feminist as "profeminists." In the interest of being philosophically inclusive, I recommend that, instead, we consider a **feminist** to be any person who believes in the fundamental equality of women and men and who actively contributes to the struggle to achieve such equality.[1]

Although it can be argued that such a broad definition of "feminist" suffers from being too inclusive, I believe that an inclusive definition is an

FEMINISM

From the French *féminisme*, this nuanced term refers to attempts to attain equal legal and political rights for women. In the broad sense, feminism includes any theory that sees the relationship between the sexes as unequal due to the subordination or oppression of women and the disparagement of women's particular experience.

FEMINIST

Any person who believes in the fundamental equality of women and men and who actively contributes to the struggle to achieve such equality. This definition is deliberately inclusive.

The association of rationality with masculinity is being challenged by contemporary women (and men) philosophers, reaffirming some of the earliest, most compelling archetypal representations of woman as a symbol of both wisdom (Athena, right) and love (Aphrodite, left). Many of these contemporary philosophers also challenge the association of femininity with emotions, pointing out that both men and women can be wise.

Now perhaps you may think it not fitting for a woman to philosophize, just as it is not fitting for her to ride horses or speak in public. But I think that some things are peculiar to a man, some to a woman, some are common to both. . . . I say that courage and justice and wisdom are common to both.

Phintys of Sparta

advantage to our philosophical search for wisdom. By insisting only that feminists recognize and resist the oppression of women, our definition can account for the extreme variety of arguments and writings put forward— by their authors—as being feminist. Our definition also has the advantage of recognizing the good intentions of many male philosophers.

As we turn to the analysis that follows, we would do well to remind ourselves that just as not all feminists are female, not all females are feminists. Susan Bordo's critique of Cartesian modernity acknowledges the fact that some modern philosophers are women. Indeed, feminists sympathetic to the basic principles of modern philosophy argue that women, like men, are equally rational beings; thus, the same legal and political standards should apply to both sexes.

Critics of modernity respond that applying a single standard of universal rationality to women's issues fails to recognize that the standard itself is a *gendered* reflection of Enlightenment values—not an expression of an objective standard of truth. Assertions of universal rationality, it is thus claimed, are merely disguised arguments on behalf of a woman's right to be like a man. Such assertions are said to overlook important social and biological differences between men and women.

One geometry cannot be more true than another. It can only be more convenient.

Henri Poincaré

The Cartesian Masculinization of Thought

Because the history of Western philosophy has been so dominated by an emphasis on logical reasoning and written argument, other components of wisdom have sometimes been given little attention. As the early Greeks developed and refined rational skills, they increasingly valued personal detachment and the suppression of traits that today we associate with maternal and caring qualities. Objectivity and emotional detachment, traits traditionally associated with masculinity, were considered essential aspects of knowledge, while subjectivity and emotional involvement were considered hindrances.

Although they speak in considerably diluted tones, there are still those who would claim that women's reason is less reliable than men's, or that it occurs in a different—perhaps even in an intuitive—manner.

Carolyn W. Korsmeyer

As noted in the First Interlude, ancient Greek philosophy developed in a series of increasingly abstract steps, until growing concern with logical consistency and rules of thinking led to theories that, though logically consistent, did not match observed facts.[2] One result of this split between common experience and the claims of early philosophers was the alienation of philosophy from the life concerns of most people. Historian of philosophy Amaury De Riencourt says, "The absolute predominance of the dissociating, analytical masculine principle in Greek thought is obvious—hence its strength and its weakness."[3]

According to feminist philosopher of culture **Susan Bordo (b. 1947)**, this "masculinizing" of modern philosophical thought reached a watershed at the beginning of the modern period. In *The Flight to Objectivity*: *Essays on Cartesianism and Culture*, Bordo argues that "Cartesian modernity is inherently linked to the repression of nature and women."[4] This repression, she suggests, is motivated by revulsion and a fear of uncertainty and mortality that modernity has traditionally associated with the daily lives of women.[5] Bordo's point is that the daily lives of women do not reflect Cartesian dualism: They are circumscribed by menstruation, childbirth, nursing, caring for others. In short, women's experiences are *embodied* experiences that cannot be abstracted into distinct mental and physical substances.

Susan Bordo

Bordo's critique of modern philosophy adds a feminist perspective to the radical sorts of criticism brought to bear on objectivity and rationality by Marx, Kierkegaard, James, and Nietzsche, to cite just those philosophers we have studied. (See Chapters 11–14.)

She Feels She's Been Swindled

Simone de Beauvoir (1908–1986) studied philosophy at the Sorbonne and taught school from 1931 until 1943, when she became a full-time writer. De Beauvoir challenged and stimulated Sartre, greatly influencing both his ideas and their written expression. Friends for most of their lives, Sartre and de Beauvoir were a unique couple whose influence extended beyond their individual works as they became role models for postwar intellectuals.

Her book *The Second Sex* is one of the most important works of contemporary feminist philosophy. In it she argues that "women are not born but are made" to see themselves as inferior—second—to men, that the lives of women are "not dictated to woman by her hormones nor predetermined by the structure of the female brain: they are shaped . . . by her situation." De Beauvoir was a superb existential feminist writer, as the following excerpt from *The Second Sex* shows:

Many of the faults for which women are reproached—

mediocrity, laziness, frivolity, servility—simply express the fact that their horizon is closed . . . [woman] has been shut up in it . . . she considers little things important for lack of any access to great things, and, furthermore, the futilities that fill her days are often of the most serious practical concern to her. . . . the occupations available to her are as empty as the pure passage of time. . . .

But no existent can be satisfied with an inessential

Philosophical Query

Do you think Cartesian dualism reflects *anyone's* life? Do you think that Cartesian dualism reflects *men's* lives more than *women's*? Discuss.

Philosophical Reconstruction and Anxiety

According to Bordo, modernity rests on "the possibility of objectivity . . . conceived by Descartes as a kind of *rebirth*, on one's own terms, this time."[6] Bordo is referring to Descartes' attempt to *reconstruct* the world based solely on his own clear and distinct ideas. She says, "We are all familiar with the dominant Cartesian themes of starting anew, alone, without influence from the past or other people, with the guidance of reason alone."[7] (The result, Bordo argues, is that objectivity, not meaning, became the chief philosophical issue; but so long as human beings are embedded in nature, embodied and subject to its rhythms, detached objectivity is impossible.)

According to Bordo, the arc of modern philosophy begins with Descartes' "project" and culminates in Kant's "discovery" that objectivity is predicated on the separation of the knower from the known, the separation of subject and object.[8] She writes:

The Cartesian reconstruction has two interrelated dimensions. On the one hand, a new model of knowledge is conceived, in which the

Why are males usually larger than females? Is it because they are hotter, and heat is productive of growth? Or is it because the male is complete in all its parts, whereas the female is defective? Or is it because the male takes a long time to achieve perfection, the female a short time?

Aristotle

role, for that immediately makes means into ends—as may be observed, for example in politicians—and the value of the means comes to be seen as an absolute value. . . . Woman is shut up in a kitchen or in a boudoir, and astonishment is expressed that her horizon is limited. Her wings are clipped and it is found deplorable that she cannot fly. Let but the future be opened to her, and she will no longer be compelled to live in the present. . . .

A free individual blames only himself for his failures, he assumes responsibility for them; but everything happens to women through the agency of others, and therefore these others are responsible for her woes. . . . She holds the entire world responsible because it has been made without her, and against her; she has been protesting against her condition since her adolescence, ever since her childhood. She has been promised compensations, she has been assured

that if she would place her fortune in man's hands, it would be returned a hundredfold—and she feels she has been swindled. She puts the whole masculine universe under indictment. Resentment is the reverse side of dependence: when one gives all, one never receives enough in return.

Simone de Beauvoir
The Second Sex, trans. H. M. Parshley (New York: Alfred A. Knopf, 1952), Part 5, Chapter 21.

purity of the intellect is guaranteed through its ability to transcend the body. On the other hand, the ontological blueprint of the order of things is refashioned. The spiritual and the corporeal are now two distinct substances which share no qualities (other than being created), permit of interaction but no merging, and are each defined precisely in opposition to the other.[9]

The result, Bordo suggests, is "the utter diremption of the natural world from the realm of the human." Most significantly:

. . . neither bodily response (the sensual or the emotional) nor associational thinking, exploring the various personal or spiritual meanings the object has for us, can tell us anything about the object "itself." . . . Thus, the specter of infantile subjectivism is overcome by the possibility of a cool, impersonal, distanced cognitive relation to the world. At the same time, the nightmare landscape of the infinite universe has become the well-lighted laboratory of modern science and philosophy.[10]

In Bordo's interpretation, Descartes' particular genius was the way in which he laid a philosophical foundation for transforming the initial experience of estrangement and loss that accompanied the sundering of the earth from its medieval location as the center of the universe into an optimistic,

The specific consciousness we call scientific, Western and modern is the long sharpened tool of the masculine mind that has discarded parts of its own substance, calling it "Eve," "female," and "inferior."

James Hillman

"Emotions May Be Helpful and Even Necessary"

Questions being raised by psychological researchers concerning exclusively male-based theories of knowledge are echoed by contemporary women philosophers. In particular, the work of **Alison Jaggar** challenges the fundamental assumptions of traditional Western theories of knowledge. Jaggar argues that emotions are vital aspects of anyone's picture of reality because they help determine what we notice or ignore, and impart degrees of interest and importance to experience. According to Jaggar, emotions select, direct, and help define observations and experiences. Yet, Jaggar notes, traditional Western philosophy has viewed emotion as inferior to reason and even viewed emotions as subversive hindrances to knowledge. Jaggar denies that a gap exists between emotion and knowledge: Far from being hindrances to the construction of knowledge, she says, "emotions may be helpful

Alison Jaggar

and even necessary." In *Love and Knowledge: Emotion in Feminist Epistemology*, she writes:

> From Plato until the present, with a few notable exceptions, reason rather than emotion has been regarded as the indispensable faculty for acquiring knowledge. . . . [Objective] testability became accepted as the hallmark of natural science; this, in turn, was viewed as the paradigm of genuine knowledge. . . . Because values and emotions

had been identified as variable and idiosyncratic, [the objective standard] stipulated that trustworthy knowledge could be established only by methods that neutralized the values and emotions of individual [thinkers].

Alison M. Jaggar
"Love and Knowledge: Emotion in Feminist Epistemology," in *Women, Knowledge, and Reality: Explorations in Feminist Philosophy*, eds. Ann Garry and Marilyn Pearsall (Boston: Unwin Hyman, 1988), p. 123ff.

Do you believe that women and men think in different ways? Do people of different ethnic backgrounds think differently? Do men from different ethnic backgrounds all think alike as men? Do rich people think differently from poor people? Discuss these issues based on your own present beliefs, and then do some research to see what different scientists and philosophers think.

REACTION FORMATION

Freudian ego-defense mechanism that attempts to prevent "dangerous" desires from being exposed and expressed by endorsing opposite attitudes and types of behavior as "barriers" against them.

objective method for understanding, dominating, and managing nature. But this transformation also required the sundering of the organic ties between the person (subject) and the world (object). Descartes accomplished this remarkable feat, Bordo says, through a kind of **reaction formation.** A reaction formation is a defense mechanism that attempts to prevent "dangerous" desires from being exposed and expressed by endorsing opposite attitudes and types of behavior as "barriers" against them. As Bordo sees it, modern philosophy, starting with Descartes, reacted to the new cosmic order with an exaggerated emphasis on objectivism and mechanism, "facilitated by an aggressive intellectual *flight* from the female cosmos and 'feminine' orientation towards the world. . . . through the . . . restructuring of knowledge and [the] world as *masculine*."[11]

From Cosmos to Machine

In sum, according to Bordo, the modern vision of the universe is a picture of a complex machine, not an organic whole (cosmos):

> This re-visioning of the universe as a *machine*— most often, a clock-work—was not the work of philosophers alone. Astronomy and anatomy had already changed the dominant picture of the movements of the heavens and the processes of the body by the time the *Meditations* were written. But it was philosophy . . . That provided the cosmology that integrated these discoveries into a consistent and unified view of nature. . . . Nature became *defined* by its lack of affiliation with divinity, with spirit. All that which is god-like or spiritual—freedom, will, and sentience—belong entirely and exclusively to *res cogitans* [the thing that thinks]. All else—the earth, the heavens, animals, the human body—is merely mechanically interacting matter.[12]

Bordo suggests that the masculinization of science involves more than just the historical fact of male dominance of the sciences. She says that "the most interesting contemporary discussions of the 'masculinist' nature of modern science describe a . . . characteristic cognitive style, an epistemological stance which is required of men *and* women working in the sciences today."[13] In her book *Reflections on Gender and Science,* Evelyn Fox Keller says that "masculine here connotes, as it so often does, autonomy, separation, and distance . . . a radical rejection of any commingling of subject and object."[14]

Bordo does not, however, see modernity as entirely negative. She suggests that:

> The feminist exposure of the gender biases in our dominant Western conceptions of science and ethics—the revelation that the history of their development, the lenses through which they see the world, their methods and priorities have been decisively shaped by the fact that it has been men who have determined their course—has come as a startling recognition to many contemporary male philosophers. Inspired by the work of [Carol] Gilligan, [Nancy] Chodorow, [Susan] Harding, and [Evelyn Fox] Keller, feminist theory has been systematically questioning the historical identification of rationality, intelligence, "good thinking," and so forth, with the masculine modes of detachment and clarity, offering alternative models of fresher, more humane, and more hopeful approaches to science and ethics.[15]

If Bordo and other critics of modernity are generally correct, the scientific, technological, and cultural advances generated by modern science and philosophy carry a high price. This price includes widespread alienation from the natural world; fear and revulsion in the face of "messy" aspects of life such as birthing, caring, and dying; and the trivialization of other *feminine* sources of knowledge and wisdom.

If a kind of Cartesian ideal were ever completely fulfilled, i.e., if the whole of nature were only what can be explained in terms of mathematical relationships—then we would look at the world with that fearful sense of alienation, with that utter loss of reality with which a future schizophrenic child looks at his mother. A machine cannot give birth.

Karl Stern

The female experience in reproduction represents a unity with nature which goes beyond the proletarian experience of interchange with nature.

Nancy Hartsock

The Problem with No Name

The problem lay buried, unspoken, for many years in the minds of American women. It was a strange stirring, a sense of dissatisfaction, a yearning that women suffered in the middle of the twentieth century in the United States. Each suburban wife struggled with it alone. As she made beds, shopped for groceries, matched slipcover material, ate peanut butter sandwiches with her children, chauffeured Cub Scouts and Brownies, lay beside her husband at night—he was afraid to ask even of herself the silent question—"Is this all?"

. . . Gradually I came to realize that the problem that has no name was shared by countless women in America. As a magazine writer I often interviewed women about problems with their children, or their marriages, or their houses, or their communities. But after a while I began to recognize the telltale signs of this other problem. I saw the same signs in suburban ranch houses and split levels on Long Island, in New Jersey, and Westchester County; in colonial houses in a small Massachusetts town; on patios in Memphis; in suburban and city apartments; in living rooms in the Midwest. Sometimes I sensed the problem, not as a reporter, but as a suburban housewife, for during this time I was also bringing up three children . . . I heard echoes of the problem in college dormitories and semi-private maternity wards . . .

Just what was this problem that has no name? What were the words women used when they tried to express it? Sometimes a woman would say, "I feel empty somehow . . . incomplete." Or she would say, "I feel as if I don't exist."

Betty Friedan
The Feminine Mystique (New York: W. W. Norton, 1963), quoted in Michael E. Adelstein and Jean G. Pival, eds., *Women's Liberation*, Perspectives Series (New York: St. Martin's Press, 1972), pp. 3–7.

The Reemergence of Other Voices

As the limits and negative effects of overemphasis on the value of objectivity and personal detachment have become increasingly apparent to growing numbers of people, converging contemporary social, political, and intellectual movements are contributing to reawakened interest in *other voices* and other approaches to doing philosophy and practicing science. Susan Bordo does not see the reemergence of other voices as a complete rejection of modern philosophy, but rather as a *complement*, a completion or enrichment:

> This is not to say that detachment, clarity, and precision will cease to have enormous value in the process of understanding. Rather, our culture needs to reconceive the status of what Descartes assigned to the shadows. Such reevaluation has been a constant, although "recessive" strain in the history of philosophy since Descartes. . . . Hume's insistence that "reason is and ought to be the slave of the passions," and, perhaps most importantly, Kant's revelation that objectivity itself is the result of human structuring, opened various doors that in retrospect now appear as critical openings.

Today women are talking to each other, recovering an oral culture, telling our life-stories, reading aloud to one another the books that have moved and healed us, analyzing the language that has lied about us, reading our own words aloud to each other . . . to name and found a culture of our own.

Adrienne Rich

Hume, for example, may now be seen as having a rightful place—along with Nietzsche . . . [and] . . . James . . . in the critical protest against the Cartesian notion that reason can and should be a "pure" realm free from contamination by emotion, instinct, will, sentiment, and value. Within this protest, we see the development both of a "naturalist" *anthropology* of the Cartesian ideals of precision, certainty, and neutrality (Nietzsche . . . and James), and a complementary *metaphysics* . . . in which "vagueness" as well as specificity, tentativeness, and valuation are honored as essential to thought.[16]

Recently published works by feminist philosophers and social scientists pose a series of interrelated questions that call into doubt the exclusive status of the traditional (masculinized) model of rationality as detached, objective knowing: Is there only one way of reasoning? Is objective reasoning the only or best way of knowing? To what extent, if any, are personal detachment and objectivity possible? Perhaps most important, when—if ever—are personal detachment and objectivity desirable? Perhaps we should base our decisions on who we really are and our actual social place.

Especially important to philosophers are discussions concerning rationality and other sources of knowledge in light of gender. Gender and biological sex are not the same, by the way. *Gender* refers to sexual orientation and includes masculine, feminine, bisexual, homosexual, lesbian, and androgynous. Some philosophers argue that any assertion of fixed gender differences contributes to divisiveness and sexism, whether it is promale or profemale, promasculine or profeminine. Then, too, there are disagreements over the extent to which gender is biological or social. That is, to what extent are gender differences and preferences socially conditioned or biologically inevitable?

Some feminist philosophers applaud what they see as the long-overdue acknowledgment of women's ways of knowing and welcome a reevaluation of traditional notions of reasonableness and rationality. Other feminist philosophers object to what they see as stigmatizing women with a special "woman's way of knowing." They fear that any so-called woman's way of knowing will become marginalized and trivialized—differentiated from a so-called "real" (masculine) way of knowing.

These important questions stretch the boundaries of philosophy when questions of knowledge and rationality involve factual issues that require both philosophical analysis and scientific scrutiny. Further, if, as some researchers suggest, men and women (as they are currently socialized) somehow experience the world differently, then our ideas about such things as moral values, human virtues, and justice may reflect these differences.

Modern Kantian moral theories of universal justice attempt to avoid just such problems of biased perspectives, including gender-bias, by adopting a single *universalized* and *impersonal* perspective meant to prevent introducing "private" considerations into moral judgments. Even so, Stanford University professor Susan Moller Okin argues, overlooked gender-bias

A sword that repelled a huge army in days past is no longer useful. Similarly, some of the dictums of the people of old may no longer be applicable in today's world.

Lie Zi

The traditional canon is elitist . . . concerned with the writing primarily of privileged white men. Women's writing, writing of people of color, people of the working class—these voices need to be brought into . . . study.

Sue Howard

The association of cognitive style with gender is in itself nothing new. We find it in ancient mythology, in archetypal psychology, in philosophical and scientific writings, and in a host of enduring popular stereotypes about men and women (for example, that women are more "intuitive," men are more "logical," etc.).

Susan Bordo

remains present in both the language and choice of examples employed in one of the most scrupulous and influential contemporary attempts to refine Kant's moral philosophy.

A Masculine Theory of Justice

In 1971, Harvard professor **John Rawls (b. 1921)** published *A Theory of Justice*, which became one of the most significant philosophical books of our time. Rawls's attempt to refine Kant's moral philosophy greatly influenced political scientists, economists, and moral philosophers. First, we'll take a look at one of the key concepts Rawls used to identify fundamental principles of "justice as fairness," then, we will look at Okin's intriguing response to Rawls's work.

According to Rawls, the fundamental principles of justice are those principles to which "free and rational" persons would agree if they were in an "original position" of equality. Of course, Rawls continued, we are not in and cannot create a position of perfect equality. How, then, he asked, can we ever determine what justice is, since any inquiry into justice will be influenced by our actual—and unequal—circumstances?

One way to deal with the limits imposed by our actual circumstances is known as a thought experiment. A **thought experiment** is a way of using our imaginations to test a hypothesis that cannot be tested in fact. As the name suggests, we "think" rather than field-test the hypothesis, using reasoned imagination to provide the necessary conditions for the experiment, and then carefully reason out the most likely consequences according to our hypothesis.

In Chapter 10 we learned that Kant had already tried to overcome the limits of personal circumstances and bias with the categorical imperative, which is supposed to overlook all merely personal considerations and inclinations. (You might want to review Kant's moral philosophy in Chapter 10.) Rawls used a thought experiment in an attempt to improve upon Kant's efforts to overcome the limits of personal concerns in ethical deliberations.

The **original position** of equality is Rawls's term for an imaginary setting in which we can identify the fundamental principles of justice from an objective, impartial perspective—as "rational agents," rather than as "interested parties." But why bother with an imaginary circumstance in the first place? Rawls has an answer: The original position can help us clarify both *what* principles we accept and *why* they are rational and just.

We "enter into the original position" by imaginatively placing ourselves behind a "veil of ignorance." As Rawls conceived it, the **veil of ignorance** is a problem-solving device that prevents us from knowing our social status, what property we own, what we like and don't like, how intelligent we are, what our talents and strengths are, "and the like." In the following passage, Rawls introduces the veil of ignorance and the original position:

The original position is not, of course, thought of as an actual historical state of affairs, much less as a primitive condition of culture. It is
understood as a purely hypothetical situation characterized so as to
lead to a certain conception of justice. . . . Among the essential features of this situation is that no one knows his place in society, his
class position or social status, nor does any one know his fortune in
the distribution of natural assets and abilities, his intelligence, strength,
and the like. I shall even assume that the parties do not know their
conceptions of the good or their special psychological propensities.
The principles of justice are chosen behind a veil of ignorance. This
assures that no one is advantaged or disadvantaged in the choices of
principles by the outcome of natural chance or the contingency of
social circumstances.[17]

In *A Theory of Justice*, Rawls argues that persons in the original position would all agree—being rational and mutually disinterested—to principles of equal political liberty and opportunity. That is, as *rational agents*
looking out for our own self-interest, we would all agree to two basic principles: (1) everyone has an equal right to "the most extensive basic liberty
compatible with a similar liberty for others," and (2) any social and economic inequalities must be such that "they are both (a) reasonably expected to be to everyone's advantage and (b) attached to positions and offices open to all."[18] When the two principles conflict, *reason directs us* to
defer to the first.

According to Rawls, "whenever social institutions satisfy these principles those engaged in them can say to one another that they are cooperat-
ing on terms to which they would agree if they were free and equal persons whose relations with respect to one another were fair."[19]

Philosophical Query

Conduct your own thought experiment by using the concept of a veil of
ignorance to write a code of conduct for college courses. Imagine that
you do not know if you are a pupil or professor, or any other personal
factors. Does the veil of ignorance aid in such tasks, or is something overlooked? Discuss.

> We are all familiar with
> the dominant Cartesian
> themes of starting anew,
> alone, without influence
> from the past or other peo-
> ple, with the guidance of
> reason alone.
>
> *Susan Bordo*

> All social primary goods—
> liberty and opportunity,
> income and wealth, and the
> bases of self-respect—are to
> be distributed equally un-
> less an unequal distribution
> of any or all of these goods
> is to the advantage of the
> least favored.
>
> *John Rawls*

Justice and Gender

In her insightful book *Justice, Gender, and the Family*, **Susan Moller Okin**
analyzes Rawls's theory of justice, with special attention to issues of gender and the family. In her powerful introduction, Okin reminds us that:

We as a society pride ourselves on our democratic values. We don't
believe people should be constrained by innate differences from being able to achieve desired positions of influence or to improve their

Susan Moller Okin

**That's an excellent suggestion, Miss Triggs.
Perhaps one of the men here would like to
make it.**

Family justice must be of
central importance for
social justice.

Susan Moller Okin

A moral theory (or family
of moral theories) that
made trust its central problem could do better justice
to men's and women's
moral intuitions than do
the going men's theories.

Annette C. Baier

well-being; equality of opportunity is our professed aim. The Pre-
amble to our Constitution stresses the importance of justice, as well
as the general welfare and the blessings of liberty. The Pledge of Allegiance asserts that our republic preserves "liberty and justice for all."

Yet substantial inequities between the sexes still exist in our society.
In economic terms, full-time working women (after some very recent
improvement) earn on average 71 percent of the earnings of full-time
working men. One-half of poor and three-fifths of chronically poor
households with dependent children are maintained by a single female
parent. The poverty rate for elderly women is nearly twice that for
elderly men.[20]

Okin goes on to point out the still disproportionate number of women in
Congress, on the Supreme Court, and so forth. She points out that women
still do most of the child rearing in this country. Even when both parents
work, the woman commonly does more of the child rearing and housekeep-
ing than the man.

Okin also reminds us that no adequate theory of justice can fail to include an analysis of justice within the family, since the family—in whatever form—is still the primary shaper of basic personality, as well as basic
attitudes of self-respect (self-esteem), gender, and race. In sum, justice cannot be separated from family experience. This includes justice for each
member of the family. Clearly, in our present society, wealth, equality, and
liberty are not evenly or justly apportioned. Okin continues:

Yet, remarkably, major contemporary theorists of justice have almost without exception ignored the situation I have just described [the status of women and all family members]. They have displayed little interest in or knowledge of the findings of feminism. They have largely bypassed the fact that the society to which their theories are supposed to pertain is heavily and deeply affected by gender, and faces difficult issues of justice stemming from its gendered past and present assumptions. Since theories of justice are centrally concerned with whether, how, or why persons should be treated differently from one another, this neglect seems inexplicable. . . . [*Justice, Gender, and the Family*] is about this remarkable case of neglect. It is also an attempt to . . . point the way toward a more fully humanist theory of justice by confronting the question, "How just is gender?"[21]

Okin argues that Rawls's analysis of justice is "ambiguous" regarding gender because, she says, he rarely indicates "how deeply and pervasively gender-structured" this society is.

Further, Okin points out, Rawls fails to mention that *Kant did not intend for his moral theory to apply to women*. Okin asserts that in his discussion of Sigmund Freud's theory of the formulation of the male superego, Rawls simply ignores the fact that Freud thought that women's moral development was *psychologically deficient*. "Thus," Okin concludes, "there is a blindness to the sexism of the tradition in which Rawls is a participant, which tends to render his terms of reference more ambiguous than they might otherwise be. A feminist reader finds it difficult not to keep asking, Does this theory apply to women?"[22]

According to Okin, Rawls's work is "ambiguous" rather than flatly sexist because he does acknowledge that sex is one of the morally relevant contingencies that are to be hidden behind the veil of ignorance. But reconsider Rawls's language regarding these contingencies in light of Okin's observations: "Among the essential features of this situation is that no one knows *his* place in society, *his* class position or social status, nor does any one know *his* fortune in the distribution of natural assets and abilities, *his* intelligence, strength, and the like" (emphasis added).[23]

Okin says that "one might think that whether or not they knew their sex might matter enough to be mentioned." "Perhaps," she suggests, "Rawls meant to cover it by his phrase 'and the like,' but it is also possible that he did not consider it significant."[24]

A Look Behind the Veil of Ignorance

Rawls hoped that the veil of ignorance could be used to "correct for" the "arbitrariness of the world" by putting people in a position to reason independently of "morally relevant contingencies" such as actual social status, talent, race, *and the like*. As "pure rational agents," they would think

Women live on the sidelines of this world; they have contact with it only through their private lives, through men, in a mediated rather than an immediate way; they have a lot more free time than men do . . . to observe, to criticize; they are used to being spectators. . . .

Simone de Beauvoir

Our ultimate goal should be a non-gendered, non-dichotomized, moral framework in which all moral concerns could be expressed. We might, with intentional irony, call this project, "demoralizing the genders."

Marilyn Friedman

Women's work has been made to seem sporadic, errant, orphaned of any tradition of its own.

Adrienne Rich

Plato's argument . . . is not valid . . . , it is irrelevant to facts about women's desires, and it is irrelevant to the injustice of sexual equality.

Julia Annas

from an identical standpoint. Each one's perspective would be the perspective of all.

Okin rightly observes that the veil of ignorance has been pierced if we retain knowledge of our gender. She thinks that:

> The significance of Rawls's central, brilliant idea, the original position, is that it forces one to question and consider traditions, customs, and institutions from all points of view, and ensures that the principles of justice will be acceptable to everyone, regardless of what position "he" ends up in. . . . The theory, in principle, avoids both the problem of domination that is inherent in theories of justice based on traditions or shared understandings and the partiality of libertarian theory to those who are talented or fortunate. For feminist readers, however, the problem of the theory as stated by Rawls himself is encapsulated in the ambiguous "he." . . . If, however, we read Rawls in such a way as to take seriously both the notion that those behind the veil of ignorance do not know what sex they are and the requirement that the family and gender system, as basic social institutions, are to be subject to scrutiny, constructive feminist criticism of these contemporary institutions follows. . . .
>
> Finally . . . if those in the original position did not know whether they were to be men or women, they would surely be concerned to establish a thoroughgoing social and economic equality between the sexes that would protect either sex from the need to pander to or servilely provide for the pleasure of the other. They would emphasize the importance of girls and boys growing up with an equal sense of respect for themselves and equal expectations of self-definition and development. . . . In general, they would be unlikely to tolerate basic social institutions that asymmetrically either forced or gave strong incentives to members of one sex to serve as sex objects for the other.
>
> . . . I reach the conclusions not only that our current gender structure is incompatible with the attainment of social justice, but also that the disappearance of gender is a prerequisite for the *complete* development of a nonsexist, fully human theory of justice.[25]

Philosophical Query

Reevaluate your response to the Philosophical Query on page 609 in light of Okin's modification of the veil of ignorance. Would ignorance of your gender alter the course syllabus? Does it add new issues? Does it change any wording? Explain.

Also consider Okin's suggestion that "the disappearance of gender" is a prerequisite for a just society. Or is that what she said? Can a gender-based society be just? Discuss.

Okin points out that Rawls's discussion is "expressed in terms of mutual disinterest and rationality"—what some feminist philosophers call the "masculine voice." And indeed, such criticism can be (and has been) leveled at many philosophers, both women and men. Not all criticism of the masculine voice is from feminists, by the way. The existentialists and sages, for instance, reject relying exclusively on an objectivistic rational ideal as distorting, inaccurate, and destructive. But some of the most consistent, compelling recent criticisms of this "masculine" perspective are being developed by feminist philosophers and psychologists.

Philosophizing in a Different Voice

In 1982, Harvard psychologist **Carol Gilligan (b. 1936)** published her groundbreaking book *In a Different Voice: Psychological Theory and Women's Development*. Gilligan's work prompted a necessary reassessment of moral reasoning. Perhaps the following passage will convey some sense of the importance and delicacy of psychological research into the area of gender-bias—and how pervasive such bias can be:

> A word, finally, about the politics and the controversy of this research. The stark fact of the all-male research sample, accepted for years as representative by psychologists studying human development, in one sense speaks for itself. That such samples were not seen long ago as problematic by women or men points to different blindnesses on the part of each sex. The fact that these samples passed the scrutiny of peer review boards, that studies of . . . moral development . . . using all-male samples were repeatedly funded and widely published in professional journals indicates that the psychological research community needs to reexamine its claims to objectivity and dispassion. If the omission of half the human population was not seen, or not seen as significant, or not spoken about as a problem (by women or men), what other omissions are not being seen? The contribution of women's thinking . . . is a different voice, a different way of speaking about relationships and about the experience of the self. The inclusion of this voice changes the map of the moral domain. Listening to girls and women, we have come to listen differently to boys and men. And we have come to think differently about human nature and the human condition, and in turn, about . . . disciplines devoted to improving human life.[26]

Gilligan's study of possible differences in the moral development of men and women distinguished between a masculine-oriented ethics of justice, such as Rawls's and Kant's, and a feminine-oriented ethics of care. In general terms, an **ethic of justice** stresses rules and rights, and an **ethic of care** stresses responsibilities and relationships. The ethic of justice is based on an expression of the traditional model of knowing that Gilligan calls

Carol Gilligan

ETHIC OF JUSTICE

Carol Gilligan's term for ethical theories that stress rules over responsibilities and relationships, and that are based on an expression of the traditional impersonal, rationalistic, objective, detached model of knowing.

ETHIC OF CARE

Carol Gilligan's term for ethical theories that stress responsibilities and relationships over rules, and that are based on "care reasoning," which depends on a sense of connectedness, or "relationship," and that is the opposite of objective detachment.

Literature is strewn with the wreckage of men who have minded beyond reason the opinions of others.

Virginia Woolf

If we would have new knowledge, we must get a whole world of new questions.

Susanne K. Langer

One race there is of men, one of gods, but from one mother we both draw our breath.

Pindar

justice reasoning. Care reasoning, by contrast, depends on a sense of connectedness, sometimes referred to as relationship, that is the opposite of objective detachment. Okin's position incorporates both justice and care; we might describe such a position as "caring justice."

Gilligan, among others, was initially troubled by the work of **Lawrence Kohlberg (1927–1987)**, which received widespread attention in education as well as in philosophical and psychological circles. Kohlberg, a prominent psychologist, identified six distinct "stages of moral development," based on years of research with male subjects. They can be summarized as:

1. Goodness is power.
2. Goodness satisfies my needs.
3. Goodness comes from pleasing and helping others.
4. Goodness is doing our duty to ensure law and order.
5. Goodness is a matter of fairness according to a social contract like the Constitution.
6. Goodness is based on universal principles of justice and equality—the ethic of justice.

In Kohlberg's scheme, reasoning at the lower levels is particularly characteristic of children, and relatively few people attain the sixth stage, even as adults.

Gilligan noted that most women remained at the three lowest levels in Kohlberg's classification. Kohlberg himself thought that, as a rule, women were excluded from the highest stages of moral development. Thus, if Kohlberg's theory is sound, then women are morally inferior to men (as Kant and Freud thought). But what if Kohlberg's theory is not sound?

As noted above, philosophy for the most part has spoken in the same masculine voice that dominates moral discourse in this culture, and until very recently, women's voices have been largely absent from the mainstream of Western philosophy. Yet the idea that women are morally inferior to men is not only intellectually repugnant, it flies in the face of actual experience. Worse yet, the issue goes beyond gender because many men do not fit the model Kohlberg described.

Traditionally, women and men whose ways of knowing do not conform to the objective model have been devalued and regularly consigned to such nonphilosophical roles as poet or religious figure. Even when this culture acknowledges that such individuals express moral insight or wisdom, their explanations and accounts are sometimes dismissed as "anecdotal" or "merely personal" by academic philosophers and social scientists. If they cannot or do not wish to speak in the voice of "objective" scientific evidence and logical argument, they may not be heard at all.

In the introduction to *In a Different Voice*, Gilligan writes:

> Over the past ten years I have been listening to people talking about morality and about themselves. Halfway through that time, I began to

hear a distinction in these voices, two ways of speaking about moral problems, two modes of describing the relationship between other and self. . . .

The different voice I describe is characterized not by gender but by theme. Its association with women is an empirical observation, and it is primarily through women's voices that I trace its development. But this association is not absolute, and the contrasts between male and female voices . . . highlight a distinction between two modes of thought and . . . focus [on] a problem of interpretation rather than represent a generalization about either sex.[27]

Gilligan suggests that because they idealized objective, logical, impersonal knowledge, philosophers have progressively developed an interest in the ethic of justice—at the expense of the ethic of care.[28] Interest in justice, she argues, has increasingly dominated Western values by restricting most moral and political discussion to issues of rights and duties. But the ethic of care is about actual relationships and intimate concerns, which cannot be confined to a set of rules and list of duties.

Gilligan points out, "The blind willingness to sacrifice people to truth, however, has always been the danger of an ethics abstracted from life. . . . It is the ethics of an adulthood that has become principled at the expense of care."[29]

Philosophical Query

Which—if any—of the philosophers you have studied this term speak in a "different voice" from the traditional "masculine voice"? Do they have anything in common? What? Do any of the philosophers speak in a "blended voice"? Who? Explain.

The Need for Caring Justice

In Western culture, the ethic of care has traditionally been associated with religious figures who transcend or ignore objective knowledge and with a feminine-nurturing-maternal orientation toward other people. Yet, with notable exceptions, philosophers have dismissed and distrusted subjective—private—emotional responses to moral problems, seeing only the dangers inherent in impulsive subjectivity. Okin, Gilligan, and others point out, however, that objectivity and detachment are as susceptible to abuse as overreliance on emotions or indiscriminate personal response.

Justice reasoning can be blind to its own biases and influences, resulting in a form of egocentrism that views a particular standard of what is reasonable as if it is the only standard. For example, when being *fully human* is taken to mean being rational, being fully human is characterized as deferring to a single objective, impersonal way of knowing. The responsible person is thus defined as one who has reached "the age of reason" and exhibits the capacity to think in an objective, impersonal, unemotional way.

I conclude then that, even granting the assumptions that natural psychological differences, and therefore role differences, between the sexes are inevitable, it does not follow that there must be sanctions enforcing correlations between roles and sex. Indeed, if individual freedom is valued, those who vary from the statistical norm should not be required to conform to it.

Joyce Trebilcot

Almost everyone will agree that there have been more geniuses for being human among women than there have been among men.

Ashley Montagu

Classical Christian spirituality viewed man as a "rational spirit." The male
alone was said to fully
possess this "human na-
ture" in its essence. The
male alone was made in the
"image of God," modeled
in his inward being after
the intellectual *Logos*. . . .
Woman was thereby mod-
eled after the rejected part
of the psyche.

*Rosemary Radford
Ruether*

Yet we all probably know "reasonable" people who lack moral wisdom
and character.

Gilligan notes that fallacious justice reasoning results in too little justice by excluding those oriented toward care from full participation in philosophy, science, law, higher education—and by denying access to the full
range of knowledge necessary for wise choices.

When we confine our standard of reasoning to the masculinized modern model, we fail to recognize wisdom as it is expressed in some Eastern,
Native American, African, and Hispanic philosophies that are not built on
the objective, rationalistic model. The result is that nontraditional philosophies tend to be classified as religions or mythologies rather than philosophies. The model of knowing in such wisdom philosophies is based on relationship (with clan, tribe, others, God, nature) and demands personal
involvement and intuitive understanding rather than objective detachment
and logical conformity.

It is a mistake, however, to equate justice reasoning with "masculine"
bias and care reasoning with "feminine" wisdom. Fallacious care reasoning can obscure the fact that the caregiver has rights and a separate point
of view. One danger is that the caregiver succumbs to a delusional view of
reality by failing to achieve any distance from others' needs and values. This
results in caregivers who become so identified with taking care of others
that they sacrifice themselves in ineffective, inappropriate ways. Gilligan
discovered, for example, that many women find it easier to care for and
help others than to apply the same standards of care and compassion to
themselves. (Men can do this, too.)

Fallacious care reasoning can also result in a variant of the character
disorder known as the *borderline personality*. The name comes from the
fact that such individuals are unable to separate themselves from others.
They lack a clearly identified borderline between themselves and other people. As a consequence, individuals suffering from borderline personality
disorder define themselves in terms of significant others; they are unable
to achieve significant objectivity or detachment in their thinking.

Gilligan characterizes the fundamental weaknesses of justice reasoning
and care reasoning as follows:

> The potential error in justice reasoning lies in its latent egocentrism,
> the tendency to confuse one's perspective with an objective standpoint
> or truth, the temptation to define others in one's own terms by putting
> oneself in their place. The potential error in care reasoning lies in the
> tendency to forget that one has terms, creating a tendency to enter
> into another's perspective and see oneself as "selfless" by defining
> oneself in others' terms. The two types of error underlie two common
> equations that signify distortions or deformations of justice and care:
> the equation of human with male, unjust in its omission of women;
> and the equation of care with self-sacrifice, uncaring in its failure to
> represent the activity and agency of care.[30]

Efforts to make the world better are often motivated by great love (care motivation) or a powerful sense of outrage (justice motivation). Care-motivated social reform results in injustice and abuse when love for the beloved group blinds us to the human qualities of their perceived oppressors. When that happens, the "other" (whether bigot, spouse abuser, or sexist) becomes demonized and thereby excluded from the realm of love. This encourages a shift of injustices, rather than a more just society.

Justice-motivated social reform results in a kind of "passive cruelty" when excessive concern for regulations, mathematically precise equality, and technical procedure blinds us to inherent disadvantages and human needs of presently oppressed groups. When justice loses touch with care, the legitimate demands of the oppressed become demonized as they are trivialized in "us-them" language that reveals contempt for their suffering by automatically characterizing their demands as "whining" or "special pleading."

Martin Luther King, Jr., perhaps the most famous exemplar of the prophetic philosophical advocate of our time, was aware of the dangers of relying exclusively on either justice or care reasoning. Consequently, his life and work reflect a compelling effort to effect positive social change without demonizing the "other," and to create justice based on universal love rather than impersonal universalized reason.

Martin Luther King, Jr.: A Prophet for Today

As we learned in the First Interlude, originally the term **prophet** referred to a person who speaks with divine guidance, who functions as a religious leader and teacher, a person who cries out for justice and mercy in the face of tyranny. Today, although the role of prophet is still fulfilled by religious figures, as we would expect, another form of prophet-advocate fulfills the role of what I characterize as a *public philosophical advocate*. A **public philosophical advocate** is a "public intellectual" who addresses current social, moral, and political issues in a personally committed way, rather than in the impersonal and detached manner of a scholar; public philosophical advocates assert moral and philosophical principles in a manner designed to reach a broad audience; they may or may not be philosophers in the strictest sense.

Martin Luther King, Jr. (1929–1968), was a prophet on all these counts. Perhaps more than any other figure in recent American history, King brought important philosophical and moral concerns into the public arena. In the process, he became a figure of reverence and contempt, idolized and ridiculed during his life, analyzed and debated in death. King had the vision, intellect, and courage to take action against injustice without demonizing

PROPHET

From the Greek roots *pro* (before) and *phanai* (to speak); originally a person who speaks with divine guidance, who functions as a religious leader and teacher; a person who cries out for justice and mercy in the face of tyranny.

PUBLIC PHILOSOPHICAL ADVOCATE

A "public intellectual" who addresses current social, moral, and political issues in a personally committed way, rather than in the impersonal and detached manner of a scholar; public philosophical advocates assert moral and philosophical principles in a manner designed to reach a broad audience; they may or may not be philosophers in the strictest sense. See also philosophical advocate.

Martin Luther King, Jr.

Rosa Parks is shown being booked into jail after her arrest for refusing to give up her bus seat to a white passenger. Speaking of civil disobedience, Martin Luther King, Jr., said, "This is not a method for cowards; it does resist."

his oppressors—a most rare, beautiful, and needful quality, indeed. King's powerful speaking skills, combined with his courageous actions on behalf of racial justice, make him a compelling exemplar of prophetic philosophy in practice.

Tracked Down by the *Zeitgeist*

In the past the civil rights groups in America have been foolishly attempting to obtain constitutional rights from the same Government that has conspired against us to deny our people these rights.

Malcolm X

Just as it is impossible to separate the sage's life from her philosophical beliefs, it is also impossible to separate the prophet from his place in history. In the case of King, that place is at the beginning of what has come to be known as the American civil rights movement.

In 1947, while attending Morehouse College, the eighteen-year-old King was licensed to preach in his father's (the Reverend Martin Luther King, Sr.) church, the Ebenezer Baptist Church of Atlanta. In 1948, King graduated from Morehouse with a bachelor's degree in sociology, and that fall he entered Crozer Theological Seminary in Chester, Pennsylvania. In 1951, he received a bachelor's degree in divinity, graduating in only three years and at the head of his class. He so impressed his professors at Crozer that they urged him to apply to the Boston University School of Theology doctoral program in systematic theology. King was accepted and received his Ph.D. in 1955. In 1954, while still working on his dissertation, he became the pastor of the prominent Dexter Avenue Baptist Church of Montgomery, Alabama.

King was barely settled into his role as an influential member of Montgomery's black community when a series of converging events changed America's view of itself forever and sparked the vision that transformed a Southern Baptist preacher into a national moral force. Two signal events galvanized and polarized the American public.

On May 17, 1954, in *Linda Brown et al. v. Board of Education of Topeka*, the U.S. Supreme Court ordered the desegregation of all public schools "with all deliberate speed." Chief Justice Earl Warren wrote the unanimous opinion that "in the field of public education the doctrine of 'separate but equal' has no place. Separate educational facilities are inherently unequal." The Court's ruling sent shock waves throughout the country, and white racist and separatist groups such as the Ku Klux Klan and White Citizens' Council initiated an escalating series of violent attacks on blacks. Shortly after the ruling, the black press in Mississippi recorded three cases of antiblack terrorism.

On December 1, 1955, Mrs. Rosa Parks, a forty-two-year-old black seamstress in Montgomery, Alabama, defied the law when she refused to yield her seat on a bus to a white man when ordered to by the bus driver. Rosa Parks was arrested, and the resulting controversy attracted national attention.[31]

Speaking of Rosa Parks, Martin Luther King, Jr., wrote:

> She was not "planted" there by the NAACP, or any other organization; she was planted there by her personal sense of dignity and self-respect. She was anchored to that seat by the accumulated indignities of days gone by and the boundless aspirations of generations yet unborn. She was a victim of both the forces of history and the forces of destiny. She had been tracked down by the *Zeitgeist*—the spirit of the time.[32]

The reaction to the *Brown* case had divided the country. When Rosa Parks refused to give up her seat on the bus a year and a half after the *Brown* decision, the South erupted with murderous racial violence: the Reverend George W. Lee was lynched in Belzoni, Mississippi, after he tried to register to vote in Humphreys County; Lamar Smith was lynched in Brookhaven, Mississippi; fourteen-year-old Emmett Till was lynched in Money, Mississippi.[33]

Character Is Destiny

Martin Luther King, Jr., acting as president of the Montgomery Improvement Association created to support Rosa Parks, led a 381-day nonviolent boycott of the Montgomery public transportation system by blacks. The boycotters initially demanded that black bus drivers be hired for buses serving mostly black areas. They also protested the many insults

A real honest effort to remove the just grievances of the 22 million Afro-Americans must be made immediately or in a short time it will be too late.

Malcolm X

You don't have to be a man to fight for freedom. All you have to do is be an intelligent human being. And automatically your intelligence makes you want freedom so badly that you'll do anything, by any means necessary, to get that freedom.

Malcolm X

If you come to doubt whether a specific person is a prophet or not, certainty can only be reached by acquaintance with his conduct, either by personal observation, or by hearsay as a matter of common knowledge.

Abu Hamid
Muhammad al-Ghazali

I'm for anybody who's for freedom. I'm for anybody who's for justice. I'm for anybody who's for equality. I'm not for anybody who tells me to sit around and wait for mine. I'm not for anybody who tells me to turn the other cheek when a cracker is busting up my jaw. I'm not for anybody who tells black people to be nonviolent while nobody is telling white people to be nonviolent.

Malcolm X

and discourtesies blacks suffered. Ultimately, the boycotters demanded an end to segregated seating. The Montgomery bus boycott was the first of many nonviolent black demonstrations aimed at securing for blacks those rights already enjoyed by whites.

During the boycott, four black churches were bombed, as well as the homes of King and another protesting black pastor, the Reverend Ralph Abernathy. Rosa Parks lost her job, as did other blacks. In spite of the lynchings, bombings, arson, and general intimidation, the push toward civil equality continued.

The Montgomery bus boycott marked a major turning point in King's life. In addition to making Martin Luther King, Jr., an internationally recognized black leader and advocate of Christian nonviolent civil disobedience, the boycott crystallized King's vision for America. Referring to that time, he said, "After prayerful consideration, I am convinced that the psychological moment has come when a concentrated drive against injustice can bring great tangible gains."[34] In short, the bus boycott showed that King's nonviolent civil disobedience *worked*.

Seizing the momentum, King founded the Southern Christian Leadership Conference (SCLC) in 1957. In 1960, he resigned from the Dexter Avenue Baptist Church to become co-pastor of his father's Ebenezer Baptist Church in Atlanta. This allowed him to devote virtually all of his time to the SCLC.

King's method of "nonviolent direct action" worked slowly and involved great struggle. It took seven years to desegregate Southern buses, for instance, and we've just noted the violence that followed Rosa Parks's refusal to give up her seat on the bus. The national fight over integrating schools took years, and remnants of that issue face us today in the form of questions regarding affirmative action, job quotas, and so forth.

In 1962, Mississippi state troopers and the nationalized Mississippi National Guard faced each other over the admission of the first black student, James Meredith, to the University of Mississippi. Many people were injured and two people killed during this particular conflict. In 1963, Alabama Governor George Wallace literally stood in the schoolhouse door to prevent two blacks from entering the University of Alabama. Ultimately, President John F. Kennedy nationalized the Alabama National Guard and used them to guarantee that the students were admitted.

Clearly, attempts to overcome racism and gain equal rights took great stamina and courage. In this context, King's efforts to *live out a philosophy* of active, direct nonviolence are especially impressive. Risking his life, surviving scorn, ridicule, beatings, and jail, King expressed a powerful moral and social philosophy that led to social changes which affect all Americans. In 1964, King received the Nobel Peace Prize.

On April 4, 1968, Martin Luther King, Jr., was assassinated in Memphis, Tennessee.

Martin Luther King, Jr., belongs to a special class of activist philosophers whose philosophies and lives are inseparable. Because King's chief concerns were social progress and improvement of the human condition for all people, his philosophy of nonviolence is expressed in dialogical sermons and lectures aimed at stirring the soul and calling the mind and body to action—not in detailed philosophical analysis or rarefied theoretical disputations.

Moral Courage

King pointed out that nonviolence is not a method of cowardice or retreat. The nonviolent resister relies on *moral force* and *moral courage* (as well as physical courage in many cases):

> First, this is not a method for cowards; it *does* resist. The nonviolent resister is just as strongly opposed to the evil against which he protests as is the person who uses violence. His method is passive or nonaggressive in the sense that he is not physically aggressive toward his opponent. But his mind and emotions are always active, constantly seeking to persuade the opponent that he is mistaken. This method is passive physically but strongly active spiritually; it is nonaggressive physically but dynamically aggressive spiritually.[35]

Active nonviolent resistance differs from passive acceptance of injustice in that nonviolent resistance *deliberately interferes* with whatever is being opposed. Refusing to move to the back of the bus, refusing to leave a segregated lunch counter, marching to protest discriminatory voter registration laws create tension by calling attention to injustice and trying to stop it.

Anyone who has seen newsreels of civil rights demonstrators being clubbed, dragged away, attacked by police dogs, or beaten back by powerful fire hoses realizes that such resistance also required considerable physical courage. Moreover, it produced a powerful effect on those who participated in it and on those who witnessed it—even in the safety and comfort of their living rooms.

King insisted that great care be taken to ensure the means used to achieve righteous goals did not tarnish those goals. The point of his nonviolent movement wasn't to achieve merely this or that specific law or right, but to create genuine social change. He knew that this required more than effective strategy—though effective strategy is also important. And he did not discount the vital importance of immediate change in the fundamental conditions of the poor of all races. The dilemma, then, was how to effect timely change without resorting to methods that violate someone else's basic rights. King insisted that no matter how reprehensible the wrong, the ends do not justify unjust means.

> The movement is based on the philosophy that ends and means must cohere. Now, this has been one of the long struggles in history, the whole idea of means and ends. Great philosophers have grappled with

Gandhi not only spoke against the caste system but he acted against it. He took "untouchables" by the hand and led them into the temples from which they had been excluded. To equal that, President Eisenhower would have taken a Negro child by the hand and led her into Central High School in Little Rock.

Martin Luther King, Jr.

Human history began with an act of disobedience, and it is not unlikely that it will be terminated by an act of obedience.

Erich Fromm

A just law is a man-made law of God. An unjust law is a code that is out of harmony with the moral law.

Martin Luther King, Jr.

Mohandas Karamchand Gandhi (1869–1948)

Mohandas Gandhi—known by the honorific term Mahatma for "great soul"—was the son of the chief minister of the Indian community of Porbanbar. His family was devoutly religious, practicing a combination of Hinduism and Jainism. After studying law in London, Gandhi went to South Africa when he was twenty-two. The racial discrimination he faced in South Africa altered his life. He became a tireless and ultimately powerful social reformer devoting himself to the abolition of all caste systems.

In 1919, Gandhi began a campaign of "passive resistance" to British rule of India. Against Gandhi's hopes, things turned violent, and Gandhi was arrested and sent to prison for two years. Gandhi led nonviolent protests in 1928 and 1940. In 1942 the British committed themselves to Indian "self-determination" at the end of World War II, and on July 17, 1948, India became an independent nation. Six months later, Gandhi was assassinated.

Gandhi was deeply impressed by the Jains' doctrine of *ahimsa* or noninjury to all living things. Among other things, Martin Luther King, Jr., was influenced by Gandhi's teaching that the means cannot be ethically isolated from the ends. The following passages are from *All Men Are Brothers*.

They say "means are after all means," I would say "means are after all everything." As the means so the end. There is no wall of separation between means and end. Indeed the Creator has given us control (and that too very limited) over means, none over the end. Realization of the goal is in exact proportion to that of the means. This is a proposition that admits of no exception. . . .

I am more concerned in preventing the brutalization of human nature than in the prevention of the sufferings of my own people. I know that people who voluntarily un-

---

If we take care of the means, we are bound to reach the end sooner or later. When once we have grasped this point final victory is beyond question. . . .

Mohandas Gandhi

---

it, and sometimes they have emerged with the idea, from Machiavelli on down, that the end justifies the means. . . .

. . . For in the long run, we must see that the end represents the means in process and the ideal in the making. In other words, we cannot believe, or we cannot go with the idea that the end justifies the means because the end is preexistent in the means. So the idea of nonviolent resistance, the philosophy of nonviolent resistance, is the philosophy which says that means must be as pure as the end, that in the long run of history, immoral destructive means cannot bring about moral and constructive ends.[36]

Philosophical Query

Apply King's doctrine of the harmony of means and ends to such current controversies as the use of violence to stop abortions, forced "outing" of gays and lesbians by gay and lesbian activists, and so forth. At some colleges, women's groups have put up posters naming "potential date rapists." When it is objected that these men have not been officially judged guilty of any wrongdoing, the activists (who are not all women) justify the risk of condemning innocent individuals by appealing to the dergo a course of suffering raise themselves and the whole of humanity; but I also know that people who become brutalized in their desperate efforts to get victory over their opponents or to exploit weaker nations or weaker men, not only drag down themselves but mankind also. And it cannot be a matter of pleasure to me or anyone else to see human nature dragged to the mire. If we are all . . . of the same God and partake of the same divine essence, we must partake of the sin of every person whether he belongs to us or to another race. You can understand how repug-

nant it must be to invoke the beast in any human being . . .

The method of passive resistance is the clearest and safest, because, if the cause is not true, it is the resisters, and they alone, who suffer.

Non-violence is the greatest force at our disposal. . . . It is mightier than the mightiest weapon of destruction . . . . Destruction is not the law of the humans. Man lives freely by his readiness to die, if need be, at the hands of his brother, never by killing him. Every murder or other injury, no matter for what cause, committed or inflicted on another is a crime against humanity. . . .

. . . I discovered in the earliest stages that pursuit of truth did not admit of violence being inflicted on one's opponent but that he must be weaned from error by patience and sympathy. For what appears to be truth to one . . . may appear to be error to another. And patience means self-suffering. So the doctrine came to mean vindication of truth, not by infliction of suffering on the opponent, but on one's self. . . .

Mahatma Gandhi
All Men Are Brothers (New York: UNESCO and Columbia University Press, 1958), III.2, 3, and 8; IV.1, 9.

good that will result from ending violence against women. What do you think of such cases? Discuss them from both pro and con viewpoints.

The Need to Practice What We Preach

King insisted repeatedly that civil disobedience must never resort to physical or emotional violence. He based his philosophy on both an ethics of justice and an ethics of caring, which he often simply referred to as *love*. By willingly suffering injustice for a truly good cause, civil dissenters could call attention to injustice and also reach out to what King called "the amazing potential goodness" in most people. Responding to violence with force—no matter how just the cause—deflects attention from the moral issues. Use of violence, for any reason, gives opponents fuel for criticism and risks harming others. The clearest moral statement, the greatest moral force, King argued, comes from active, courageous resistance, accompanied by a willingness to suffer when necessary:

> Those who adhere to or follow this philosophy must follow a consistent principle of noninjury. They must consistently refuse to inflict injury upon another. . . . Now this has an external aspect and it has

The highest result of education is tolerance.

Helen Keller

During the civil rights movement, the evening news on television regularly revealed the ugliness of racism and the moral power of civil disobedience. Scenes of passive, nonviolent resistors being hosed, beaten, and attacked by police dogs awakened the conscience of the nation (at least for a time).

There's only one way to be independent. There's only one way to be free. It's not something that someone gives you. It's something that you take. Nobody can give you independence. Nobody can give you freedom. Nobody can give you equality or justice or anything.

Malcolm X

an internal one. From the external point of view it means the individuals involved must avoid external physical violence. If they are hit in the process, they avoid external physical violence at every point. But it also means they avoid internal violence of the spirit. This is why the love ethic stands so high. . . .

. . . There is something else: that one seeks to defeat the unjust system, rather than individuals who are caught in that system.[37]

King believed that the power of self-chosen, carefully directed sacrifice and suffering could reform society by calling to the goodness that already exists in most people. He believed that the general population would ultimately respond to the abuses heaped on civil rights protesters, that—when clearly exposed—the horrible and unjust sufferings of the protesters would capture the public's attention. Once the public was paying attention, it could be educated and informed; once awakened, the public's sense of justice could be turned from such immediate concerns as lynchings, bombings, hosings, and beatings to other, deeper, historical patterns of injustice.

The importance of this cause, King reminded civil dissenters, required a most scrupulous strategy. Opponents of civil rights reform could not be given any opportunity to evade their responsibilities by citing demonstrators for acts of violence or injustice—thus King's clear, strong stance regarding self-defense and willingness to suffer:

In a nonviolent demonstration, self-defense must be approached from quite another perspective. One must remember that the cause of the demonstration is some exploitation or form of oppression that has made it necessary for men of courage and good will to demonstrate against the evil. For example, a demonstration against the evil of de facto school segregation is based on the awareness that a child's mind is crippled by inadequate educational opportunity. The demonstrator agrees that it is better for him to suffer publicly for a short time to end the crippling evil of school segregation than to have generation after generation of children suffer in ignorance.

In such a demonstration the point is made that schools are inadequate. This is the evil to which one seeks to point; anything else detracts from that point and interferes with confrontation of the primary evil against which one demonstrates. Of course, no one wants to suffer and be hurt. But it is more important to get at the cause than to be safe. It is better to shed a little blood from a blow on the head or a rock thrown by an angry mob than to have children by the thousands grow up reading at a fifth- or sixth-grade level.

It is always amusing to me when a Negro man says that he can't demonstrate with us because if someone hit him he would fight back. Here is a man whose children are being plagued by rats and roaches, whose wife is robbed daily at overpriced ghetto food stores, who himself is working for about two-thirds the pay of a white person doing a similar job and with similar skills, and in spite of all this daily suffering it takes someone spitting on him or calling him a nigger to make him want to fight.

. . . When violence is tolerated even as a means of self-defense there is grave danger that in the fervor of emotion the main fight will be lost over the question of self-defense.

When my home was bombed in 1955 in Montgomery, many men wanted to retaliate, to place an armed guard on my home. But the issue there was not my life, but whether Negroes would achieve first-class treatment on the city's buses. Had we become distracted by the question of my safety we would have lost the moral offensive and sunk to the level of our oppressors.

I must continue by faith or it is too great a burden to bear and violence, even in self-defense, creates more problems than it solves. Only a refusal to hate or kill can put an end to the chain of violence in the world and lead us toward a community where men can live together without fear. Our goal is to create a beloved community and this will require a qualitative change in our souls as well as a quantitative change in our lives.[38]

> We must never forget that everything Hitler did in Germany was "legal." . . . It was "illegal" to aid and comfort a Jew in Hitler's Germany. But I am sure that if I had lived in Germany during that time I would have aided and comforted my Jewish brothers even though it was illegal.
>
> *Martin Luther King, Jr.*

> They may have the gas ovens built before you realize that they're already hot.
>
> *Malcolm X*

Philosophical Query

Passive moral force may be as difficult as it is effective. The movie biography *Gandhi* effectively captures both aspects of nonviolent resistance, as do documentary films of civil rights demonstrations in the 1960s.

Compare nonviolent resistance with riots and spontaneous violent out-bursts such as those following the first Rodney King beating verdicts in 1992. Discuss the advantages and disadvantages of Rodney King's position. Is it realistic in today's world? Explain.

"If Not Now, When?"

To those who counseled patience—suggesting that conditions would improve if the protesters followed procedures—and who asked the courts for justice, spoke politely, and stated their case clearly, King argued that time is a luxury to a starving child, a luxury to any person denied basic rights, a luxury to an innocent person in jail, a luxury to a poor person in need of medical care, a luxury to the homeless.

We know from experience that freedom is never voluntarily given by the oppressor; it must be demanded by the oppressed. Frankly, I have never engaged in a direct action movement that was "well-timed," according to the timetable of those who have not suffered unduly from the disease of segregation. For years now I have heard the word "Wait!" It rings in the ears of every Negro with a piercing familiarity. . . . I guess it is easy for those who have never felt the stinging darts of segregation to say, "Wait." But when you have seen vicious mobs lynch your mothers and fathers at will and drown your sisters and brothers at whim; when you have seen hate-filled policemen curse, kick, brutalize and even kill your black brothers and sisters with impunity; when you see the vast majority of your twenty million Negro brothers smothering in an airtight cage of poverty in the midst of an affluent society; when you suddenly find your tongue twisted and your speech stammering as you seek to explain to your six-year-old daughter why she can't go to the public amusement park that has just been advertised on television, and see tears welling up in her little eyes when she is told that Funtown is closed to colored children, and see the depressing clouds of inferiority begin to form in her little mental sky, and see her begin to distort her little personality by unconsciously developing a bitterness toward white people; when you have to concoct an answer for a five-year-old son asking in agonizing pathos: "Daddy, why do white people treat colored people so mean?"; when you take a cross-country drive and find it necessary to sleep night after night in the uncomfortable corners of your automobile because no motel will accept you; when you are humiliated day in and day out by nagging signs reading "white" and "colored"; when your first name becomes "nigger" and your middle name becomes "boy" (however old you are) and your last name becomes "John," and when your wife and mother are never given the respected title "Mrs."; when you

They approach me in a half-hesitant sort of way, eye me curiously or compassionately, and then, instead of saying directly, How does it feel to be a problem? they say I know an excellent colored man in my town . . . or, Do not these Southern outrages make your blood boil? At these I smile, or am interested, or reduce the boiling to a simmer, as the question may require. To the real question, How does it feel to be a problem? I answer seldom a word.

W. E. B. Du Bois

Under a government which imprisons any unjustly, the true place for a just man is also in prison.

Henry David Thoreau

are harried by day and haunted at night by the fact you are a Negro, living constantly at tiptoe stance never quite knowing what to expect next, and plagued with inner fears and outer resentments; when you are forever fighting a degenerating sense of "nobodiness": then you will understand why we find it difficult to wait. There comes a time when endurance runs over, and men are no longer willing to be plunged into an abyss of injustice where they experience the blackness of corroding despair. I hope, sirs, you can understand our legitimate and unavoidable impatience.[39]

Creative Moral Tension

To those who argued for negotiation rather than confrontation, King replied that negotiation was the very essence of active nonviolent resistance. With time an indefensible luxury, with the law slow to act—sometimes the law was itself the source of injustice—with violence and self-defense ruled out as counterproductive and likely to create new abuses, the only course left for decent people was nonviolent direct action. Good people must be awakened from their moral slumber; the ability to live at peace in the midst of great injustice must be shattered. Complacency must be set aside, conscience must be aroused. But how? King's answer was to create the kind of moral tension that flows from genuine philosophical advocacy, the kind of advocacy that fuses the character of the advocate with her philosophical principles, producing precisely the kind of moral "shock" Socrates used to awaken his people to the injustices of their time:

> Nonviolent direct action seeks to create such a crisis and establish such creative tension that a community that has constantly refused to negotiate is forced to confront the issue. It seeks so to dramatize the issue that it can no longer be ignored. . . . This may sound rather shocking. But I must confess that I am not afraid of the word tension. I have earnestly worked and preached against violent tension, but there is a type of constructive nonviolent tension that is necessary for growth. Just as Socrates felt that it was necessary to create a tension in the mind so that individuals could rise from the bondage of myths and half-truths to the unfettered realm of creative analysis and objective appraisal, we must see the need of having nonviolent gadflies to create the kind of tension in society that will help men to rise from the dark depths of prejudice and racism to the majestic heights of understanding and brotherhood. So the purpose of direct action is to create a situation so crisis-packed that it will inevitably open the door to negotiation. We, therefore, concur with you in your call for negotiation. Too long has our beloved Southland been bogged down in the tragic attempt to live in monologue rather than dialogue.[40]

Now I'm not criticizing those here who are non-violent. I think everybody should do it the way they feel best, and I congratulate anybody who can be non-violent in the face of all that kind of action in that part of the world.

Malcolm X

Shallow understanding from people of good will is more frustrating than absolute misunderstanding from people of ill will. Lukewarm acceptance is much more bewildering than outright rejection.

Martin Luther King, Jr.

You Have to Speak the Language of the Brute

Malcolm X (1925–1965) spoke a different prophetic language than Martin Luther King, Jr. Malcolm X did not rule out the use of force in self-defense or the pursuit of justice. Whereas King's spiritual roots lay in Christian doctrine, Malcolm X found his voice in Islam. Born Malcolm Little, the seventh son of a Baptist minister, Malcolm X's father was brutally murdered in 1931, most likely by racists. His mother struggled to hold her family together, but circumstances eventually wore her down. As Malcolm's mother's emotional condition deteriorated, state officials sent him to live with a friend's family. In 1927, his mother was sent to a mental hospital in Kalamazoo, where she remained for nearly 26 years.

Malcolm Little dropped out of school when he was 15 and was convicted of burglary when he was 21. While in prison, he converted to the Nation of Islam (the Black Muslims). In 1952, he left prison and adopted the name Malcolm X. For twelve years, Malcolm X was an effective supporter of and activist for the Mus-

Malcolm X

lim cause. By 1964, Malcolm X was second only to Elijah Muhammed, the leader of the Nation of Islam, and tensions developed between the two men. Malcolm X had become the most powerful and brilliant voice of the black nationalist movement. The black nationalists believed that blacks must resist all efforts to subordinate them and must learn to control their own destinies.

Malcolm X left the Nation of Islam in 1964 and founded first the Muslim Mosque, Inc. and then the nonreligious Organization of Afro-American Unity. He made two trips to Africa and the Middle East in 1964, including a visit to Mecca. At two-thirty

in the morning on February 14, 1965, someone threw Molotov cocktails at Malcolm X's house. The explosion was strong enough to cause extensive damage. Though terrified, Malcolm X's family was unharmed. One week later, during a February 21, 1965, meeting of the Organization of Afro-American Unity, Malcolm X—by then known as Malik El-Shabazz—was shot and killed in the Audubon Ballroom in Harlem.

At his death, Malcolm X was both a hero and a villain to blacks (and many whites) in America and around the world. In the more than thirty years that have passed since his death, his reputation and stature have grown to nearly rival that of his fellow prophet, Martin Luther King, Jr.

Malcolm X distinguished between separation and segregation. He insisted that freedom for black people could only come through independence from white America, through *separatism*:

> Segregation is when your life and liberty are controlled, regulated, by someone else.

King said that moral tension is not *created* by nonviolent resisters; it is *exposed*:

> Actually, we who engage in nonviolent direct action are not the creators of tension. We merely bring to the surface the hidden tension that is already alive. We bring it out in the open where it can be seen and dealt with. Like a boil that can never be cured as long as it is covered up but must be opened with all its pus-flowing ugliness to the natural medicines of air and light, injustice must likewise be exposed,

To segregate means to control. Segregation is that which is forced upon inferiors by superiors. But separation is that which is done voluntarily, by two equals—for the good of both!

The universal law of justice is sufficient to bring judgment upon the American whites who are guilty of racism. The same law will also punish those who have benefitted from the racist practices of their forefathers and have done nothing to atone for the "sins of their fathers." Just look around on this earth today and see the increasing troubles this generation of American whites is having. . . . it is not necessary to look for their victim—the Afro-American—to seek revenge. The very conditions the American whites created are already plaguing them into insanity and death.

But when [people] get angry, they bring about a change. When they get angry, they aren't interested in logic, they aren't interested in odds, they aren't interested in consequences. When they get angry, they realize the condition that they're in—that their suffering is unjust, immoral, illegal, and that anything they do to correct it or eliminate it, they're justified. When you develop that type of anger and speak in that voice, then we'll get some kind of respect and recognition, and some changes from these people who have been promising us falsely for far too long.

. . . So you have to speak their language . . . the language of brutality. . . . the language of a brute, the language of someone who has no sense of morality, who absolutely ignores law—when you and I learn how to speak [this] language, then we can communicate. But we will never communicate . . . while you and I are running around with this little chicken-picking type of language. . . .

Let's learn [the racist's] language. If his language is with a shotgun, get a shotgun. Yes, I said if he only understands the language of a rifle, get a rifle. If he only understands the language of a rope, get a rope. But don't waste time talking the wrong language to a man if you really want to communicate with him. Speak his language—there's nothing wrong with that. If something was wrong with that language, the federal government would have stopped the cracker from speaking it to you and me.

Malcolm X
The Autobiography of Malcolm X (New York: Grove Press, 1964), p. 246.

Malcolm X
"Racism: The Cancer That Is Destroying America," written for the *Egyptian Gazette*, August 25, 1964, in *Malcolm X: The Man and His Times*, ed. John Henrik Clarke (New York: Macmillan Company, 1969), pp. 302–306.

Malcolm X
"With Mrs. Fannie Lou Hamer," in *Malcolm X Speaks: Selected Speeches and Statements*, ed. George Breitman (New York: Grove Weidenfeld, 1965), pp. 107–108.

with all of the tension its exposing creates, to the light of human conscience and the air of national opinion before it can be cured.[41]

A Prophetic Framework for Today

Cornel West is an example of a public philosophical advocate who regards philosophy as a "weapon that should be used in the arena of social action—to clarify issues and to help build progressive alliances across racial

You get freedom by letting
your enemy know that
you'll do anything to get
your freedom; then you'll
get it. It's the only way
you'll get it.

Malcolm X

lines."[42] Formerly a professor of religion and director of Afro-American Studies at Princeton University, West currently teaches philosophy and religion at Harvard and writes general interest books on cultural and philosophical issues. He refers to himself as "a religious and intellectual freedom fighter."

West argues that the old framework of "racial reasoning" needs to be dismantled; in its place he calls for a *prophetic framework*:

> This new framework should be a prophetic one of moral reasoning . . . a prophetic viewpoint bases mature black self-love on the moral quality of black responses to undeniable racist degradation in the American past and present. . . .
>
> Instead of a closing-ranks mentality, a prophetic framework encourages a coalition strategy that solicits genuine solidarity with those deeply committed to antiracist struggle. . . .
>
> Such coalitions are important precisely because they not only enhance the plight of black people but also because they enrich the quality of life in America. . . . Where there is no vision, the people perish; where there is no framework of moral reasoning, the people close ranks in a war of all against all.[43]

So where are we today—all of us, every age, gender, color, size, and shape of us? Can the voice of wisdom be heard over the din of anger, confusion, materialistic seduction, economic fear, nearly tribal identification with some particular feature of ourselves? Of course, no one knows for sure whether or not wisdom can be heard by the masses, but I believe that there is merit in West's efforts to take philosophy out of the academy and into the streets.

In *Race Matters*, for example, West attempts to construct a prophetic framework that can speak to "everyday people" in a voice that will reach beyond our impulses to identify with some divisive aspect of ourselves. In the passage below, he writes in the prophetic voice to point us toward a special kind of self-actualization or *psychic conversion*. Here, West writes as a prophet showing angry black people a way to build on their anger. West does not reject the experience of outrage over injustice. He does not trivialize or deny it. Instead, he recasts it into what he calls a prophetic framework:

I feel like a man who has
been asleep somewhat and
under someone else's con-
trol. I feel what I'm thinking and saying now is for
myself.

Malcolm X

> If we are to build on the best of Malcolm X, we must preserve and expand his notion of psychic conversion that cements networks and groups . . . [Our] visions, analyses, and strategies never lose sight of black rage, yet they focus this rage where it belongs: on any form of racism, sexism, homophobia, or economic injustice that impedes the opportunities of "everyday people" . . . to live lives of dignity and decency. For example, poverty can be as much a target of rage as degraded identity.

. . . This kind of critical and democratic sensibility flies in the face of any policing of borders and boundaries of "blackness," "maleness," "femaleness," or "whiteness."[44]

Commentary

It is too soon to tell whether or not feminism or prophetic philosophical advocacy will produce new philosophical archetypes. But we can reasonably expect that some of the topics touched on in this chapter will continue to attract serious philosophical attention. Complex questions concerning the effects of gender, race, and social climate on philosophizing are not easily answered. Indeed, some of these issues hearken back to issues raised by Socrates in his encounters with Sophists.

As long as impersonal, objective knowing is considered the highest type of knowledge, emotional, intuitive, personal ways of knowing and responding to life's demands will be seen as inadequate—if not dangerous. Yet care reasoning is not inferior to justice reasoning. Clearly, mere caring is not an adequate basis for the best life, nor can justice reasoning alone provide either sufficient justice or adequate care. Consider how so many of the major problems facing us today involve both care and justice: health care, homelessness, hunger, poverty, unadopted children.

Although our society has one of the most complicated sets of laws defining rights ever devised, we are discovering that emphasis on rights without equal emphasis on real caring creates a legalistic atmosphere of petty resentments and continually increasing demands for more rights. All around us we see the need for a dialogue between the voice of justice and the voice of care. Even so, public emotional responses are still seen as immature or childishly out of place by many people in politics, education, science, and philosophy. We see signs of the tension between "emotions" and "reason," and considerations of both justice and care throughout society.

The last few years have witnessed growing discouragement about race in America. Fueled by the persistence of racism and an apparently ever-widening gap between the haves and the have-nots, contemporary social reformers and rights activists seem to have rejected Martin Luther King, Jr.'s method of active, nonviolent moral resistance to injustice in favor of more direct confrontation, be it economic, legislative, or rhetorical. King's assassination, coupled with sweeping civil rights legislation, all but stopped widespread use of nonviolent resistance to injustice.

Ironically, isolated improvements in education, employment, and social opportunities for many blacks, women, and other oppressed groups may have actually slowed racial and social progress because a decline in the most obvious forms of racism and sexism has led many Americans to conclude

May the gods grant you all things which your heart desires . . . , and may they give you a home with gracious concord, for there is nothing greater and better than this—when a husband and wife keep a household in oneness of mind, a great woe to their enemies and joy to their friends, and win high renown.

Homer

Hell is when you don't have justice!

Malcolm X

that all major racial and gender problems have been solved. Events of recent years show otherwise.

Cornel West's suggestion that we can all benefit by *actively resisting* any form of injustice that "impedes the opportunities of 'everyday people'" strikes at the taproot of most types of prejudice, social insecurity, and divisiveness. West reminds us that "poverty can be as much a target of rage as degraded identity." Our greatest danger lies not in being angry at gross injustice, but in being too comfortable while others suffer unnecessarily.

Before giving in to despair or concluding that we have made all the social progress we can, we must remember that King's program of moral repair was cut down before it really flowered. We have yet to experience widespread, genuine, significant, nonviolent resistance to all forms of injustice. For that, we need prophets who can help us see that all forms of prejudice, homelessness, poverty, lack of opportunity, inferior education, and social decay are wrong in and of themselves—not because they affect this or that class of people, but because they affect *human beings*. King's great dream included everybody.

Martin Luther King, Jr.'s most famous speech, "I Have a Dream," is the best known contemporary example of the prophetic voice. Delivered in front of the Lincoln Memorial in Washington, D.C., on August 28, 1963, "I Have a Dream," officially the keynote address for the great civil rights march on Washington, transcended its ceremonial function.

The thousands of people present, and the millions watching on television, witnessed an epiphany. King seemed to speak for thousands of dead slaves, for millions of oppressed black people in America, and, ultimately, for all oppressed and powerless people everywhere. With the power of a prophet, Martin Luther King, Jr., still speaks across time to the goodness and wisdom in most of us. If you have not seen and heard a recording of this remarkable speech, you owe it to yourself to do so. As compelling as King's words are, the written speech is but a pale reflection of King's delivery—*de profundis*, from the depths of his being to, let us hope, the depths of ours:

> I have a dream that one day on the red hills of Georgia, sons of former slaves and sons of former slave-owners will be able to sit down together at the table of brotherhood. . . .
>
> I have a dream my four little children will one day live in a nation where they will not be judged by the color of their skin but by the content of their character. I have a dream today!
>
> I have a dream that one day . . . little black boys and little black girls will be able to join hands with little white boys and little white girls as sisters and brothers. I have a dream today!
>
> I have a dream that one day every valley shall be exalted, every hill and mountain shall be made low, the rough places shall be made plain, and the crooked places shall be made straight and the glory of the Lord will be revealed and all flesh shall see it together.

I still believe that standing up for the truth of God is the greatest thing in the world. This is the end of life. The end of life is not to be happy. The end of life is not to achieve pleasure and avoid pain. The end of life is to do the will of God, come what may.

Martin Luther King, Jr.

If ever America undergoes great revolutions, they will be brought about by the presence of the black race on the soil of the United States—that is to say, they will owe their origin, not to the equality, but to the inequality of conditions.

Alexis de Tocqueville

. . . With this faith we will be able to work together, to pray together, to struggle together, to go to jail together, to stand up for freedom together, knowing that we will be free one day. This will be the
day when all of God's children will be able to sing with new meaning—"my country 'tis of thee; sweet land of liberty; of thee I sing;
land where my fathers died, land of the pilgrim's pride; from every
mountain side, let freedom ring"—and if America is to become a
great nation, this must become true. . . .

And when we allow freedom to ring, when we let it ring from every
village and hamlet, from every state and city, we will be able to speed
up that day when all of God's children—black men and white men,
Jews and Gentiles, Catholics and Protestants—will be able to join
hands and to sing in the words of the old Negro spiritual, "Free at
last, free at last; thank God almighty, we are free at last."[45]

> The society of money and
> exploitation has never been
> charged, so far as I know,
> with assuring the triumph
> of freedom and justice.
>
> *Albert Camus*

Summary of Main Points

1. A philosophical advocate is a philosopher whose work identifies, clarifies, and actively opposes a perceived injustice; philosophical advocates give philosophical credence to personal experience based on gender, ethnic background, or social status.

2. One current critique of modern philosophy holds that, with rare exceptions, Western philosophers have failed to recognize that they have personal, social, gendered, and ethnic perspectives. Consequently, some modern and contemporary philosophers remain blind to the fact that their philosophy reflects the interests of only a small portion of the human community. According to certain feminist philosophers, one source of this blindness is the masculinization of philosophy.

3. In the narrowest sense, feminism refers to attempts to attain equal legal and political rights for women. In the broadest sense, feminism refers to any theory that sees the relationship between the sexes as unequal due to the oppression of women and the disparagement of women's particular experience, and that aims to identify and remedy the sources

of gender inequality and oppression. A feminist is any person who believes in the fundamental equality of women and men and who actively contributes to the struggle to achieve such equality.

4. According to Susan Bordo, a "masculinizing" of modern philosophical thought reached a watershed at the beginning of the modern period. Bordo asserts that Cartesian modernity is inherently linked to the repression of both nature and women. Bordo argues that the daily lives of women do not reflect Cartesian dualism because women's experiences are embodied experiences that cannot be abstracted into distinct mental and physical substances.

5. Bordo suggests that modern philosophy began with an exaggerated emphasis on objectivism and mechanism as a kind of reaction formation to a new cosmic order. The result, she says, was a flight from the feminine and a restructuring of knowledge and the world as masculine.

6. As the limits and negative effects of over-emphasis on the values of objectivity and

personal detachment have become increasingly apparent to growing numbers of people, converging contemporary social, political, and intellectual movements are contributing to reawakened interest in other voices and other approaches to doing philosophy and practicing science.

7. John Rawls is an influential modern philosopher who has constructed a theory of justice designed to overcome the limits of personal bias that prevent us from basing our moral and social values on objective and impartial rational principles.

8. In a feminist analysis of Rawls, Stanford University professor Susan Moller Okin argues that overlooked gender-bias remains present in both the language and choice of examples employed in Rawls's influential attempt to refine Kant's modern moral philosophy. Okin analyzes Rawls's theory of justice with special attention to issues of gender and the family, arguing that Rawls's position is "ambiguous" regarding gender because he rarely indicates how deeply and pervasively gender-structured this society is.

9. Troubled by the work of Lawrence Kohlberg, Harvard psychologist Carol Gilligan's research into moral development has led her to distinguish between a masculine-oriented ethic of justice, such as Rawls's, and a feminine-oriented ethic of care. Gilligan suggests that interest in universalized justice dominates Western values by restricting most moral and political discussion to issues of rights and duties. The ethic of care, in contrast, is about actual relationships and intimate concerns, which cannot be confined to a set of rules and list of duties.

10. Gilligan says that fallacious justice reasoning results in too little justice by excluding those oriented toward care from full participation in philosophy, science, law, and higher education—and by denying access to the full range of knowledge necessary for wise choices. Fallacious care reasoning can obscure the fact that the caregiver has rights and a point of view, too; this results in caregivers who become so identified with taking care of others that they sacrifice themselves in ineffective, inappropriate ways.

11. Martin Luther King, Jr. (1929–1968), is an example of a public philosophical advocate, a public intellectual who addresses current social, moral, and political issues in a personally committed way, rather than in the impersonal and detached manner of a scholar. Public philosophical advocates assert moral and philosophical principles in a manner designed to reach a broad audience. They may or may not be philosophers in the strictest sense.

12. King practiced a form of nonviolent direct action. Active nonviolent resistance differs from passive acceptance of injustice in that nonviolent resistance deliberately interferes with whatever is being opposed. King believed that the power of self-chosen, carefully directed sacrifice and suffering could reform society by calling to the goodness that exists in most people. He claimed that most people would eventually respond to the abuses heaped on civil rights protesters, as the horrible and unjust sufferings of the protesters would capture the public's attention and appeal to a widespread, if slumbering, sense of justice.

13. Cornel West is a Harvard professor and public philosophical advocate who argues that the old framework of racial reasoning needs to be dismantled. In its place he calls for a prophetic framework that, he says, "flies in the face of any policing of borders and boundaries of 'blackness,' 'maleness,' 'femaleness,' or 'whiteness.'"

Study Questions

1. What is philosophical advocacy? What philosophical issues are associated with the problem of advocacy?

2. Use the notion of postmodernity to summarize the critique of modern philosophy.

3. What is feminism? Can men be feminists?

4. Explain what Susan Bordo means by "the Cartesian masculinization" of philosophy.

5. What is a "thought experiment"? Give an example of one and explain how it works.

6. What is the "original position"?

7. What is the "veil of ignorance"?

8. What is the relationship between the original position and the veil of ignorance?

9. In what sense is John Rawls's *A Theory of Justice* an elaboration on Kant's moral philosophy?

10. Why does Susan Moller Okin say that Rawls's theory of justice is ambiguous?

11. What is Okin's chief criticism of Rawls?

12. What is the "different voice" Carol Gilligan refers to? What is its significance?

13. Compare and contrast the ethic of justice with the ethic of care.

14. What was Lawrence Kohlberg's theory of moral development? What was Gilligan's criticism of it?

15. Describe fallacious justice reasoning.

16. Describe fallacious care reasoning.

17. Who are Linda Brown and Rosa Parks, and what is their significance to the American civil rights movement?

18. What is "active nonviolent resistance"? What is "creative moral tension"? How are they related?

19. What was King's position regarding means and ends? Why was the issue so important to him?

20. Discuss King's views on self-defense during protest activities.

21. What is what Cornel West refers to as a "new prophetic framework"?

Τῶν ὄντων τὰ μέν ἐστιν ἐφ' ἡμῖν,
ἐφ' ἡμῖν. ἐφ' ἡμῖν μὲν ὑπόληψις, ὁρμή,
σις καὶ ἑνὶ λόγῳ ὅσα ἡμέτερα ἔργα· ο
δὲ τὸ σῶμα, ἡ κτῆσις, δόξαι, ἀρχαὶ κ
καὶ τὰ μ
φύσει ἐλεύθερον κώλυτα, ἀπα
τα δὲ οὐκ ἐφ' ἡμῖν ἀσθενῆ, δοῦλα, κω
τρια· μέμνησο οὖν, ὅτι, ἐὰν τὰ φύσει
ερα οἰηθῇς καὶ τὰ ἀλλότρια ἴδια, ἐμ
πενθήσεις, ταραχθήσῃ, μέμψῃ καὶ
νθρώπους, ἐὰν δὲ τὸ σὸν μόνον οἰηθ
τὸ δὲ ἀλλότριον, ὥσπερ ἐστίν, ἀλλ
σε ἀναγκάσει οὐδέποτε, οὐδείς σε κω
έμψῃ οὐδένα, οὐκ ἐγκαλέσεις τινί,
εις οὐδὲ ἕν, ἐχθρὸν οὐχ ἕξεις,[1] οὐδ
ει, οὐδὲ γὰρ βλαβερόν τι πείσῃ.

Continuative

While we're waiting to live, life passes us by.
Pierre Hadot

I have not written *Archetypes of Wisdom* just to convey philosophical facts and arguments, but also to evoke philosophical yearnings that most of us experience—but don't always recognize as being philosophical. I can think of no better way to say "Fare thee well" than to encourage you not to diminish, forget, or forsake the love of wisdom. Think of this brief Continuative as a personal invitation to keep company with the sages.

I hope that in addition to any intellectual satisfaction you have found in philosophy, you have also *experienced* something special: a sense of the majesty of the human condition that is simultaneously poignant, profound, encouraging, humbling, and comforting. The special experience I am referring to evokes a longing to be a better, wiser person—not in any specific way, but in a fundamental way. This longing is the *love of wisdom*, and it triggers a "felt need" for an honest vision of the human condition and of our particular place in it.

Once felt, the need to see the human condition and our particular place in it "as a whole" never leaves us. The need to find meaning in a capricious, dangerous world never leaves us. Life assaults us with questions of choice, value, meaning—*philosophical* questions: issues of fairness; choices among "evils"; existential conditions that demand action; forced choices that, once made, obliterate all other possibilities. Highly specialized professional philosophers properly see themselves as scholars rather than sages. Scholars and other experts abound, but sages are rare.

Today, the public function of the *sophos*, or sage, has been taken over by the priest, the scientist, the psychologist, and the all-too-eager "celebrity guru." Every year seems to produce another celebrity guru, another blockbuster book about the soul, wisdom, metaphysics, ancient secrets, past lives, angels, wise "entities," "simple secrets of happiness." The 1997 mass suicide of more than thirty members of the Heaven's Gate cult is but one dramatic example of the lengths people will go to in order to fulfill their longing for meaning. Media reports stressed how "intelligent" and "successful" the dead Heaven's Gate cult members were. Commentators

Discourse about philosophy is not the same thing as philosophy.

Pierre Hadot

Discourse on virtue and they pass by in droves; whistle and dance the shimmy and you've got an audience.

Diogenes

Without philosophy the
mind is sickly.

Seneca

expressed surprise and dismay that such intelligent and successful people
could be so gullible, so "lost."

What the media reports did not stress was something known to the sages
for at least two thousand years: Without wisdom, intelligence has no guide.
When Empedocles told Xenophanes that it was impossible to find a wise
man, Xenophanes is said to have replied: "Naturally, for it takes a wise
man to recognize a wise man."

Wisdom Query

Imagine Socrates, Epictetus, and Diogenes wandering through a modern
bookstore. Imagine them channel-surfing or roaming the Internet. Describe a detailed scenario—including philosophical conversations and
comments—in which these sages confront today's claimants to wisdom.
Would they be impressed? Angry? Amused? Saddened? If you feel up to
it, generate a rational, respectful discussion of specific books, guru figures, "philosophical" belief systems. This is dangerous stuff—but it's also
invigorating and important stuff. (Try using other philosophers, too.)

The Unifying Function of Wisdom

There is, I assure you, a
medical art for the soul. It
is philosophy, whose aid
need not be sought, as in
bodily diseases, from outside ourselves. We must
endeavor with all our re-
sources and all our strength
to become capable of doc-
toring ourselves.

Cicero

It is tempting for some sophisticated Americans to dismiss the search for
wisdom as a form of sophomoric naïveté and self-indulgence—or to ro-
manticize it as the cure-all for the ills of our confused, technological,
crowded society. Both views miss the true splendor and power of one important aspect of searching for wisdom: the *therapeutic* unifying function
of seriously valuing such a search. One of the best ways to achieve this
therapeutic effect is to make philosophical reading and reflection a regular part of our lives—as regular as exercise, recreation, and work. Without
deluding ourselves or trying to become sages ourselves, we can nonetheless join the sages by living our own examined lives.

Stories about sages and philosophers take the need for wisdom seriously, a need that this society tends to ignore or trivialize. In the following
passage, Denise L. Carmody and John T. Carmody capture the problem of
resurrecting respect for wisdom in today's world, and suggest one direction:

> . . . You do not like . . . quirky phrases? Paradoxes put you off? Ah
> well, no . . . sage ever promised you a garden of platitudes. . . . It is
> not cruelty that makes good gurus demanding. It is unusual kindness.
> In the spiritual life you become what you do . . . outer persona and
> inner self must come closer and closer together.
>
> What doth it profit a person if she can assemble any stereo and
> never hears the music of the spheres? What doth it profit a person to
> place all his energies in the stock market? Stereos and the stock mar-

ket have their place—all the . . . sages allow them. What the . . . sages do not allow them is primacy of place. . . . To hear the Tao [Logos, Truth, Wisdom] in the morning or in the evening, to die content, one must vacate assembling and selling. The business of life is not business. The business of life is being. . . . It does not matter that many of our schools know nothing of such . . . wisdom. The college catalogue is seldom a great book. Real learning occurs in dark nights and painful passages. Wisdom to live goes far below figures and facts.

. . . If today you would possess your soul, you must empty it of what is tawdry. If today you would hear the [wisdom], you must attune your inner ear.

Does the . . . sage have a distinctive message for today's students . . .? Perhaps so. If the students come from the West they likely have been touched by [a] loss of confidence in wisdom . . . people who speak authoritatively about enlightenment, persuasively incarnate [wisdom], are few and far between. So, an increasingly influential argument has arisen. "Since so few wise people appear in our midst," the argument runs, "wisdom must be an endangered species, going the way of the dodo. Evolution must be in the hands of the technicians . . . shouting 'can do!'" Swiftly and surely, the . . . sages rebut this argument. Let [the sage] occupy your mind a half-hour and the marines will lie high and dry. "What can you do?" [the sage] politely asks. "What is the end of all your technique? If your graphs do not bring you beauty, your tanks do not win you peace, why all your plotting and piloting?"[1]

Like the Carmodys, the late historian of philosophy Will Durant believed that without wisdom, technological progress and social "success" will only confuse us and make us unhappier than before:

Human conduct and belief are now undergoing transformations profounder and more disturbing than any since the appearance of wealth and philosophy put an end to the traditional religion of the Greeks. It is the age of Socrates again: our moral life is threatened, and our intellectual life is quickened and enlarged by the disintegration of ancient customs and beliefs. Everything is new and experimental in our ideas and our actions; nothing is established or certain any more. The rate, complexity, and variety of change in our time are without precedent . . . all forms about us are altered, from the tools that complicate our toil, to the wheels that whirl us restlessly about the earth, to the innovations in our sexual relationships, and to the hard disillusionment of our souls. . . .

Our culture is superficial today, and our knowledge dangerous, because we are rich in mechanisms and poor in purposes. The balance of mind which once came of a warm religious faith is gone; science has taken from us the supernatural bases of our morality, and all the world seems consumed in a disorderly individualism that reflects the

To be truly commercial is to do well that which should not be done at all.

Gore Vidal

The untrained mind shivers with excitement at everything it hears.

Heraclitus

Truth, or wisdom if you will, cannot be identified by committees or social institutions, and technology is only a new name for mechanism. Wisdom is revealed socially: in our families, friendships, and consciously honored commitments.

Guiseppe Vargasini

chaotic fragmentation of our character. . . . We move about the earth with unprecedented speed, but we do not know, and have not thought, where we are going, or whether we shall find any happiness there for our harassed souls. We are being destroyed by our knowledge, which has made us drunk with our power. And we shall not be saved without wisdom.[2]

In a remarkably insightful and timeless passage, the Taoist sage Chuang-tzu speaks across generations and cultures:

There is often chaos in the world, and the love of knowledge is ever at the bottom of it. For all men strive to grasp what they do not know, while none strive to grasp what they already know. . . . Thus, above, the splendor of the heavenly bodies is dimmed; below, the power of land and water is burned up, while in between the influence of the four seasons is upset. There is not one tiny worm that moves on earth or an insect that flies in the air but has lost its original nature. Such indeed is the world chaos caused by the desire for knowledge![3]

> Philosophy heals human diseases, diseases produced by false beliefs. Its arguments are to the soul as the doctor's remedies are to the body.
>
> *Martha C. Nussbaum*

Philosophy as a Way of Life

Pierre Hadot's *Philosophy as a Way of Life* is one of my favorite books. In it, Hadot, Professor Emeritus of the History of Hellenistic and Roman Thought at the Collège de France, presents a distillation of his accumulated knowledge and experience as a professional scholar and lover of wisdom. He takes seriously the sage's goal that philosophy become a way of life. Although technical and scholarly, Hadot's text contains many powerful passages that capture the richness of lived philosophy, the therapeutic action of philosophy done out of love of wisdom.

According to Hadot, the true philosopher

knows that the normal, natural state of [human beings] should be wisdom, for wisdom is nothing more than the vision of things as they are, the vision of the cosmos as it is in the light of reason, and wisdom is also nothing more than the mode of being and living that should correspond to this vision. But the philosopher also knows that this wisdom is an ideal state, almost inaccessible. For such a [lover of wisdom], daily life, as it is organized and lived by other [people], must necessarily appear abnormal, like a state of madness, unconsciousness, and ignorance of reality. . . . And it is precisely in this daily life that [lovers of wisdom] must seek to attain that way of life which is utterly foreign to the everyday world. The result is a perpetual conflict between the philosopher's effort to see things as they are from the standpoint of universal nature and the conventional

> The history of philosophy is a history of misfits; but, then, who in her right mind would have wanted to "fit in" with Caligula's court, Stalin's sadists, or Hitler's thugs? "Normal" is hardly a term of high praise.
>
> *Sir Ross Delbert-Fetters*

vision of things underlying human society, a conflict between the life one should live and the customs and conventions of daily life. This conflict can never be totally resolved.[4]

Even though Hadot asserts that the conflict between wisdom and "the world" can never be totally resolved, he nonetheless promises what the sages have always promised: Life is better with philosophy than without it, and if wisdom is hard to define precisely, it is still worth seeking because taking wisdom seriously raises our sights, requires more of us than does abandoning the search. Whatever wisdom is or is not, we do know that technology, possessions, fame, fortune, high grades, attractive figures, and disease-free years are not enough to make life meaningful. As attractive and pleasing as these things can be, nothing external can make us happy if being happy means more than "satisfied" or "pleased." In one form or another, this is the teaching of Socrates, Epicurus, Epictetus, Marcus Aurelius, Buddha, Jesus, Muhammad, Kierkegaard, our grandparents, pastors, and wiser elders. Who are we to refute the teachings of the wise? (But how wise is it to accept such teachings without testing and questioning them?)

Philosophical Remembering

In his book *The Heart of Philosophy*, contemporary philosopher Jacob Needleman writes:

> Man cannot live without philosophy. This is not a figure of speech, but a literal fact that [can] be demonstrated. . . . There is a yearning in the human heart that is nourished only by real philosophy and without this nourishment man dies as surely as if he were deprived of food or air. But this part of the human psyche is not known or honored in our culture. When it does break through to our awareness, it is either ignored or treated as though it were something else. It is given wrong names; it is not cared for; it is crushed. And eventually, it may withdraw altogether, never again to appear. When this happens, man becomes a thing. No matter what he accomplishes or what he performs, he has in fact lost his real possibility. He is dead.
>
> The fear of this inner death has begun to surface in the modern world. In quiet moments, an individual senses this fear of dying inwardly and sees that all the other fears of his life—his physical and psychological fears—are in no way related to it. At the same time, he senses—along with this fear—a yearning or love unknown to him in his ordinary life. He sees that none of the other loves of his life—his family, his work, perhaps not even his God—are related to that yearning for something he cannot name. And he wonders what he can do to heal this profound division in himself between the wish for being and his psychosocial needs. Neither ordinary religion, nor therapy, nor social action, nor adventure, nor work, nor art can bridge these

Think about these and related matters day and night, by yourself and in company with someone like yourself. If you do, you will never experience anxiety, waking or sleeping, but you will live like a god among men. For a human being who lives in the midst of immortal blessings is in no way like mortal man!

Epicurus

We need to make sure that philosophy and the search for wisdom are regular parts of our lives, lest we forget what really matters.

Douglas J. Soccio

Receive each moment of accumulating time as though it came about by an incredible stroke of luck.

Pierre Hadot

We should exercise ourselves with realities, not with dialectical speculations, like a man who has devoured some textbook on harmonics, but has never put his knowledge into practice. Likewise, we must not be like those who can astonish their onlookers by their skill in syllogistic argumentation, but who, when it comes to their own lives, contradict their own teachings.

Polemon

two fundamental notions for him. But no sooner does a man move into the activities of his life than this division within himself is forgotten.

What will help him remember? For it is absolutely essential that he remember this truth about himself. If he does not, he will be absorbed by the external forces of nature and society. He will be "lived" by the emotions, opinions, obligations, terrors, promises, programs, and conflicts that comprise the day-to-day life of every human being. He will forget that there are actually two separate lives within him and that these disparate lives need to be related to each other. He will strive for happiness, creativity, love, service to the higher; for vitality, commitment, honor; for understanding, health, integrity; for safety, exhilaration, passionate involvement—but nothing of this will be possible for him in the state of metaphysical forgetfulness. As long as he does not remember the real twofold structure of his being, he and the life around him will form themselves into a tissue of illusion.

The function of philosophy in human life is to help man remember. *It has no other task*. And anything that calls itself philosophy which does not serve this function is simply not philosophy.

But modern man has strayed so far from philosophy that he no longer even knows what this sort of remembering is. We think of memory only as mental recall because the experience of deep memory has vanished from our lives. Therefore, I ask you not to turn to the dictionary or to modern psychological texts for clarification about remembering. It is not something that can be defined right at the outset; its meaning will emerge as we proceed [in our search for wisdom]—this I promise.[5]

In the following passage, Pierre Hadot suggests a way to deal with what Needleman characterizes as the "twofold structure" of our being:

The trick is to maintain oneself on the level of reason, and not allow oneself to be blinded by political passions, anger, resentments, or prejudices. To be sure, there is an equilibrium—almost impossible to achieve—between the inner peace brought about by wisdom, and the passions to which the sight of the injustices, sufferings, and misery of mankind cannot help but give rise. Wisdom, however, consists in precisely such an equilibrium, and inner peace is indispensable for efficacious action.

Such is the lesson of ancient philosophy: an invitation to each human being to transform himself. Philosophy is a conversion, a transformation of one's way of being and living, and a quest for wisdom. This is not an easy matter. As Spinoza wrote at the end of the *Ethics*:

If the way which I have pointed out as leading to this result seems exceedingly hard, it may nevertheless be discovered. It must indeed be hard, since it is so seldom found. How would it be possible, if salvation were easy to find, and could without great labour be found, that it should be neglected by almost everybody? But all excellent things are as difficult as they are rare.[6]

Let Philosophy Touch Your Heart

Hadot reminds us that part of the difficulty Spinoza recognizes is due to the very nature of the human condition:

> Everything which is "technical" in the broad sense of the term, whether we are talking about the exact sciences or the humanistic sciences, is perfectly able to be communicated by teaching or conversation. But everything that touches the domain of the existential—which is what is most important for human beings—for instance, our feeling of existence, our impressions when faced by death, our perception of nature, our sensations . . . is not directly communicable. The phrases we use to describe them are conventional and banal; we realize this when we try to console someone over the loss of a loved one. That's why it often happens that a poem or a biography are more philosophical than a philosophical treatise, simply because they allow us to glimpse this unsayable in an indirect way.[7]

Passages from many philosophical masterpieces are included throughout *Archetypes of Wisdom*. Others are listed in the Bibliography of Interesting Sources. I find myself returning again and again to a select few for consolation, encouragement, and wisdom. Following are selections from four of my favorite philosophical writers: Chuang-tzu, Viktor Frankl, Philo Judaeus (first century), and Epictetus. I hope that they move and inspire you, and that philosophy—in some form or other—becomes a regular, enriching part of your life.

From *The Chuang-tzu*:

> Suppose you and I argue. If you beat me instead of my beating you, are you really right and am I really wrong? If I beat you instead of your beating me, am I really right and are you really wrong? Or are we both partly right and partly wrong? Or are we both wholly right and wholly wrong? Since between us neither you nor I know which is right, others are naturally in the dark. Whom shall we ask to arbitrate? If we ask someone who agrees with you, since he has already agreed with you, how can he arbitrate? If we ask someone who has already agreed with me, how can he arbitrate? If we ask someone who disagrees with both you and me to arbitrate, since he has already disagreed with you and me, how can he arbitrate? If we ask someone who agrees with both you and me to arbitrate, since he has already agreed with you and me, how can he arbitrate? Thus, among

Wisdom has never been a social norm; talking about wisdom, on the other hand, seems to be.

Guiseppe Vargasini

The lessons of wisdom are not new, just hard to take sometimes—and easy to forget when things are going well.

Douglas J. Soccio

you, me, and others, none knows which is right. Shall we wait for still others?[8]

From Viktor Frankl's *Man's Search for Meaning:*

When we are no longer able to change a situation—just think of an incurable disease such as inoperable cancer—we are challenged to change ourselves.

Let me cite a clear-cut example: Once, an elderly general practitioner consulted me because of his severe depression. He could not overcome the loss of his wife who had died two years before and whom he loved above all else. Now, how could I help him? What should I tell him? Well, I refrained from telling him anything but instead confronted him with the question, "What would have happened, Doctor, if you had died first, and your wife had been the one to survive you?" "Oh," he said, "for her this would have been terrible; how she would have suffered!" Whereupon I replied, "You, see, Doctor, such a suffering has been spared her, and it was you who have spared her this suffering—to be sure, at the price that now you have to survive and mourn her." He said no word but shook my hand and calmly left my office. In some way, suffering ceases to be suffering at the moment it finds a meaning, such as the meaning of a sacrifice.[9]

From *On the Special Laws* by Philo Judaeus:

Every person—whether Greek or Barbarian—who is *in training for wisdom,* leading a blameless, irreproachable life, chooses neither to commit injustice nor return it unto others, but to avoid the company of busybodies, and hold in contempt the places where they spend their time—courts, councils, marketplaces, assemblies—in short, every kind of meeting or reunion of thoughtless people. As their goal is a life of peace and serenity, they contemplate nature and everything found within her: they attentively explore the earth, the sea, the air, the sky, and every nature found therein. In thought, they accompany the moon, the sun, and the rotations of the other stars, whether fixed or wandering. Their bodies remain on earth, but they give wings to their souls, so that, rising into the ether, they may observe the powers which dwell there, as is fitting for those who have truly become citizens of the world. Such people consider the whole world as their city, and its citizens are the companions of wisdom; they have received their civic rights from virtue, which has been entrusted with presiding over the universal commonwealth. Thus, filled with every excellence, they are accustomed no longer to take account of physical discomforts or exterior evils, and they train themselves to be indifferent to indifferent things; they are armed against both pleasures and desires, and, in short, they always strive to keep themselves above passions . . . they do not give in under the blows of fate, because they have calculated its attacks in advance (for foresight makes easier to bear even

---

Whether or not the world is ruled by reason (and thus by providence), don't *you* act unreasonably.

Marcus Aurelius

"What is the fruit of your doctrines?" Epictetus was asked. His reply was three crisp words: "Tranquillity, Fearlessness, and Freedom." I'll never let go of that. I've moved "inside."

James Bond Stockdale

It is one thing to remember, another to know.

Seneca

the most difficult of the things that happen against our will; since then the mind no longer supposes what happens to be strange and novel, but its perception of them is dulled, as if it had to do with old and worn-out things). It is obvious that people such as these, who find their joy in virtue, celebrate a festival their whole life long. To be sure, there is only a small number of such people; they are like embers of wisdom kept smouldering in our cities, so that virtue may not be altogether snuffed out and disappear from our race. But if only people everywhere felt the same way as this small number, and became as nature meant for them to be: blameless, irreproachable, and *lovers of wisdom*, rejoicing in the beautiful just because it *is* beautiful, and considering that there is no other good besides it . . . then our cities would be brimful of happiness. They would know nothing of the things that cause grief and fear, but would be so filled with the causes of joy and well-being that there would be no single moment in which they would not lead a life full of joyful laughter; indeed, the whole cycle of the year would be a festival for them.[10]

I have probably read the small collection of teachings of Epictetus known as *The Enchiridion* more than any other book. I think so highly of it that I have handed out countless copies to students, friends, and family members. You will recall that the handbook was originally compiled for Roman soldiers to carry on long, difficult military campaigns. We might also think of it as a handbook to carry and consult in our daily campaign against the confusions, deceptions, and distractions of modern life. Let me say, "Fare thee well, philosopher" with a message from Epictetus:

How long do you put off thinking yourself worthy of the best things, and [worthy of] never going against the definitive capacity of reason? You have received the philosophical propositions that you ought to agree to and you have agreed to them. Then what sort of teacher are you still waiting for, that you put off improving yourself until he comes? You are not a [child] anymore, but already . . . full grown. . . . If you now neglect things and are lazy and are always making delay after delay and set one day after another as the day for paying attention to yourself, then without realizing it you will make no progress but will end up a non-philosopher all through life and death. So decide now that you are worthy of living as a full-grown [human being] who is making progress, and make everything that seems best be a law you cannot go against. And if you meet with any hardship or anything pleasant or reputable or disreputable, then remember that the contest is now and the Olympic games are now and you cannot put things off any more and that your progress is made or destroyed by a single day and a single action. Socrates became fully perfect in this way. . . . You, even if you are not yet Socrates, ought to live as one wanting to be [like] Socrates.[11]

The medicines for the soul were discovered by the ancients—but it is our job to find out how to apply them and when. Our predecessors accomplished a lot, but not everything

Seneca

Douglas Soccio

Notes

Chapter 1
Philosophy and the Search for Wisdom

1. Mary Ellen Waithe, *Introduction to the Series, A History of Women Philosophers*, vol. 1, 600 B.C.–500 A.D., ed. Mary Ellen Waithe (Dordrecht: Martinus Nijhoff Publishers, 1987), pp. IX–X.
2. "Newsmakers," *Los Angeles Times*, December 29, 1989.
3. Albert Hakim, *A Historical Introduction to Philosophy* (New York: Macmillan, 1987), pp. viff.
4. Will Durant, *The Mansions of Philosophy: A Survey of Human Life and Destiny* (New York: Simon & Schuster, 1929), pp. vii, viii, xff.

Overview of Classical Themes

1. W. T. Jones, *A History of Western Philosophy: The Classical Mind*, 2nd ed. (New York: Harcourt Brace Jovanovich, 1970), p. 2.

First Interlude
The Presocratic Sophos

1. Mircea Eliade, *Shamanism* (Princeton, N.J.: Princeton University Press, 1964), pp. 3–13. See also Denise L. Carmody and John T. Carmody, *Eastern Ways to the Center: An Introduction to Religions of the West* (Belmont, Calif.: Wadsworth Publishing, 1981), pp. 9–11.
2. Carmody and Carmody, *Eastern Ways to the Center*, pp. 9–11.
3. See Denise L. Carmody and John T. Carmody, *Western Ways to the Center: An Introduction to Religions of the West* (Belmont, Calif.: Wadsworth Publishing, 1981), pp. 210–213.
4. Pierre Hadot, *Philosophy as a Way of Life*, trans. Arnold I. Davidson (Oxford: Blackwell, 1995), pp. 56–61.
5. Ibid., p. 57.
6. Ibid.
7. Christopher Janaway, "Ancient Greek Philosophy I: The Pre-Socratics and Plato," in *Philosophy: A Guide Through the Subject*, ed. A. C. Grayling (Oxford: Oxford University Press, 1995), p. 338.
8. Plato, *Theatetus*, 174A, trans. F. M. Cornford in *The Collected Dialogues of Plato: Including the Letters* (New York: Pantheon Books, 1961), p. 879.
9. Aristotle, *Metaphysics*, M'Mahon trans., pp. i, 3.
10. J. Barnes, *The Presocratic Philosophers: Arguments of the Philosophers* (London, 1989), p. 72.
11. Ibid., p. 74.
12. Will Durant, *The Story of Civilization, vol. 2: The Life of Greece* (New York: Simon and Schuster, 1966), pp. 138–139.
13. Janaway, p. 342.
14. Plato, *Parmenides*, 127A, in Cornford, *The Collected Dialogues of Plato*, p. 921.
15. Plato, *Parmenides*, Fragment 3, Freeman trans., in Giovanni Reale, *A History of Ancient Philosophy, vol. 1: From the Origins to Socrates*, trans. John R. Catan (Albany, N.Y.: State University of New York Press, 1987), p. 84.
16. Reale, p. 87.
17. W. T. Jones, *The Classical Mind: A History of Western Philosophy*, 2nd ed. (New York: Harcourt Brace Jovanovich, 1970), pp. 21–22.
18. Theophrastus, quoted in G. S. Kirk and J. E. Raven, *The Presocratic Philosophers* (Cambridge, England: Cambridge University Press, 1957), p. 344.
19. Kirk and Raven, p. 345.
20. Jones, p. 27.
21. Anaxagoras, Frg. 10; Kirk and Raven, p. 378.
22. Jones, p. 29; Peter Angeles, *Dictionary of Philosophy* (New York: Barnes & Noble Books, 1981), p. 191.
23. Reale, p. 114.
24. Anaxagoras, Frg. 12; Reale, p. 114.
25. Anaxagoras, Frg. 11; Burnet, *Early Greek Philosophy, 4th ed.* (London, 1930), p. 259.
26. Anaxagoras, Frg. 21, Jones, p. 29.
27. Charles H. Kahn, *The Art and Thought of Heraclitus* (Cambridge, England: Cambridge University Press, 1979), pp. 1–3.
28. Reale, p. 53.
29. Janaway, p. 343.
30. Reale, p. 53.
31. Heraclitus, Frg. 23, *Herakleitos and Diogenes*, trans. Guy Davenport (San Francisco: Grey Fox Press, 1979), p. 15.
32. Jones, p. 16.
33. Heraclitus, Frg. 116; Davenport, p. 31.
34. Heraclitus, Frg. 117; Davenport, p. 31.
35. Heraclitus, Frgs. 25, 26, 27, 98, and 99; Davenport, pp. 15, 55.
36. Amaury de Riencourt, *Sex and Power in History* (New York: David McKay, 1974), p. 97ff.
37. Ibid., p. 99.

Chapter 2
The Sophist: Protagoras

1. Plato, *The Republic*, trans. H. D. P. Lee (London: Penguin, 1955), bk. 7, sec. 6.
2. See W. K. C. Guthrie, *The Sophists* (Cambridge, England: Cambridge University Press, 1971); Giovanni Reale, *From the Origins to Socrates*; Will Durant, *The Story of Civilization, vol. 2: The Life of Greece* (New York: Simon & Schuster, 1939); Frederick Copleston, S.J., *A History of Philosophy, vol. 1: Greece and Rome* (New York: Image, 1985).
3. Will Durant, *The Story of Philosophy* (New York: Simon & Schuster, 1953), p. 358.
4. Guthrie, *The Sophists*, p. 35.
5. Plato, *The Sophist*, 231D–E, in Reale, *From the Origins to Socrates*, p. 149; emphasis added.
6. Xenophon, *Memorabilia*, trans. E. C. Marchant, in *Xenophon, Memorabilia and Oeconomics* (London and Cambridge, Mass.: Loeb Classical Library, 1959), bk. 1, sec. 6, line 13.
7. Plato, *Theaetetus*, trans. F. M. Cornford, 151E–152A, in Reale, *From the Origins to Socrates*, p. 157.

8. Gregory Vlastos, *Protagoras* (Indianapolis, Ind.: Bobbs-Merrill, Library of Liberal Arts ed., 1956), pp. xii–xvi, xviii–xix.
9. Plato, *Theaetetus*, 166D, in Reale, *From the Origins to Socrates*, pp. 160ff.
10. Plato, *Gorgias*, trans. W. C. Helmbold (Indianapolis, Ind.: Bobbs-Merrill, Library of Liberal Arts ed., 1952), pp. 482–486.
11. Ibid., p. 457B.

Chapter 3
The Wise Man: Socrates

1. W. K. C. Guthrie, *Socrates* (Cambridge, England: Cambridge University Press, 1971), p. 6.
2. Plato, *Phaedo*, 60C–D, trans. Benjamin Jowett, in *The Dialogues of Plato*, 3rd ed. (Oxford: Clarendon Press, 1892).
3. Guthrie, *Socrates*, p. 4.
4. Ibid.
5. Xenophon, *Symposium*, trans. E. C. Marchant (London and Cambridge, Mass.: Loeb Classical Library, 1959), ch. 2, line 18.
6. Plato, *Gorgias*, 470E, in Reale, *From the Origins to Socrates*, p. 219.
7. Xenophon, *Symposium*, ch. 5, in Guthrie, *Socrates*, pp. 67–68.
8. Xenophon, *Memorabilia*, bk. 1, sec. 6, line 10, in Reale, *From the Origins to Socrates*, p. 216.
9. Ibid., sec. 2, lines 29–30. See also Mary Renault's novel, *The Last of the Wine* (New York: New English Library paperback, 1968), pp. 120ff.
10. Xenophon, *Memorabilia*, bk. 4, sec. 5, lines 9ff., in Reale, *From the Origins to Socrates*, p. 218.
11. Plato, *Apology*, 34D, trans. Benjamin Jowett, in *The Dialogues of Plato: Phaedo*, 60A.
12. Durant, *Life of Greece*, p. 367.
13. Karl Jaspers, *Socrates, Buddha, Confucius, Jesus: The Paradigmatic Individuals*, trans. Ralph Manheim, ed. Hannah Arendt (New York: Harcourt Brace Jovanovich, Harvest paperback, 1962), p. 87.
14. Pierre Hadot, *Philosophy as a Way of Life*, trans. Arnold I. Davidson (Oxford: Blackwell, 1995), 147.
15. Plato, *Apology*, 17A.
16. Plato, *The Republic*, trans. H. D. P. Lee (London: Penguin, 1955), bk. I, sec. 3, lines 336–339.
17. Reale, *A History of Ancient Philosophy*, p. 202.
18. Plato, *Apology*, 21B–E.
19. Plato, *Apology*, 20C.
20. Ibid., 22D, 23A.
21. Plato, *Apology*, 29–30.
22. Plato, *Gorgias*, W. C. Helmbold trans., 468b–c.
23. Plato, *Protagoras*, 345e, Benjamin Jowett trans., Martin Ostwald revision (Indianapolis, Ind.: Bobbs-Merrill, 1956), p. 49.
24. Plato, *Meno*, 87–89, Jowett trans. in *Plato's Meno: Text and Criticism*, eds. Alexander Sesonske and Noel Fleming (Belmont, Calif.: Wadsworth Publishing, 1965), pp. 24–26.
25. Plato, *Meno*, Jowett trans., 77b–78b.
26. Plato, *Apology*, 40A.
27. Plato, *Phaedo*, 115Dff.
28. Ibid., 117Bff.

Chapter 4
The Philosopher-King: Plato

1. Diogenes Laërtius, *Life of Plato*, in *Lives of Eminent Philosophers*, trans. R. H. Hicks (Cambridge, Mass.: Harvard University Press, 1925).
2. Plato, *Letter: VII*, 324E, trans. L. A. Post, in *Plato: The Collected Dialogues*, p. 1575.
3. See A. W. Levi, "Ancient Philosophy: The Age of the Aristocrat," Chapter 2 in *Philosophy as Social Expression* (Chicago: University of Chicago Press, 1974), for a full discussion of the influence of social class on Plato.
4. Ibid., p. 66.
5. Plato, *Letter: VII*, 325D–326B, p. 1576.
6. A. E. Taylor, *Plato: The Man and His Works* (London: Methuen, 1966), pp. 6ff.
7. Christopher Janaway, "Ancient Greek Philosophy I: The Pre-Socratics and Plato," in *Philosophy: A Guide Through the Subject*, ed. A. C. Grayling (Oxford: Oxford University Press, 1995), pp. 378, 380. In the *Parmenides*, Plato revisits some of the difficult questions generated by the theory of forms.
8. Janaway, p. 378.
9. Peter A. Angeles, *Dictionary of Philosophy* (New York: Barnes & Noble Books, 1981), p. 124.
10. Plato, *Timaeus*, 27D–28A, trans. Benjamin Jowett, in *The Dialogues of Plato*, 3rd ed. (Oxford: Clarendon Press, 1892).
11. Plato, *The Republic*, 506, pp. 269–270.
12. This characterization of the lowest level goes beyond what Plato says in this section, but is required considering what he does say in the Allegory of the Cave and in Book X about poetry and art.
13. Plato, *The Republic*, 510–511, pp. 276–277.
14. Plato, *The Republic*, 508–509, pp. 272–273.
15. Plato, *The Republic*, 511, p. 278.
16. Plato, *The Republic*, bk.VII: 516, pp. 278–281.
17. Plato, *The Republic*, 516–517, pp. 281–282.
18. Plato, *The Republic*, bk. I, Prelude, pp. 327–328.
19. H. D. P. Lee, introduction to Plato, *The Republic*, p. 87.
20. B. A. G. Fuller, *History of Greek Philosophy*, vol. 2 (New York: Henry Holt, 1931), p. 214.
21. Plato, *The Republic*, bk. II, 363, pp. 94ff.
22. Taylor, *Plato: The Man and His Works*, p. 270.
23. Plato, *The Republic*, bk. IV, 442E–443A, p. 194.
24. Ibid., bk. VIII, sec. 6, p. 326.
25. Ibid., 555C, p. 327.
26. Ibid., 557, pp. 329ff.
27. Ibid., p. 330.
28. Ibid., p. 331.
29. Ibid., 561, p. 334.
30. Ibid., 563, pp. 336–337.
31. Ibid., bk. IX, 573–574, pp. 346ff.

Chapter 5
The Naturalist: Aristotle

1. In the 1970s, psychologists Daniel Levinson and G. E. Vailant identified something called a "mid-life crisis," which, they claimed, prompted major disruptions in men's lives. Since then, other psychologists, like Carol Gilligan (see Chapter 15), have pointed out that in mid-life both men and women try to establish better balance in their

lives. Earlier, Erik Erikson had proposed a theory of personal development based on psychosocial stages. He coined the term "identity crisis" to characterize typical changes during adolescence. See Phillip G. Zimbardo, *Psychology and Life*, 12th ed. (Glenview, Ill.: Scott, Foresman, 1988), pp. 98–99.

2. Durant, *Life of Greece*, p. 526.
3. Diogenes Läertius, *Life of Plato*, sec. 25.
4. Samuel Enoch Stumpf, *Philosophy: History and Problems*, 4th ed. (New York: McGraw-Hill, 1989), bk. 1, p. 83.
5. Durant, *Life of Greece*, p. 525.
6. W. T. Jones, *The Classical Mind*, 2nd ed. (New York: Harcourt Brace Jovanovich), 1970, p. 219.
7. Aristotle, *Metaphysics*, bk. 7, ch. 1, 1028A10.
8. Aristotle, *Physics*, bk. 2, ch. 7.
9. Ibid., bk. 2, ch. 1, 93A10.
10. Ibid., 193A36–193B6.
11. Ibid., bk. 2, ch. 7, 198A, pp. 33–35.
12. Aristotle, *Physics*, bk. 2, ch. 8, sec. 199b, line 15, trans. Phillip Wheelwright, in *Aristotle* (New York: Odyssey, 1951).
13. Sir David Ross, *Aristotle* (London: Methuen, 1966), p. 129.
14. Aristotle, *Nicomachean Ethics*, bk. 1, 1094A, trans. J. C. Welldon, in *Philosophers Speak for Themselves*, ed. T. V. Smith (Chicago: University of Chicago Press, 1934).
15. Ibid., 1094B.
16. Ibid., 1095A.
17. Ibid., 1095B.
18. Ibid., 1096A.
19. Ibid., 1095B.
20. This treatment of eudaimonia is based in part on material found in Burton F. Porter, *Reasons for Living: A Basic Ethics* (New York: Macmillan, 1988), pp. 204–207.
21. Aristotle, *Nicomachean Ethics*, bk. 1, 1095Bff, trans. J. C. Welldon, in *Philosophers Speak for Themselves*.
22. Aristotle, *Nicomachean Ethics*, 1103B30, trans. Martin Ostwald (Indianapolis, Ind.: Library of Liberal Arts, 1962).
23. Ibid., 1104A13.
24. Ibid., 1104Aff.
25. Aristotle, *Nicomachean Ethics*, 1103A17ff, trans. W. D. Ross, in *Basic Works of Aristotle*, p. 952.
26. Aristotle, *Nicomachean Ethics*, trans. Martin Ostwald, 1143B22.
27. Ibid., 1144A6.
28. Ibid., 1106B15.
29. I am indebted to Burton F. Porter's *Reasons for Living* for excellent examples of recent trends in self-realization.
30. Abraham Maslow, *Motivation and Personality* (New York: Harper & Row, 1970), p. 279.
31. Carl Rogers, *On Becoming a Person* (Boston: Houghton Mifflin, 1961), pp. 187ff.
32. Ibid., p. 195.
33. Thomas Merton, *New Seeds of Contemplation* (New York: New Directions, 1961), p. 98.

Second Interlude

The Hedonist

1. *Newsweek*, January 15, 1990.
2. Lin Yutang, *The Importance of Living* (New York: John Day, 1937), p. 127.
3. Christopher Lasch, *The Culture of Narcissism: American Life in an Age of Diminishing Expectations* (New York: W. W. Norton, 1979), quoted in Christina Sommers and Fred Sommers, *Vice and Virtue in Everyday Life*, pp. 644–665.

4. Xenophon, *Memorabilia*, bk. 2, sec. 1, line 11, trans. E. C. Marchant.
5. Epicurus, Frg. 221, in Giovanni Reale, *A History of Ancient Philosophy, vol. 3: The Systems of the Hellenistic Age*, ed. and trans. John R. Catan (Albany, N.Y.: State University of New York Press, 1985), p. 111.
6. Reale, *Systems of the Hellenistic Age*, p. 113.
7. Ibid.
8. Durant, *Life of Greece*, p. 645.
9. Robert F. Davidson, *Philosophies Men Live By* (New York: Holt, Rinehart, and Winston, 1974), p. 36.
10. Stobaeus, *Anthology*, bk. 3, sec. 17, line 33, in Reale, *Systems of the Hellenistic Age*, p. 170.
11. Epicurus, Frg. 138, trans. G. Murray, in *History of Greek Religion* (Oxford: Oxford University Press, 1930), p. 141.
12. Diogenes Läertius, *Epicurus*, sec. 10, in *Lives of Eminent Philosophers*, trans. R. Hicks.
13. Epicurus, *Letter to Herodotus 38*, in Reale, *Systems of the Hellenistic Age*, p. 134.
14. Epicurus, *Letter to Herodotus 67*, in Reale, *Systems of the Hellenistic Age*, p. 151.
15. Lin Yutang, *The Importance of Living*, pp. 25ff.
16. Epicurus, *Letter to Menoceceus*, trans. George D. Strodach, quoted in *Hellenistic Philosophy*, ed. Herman Shapiro and Edwin M. Curley (New York: Modern Library, 1965), p. 5.
17. Epicurus, *Leading Doctrine*, trans. George K. Strodach, in *Hellenistic Philosophy*, p. 10.
18. Epicurus, *Letter to Menoceceus*, p. 6.
19. Ibid., pp. 7ff.
20. Ibid., p. 8.
21. Reale, *Systems of the Hellenistic Age*, p. 178.
22. Ibid.
23. Epicurus, *Sententiae Vaticanae 78*, trans. W. Y. Oates, in Reale, *Systems of the Hellenistic Age*, p. 179.
24. Epicurus, *Principal Doctrines 23*, quoted in Reale, *Systems of the Hellenistic Age*, p. 179.
25. Epicurus, *Principal Doctrines 39*, p. 179.
26. Epicurus, *Sententiae Vaticanae*, p. 179.
27. Epicurus, *Letter to Menoceceus*, p. 8.

Chapter 6

The Stoic: Epictetus and Marcus Aurelius

1. Epicurus, *Principal Doctrines*, 4.
2. Epictetus, *Discourses*, trans. P. E. Matheson (Oxford: Clarendon Press, 1916), in William Sahakian and Mabel Lewis Sahakian, *Realms of Philosophy* (Cambridge, Mass.: Schenkman, 1965), p. 133.
3. Epictetus, *Handbook of Epictetus*, trans. Nicholas P. White (Indianapolis, Ind.: Hackett, 1983), p. 13.
4. This sketch of Epictetus's life is based on Philip Hallie's entry on Epictetus in *The Encyclopedia of Philosophy*, vol. 3, ed. Paul Edwards et al. (New York: Macmillan and the Free Press, 1967), p. 1.
5. Marcus Aurelius, *Meditations*, bk. 7, sec. 54, trans. George Long, in *Plato, Epictetus, Marcus Aurelius* (Harvard Classics ed.) (New York: P. Collier & Son, 1937).
6. Ibid., bk. 6, sec. 2.
7. Ibid., bk. 7, sec. 58, 59.
8. From Maxwell Staniforth's entry in *Encyclopedia of Philosophy*, vol. 5, p. 156.
9. Seneca, "On Tranquility," in *The Stoic Philosophy of Seneca*, trans. Moses Hadas (New York: W. W. Norton, 1958), p. 93.

10. Epictetus, *Enchiridion*, sec. 27, trans. George Long, in *The Discourses of Epictetus with the Encheiridion and Fragments* (New York: A. L. Burt, 1929).
11. Seneca, *Letter 41*, in *Stoic Philosophy of Seneca*, p. 188.
12. Ibid.
13. Marcus Aurelius, *Meditations*, bk. 7, sec. 22, 23, 25, trans. Maxwell Staniforth (Middlesex: Penguin Books, 1970).
14. Ibid.
15. Seneca, "On Self-Control," trans. Gunmere, in *Philosophers Speak for Themselves*, pp. 623ff.
16. Epictetus, *Enchiridion*, sec. 1.
17. Ibid., sec. 4.
18. Ibid., sec. 1.
19. Ibid.
20. Ibid., sec. 30.
21. Ibid., sec. 25.
22. Seneca, "On Providence," in *Stoic Philosophy of Seneca*, p. 37.
23. Ibid., pp. 38–39.
24. William Glasser, *Positive Addiction* (New York: Harper & Row, 1976), p. 1.
25. Albert Ellis, *Humanistic Psychotherapy*, ed. Edward Sagarin (New York: McGraw-Hill, 1973), p. 32.
26. Ibid., p. 32.
27. Albert Ellis and Robert A. Harper, *A New Guide to Rational Living* (North Hollywood, Calif.: Wilshire Books, 1978), p. 5.
28. Ibid., pp. 178–79.
29. Viktor E. Frankl, *Man's Search for Meaning: An Introduction to Logotherapy* (New York: Pocket Books, 1963), p. 178.
30. Ibid., p. 179.
31. Viktor E. Frankl, "Logotherapy and the Challenge of Suffering," in *Psychotherapy and Existentialism: Selected Papers by Viktor E. Frankl* (New York: Simon & Schuster, 1967), p. 90.
32. James Bond Stockdale, "The World of Epictetus," *Atlantic Monthly*, April 1978, reprinted in Sommers and Sommers, *Vice and Virtue in Everyday Life*, pp. 592–593.
33. James Bond Stockdale, *Epictetus' Enchiridion*, in *Text and Teaching: The Search for Human Excellence*, ed. Michael J. Collins and Frances J. Ambosio (Washington, D.C.: Georgetown University Press, 1991), pp. 39–42.

Chapter 7

The Scholar: Thomas Aquinas

1. W. T. Jones, *A History of Western Philosophy: The Medieval Mind*, 2nd ed. (New York: Harcourt Brace Jovanovich, 1969), p. 2.
2. Vernon J. Bourke, in *Aquinas' Search for Wisdom* (Milwaukee, Wisc.: Bruce, 1965), identifies discrepancies in many biographical sketches of Thomas Aquinas, since most are based on William of Tocco. Bourke points out that all we know for sure is that Thomas was born between 1220 and 1227. The commonly cited date of 1225 originated with Tocco and cannot be verified.
3. Bourke, *Aquinas' Search for Wisdom*, p. 18.
4. Levi, *Philosophy as Social Expression*, p. 106.
5. William of Tocco in Bourke, *Aquinas' Search for Wisdom*, p. 37.
6. See "The Age of the Saint" in Levi, *Philosophy as Social Expression*.
7. Ibid.

8. Martin Grabmann, *Die Geschichte der Scholastichen Methode* (1957), trans. A. W. Levi, quoted in *Philosophy as Social Expression*, p. 125.
9. Based on Peter A. Angeles, *Dictionary of Philosophy* (New York: Barnes & Noble Books, 1981), p. 250.
10. Levi, *Philosophy as Social Expression*, pp. 122ff.
11. Ibid., p. 124.
12. From Thomas Aquinas's commentary on Aristotle's Metaphysics, quoted in Levi, *Philosophy as Social Expression*, p. 102.
13. "More Turning to Prayer to Handle Life: Spiritual Path Often Leads Outside Church," *Sacramento Bee*, March 11, 1990.
14. The Five Ways are found in *Summa Theologica*, trans. Dominican Fathers, *Basic Writings of Saint Thomas Aquinas*, ed. A. C. Pegis (New York: Random House, 1945), part 1, ques. 2, art. 3.
15. Ibid.
16. Ibid.
17. Ibid.
18. Ibid.
19. Jones, *The Medieval Mind*, pp. 220ff.
20. Thomas Aquinas, *Summa contra Gentiles*, trans. English Dominican Fathers (London: Bunns Oates, 1924), part 3, ques. 25.

Overview of Modern Themes

1. Martin Luther, *A Treatise on Christian Liberty*, trans. W. A. Lambert, in *Works of Martin Luther*, vol. 2 (Philadelphia: A. J. Holman, 1915), p. 318.
2. Quoted in William K. Hartmann, *Astronomy: The Cosmic Journey* (Belmont, Calif.: Wadsworth Publishing, 1991), p. 64.

Chapter 8

The Rationalist: René Descartes

1. *The Philosophical Works of Descartes*, vol. 1, trans. Elizabeth Haldane and G. R. T. Ross (Cambridge, England: Cambridge University Press, 1931; reprint, New York: Dover, 1931), p. 87.
2. Quoted in Levi, *Philosophy as Social Expression*, p. 185.
3. René Descartes, *Discourse on Method*, in *Philosophical Works*, vol. 1, p. 83.
4. Descartes, *Rules for the Direction of the Mind*, in *Philosophical Works*, vol. 1, p. 6.
5. Ibid., pp. 9, 14.
6. Descartes, *Discourse on Method*, p. 88.
7. Ibid., pp. 81ff.
8. Descartes, *Meditation I*, in *Philosophical Works*, vol. 1, pp. 144–145.
9. Ibid., pp. 145–146.
10. Ibid., p. 148.
11. Descartes, *Meditation II*, in *Philosophical Works*, vol. 1, p. 150.
12. Ibid., pp. 151–53.
13. Descartes, *Meditation III*, in *Philosophical Works*, vol. 1, p. 159.
14. Ibid., p. 165.
15. Ibid., p. 166.
16. Ibid., p. 169.
17. Ibid., p. 170.
18. Ibid., pp. 170–171.
19. Descartes, *Meditation VI*, in *Philosophical Works*, vol. 1, p. 185.

20. Ibid., p. 191.
21. Ibid., p. 195.
22. Gilbert Ryle, *The Concept of Mind* (New York: Harper & Row, 1941), p. 11.
23. Descartes, *Meditation VI*, in *Philosophical Works*, vol. 1, p. 192.

Third Interlude

The Buddha

1. The brief sketch that follows is based on Nancy Wilson Ross, *Buddhism: A Way of Life and Thought* (New York: Vintage, 1981); see also Edward Conze, *Buddhism: Its Essence and Development* (New York: Harper Torchbooks, 1965), *Stories of the Buddha: Being Selections from the Jataka*, trans. and ed. by Caroline A. F. Rhys Davids (New York: Dover Publications, 1989), and Richard H. Robinson and Willard L. Johnson, *The Buddhist Religion* (Encino, Calif.: Dickenson, 1977).
2. Ross., *Buddhism*, p. 6.
3. Ibid., p. 10.
4. Ibid., p. 18.
5. Ibid.
6. Ibid., p. 33.
7. The Buddha, "The Discourse on Universal Love," in Ross, *Buddhism*, p. 32.
8. Ross, *Buddhism*, p. 26.
9. Padmasiri de Silva, "Buddhist Ethics," in *A Companion to Ethics*, ed. Peter Singer (Oxford: Basil Blackwell, 1993), p. 64.
10. Ibid., p. 58.
11. Ibid., pp. 59–60.
12. Ibid, p. 61, and "Basic Original Doctrines Essential to Zen," by Rev. Master P.T.N.H. Jiyu-Kennett, M.O.B.C. In Jiyu-Kennett, *Zen Is Eternal Life* (Mt. Shasta, Calif.: Shasta Abbey Press, 1987), p. 9.
13. Ross, *Buddhism*, pp. 23ff.
14. Modified from Ross, *Buddhism*, p. 24.
15. See Ross, *Buddhism*, pp. 24ff.
16. Ibid., p. 35.
17. De Silva, p. 65.
18. Ibid., p. 65.
19. Ross, *Buddhism*, p. 26.
20. Ibid., p. 26f.
21. Ibid., p. 27.
22. Ibid., p. 37.
23. De Silva, Ibid., p. 66.
24. Ibid.
25. A. Burtt, ed., *The Teachings of the Compassionate Buddha* (New York: Mentor, 1982), pp. 202ff.
26. Ibid., pp. 34ff, 36.
27. Ibid., p. 204.

Chapter 9

The Skeptic: David Hume

1. H. R. Fox Bourne, *The Life of John Locke*, vol. 1 (New York: Harper, 1876), pp. 200–201.
2. John Locke, "Epistle to the Reader," in *An Essay Concerning Human Understanding*, ed. A. C. Fraser (Oxford: Clarendon Press, 1894), p. 9.
3. John Locke, "The Art of Medicine" (a paper written in 1669), quoted in Fox Bourne, vol. I, p. 224, and John Locke, *An Essay Concerning Human Understanding*, ed. A. C. Fraser (Oxford: Clarendon Press, 1894), bk. 4, ch. 7, sec. 11.
4. Ibid., bk. 1, ch. 3, sec. 24–25.
5. Ibid., bk. 2, ch. 11, sec. 17.
6. Ibid., bk. 2, ch. 1, sec. 2.
7. Ibid., bk. 2, ch. 23, sec. 1.
8. Ibid., sec. 2.
9. Ibid., sec. 3.
10. Ibid., sec. 5.
11. Ibid. sec. 29.
12. George Berkeley, *Three Dialogues Between Hylas and Philonous*, in *Selections*, ed. Mary W. Calkins (New York: Scribner's, 1957), pp. 268–269.
13. Ibid., pp. 238–239.
14. George Berkeley, *A Treatise Concerning the Principles of Human Knowledge*, in *The Works of George Berkeley*, vol. 1, ed. A. C. Fraser (Oxford: Clarendon Press, 1901), part 1, sec. 3.
15. Ernest C. Mossner, *Life of David Hume* (1954; reprint, Oxford: Clarendon Press, 1970), p. 51.
16. Thomas H. Huxley, *Hume* (New York, 1901), p. 3.
17. Mossner, *Life of David Hume*, p. 94.
18. Richard Watson, *The Philosopher's Diet: How to Lose Weight and Change the World* (Boston: Atlantic Monthly Press, 1985), p. 97.
19. Mossner, *Life of David Hume*, p. 111.
20. Ibid., p. 213.
21. Ibid., pp. 223, 318.
22. David Hume, "My Own Life," in *Dialogues Concerning Natural Religion*, ed. Henry D. Aiken (New York: Hafner, 1948), p. 239.
23. Mossner, *Life of David Hume*, p. 568.
24. Hume, "My Own Life," p. 239.
25. Ibid., p. 244.
26. Mossner, *Life of David Hume*, pp. 598–600.
27. David Hume, *An Enquiry Concerning Human Understanding*, ed. L. A. Selby-Bigge (Oxford: Clarendon Press, 1894), sec. 2.
28. Ibid.
29. I owe using the idea of God to illustrate the empirical criterion of meaning to Robert Paul Wolff's *About Philosophy*.
30. David Hume, *A Treatise of Human Nature*, ed. L. A. Selby-Bigge (Oxford: Clarendon Press, 1896), bk. 1, part 4, sec. 6.
31. Ibid.
32. Ibid.
33. Hume, *Enquiry Concerning Human Understanding*, bk. 12, part 1.
34. Hume, *Treatise*, bk. 1, part 4, sec. 2.
35. Ibid.
36. Hume, *Enquiry Concerning Human Understanding*, sec. 7, parts 1, 2.
37. Hume, *Dialogues Concerning Human Religion*, ed. Norman Kemp-Smith (Edinburgh: Nelson, 1947), part 2.
38. Ibid., part 11, and *Enquiry Concerning Human Understanding*, sec. 1.
39. *Dialogues*, parts 10, 11.
40. Ibid., part 7.
41. Ibid.
42. Ibid., bk. II, § III.
43. David Hume, *An Enquiry Concerning the Principles of Morals*, ed. L. A. Selby-Bigge (Oxford: Clarendon Press, 1894), *Appendix I*.
44. Ibid., § I.

45. Hume, *Treatise*, bk. 2, part 3, sec. 3.
46. Hume, *Treatise*, bk. 3, part 1, sec. 1.
47. Hume, *An Enquiry Concerning the Principles of Morals*, § I.
48. Hume, *Treatise*, bk. 3, part 1, sec. 2.
49. Hume, *An Enquiry Concerning the Principles of Morals*, Appendix II.
50. Ibid.
51. Ibid.
52. Hume, *Dialogues*, parts 10, 11.
53. Hume, *Treatise*, bk. 1, part 4, sec. 7.
54. Hume, *Enquiry Concerning Human Understanding*, part 1.

Chapter 10

The Universalist: Immanuel Kant

1. In A. D. Lindsay, *Kant* (London: Oxford University Press, 1934), p. 2.
2. Henry Thomas and Dana Lee Thomas, *Living Biographies of Great Philosophers* (Garden City, N.Y.: Blue Ribbon Books, 1941), p. 191.
3. In Josiah Royce, *The Spirit of Modern Philosophy* (Boston: Houghton Mifflin, 1892), p. 108.
4. Ben-Ami Scharfstein, *The Philosophers: Their Lives and the Nature of Their Thought* (New York: Oxford University Press, 1980), pp. 210–230.
5. R. B. Jachmann, in *Immanuel Kant: Sein Leben in Darstellungen von Zietgenossen*, ed. Felix Gross (Berlin: DeutscheBibliothek, 1912), trans. Ben-Ami Scharfstein, 9th letter, pp. 171–173.
6. Scharfstein, *The Philosophers*, pp. 214–215ff.
7. Thomas and Thomas, *Living Biographies*, p. 198.
8. Norman Kemp Smith, *Commentary to Kant's "Critique of Pure Reason"* (London: Macmillan, 1923), p. xix.
9. Immanuel Kant, preface to 1st ed. of *Critique of Pure Reason*, trans. Norman Kemp Smith (London: Macmillan, 1929), p. 13.
10. Thomas and Thomas, *Living Biographies*, p. 196.
11. Friedrich Schiller, *Poems in Works* (London, 1901).
12. Immanuel Kant, *Religion Within the Limits of Reason Alone*, trans. T. H. Greene and H. H. Hudson (Chicago: Open Court, 1934), p. xxxiv.
13. Quoted in Will Durant, *The Story of Civilization, vol. 10: Reason and Revolution* (New York: Simon & Schuster, 1967), p. 547.
14. Crane Brinton, *The Portable Age of Reason Reader* (New York: Viking, 1956), p. 1.
15. W. T. Jones, *A History of Western Philosophy: Kant and the Nineteenth Century*, rev. 2nd ed. (New York: Harcourt Brace Jovanovich, 1975), p. 1.
16. Immanuel Kant, *What Is Enlightenment?*, trans. W. T. Jones, in *Immanuel Kant Werke*, vol. 4, ed. E. Cassirer (Berlin: E. Cassirer, 1922), pp. 169ff.
17. Quoted by Robert Paul Wolff in *About Philosophy*, p. 358.
18. Immanuel Kant, *Prolegomena to Any Future Metaphysics*, trans. Lewis White Beck (Indianapolis, Ind.: Liberal Arts Press, 1950), intro., pp. 5–6.
19. See Jones, *Kant and the Nineteenth Century*, pp. 19ff.
20. Immanuel Kant, *Critique of Pure Reason*, 2nd ed., trans. Norman Kemp Smith, unabridged ed. (New York: St. Martin's Press, 1929), pp. 41–42.
21. Ibid., p. 532.
22. Ibid., pp. 557ff.
23. Ibid., pp. 558ff.
24. Ibid., p. 559.
25. Roger Scruton, "The Rationalists and Kant," in *Philosophy: A Guide Through The Subject*, ed. A. C. Grayling (Oxford: Oxford University Press, 1995), p. 475.
26. Ibid., pp. 475–476.
27. See Immanuel Kant, *Critique of Practical Reason and Other Essays*, trans. Lewis White Beck (Chicago: University of Chicago Press, 1949), p. 8, B, ix.
28. S. Körner, *Kant* (Baltimore: Penguin, 1955), pp. 129ff.
29. Immanuel Kant, *Fundamental Principles of the Metaphysics of Morals*, trans. T. K. Abbott (London: Longmans, Green, 1927), sec. 1, p. 10.
30. Ibid., p. 16.
31. Ibid., p. 17.
32. Ibid., sec. 2, p. 36.
33. Ibid., sec. 1, p. 18.
34. Mary Corey, "Cheating Common for Many," *Redding (Calif.) Record-Searchlight*, May 25, 1990.
35. Kant, *Metaphysics of Morals*, sec. 2, pp. 46–47.
36. H. J. Paton, trans., *Kant's Groundwork of the Metaphysics of Morals*, 3rd ed. (New York: Harper & Row Torchbook, 1964), p. 96.

Chapter 11

The Materialist: Karl Marx

1. Quoted in Isaiah Berlin, *Karl Marx* (New York: Oxford University Press, 1939), p. 73.
2. Condensed from "Karl Marx's Funeral," in Robert Payne, *Marx* (New York: Simon & Schuster, 1968), pp. 500–502.
3. Karl Marx, *Critique of Political Economy*, trans. N. I. Stone, in *Marx and Engels: Selected Works*, vol. 1 (Moscow: Foreign Languages Publishing House, 1955), pp. 362–364.
4. In Sidney Hook, *Towards the Understanding of Karl Marx* (New York: John Day, 1932), pp. 80–81, and "Theses on Feuerbach, III," in *Karl Marx and Friedrich Engels on Religion*, ed. Reinhold Niebuhr (New York: Schocken Books, 1964), p. 70.
5. Karl Marx, *Economic and Philosophic Manuscripts*, trans. T. B. Bottomore, in Erich Fromm, *Marx's Concept of Man* (New York: Ungar, 1961), p. 181.
6. Karl Marx, *Critique of Political Economy*, trans. N. I. Stone (Chicago: C. H. Kerr, 1911), p. 11.
7. Karl Marx and Friedrich Engels, *Manifesto of the Communist Party*, 1888 ed., reprinted in Avrum Stroll and Richard H. Popkin, *Introductory Readings in Philosophy* (New York: Holt, Rinehart, and Winston, 1972), p. 412.
8. Ibid., p. 413.
9. Ibid., p. 415.
10. Ibid.
11. Ibid., pp. 415ff.
12. Ibid., p. 416.
13. Ibid., pp. 416–417.
14. Ibid., p. 418.
15. Karl Marx, *Economic and Philosophic Manuscripts* (1844), in *Writings of the Young Marx on Philosophy and Society*, ed. and trans. Loyd D. Easton and Kurt H. Guddat (Garden City, N.Y.: Anchor Doubleday, 1967), p. 290.
16. Ibid., p. 292.
17. Ibid., p. 294.
18. Herbert Marcuse, *One-Dimensional Man: Studies in the Ideology of Advanced Industrial Society* (Boston: Beacon Press, 1964), pp. x, xiv.
19. Erich Fromm, *The Art of Loving* (1956; reprint, New York: Perennial Library, 1974), pp. 70–71, 72–73, 89.

Fourth Interlude

The Utilitarians

1. Jones, *Kant and the Nineteenth Century*, p. 162.
2. Thomas Malthus, *An Essay on the Principle of Population as It Affects the Future Improvement of Society* (London, 1798), p. 4.
3. Jeremy Bentham, *An Introduction to Principles of Morals and Legislation* (Oxford: Oxford University Press, 1823 ed.), ch. 1, sec. 1.
4. A. Bain, *John Stuart Mill* (1882; reprint, New York: Augustus M. Kelley, 1966), p. 334.
5. B. Mazlish, *James and John Stuart Mill* (New York: Basic Books, 1975), p. 66.
6. John Stuart Mill, *Autobiography*, ed. J. D. Stillinger (London: Oxford University Press, 1971), pp. 6, 9.
7. John Stuart Mill, *Autobiography* (New York: Columbia University Press, 1924), pp. 21–22.
8. Mill, *Autobiography*, ed. J. D. Stillinger, p. 20.
9. Ibid., p. 33, note 3.
10. Mazlish, *James and John Stuart Mill*, pp. 201–202, and M. St. John Packe, *The Life of John Stuart Mill* (London: Stecker & Warburg, 1954), pp. 66–68.
11. Mill, *Autobiography*, ed. J. D. Stillinger, pp. 32, 33, note 3.
12. Mill, *Autobiography* (Columbia), pp. 97–98.
13. Mill, *Autobiography*, ed. J. D. Stillinger, pp. 83–84.
14. Ibid., p. 85.
15. Mill, *Autobiography* (Columbia), p. 122.
16. Lewis S. Feuer, "John Stuart Mill as a Sociologist: The Unwritten Ethology," in John Stuart Mill, *On Socialism* (1879; reprint, Buffalo, N.Y.: Prometheus Books, 1987), p. 10.
17. Jeremy Bentham, *The Rationale of Reward*, in *The Works of Jeremy Bentham* (Edinburgh: Tait, 1838–1843), part 2, sec. 1, p. 253.
18. John Stuart Mill, *Utilitarianism*, Chapter 2, "What Utilitarianism Is," in *The Utilitarians* (Garden City, N.Y.: Dolphin Books, 1961), p. 407.
19. Ibid., pp. 408–409.
20. Ibid., p. 409.
21. Ibid., pp. 410–411.
22. Ibid., p. 418.
23. Ibid., pp. 412–413.
24. Ibid., pp. 414–415.
25. Ibid., p. 415.
26. Ibid., pp. 415ff.
27. Ibid., p. 416.
28. Mill, *Utilitarianism*, Chapter 3, p. 437.
29. Mill, *Autobiography* (Columbia), p. 100.

Chapter 12

The Existentialist: Søren Kierkegaard and Jean-Paul Sartre

1. Samuel Enoch Stumpf, *Philosophy*, bk. 1, p. 475.
2. Søren Kierkegaard, *The Journals of Søren Kierkegaard*, trans. Alexander Dru (New York: Oxford University Press, 1938), p. 94.
3. Søren Kierkegaard, *The Point of View for My Work as an Author*, conclusion (abridged), trans. Walter K. Lowrie, in *A Kierkegaard Anthology*, ed. Robert Bretall (New York: Modern Library, 1946), pp. 337, 339.
4. Kierkegaard, *Journals*, p. 4.

5. Kierkegaard, *Concluding Unscientific Postscript*, trans. D. F. Swenson, L. M. Swenson, and W. K. Lowrie, 1846 ed., in *A Kierkegaard Anthology*, p. 276, and *The Journals of Kierkegaard*, trans. and ed. Alexander Dru (London: Collins, 1958), p. 46.
6. Søren Kierkegaard, *Either/Or, vol. 1: Diapsalmata*, trans. D. F. Swenson, L. M. Swenson, and W. K. Lowrie, in *A Kierkegaard Anthology*, p. 33.
7. William Barrett, *Irrational Man: A Study in Existential Philosophy* (Garden City, N.Y.: Doubleday Anchor, 1958), p. 173.
8. Søren Kierkegaard, "The Individual and the Public," in *The Present Age*, trans. Alexander Dru, in *A Kierkegaard Anthology*, pp. 260–261.
9. Ibid., p. 263.
10. Robert Bly, *The Sibling Society*, Reading, Mass.: Addison-Wesley, 1996, pp. vii–viii.
11. Cited in Albert Camus and Jean-Paul Sartre, *Camus and Sartre* (New York: Dell, 1972), p. 71.
12. Jean-Paul Sartre, *The Words*, trans. Bernard Frechtman (New York: Fawcett World Library, 1966), p. 52.
13. Ibid., p. 25.
14. Jean-Paul Sartre, *Nausea*, trans. L. Alexander (New York: New Directions, 1959), p. 227.
15. Ibid., p. 173.
16. Jean-Paul Sartre, *What Is Literature?*, trans. Bernard Frechtman (New York: Philosophical Library, 1949), p. 217.
17. Jean-Paul Sartre, *Critique of Dialectical Reason*, trans. H. E. Barnes (New York: Vintage, 1960), p. 24.
18. Ibid., p. 25.
19. Jean-Paul Sartre, *Existentialism Is a Humanism*, trans. Bernard Frechtman, 1957, in *The Fabric of Existentialism: Philosophical and Literary Sources*, ed. Richard Gill and Ernest Sherman (Englewood Cliffs, N.J.: Prentice-Hall, 1973), p. 523.
20. Ibid., pp. 523–524.
21. Ibid., p. 524.
22. Ibid., pp. 524–525.
23. Ibid., p. 525.
24. See W. T. Jones, *The Twentieth Century to Wittgenstein and Sartre: A History of Western Philosophy*, rev. 2nd ed. (San Diego, Calif.: Harcourt Brace Jovanovich, 1975), p. 356.
25. Jean-Paul Sartre, *Being and Nothingness*, trans. H. E. Barnes (New York: Philosophical Library, 1956), pp. 476–479.
26. Sartre, *Existentialism Is a Humanism*, p. 522.
27. Ibid.
28. Ibid., pp. 522–523.
29. Ibid., pp. 525–526.
30. Ibid., pp. 526–527.
31. Ibid., p. 527.
32. Ibid.
33. Ibid., p. 528.

Chapter 13

The Pragmatist: William James

1. G. W. Allen, *William James: A Biography* (New York: Viking, 1967), p. 134.
2. Ibid., p. 163.
3. Ibid., pp. 168–169.
4. Ralph Barton Perry, *The Thought and Character of William James* (Cambridge, Mass.: Harvard University Press, 1948), p. 386.

5. Allen, *William James*, pp. 214–220.
6. Guy W. Stroh, *American Philosophy from Edwards to Dewey: An Introduction* (Princeton, N.J.: Van Nostrand, 1968), p. 123.
7. Perry, *The Thought and Character of William James*, p. 300.
8. Ibid.
9. Quoted in Robert F. Davidson, *Philosophies Men Live By*, p. 296.
10. Charles Sanders Peirce, *Collected Papers of Charles Sanders Peirce, vol. 5*, ed. Charles Hartshorne and Paul Weiss (Cambridge, Mass.: Harvard University Press, 1931–1935), pp. 276ff.
11. Ibid., pp. 284ff.
12. Ibid., p. 6.
13. Ibid., pp. 272–273, 259–262.
14. William James, *The Will to Believe and Other Essays in Popular Philosophy* (1897; reprinted in *Human Immortality: Two Supposed Objections to the Doctrine*, New York: Dover, 1956, pp. 146–147).
15. Ibid., p. 177.
16. William James, *Pragmatism*, 1907 text, in *William James: Writings 1902–1910* (New York: Library of America, 1987), pp. 573ff.
17. Ibid., pp. 489, 490, 491.
18. James, *The Will to Believe*, pp. 28, 30.
19. William James, *Pragmatism* (New York: Longmans, Green, 1907), p. 58.
20. Ibid., pp. 59–64.
21. Ibid., p. 64.
22. William James, "The Dilemma of Determinism," in *The Will to Believe*, p. 150.
23. Ibid., pp. 161–163.
24. William James, "Some Problems in Philosophy," in *The Moral Equivalent of War and Other Essays*, ed. John K. Roth (New York: Harper & Row, 1971), p. 164.
25. William James, "The Dilemma of Determinism," in *The Will to Believe*, pp. 146–147.
26. James, *The Will to Believe*, p. 31.
27. Ibid., pp. 200–201.
28. William James, "Is Life Worth Living?" an address to the Harvard Young Men's Christian Association, published in *International Journal of Ethics*, October 1895, and in Robert F. Davidson, ed., *The Search for Meaning in Life: Readings in Philosophy* (New York: Holt, Rinehart, and Winston, 1962), p. 61.
29. William James, "The Moral Philosopher and Moral Life," in *The Will to Believe*, pp. 211ff.
30. William James, *The Varieties of Religious Experience* (New York: Longmans, Green, 1902), pp. 525, 516–517.
31. James, *The Varieties of Religious Experience*, in *William James: Writings 1902–1910*, p. 88.
32. Ibid., p. 124.
33. Ibid., p. 127.
34. Ibid., p. 152.
35. Ibid., pp. 213–215.
36. Ibid., p. 310.
37. Ibid., pp. 325ff.
38. Ibid., pp. 349–350.
39. William James, "A Pluralistic Mystic," cited in Dmitri Tymoczko, "The Nitrous Oxide Philosopher," *Atlantic Monthly*, May 1996, p. 98–99.
40. Quoted in Tymoczko, p. 100.
41. James, *The Will to Believe.*, pp. 202ff.
42. W. T. Jones, *Kant and the Nineteenth Century: A History of Western Philosophy*, rev. 2nd ed. (New York: Harcourt Brace Jovanovich, 1975), p. 323.
43. James, *The Will to Believe*, p. 320.
44. Ibid., p. 18–19.
45. James, *The Varieties of Religious Experience*, p. 26.
46. Tymoczko, pp. 99–100.
47. Ibid., pp. 99–100.
48. James, "Is Life Worth Living?" p. 53.

Overview of Postmodern Themes

1. Lawrence Cahoone, ed., *From Modernism to Postmodernism: An Anthology* (Cambridge, Mass.: Blackwell, 1966), p. 1.

Chapter 14

The Anti-Philosopher: Friedrich Nietzsche

1. Friedrich Nietzsche, *The Will to Power*, ed. Walter Kaufmann, trans. Walter Kaufmann and R. J. Hollingdale (New York: Vintage, 1967), p. 3.
2. Friedrich Nietzsche, *The Birth of Tragedy*, trans. W. A. Haussmann (New York: Russell & Russell, 1964), p. xvii.
3. Letter from Friedrich Ritschl in *The Portable Nietzsche*, trans. Walter Kaufmann (New York: Penguin, 1968), pp. 8–9.
4. R. J. Hollingdale, introduction to his translation of *Thus Spake Zarathustra* (Baltimore, Md.: Penguin, 1967), p. 26.
5. Friedrich Nietzsche, *Ecce Homo*, quoted in *Thus Spake Zarathustra*, trans. Thomas Cotton (New York: Modern Library, 1967), pp. 18–19.
6. Friedrich Nietzsche, *Ecce Homo*, in *The Portable Nietzsche*, p. 298.
7. Stefan Zweig, quoted in *The Portable Nietzsche*, p. 104.
8. Friedrich Nietzsche, "Attempt at a Self-Criticism," in *The Birth of Tragedy*, trans. Walter Kaufmann (New York: Vintage Books, 1967), § 3, pp. 19–20.
9. Quoted in Karl Jaspers, *Nietzsche: An Introduction to the Understanding of His Philosophical Activity* (Tucson, Ariz.: University of Arizona Press, 1965), p. 56.
10. Nietzsche, letter to Franz Overbeck, quoted in Jaspers, *Nietzsche*, p. 87.
11. Nietzsche, "Attempt at a Self-Criticism," § 5, p. 23.
12. Alexander Nehamas, *Nietzsche: Life as Literature* (Cambridge, Mass.: Harvard University Press, 1985), p. 2.
13. Friedrich Nietzsche, "On Truth and Lie in an Extra-Moral Sense," in *The Portable Nietzsche*, pp. 42, 44.
14. Friedrich Nietzsche, *On the Genealogy of Morals* in *On the Genealogy of Morals and Ecce Homo*, ed. Walter Kaufmann, trans. Walter Kaufmann and R. J. Hollingdale (New York: Vintage, 1969), Third Essay, § 26, pp. 158–159.
15. Nietzsche, *Thus Spake Zarathustra*, "Of Self-Overcoming," pp. 136, 137, 138.
16. Friedrich Nietzsche, *Daybreak* § 356, in Philip Novak, *The Vision of Nietzsche* (Rockport, Mass.: Element, 1996), p. 31.
17. Philip Novak, *The Vision of Nietzsche*, pp. 8–9.
18. Nietzsche, *The Will to Power*, § 1067, pp. 549–550.
19. Nietzsche, *On the Genealogy of Morals*, Third Essay, § 25, pp. 155–156.
20. Friedrich Nietzsche, "The Natural History of Morals," Part Five of *Beyond Good and Evil*, trans. Walter Kaufmann and R. J. Hollingdale, § 186, in Cahoone, pp. 104–105.

21. Ibid.
22. Nietzsche, *Daybreak* § 3, Novak, p. 69.
23. Nietzsche, *On the Genealogy of Morals*, Third Essay, § 19, pp. 136–137.
24. Friedrich Nietzsche, *Ecce Homo*, "Why I Am a Destiny," § 6, in *On the Genealogy of Morals and Ecce Homo*, ed. Walter Kaufmann, trans. Walter Kaufmann and R. J. Hollingdale (New York: Vintage, 1969), p. 331.
25. Nietzsche, "Why I Am a Destiny," § 7, p. 332.
26. Nietzsche, *Beyond Good and Evil*, § 190, in Cahoone, p. 108.
27. Nietzsche, *Daybreak*, § 131, p. 78.
28. Nietzsche, *Beyond Good and Evil*, § 198, in Cahoone, p. 113.
29. Ibid., § 201, p. 117.
30. Friedrich Nietzsche, *The Gay Science*, trans. Walter Kaufmann (New York: Vintage Books, 1974), bk. 3, § 125, p. 181.
31. Ibid.
32. Nietzsche, *The Will to Power*, § 2, pp. 3–4.
33. Nietzsche, *Thus Spoke Zarathustra*, in *The Portable Nietzsche*, pp. 199–200.
34. Nietzsche, *The Gay Science*, § 343, p. 279.
35. Quoted in Jaspers, *Nietzsche*, p. 162.
36. Nietzsche, *Thus Spoke Zarathustra*, in *The Portable Nietzsche*, p. 398.
37. Nietzsche, *Toward a Genealogy of Morals*, Kaufmann trans., "Good and Evil Versus Good and Bad," sec. 10, in *The Portable Nietzsche*, pp. 451–452.
38. Ibid.
39. Nietzsche, *Thus Spoke Zarathustra*, in *The Portable Nietzsche*, pp. 124–128.
40. Novak, p. 20.
41. Nietzsche, *Thus Spake Zarathustra*, Kaufmann and Hollingdale, p. 208.
42. Nietzsche, *The Gay Science*, § 341, in Novak, p. 156.
43. Ibid., pp. 156–157.
44. Friedrich Nietzsche, *Twilight of the Idols*, "Four Great Errors," § 8, in *Twilight of the Idols* and *The Anti-Christ*, trans. R. J. Hollingdale (Middlesex: Penguin Books, 1968), p. 54.
45. Nietzsche, *Ecce Homo*, "Why I Am So Clever," § 10, p. 258.
46. Nietzsche, *The Gay Science*, § 276, Novak, p. 160.

Chapter 15

Emerging Archetypes

1. This definitional material is based, in part, on Susan Mendus's "Feminism," in *The Oxford Companion to Philosophy*, ed. Ted Honderich (Oxford: Oxford University Press, 1995), pp. 270–272.
2. Amaury de Riencourt, *Sex and Power in History* (New York: David McKay, 1974), pp. 97ff.
3. Ibid., p. 99.
4. Cahoone, p. 638.
5. See "The Cartesian Masculinization of Thought" in Susan Bordo, *The Flight to Objectivity: Essays on Cartesianism and Culture* (Albany, N.Y.: State University of New York Press, 1987), pp. 97–118, in Cahoone, pp. 638–660.
6. Susan Bordo, "The Cartesian Masculinization of Thought," Chapter 6 of *The Flight to Objectivity: Essays on Cartesianism and Culture* (Albany, N.Y.: State Univer-

sity of New York Press, 1987), pp. 97–118, in Cahoone, p. 638. Notes have been deleted in all Bordo passages.
7. Ibid.
8. Ibid., p. 640.
9. Ibid.
10. Ibid.
11. Bordo, in Cahoone, p. 641.
12. Bordo, in Cahoone, p. 643.
13. Bordo, in Cahoone, p. 645.
14. Evelyn Fox Keller, *Reflections on Gender and Science* (New Haven, Conn.: Yale University Press, 1985), p. 79.
15. Bordo, p. 656.
16. Bordo, pp. 656–657.
17. John Rawls, *A Theory of Justice* (Cambridge, Mass.: Harvard University Press, 1971), p. 12.
18. Ibid., pp. 60–61.
19. Ibid., p. 13.
20. Susan Moller Okin, *Justice, Gender, and the Family* (New York: Basic Books, 1989), p. 3.
21. Ibid., p. 8.
22. Ibid., p. 91.
23. Rawls, *A Theory of Justice*, p. 12.
24. Okin, *Justice, Gender, and the Family*, p. 91.
25. Ibid., pp. 101, 104–105.
26. Carol Gilligan, *Mapping the Moral Domain: A Contribution of Women's Thinking to Psychological Theory and Education*, ed. Carol Gilligan, Janie Victoria Ward, and Jill McLean Taylor, with Betty Baridge (Cambridge, Mass.: Center for the Study of Gender Education and Human Development, distributed by Harvard University Press, 1988), p. v.
27. Carol Gilligan, *In a Different Voice: Psychological Theory and Women's Development* (Cambridge, Mass.: Harvard University Press, 1982), pp. 1–2.
28. See Carol Gilligan's preface to *Mapping the Moral Domain*.
29. Gilligan, *In a Different Voice*, pp. 104–105.
30. Carol Gilligan, "Moral Orientation and Moral Development," in *Women and Moral Theory*, ed. Eva Feder Kittay and Diane T. Mayers (Totowa, N.J.: Rowman and Littlefield, 1987), pp. 19–33.
31. James M. Washington, ed., *A Testament of Hope: The Essential Writings of Martin Luther King, Jr.* (San Francisco: Harper & Row, 1986), pp. xviii–xix.
32. Martin Luther King, Jr., *Stride Toward Freedom: The Montgomery Story* (New York: Harper & Row, 1958), p. 29.
33. Washington, *Testament of Hope*, p. xix.
34. Quoted in Sydney E. Ahlstrom, "The Radical Turn in Theology and Ethics: Why It Occurred in the 1960s," *Annals of the American Academy of Political and Social Science 387* (January 1970), p. 10.
35. Martin Luther King, Jr., *Christian Century 74*, February 6, 1957, p. 166.
36. Martin Luther King, Jr., "Love, Law and Civil Disobedience," address before the Fellowship of the Concerned, November 16, 1961, in Washington, *Testament of Hope*, p. 45.
37. Ibid., pp. 46–47.
38. Martin Luther King, Jr., "Nonviolence: The Only Road to Freedom," in Washington, *Testament of Hope*, pp. 57–58.
39. Martin Luther King, Jr., "Letter from Birming-ham Jail," in Washington, *Testament of Hope*, pp. 292–293.
40. Ibid., pp. 291–292.
41. Ibid., pp. 295–296.

42. Jervis Anderson, "The Public Intellectual," *New Yorker*, January 17, 1994, p. 40.

43. Cornel West, *Race Matters* (Boston: Beacon Press, 1993), pp. 28–29, 31.

44. West, pp. 104–105.

45. Martin Luther King, Jr., "I Have a Dream," in Washington, *Testament of Hope*, pp. 219–220.

Continuative

1. Denise L. Carmody and John T. Carmody, *Eastern Ways to the Center: An Introduction to Religions of the West* (Belmont, Calif.: Wadsworth Publishing, 1981), pp. 201–203.

2. Will Durant, *The Mansions of Philosophy: A Survey of Human Life and Destiny* (Garden City, N.Y.: Simon and Schuster, 1929), pp. vii, viii, xff.

3. Chuang-tzu, *The Chuang-Tzu*, in Wing-Tsit Chan, trans. and comp., *A Source Book in Chinese Philosophy* (Princeton, N.J.: Princeton University Press, 1963), p. 180.

4. Pierre Hadot, *Philosophy as a Way of Life*, p. 58.

5. Jacob Needleman, *The Heart of Philosophy* (New York: Alfred A. Knopf, 1982), pp. 3–4ff.

6. Hadot, p. 274.

7. Ibid., p. 285.

8. Chuang-tzu in Chan, pp. 189–190.

9. Viktor E. Frankl, *Man's Search for Meaning: An Introduction to Logotherapy*, p. 135.

10. Philo Judeaus, *On the Special Laws* in *Philo*, trans. F. H. Colson and G. H. Whitaker (London and Cambridge, Mass.: Loeb Classical Library, 1962), vol. 2, pp. 44–48.

11. Epictetus, *Handbook of Epictetus*, trans. Nicholas P. White, pp. 28ff.

Glossary

This Glossary contains all of the terms defined in the margins of the text (and a few additional key terms). Chapter and page number notations for margin definitions are indicated in parentheses. Consult the index for terms and concepts not listed here.

A posteriori knowledge Empirical knowledge derived from sense experience and not regarded as universal because the conditions under which it is acquired change, perceivers vary, and factual relationships change. (Ch. 8, p. 296)

A priori ideas (or innate ideas) Truths, not derived from observation or experiment, characterized as being certain, deductive, universally true, and independent of all experience. See also Innate ideas. (Ch. 8, p. 290; see also Ch. 9, p. 344)

A priori knowledge Derived from reason without reference to sense experience. Examples include: "All triangles contain 180°" and "Every event has a cause." (Ch. 8, p. 296)

Absolute idealism, see Idealism (absolute or Hegelian)

Aesthetics Branch of philosophy that studies all forms of art. (Ch. 1, p. 9)

Alienated life Unconscious, unspontaneous, and unfulfilled life; deprived of fundamental conditions necessary for self-actualization. (Ch. 11, p. 441)

Alienation According to Marx, condition of workers separated from the products of their labor; primarily an objective state, but can also refer to not feeling "at one" with the product of labor. (Ch. 11, p. 439)

Altruism From Latin for "other," the capacity to promote the welfare of others; opposed to egoism. (Fourth Interlude, p. 467)

Amor fati Nietzsche's term meaning "the love of fate"; expressed as joyous affirmation of the eternal recurrence and delight that everything is exactly as and what it is. (Ch. 14, p. 588)

Amoral, see Nonmoral

Anachronism, see Fallacy of anachronism

Anguish Term Sartre uses to describe the awareness that even our most seemingly private and individual choices involve all people; by choosing to be this or that type of person, we create an image of the way others ought to be; not to be confused with Kant's categorical imperative. (Ch. 12, p. 503)

Anti-philosopher A radical critic of the techniques and doctrines of modern science and philosophy. The anti-philosopher disputes the possibility of objectivity and universality and rejects the absolute authority of reason; anti-philosophers also reject the possibility of a *neutral stance* or *perspectiveless perspective*. (Ch. 14, p. 567)

Apeiron According to Anaximander, the first principle from which all existing things develop, a vast "Indefinite-Infinite"; the apeiron is an infinite mass of forces with no specific qualities. (First Interlude, p. 37)

Archetypal individual (or paradigmatic individual) A special class of teachers, philosophers, and religious figures whose nature becomes a standard by which a culture judges the "ideal" human being; a rare human being whose very nature represents something elemental about the human condition. (Ch. 3, p. 83)

Archetype Basic image that represents our conception of the essence of a certain type of person; according to psychologist C. G. Jung, some of the images have been shared by the whole human race from the earliest times. (Ch. 1, p. 10)

Archetype (philosophical) A philosopher who represents an original or influential point of view in a way that significantly affects philosophers and nonphilosophers: cynic, saint, pessimist, optimist, atheist, rationalist, idealist, and so on. (Ch. 1, p. 10)

Argument from design, see Teleological argument

Argument from gradation Argument for the existence of God based on the idea that being progresses from inanimate objects to increasingly complex animated creatures, culminating in a qualitatively unique God; Aristotelian argument that forms the basis for the fourth of Aquinas's Five Ways. (Ch. 7, p. 265)

Argument from motion Attempt to prove the existence of God based on the reasoning that in order to avoid an infinite regress, there must be an Unmoved Mover capable of imparting motion to all other things; Aristotelian argument that forms the basis for the first of Thomas Aquinas's Five Ways. (Ch. 7, p. 262)

Argument from necessity Argument for the existence of God based on the idea that if nothing had ever existed, nothing would always exist; therefore, there is something whose existence is necessary (an eternal something); Aristotelian argument that forms the basis for the third of Aquinas's Five Ways. (Ch. 7, p. 264)

Ascetic Individual who turns away from pleasure and severely limits all sensual appetites in order to achieve salvation or peace of mind. (Third Interlude, p. 316)

Atomism Early Greek philosophy developed by Leucippus and Democritus and later refined by Epicurus and Lucretius; materialistic view that the universe consists entirely of empty space and ultimately simple entities that combine to form objects. (First Interlude, p. 44)

Atoms From the Greek *atomos*, meaning "indivisible," "having no parts," or "uncuttable"; minute material particles; the ultimate material constituents of all things. Atoms have such properties as size, shape, position, arrangement (combination), and motion, but lack qualities like color, taste, temperature, or smell. (First Interlude, p. 44)

Authenticity Subjective condition of an individual living honestly and courageously in the moment, refusing to make excuses, and not relying on groups or institutions for meaning and purpose. (Ch. 12, p. 482)

Axiology Branch of philosophy that studies values in general. (Ch. 1, p. 8)

Barbarian From a rude "bar-bar" noise used to mock dialects considered crude by the ancient Athenians; originally referred to other cultures considered "less than human" or uncivilized. (Ch. 2, p. 55)

Belief Conviction or trust that a claim is true; an individual's subjective mental state; distinct from knowledge. (Ch. 1, p. 15)

Belief (mere) A conviction that something is true for which the only evidence is the sincerity of the believer. (Ch. 1, p. 15)

Bodhisattva An enlightened being who voluntarily postponed his own nirvana in order to help all other conscious life-forms find "supreme release"; not a savior. (Third Interlude, p. 321)

Bourgeoisie All those who do not produce anything, yet who own and control the means of production. (Ch. 11, p. 425)

Bundle theory of the self Humean theory that there is no fixed "self," but that the "self" is merely a "bundle of perceptions"; a "self" is merely a habitual way of discussing certain perceptions. (Ch. 9, p. 361)

Capitalism Economic system in which the means of production and distribution are all (or mostly) privately owned and operated for profit under fully competitive conditions; tends to be accompanied by concentration of wealth and growth of great corporations. (Ch. 11, p. 430)

Categorical imperative According to Kant, a command that is universally binding on all rational creatures; the ultimate foundation of all moral law: "Act as if the maxim of thy action were to become a universal law of nature." (Ch. 10, p. 406)

Character From the Greek *charakter*, a word derived from *charassein*, "to make sharp" or "to engrave," character refers to the sum total of a person's traits, including behavior, habits, likes and dislikes, capacities, potentials, and so on; a key element of Aristotelian ethics and psychology, meaning the overall (generally fixed) nature or tone of a person's habits. (Ch. 5, p. 180)

Cogito, ergo sum Latin version of Descartes' famous sentence "I think, therefore I am." (Ch. 8, p. 302)

Coherence theory of truth Truth test in which new or unclear ideas are evaluated in terms of rational or logical consistency and in relation to already established truths. (Ch. 8, p. 290)

Co-opted In Marxian social analysis, co-option occurs when workers identify with the economic system that oppresses them by confusing the remote possibility of accumulating wealth with their actual living and working conditions; being co-opted also refers to anyone who is somehow convinced to further interests that are to her or his ultimate disadvantage. (Ch. 11, p. 436)

Copy theory of truth, see Correspondence theory of truth

Correspondence theory of truth Truth test that holds that an idea (or belief or thought) is true if whatever it refers to actually exists (corresponds to a fact). Sometimes referred to as copy theory of truth. (Ch. 9, p. 344)

Cosmological argument From the Greek word *kosmos*, meaning "world," "universe," or "orderly structure," argument for the existence of God that since it is impossible for any natural thing to be the complete and sufficient source of its own existence, there must be an Uncaused Cause capable of imparting existence to all other things; Aristotelian argument that forms the basis for the second of Aquinas's Five Ways. (Ch. 7, p. 263)

Cosmos Greek term for "ordered whole"; first used by the Pythagoreans to characterize the universe as an ordered whole consisting of harmonies of contrasting elements. (First Interlude, p. 48)

Critical philosophy Kant's term for his effort to assess the nature and limits of "pure reason" unadulterated by experience in order to identify the actual relationship of the mind to knowledge. (Ch. 10, p. 394)

Cynic Individual who lives an austere, unconventional life based on Cynic doctrine. (Ch. 6, p. 216)

Cynicism Philosophy based on the belief that the very essence of civilization is corrupt and that civilization destroys individuals by making them soft and subject to the whims of fortune. (Ch. 6, p. 215)

Despair   Sartrean term referring to the refusal to base choices and actions on possibilities; the condition of confining ourselves to what directly falls under our present influence and control. (Ch. 12, p. 505)

Determinism   Belief that everything that happens must happen exactly the way it does because all matter is governed by cause and effect and follows laws of nature. (Ch. 13, p. 530)

Dialectic (Hegelian)   According to Hegel, a three-step pattern in which an original idea, known as a thesis, struggles with a contrary idea, known as the antithesis, to produce a new synthesis that combines elements of both. (Ch. 11, p. 419)

Dialectic (Socratic), see Socratic method

Dialectical process (Hegelian)   Internally governed evolutionary cycle in which progress occurs as the result of a struggle between two opposing conditions. (Ch. 11, p. 424)

Dualism   Any philosophical position that divides existence into two completely distinct, independent, unique substances. (Ch. 8, p. 308; see also Ch. 4, p. 123f)

Dualism (epistemological)   The view that knowing consists of two distinct aspects: the knower and the known. (Ch. 9, p. 348)

Economic (as used by Marx)   Term Marx used to refer to the complete array of social relationships and arrangements that constitute a particular social order. (Ch. 11, p. 428)

Efficient Cause (Aristotle)   The "triggering cause" that initiates activity; the substance by which a change is brought about; close to the contemporary meaning of cause; third of Aristotle's "four causes." (Ch. 5, p. 168)

Egocentric predicament   Problem generated by epistemological dualism: If all knowledge comes in the form of my own ideas, how can I verify the existence of anything external to them? (Ch. 9, p. 348)

Egoism   Belief that self-interest is or ought to be the basis of all deliberate action; psychological egoists deny that altruism is even possible. See Altruism. (Fourth Interlude, pp. 456–457)

Eightfold path   Buddha's prescription for rooting out suffering: 1) right understanding; 2) right purpose; 3) right speech; 4) right conduct; 5) right livelihood; 6) right effort; 7) right mindfulness; 8) right meditation. (Third Interlude, p. 328)

Empirical criterion of meaning   Meaningful ideas are those that can be traced back to sense experience (impressions); beliefs that cannot be reduced to sense experience are not "ideas" at all, but meaningless utterances. (Ch. 9, p. 359)

Empiricism   Belief that all knowledge is ultimately derived from the senses (experience) and that all ideas can be traced to sense data. (Ch. 9, p. 342)

Entelechy   From the Greek, "having its end within itself": according to Aristotle, an inner urge that drives all things to blossom into their own unique selves; inner order or design that governs all natural processes. (Ch. 5, p. 169)

Epicurean fallacy   Error of confusing the active pursuit of specialized pleasures with Epicurus's philosophy of disciplined moderation and restraint. (Second Interlude, p. 209)

Epistemological dualism, see Dualism (epistemological)

Epistemology   Branch of philosophy that studies the nature and possibility of knowledge. (Ch. 1, p. 8)

Esse est percipi   Latin for Berkeley's belief that "to be is to be perceived." (Ch. 9, p. 352)

Eternal recurrence   Nietzschean idea that everything that is happening now will one day happen again—in exactly the same way. Based on principles of Newtonian physics and Darwinian evolution, the doctrine holds that every possible configuration of the universe must have already occurred an infinite number of times. (Ch. 14, p. 587)

Ethic of care   Carol Gilligan's term for ethical theories that stress responsibilities and relationships over rules, and that are based on "care reasoning," which depends on a sense of connectedness, or "relationship," and that is the opposite of objective detachment. (Ch. 15, p. 613)

Ethic of justice   Carol Gilligan's term for ethical theories that stress rules over responsibilities and relationships, and that are based on an expression of the traditional impersonal, rationalistic, objective, detached model of knowing. (Ch. 15, p. 613)

Ethics   Branch of philosophy concerned with the good life and with moral value and moral reasoning. (Ch. 1, p. 9)

Ethnocentrism   From Greek roots meaning "the race is the center"; belief that the customs and beliefs of one's own culture are inherently superior to all others. (Ch. 2, p. 54)

Eudaimonia   Often translated as happiness; term Aristotle used to refer to fully realized existence; state of being fully aware, vital, alert. (Ch. 5, p. 176)

Existentialism   Term used to refer to any philosophy that emphasizes fundamental questions of meaning and choice as they affect existing individuals; existential themes include choice, freedom, identity, alienation, inauthenticity, despair, and awareness of our own mortality. (Ch. 12, p. 477)

Fallacy of anachronism   Error in reasoning that results from uncritically and rigidly applying contemporary values to past practices and ideas. (Overview of Classical Themes, p. 28)

False authority (fallacy of) The error in reasoning that results from accepting the word of experts who are speaking outside their proper fields or uncritically relying on the testimony of others without checking it against our own experiences and reason. (Ch. 8, p. 289)

Feminism From the French *féminisme*, this nuanced term refers to attempts to attain equal legal and political rights for women. In the broad sense, feminism includes any theory that sees the relationship between the sexes as unequal due to the subordination or oppression of women and the disparagement of women's particular experience. (Ch. 15, p. 599)

Feminist Any person who believes in the fundamental equality of women and men and who actively contributes to the struggle to achieve such equality. This definition is deliberately inclusive. (Ch. 15, p. 599)

Final Cause (Aristotle) That for which an activity or process takes place; a thing's very reason for being (*raison d'être*); fourth of Aristotle's "four causes." (Ch. 5, p. 168)

Forces of production In philosophical Marxism, the forces of production are factories, equipment, technology, knowledge, and skill; a part of the substructure of society. (Ch. 11, p. 429)

Forlornness Jean-Paul Sartre's term for his belief that we face life alone, without God, without certainty, with only absolute freedom and the responsibility that accompanies it. (Ch. 12, p. 498)

Form (Aristotle) From the Greek word for essence (*ousia*), that which is in matter and makes a thing what it is; can be abstracted from matter but cannot exist independently of matter. (Ch. 5, p. 163)

Formal Cause (Aristotle) The shape, or form, into which matter is changed; second of Aristotle's "four causes." (Ch. 5, p. 167)

Forms, see Platonic forms

Four Noble Truths Foundation of Buddha's teachings: 1) to exist is to suffer; 2) self-centeredness is the chief cause of human suffering; 3) the cause of suffering can be understood and rooted out; 4) suffering can be alleviated by following the Eightfold Path. (Third Interlude, p. 327)

Functionalist theory of morality Moral position that right and wrong can be understood only in terms of their effect on anything's natural function; each kind of thing has a natural purpose or function. (Ch. 4, p. 142)

Hedonism From the Greek root for "pleasure," the general term for any philosophy that says pleasure = good and pain = evil. (Second Interlude, p. 192)

Hedonism (Cyrenaic) Philosophy that advocates the unreflective pursuit of intense, immediate pleasure; makes no qualitative distinctions among pleasures. (Second Interlude, p. 195)

Hedonism (ethical) The belief that though it is possible to deliberately avoid pleasure or choose pain, it is morally wrong to do so. (Second Interlude, p. 192)

Hedonism (psychological) The belief that all decisions are based on considerations of pleasure and pain because it is psychologically impossible for human beings to do otherwise. (Second Interlude, p. 192)

Hedonistic paradox The harder we try to be happy, the harder it is to be happy. (Second Interlude, p. 212)

Hedonistic utility Principle of maximizing pleasure and minimizing pain. (Second Interlude, p. 198)

Hypothetical imperatives Propositions that tell us what to do under specific, variable conditions. (Ch. 10, p. 405)

Idealism (absolute or Hegelian) Term used to identify Hegel's particular form of German idealism; a monistic philosophy that is based on an all-encompassing Absolute Spirit that is self-actualizing into perfection; Reality (Absolute Mind or Absolute Spirit) is independent of any individual's mind; not to be confused with Berkeleian idealism (immaterialism), in which objective reality is said to exist in the individual's mind. (Ch. 11, p. 419)

Idealism (immaterialism) Belief that only ideas (mental states) exist; the material world is fiction—it does not exist. (Ch. 9, p. 350)

Immoral Morally wrong, bad, or not right; a moral value judgment or prescriptive claim. (Ch. 10, p. 381)

Inauthenticity Condition that results when the nature and needs of the individual are ignored, denied, and obscured, or sacrificed for institutions, abstractions, or groups. (Ch. 12, p. 481)

Inductive reasoning Reasoning pattern that proceeds from the particular to the general or from some to all and results in generalized rules or principles established with degrees of probability. (Ch. 9, p. 365)

Innate ideas Ideas present in the mind at birth. See A priori ideas. (Ch. 9, p. 344; see also Ch. 8, p. 290)

Instrumental theory of morality Moral position that right and wrong must be determined by the consequences of acts; right and wrong viewed as means (instruments) for getting something else. (Ch. 4, p. 141)

Intellectualism Term used to refer to the claim that behavior is always controlled by beliefs about what is good and the means to that good. (Ch. 3, p. 104)

Irony Communication on at least two levels, a literal or obvious level and a hidden or real level; favored by

Socrates as a technique for keeping his listeners alert and involved. (Ch. 3, p. 87)

Justice (Platonic)   Excellence of function for the whole; in a just society, each individual performs his or her natural function according to class; in a just individual, reason rules the spirit and the appetites. (Ch. 4, p. 145)

Kantian formalism (also known as Kantian idealism and transcendental idealism)   Theory that knowledge is the result of the interaction between the mind and sensation, and is structured by regulative ideas called categories. (Ch. 10, p. 392)

Kantian idealism, see Kantian formalism

Karma   From the Pali *kamma*, according to Buddhist tradition, the law of moral causation (moral cause and effect); it includes past and present actions, and is not to be confused with fate or predestination; good or bad karma results from our own actions. (Third Interlude, p. 326)

Knowledge   Justified true belief. (Ch. 1, p. 15)

Knowledge, see A posteriori knowledge

Knowledge, see A priori knowledge

Knowledge (practical)   Consists of skills needed to do things like play the piano, use a bandsaw, remove a tumor, or bake a cake. (Ch. 1, p. 18)

Knowledge (theoretical)   The accurate compilation and assessment of factual and systematic relationships. (Ch. 1, p. 18)

Law of contradiction (sometimes known as the law of noncontradiction)   Rule of inference that says no statement can be both true and false at the same time and under the same conditions. (Ch. 7, p. 252)

Law of noncontradiction, see Law of contradiction

Logic   Branch of philosophy that studies the rules of correct reasoning. (Ch. 1, p. 9)

Logos   One of the richest and most complex terms in ancient philosophy; associated meanings include: "intelligence," "speech," "discourse," "thought," "reason," "word," "meaning"; the root of "log" (record), "logo," "logic," and the "ology" suffix found in terms like sociology and physiology; according to Heraclitus, the rule according to which all things are accomplished and the law that is found in all things; according to the Stoics, World Reason, also referred to as Cosmic Mind, God, Zeus, Nature, Fate: the force that governs the world. (First Interlude, p. 47; see also Ch. 6, p. 224)

Logos (Stoic)   According to Stoic doctrine, World Reason, also referred to as Cosmic Mind, God, Zeus, Nature, Providence, Cosmic Meaning, Fate; force that governs the universe. (Ch. 6, p. 224; see also First Interlude, p. 47)

Master morality   In Nietzschean philosophy, the aesthetic honor code of the overman; morality that looks only to the authentic individual (overman) for values that transcend the slave's good–evil dichotomy with: glorious–degrading, honorable–dishonorable, refined–vulgar, and so on; "good" equals "noble" and "evil" equals "vulgar." (Ch. 14, p. 584)

Material Cause (Aristotle)   The material (substance) from which a thing comes, and in which change occurs; first of Aristotle's "four causes." (Ch. 5, p. 167)

Materialism   Belief that everything is composed of matter (and energy) and can be explained by physical laws, that all human activity can be understood as the natural behavior of matter according to mechanical laws, and that thinking is merely a complex form of behaving: the body is a fleshy machine. Also known as behaviorism, mechanism, or reductionism. (Ch. 8, p. 307)

Materialism (Marxian)   Form of social determinism based on a reciprocal relationship between individuals and their environment; distinguished from strict materialism and hard determinism. (Ch. 11, p. 428)

Matter (Aristotelian)   From the Greek word *hyle*, the common material found in a variety of things; it has no distinct characteristics until some form is imparted to it or until the form inherent in a thing becomes actualized. (Ch. 5, p. 163)

Mean   From the Latin *medius*, the midpoint between two other points; for Aristotle, moral virtue was characterized as a mean between too little (deficiency) and too much (excess). (Ch. 5, p. 181)

Means of production   In philosophical Marxism, the means of production include natural resources such as water, coal, land, and so forth; a part of the substructure of society. (Ch. 11, p. 429)

Mere belief, see Belief (mere)

Metaphysics   Branch of philosophy that addresses the problem of what is real. (Ch. 1, p. 8)

Methodic doubt   Cartesian strategy of deliberately doubting everything it is possible to doubt in the least degree so that what remains will be known with absolute certainty. (Ch. 8, p. 295)

Modernity   The historical period of nineteenth- and twentieth-century nation-states and a corresponding set of cultural conditions and beliefs dominated by Enlightenment ideals including: faith in science, objective truth and rationality, expectations of inevitable progress, political democracy, capitalism, urbanization, mass literacy, mass media, mass culture, antitraditionalism, large-scale industrial enterprise, individualism, and secularization. (Ch. 14, p. 557)

Monism General name for the belief that everything consists of only one, ultimate, unique substance such as matter or spirit. (First Interlude, p. 36; see also Ch. 8, p. 308)

Moral From the Latin *moralis*, meaning "custom," "manner," or "conduct," refers to what people consider good or bad, right or wrong; used descriptively as a contrast to amoral or nonmoral and prescriptively as a contrast to immoral. (Ch. 10, p. 381)

Moralistic (being) Being moralistic consists of expressing commonplace moral sentiments that conflict with one's behavior, and equating moral sentimentality with virtuous living; a form of hypocrisy that resembles a reaction formation. (Ch. 14, p. 572)

Mysticism (Jamesean) According to James, a way of thinking that views everything in terms of a powerful religious experience; cognitive result of being reborn. (Ch. 13, p. 539)

Mystification Use of cloudy abstractions to create elaborate metaphysical systems that distract us from concrete material reality. (Ch. 11, p. 427)

Naturalism Belief that reality consists of the natural world; denial of the existence of a separate supernatural order of reality; belief that nature follows orderly, discoverable laws. (Ch. 5, p. 160)

Nietzschean perspectivism The contention that every view is only one among many possible interpretations, including, especially, Nietzschean perspectivism, which itself is just one interpretation among many interpretations. (Ch. 14, p. 566)

Nihilism From Latin for "nothing"; belief that the universe lacks meaning and purpose. (Ch. 14, p. 577)

Nirvana Annihilation of the ego; a state of emptiness or "no-thing-ness"; "pure consciousness" that leads to release from suffering while remaining conscious. (Third Interlude, p. 320)

Nonmoral (amoral) Not pertaining to moral; a value-neutral descriptive claim or classification. (Ch. 10, p. 381)

Noumenal reality Kant's term for reality as it is, independent of our perceptions; what is commonly called "objective reality." (Ch. 10, p. 394)

Nous From the Greek word for "mind"; according to Anaxagoras, "the all-pervading Mind which imposes (brings about) an intelligible pattern in an otherwise unintelligible universe"; a material being that affects all things without being in them. (First Interlude, p. 42)

Ontological argument An attempt to prove the existence of God either by referring to the meaning of the word *God* when it is understood a certain way or by referring to the purportedly unique quality of the concept of God. (Ch. 8, p. 305)

Original position John Rawls's imaginary setting in which we can identify the fundamental principles of justice from an objective, impartial perspective, as rational agents, rather than as "interested parties"; similar to the "state of nature" in the social contract theories of Thomas Hobbes, Jean-Jacques Rousseau, and John Locke. (Ch. 15, p. 608)

Overman Nietzsche's "higher type," a more-than-human being who will emerge only by overcoming the false idols of conventional morality and religion; announced in *Thus Spake Zarathustra*. (Ch. 14, p. 578)

Paradigmatic individual, see Archetypal individual

Perspectivism, see Nietzschean perspectivism

Pessimism Schopenhauer's theory that life is disappointing and that for every satisfied desire, new desires emerge; our only hope is detachment and withdrawal. (Ch. 14, p. 559)

Phenomenal reality Kant's term for the world as we experience it. (Ch. 10, p. 394)

Phenomenology Philosophical method of analysis developed by Edmund Husserl; using purely descriptive statements, phenomenology tries to provide a "descriptive analysis" of consciousness in all its forms, stressing the concrete rather than the abstract and experienced facts rather than theory, in order to reveal the "essence" of human consciousness. (Ch. 12, p. 492)

Philophaster A pretender or dabbler in philosophy. (Ch. 1, p. 14)

Philosophical advocate Philosopher whose work identifies, clarifies, and actively opposes a perceived injustice; philosophical advocates give philosophical credence to personal experience based on gender, ethnic background, or social status. See also Public philosophical advocate. (Ch. 15, p. 594)

Philosophical archetype, see Archetype (philosophical)

Philosophy From Greek roots meaning "the love of wisdom." (Ch. 1, p. 2)

Philosophy (political) Branch of philosophy concerned with the state and issues of sovereignty. (Ch. 1, p. 9)

Philosophy (social) Branch of philosophy concerned with social institutions and relations. (Ch. 1, p. 9)

Platonic forms Independently existing, nonspatial, nontemporal "somethings" known only through thought and that cannot be known through the senses; independently existing objects of thought; that which makes a particular thing uniquely and essentially what it is. (Ch. 4, p. 124)

Platonic virtue, see Virtue (Platonic)

Plenitude, see Principle of plenitude

Pluralism   The belief that there exist many realities or substances. (First Interlude, p. 41; see also Ch. 8, p. 308)

Pneuma   According to Anaximenes, the ultimate, pervasive spirit that holds the world together; all things are produced by either "rarefaction" of the *pneuma*, which creates fire, or condensation of the *pneuma*, which creates—in order of density—wind, cloud, water, earth, and stone. (First Interlude, p. 37)

Practical imperative (or principle of dignity)   Kant's formulation of the Categorical Imperative based on the concept of dignity: "Act in such a way that you always treat humanity, whether in your own person or in the person of another, never simply as a means but always at the same time as an end." (Ch. 10, p. 410)

Practical knowledge, see Knowledge (practical)

Practical reason, see Reason (practical)

Pragmatic paradox   Pragmatism works only if we believe that our ideas are true according to nonpragmatic criteria. (Ch. 13, p. 545)

Pragmatism   From the Greek for "deed"; ideas have meaning or truth value to the extent that they produce practical results and effectively further our aims; empirically based philosophy that defines knowledge and truth in terms of practical consequences. (Ch. 13, p. 514; see also Ch. 2, p. 63)

Primary qualities   According to Locke, objective sensible qualities that exist independently of any perceiver; shape, size, location, and motion are examples of primary qualities. (Ch. 9, p. 347)

Principle of dignity, see Practical imperative

Principle of plenitude   The name given by American historian of ideas Arthur O. Lovejoy (1873–1962) to the metaphysical principle that, given infinity, any real possibility must occur (at least once). (Ch. 7, p. 264)

Principle of sufficient reason   The principle that nothing happens without a reason; consequently, no adequate theory or explanation can contain any brute, crude, unexplained facts. First specifically encountered in the work of the medieval philosopher Peter Abelard (1079–1142), it is usually associated with the rationalist philosopher Gottfried Wilhelm Leibniz (1646–1716), who used it in his famous "best of all possible worlds" argument. (First Interlude, p. 31; see also Ch. 7, p. 264)

Principle of utility, see Utility (principle of)

Principles of reason (or rules of inference)   Principles such as the law of contradiction that define the limits of rationality by their very structure and that cannot be rationally refuted since we rely on them in order to reason. (Ch. 7, p. 251)

Problem of evil   If God can prevent the suffering of the innocent, yet chooses not to, He is not good. If God chooses to prevent the suffering, but cannot, He is not omnipotent. If God cannot recognize the suffering of the innocent, He is not wise. (Ch. 7, p. 271)

Proletariat   All those whose labor produces goods and provides essential services, yet who do not own the means of production. (Ch. 11, p. 425)

Prophet   From the Greek roots *pro* (before) and *phanai* (to speak); originally a person who speaks with divine guidance, who functions as a religious leader and teacher; a person who cries out for justice and mercy in the face of tyranny. (First Interlude, p. 32; see also Ch. 15, p. 617)

Psyche   Greek for "soul"; in today's terms, combination of mind and soul, including capacity for reflective thinking. (Ch. 3, p. 95)

Public philosophical advocate   A "public intellectual" who addresses current social, moral, and political issues in a personally committed way, rather than in the impersonal and detached manner of a scholar; public philosophical advocates assert moral and philosophical principles in a manner designed to reach a broad audience; they may or may not be philosophers in the strictest sense. See also Philosophical advocate. (Ch. 15, p. 617)

Qualities, see Primary qualities and Secondary qualities

Rational discourse   The interplay of carefully argued ideas; the use of reason to order, clarify, and identify reality and truth according to agreed-upon standards of verification. (First Interlude, p. 36)

Reaction formation   Freudian ego defense mechanism that attempts to prevent "dangerous" desires from being exposed and expressed by endorsing opposite attitudes and types of behavior as "barriers" against them. (Ch. 14, p. 572; see also Ch. 15, p. 604)

Reason (practical)   According to Kant, moral function of reason that produces religious feelings and intuitions based on knowledge of moral conduct. (Ch. 10, p. 399)

Reason (theoretical)   According to Kant, a function of reason confined to the empirical, phenomenal world. (Ch. 10, p. 399)

Reductio ad absurdum   From the Latin for "reduce to absurdity"; form of argument that refutes an opponent's position by showing that accepting it leads to absurd, unacceptable, or contradictory conclusions because: 1) accepting it leads to a logical contradiction, or 2) it leads to a logical conclusion that is somehow obviously ridiculous because it offends either our reason or common sense. (First Interlude, p. 40; for examples, see Zeno's Paradoxes, First Interlude, pp. 40–41, and Hume's The Limits of Theology, Ch. 9, pp. 366ff)

Regulative ideas In Kantian philosophy, a special class of transcendental ideas that bridges the gap between the phenomenal and noumenal worlds: the ideas of self, cosmos (totality), and God. (Ch. 10, p. 395)

Relationships of production In philosophical Marxism, relationships of production consist of who does what, who owns what, and how this affects members of both groups; a part of the substructure of society. (Ch. 11, p. 429)

Relativism Belief that knowledge is determined by specific qualities of the observer, including age, race, gender, cultural conditioning. (Ch. 1, p. 16; see also Ch. 2, p. 58)

Ressentiment French for "resentment"; term used in Nietzschean philosophy for a deep form of psychically polluting resentment that generates slave morality; the dominant emotion of the underman. (Ch. 14, p. 582)

Rules of inference, see Principles of reason

Sage Derived from the Latin *sapiens*, meaning "wise"; in Asian traditions, an archetypal figure who combines religious inspiration with a love of wisdom; gurus, *yogis*, and Zen *roshis* are examples of sages; in Western traditions, the *sophos* and Hasidic *rebbe* fulfill the role of sage. (First Interlude, p. 31)

Saintliness According to James, a way of life devoted exclusively to a heightened religious consciousness; behavioral result of being reborn. (Ch. 13, p. 539)

Scholasticism Christian philosophy that dominated medieval Europe from about A.D. 1000 to 1300, stressing logical and linguistic analysis of texts and arguments in order to produce a systematic statement and defense of Christian beliefs. (Ch. 7, p. 258)

Scientism The belief that the methods of the natural sciences apply to all areas of knowledge, and that only they can overcome the vagaries of prescientific superstition, religion, and metaphysics. (Ch. 14, p. 568)

Secondary qualities According to Locke, subjective qualities whose existence depends on a perceiver; color, sound, taste, and texture are examples of secondary qualities. (Ch. 9, p. 347)

Self-fulfilling prophecy A belief that affects events in such a way that it causes itself to be true; such as the student who does poorly on an exam because she expects to fail it. (Ch. 13, p. 545)

Shaman A specialist in techniques for making contact with the sacred forces that govern the world by going "outside of" him- or herself; in tribal cultures the shaman usually receives wisdom through a public initiation ceremony that involves "ritualized suffering" and ecstatic trance, though in some cultures the gods come to the shaman. (First Interlude, p. 31)

Skeptic From the Greek *skeptesthai*, "to consider or examine," a person who demands clear, observable, undoubtable evidence before accepting any knowledge claims as true. (Ch. 9, p. 340)

Slave morality In Nietzschean philosophy, a distortion of the will to power in which the characteristics of the inferior type (underman) are praised as virtues, while the characteristics of the superior type (overman) are condemned as arrogance and coldheartedness; a morality of inhibitions, equality, restrictive duties, and "bad conscience." (Ch. 14, p. 581)

Socratic dialectic, see Socratic method

Socratic method (or Socratic dialectic) Question-and-answer technique perfected by Socrates to draw truth out of his pupils. (Ch. 3, p. 86)

Sophistry The teachings and practices of the original Sophists; modern usage refers to subtle, plausible, but fallacious reasoning used to persuade rather than discover truth. (Ch. 2, p. 57)

Sophists Fifth-century B.C. paid teachers of rhetoric; relativists who taught that might makes right, truth is a matter of appearance and convention, and power is the ultimate value. (Ch. 2, p. 56)

Sophos Sage or wise man; term applied to the first philosophers; from the Greek word for "wise." See Sage. (First Interlude, p. 33)

Sophrosyne Wisdom as moderation; hitting the mark; quality of finding the mean between excess and deficiency. (Ch. 5, p. 178)

Species-life Fully human life lived productively and consciously; not alienated. (Ch. 11, p. 441)

Stoic Individual who attempts to live according to Stoic doctrine. See Stoicism. (Ch. 6, p. 214)

Stoicism Philosophy that counsels self-control, detachment, and acceptance of one's fate as identified by the objective use of reason. (Ch. 6, p. 214)

Subjectivism Belief that we can know only our own sensations, not their objective causes. (Second Interlude, p. 197)

Substructure of society In philosophical Marxism, the material substructure or base of society determines the nature of all social relationships, as well as religions, art, philosophies, literature, science, and government. (Ch. 11, p. 428)

Sufficient reason, see Principle of sufficient reason

Superstructure of society According to philosophical Marxism, the superstructure of a culture consists of the ideas and institutions (religious beliefs, educational systems, philosophies, the arts, and so on) compatible with and produced by the material substructure of the society. (Ch. 11, p. 429)

Surplus value   Term Marx used to refer to the capital accumulated by owners; the result of keeping prices higher than the costs of production at the expense of workers. (Ch. 11, p. 431)

Tabula rasa   Latin expression for a "clean slate," used by John Locke to challenge the possibility of innate ideas by characterizing the mind at birth as a blank tablet or clean slate. (Ch. 9, p. 346)

Techne   From the Greek for "art," "skill," "craft," "technique," "trade," "system," or "method of doing something"; root of English words such as "technique," "technical," and "technology"; term Socrates used when he asserted that virtue (*arete*) is knowledge or wisdom (*techne*). (Ch. 3, p. 102)

Teleological argument   Also called the argument from design, this widely known argument for the existence of God claims that the universe manifests order and purpose that can only be the result of a conscious intelligence (God); Aristotelian argument that forms the basis for the fifth of Aquinas's Five Ways and the basis of William Paley's watchmaker argument. (Ch. 7, p. 267)

Teleological thinking   Way of explaining things in terms of their ultimate goals; understanding things functionally in terms of the relationship of the parts to the whole. (Ch. 5, p. 174)

Theology   From the Greek *theos* (God) and *logos* (study of), "talking about God" or "the study or science of God." (Ch. 7, p. 249)

Thought experiment   A way of using our imaginations to test a hypothesis; we "think" rather than field-test a hypothesis, using reasoned imagination to provide the necessary conditions for the "experiment," and carefully reasoning out the most likely consequences according to our hypothesis. (Ch. 15, p. 608)

Timeless questions   Questions concerning ultimate values, general principles, and the very nature of reality, knowledge, justice, happiness, truth, God, beauty, and morality; asked in virtually every culture. (Ch. 1, p. 7)

Timely questions   Questions involving issues that are important to a particular time or place. (Ch. 1, p. 6)

Tragic optimism   According to Nietzsche, the sense of joy and vitality that accompanies the superior individual's clear-sighted imposition of his own freely chosen values on a meaningless world. (Ch. 14, p. 561)

Transcendental idealism, see Kantian formalism

Tyranny   Form of government in which all power rests in a single individual, known as the tyrant. (Ch. 4, p. 147)

Ultimate ends   Goals that are valued for their own sake, not as means to something else. (Ch. 1, p. 5)

Underman   Term Nietzsche uses for the type of person who cannot face being alone in a godless universe, an inferior individual seeking safety and identity in a group or from another; characterized by resentment and hypocrisy. (Ch. 14, p. 580)

Utility (principle of)   Always act to promote the greatest happiness for the greatest number. (Fourth Interlude, p. 455)

Utopia   Term for a perfect or ideal society derived from Sir Thomas More's 1516 novel of the same name; the word was created from the Greek root meaning "nowhere." (Ch. 4, p. 145)

Veil of ignorance   John Rawls's mechanism for imaginatively entering into the original position by avoiding all personal considerations in the process of determining principles of justice; the veil of ignorance is a problem-solving device that prevents us from knowing our social status, what property we own, what we like and don't like, how intelligent we are, what our talents and strengths are, and so on. (Ch. 15, p. 608)

Virtue   From the Greek *arete*, meaning "that at which something excels" or "excellence of function." (Ch. 3, p. 102)

Virtue (Platonic)   Excellence of function. (Ch. 4, p. 143)

Void (the)   Democritus's term for no-thing (no-bodies); empty space in Atomist theory. (First Interlude, p. 45)

Will to power   Nietzsche's term for what he thought is a universal desire to control others and impose our values on them. (Ch. 14, p. 559)

Willed ignorance   An attitude of indifference to the possibility of error or enlightenment that holds on to beliefs regardless of the facts. (Ch. 1, p. 16)

Wisdom   General knowledge of what does and does not produce human happiness, including the difference between right and wrong, combined with the desire and ability to act in basic accord with that knowledge. (Ch. 1, p. 18)

Bibliography of Interesting Sources

This list highlights some especially well-written, interesting, and important books that supplement the material covered in *Archetypes of Wisdom*, third edition. Not only are they philosophically valuable, most of them are "good reads." As a general rule, this list does not duplicate the main philosophical sources cited in the text, since these are fully annotated in the Notes section. Regardless of their publication dates, the vast majority of works listed below are available in many large bookstores and college libraries. If your college library does not own a particular book, it can probably get it for you through an interlibrary loan arrangement.

General Sources

Angeles, Peter A. *Dictionary of Philosophy*. New York: Barnes & Noble Books, 1981. A clear, readable, and comprehensive dictionary useful for instructors and students.

Blackburn, Simon. *The Oxford Dictionary of Philosophy*. Oxford, England: Oxford University Press, 1994. This witty, up-to-date, and authoritative philosophical dictionary includes excellent cross-references.

Bunnin, Nicholas, and E. P. Tsui-James, eds. *The Blackwell Companion to Philosophy*. Oxford, England: Blackwell, 1996. Although presented as a textbook, this is an excellent reference book for the serious philosopher: technical, thorough, and carefully edited.

Copleston, Frederick, S. J. *A History of Philosophy*. New York: Doubleday, Image ed., 1985. Copleston's strength is his ability to summarize and explain other philosophers' ideas without intruding. His own editorial comments are always clearly identified.

Edwards, Paul, ed. in chief. *The Encyclopedia of Philosophy*. New York: Macmillan & The Free Press, 1967. Two versions of this indispensable source are available, the regular edition of eight separate volumes and a four-volume "student edition" that contains exactly the same material.

Honderich, Ted, ed. *The Oxford Companion to Philosophy*. Oxford, England: Oxford University Press, 1995. Checking in at a massive 1,009 pages, Honderich's text is one of the most thorough single-volume reference books available—nearly an encyclopedia.

Mautner, Thomas, ed. *A Dictionary of Philosophy*. Oxford, England: Blackwell, 1996. This dictionary contains entries from more than one hundred distinguished philosophers.

Singer, Peter, ed. *A Companion to Ethics*. Oxford, England: Blackwell, 1993. This solid addition to the Blackwell Companions to Philosophy series consists of 47 entries written by some of today's leading philosophers; entries include up-to-date bibliographies.

Chapter 1

Philosophy and the Search for Wisdom

Gaarder, Jostein. *Sophie's World*. New York: Farrar, Straus Giroux, 1994. Paulette Møller's excellent translation of Gaarder's delightful story of an 18-year-old girl's intriguing introduction to philosophy is highly recommended.

Needleman, Jacob. *The Heart of Philosophy*. New York: Knopf, 1982. Needleman's adventures teaching philosophy through dialogue to high school students and their parents produced intriguing ideas about education, society, and the need for philosophy.

Rand, Ayn. *Philosophy: Who Needs It?* The Ayn Rand Library, vol. 1. New York: Signet, 1982. Rand ranks as one of the few best-selling philosophical writers of recent years. In this collection of essays, she argues for her own objectivist philosophy. Even when her argument is weak, her confrontational style raises questions about the value of philosophy rarely asked in popular literature.

First Interlude

The Presocratic Sophos

Grant, Michael. *The Classical Greeks*. New York: Scribner's, 1989. This nicely written history of classical Greece often reads like a novel. Good index, useful for selective research.

Kirk, G. S., J. E. Raven, and M. Schofield. *The Presocratic Philosophers*. Cambridge, England: Cambridge University Press, 1983. Perhaps the best single volume of commentary and original sources in this area.

Chapter 2

The Sophist: Protagoras

Guthrie, W. K. C. *The Sophists*. Cambridge, England: Cambridge University Press, 1971. Thorough, major source of general information. Best read in conjunction with a general history of the period.

Henry, Jules. *Culture Against Man*. New York: Vintage Books, 1963. The section on advertising as a philosophical system, though dated in its examples, is a stinging indictment of modern sophistry.

Plato. *The Collected Dialogues*. Edith Hamilton and Huntington Cairns, eds. New York: Pantheon Books, Bollingen Series LXXI, 1966. See especially *Gorgias*, *Protagoras*, *Republic*, and *Sophist*. Good, basic collection of Plato's dialogues, including the *Letters*.

Chapter 3

The Wise Man: Socrates

Guthrie, W. K. C. *Socrates*. Cambridge, England: Cambridge University Press, 1971. Comprehensive survey of Socrates' life and philosophy. Sophisticated reading level, but valuable source for research papers.

Jaspers, Karl. *Socrates, Buddha, Confucius, Jesus: The Paradigmatic Individuals*. Hannah Arendt, ed. Ralph Manheim, trans. New York: Harcourt Brace Jovanovich, 1962. This excerpt from Jaspers's history of philosophy presents his fascinating notion of the paradigmatic individual. Worth tracking down for those interested in wise people.

Plato. *Five Dialogues (Euthyphro, Apology, Crito, Meno, Phaedo)*. G. M. A. Grube, trans. Indianapolis, Ind.: Hackett, 1981. Excellent translation at an affordable price.

Stone, I. F. *The Trial of Socrates*. Toronto: Little, Brown, 1988. Valuable as an alternative view of Socrates and as an example of a first-rate mind driven by wonder. Working outside the academic establishment, Stone, like Joseph Campbell, reminds us of the virtues of curiosity and independence.

Chapter 4
The Philosopher-King: Plato

Levi, A. W. *Philosophy as Social Expression*. Chicago: University of Chicago Press, 1974. See Chapter 2, "Ancient Philosophy: The Age of the Aristocrat," for a full discussion of the influence of social class on Plato.

Taylor, A. E. *Plato: The Man and His Work*. London: Methuen, 1966. Scholarly and sometimes difficult, but useful for research papers.

Chapter 5
The Naturalist: Aristotle

Andrews, Lewis M. *To Thine Own Self Be True: The Rebirth of Values in the New Ethical Theory*. New York: Doubleday/Anchor Press, 1987. Intriguing blend of philosophy and psychology. Andrews's ethical therapy is based on universal moral principles derived from Plato and Aristotle.

Horney, Karen. *Neurosis and Human Growth: The Struggle Toward Self-Realization*. New York: W. W. Norton, 1950. Norton has recently reissued a comprehensive collection of Horney's work in inexpensive paperback editions. *Neurosis and Human Growth* is her clear, penetrating discussion of self-realization in contemporary terms. One of the best.

MacIntyre, Alasdair. *After Virtue*. Notre Dame, Ind.: University of Notre Dame Press, 1981. MacIntyre argues that virtues are necessary for society and human development. An impressive assessment of excellence and community.

Maslow, Abraham H. *Toward a Psychology of Being*. New York: D. Van Nostrand, 1968. Though aptly criticized for lacking precise, scientific criteria, Maslow's theory of the ever-developing self has a certain intuitive appeal.

Merton, Thomas. *New Seeds of Contemplation*. New York: New Directions, 1961. This is one of Merton's best, a rare combination of literature, philosophy, psychology, and Catholic theology. This book is a little gem.

Second Interlude
The Hedonist

Lasch, Christopher. *The Culture of Narcissism: American Life in an Age of Diminishing Expectations*. New York: W. W. Norton, 1979. Interesting, troubling analysis of contemporary culture by a social historian.

Lin Yutang. *The Importance of Living*. New York: William Morrow, 1937, 1965. A genuinely delightful book that raises questions about what's important and what's not.

Some dated passages, but much of this is elegant, pleasant, everything a hedonist looks for. William Morrow's 1996 hardcover edition of this gem is itself appropriately elegant. An excellent edition.

Watts, Alan. *Does It Matter?* New York: Vintage Books, 1970. Effective example of "popular philosophy," this overlooked collection of essays raises philosophical issues that may be obscured by Watts's playful, polished style.

Chapter 6
The Stoic: Epictetus and Marcus Aurelius

Epictetus. *Handbook of Epictetus*. Nicholas P. White, trans. Indianapolis, Ind.: Hackett, 1983. First-rate translation, inexpensive edition.

Frankl, Viktor E. *Man's Search for Meaning: An Introduction to Logotherapy*. New York: Pocket Books, 1963. A modern classic. Frankl's account of his concentration camp experiences is harrowing, and the conversion of those experiences into a form of philosophical therapy is inspiring. Almost qualifies as required reading.

Lippmann, Walter. *A Preface to Morals*. 1929. Reprint. New Brunswick, N.J.: Transaction Books, 1982. Though dated, the opening and closing chapters present a stirring Stoic analysis of American culture.

Marcus Aurelius. *The Meditations*. G. M. A. Grube, trans. Indianapolis, Ind.: Hackett, 1983. Good, contemporary translation of one of the finest works of philosophy in the Western tradition. A number of editions of George Long's elegant Victorian translation are widely available as well. Truly timeless.

Seneca. *The Stoic Philosophy of Seneca*. Moses Hadas, trans. New York: W. W. Norton, 1958. This excellent translation is still available as a paperback reprint. Seneca's letters remain edifying.

Stockdale, Jim. *Thoughts of a Philosophical Fighter Pilot*. Stanford, Calif.: Hoover Institution Press, 1995. An inspiring and accessible collection of essays, articles, lectures, and speeches focusing on the human capacity for meeting adversity with courage, dignity, and wisdom; Stockdale may be the Epictetus of our time.

Chapter 7
The Scholar: Thomas Aquinas

Augustine. *Confessions*. R. S. Pine-Coffin, trans. Middlesex, England: Penguin Books, 1961. The first "autobiography" as such. You'll be surprised how contemporary Augustine sounds in this honest, introspective blend of philosophy and journal writing.

Hick, John. *Philosophy of Religion*. 3d ed. Englewood Cliffs, N.J.: Prentice-Hall, 1983. Introduction to philosophical questions raised by religion.

Kaufmann, Walter. *The Faith of a Heretic*. New York: New American Library, 1978. Stimulating, powerful analysis and attack on theology.

Lewis, C. S. *Mere Christianity*. New York: Macmillan, 1976. One of the most popular examples of contemporary apologetics. Lewis attempts to construct a rational argument for Christianity. Quite interesting.

Russell, Bertrand. *Why I Am Not a Christian, and Other Essays on Religion and Related Subjects*. New York: Simon & Schuster, 1957. Russell's tightly argued but clear account of his objections to Christianity. Intelligent atheism at its best.

Chapter 8

The Rationalist: René Descartes

Churchland, Paul M. *Matter and Consciousness: A Contemporary Introduction to the Philosophy of Mind*. Cambridge, Mass.: MIT Press, 1988. Sophisticated survey of the philosophy of mind. Good resource for dedicated students that should be especially appealing to science and psychology majors.

Descartes, René. *Objections and Replies* to Descartes' *Meditations*, in *The Philosophical Works of Descartes*, vol. 2. Elizabeth S. Haldane and G. R. T. Ross, trans. Cambridge, England: Cambridge University Press, 1968. This witty exchange of letters between Descartes and Hobbes (and others) is philosophically important and has the added virtue of showing us philosophy in action.

Frankfurt, Harry G. *Demons, Dreamers, and Madmen: The Defense of Reason in Descartes's Meditations*. Indianapolis, Ind.: Bobbs-Merrill, 1970. Detailed, tightly reasoned assessment of Descartes' method of doubt.

Ryle, Gilbert. *The Concept of Mind*. New York: Barnes & Noble Books, 1949. Important work in the analytic tradition. Quite readable introduction to early analytic method.

Sesonske, Alexander, and Noel Fleming, eds. *Meta-Meditations: Studies in Descartes*. Belmont, Calif.: Wadsworth, 1965. Variety of articles concerning the evil genius, dreaming, and other Cartesian themes, many accessible to uninitiated readers.

Third Interlude

The Buddha

Bankei. *The Unborn*. Norman Waddell, trans. San Francisco: North Point Press, 1984. Delightful collections of talks and sermons by a seventeenth-century Japanese sage. Bankei's wisdom is funny, profound, and relevant. An excellent introduction to Buddhism without technical language.

Benares, Camden. *Zen Without Zen Masters*. Berkeley, Calif.: And/Or Press, 1977. Bizarre collection of Buddhist-like tales, most with punch lines. A kind of stand-up comedy approach to philosophy.

Chan, Wing-Tsit, trans. and comp. *A Source Book in Chinese Philosophy*. Princeton, N.J.: Princeton University Press. A bargain in more ways than one. Chan's collection and commentaries are among the best introductions to Chinese philosophy. Modestly priced, worth having.

Hesse, Hermann. *Siddhartha*. Hilda Rosner, trans. Toronto: Bantam, 1951. An easy-to-read fictionalized account of the Buddha's life by a gifted storyteller.

Lao-tzu. *The Wisdom of Laotse*. Lin Yutang, trans. and ed. New York: Modern Library, 1948. This is one of my favorite books. It's a modestly priced little hardback containing excellent translations of both Lao-tzu and Chuang-tzu. Wise and witty.

Maugham, W. Somerset. *The Razor's Edge*. New York: Penguin, 1979. A classic of spiritual discovery.

Pirsig, Robert. *Zen and the Art of Motorcycle Maintenance: An Inquiry into Values*. New York: Morrow, 1974. A remarkably moving book that works on many levels. It's about motorcycles, parenthood, traveling, mental breakdowns, values, Plato, Buddhism, courage, loneliness, and wisdom.

Suzuki, D. T. *An Introduction to Zen Buddhism*. New York: Grove Press, 1964. This short collection of essays is a good introduction to Buddhism for the curious general reader.

If it piques your interest, then you will want to turn to Suzuki's longer works.

Chapter 9

The Skeptic: David Hume

Annas, Julia, and Jonathan Barnes. *The Modes of Scepticism: Ancient Texts and Modern Interpretations*. Cambridge, England: Cambridge University Press, 1985. First-rate contemporary look at skepticism.

Hallie, Phillip P. "Classical Scepticism—A Polemical Introduction." In Sextus Empiricus, *Selections from the Major Writings on Scepticism, Man, & God*, Phillip P. Hallie, ed., Sanford G. Etheridge, trans. Indianapolis, Ind.: Hackett, 1985. Lucid commentary on classical skepticism.

Naess, Arne. *Scepticism*. London: George Allen & Unwin, 1968. Supportive analysis of classical skepticism.

Russell, Bertrand. *Our Knowledge of the External World*. Chicago: Open Court, 1915. First-rate assessment of some fundamental epistemological problems.

Santayana, George. *Scepticism and Animal Faith*. 1923. Reprint. New York: Dover, 1955. Santayana's challenge to skepticism is an excellent example of precise thinking presented in nontechnical terms. Very well written.

Watson, Richard. *The Philosopher's Diet: How to Lose Weight and Change the World*. Boston: Atlantic Monthly Press, 1985. Watson talks about diets, exercise, philosophy, and David Hume in a powerful, witty, surprisingly effective manner. This is a delightful book you'll want to reread. A refreshing change of pace.

Chapter 10

The Universalist: Immanuel Kant

Kant, Immanuel. *Kant Selections*. Lewis White Beck, ed. New York: Scribner's/Macmillan, 1988. Excellent set of readings and editorial introductions.

Körner, S. *Kant*. Baltimore: Penguin, 1955. Basic study of Kant, good as a resource.

Paton, H. J. *The Categorical Imperative*. London: Hutchinson, 1946. Helpful commentaries on Kantian ethics.

Wellman, Carl. *Morals and Ethics*. Englewood Cliffs, N.J.: Prentice-Hall, 1988. Good introduction to moral philosophy.

Chapter 11

The Materialist: Karl Marx

Fromm, Erich. *The Art of Loving*. 1956. Reprint. New York: Perennial Library, 1974. Another good book with a potentially misleading title. This is not a self-help book; it's much more. The chapter on the disintegration of love is a superb humanistic analysis of modern capitalism.

Marcuse, Herbert. *One-Dimensional Man: Studies in the Ideology of Advanced Industrial Society*. Boston: Beacon Press, 1964. Powerful critique of modern capitalism.

Marx, Karl. *Marx Selections*. Allen Wood, ed. New York: Scribner's/Macmillan. Fine selection of material accompanied by editorial comments.

Fourth Interlude

The Utilitarians

Mill, John Stuart. *Autobiography*. New York: Columbia University Press, 1924. A classic autobiography.

Nagel, Thomas. *The Possibility of Altruism*. Oxford: Claren-don Press, 1970. Sophisticated analysis of egoism.

Narveson, Jan. *Morality and Utility*. Baltimore, Md.: Johns Hopkins Press, 1967. Sophisticated defense of basic utili-tarianism. Chapters 1 and 3 are quite good.

Chapter 12

The Existentialist: Søren Kierkegaard and Jean-Paul Sartre

Barrett, William. *Irrational Man: A Study in Existential Phi-losophy*. Garden City, N.Y.: Doubleday/Anchor Books, 1962. Impressive analysis of the contemporary intellectual and social scene.

Kaufmann, Walter, ed. *Existentialism from Dostoevsky to Sartre*. New York: New American Library, 1975. Excellent anthology with a first-rate introduction.

Slater, Phillip. *The Pursuit of Loneliness*. Boston: Beacon Press, 1970. Influential and readable assessment of the relation-ship between self-chosen reliance on technology and qual-ity of life. Disturbing and moving.

Unamuno, Miguel de. *The Tragic Sense of Life in Men and in Peoples*. 1913. Reprint. New York: Dover, 1954. Spanish philosopher's compelling plea for passion over rationalism, heart over head. Sophisticated but worth the effort, espe-cially the first chapter.

Weil, Simone. *The Need for Roots*. Arthur Wills, trans. New York: Harper/Colophon, 1971. Brilliant analysis of mod-ern culture and the need for charity by a remarkable woman, noted for both her brilliance and her sanctity.

Wilson, Colin. *The Outsider*. New York: Delta Books, 1956. This modern classic of alienation is still widely available. Of special interest to literature majors.

Chapter 13

The Pragmatist: William James

James, William. *William James: Writings 1902–1910*. New York: Literary Classics of the United States, Library of America–vol. 38, 1987. Excellent edition, though both Collier and Dover have inexpensive paperback editions available of *The Will to Believe* and *Varieties of Religious Experience*.

Stroh, Guy W. *American Philosophy from Edwards to Dewey: An Introduction*. Princeton, N.J.: D. Van Nostrand, 1968. Short but thorough survey of the highlights of American philosophy.

Chapter 14

The Anti-Philosopher: Friedrich Nietzsche

Kaufmann, Walter. *Without Guilt and Justice: From Decido-phobia to Autonomy*. New York: Delta Books, 1973. Kaufmann's attempt to construct a Nietzschean ethic is easy to read and guaranteed to get you thinking about contemporary values. His assessment of the various strate-gies of "decidophobia" (fear of making decisions) is espe-cially effective.

MacIntyre, Ben. *Forgotten Fatherland: The Search for Elisa-beth Nietzsche*. New York: Farrar, Straus Giroux, 1992. This fascinating account of efforts to establish a "New Germany" in South America raises disturbing questions about ways that Nietzsche's sister distorted her brother's reputation.

Nietzsche, Friedrich. *The Portable Nietzsche*. Walter Kauf-mann, ed. and trans. New York: Penguin, 1968. A "best buy," this handy collection includes Kaufmann's helpful comments.

Chapter 15

Emerging Archetypes

Anderson, Bonnie S., and Judith P. Zinsser. *A History of Their Own: Women in Europe from Prehistory to the Present*, vol. 1. New York: Harper & Row, 1988.

Baldwin, James. *Nobody Knows My Name: More Notes of a Native Son*. New York: Dial Press, 1961. Collection of essays by the brilliant social observer, touching and frightening.

Belenky, Mary Field, Blythe McVicker Clinchy, Nancy Rule Goldberger, and Jill Mattuck Tarule. *Women's Ways of Knowing: The Development of Self, Voice, and Mind*. New York: Basic Books, 1986.

Ellison, Ralph. *Invisible Man*. New York: Random House, 1952. Powerful novel about being socially, politically, and economically "invisible" in a racist culture.

Friedan, Betty. *The Feminine Mystique*. New York: W. W. Norton, 1963. Friedan's moving description of "the prob-lem with no name" awakened America to what became the contemporary women's movement.

Jaggar, Alison M., and Susan R. Bordo, eds. *Gender/Body/Knowledge: Feminist Reconstructions of Being and Know-ing*. New Brunswick, N.J.: Rutgers University Press, 1989. Sophisticated anthology of current feminist analyses of epistemological and metaphysical issues.

King, Martin Luther, Jr. *A Testament of Hope: The Essential Writings of Martin Luther King, Jr*. James M. Washington, ed. New York: Harper & Row, 1986. All of King's impor-tant speeches, essays, and books are included. An impres-sive collection.

Malcolm X. *Autobiography*. New York: Grove Press, 1965. Stunning work by an activist who challenged both blacks and whites.

Okin, Susan Moller. *Justice, Gender, and the Family*. New York: Basic Books, 1989. Disturbing (in a valuable way) challenge to John Rawls's influential theory of justice, and the possibility of gender-free rationality. Excellent discus-sion of "original position" reasoning.

Continuative

Davies, Roberton. *The Cunning Man*. New York: Penguin Books, 1994. A truly magnificent novel, Davies' last book presents a fine account of the journey from intelligence to wisdom; the fictional Jonathan Hullah is warm, wise, and kind. The sort of book you can't wait to finish but don't want to end.

Hadot, Pierre. *Philosophy as a Way of Life*, trans. Arnold I. Davidson, Oxford, England: Blackwell, 1995. Hadot's book deserves wider attention than it has received. This valedictory statement by one of our era's premiere intellec-tuals combines the scholarly authority of a lifetime with passion, spiritual depth, and superlative philosophical taste. I recommend it without qualification. A "must read" for anyone even remotely interested in the *sophos*.

Index of Margin Quotes

Index

Credits

Quotations

The numbers in parentheses after each entry are the page numbers on which the material appears.

From Pierre Hadot in *Philosophy as a Way of* Life, translated by Arnold I. Davidson, Blackwell, 1995. Reprinted by permission of the publisher. (34, 86, 640–641, 642–643) From *Protagoras* by Plato, Benjamin Jowett, translator; revised translation by Martin Ostwald. Copyright © 1956 by Macmillan Publishing Company; copyright © renewed 1984. Used by permission. (62–65) From *Xenophon: Memorabilia and Oeconomics*, translated by E. C. Marchant, Harvard University Press, 1923. Used by permission. (79–81) From *The Republic* by Plato, translated by Desmond Lee, Penguin Classics, 1955. Copyright © 1973, 1974, 1987 H. D. P. Lee. Used by permission. (131) From *Translations from the* Chinese by Arthur Waley. Copyright 1919 and renewed 1947 by Arthur Waley. Used by permission of Alfred A. Knopf, Inc., and Unwin Hyman, HarperCollins Publishers Limited. (193) From *The Importance of Living* by Lin Yutang. Copyright © 1965 by Lin Yutang. Used by permission of H. J. Lin. (196) From "Letter to Menoceceus" by Epicurus, in *Readings in Hellenistic Philosophy*, Shapiro and Curley, eds., Northwestern University Press, 1963. Used by permission. (205–208) From *Does It Matter?* by Alan Watts. Copyright © 1968, 1969, 1970 by Alan Watts. Used by permission of Pantheon Books, a division of Random House, Inc. (210–211) From *Herakleitos and Diogenes* by Guy Davenport, Grey Fox Press, 1979. Used by permission of the author. (216) From *A New Guide to Rational Living* by Albert Ellis and Robert A. Harper, Wilshire Book Company, 1978. Used by permission of Albert Ellis. (238) From *Man's Search for Meaning* by Viktor E. Frankl, Pocket Books, 1963. Used by permission of Beacon Press. (240) From "The World of Epictetus" by James B. Stockdale, *Atlantic Monthly,* April 1978. Used by permission of the author. (241–242) From *Epictetus' Enchiridion* © 1991 by James Bond Stockdale. Reprinted by permission of the author. (243–244) From *Discourse on Method Meditations* and *Rules for the Direction of the Mind* by René Descartes, translated by Haldane and Ross, Cambridge University Press, 1931. Used by permission. (289–294) From *The Way of Lao Tzu: Tao-te Ching*, translated by Wing-tsit Chan. Copyright © 1963 Macmillan Publishing Company, Inc. Used by permission. (331) From *A Source Book in Chinese Philosophy* translated by Wing-tsit Chan, Prentice-Hall, 1963. Used by permission. (331) From *Buddhism: A Way of Life and Thought* by Nancy Wilson Ross. Copyright © 1980 Nancy Wilson Ross. Used by permission of Alfred A. Knopf, Inc. (333) From *The Teachings of the Compassionate Buddha* by E. A. Burtt, Mentor Edition, 1982. Used by permission of the Estate of E. A. Burtt. (337) From *Dialogues Concerning Natural Religion* by David Hume, edited by Norman Kemp-Smith, Bobbs-Merrill, 1947. Used by permission of Thomas Nelson & Sons Limited. (367–381) From *Economic and Philosophic Manuscripts* by Karl Marx in *Writings of the Young Marx on Philosophy and Society*, edited and translated by Loyd D. Easton and Kurt H. G. Guddat, Anchor Doubleday Edition, 1967. Used by permission of Loyd D. Easton and Mrs. Kurt H. Guddat. (440–442) From *The Art of Loving* by Erich Fromm. Copyright © 1956 Erich Fromm. Used by permission of HarperCollins Publishers, Inc. (445–446) From *A Kierkegaard Anthology* edited by Robert Bretall, The Modern Library, 1946. Used by permission of Princeton University Press. (482–489) From *Nausea* by Jean Paul Sartre. Copyright © 1964 New Directions Publishing Corporation. Reprinted by permission of the publisher. (493) From Jean-Paul Sartre, *Existentialism Is a Humanism*, translated by Bernard Frechtman; copyright 1957 Philosophical Library, Inc. Used by permission of Philosophical Library, Inc. (498, 500) From *The Portable Nietzsche* by Walter Kaufman. Copyright © 1954 The Viking Press, renewed 1982 Viking Penguin. Used by permission of Viking Penguin, a division of Penguin Books USA, Inc. (560–564) From *The Gay Science* by Friedrich Nietzsche, translated by Walter Kaufman. Copyright © 1974 Random House, Inc. Used by permission. (576–577) From *Justice, Gender and the Family* by Susan Moller Okin. © 1989 by Basic Books, Inc. Reprinted by permission of Basic Books, a division of HarperCollins Publishers, Inc. (610–611) From *A Testament of Hope: The Essential Readings of Martin Luther King, Jr.*, edited by James M. Washington. Copyright © 1986 by Coretta Scott King. Reprinted by arrangement with The Heirs to the Estate of Martin Luther King, Jr. c/o Joan Daves Agency as agent for the proprietor. (621, 623–625) From "Letter from Birmingham Jail" in *Why We Can't Wait* by Martin Luther King, Jr. Copyright © 1963, 1964 by Martin Luther King, Jr. Reprinted by arrangement with The Heirs to the Estate of Martin Luther King, Jr. c/o Joan Daves Agency as agent for the proprietor. (626–629) From "I Have a Dream" by Martin Luther King, Jr., in *A Testament of Hope*, Harper & Row Publishers, 1986. Copyright 1963 Martin Luther King, Jr. Reprinted with The Heirs to the Estate of Martin Luther King, Jr. c/o Joan Daves Agency as agent for the proprietor. (632–633) *Postscript*: From *The Handbook of Epictetus*, translated by Nicholas P. White, Hackett Publishing Company, 1983. Used by permission. (645)

Pictures

p. 1: From the *Encheiridion* by Epictetus, Vol. II. Translated by W. A. Oldfather © 1928 Harvard University Press, Cambridge, Mass. Reprinted by permission of the publishers and the Loeb Classical Library; p. 5: © Agence France-Presse; p. 11: (left) Raphael, detail from *The School of Athens* (1510–1511), The Vatican, Rome. Photo © Scala/Art Resource, N.Y.; (right) © Leonard Freed/Magnum; p. 27: Corbis-Bettmann; p. 36: photo © AKG London; p. 50: © Anglo-Australian Telescope Board, courtesy David Malin; p. 52: from Lucretius, *De Rerum Natura*, Ms. 11912, folio 2. Courtesy The British Library, London; p. 59: © Gilles Peress/Magnum; p. 64: © Eli Reed/Magnum; p. 65: © AP/Wide World Photos; p. 75: from the *Apology* by Plato, Vol. I. Translated by H. N. Fowler © 1914 Harvard University Press, Cambridge, Mass. Reprinted by permission of the publishers and the Loeb Classical Library; p. 78: The Granger Collection; p. 90: © Ted Soqui/Impact Visuals; p. 99: © Evan Agostini/Gamma-Liaison; p. 110: The Metropolitan Museum of Art, New York. Wolfe Fund, 1931; p. 115: from the *Republic* by Plato, Vol. VI. Translated by Paul Shorey © 1930 Harvard University Press, Cambridge, Mass. Reprinted by permission of the publishers and the Loeb Classical Library; p. 121: photo © Scala/Art Resource, N.Y.; p. 137 © Dick Cole & Associates; p. 144: © Paul Fortin/Stock, Boston; p. 149: (left) © Ian Shaw/Tony Stone Images; p. 149: (right) © Linda Rosier/Impact Visuals; p. 155: from *The Athenian Constitution* by Aristotle, c. 329–324 B.C. The British Museum, London. Photo © AKG London; p. 159: photo © AKG London; p. 177: © Virginia Blaisdell/Stock, Boston; p. 179: © Mel Rosenthal/The Image Works; p. 194: © Mark Peterson/Saba; p. 196: Corbis-Bettmann; p. 203: © Anna Kaufman Moon/Stock, Boston; p. 205: © Magnum; p. 209: © David F. Hughes/The Picture Cube; p. 213: Boethius, *De Consolatione philosophiae* (dedication page). Tours or Angers, c. 1465, by the Coetivity Master (Henri de Vulcop?) Ms. 222, f.1. The Pierpont Morgan Library, New York/Art Resource, N.Y.; p. 217: *Diogenes and Alexander the Great*, First Century A.D. Villa Albani, Rome. Photo © Alinari/Art Resource, N.Y.; p. 218: © Mike Maple/Woodfin Camp & Associates; p. 223: (left) Photofest; p. 223: (right) © Marcel Thomas/Sipa Press; p. 225: © Frédéric Brenner/Courtesy Howard Greenberg Gallery, New York; p. 228: © Roberto Soncin-Gerometta/Photo 20-20; p. 231: © Matthew Neal McVay/Stock, Boston; p. 234: © Gilles Peress/Magnum; p. 235: © Frank Siteman/Stock, Boston; p. 241: © Corbis-Bettmann; p. 247: *Philosophy with Aristotle, Plato, Socrates and Seneca*. Bartolomeo da Bologna di Bartoli. Panegyrique de Bruzio Visconti. Ms. 599/1426, fol. 6v. Fourteenth century. Musée Condé, Chantilly, France. Photo © Giraudon/Art Resource, N.Y.; p. 251: courtesy The Bodleian Library, Oxford; p. 256: Mary Evans Picture Library, London; p. 266: © Frank Siteman/Stock, Boston; p. 272: © Sebastião Salgado/Magnum; p. 280:

courtesy The Bancroft Library, University of California at Berkeley; p. 281: Corbis-Bettmann; p. 282: The Granger Collection; p. 285: letter from Descartes to Père Mersenne. Photo © Roger-Viollet, Paris; p. 292: © Robert Brenner/PhotoEdit; p. 317: Alex Milovsky, from *Natural History*; p. 322: Corbis-Bettmann; p. 335: The National Palace Museum, Taiwan; p. 339: A late and unpublished revision of a passage from *The History of England* by David Hume. Courtesy of the Librarian, The Royal Society of Edinburgh; p. 341: © Bruce Flynn/Stock, Boston; p. 362: © Joe Munroe/Photo Researchers; p. 376: (left) © Bob Thomas/Tony Stone Images; p. 376: (right) © James D. Wilson/Gamma-Liaison; p. 380: *To Eternal Peace* by Immanuel Kant (1795). Photo © AKG London; p. 387: from *A Diderot Pictorial Encyclopedia of Trades and Industry*, Dover Publications; p. 388: Corbis-Bettmann; p. 389: © Frank Capri/Saga/Archive Photos; p. 408: © Michael Dwyer/Stock, Boston; p. 416: A page from *The Communist Manifesto* (1848) by Karl Marx. Photo © AKG London; p. 426: photo © AKG London; p. 432: © Harvey Finkel/Impact Visuals; p. 456: © Viviane Moos/Saba; p. 464: (left) © David Young-Wolff/PhotoEdit; p. 464: (right) © Christa Armstrong; p. 467: © Jonathan Nourok/Tony Stone Images; p. 471: © Spencer Grant/Photo Researchers; p. 474: first page from *The Stages on Life's Way: Lectori Benevolo!* by Søren Kierkegaard. Courtesy The Royal Library, Copenhagen; p. 478: © AP/Wide World Photos; p. 479: © Mark Richards/PhotoEdit; p. 485: (top left) © Lincoln Potter/Gamma-Liaison; p. 485: (top right) © James Wilson/Woodfin Camp & Associates; p. 485: (bottom) © Bob Mahoney/The Image Works; p. 491: © Paul Lowe/Magnum; p. 495: © AP/Wide World Photos; p. 499: The Art Institute of Chicago. © 1997 ARS, New York/ADAGP;

p. 513: from *The Will to Believe* by William James. Ms. Am 1092.5, p. 62. Reprinted by permission of The Houghton Library, Harvard University; p. 515: courtesy The University of Pennsylvania School of Medicine; p. 527: © F. M. Kearney/Impact Visuals; p. 528: © Costa Manos/Magnum; p. 529: © Gale Zucker/Stock, Boston; p. 540: © Mary Ellen Mark/Library; p. 551: (left) © Andrew Syred/Science Photo Library/Photo Researchers; p. 551: (right) © Chris Bjornberg/Photo Researchers; p. 552: © Tony Stone Images/The Hulton Getty Picture Collection Ltd.; p. 554: The Metropolitan Museum of Art, New York. George A. Hearn Fund, 1956; p. 556: *The Case Wagner* (1888) by Friedrich Nietzsche. Universitätsbibliothek, Basel. Photo © AKG London; p. 560: The Kunsthalle, Hamburg; p. 562: courtesy Verlag Montabella, St. Moritz; p. 565: courtesy Goethe-Schiller Archiv, Stiftung Weimarer Klassik, Weimar; p. 578: © AP/Wide World Photos; p. 581: © Ron Sherman/Tony Stone Images; p. 582: © Danny Lyon/Magnum; p. 585: courtesy Goethe-Schiller Archiv, Stiftung Weimarer Klassik, Weimar; p. 593: from *Propagandizing Religion*, a 1954 sermon by Rev. Dr. Martin Luther King, Jr. Reprinted by arrangement with The Heirs to the Estate of Martin Luther King, Jr., c/o Writers House, Inc., as agent for the proprietor. Copyright © 1954, 1957 by Martin Luther King, Jr., copyright renewed 1984 by Coretta Scott King; p. 599: © Mike Ramirez/Copley News Service; p. 600: (left) Hans Holbein, *Venus and Cupid*, photo © AKG London; p. 600: (right) Hans Jordaens, *Minerva Visiting the Muses on Mount Helicon*, photo © Bridgeman Art Library/London; p. 618: © AP/Wide World Photos; p. 624: © Charles Moore/Black Star.

Fold here

CUT PAGE OUT

Fold here

NO POSTAGE
NECESSARY
IF MAILED
IN THE
UNITED STATES

BUSINESS REPLY MAIL

FIRST CLASS   PERMIT NO. 34   BELMONT, CA

Postage will be paid by addressee

Douglas Soccio
Wadsworth Publishing Company
10 Davis Drive
Belmont, CA 94002

To the owner of this book

I hope that you have enjoyed *Archetypes of Wisdom*, third edition, as much as I enjoyed writing it. I would like to know as much about your experience as you would care to offer. Only through your comments and those of others can I learn how to make this a better text for future readers.

School _____   Your instructor's name _____

City _____   State _____

1. What did you like most about *Archetypes of Wisdom*? _____

_____

_____

_____

2. Do you have any recommendations for ways to improve the next edition of this text? _____

_____

_____

_____

3. In the space below or in a separate letter, please write any other comments you have about the book. (For example, were any chapters or concepts particularly difficult?) I'd be delighted to hear from you! _____

_____

_____

_____

_____

_____

_____

_____

_____

_____

_____

_____

_____

_____

_____

Optional:

Your name/address: _____   Date _____

_____

_____

May Wadsworth quote you, either in promotion for *Archetypes of Wisdom* or in future publishing ventures?

Yes ☐   No ☐

Thank you!